Behavior in Organizations

An Experiental Approach

Seventh Edition

Behavior in Organizations

An Experiental Approach

Seventh Edition

A. B. (RAMI) SHANI, PhD
Professor of Organizational Behavior and Management

JAMES B. LAU, PhD
Professor Emeritus

Both of California Polytechnic State University
San Luis Obispo

Boston   Burr Ridge, IL   Dubuque, IA   Madison, WI   New York   San Francisco   St. Louis
Bangkok   Bogotá   Caracas   Lisbon   London   Madrid
Mexico City   Milan   New Delhi   Seoul   Singapore   Sydney   Taipei   Toronto

McGraw-Hill Higher Education

A Division of The **McGraw-Hill** *Companies*

BEHAVIOR IN ORGANIZATIONS: AN EXPERIENTIAL APPROACH

Copyright © 2000, 1996, 1992, 1988, 1984, 1978, and 1975 by The McGraw-Hill Companies, Inc. All rights reserved. Printed in the United States of America. Except as permitted under the United States Copyright Act of 1976, no part of this publication may be reproduced or distributed in any form or by any means, or stored in a database or retrieval system, without the prior written permission of the publisher.

This book is printed on acid-free paper.

domestic   3 4 5 6 7 8 9 0 QPD/QPD 9 0 9 8 7 6 5 4 3 2 1
international 1 2 3 4 5 6 7 8 9 0 QPD/QPD 9 0 9 8 7 6 5 4 3 2 1 0 9

ISBN 0-07-228461-7

Vice president/Editor-in-chief: *Michael W. Junior*
Publisher: *Craig S. Beytien*
Senior sponsoring editor: *John E. Biernat*
Editorial coordinator: *Erin Riley*
Marketing manager: *Kenyetta Giles Haynes*
Project manager: *Pat Frederickson*
Production supervisor: *Kari Geltemeyer*
Designer: *Jennifer McQueen Hollingsworth*
Cover illustration: *Paul Turnbaugh*
Compositor: *Electronic Publishing Services, Inc., TN*
Typeface: *10/12 Times Roman*
Printer: *Quebecor Printing Book Group/Dubuque*

Library of Congress Cataloging-in-Publication Data

Shani, Abraham B.
    Behavior in organizations : an experiential approach / A.B. (Rami)
  Shani, James B. Lau. — 7th ed.
        p.   cm.
    Includes bibliographical references and index.
    ISBN 0-07-228461-7
    1. Organizational behavior. 2. Group relations training.
  I. Lau, James Brownlee, 1916– .
  HD58.7.S476   2000
  302.3'5—dc21   99–26768

INTERNATIONAL EDITION   ISBN 0-07-116989-X
Copyright © 2000. Exclusive rights by The McGraw-Hill Companies, Inc. for manufacture and export. This book cannot be re-exported from the country to which it is consigned by McGraw-Hill. The International Edition is not available in North America.

http://www.mhhe.com

Acknowledgments

The seventh edition of this book is the outcome of ongoing dialogues with colleagues, students, and managers, all of whom share the fascination with fostering adult learning and discovery. We wish to acknowledge the many scholars, managers, and researchers who contributed to the text. We are indebted to all those individuals who granted permission for the use of figures, tables, cases, simulations, and activities. The rich input from many of the adopters of the book on how to continuously improve this product is appreciated. Their support gave us the vote of confidence to carry out this revision.

The book was shaped significantly by three colleagues: David Peach and Michael Stebbins at CalPoly State University and Roger Conway at the Center for Creative Leadership, San Diego. They have shared and put into practice a common belief that experiential learning is a synergistic and exhilarating way to teach and learn about organizational behavior and management. Rebecca Ellis, Kay Glasgow, James Sena, Allan Bird, Dan Hawthorne, Denise Mortorff, and Candis Williams at CalPoly; Robert Grant at Georgetown University; Torbjorn Stjernberg, Bengt Stymne, Jan Lowstedt, and Peter Docherty at the Stockholm School of Economics; Dov Eden, Asya Pazy, and Mina Westman at Tel-Aviv University; David Kolb and William Pasmore at Case Western Reserve University; Mary Ann Hazen at the University of Detroit; Thom Sepic at Pacific Lutheran University; Gervase Bushe at Simon Fraser University; Harvey Kolodny at the University of Toronto; and Yoram Mitki at Ruppin Institute have exchanged ideas, materials, and views with the authors over the years, many of which are reflected in the book.

As with the previous editions, our primary indebtedness is to our students who were involved in the origination, testing, and evaluation of most of the educational aspects of this text. We personally thank the following students—some of whom are now faculty members—for their direct contributions and suggestions that have been integrated into the text: Anna Cunningham, Jennifer Fashing, Ian Keoki Ikemori, Maria-Elena (Mar) Radriguez, Martin Rogberg, Chris Roth, Anjali Saraf, Carol Sexton, James Sundali, and Jeff Trailer.

We would like to thank the following colleagues for the many suggestions they provided in reviewing the book.

Seventh Edition Reviewers

Brad Brown, *University of Virginia*

Anthony Buono, *Bentley College*

Anne Cowden, *California State University—Sacramento*

Dan Hawthorne, *California Polytechnic State University—San Luis Obispo*

Bruce Johnson, *Gustavus Adolphus College*

Previous Reviewers

John R. Aiello, *Rutgers University*

Gerald L. Arffa, *Indiana University-Purdue University at Indianapolis*

Jane Burman-Holtom, *University of Florida*

James W. Carr, *West Georgia College*

Christine Clements, *North Dakota State University*

Elaine D. Guertler, *Augustana College*

Jane Humble, *Arizona State University*

Esther Long, *University of West Florida*

Chris Poulson, *California State Poly U-Pomona*

Charles Smith, *University of Southern Maine*

David Turnipseed, *Indiana University-Purdue University at Fort Wayne*

Finally, our thanks to our families—Elaine, Talia, Liat, Leora, and Arlene—who, over the years, have listened, watched, and continuously supported us as we tried to bring every new edition to completion.

A. B. (Rami) Shani
James B. Lau

Contents in Brief

Contents

List of Activities

List of Cases

List of WWW Activities

Introduction

We live in an era in which the labor market and work are changing at a very fast pace. Development in new technology are helping to make the world turn faster and faster. Internationalization and the flow of information have altered the social and economic conditions both for nations as a whole and for individual employees and employers. As such, understanding the context of work, the nature of work, the nature of human behavior, and the nature of organizational behavior becomes critical as we enter the 21st century.

The first edition of this book was published in the early 1970s, when there were few textbooks in organizational behavior (OB). And only a handful of educators recognized the need to teach OB experientially. Twenty-five years later, as we complete the seventh edition of this book, the Organizational Behavior Division is the Academy of Management's largest division, the Organizational Behavior Teaching Society has 500 active members, some scholarly journals have incorporated the term *organizational behavior* into their titles, and many basic textbooks are available on this subject. The original textbook launched what has become a continuing enterprise, the essence of which was to learn about organizational behavior in an experiential way and to go beyond trying to summarize the existing and growing body of knowledge.

We have used the OB approach in this text by focusing first on design and second on classroom management practices. A current OB emphasis is to influence behavior and outcome through use of design (the subject of Module 13), whether it be architectural, organization, work, or job design. We have designed a management workshop for this OB course to achieve our learning objectives. We have selected certain learning methods and sequences to implement the design. And we provide guidance for classroom management practices that creates a learning community in which behavioral and intellectual change occurs. In this sense the instructors are managers of the educational design, the learning processes, the classroom, and the learning community, using the OB methods in which they are instructing the students. As managers, instructors are models of their own OB instruction.

As with the six preceding editions, the seventh edition of *Behavior in Organization* is designed first and foremost to meet needs that other texts do not satisfy. There are many continuities with prior editions, but some important changes freshen and update the text. We revised the overall design to include 15 core modules in the book and five advanced modules on the Web site. Each module is designed to stand alone so that the instructor can have more freedom to develop the overall structure of his or her course. We organized the book into four major parts: managing the context; managing teams; managing individuals; and managing work design, culture, and change. We strived to improve the balance between experiential activities, cases, and theoretical knowledge for each part and module, and we added two new modules—"Organization Culture, Symbolism, and Effectiveness" and "Stress and the Management of Stress"—to cover these important topics. We've deleted a few cases and activities and added 25 new activities and seven new cases.

Major continuities with previous editions include our basic approach, aims, and emphasis. As before, the text is intended for use in an experiential learning course for undergraduate or graduate business administration students in a required organizational behavior core course. Thus we provide basic coverage of essential OB topics. These topics are often taught solely by lectures and readings, a cognitive approach primarily emphasizing content. Content-based approaches do not deal adequately with the need for student involvement, nor do they help students acquire behavioral skills. In contrast, *Behavior in Organizations* emphasizes involvement exercises to help students quickly and effectively enter the process of thinking about behavior, applying concepts, and developing their own expertise. Lectures and readings are intended to bolster this process orientation. At the graduate level we usually supplement our book with a book of readings.

Experiential methods provide a powerful stimulus for learning, growth, and change by helping participants focus on their own behaviors and reactions as data. For this very reason, some students may at first be uncomfortable about encountering experiential methods in a required course. (In contrast, students who have elected such courses are often eager and excited by experiential learning—or, if they find it threatening, they can quickly drop the course.) To help students deal with this problem, we begin with more structured, less personal exercises that are readily recognized as relevant to human effectiveness in organizational settings. Personal growth and self-understanding activities are introduced later in the text, after students have had enough experience to become more comfortable and ready for them.

This edition also retains its emphasis on bringing to the university classroom the type of training that supervisors, managers, and executives experience in management development programs. It includes methods of adult education such as team activities, role playing, case studies, in-baskets, and other simulation exercises. Managers generally will not sit through many lectures, nor do they find time for long reading assignments. But action-oriented exercises that provide a new conceptual input and permit them to apply their experience and share it with others are undertaken with great energy and involvement. Most of the activities in this text (or others similar to them) have been used successfully with supervisors, managers, and executives in education programs in our major industries and government agencies.

Since one of our objectives is to bring what is being done in management education into the college classroom in a basic course, there has been no attempt to be highly original in content or activities. Many activities have been written by the authors but are similar to others already in use. In this edition we have been fortunate to be able to include fresh activities and case studies written by creative colleagues. The theoretical and conceptual writings that integrate the activities are basic organizational behavior theory. Both theory and activities are intended to present an eclectic approach, and we make no attempt to take a position of advocacy except for the experiential approach.

Alternative Plans for Using the Text

The design of the text allows instructors to adapt the course to the conditions under which they are teaching and the type of students with whom they work. It can be used in classes with time blocks of 1, 1½, 2, 3, or 4 hours by planning the activities and readings accordingly. The workload can also be adjusted for desired depth of coverage by following one of the three plans suggested in Figure A.

**Figure A
Alternative Course Designs for Using This Text**

Plan A: Complete selected activties and readings with classroom discussion.
Plan B: Complete plan A and add the outside-of-class team task project. See WWW site "plan B."
Plan C: Complete plan A and add the in-class and outside-of-class team tasks.
    See WWW site "plan C."

Plan A can be used when no homework is required other than the modules, activities, and case studies in the text or Web site. A basic supervisory or management course is frequently conducted in this manner. Plan B can provide the richest and most challenging approach. The teams complete an outside-of-class task project lasting throughout the course, which allows for the skills development and the application of course concepts to team members' own behavior. Plan C has the same objectives but no task project; team activities are limited to classroom exercises and several outside preparatory meetings. The time requirements of plan B make it more appropriate for a semester course, while plan C can be readily completed in a quarter course.

The Course Topics

This course includes 15 modules in the text and 5 advanced modules on the Web. The modules have been arranged to utilize the appropriate learning methods and to provide a generally logical development of the theory and concepts. Several considerations were important in the design.

Involvement learning proceeds best when it starts with the first class session and continues with growing intensity, particularly early in the course. Because students come with the expectation that the classroom is a lecturer–listener, chairs-in-a-row environment, they will quickly lapse into that mode if the course structure does not avoid it. Thus there are class activities in the introductory modules. Students use their own experience to define organizational behavior (Module 1), and the classroom climate is established through dialoguing (Module 2).

Reinforcement and opportunities to apply learning are provided for by introducing major concepts early and studying their various aspects throughout the course. Thus the small group, a primary focus of the text, is introduced at the end of Module 2 and returned to at intervals throughout the course. Group processes and group skills are integrated throughout the duration of the course with a specific module (Module 5 on team problem solving and decision making halfway through the course; Module 6 on group dynamics, and Module 7 on team building). In courses that adopt plans B or C, which require group projects, student groups can apply new theory and concepts to their own project teams throughout the course. Four-pervasive core concepts—communication, motivation, perception, and personality—are discussed throughout the text in conjunction with other topics. This learning is integrated when the topics are addressed directly in later modules (Module 9 for personality, Module 10 for motivation, Module 11 for perception, and Module 12 for communication).

The general logical sequence of material follows the progression from the exploration of the context in which human behavior occurs to the understanding of team behavior, which seems to have become one of the most dominant features of organizations. We proceed to focus on individual behavior issues and back to the macro-level issues of work design, organizational culture, symbolism, effectiveness, change, and development.

The test is divided into four parts. Statements at the beginning of each part provide previews of the coming modules and, in Parts 2 through 4, also provide a review of material already covered. A more complete understanding of the subject areas and the learning methods of the entire text can be achieved by reading through these statements at the beginning of Parts 1 through 4.

The Web site for this book is an integral part of the learning endeavor. For each module the Web site includes additional optional activities that the instructor can integrate into the learning process. Some of the activities on the Web site provide links to other sites. The Web site also includes five advanced modules, which the instructor might choose to incorporate into the course.

Human behavior in organizations is both fascinating and important to understand. It surrounds and concerns us all, and affects every aspect of our lives. Moreover, it is the heart of effective management. Students respond with great eagerness to organizational behavior concepts in a properly designed course. Their enthusiasm offers the quickest route to the working skills they will find essential in the organizational world. This text's main aim is to help them succeed.

Note to Participants

Please do not read ahead in this book unless the assignment at the end of the module or the instructor specifically instructs you to do so. The format of this book is to start many modules with an activity and then to develop the concepts and theories, using your experience as data. If you look at the activities ahead of time, some of the spontaneity of participation will be lost. You will miss out on the enjoyment and on an important part of the learning as well.

Behavior in Organizations

An Experiental Approach

Seventh Edition

Part 1

Managing the Context

The exploration of behavioral issues in the context of the work organization is the focus of this course. The dual objectives set forth are individual and team learning. As such we are concerned with *how* you learn as well as *what* you learn about human behavior in organizations. The how and the what are closely connected in this course because so much of what you will learn is a process: a different way of looking at your own experience, a deeper way of understanding the power of attitudes or expectations, or a new awareness of how people experience work organizations. Management education strives to provide viewpoints and learn-by-doing methods that help participants walk through new learning. We use experience in this way. Your own experiences in this course will be the basic data to build your understanding. The activities of this course are structured to help you understand the behavior of people in organizations.

Management and executive workshops often spend the first hours or days developing a sense of community and deciding how to use experience and the interactions of participants for maximum learning. The workshop becomes a *learning community*— a community in this sense refers to a group of people with common interests, values, and purposes who meet regularly; it suggests supportiveness; it implies exchange of information as a primary process of community integration. Workshop participants find out about one another and about the faculty, become part of a team, and learn more effective ways of interacting.

The climate that best promotes learning is one in which participants support one another; are open with one another about their responses; and are willing to confront or compare different responses, insights, and experiences. Learning to learn is important enough (and difficult enough) for managers to spend time building such a climate systematically. We too will spend time learning to learn and creating an appropriate climate. A key aspect of this sort of learning environment involves learning how to effectively utilize our own experiences and those of others.

Part 1 of this book is designed to accomplish these ends. Allocating the limited classroom time available for lectures and exercises is a continuous struggle for instructors using the experiential learning approach. The assumption in this "workshop model" is that class time will be used primarily for examining more intently a limited number of theories and concepts at the sacrifice of extensive content coverage in lectures and readings. However, many students feel the need for more complete cognitive learning. The modules lay the foundation for content learning. The references and endnotes provide a window into the extensive material available to enhance knowledge and understanding of the topics covered in the organizational behavior area.

Preview of Part 1

The learning climate of the classroom is developed in the first two modules. In Module 1 and Activity 1–1, class members participate in a triad exercise in which each tells of an experience from his or her work. A number of participants then relate their experiences to the entire class. From these experiences, the professor constructs the topic areas of organizational behavior for the class to demonstrate that the behavioral study of the course has immediate relevance to everyone. Activity 1–2 provides an opportunity to explore the experience of individual differences at the workplace. The experiential learning orientation in this course and the systems approach at the workplace is followed by a historical review of the evolution of the organizational behavior field. Activity 1–3 provides an opportunity to explore organization behavior topics on the World Wide Web.

In Module 2 and Activity 2–1, an open communication dialogue enables participants to examine the assumptions of the students and the professor that are relevant to the course and its learning goals. Content and process learning are discussed, and the first activity is used as an illustration to enhance understanding of process (experiential) learning. The role of the participant as a coach and contributor to the learning of others gets special emphasis. A review of expectations is followed by a discussion of the adult learner; experiential learning; individual, team, and organizational learning; and appreciative inquiry. The values of the learning community model are also discussed. Activity 2–2 provides an opportunity for individuals to diagnose their learning style and a way for teams to explore similarities, differences, and team learning. Optional Activity 2–4, on the WWW site, provides an opportunity for the learner (1) to articulate individual learning objectives, performance goals, potential obstacles, and specific action statements in a contract and (2) to have the contract co-signed with the instructor.

Once the classroom learning climate is established, participants are assigned to working teams. Activity 2–3 fosters team dialogue around the development of the team's name and the creation of the team's logo. The next substantive area focuses on management and leadership. We start Module 3 with Activities 3–1 or 3–4, which explore the meaning of leadership and management based on your own experiences. From these experiences your instructor will develop the topic areas of leadership and management. The multifaceted definition of leadership is followed by a synopsis of the debate on the differences between leadership and management. Next we review different schools of leadership thoughts. Last, current themes and challenges are discussed. Activities 3–2 and 3–5 provide alternative leadership diagnostic instruments, each of which is based in a different theory of leadership. The first case study, "Donny Is My Leader," is introduced as an important learning tool for facilitating the exploration of the organizational behavior topic—leadership and managerial challenges at the workplace.

Module 4 concludes this section by providing a conceptual framework and analytical tools to begin the investigation of the organizational context in which human behavior takes place. The organization is viewed as an open system. Activity 4–1 provides an opportunity to compare two types of organizations and explore some key elements of organizations. The systems view of organizations is introduced as an alternative basic cognitive roadmap. Next we discuss characteristics of human and formal organizations. Two conceptual tools—the "Operational Blueprint" (Figure 4–2), "Actors Playing Their Roles" (Figure 4–3)—and an integrative road map (Figure 4–4) are provided for the analysis of the work organization. Activities 4–3 and 4–4 on the WWW provide additional opportunities to explore the nature and key characteristics of organizations and their management.

The establishment of the learning method and climate through interaction exercises and the introduction of the framework of the content areas to be studied should satisfactorily prepare course participants for Part 2, which deals with the core concepts in understanding and managing team behavior.

1 Organizational Behavior: Historical and Global Context

Learning Objectives

After completing this module, you should be able to

1. Define the field of organizational behavior.
2. Summarize the historical evolution of the field.
3. Briefly describe the systems approach to understanding, managing, and directing people in organizations.
4. State the four levels of improving organizational effectiveness.
5. Explain the relationship between rationality and irrationality in management.
6. Describe the objectives of the course.

Module Outline

Premodule Preparation

Activity 1–1: Defining Organizational Behavior

Objectives:

a. To identify course topic areas from your own work experiences.

b. To introduce involvement learning and to begin building the learning environment.

c. To introduce the communication skills of sharing, listening, and paraphrasing.

Task 1:

Your past work experiences often make interesting case studies. The worksheet for Activity 1–1 presents three alternatives for selecting your case study. Your professor will assign one of these to the entire class or divide the class into three groups, one for each alternative. Use the worksheet for Activity 1–1 to make notes on your case study. (Time: Individuals have 5 minutes to think about their experiences and jot down notes.)

Task 2:

Participants form triads. Member A tells his or her case study and what it illustrates to member B. Member B listens carefully and paraphrases back to A the story and what it illustrates. Member B must convince member A that B has understood fully what A was trying to communicate. Member C is the observer and remains silent during the process (a role many find difficult). Member B tells an experience to member C while A observes. Member C tells an experience to member A while B observes. (Time: Each person will have 5 minutes to relate a case study and have it paraphrased back by the listener. The instructor will call out the time at the end of each 5-minute interval to allow for equal "airtime" among participants. Total time: 15 minutes.)

Task 3:

Each group selects a member to relate his or her case study to the class. The instructor briefly analyzes for the class how the incident fits in with some topic to be studied in the course, such as motivation or leadership style. Topic areas are listed on the board.

Task 4:

Questions for discussion: What are the general character and tone of the stories you have heard? What are the implications of these findings for managers who have the responsibility for persons similar to those in this class?

Worksheet for Activity 1–1

Make notes below on your case study for the alternative you were assigned for task 1.

Alternative 1: Describe an experience in a past work situation that you think illustrates something about human relations in organizations. What does it illustrate?

Alternative 2: Describe a difficult problem you encountered while working. What caused the problem? What was done or could have been done to reduce or overcome the problem?

Alternative 3: Describe a work experience that illustrated good management. What happened? Why was it good? How did it affect you?

Introduction

We always have dialogues with participants during our opening class sessions to determine how they perceive our course of study. They generally ask two questions: What can I get out of a course in organizational behavior? and Will I learn something that I really can use? Fair questions.

In response we say first that this course is an experiential learning course, meaning that the interactive exercises focus on developing skills and attitudes that will carry into the future. For instance, one of our MBA students of 20 years ago, who is now among the top executives at a global corporation, told us recently, "If students learn nothing more than how to cope with 'groupthink,' they will be far ahead." He went on to say that he frequently makes a "groupthink assessment" before bringing executive team decisions to a final conclusion.

Another of our past participants, now with one of the big accounting houses, commented, "The dialoguing sequence model we used in class is a basic requirement for working with clients. If you do not know how a client perceives your role or how he is perceiving what you are attempting, serious misunderstandings can complicate the progress of your activities. You must complete this dialoguing process at the beginning of the relationship and revisit it at appropriate times."

An experiential course in organizational behavior should focus directly on you and the interactions of your behavior with that of others. At the more personal level, you will want to know what you can learn that will help you become more effective in achieving your goals as you confront that exciting, nevertheless scary, world of accelerating change—a topic that is useful to think about for a minute.

We live at a time when global warming and global turbulence, related to climate variability, bulging populations, and technological growth, are coinciding with industrial globalization. The media are constantly forecasting the period of the millennium to be one of incredible technological change that will reshape, re-form, and reengineer corporations. As globalization occurs, the interaction of the financial markets make regional areas more interdependent and, of course, more vulnerable to problems of ailing areas, such as the depression in East Asia during the 1990s.

This environment means you are looking forward to a career pathway wending its way through a number of organizations, most of which are continually reshaping themselves on a dynamic basis. You can see evidence of this trend in the high-tech industries in which many new companies merge with or are taken over by others, or disappear, in a very short time. Those investing in the stock market of the late 1990s found that the areas for future growth and financial gains were in the high-tech fields; however, investors also found a high price variability and companies ravishing one another as creativity produced market changes and opportunities.

Returning to the focus of what you may learn that will help you cope with change, we will discuss what we believe to be some primary areas of concern. We realize that you are already familiar with many aspects of these areas; however, learning better-defined concepts and developing related behavioral skills is something many executives find sufficiently meaningful to study at university graduate programs. Behavioral skills and understandings require continuous renewal and awareness.

Let us start with a viewpoint, or a way to think about organizations. When you enter the world of Exxon or the world of General Electric or of Disney, you are entering a community that by design and evolution meets the primary purposes of the corporation and the people involved. The community is set upon a blueprint, a hardwired substructure of interrelated roles that assure the desired outputs of the corporation. The manner in which each organizational community has evolved and emerged is unique and distinct, and the character of the total complex of interactions is referred to as a *culture*. (Sometimes we hear that two recently merged corporations had such a culture clash that they had to break up again.)

Because a corporation is a community, rather than just an organization of people carrying out their functional roles, managers wear many hats. In a sense they may be mayors concerned for the welfare and needs of the workers and charged with supporting the value system of "what this company stands for." Or managers may be seen as educators attending to the learning needs and professional and skills development of employees. Or as coaches or as mentors.

So when you report to the world of Exxon or Corporation X, you have an obligation to yourself and your company to learn the culture—that is, the behavioral expectations, the value systems, and the role relationships.

Once underway in this venture, probably the most useful analytical concept is perception: people perceive the world differently, depending in part on where they are standing on the landscape. The Exxons and the General Electrics may perceive the world very differently—obviously because of their dissimilar products, markets, and so on, but you will also find many other factors at play. And within each organization people in different departments, for example, sales, engineering, marketing, production, will perceive the same topic of discussion very differently. And carrying this right down to interpersonal dialoguing, two people often perceive the same activities differently. Now this does not sound profound. What is profound is that every day in every way, these differences in perception cause breakdowns, misunderstandings, inefficiencies, and ineffectiveness; and the parties involved do not realize that they are not perceiving the topic of discussion in the same way. Perceptual differences can be incredible barriers to communication. Corporations often have professionals who accelerate relationships or overcome conflicts between departments and groups by first working out differences in perceptions between the parties. Participants in this course have indicated that the interpersonal dialoguing exercises and units are among the most rewarding learning areas—which brings us the subject of communication.

Surveys have consistently shown that when managers are asked what additional areas of education and training universities should provide to prepare students better for employment in their organization, the most frequent reply is that greater communication and team skills are needed. In this course, having recognized perceptual differences as a major deterrent to organizational and interpersonal effectiveness, we focus on communication as a means through which barriers can be avoided and overcome. *Communications* means not only the transmission of hard data needed to perform tasks but the softer-ware of viewpoints, attitudes, emotions, and feelings. The greater your awareness of how communication can occur effectively in the organization, between groups, within groups, and in interpersonal interactions, the more able you will be. For instance, if you carry away from this course nothing more than the skills and understanding of the value of interpersonal dialoguing, you will find lifelong application for your learning, not only in your work but also in your personal life.

You will learn that perception and communication are basic, interrelated aspects of behavior in organizations, but even more basic is the third concept that holds them together: motivation. Much of what is perceived depends on the underlying motivation of the parties involved; for example, their goals, or what they want to achieve, will largely determine how they perceive the activity about which they are communicating. The human organization of a corporation can be regarded as a reservoir of energy arising from what people bring to work, their motivational needs, and what the work situation, in addition, creates and shapes. Understanding the motivation to work, and how technology such as work-design systems can shape it, is important. Equally important to understand is the concept of frustration. Managerial practices or work systems that set up barriers to achieving goals or that do not permit needed innovation can have dire consequences such as inefficiencies and antiorganizational activities. Knowing what "turns people off" is as important as knowing what "turns people on."

Moving down from the total organization to work groups, the area of team skills presents one of the best arenas for individual learning. If you improve your understanding of how you function in a team, learn how others in your team perceive your skills, and find roles with which you are most comfortable in groups, the results will be impressive. For instance, understanding that people play many informal roles in groups and that it is important to be able to play a number of these yourself. If you are not the group leader and desire to facilitate progress, you may move the group forward by performing roles such as "definer of goals," "summarizer," or "clarifier," and others.

In addition, becoming sensitive to small group dynamics is an asset. Knowing that whenever two or more people come together to perform a task, the web of group dynamics begins to spin. Knowing that shared expectations, or norms, roles, and sub-structuring into dyads and triads spontaneously occur not only provides you with the advantage of understanding what is going on but also presents an opportunity to influence or shape the development of that group.

Finally, we see as the most important area of learning for you as you wind your way through one or many careers in this kaleidoscopic period of change to be that of personal growth. Every professional needs not only improved, updated skills to stay current but also—and above everything else—the attitudes and viewpoints to cope with change. Most basic of these is, If I don't achieve what I want, it is my own fault. With this attitude goes the practice of setting goals, of coping with barriers, of regrouping and cutting losses when failure occurs, and of moving on to the redefined goals. Wasting energy on or blaming others or the system does not move one on to new challenges. Taking responsibility for your own career—directing your energy into renewed plans—is the most basic personal learning.

The preceding concepts are selected from the following three areas of emphasis in this course:

- The body of knowledge, theory, concepts, and research of organizational behavior.
- Behavioral skills development.
- Organizational behavior (OB) technology, or the means by which managers and behavioral specialists can design and change organizations and work systems to achieve human effectiveness.

Obviously, all the areas of learning described in this introduction are overwhelming for one humble course. But this is what the course is about. You can take away a good deal or maybe just one idea or a different analytical road map to explore the nature of behavior dynamics in the workplace. Your personal choice of how much you invest in the course will have a direct effect on what you'll take from this learning opportunity.

The Systems Approach to Organizational Behavior

The Experience of Work

The work experiences described by participants in Activity 1–1 illustrate numerous topics to be discussed in this book. They include behavior of bosses, relationships with fellow workers, what makes people want to and not want to perform well, and communication problems. We can organize these subjects into a conceptual framework that will make organizational behavior easier to study in a systematic way by using the idea of effectiveness. **Effectiveness** as we will use it means the ability to achieve goals. Organizations and all groupings of people within them perform tasks to achieve goals. Organizational behavior provides guidelines for defining goals and methods for augmenting the process of attaining them. To organize the learning process, we use a systems approach to understanding, predicting, and managing people in organizations. Later we devote a complete module to the development of the systems analytical view of work and organizations. For this stage we define a **system** as an arrangement of interrelated parts.

Initial Framework

As an initial framework we use the systems approach to study the collection of people making up an organization. The total unit is a system and the interacting groupings and individuals within are subsystems. We can create a systems approach to effectiveness as follows:

1. *Total organizational effectiveness.* This includes a definition of the overall purposes and goals of the organization. Thus business organizations must continuously determine whether they are in the right business to avoid becoming obsolete in a changing environment. Smalltown newspapers, for example, recently finding they could not survive solely as a press, have redefined their role to be that of distributor of advertising brochures. Management practices to divide up the responsibilities of all subunits may include managing by output. Practices that focus on continuous improvements and the improvement of service and product quality—Total Quality Management—are discussed in terms of total system effectiveness. Integrating people of diverse professions, skills, and cultural backgrounds into a harmoniously operating company may require leadership skills similar to those of a symphony conductor. Climate building provides a supportive environment for workers. Designing procedures for use of technology as well as providing education and training, particularly for managers, are other examples.

2. *Intergroup effectiveness.* Groups coordinating their processes to achieve company objectives must have well-developed methods of communication. Procedures for conflict prevention and resolution need to be understood and practiced by interacting subsystems.

3. *Team effectiveness.* Small group skills related to teamwork design, goal setting, problem solving and creativity, communication, decision making, and conflict resolution must be used. Self-managed teams, virtual teams, and cross-functional teams are currently emerging as a specific organized form of teams. Regardless of the specific team form, team skills require education and practice by both leaders and teams.

4. *Individual effectiveness.* Models of leadership styles appropriate for a specific organization are an important ingredient of managerial education and practice. The ability to perform well is the obvious focus for individual employees. But to go beyond that we must be concerned with the personal growth and development of all personnel. Skills in goal setting and interpersonal communication as well as attitudes toward failure and success are of prime relevance for the individual who must ever face a turbulent work world that is always undergoing restructuring. Motivation to work is the driving force around which all other aspects of individual effectiveness can be viewed.

Understanding behavior in organizations can start with the total system and delve down into the subsystems or with the individual and work out into groups, on up to the whole. The specific order of the learning journey can vary from individual to individual and from situation to situation.

Rationality in Managing

In attempting to define our area of study, a special comment should be made about rationality. Typically, managers look at employee behavior from the viewpoint of how people ought to behave. People should make sense, they should do what they are supposed to do, and they should do what is good for the organization. After all, the basic definition of an organization is a rational model: people gathered together to achieve a purpose. Only logic, rationality, and objectivity—what makes common sense—can achieve that purpose. Specialty areas of business management, such as finance, engineering, marketing, accounting, and law, are based on rational, logical models. Thus, **rationality** is a process that is based on logic and reason. When executives and managers participate in workshops and when students come to courses in organizational behavior, someone almost always makes the comment that understanding behavior is just a matter of common sense.

If rationality were our only concern in this field, there would be no reason to study behavior. Managers would simply plan, organize, direct, and control. But as shown in Figure 1–1, rationality is just the tip of the iceberg. Below the water line are forces that are potent generators of behavior: emotions, feelings, needs, stress reactions, impulsiveness, energy, creativity, conformity forces, loyalties, and groupthink, just to mention a few. Are we saying that managers do not know what is below that water

**Figure 1–1
Rational Behavior Is Only
the Tip of the Iceberg**

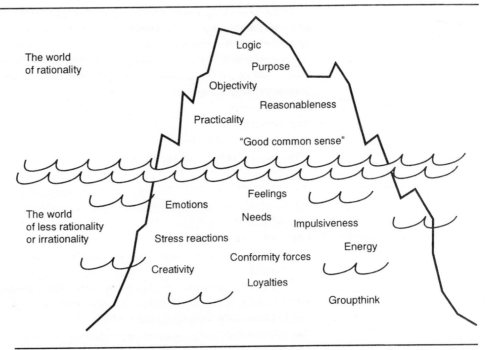

The study of organizational behavior focuses heavily on the less rational aspects of human action and interactions to understand why people do not always behave according to the rational model of organizations.

level? Not at all. The problem is that managers are so involved in the rational model they often fail to take into account, or understand, the less rational forces. They are so involved with tasks, purposes, goals, deadlines, and balance sheets that they can become blinded to the realities below the surface until some eruption occurs.

An outstanding example is the *Challenger* space shuttle disaster. The blue-ribbon commission investigating the explosion came to this conclusion: "If the decision makers had known all of the facts, it is highly unlikely they would have decided to launch." Thus management broke one of the oldest rules in the management book. Why? Many newspaper articles at the time reported that the entire management staff had become mesmerized by past successes. Information and dissent did not flow up the ladder to give input to the final decision makers. The objections to the launch by engineers who were aware of the shuttle's weaknesses were overruled and top management did not get the message. When we study groupthink later in the course, we will have more to say about this subject, but for now our point is that the so-called mesmerizing factor does not belong to the world of rationality; it is below the water line in Figure 1–1.

Unions would probably not arise if managers were more fully aware and responsive to the behaviors at the bottom of the iceberg. Astronauts experienced a disastrous shock to their trust in their organization when they learned that management had not informed them of the long-standing problem with the O-rings in the shuttle's boosters, which turned out to be a factor in the blowup of the *Challenger.* When this information was disclosed, the astronauts' representative made a number of protest speeches on their behalf.

It is fascinating to watch students in these courses switch perceptions from employee to management viewpoints and in the process completely forget or ignore what is below the water line. When students are engaged in task 1 from Activity 1–1 on defining human relations in business, more than 90 percent of their examples are negative experiences that illustrate how little concern managers have for the factors below the water line. Yet by the time they assume the role of managers taking remedial action at a later stage in the course, they most always design solutions that take only the rational factors into consideration; they assume workers should respond rationally to management direction.

Our hope, an improbable one, is that managers will develop viewpoints that (1) maximize the human assets of employees for purposes of economic gain and (2) humanistically focus on quality. This presumes a more integrated awareness of the rational and irrational forces. In turn, we hope that employees develop more trust and understanding of the rational model, which is essential to help our industries become productive and competitive.

Organizational Behavior: Historical Evolution

Although discussions about management, administration, organization, and organizing can be traced to ancient Greek, Egyptian, and biblical times, the study of management and organizational behavior as a distinct and separate field has largely been confined to the beginning of the 20th century. Today's theories are an integral part of the logical and natural evolution in management thought and practice. The systematic theorizing of the field has been clustered in many ways. For our purpose we follow the sociology of knowledge perspective that proposed four clusters: prescientific (pre-1880s), classical (1880s–1930s), neoclassical (1930s–1960s), and modern (1960s–present).[1] Figure 1–2 captures the essence of each era.

The Prescientific Era (pre-1880s)

The **prescientific era** is characterized by little systematic theorizing about management and organizations. Yet we find Jethro's advice to Moses to delegate authority over the tribes of Israel along hierarchical lines around 1491 B.C. Sun Tzu's *The Art of War* (written in 500 B.C.) recognizes the need for hierarchical organizations, interorganizational communications, and staff planning. Socrates' work, around 44 B.C., argues for the universality of management as an art unto itself. Aristotle, around 360 B.C., asserts that the nature and power of executive functions must reflect a specific cultural environment. Xenophon, around 370 B.C., records and describes the Greek shoe factory focus on the advantages of the division of labor. Machiavelli's *The Discourses* (1513) and *The Prince* (1532) focus on both the principles of unity of command and how to succeed as a leader. Adam Smith's *The Wealth of Nations* (1776) describes the optimal organization of a pin factory and focuses on the economic rationale for the division of labor and the factory system.[2] The ruling class in the preindustrial societies perceived work, trade, and commerce as being beneath its dignity, something to be accomplished by slaves and "low level" classes.[3] The sources of authority were based on long-standing institutions and procedures that citizens of these societies perceived as legitimate. Most individuals obeyed the ruling elite in accordance with traditional customs.[4]

The Classical Era (1880s–1930s)

The **classical era** of management thought evolved between the end of the 19th century and into the beginning of the 20th. The transition from agrarian to industrial society coupled with the changing economic, social, and technological environment established the condition to begin the systematic study of management and organizations. The focus of the early studies centered on the search for alternative ways to organize and structure the industrial organization; the way to organize, delegate, and coordinate work; and the ways to motivate people who work within the emerging organizational structures. Three dominant schools can be identified in this era:

The **scientific management school** led by Frederick Taylor focused on the measurement of work. It followed four basic principles of organization and management with the aim of creating the most effective way to carry out work tasks. The four basic principles included finding the one best way to do each job, the scientific selection of individuals for the position, the development of financial incentives to ensure that the work is carried out as required, and the establishment of functional foremanship.[5]

Figure 1–2　　　　　　　**Historical Evolution of Management Thought: A Brief Road Map**

	Period			
	Prescientific pre-1880s	Classical 1880–1930s	Neoclassical 1930–1960s	Modern 1960–present
Emerging schools of thought		• Scientific management • Administrative school • Structuralist school	• Human relations school • Behavior schools: 　- Group dynamics 　- Leadership 　- Decision making	• Systems school • Sociotechnical system school • Management science school • Contingency school
Focus/emphasis	• Basic principles for nature and society • The position of authority and order in society • Economic rationale • Division of labor (early development)	• Basic principles of organizing and managing the most effective firm • The basic functions of managers • Characteristics of "the ideal type of an organization"	• Organizations are cooperative systems • Informal roles and norms influence individual performance • Work group dynamics influence individual and group performance • Leadership styles affect individual and group behavior • Decision-making styles influence performance	• Organization is a system composed of subsystems • Organization as an open system composed of social, technological, and environmental subsystems • Use of quantitative methods to solve organization and managing issues • Exploration of alternative organization design configurations and managerial actions for changing situations
Representative scholars	• Jethro (Moses' father-in-law) • Sun Tzu • Socrates, Aristotle • Xenophon • Machiavelli • Adam Smith	• Taylor • Fayol • Gulick • Weber	• Berbard • Roethlisberger • Lewin • McGregor • Maslow	• Bertalanffy • Katz and Kahn • Emery and Trist • Thompson • Lorsch and Lawrence • Galbraith

The **administrative school** led by Henry Fayol focused on the functions of management. Five basic functions of management were identified: planning, organizing, commanding, coordinating, and controlling.[6]

The **structuralist school** led by Max Weber focused on the basic tenets of the ideal type of organization, the bureaucratic model, as the most effective way to organize and manage organizations. The model emphasized order via a system of rules and procedures, rational-legal authority, division of labor based on functional specialization, a well-defined hierarchy, differentiation between organizational functions, rationality, uniformity, and administrative consistency.

The Neoclassical Era (1930s–1960s)

The **neoclassical era** is characterized by direct challenges to the classical schools, their assumptions, and their implications. The neoclassical theories focused on the dimension of human interaction, which the classical schools neglected. During this era behavioral science theories were introduced and integrated with management thought. The theories are anchored in two major sources: (1) social psychologists and sociologists who focused on human interactions and human relations within groups (the human relations or the group dynamics schools) and (2) psychologists who focused on individual behavior in different settings (the behavioral science school).

The **human relations school** argued that organizations are cooperative systems and not the product of mechanical engineering.[7] The first large-scale empirical studies that focused on the relations between productivity and social interaction were conducted at the Hawthorne plant of the Western Electric Company. They illustrated the importance of workers' attitudes and feelings and argued that informal roles and norms influence individual performance.[8]

The **behavioral science schools** include three clusters of theories that were an outgrowth of the human relations school and focused on individual behavior within work groups:

Group dynamics focused on the effect of work group dynamics on individual and group performance.

Leadership stressed the importance of groups having both task and social leaders, differentiated between Theory X and Theory Y management, and identified different theories of leadership and leadership styles.

Decision making focused on the degree of individual involvement in decision making and its influence on performance. The contributions of these schools to our understanding of human behavior is discussed in depth in the appropriate modules throughout this book.

The Modern Era (1960s–Present)

The **modern era**—or what some call contemporary management and organization era—is characterized by an increased emphasis on integration of some key elements of the classical and neoclassical eras. The underlying assumption is that organizations are systems composed of interrelated and interdependent components that function within an environmental context. Throughout this course we explore in depth many key elements of the modern era schools of thoughts. Four clusters of schools can be delineated: systems, sociotechnical systems, management science, and contingency.

The **systems school** is anchored in general systems theory. The organization is viewed as a system composed of subsystems or subunits that are mutually dependent on one another and that continuously interact. General systems theory concepts such as holism, equifinality, equilibrium, input, transformation, output, and feedback provide the foundation for this school of thought (to be discussed in a later module).[9]

The **sociotechnical systems school** at the most basic level believes that every organization is made up of a social subsystem (the people) using tools, techniques, and knowledge (the technical subsystem) to produce a product or a service valued by the environmental subsystem. This school further argues that the degree to which the technical subsystem and the social subsystem are designed with respect to each other and the environmental subsystem determines how successful and competitive the organization will be.[10]

The orientation of the **management science school** and operational research school is to apply quantitative techniques, methods, and technologies to organization and management issues. The emphasis of this problem-solving approach is relatively narrow; it centers on merging strategic concern for planning and forecasting with the administrative concern for organizational objectives and goal accomplishment. Recently, the field of management science expanded its focus to include advanced technologies such as computer-integrated manufacturing, flexible manufacturing systems, and new manufacturing and integrated orientations such as just-in-time, total quality management, and reengineering.[11]

The **contingency school** seeks (1) to understand the relationships within and among subsystems as well as between the organization and its environment and (2) to define patterns of relationships or configurations of variables. The essence of this orientation is that there is "no one best way" and that there is a middle ground between "universal principles" and "it all depends." Furthermore, the emphasis is on the degree of fit between organizational processes and characteristics of the situation. Contingency views are ultimately directed toward suggesting organizational designs and managerial actions most appropriate for specific situations.[12]

Organizational Behavior: A Working Definition

Organizational behavior, to define it most broadly, is the utilization of theory and methods of multiple academic disciplines (such as anthropology, biology, economics, political science, psychology, social psychology, and psychology) for understanding and influencing the behavior of people in organizations. Definitions of organizational behavior vary widely because the field has evolved with parallel developments in the social sciences, the behavioral sciences, and management and human relations courses in schools of business. One large frame of reference focuses on the differences between organizations without people and people without organizations. The former, the realm of organizational sociology, relates to organizations as systems interacting with their environment; the latter, the realm of psychology, relates to human relations in work situations. More recent approaches have emphasized the need for integrating these two realms to account for the great variability among people, tasks, and environment. Another point of focus is the macro–micro perspective. The *macro view* emphasizes the big picture, such as the entire organization and its relationships to the environment. The *micro view* considers smaller units, such as the individual, work groups, or work systems. This text works with the micro initially and moves on to the macro as the course progresses.

Objectives of the Course

Our aims for the course are high. To the extent possible in a one-quarter or one-semester experience, we'd like you to achieve the following:

- Knowledge of behavioral science theory and concepts useful in organizations, with special emphasis on small group theory.
- Knowledge of methods and techniques that are helpful in developing effectiveness in individuals, teams, and organizations.
- Appreciation of diversity; its dynamics; and its impact on individual, team, and organizational effectiveness.
- Understanding of how perceptual distortion affects communication, motivation, and human dynamics in organizations.
- Understanding of the potential cause-and-effect relationships among motivation; perception; communication; and the management processes of work design, team design, organizational culture, and effectiveness.
- Ability to effectively use team skills, such as group problem solving and decision making.
- Ability to analyze diverse management situations and your own experience while utilizing course concepts.
- Improved skills in personal goal setting and interpersonal communications.
- Better awareness of your own behavior in different work settings.
- Understanding of the process of change and the management of change in organizations.

Our overall intent is to emphasize skills development, understanding, and knowledge that you can use.

Summary

We started our textbook with the focus on the individual in the workplace. We have introduced the course by examining your own experience with human behavior in organizations. We have suggested that the diversity of people's experiences in organizations typically includes many problems that affect individual, group, and organizational performance and the sense of satisfaction or dissatisfaction felt. Both task and human dimensions are important for understanding organizational effectiveness. Such topics as fair treatment, good supervision, effective communication, and motivation are closely interwoven. This situation implies that an effective theoretical framework must deal with both task and human dimensions of effectiveness and must include all four levels of behavior: individual, group, intergroup, and organizational. This approach is known as the systems approach to organizational behavior, which will serve as an overall framework for the learning process of this book. Objectives of the course are drawn from this theoretical approach but emphasize improving effectiveness in real organizations, not just academic knowledge. In addition, we stressed that our studies will include the "irrational" as well as the rational factors in behavior (see Figure 1–1), the latter being the perceptual window through which management typically views employee conduct.

Organizational behavior is an interdisciplinary field of study. While the study of organizational behavior is relatively young, issues of human behavior in the context of work, organization, and management can be traced to ancient Greek, Egyptian, and biblical thought. We have provided a brief review of the historical evolution of management thought. Following the sociology of knowledge perspective, we identified four clusters of thoughts: the prescientific, classical, neoclassical, and modern eras. In each era we briefly discussed the major schools of organization and management thought with their focus and emphases.

Because our approach to learning stresses involvement, the first activity helped integrate your experience with organizational behavior ideas. Your experience, perceptions, and reactions will continue to be a key part of this course. In Activity 1–1 we saw that individuals' experiences offer important data that we can draw upon to increase our understanding. We saw that many common experiences and perceptions were widely shared among participants and that, even so, effective communication can be difficult. The communication skills of listening, paraphrasing, and sharing were explicitly related to participants' attitudes and responses to one another. We saw that differences can be either useful or troublesome, depending on how they are handled. Finally, we began the process of applying organizational behavior knowledge directly to your own experience. We will build on these experiences throughout the course. Activity 1–2 that follows provides another opportunity to illustrate how individual experiences can be used as an important database for understanding and discovery. This activity begins the systematic exploration of human diversity and the implications of diversity in the context of organizational behavior.

Key Terms and Concepts

Behavioral science school

Classical era

Contingency school

Effectiveness

Human relations school

Management

Management science school

Modern era

Neoclassical era

Organizational behavior

Prescientific era

Rationality

Scientific management school

Sociotechnical systems school

Structuralist school

System

Systems school

Study Questions

1. What are the three areas of emphasis in this course?

2. What is a "learning community"? In what way did Activity 1–1 ("Defining Organizational Behavior") contribute to the development of the classroom learning community?

3. What is the "systems approach" to studying organizational behavior?

4. Why do we emphasize "irrational" as well as rational aspects of behavior?

5. Review the historical evolution of organizational behavior. Select any two schools of thought that you feel influenced our understanding of individual behavior the most. Provide the reasoning for your choice.

6. Review the goals of the course. Select the two that you feel have the greatest potential for improving your learning at this time. Name the two and give the reasons.

Endnotes

1. Many scholars examined the evolution of management thought in the context of the evolution of the society. Among them we find R. Miles, *Theories of Management,* (New York: McGraw-Hill, 1975); D. A. Nadler and M. L. Tushman, *Competing by Design,* (New York: Oxford University Press, 1997); T. Parsons and N. Smelser, *Economy & Society,* (London: Routledge & Kegan, 1956); C. Perrow, "The Short & Glorious History of Organizational Theory," *Organizational Dynamics* (Summer 1973), pp. 2–15; M. Weber, *The Theory of Social & Economic Organization,* (New York: Free Press, 1947); D. Wern, *The Evolution of Management Thought,* (New York: Wiley, 1979).

2. A nice summary of the chronology of organization theory is found in J. M. Shafritz and J. S. Ott, *Classics of Organization Theory,* (Chicago: Dorsey, 1987).

3. See, for example, Parsons and Smelser, *Economy & Society.*

4. See, for example, J. Bowditch and A. Buono, *A Primer on Organizational Behavior,* (New York: Wiley, 1998).

5. F. Taylor, *The Principles of Scientific Management,* (New York: Harper & Brothers, 1911).

6. H. Fayol, *General and Industrial Management,* (London: Pitman, 1916).

7. C. I. Barnard, *The Function of the Executive,* (Cambridge, MA: Harvard Press, 1938).

8. F. J. Roethlisberger and W. Dickson, *Management and the Worker,* (Cambridge, MA: Harvard Press, 1938).

9. L. Bertalanffy, *General Systems Theory: Foundations, Development, and Applications,* (New York: Braziller, 1967).

10. For a full description of the sociotechnical systems school of thought, see F. E. Emery, *Some Characteristics of Sociotechnical Systems,* (London: Tavistock, 1959); W. A. Pasmore, *Designing Effective Organizations: Sociotechnical System Perspective,* (New York: Wiley, 1988); J. C. Taylor and D. F. Felton, *Performance by Design: Sociotechnical Systems in North America,* (Reading, MA: Addison-Wesley, 1994); A. Majchrzak, "What to Do When You Can't Have It All: Toward a Theory of Sociotechnical Dependencies," *Human Relations* 50, no. 5 (1997), pp. 535–65; E. L. Trist, "Sociotechnical System Perspective," in A. H. Van de Ven and W. F. Joyce (eds.), *Perspectives on Organization Design & Behavior,* (New York: Wiley, 1982), pp. 19–75.

11. See, for example, C. W. Churchman, R. L. Ackoff, and E. L. Arnoff, *Introduction to Operations Research* (New York: Wiley, 1961); N. Slack, *The Manufacturing Advantage,* (Oxfordshire, England: Management Books 2000 Ltd., 1998).

12. See, for example, J. R. Galbraith, *Designing Organizations,* (San Francisco: Jossey-Bass, 1995); D. A. Nadler and M. L. Tushman,   (New York: Oxford University Press, 1997).

Objectives:

Activity 1–2:
Initial Exploration
of Diversity

a. To identify individual differences.

b. To introduce the range and basic sources of diversity.

c. To explore issues associated with the management of diversity.

Task 1:

We all feel that in some way we are different from others. The worksheet for Activity 1–2 asks you to explore the differences. Use the worksheet to take notes. (Time: 5 minutes for individuals to think about their experience and jot down notes)

Task 2:

Each participant shares these thoughts with a small group. After each has done so, discuss what common elements seem to emerge. Have a spokesperson make a list.

Task 3:

The spokesperson reports findings to the class.

Name _____ Date _____

Worksheet for Activity 1–2

1. Drawing from your cumulative experiences, identify and describe one important way in which you feel different from most of the people in your office, on your team, in this class, in your family, or among your friends.

laid bAck

I like to lAugh
(HAppy-Go-Lucky)

For the most part, I feel comfortable speaking in front of A group

2. How do you feel about this difference?

3. What might be the source or sources of the difference?

4. What are the positive and negative consequences of this difference?

5. What are the managerial implications for managing the difference?

2

Learning, Expectations, and Appreciative Inquiry

Learning Objectives

After completing this module, you should be able to

1. Explain the importance of managing expectations, dialoguing, and appreciative inquiry.
2. Describe the role of expectations, expectations discrepancies, and self-fulfilling prophecies in organizational settings.
3. Appreciate the process and the importance of developing a "psychological contract."
4. Explain the relationship between expectation, learning, experiential learning, appreciative inquiry, and self-learning competency.
5. Explain the basic assumptions about the adult as learner.
6. Appreciate the roles of the participant and the instructor in an experiential learning–based course.

Module Outline

Premodule Preparation
    Activity 2–1: Organizational Dialoguing about Teams, Learning, and Expectations
Introduction
    Diversity and Expectations
    The Psychological Contract
Expectations and Self-Fulfilling Prophecy
    Expectations Discrepancies
Expectations and Individual, Team, and Organizational Learning
    Learning
    Self-Learning Competency
The Adult Learner, Experiential Learning, and Appreciative Inquiry
    Experiential Learning Process
    Rationale for Learning by Involvement

Premodule Preparation

Activity 2–1:
Organizational
Dialoguing about
Teams, Learning,
and Expectations

Objectives:

a. To help you understand the learning goals and methods of the course, the instructor's viewpoints about the course, and other participants' learning needs and attitudes in several areas.

b. To help the instructor understand your viewpoints, attitudes, and needs.

c. To build the classroom learning climate by involvement learning and dialoguing.

Task 1:

Individuals, while reflecting on their learning goals and this specific course, should write a few notes in response to the following five questions:

a. What things would you like to learn, study, or have emphasized in this course on human behavior in organizations?

b. What doubts or concerns do you have about this course? What are some things you would not like to study or have happen in the course?

c. What are your viewpoints toward college life, college education, or your major course of study that might influence your attitudes toward this course?

d. What was your best group learning experience? What was great about it?

e. What was your worst group learning experience? What made it that way?

In general, these questions are to bring out any factors that may account for your expectations, hopes, or doubts for the course. These may be directly related to the subject of study, but they may also be related to the life you are experiencing on campus or in the larger environment. Feel free to express any views. Your representative does not have to identify who said what. (Time: 15 to 20 minutes)

Task 2 (To Be Completed in Class):

Participants will form work groups of five to seven members (no larger). Individuals are to share their responses to the five questions in task 1. Each group will elect a representative and keep notes of the discussion. Each group is to prepare its answer to the five questions. (Time: 15 to 20 minutes)

Task 3:

Representatives from the groups will meet in a fishbowl circle in the center of the room to report and discuss their groups' viewpoints. The instructor will raise issues for clarity and understanding after they have completed their discussion, but will not respond at this point. (Time: 10 to 15 minutes)

Task 4:

Work groups will choose a second representative for this task. Groups will prepare a list of questions you would like to have the instructor answer to help you understand his or her expectations and attitudes about the course (such as learning approach, education, background, satisfactions or frustrations gained from teaching, or what the instructor hopes to see participants gain from the course). Any questions that will help you get to know the instructor or understand the course and how it is to be conducted are appropriate. The instructor's expectations of students should be probed here. Try to prepare confrontational questions such as those a good television interviewer would use. (Time: 10 minutes)

Task 5:

Put the instructor on the hot seat. Representatives will meet in a circle with the instructor. Each poses one question at a time until all have been answered. (Time: 15 to 20 minutes)

Introduction

The increasing diversity of the workplace brings to the forefront one of the basic and most persistent problems of organizational life. Individuals see situations, issues, or goals differently, depending on their particular perspectives, experiences, educational and cultural backgrounds, personality traits, competencies and skills, and biases—yet everyone typically assumes that everyone else sees things as they do. We fail to take into account that what seems "obvious" and "common sense" to us may appear bizarre and inexplicable to others. Or lacking some key piece of information to interpret the situation, someone may come to a resoundingly different conclusion about data that others agree upon. Neither the problem nor its recognition is new. One classic study in 1966 showed relatively low agreement between bosses and subordinates on what subordinates' job duties were and very low agreement on what obstacles were faced in accomplishing these duties.[1] In another study, carried out over 30 years ago, 80 percent of supervisors said they "very often" praised good performance, but only 14 percent of their employees agreed.[2] Similar results are found widely both in formal research and in studies of contemporary organizations by consultants.

Diversity and Expectations

The difficulties described above seem typical of human interactions and interpersonal relations at work, at school, in social settings, and even in the family. Yet we seldom discuss the assumptions and beliefs on which we base our behavior, so it's often difficult to identify the causes of the failures, let alone to deal effectively with them. But whether they're discussed or ignored, underlying assumptions and beliefs have a powerful effect on our behavior. Two people with contradictory expectations of one another are probably doomed to ongoing conflict. Such conflict can result in low productivity, alienation, absenteeism, dissatisfaction with work in the organization, or even divorce in marriage.

As the workforce becomes more diverse, are there some things that have to be done differently to more fully utilize human potential? We think yes. Are we trapped in our own assumptions and beliefs, forever separated from others? We think not. Methods exist to improve understanding and communication within a diverse workforce by creating shared assumptions, thus enabling common interpretations. **Communication dialoguing** and **appreciative inquiry** are two ways to overcome diversity and contradictory expectations by bringing similarities and differences in perspective out into the open. They can then be discussed, modified by other data or new interpretations, and shared. The premodule activity uses a form of dialoguing to develop an effective learning climate in the classroom. Figure 2–1 diagrams this dialoguing process as it might exist between a boss and employees or between a professor and students. Somewhat different methods might be used in business, but the shared exchange of perspectives and expectations would be visible there as well. For instance, an employee might explicitly inquire about the boss's expectations for a project or report, about the extent of his or her discretion, or the flexibility possible in time schedules. Such exchange is the foundation for understanding, trust, and, thus, effective working relations. Successful managers and employees use this exchange frequently.

The Psychological Contract

The premodule Activity 2–4W initiates a set of understandings between you and the instructor on (1) the educational program for this course and (2) the conduct and attitudes of those who will take part in it. In a sense it is a **psychological contract** we hope to follow. Activity 2–4W ("Personal Learning Statement") that can be found on the WWW will make the learning contract more explicit. Edgar Schein applies this idea to an agreement between the individual and an organization when he says:

The notion of a psychological contract implies that the individuals have a variety of expectations of the organization and that the organization has a variety of expectations of them. These expectations not only cover how much work is to be performed for how much pay, but also involve the whole pattern of rights, privileges, and obligations between worker and organization.[3]

Figure 2–1
Dialoguing to Overcome
Differences in Expectations
in Business or the
Classroom

In Business

- My expectations of what subordinates should, ought, and must do.
- My managerial philosophy.
- What I hope subordinates will get from the workplace.
- What I want from the workplace.

- Our expectations of what bosses and organizations should, ought, and must do.
- Our attitudes towards work, the workplace, bosses, and peers.
- Our goals—what we want out of our work, jobs, and the organization.

In the Classroom

- My expectations of what students should, ought, and must do.
- My educational philosophy.
- What I hope students will get out of this course.
- What I want from the course.

- Our expectations of what instructors should, ought, and must do.
- Our attitudes towards education, professors, and college life.
- What we want out of college.

The clearer these expectations are to both sides, the more coordination and cooperation are possible. The psychological contract is a dynamic, living process in that it needs to be adjusted to trends and ongoing activities. The model in Activity 2–1 makes a continuous flow of communication between instructor and participants possible. This means that a value system that includes some degree of openness and trust must exist as part of the organizational culture. We might say that organizations need a fair conditioning system, meaning a continuous and open flow of communication in which fairness—fair treatment—is an essential ingredient. Activity 2–4W in this module was created both as a learning tool and as an experiential mechanism to help you develop a psychological contract between you and your instructor.

Expectations and Self-Fulfilling Prophecy

Expectations Discrepancies

Recent research indicates that many organizational problems can be traced to expectations discrepancies. Interpersonal dialoguing is seen as a managerial tool to bridge the discrepancy gap. Raising managerial expectations about employees' abilities and performances can improve performance and boost productivity. Hence productivity as a self-fulfilling prophecy presents a variety of unique possibilities for crafting desired behavior and outcomes in the workplace.

Based on the experience of working with several organizations, Livingston concluded that (1) what a manager expects of his subordinates and the way he treats them largely determine their performances and career progress, (2) a unique characteristic of superior managers is their ability to create high-performance expectations that subordinates fulfill, (3) less effective managers fail to develop similar expectations and, as a consequence, the productivity of their subordinates suffers, and (4) subordinates, more often than not, appear to do what they believe they are expected to do.[4]

The **self-fulfilling prophecy (Pygmalion)** has been attracting growing interest in the past decade. Self-fulfilling prophecy (SFP) is described as a three-stage process beginning with a person's belief that a certain event will occur. In the second stage this expectation or "prophecy" leads to some new behavior that the person would not have performed were it not for the expectation. In the third stage the expected event occurs and the prophecy is fulfilled.[5] The phenomenon of self-fulfilling prophecies has become widely recognized in the behavioral, social, educational, and organizational sciences. Recent empirical studies shed light on the multiple dimensions of the phenomenon and its important role in the context of work. For example, a set of studies carried out by Eden and his colleagues demonstrated empirically that high expectations resulted in improved performance, raised self-expectancy, increased overall satisfaction, and improved leadership, which in turn augmented subordinates' productivity. Furthermore, Eden envisions managers as prophets. He argues that managers as prophets expect certain things to happen and then act in ways to fulfill their expectations.[6] The relationship between expectancy and learning, leadership, group behavior, motivation, perception, and performance is addressed in the succeeding modules.

At this point we will continue to clarify expectations and to build the psychological contract by discussing our view about learning, the adult learner, learning competencies, team learning, organizational learning, the learning community, and appreciative inquiry. Your awareness of these is important not only for understanding the course but also for learning techniques and competencies that you can acquire and apply later when you are supervising people.

Expectations and Individual, Team, and Organizational Learning

Learning

The quality of individual and collective learning (team and organizational) is a key determinant of organizational success.[7] A recent set of studies argued that the ability to learn faster than the competitors may be the only sustainable competitive advantage.[8] Rapid and continuing changes of the workplace foster the preoccupation of most human beings with learning and the need to learn—just to survive. The expectations that individuals must be willing to learn are increasing. **Learning** is defined as the process whereby new skills, knowledge, ability, and attitudes are created through the transformation of experience.[9] At the most basic level, organizations expect individuals to learn productive work behaviors. Furthermore, individuals and organizations alike must learn to adapt to the new rules of the game and the ever changing and increasingly diverse global business environment. The major challenge that organizations face has to do with providing learning experiences in an environment that will promote employee behaviors desired by the organization.

Three levels of learning occur in organizations: individual, team, and organization. **Individual learning** refers to the change of skills, insights, knowledge, attitudes, and values acquired by a person through self-study, technology-based instruction, insight, and observation. Group or **team learning** alludes to the increase in knowledge, skills, and competencies that is accomplished by and within groups.[10] **Organization learning** refers to the principles, activities, processes, and structures that enable the organization to create, acquire, and transfer knowledge to continuously improve products, services, practices, processes, and financial results.[11] (The areas of team learning and organization learning receive focused attention later in the book.)

Self-Learning Competency

The most critical skill that an individual must acquire is **self-learning competency.** Self-learning competency enables people to learn actively in a variety of situations. This means, for example, that people have the skills to apply knowledge gained in one situation to other situations.

This competency makes people aware of, and open to, learning opportunities in their day to day experiences. A workforce possessing this competency sees learning as an everyday natural occurrence. This kind of workforce is able to exploit learning opportunities which arise "on the job," as well as make effective use of formal structured learning experiences, open learning and multimedia delivery systems.[12]

Self refers to the fact that the learner must take primary responsibility for his or her own learning and that learning is an inner activity. *Competency* is meant to focus on the development of independent self-learners as a goal of training as distinct from the narrower use of the term *self-learning,* which refers to "individualized delivery systems," often using computer-based packages. As we can see, self-learning is related to self-motivation, self-awareness, and self-control. It presupposes that the learners are interested in learning. Further, knowing oneself and having the ability for planning and a sense of commitment seem critical.

Skills that the adult learner must master to develop self-learning competency include the ability to engage in divergent thinking and the ability to be in touch with curiosities; the ability to perceive one's self objectively and accept feedback about one's performance nondefensively; the ability to diagnose one's learning needs in the light of models of competencies required for performing life roles; the ability to formulate learning objectives in terms that describe performance outcomes; the ability to identify human, material, and experiential resources for accomplishing various kinds of learning objectives; the ability to design a plan of strategies and carry out the plan systematically while utilizing the appropriate learning resources effectively; and the ability to collect evidence of the accomplishment of learning objectives and have it validated through performance.[13]

The Adult Learner, Experiential Learning, and Appreciative Inquiry

This book, and the learning that it attempts to foster, is based on a few assumptions about adults as learners:[14] (1) Adults have a need to be self-directed in establishing and implementing their learning goals. (2) Adults desire to integrate their past experiences with new learning. (3) Adults have a dominant and a preferred learning style. (4) Adults can modify their learning processes to suit changing needs and conditions. (5) Learning is a continuous lifelong process that is grounded in experience.

Experiential Learning Process

As can be seen from the preceding set of assumptions, the guiding approach to this book is **experiential learning.**[15] That is,

Learning, growth, and change are facilitated by an integrated process that begins with here-and-now experience followed by collection of data and observation about the experience. These observations are assimilated with previous knowledge into a "theory" from which new implications for actions can be deduced. These implications then serve as guides in acting to create new experiences.[16]

A few variations of experiential learning theories and models can be found in the literature. One school of thought argues that learning occurs not only through thinking and cognition but also through experience and affect or feeling.[17] Furthermore, two dimensions of learning were identified: for David Kolb the dimensions are *concrete to abstract* and *reflective observation to active experimentation,* and for Kenneth Murrell the dimensions are *abstract to concrete* and *affective to cognitive.* The two sets of dimensions create a matrix upon which one can plot his or her style via the response to a pencil-and-paper instrument. Activity 2–3 at the end of this module provides an opportunity to map your learning style, using Murrell's instrument and matrix. The other school of thought focuses on work-based learning.[18] The two dimensions advanced by Joseph Raelin are knowledge (from explicit to tacit) and learning (from theory to practice). These two dimensions create a somewhat different matrix. Despite their differences, all experiential learning schools of thought strongly advocate the importance of the learner's active involvement in the learning process.

Rationale for Learning by Involvement

So far the course has been developed almost entirely by interaction exercises. Involvement methods (developed widely in business and government workshops for training managers, supervisors, and executives) are designed for adult education. The basis for learning is not simply the instructor or a textbook. Instead, the course is built around using the participants' own experiences, both before and during the course. Participants are involved in sharing with one another what they have learned in the process of working with others. Exercises or experiences allow participants to apply the insights of theory in practice, to try alternative methods, and to experience first-hand the situations and issues they are studying. In essence, the participants use their own experiences as a laboratory for exploring how people behave in organizations. Team interactions examine different perspectives; solutions naturally arise out of diverse backgrounds and experiences. Even more important, teams provide a rich resource for participants to draw upon; team members learn from one another just as they learn from the instructor and text. This approach to learning is participant centered rather than instructor centered. The instructor's role is that of facilitator of learning as well as specialist or expert.

Most large companies—such as IBM, Ford, Intel, Digital Equipment, General Motors, AT&T, and General Electric—regularly use these workshop methods for management education and training. So do federal government agencies such as the IRS, National Park Service, Forest Service, CIA, and Office of Personnel Management. The methods are widely used by consultants and management institutes that specialize in education of executives and managers. We have used all of the activities in this book (or variants of them) with various levels of management in business and government as well as with undergraduate, MBA, and executive MBA students.

After completing Activity 2–1, participants often express their hopes that the course will provide them with understanding and skills that will be useful in the real world of work and, more important, in their personal and university life at present. The fact that managers and executives testify that they get practical, useful learning from workshops conducted within their corporations indicates that the involvement method is on target.

Involvement Learning Methods

Involvement-process learning, the central approach in this course, places primary emphasis on the process of interaction and thinking, rather than on rote memory of factual content of the area being studied. In contrast, **content learning** is learning based on knowledge, facts, and theory only, which serve as the database for analysis and reasoning. Application of ideas, experience in the subject, and attention to participants' responses are crucial in process learning. We chose this approach because we believe it is more effective for three reasons. First, content or subject matter is proliferating so rapidly that knowledge soon becomes outdated. Keeping current will be a lifelong process for any manager. Second, changes in attitudes and behavior (that is, real learning) come about by doing and understanding, not just by knowing intellectually. Third, the most effective learning is learning in which the student participates knowledgeably. Since the effective manager will have to continue to learn in a self-directed manner, learning how to learn from his or her own experience acquires a special importance. For each of these issues, involvement learning has proven superior to content-oriented approaches.

Your experience is important because ultimately *you* must apply and interpret whatever you learn. So we start here. There's no substitute for experience in this as in other matters. You cannot really understand what honey tastes like until you have tasted it, and you cannot comprehend group problem solving until you have been involved and seen it work. You may read a book on skiing or tennis that is very helpful, but you won't really develop skill in your sport until you've practiced it. The same thing could be said about sex—no amount of intellectualizing or theoretical knowledge will substitute for actual experience. So it is with the knowledge of people and interactions that are our subjects. Some differences between involvement learning and content learning are shown in Figure 2–2.

**Figure 2–2
Some Differences between
Types of Learning and
Methods Used in Process-
Involvement and Content
Courses**

Process-Involvement Learning	Content Learning
Ways of thinking	Theories and concepts
Inductive reasoning	Knowledge
Deductive reasoning	Facts
Viewpoints (for example, change as a way of life)	Database for reasoning
Models	
Application of theories and concepts	
Skills	
Interaction	
Communications	
Working with feelings and emotions	
Learning-to-learn skills	
Methods of instruction	*Methods of instruction*
Involvement exercises	Reading
Group exercises	Lecturing
Application case studies	Discussion
Role playing	
Discussion	

The Special Role of the Participant

In an involvement learning course, "students" are participants as well. This condition implies a dual role—that of learning from others and that of contributing to the learning of others. Your views, your interactions, your reactions to others, and your ideas are the essential database from which others gain knowledge and develop skills and viewpoints. We assume the classroom activities are where the primary learning takes place, and the textbook only reinforces that process. Therefore, if you are interacting and sharing your views with others, you are providing them with an opportunity to learn. In a sense you are a coach for your fellow participants, just as you will coach your employees in your future role as a manager.

Appreciative Inquiry

The experiential learning approach is anchored in a systematic collaborative inquiry process into one's own experience. During the last 10 years, *appreciative inquiry* has been developed and advanced as a theory and method for system's learning and development. So, what is appreciative inquiry?

Ap-pre' ci-ate, v., 1. Valuing; the act of recognizing the best in people or the world around us; affirming past and present strengths, successes, and potentials; to perceive those things that give life (health, vitality, excellence) to living systems. 2. To increase in value, for example, the economy has appreciated in value. Synonyms: valuing, prizing, esteeming, and honoring.

In-quire', v., 1. The act of exploration and discovery. 2. To ask questions; to be open to seeing new potentials and possibilities. Synonyms: discovery, search, systematic exploration, and study.[19]

At the foundation of appreciative inquiry is the coinquiry between two or more individuals for the best in people, their organizations, and the relevant world around them. "In its broadest sense, it involves systematic discovery of what gives life to a living system when it is most alive, most effective, and most constructively capable in economic, ecological, and human terms."[20] As such an integral part of experiential learning is the spirit of appreciative inquiry. We would like individuals to begin to explore the thinking behind their views, the deeper assumptions they may hold, and the evidence they have that leads them to these views with the utmost respect to individual differences. So it will be fair to begin to ask other questions such as, What leads you to say or believe this? or What makes you ask about this?

In his attempt to clarify further, David Cooperrider differentiates between problem solving and appreciative inquiry. Problem solving includes identification of the problem, analysis of the causes, analysis and possible solutions, and action planning;

**Figure 2–3
Appreciative
Inquiry 4-D Cycle**

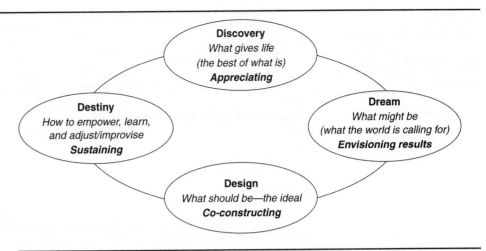

Source: Adapted from D. L. Cooperrider and D. Whitney, "A Positive Revolution in Change: Appreciative Inquiry," 1998.

appreciative inquiry includes appreciating and valuing the best of what is, envisioning what might be, and dialoguing on what should be. Appreciative inquiry can be viewed as a cycle composed of four basic elements: *discovery* (what gives life), or the best of what is—appreciating; *dream* (what might be), or what the world is calling for—envisioning results; *design* (what should be—the ideal)—co-constructing, and *destiny* (how to empower, learn, and adjust/improvise)—sustaining. Figure 2–3 illustrates the appreciative inquiry cycle.

Developing a Learning Community

Our approach views the classroom as a dynamic learning community/organization that is guided by appreciative inquiry. We strive to develop a learning organization. As we saw earlier, a learning system is characterized by a particular culture, climate, managerial/instructional style, and capacity that enable the entity to improve itself systematically. As such the system is guided by a set of principles, activities, processes, and structures that enable it to realize the potential inherent in its human capital's knowledge and experience. In the first two activities of this course, our efforts were aimed at developing the interaction and communication atmosphere conducive to learning and the establishment of the foundations for a climate conducive to appreciative inquiry. Some special requirements for the learning organization include

1. Mutual respect.
2. Appreciation of individual differences and uniqueness.
3. Two-way communication and influence.
4. Openness in expressing views, feelings, and emotions. Tell it like it is, but do so with a respect for others, whose views may differ.
5. Supportiveness. When you are in agreement with others, give them your support. But also learn to express differences without offending. Often two people in conflict are 90 percent in agreement but focus only on their differences. Acknowledging areas of agreement can help provide the basis for a satisfactory resolution, making each person more inclined to consider the validity of the other's view.
6. Recognition that conflict can be creative when differences are expressed appropriately. Differences can lead to new and better perspectives and new bases for acceptable solutions.
7. Effective confrontation:
   a. Have you the courage to express your own convictions?
   b. Can you take feedback as well as give it usefully?
   c. Are you overly concerned about disagreement or disapproval?

    d. Are you willing to risk learning and change?

    e. Are you using your share of the air time, not too much nor too little?

8. Tolerance for ambiguity, the willingness to explore uncertain issues (which includes most important issues), rather than leaping to what H. L. Mencken called the simple, obvious—and wrong—solution that typically presents itself for every complex problem.

Caution: How much openness is desirable? How much confrontation? How can you effectively protect yourself and others from undue intrusion?

Summary

Differences in perception and expectations among individuals, groups, or levels of the hierarchy of an organization can be sources of conflict and frustration for all concerned. Organizational dialoguing and appreciative inquiry are methods used to explore differences and similarities in expectations in these interface situations and to develop a "psychological contract." In Activity 2–1 dialoguing focuses on instructor–participant expectations relevant to the goals and methods of the course, an additional purpose being to develop the classroom climate and interaction patterns that will facilitate learning. Activity 2–4W takes the psychological contract one step further: individuals refine and articulate their learning objectives, goals, potential roadblocks, and desired outcome. The instructor reviews and co-signs the student learning contract. Activity 2–2 provides you with the opportunity to diagnose your learning style, begin the appreciative inquiry process, and appreciate individual differences in your team as they pertain to the individual learning styles. Activity 2–3 takes expectations from the individual level to the team level. Each team is asked to create a name and logo that capture its essence. This activity sets in motion the formation of team identity. Overall the first eight activities of the course illustrate the advantage of appreciative inquiry for attitudinal and behavioral learning, with primary emphasis on the process of interaction and thinking rather than on the pure factual content of the area being studied.

Key Terms and Concepts

Adult learner

Appreciative inquiry

Communication dialoguing

Content learning

Expectations

Experiential learning

Individual learning

Involvement-process learning

Learning

Learning community

Organization learning

Process learning

Psychological contract

Self-efficacy

Self-fulfilling prophecy (Pygmalion)

Self-learning competency

Team learning

Study Questions

1. What does "managing expectations" mean?

2. What is a psychological contract? What is its relationship to Activities 2–1, 2–3, and 2–4W?

3. How did Activities 2–1 and 2–3 contribute to the development of the learning community?

4. Describe the roles of expectations, expectations discrepancies, and self-fulfilling prophecy in organizational settings.

5. Explain the relationship between expectation, self-efficacy, learning, experiential learning, and self-learning competency.

6. Discuss the relationship between appreciative inquiry and experiential learning.

7. What is the difference between process and content learning? Why do we emphasize this distinction?

8. Explain the basic assumptions about the adult as learner.

9. What are the roles of participants and instructors in an appreciative inquiry–based course?

Endnotes

1. A. S. Tannenbaum, *Social Psychology of the Work Organization,* (Belmont, CA: Wadsworth, 1966), p. 47.

2. R. Likert, *New Patterns of Management,* (New York: McGraw-Hill, 1961), p. 91.

3. E. H. Schein, *Organizational Psychology,* (Englewood Cliffs, NJ: Prentice-Hall, 1970), p. 12.

4. J. S. Livingston, "Pygmalion in Management," *Harvard Business Review* 47, no. 4 (1969), pp. 81–89; J. S. Livingston, "Retrospective Commentary," *Harvard Business Review,* September-October 1988, p. 125.

5. The original scientific work on SFP was conducted by Robert K. Merton and reported in R. K. Merton, "The Self-Fulfilling Prophecy," *Antioch Review* 8 (1948), pp. 193–210. Dov Eden's research provides a holistic understanding of the phenomenon, part of which is published in D. Eden, *Pygmalion in Management,* (Lexington, MA: Lexington Books, 1990). A recent study demonstrated the effect of self-fulfilling prophecy on seasickness and performance. See D. Eden and Y. Zuk, "Seasickness as a Self-Fulfilling Prophecy: A Field Experiment on Self-Efficacy and Performance at Sea," *Journal of Applied Psychology* 80 (1995), pp. 628–35; D. Eden, "Implanting Pygmalion Leadership Style through Training: Seven True Experiments," paper presented at the 13th annual meeting of the Society for Industrial and Organizational Psychology, Dallas, Texas, April 24–26, 1998.

6. See, for example, D. Eden and G. Ravid, "Pygmalion vs. Self-Expectancy: Effects of Instructor- and Self-Expectancy on Trainee Performance," *Organizational Behavior and Human Performance* 30 (1982), pp. 351–64; D. Eden and A. B. Shani, "Pygmalion Goes to Boot Camp: Expectancy, Leadership, and Trainee Performance," *Journal of Applied Psychology* 67 (1982), pp. 194–99.

7. J. Hayes and C. W. Allinson, "Cognitive Style and the Theory and Practice of Individual and Collective Learning in Organizations," *Human Relations* 51, no. 7 (1998), pp. 847–71.

8. De Geus, "Planning as Learning," *Harvard Business Review,* March–April 1998, pp. 71–80; B. Guns, *The Faster Learning Organization,* (San Francisco: Jossey-Bass, 1997).

9. While many definitions of learning can be found in the literature, for our purpose we have modified Kolb's definition that can be found in D. A. Kolb, *Experiential Learning,* (Englewood Cliffs, NJ: Prentice-Hall, 1984), p. 38.

10. M. J. Marquardt, *Building the Learning Organization,* (New York: McGraw-Hill, 1996).

11. A. B. (Rami) Shani and Y. Mitki, "Creating the Learning Organization: Beyond Mechanisms," in B. Golembiewski (ed.), *Handbook of Organizational Consultation,* 2nd ed., (New York: Marcel Dekker, Inc. 1999).

12. B. Nahan, *Developing People's Ability to Learn,* (Brussels' European Interuniversity Press, 1991), p. 16.

13. Adapted from Knowles, *The Adult Learner: A Neglected Species.*

14. For an in-depth discussion on adults as learners, see M. Knowles, *Self-Directed Learning: A Guide for Learners and Teachers,* (Chicago: Association Press, 1975); M. Knowles, *The Modern Practice of Adult Education: From Pedagogy to Andragogy,* (Chicago: Association Press, 1980).

15. The theoretical foundation for experiential learning theory can be found in the works of K. Lewin, *Field Theory in Social Science,* (New York: Harper & Row, 1951); J. Dewey, *Experience* *and Education,* (New York: G. P. Putnam Books, 1938); J. Piaget, *Play, Dreams and Imitation in Childhood,* (New York: W. W. Norton, 1951); C. Argyris and D. Schon, *Organizational Learning: A Theory of Action,* (Reading, MA: Addison-Wesley, 1978); Kolb, *Experiential Learning.*

16. Kolb, *Experiential Learning,* p. 26.

17. D. A. Kolb, *Experiential Learning,* (Englewood Cliffs, NJ: Prentice-Hall, 1984); K. L. Murrell, *The Learning-Model Instrument: An Instrument Based on the Learning Model for Managers,* (Chicago: Metrex, 1998).

18. J. A. Raelin, "A Model of Work-Based Learning," *Organization Science* 8, no. 6 (1997), pp. 563–78.

19. More than 10 years ago D. L. Cooperrider began to develop the theory and vision for appreciative inquiry and organizational life. Since then many reports have discussed the utilization of appreciative inquiry in different organizations, systems, and countries. See, for example, D. L. Cooperrider and S. Srivastva, "Appreciative Inquiry and Organizational Life," in W. A. Pasmore and W. Woodman (eds.), *Research in Organization Change and Development,* vol. 1, (Greenwich, CT: JAI Press, 1987), pp. 129–69; G. R. Bushe, "Advances in Appreciative Inquiry as a Team Development Intervention," *Organization Development Journal* 13, no. 3 (1995), pp. 2–22; F. J. Barrett, "Creating Appreciative Learning Cultures," *Organizational Dynamics* 24, no. 1 (1995), pp. 36–49; D. L. Cooperrider and D. Whitney (1998) "A Positive Revolution in Change: Appreciative Inquiry," Weatherhead School of Management, Case Western Reserve University, Cleveland, OH. For a comprehensive and systematic review of the literature, see R. T. Golembiewski, "Appreciating Appreciative Inquiry," in R. Woodman and W. Pasmore (eds.), *Research in Organization Change and Development,* vol. 11, (Greenwich, CT: JAI Press, 1999), pp. 1–45.

20. Cooperrider and Srivastva, ibid.

Activity 2–2: **Individual Learning Style: Diagnosis and Appreciation of Individual Differences**	*Objectives:* **a.** To allow you to examine your own learning style. **b.** To provide you and your team an opportunity to get to know each other via the appreciative inquiry learning process. **c.** To continue with the development of team and community learning environments.

Name _____   Date _____

The Learning Model Instrument*

Task 1 (Individual Activity):

Step 1: For each statement choose the response that is more nearly true for you. Place an X on the blank that corresponds to that response.

1. When meeting people, I prefer
   - ____ (a) to think and speculate on what they are like.
   - ____ (b) to interact directly and to ask them questions.

2. When presented with a problem, I prefer
   - ____ (a) to jump right in and work on a solution.
   - ____ (b) to think through and evaluate possible ways to solve the problem.

3. I enjoy sports more when
   - ____ (a) I am watching a good game.
   - ____ (b) I am actively participating.

4. Before taking a vacation, I prefer
   - ____ (a) to rush at the last minute and give little thought beforehand to what I will do while on vacation.
   - ____ (b) to plan early and daydream about how I will spend my vacation.

5. When enrolled in courses, I prefer
   - ____ (a) to plan how to do my homework before actually attacking the assignment.
   - ____ (b) to immediately become involved in doing the assignment.

6. When I receive information that requires action, I prefer
   - ____ (a) to take action immediately.
   - ____ (b) to organize the information and determine what type of action would be most appropriate.

7. When presented with a number of alternatives for action, I prefer
   - ____ (a) to determine how the alternatives relate to one another and analyze the consequences of each.
   - ____ (b) to select the one that looks best and implement it.

8. When I awake every morning, I prefer
   - ____ (a) to expect to accomplish some worthwhile work without considering what the individual tasks may entail.
   - ____ (b) to plan a schedule for the tasks I expect to do that day.

9. After a full day's work, I prefer
   - ____ (a) to reflect back on what I accomplished and think of how to make time the next day for unfinished tasks.
   - ____ (b) to relax with some type of recreation and not think about my job.

10. After choosing the above response, I
    - ____ (a) prefer to continue and complete this instrument.
    - ____ (b) am curious about how my responses will be interpreted and would prefer some feedback before continuing with the instrument.

11. When I learn something, I am usually
    - ____ (a) thinking about it.
    - ____ (b) right in the middle of doing it.

12. I learn best when
    - ____ (a) I am dealing with messy real-world issues.
    - ____ (b) concepts are clear and well organized.

13. In order to retain something I have learned, I must
    - ____ (a) periodically review it in my mind.
    - ____ (b) practice it or try to apply the information.

14. In teaching others how to do something, I first
    - ____ (a) demonstrate the task.
    - ____ (b) explain the task.

*Copyright by Kenneth L. Murrell. All rights reserved, and no reproduction should be made without the expressed approval of Professor Murrell, University of West Florida. We appreciate Professor Murrell's permission to include this activity in this textbook.

15. My favorite way to learn to do something is

____ (a) reading a book of instructions or enrolling in a class.

____ (b) trying to do it *and learning* from my mistakes.

16. When I become emotionally involved with something, I usually

____ (a) let my feelings take the lead and then decide what to do.

____ (b) control my feelings and try to analyze the situation.

17. If I were meeting jointly with several experts on a subject, I would prefer

____ (a) to ask each of them for his or her opinion.

____ (b) to interact with them and share our ideas and feelings.

18. When I am asked to relate information to a group of people, I prefer

____ (a) not to have an outline, but to interact with them and become involved in an extemporaneous conversation.

____ (b) to prepare notes and know exactly what I am going to say.

19. Experience is

____ (a) a guide for building theories.

____ (b) the best teacher.

20. People learn easier when they are

____ (a) doing work on the job.

____ (b) in a class taught by an expert.

Name _____ Date _____

The Learning Model Instrument Scoring Sheet

Step 2: Transfer your responses by writing either *a* or *b* in the blank that corresponds to each item in the Learning Model Instrument.

	Abstract/Concrete			Cognitive/Affective	
	Column 1	Column 2		Column 3	Column 4
	1. _____	2. _____		11. _____	12. _____
	3. _____	4. _____		13. _____	14. _____
	5. _____	6. _____		15. _____	16. _____
	7. _____	8. _____		17. _____	18. _____
	9. _____	10. _____		19. _____	20. _____
Total circles	_____	_____		_____	_____
Grand totals	_____			_____	

Step 3: Now circle every *a* in column 1 and in column 4. Then circle every *b* in column 2 and column 3. Next total the circles in each of the four columns. Then add the totals of columns 1 and 2; plot this grand total on the vertical axis of the Learning Model for Managers and draw a horizontal line through the point. Now add the totals of columns 3 and 4; plot that grand total on the horizontal axis of the model and draw a vertical line through the point. The intersection of these two lines indicates the domain of your preferred learning style.

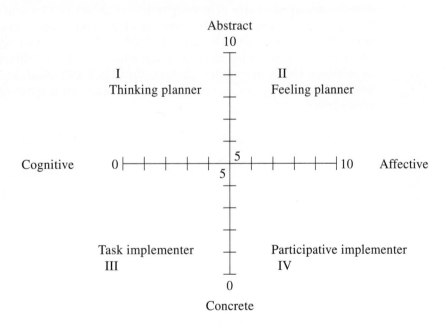

The Learning Model for Managers

The Learning Model Instrument Interpretation Sheet

The cognitive-affective axis or continuum represents the range of ways in which people learn. Cognitive learning includes learning that is structured around either rote storing of knowledge, intellectual abilities and skills, or both. Affective learning includes learning from experience, from feelings about the experience, and from one's own emotions.

The concrete-abstract axis or continuum represents the range of ways in which people experience life. When people experience life abstractly, they detach themselves from the immediacy of the situation and theorize about it. If they experience life concretely, they respond to the situation directly with little subsequent contemplation.

The two axes divide the model into four parts or domains. Most people experience life and learn from it in all four domains but have a preference for a particular domain. Liberal arts education has typically concentrated on abstract learning (domains I and II), whereas vocational and on-the-job training usually takes place in the lower quadrants, particularly domain III.

Occupations representative of the four styles include the following: domain I, philosopher or chief executive officer; domain II, poet or journalist; domain III, architect or engineer, domain IV, psychologist, supervisor, or team leader.

Managerial jobs require an ability to learn in all four domains, and a manager's development depends on his or her ability to learn both cognitively and effectively. Thus management education and development demand the opportunity for the participants to learn how to learn in each domain.

Team Learning to Organizational Learning

Since each individual has a unique learning style, teams will be composed of a variety of learning strengths. This diversity can be an advantage for a well-integrated team, assuming there is built-in mutual respect for the inherent differences. In planning and decision making, the range of learning styles can greatly add value to the process. Organizations like teams can take advantage of different learning styles to organize around particular strengths. Operating decisions and strategic thinking both can be enriched if the organization makes a special effort to value the learning differences of its members. Ideally in these fast changing times, both individuals and organizations will learn to learn better together by understanding and using different learning styles shown here.

Task 2 (Team Activity):

Individuals are to meet in their teams, share scores, and explore their meaning. The following is a suggestion on how to conduct the sharing and begin the appreciative inquiry process.

■ Each person, in turn, should share with the group his or her thoughts on the following three topics:

    a. How do you characterize the way in which you learn? Do your learning profile scores seem valid to you? Why?

    b. What are some of your greatest strengths as a learner?

    c. What might be a learning strength (competence or skill) that you would want to develop?

    d. How could the team and/or learning community help you acquire that desired learning strength?

■ Other team members may ask clarifying questions as each individual speaks. However, the team should budget its time carefully to provide each team member with the airtime to share his or her insights.

■ A spokesperson for each team will provide a brief report to the total class on the main points of the team's discussion.

Activity 2–3:
Group Dialoguing:
The Development of a
Team Name and Logo

Objective:

To help the newly formed teams begin to develop a distinct identity.

Task 1:

The newly assigned team is to get together and brainstorm about a name for itself. The name that the group agrees on is going to be the team's name throughout the course. You might want to choose a name that reflects who you are, that you can be proud of, and that reflects what you would like to become as a team.

Task 2:

Working together as a group, your assignment is to create a team logo, on a regular-size page, that captures creatively who you are. Your team logo is due at the beginning of the next class session.

Task 3:

A group spokesperson will be asked to share with the rest of the learning community your team's name, its logo, and how they were developed or created.

3

Leadership, the Manager and the Firm

Learning Objectives

After completing this module, you should be able to

1. Explain what leadership is and what role it plays in organizational life.
2. Identify the different leadership schools of thought and their contribution to our understanding of leadership.
3. Gain insights into your own leadership style, its effect on others, and its effectiveness.
4. Explore the impact of technology, globalization, diversity, and culture on leadership.

Module Outline

*Our colleague, Roger Conway, Center for Creative Leadership, San Diego, California, took the lead on the revision of this module. We are grateful to Dr. Conway.

Premodule Preparation

**Activity 3–1:
Exploring the
Meaning of
Leadership**

Objective:

To help you explore the meaning of leadership based on your own experience.

Task 1:

Write down the following:

a. Your favorite fictional hero or leader (from a book, movie, or TV show).

b. Your favorite real-life leader.

c. Your favorite boss, coach, or teacher.

Task 2:

Try to think about each name on your list in terms of any image that occurs to you—a food, plant, animal, bird, musical instrument, and so on. Choose an image for each name on your list.

Task 3:

Reflect on the images that you have chosen and write down few thoughts on the following topics:

a. What the images mean to you.

b. Why you have selected them.

c. What it is about the style, behavior, and personality of the person that brings these images to mind.

d. Are the images positive? negative? neutral?

e. What are the images' strengths? weaknesses?

f. Do they capture the essence of the person's impact and behavior? If not, what additional images would you choose to capture the person's behavior?

Task 4:

Each participant will share one of his or her chosen leaders with the team. As a team, explore the meaning of the images based on the items in task 3. Capture the common elements that emerge and have a spokesperson keep a list.

Task 5:

Spokespersons will report findings to the class, and the instructor will lead a class discussion about the meaning of leadership and its key features.

Introduction

The phenomenon of leadership has been around since antiquity. Yet the systematic study of leadership and management did not begin until the 1930s.[1]

Leadership and management are very much on everyone's mind today. Institutions and organizations are struggling as they face increasingly turbulent times. Leading and managing occur at the federal government level in Washington, D.C.; at the corporate level as foreign competition increases; and in religious institutions, schools, courts, museums, hospitals, computer-integrated manufacturing facilities, and other institutions that all seem to be in the midst of change and an uncertain future. As the challenges of managing and leading increase, so does our need to understand the unique features of leaders, the leadership process, and managerial and leadership dynamics in the context of behavior in organizations.

Module 2 opened the discussion of organizational behavior with exercises demonstrating key aspects of the involvement learning process. We began with a discussion of what organizational behavior was, drawn from participants' own experiences. We then moved to creating a climate for learning, based on communication and trust building. Module 3 turns to a key contextual dimension of organizational behavior—leadership. Leadership is most comprehensible as an aspect of individual effectiveness. The leader's own effectiveness is individual; in exercising leadership, interpersonal effectiveness is involved. However, contemporary leadership includes encouraging employees to look beyond their self-interests to larger concerns. Leaders have new visions of organizational success, and they influence others to bring about change. Activity 3–1 focuses on the exploration of some of the tenets of leadership in the context of individual, interpersonal, team, and organizational effectiveness.

Leadership: An Overview

Leadership Defined

Group discussions of leadership are fascinating, whether the participants are business executives, college students, or academics. Many executives believe strongly that when it comes to leadership, "you've either got it or you haven't." But when it comes to defining what it is you've got or haven't got, they can't agree. In contrast, academic views of leadership range from the benign "we don't really know what it is" to rigorous definitions based on very narrow research. In 1974 Stogdill concluded that "there are almost as many definitions of leadership as there are persons who have attempted to define the concept."[2] Three massive reviews by Bass[3] and Yukl[4,5] provide excellent surveys of the leadership literature and help to clear the air. Yukl notes that while conceptual disagreements are deep, most definitions emphasize leadership as an *influence process*. Beyond this common theme, researchers disagree on many other aspects, including how leaders are identified, who exerts influence, how leaders differ from followers, and which elements in the work situation influence leader behavior. Sample definitions of **leadership** include

1. Leadership is the behavior of an individual when he or she is directing the activities of a group toward a shared goal.[6]
2. Leadership is interpersonal influence, exercised in a situation, and directed, through the communication process, toward the attainment of a specified goal or goals.[7]
3. Leadership is the influential increment over and above mechanical compliance with the routine directives of the organization.[8]
4. Leadership appears to be the art of getting others to want to do something that you are convinced should be done.[9]
5. Leadership is broadly defined as influence processes affecting the interpretation of events for followers, the choice of objectives for the group or organization, the organization of work activities to accomplish the objectives, the motivation of followers to achieve the objectives, the maintenance of cooperative relationships and teamwork, and the enlistment of support and cooperation from people outside the group or organization.[10]
6. Leadership is an activity or set of activities, observable to others, that occurs in a group, organization, or institution involving a leader and followers who willingly subscribe to common purposes and work together to achieve them.[11]

The Leadership-versus-Management Debate

Yet not all employees and managers exercise leadership. Bernard Bass, a leadership scholar, concludes that "leaders manage and managers lead, but the two activities are not synonymous."[12] Some scholars argue that although management and leadership overlap, each entails a unique set of activities or functions. Certainly, if a leader is loosely defined as a person who influences others in any manner, then the person can be a leader without being a manager. Also, a person can be manager but can fail to lead. Managers have numerous roles and activities to carry out, and leadership activities relate only to a subset of the larger managerial functions and activities.[13] These distinctions are well accepted and have not been part of the debate. The controversy concerns the notion that leading and managing are qualitatively different or mutually exclusive.

The first writer to take a hard line on this issue was Abraham Zaleznik, when his landmark article was published in *Harvard Business Review* in 1977.[14] Zaleznik argues that managers carry out responsibilities, exercise authority, and worry about how things get done, whereas leaders are concerned with understanding people's beliefs and gaining their commitment. Managers and leaders differ in what they attend to and in how they think, work, and interact. Zaleznik believes that these differences stem from unequal developmental paths, from childhood to adulthood. Essentially, leaders have encountered major hardships or events in stark contrast to the orderly upbringing of the typical manager. Leaders have achieved separateness, which enables them to dream up ideas and to stimulate others to work hard to bring these dreams into reality. In contrast, managers are process oriented and believe that good systems and processes produce good results.[15] In a related argument, Kotter states that leadership is about coping with change, whereas management is about coping with complexity.[16] Warren Bennis believes that the difference between leaders and managers is the ability to master the context rather than surrender to it: "The manager does things right; the leader does the right thing."[17] Figure 3–1 summarizes the unique features of both management and leadership.

**Figure 3–1
A Comparative Summary of Leadership and Management Features**

Management

Carrying out traditional management functions:
    Planning, budgeting, organizing, staffing, problem solving, and control.
Assuming roles as required:*
    Interpersonal roles of symbolic figurehead, liaison with key people, supervisor of employees.
    Informational roles of information monitor, information disseminator, and spokesperson.
    Decision-making roles of innovator within the unit, disturbance handler, resource allocator, and negotiator.

Leadership

Challenging the status quo.
Developing vision and setting direction.
Developing strategies for producing changes toward the new vision.
Communicating the new direction and getting people involved.
Motivating and inspiring others.

---

*From H. Mintzberg, "The Manager's Job: Folklore and Fact," *Harvard Business Review,* July–August 1975.

The response to the writers who claimed a distinction between leadership and management was immediate and strong. Many executives and academicians see considerable overlap between leadership and management activities and preoccupations, and they believe that it is wrong to assume that a person cannot be good at both. Certainly, there is little or no research to support the notion that selected people can be classified as leaders rather than as managers or that managers cannot adopt visionary behaviors when they are required for success. We maintain that it is important for all managers and supervisors to establish themselves as leaders. Further, team-based organization designs are extending leadership functions to work groups and cross-department teams in most modern organizations. There is opportunity for more innovation and critical thinking at all levels of the organization.

We will not argue that leadership and management are mutually exclusive, but they are distinct. We will draw from Clark and Clark[18] that choosing to lead is an intentional act—not everyone is willing to fully accept the responsibilities and burdens of leadership or perceive him- or herself as a leader. Leadership skills can be developed and enhanced at any developmental stage of one's career—the earlier this decision is made, the more likely that those skills will develop to their potential. The decision to lead can have a more dynamic impact on future outcomes based on an early intentional decision. The process of leading involves a progression from low- to high-stakes adventures or trials that generate rich feedback with which to self-monitor behavior and its impact. The later in life the decision to lead is made, the higher the risk of failure both in terms of what is at stake and the degree to which the world around us will tolerate our experimentation. The argument that maturational readiness presents itself in the late teens and diminishes dramatically by the late 20s has an intuitive logic. The discussion of the challenge and opportunity of leadership is very timely among college students and needs the same care and deliberate engagement as the earlier proverbial discussion of the "birds and bees."

Many people choose not to lead, but to "boss"; they view their group members as inferior, undisciplined, untrainable, and requiring "management." We surmise that there may be as much tyranny today as the world has ever seen. However, it is widely condoned as the necessary tyranny of the foreman getting the job done, the enforcement of rules by the bureaucrat preventing disorder, the control of thugs by the police protecting the populace, or the right of the "big people" dominating "little people." Our comics and cartoonists find this form of tyranny a dependable source for plying their trade.[19]

Role Behaviors

Behavioral science investigations of leadership now cover more than 50 years. Personality, traits, attitudes, role behaviors, and situational factors (among others) have been used as the basis for leadership studies. What emerges from all of this is, frankly, less than one might hope. It is difficult to identify traits or characteristics an individual must possess to be a successful leader. Little progress has been made in identifying future leaders on the basis of personality, traits, or attitudes, even though these factors are apparently important. In leadership, as in other aspects of human behavior, complexity dictates that there is no single "one best way," however much we might wish it. Instead, contingent approaches, depending on circumstances, seem more likely. Current research is aimed at identifying the circumstances. One of the more meaningful ways of understanding and studying leadership is in terms of **role behaviors,** which we emphasize in this text.

Roles are patterns of behavior an individual learns in order to perform tasks and relate to people while fulfilling the responsibilities of a given position. Thus a manager must learn the skills and acquire the knowledge necessary to accomplish duties and relate to superiors, peers, and subordinates. Focusing on role behaviors has several advantages.

First, it is possible to study what more competent managers do to get results and to involve people in the performance of their work. The patterns of these behaviors and the assumptions upon which they are based are frequently referred to as managerial style. There are different styles of management; one may be successful under one set of conditions, while another may work better under other circumstances. What works in the electronics industry may not work in the steel industry. What works in the military may not work in NASA, and what works in NASA may not work at a university. Different styles are needed to achieve results in different work environments.

Second, while it is difficult to change personality or traits, it is assumed that most people, to some degree, can learn the role behaviors of different leadership styles. Role behaviors are determined in part by attitudes, assumptions, knowledge, and skills, all of which can be learned. Research knowledge has provided the substance for leadership training and management development programs and for courses such as this one.

Third, role behaviors are part of a systems approach to understanding effectiveness at the four levels of behavior targeted by this course. The managerial role is related to those of superiors, subordinates, and peers, and to those of the small group or team. The small group behaviors are in turn a subsystem of activities related to other teams or subsystems, and these are integrated into the total system of organization. Understanding leadership styles calls for an understanding of team style and organization style—concepts that are developed in future chapters.

Leadership Style

We have chosen role behaviors as our focus for the study of leadership, but when we turn to a definition of leadership style, it will be in terms of attitudes and beliefs. The reason is that our expectations and assumptions about people are based upon our belief systems. Role behaviors may be what we see people actually do, but what people actually do is based upon what they believe or assume should be done when acting out their roles in a particular set of circumstances.

Leadership style, as we use it here, refers to a pattern of philosophy, beliefs, attitudes, feelings, and assumptions about leadership that affect the individual's behavior when managing people. More specifically, style refers to the individual's expectations about how to use a leadership position both to participate and to involve other people in the achievement of results. This will become clearer with some examples. If you believe that people are basically "no damned good" and that they'll do as little as possible if you let them get away with it, then as a supervisor you'll seek to control people closely. You may have the image of yourself as "the boss" who spends much time checking up on what people are doing. A contrary set of assumptions holds that people are responsible, if given the opportunity for self-direction, and that they work as naturally as they play. If you hold these beliefs, your image of yourself as a supervisor may emphasize helping or coordinating people's efforts—you may concentrate on planning so that employees can act autonomously within the guidelines you set down. The main point is that your attitudes, expectations, and assumptions about yourself, your position, and the appropriate behavior for dealing with your employees will have a major impact on how you behave as a manager. In our sense you have role behavior models in your head that determine how you behave.

Leadership Style and Culture

Styles of managing cannot be separated from the general culture in which they occur. The style of management would be expected to be consistent with the national character of a country. The autocratic style, with its highly directive involvement by management and a strongly conforming involvement by employees, is apparently more acceptable in societies more structured than the United States. Generally, family style also can be fitted into the models used here. For instance, parents can take the disciplinary role of the autocratic style with their children, or they can place major emphasis on conforming to the community, which parallels the emphasis on system in the corporate style. They can overindulge their young as the permissive style does employees; they can neglect them and assume little responsibility, like the retired-on-the-job type; or they can produce a supportive, problem-solving environment so the offspring can assume the responsibility for their own self-direction as they gain competence, as in the professional-transformational manager style.

Most managers believe that they must adapt their style of leadership to the culture of the employees; that is, they believe that leadership is culturally contingent.[20] The interrelationship between lifestyles and the culture or subcultures of a country is also similar to the interrelationship between leadership style and organizational style. They tend to be consistent with and reinforce one another. The study of leadership and its unique dynamics have attracted scholars from a variety of disciplines. Each school of thought contributed insight into this complex phenomenon. In the next section we examine some of these perspectives.

Leadership: Multiple Views

The study of leadership in the behavioral sciences now covers more than six decades. Personality, physical appearance, attitudes, behavior, and other factors have been studied as the basis for leadership and leadership success. A few distinct models have emerged.

Researchers initially thought that personal traits would identify leaders and explain different levels of success. Later studies focused on the leader's behavior as viewed by subordinates and related different behavior with the effectiveness of work units. More recently, some researchers have studied elements in the situations that influence the traits, behavior, and end results. Simply put, they believe that some people function better in certain situations or that leader behavior must adjust to reflect the peculiar demands of each situation. Next we explore the different schools of thought on leadership.

Leadership Traits and Skills

Between 1920 and 1950 researchers hoped to discover how individual traits are connected to leadership effectiveness. The "natural born leader" concept seemed a logical basis for investigation. According to the leadership trait concept, leaders naturally possess traits that set them apart from other people. Thus height, appearance, personality, intelligence, race, sex, and other traits were used to explain the emergence of leaders and leadership effectiveness. This line of thinking produced few significant results. The trait theories were dealt a significant blow by leadership scholar Ralph Stogdill, who—after a thorough review of the research literature—concluded, "A person does not become a leader by virtues of the possession of some combination of traits."[21] Since Stogdill's pronouncement much more research has been conducted. Kirkpatrick and Locke now assert that traits do matter.[22] They have identified six traits:

1. Drive: achievement, ambition, energy, tenacity, and initiative.
2. Leadership motivation (personalized versus socialized).
3. Honesty and integrity.
4. Self-confidence (including emotional stability).
5. Cognitive ability: intelligence and the perception of intelligence.
6. Knowledge of the business.

Skills are also predictors of leadership effectiveness. Depending on the organizational level, different mixes of technical skills, conceptual skills, and interpersonal skills are needed for success. At the lowest organizational levels, technical and interpersonal skills are very important, while at the highest levels, conceptual and administrative knowledge and skills are most required. Skills such as analytical ability, persuasiveness, memory for details, tact, and empathy are helpful in all leadership positions.

A recent summary of research in the area of leadership traits[23] draws the following conclusions: (1) The traits of physical energy, intelligence greater than the average intelligence of followers, self-confidence, and achievement motivation and the motives of the leader were found to consistently differentiate leaders from one another. (2) The effects of the traits on leader behavior and leader effectiveness are enhanced to a great extent by the relevance of the traits to the situation in which the leader functions.

Leadership Behavior

As a reaction to some of the early studies on the trait approach, three influential independent groups of researchers—at Harvard University, Ohio State University, and University of Michigan—began studying the behavior of leaders by asking individuals in field settings to describe the behavior of individuals in positions of authority and relating the responses to different criteria of leader effectiveness.

The Ohio State Leadership Studies identified 1,800 specific examples of leadership behavior resulting in 150 questionnaire items of important leadership functions.[24] The approach was to ask subordinates to describe their immediate supervisor using the survey items. Two factors emerged as important general dimensions of leadership:

consideration and initiating structure. Consideration covers a wide variety of behaviors related to the treatment of people, including showing concern for subordinates, looking out for their welfare, and acting in a friendly supportive manner. Finding time to listen to subordinates' problems and consulting with subordinates on important issues before making decisions are good examples of consideration. Initiating structure is a task-related dimension. It also covers a wide variety of behaviors, including defining roles and guiding subordinates toward attainment of work-group goals. Assignment of work, attention to standards of performance, and emphasis on deadlines are examples of initiating structure. The differences in the two dimensions can be reduced to concern for people and concern for task completion. This distinction has survived over the years as a major element in leadership models and studies.

In roughly the same time period (the 1950s), a second major program was launched, at the University of Michigan. The research methods of that program included interviews and questionnaires; its objective was to determine whether leaders of high-production units behaved differently from leaders of low-production units. The essence of the findings was that effective leaders performed different work than their subordinates, concentrating on planning and scheduling of work, coordinating projects, and offering various types of support. Effective supervisors were also relationship oriented, showing trust and confidence, trying to understand subordinates' problems, and helping to develop their potential.[25] The early Michigan studies identified task- and people-oriented behaviors that were surprisingly similar to those found in the Ohio State studies. They also concluded that successful leaders emphasize participation in decision making and rely on group discussions in place of one-on-one supervision. An extension of these findings was that most leadership functions can be carried out by the subordinates as well as the manager.

By the 1960s the University of Michigan model had been advanced to include five leadership dimensions, and the leadership questionnaire had been used in hundreds of organization-climate studies in both the public and private sectors.[26] Activity 3–2 at the end of this module provides an insight and demonstrates the practical use of the Michigan model.

Case Example of the Michigan Behavioral Approach

During a recent management conference, the CEO of a large private gerontological institue asked the program directors for feedback on his performance as boss. He felt comfortable making the request because he had a history of good rapport with all of the directors. The directors managed legal, psychosocial (therapy), community program, research, and educational services for senior citizens at a central facility within a large metropolitan area.

The consultant proposed the Michigan leadership model as an initial basis for discussion. Each director was asked to anonymously rate the CEO on a continuum from two stars (high score), one star, one flag, and two flags (low score) for each of the five Michigan leadership dimensions. The directors complied. The tally of the scores appears in the following chart.

☆ ☆ ☆ ☆ ☆	Leadership support	(all stars)
⚑ ⚑ ⚑	Team facilitation	(three flags)
⚑ ⚑ ⚑	Work facilitation	(three flags)
☆ ⚑ ⚑ ⚑	Goal emphasis	(mostly flags)
☆ ☆ ☆ ☆	Upward influence	(all stars)

"That's awful!" exclaimed the CEO. "The profile is so unbalanced. It appears that I don't promote teamwork and that I'm bad at helping with the work."

The ensuing discussion helped clarify the CEO's scores. One director mentioned that the CEO seldom called staff meetings, and the management conference was the first team-oriented activity in years. It was noted that the CEO spent little time advising the directors on day-to-day work matters, and he left the program goals up to each division. In contrast, the CEO spent most of his time representing the institute to the outside community, corporate sponsors, and other national gerontological organizations. Nevertheless, the CEO was available on a personal basis to meet with each director. An excellent communicator, the CEO was in high demand as a conference speaker and was highly involved with professional societies.

As the team discussed work demands, it became clear that the CEO's skills and behavior matched the requirements of the top-executive position. The directors valued his openness and personal support, but they believed he was not qualified to give technical advice regarding many of their respective functions. In fact, his help in facilitating their work was not needed or welcomed. The directors thought the CEO functioned best as a generalist, and they were delighted with his successful fund-raising activities. His outside focus produced a steady stream of donations to the institute, providing a measure of security to its employees. While they appreciated his contributions, the directors felt some changes were in order regarding goals and teamwork. The exercise ended with agreement on action steps for setting more institutewide goals and planning additional managerial meetings. In brief, the exercise affirmed the CEO's strengths and resulted in a few action steps to strengthen the team.

Situational Theories of Leadership

So far, although we have discussed the possibility that leadership behavior depends on the situation, we have not identified the factors in the situation that might influence the leader. The situational approach emphasizes that leaders may not have the required authority and discretion to make decisions, may not possess technical expertise in the unit managed, may be new to the subordinates in the work group, and may face other factors that make it easy or tough to manage. Do leaders behave differently in very unfavorable circumstances than they do in "normal" assignments? Situational theories attempt to discover aspects of the situation that influence behavior and explain how different leaders respond. To illustrate the factors to consider in understanding the situational approach, we turn to Fred Fiedler's contingency theory.[27]

Fiedler's Contingency Model

Fiedler's theory provides some insight into certain aspects of directive and nondirective styles of leadership. The focus is on designing the managerial position to match the motivational and personality characteristics of the manager. Fiedler's work is meaningful for two reasons: interesting managerial implications can be drawn from the theory, and it provides an opportunity to examine important research questions, such as those on the questionnaire in Activity 3–5, "**Least Preferred Co-worker (LPC) Scale,**" which can be found on the Web site.

An individual's managerial style is defined with reference to his or her score on the Least Preferred Co-worker (LPC) Scale, an exercise consisting of 18 pairs of bipolar adjectives. The manager is asked to choose the adjectives that most accurately describe the individual with whom he has worked least well. Those who receive a "high" score on the scale are defined as relationship motivated: the score indicates that they obtain satisfaction from working with others. Individuals whose scores fall at the other extreme are said to be task motivated.

The second part of the contingency model—situational control—has three components. In descending order of importance they are (1) leader–member relations—the support and loyalty obtained from the work group; (2) task structure—the clarity with which critical task components (goals, methods, and standards of performance) are defined; and (3) position power—the degree of power bestowed by the organization to reward and punish subordinates.

Fiedler posits that task-motivated (low LPC) leaders perform best in situations in which they have either very much or very little situational control; relationship-motivated (high LPC) leaders perform best in situations allowing them moderate control and influence. In leader-match training the individual's leadership style and situational control are identified, and the individual is offered strategies for changing critical components of the situation rather than suggestions for modifying his or her personality. The contingency model assumes that the manager's behaviors and personal characteristics are more difficult to change than is the work situation.[28]

Research Design and Results: The design of Fiedler's research was to form work groups, each of which had some combination of the three job situation variables. Eight different combinations were used. (See Figure 3–2.) Thus the first would have a work group that made good leader-member relations possible, had a structured task, and was one in which the leader had strong position power. Numerous relationship-motivated (high-LPC) leaders and task-motivated (low LPC) leaders were used to manage all eight variations to see whether the style of leadership made a difference in the group performance.

The results from a research project with such an extensive design were complicated and difficult to interpret. Figure 3–3 provides a broad summary of the findings. The high-control situation represents regions 1 and 2 of the eight categories in Figure 3–2, the low-control situation represents regions 7 and 8, while the moderate-control regions are near the center.

Figure 3–2   **Types of Job Situations for Leaders**

	1	2	3	4	5	6	7	8
Leader–member relations	Good	Good	Good	Good	Poor	Poor	Poor	Poor
Task structure	High	High	Low	Low	High	High	Low	Low
Leader position power	Strong	Weak	Strong	Weak	Strong	Weak	Strong	Weak

Adapted from F. E. Fiedler, "The Leadership Game: Matching the Man to the Situation," *Organizational Dynamics,* Winter 1976. © 1976 American Management Association, New York. All rights reserved. Reprinted by permission of the publisher.

Figure 3–3   **Summary of Leadership Style, Behavior, and Performance in Varying Situations**

Leader Type	Situational Control		
	High Control	**Moderate Control**	**Low Control**
High LPC (relationship motivated)	Behavior: Somewhat autocratic, aloof, and self-centered. Seemingly concerned with task	Behavior: Considerate, open, and participative	Behavior: Anxious, tentative, overly concerned with interpersonal relations
	Performance: Poor	Performance: Good	Performance: Poor
Low LPC (task motivated)	Behavior: Considerate and supportive	Behavior: Tense and task focused	Behavior: Directive, task focused, and serious
	Performance: Good	Performance: Poor	Performance: Relatively good

Reprinted from F. E. Fiedler and M. M. Chemers with L. Mahar, *Improving Leadership Effectiveness: The Leader Match Concept,* (New York: John Wiley & Sons, 1976), p. 136.

Hersey and Blanchard's Situational Leadership

The situational leadership model developed by Hersey and Blanchard is widely used in corporate training, the military, and other government agencies in the United States. "It has been a major factor in training and development programs for more than 400 of the *Fortune* 500 companies, such as Bank of America, Caterpillar, IBM, Mobil Oil, Union 76, and Xerox."[29] This model owes its origins to the Ohio State studies and uses concepts similar to initiating structure (task behavior) and consideration (relationship behavior). The model emphasizes behavior that is observable as opposed to attitudes.

Situational leadership asserts that there is no one correct style of leadership with a single set of accompanying behaviors. They contend that the leader must respond to the environmental stimulus with appropriate sets of task and relationship behaviors based on followers' behavior and environmental context. They propose four possible sets of behaviors:

S1: high-task and low-relationship behaviors in response to followers who are unable and unwilling or insecure.

S2: high-task and high-relationship behaviors in response to followers who are unable and willing or confident.

S3: high-relationship and low-task behaviors in response to followers who are able but unwilling or insecure.

S4: low-relationship and low-task behaviors in response to followers who are able and willing or confident.

"**Task behavior** is defined as the extent to which the leader engages in spelling out duties and responsibilities of an individual or group."[30]

"**Relationship behavior** is defined as the extent to which the leader engages in two-way or multiway communication." The behaviors include listening, facilitating, and supportive behaviors.[31] Figure 3–4 respresents the range of leader behavior in response to follower readiness.

Path–Goal Theory

A third situational approach that has generated considerable interest is **path–goal theory.**[32] This approach is unique because it combines leadership with motivation theory. (See Module 10.) Path–goal theory suggests that leaders motivate subordinates to achieve high performance by showing them the path to reach valued goals or results. When the tasks along the way have been performed and the goals reached, rewards follow. The leader's role is to show a clear path and to help eliminate barriers to achievement of the goals.

Path–goal theory starts with this simple scenario, but it becomes increasingly complex when leadership style enters the picture. Leadership style was defined earlier in this module as a pattern of philosophy, beliefs, and assumptions about leadership that affects the individual's behavior when managing people. Path–goal theory includes four leadership styles: **directive leadership,** which is similar to the Ohio State concept of initiating structure; **supportive leadership,** which is similar to the concept of consideration; **participative leadership,** which emphasizes consultation with subordinates before decisions are made; and **achievement-oriented leadership,** where the leader is preoccupied with setting challenging goals for the work group. Leader style and behavior interact with several contingency factors to determine the employee's job performance and satisfaction. Figure 3–5 summarizes the contingency and outcome factors involved.

Path–goal theory is difficult to summarize given the number of contingency factors involved. Three subordinate characteristics are covered by the model, including ability, attitude toward authoritarianism, and preference for self-control or internal control (in contrast to control by others). These characteristics influence how subordinates perceive the leader's behavior. For example, people who have an internal locus of control prefer participative leaders; those who are high in authoritarianism react positively to directive leadership. Background factors such as the nature of the task and rewards also come into play. If subordinates know how to do the job and the task is routine, then the path to the goal is clear and the best style may be supportive. When tasks are uncertain, a more directive style of leadership may be welcomed by subordinates. The leader's task is to reduce uncertainty by clarifying either the desired results or the tasks to accomplish them. Also, the leader must remove barriers to performance and attempt to influence attitudes about tasks, goals, and rewards.

Path–goal theory is complex and difficult to study. Most researchers have focused on a few aspects of the complete theory, and the results have been mixed.[33] The principal contributions of this approach have been an expanded search for relevant contingency factors and clarification of ways that managers can influence employee motivation and performance. It suggests that managers can determine the best mix of behavior to apply in guiding subordinates toward improved effort, performance, and

Figure 3–4

Hersey and Blanchard's Situational Leadership Model

Task behavior

The extent to which the leader engages defining roles—that is, telling what, how, when, where, and, if more than one person, who is to do what in:

- Goal setting
- Organizing
- Establishing time lines
- Directing
- Controlling

Relationship behavior

The extent to which a leader engages in two-way (multiway) communication, listening, facilitating behaviors, and socioemotional support:

- Giving support
- Communicating
- Facilitating interactions
- Active listening
- Providing feedback

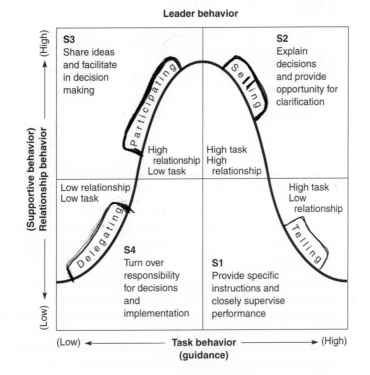

Decision styles

1. Leader-made decision
2. Leader-made decision with dialogue and/or explanation
3. Leader/follower-made decision or follower-made decision with encouragement from leader
4. Follower-made decision

Follower readiness

High	Moderate		Low
R4	R3	R2	R1
Able and willing or confident	Able but unwilling or insecure	Unable but willing or confident	Unable and unwilling or insecure

Follower directed | Leader directed

Ability: has the necessary knowledge, experience, and skill

Willingness: has the necessary confidence, commitment, motivation

When a leader behavior is used appropriately with its corresponding level of readiness, it is termed a *high-probability match.* The following are descriptors that can be useful for situational leadership for specific applications:

S1	S2	S3	S4
Telling	Selling	Participating	Delegating
Guiding	Explaining	Encouraging	Observing
Directing	Clarifying	Collaborating	Monitoring
Establishing	Persuading	Committing	Fulfilling

Source: P. Hersey and K. Blanchard, *Management of Organizational Behavior: Utilizing Human Behavior,* 6th ed., (Escondido, CA: Center for Leadership Studies, 1988), p. 207. Reprinted with permission. All rights reserved.

satisfaction. This is a dramatic shift away from Fiedler's contingency theory, where leadership style is considered to be relatively fixed and the solution may be to change leaders or aspects of the work situation.

Personality Assessment Theory

The best way to forecast leadership is to use a combination of measurements of cognitive ability, personality, simulations, role play, and multirater instruments and techniques according to Hogan, Curphy, and Hogan.[34] It is generally acknowledged that personality assessments alone cannot be used to forecast leadership, but these authors assert that they can play a very useful role in predicting leaders' behavior.

Figure 3–5
Path–Goal View of
Leadership Dynamics

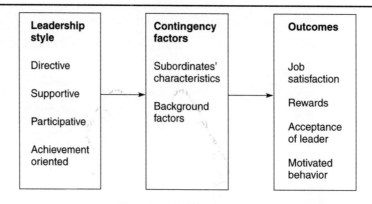

They specifically advance the "big five dimensions of personality" as a substantial enhancement of personality research. The components of the big five dimensions of personality are surgency, emotional stability, conscientiousness, agreeableness, and intellectance.

"Surgency measures the degree to which an individual is sociable, gregarious, assertive, and leaderlike versus quiet, reserved, mannerly, and withdrawn."[35]

Emotional stability is concerned with "the extent to which individuals are calm, steady, cool, and self-confident versus anxious, insecure, worried, and emotional."[36]

Conscientiousness "differentiates individuals who are hard working, persevering, organized, and responsible from those who are impulsive, irresponsible, undependable, and lazy."[37]

"Agreeableness measures the degree to which individuals are sympathetic, cooperative, good-natured, and warm versus grumpy, unpleasant, disagreeable, and cold."[38]

Intellectance "concerns the extent to which an individual is imaginative, cultured, broad minded, and curious versus concrete minded, practical, and has narrow interests."[39]

We will explore the big five theory in more depth in Module 9 that focuses on individual personality. In the context of leadership, utilizing the basic definitions of the five factors, the authors revisit the work of Stogdill, Bent, Bray, and Howard to find support for their assertion of personality determinants of leadership.[40] The above dimensions form a continuum with each definition starting with the most positive attributes and ending with negative attributes. It is the researchers' assertion that the dimensions' positive end of the continuum directly correlate with managerial advancement and positive observer ratings of leaders. They argue further that these positive dimensions equate to effective group and team leadership.

Fitzgerald and Kirby present a review of research based on the Myers-Briggs Type Indicator (MBTI), an instrument similar to big five instruments like the NEO-PI. They offer insights into the most common preferences among male and female college graduates versus those of managers in business and industry (and also by geographical region). The researchers do not argue for a cause-and-effect relationship between type and success in a field of endeavor, but rather report on the high incidences of specific types in management positions. Furthermore, they elaborate on how type preferences impact the practice of leadership and the need to be aware of how one's own style impacts his or her leadership.[41]

Charismatic Leadership

Some leaders in the public eye such as GE's Jack Welch, Virgin's Richard Branson, and AAB's Percy Barnevik are frequently in the business press and are usually associated with an incredible capacity to move followers to action by shear force of personality. They are often described as being **charismatic leaders.** "Charismatic leaders are those who by force of personality have great influence on others.[42] While many visions of charismatic leadership might present themselves, researchers have asked which characteristics of charismatic leadership have a real impact. Shamir et al.[43] identify three categories of charismatic leadership. The three components of charisma were examined by researchers studying military units: the leader's emphasis of ideology, emphasis of collective identity, and modeling of exemplary behavior. The researchers looked for impacts on such dimensions as willingness to sacrifice, attachment to the unit, high levels of cohesiveness and discipline, and performance as appraised by the leader's supervisor. On the dimensions of self-sacrifice and attachment to the unit, individuals were affected only by the leader's emphasis on the unit's collective identity. Interestingly, a leader's perceptions were more positively impacted by his or her ideological emphasis and modeling of exemplary behavior.[44] Charismatic leaders lead up and down; the impacts of this study point to different dimensions of charisma that might be effective for different audiences.

Transformational Leadership

The 1980s environment brought revolutionary change to many American businesses, and the pace of change is accelerating according to political and economic developments in Europe, the Middle East, and other locations. The 1990s environment is expected to continue to emphasize the transformation and revitalization of public and private institutions. Deeply entrenched differences between management and labor, between environmentalists and businesses, and between universities and constituent organizations are being reevaluated according to the changing power of nations and increasing economic competition. In light of these unprecedented changes, transformational leadership can be viewed as vital to the survival and growth of organizations, and it is a timely topic for further discussion. Yukl refers to **transformational leadership** as the process of influencing major changes in the attitudes and assumptions of the organization's members and building commitment for the organization's mission or objectives.[45]

While the literature on transformational leadership is naturally focused on CEOs and top management, transformational leadership commonly involves the actions of leaders at all levels, not just those at the top. Bass defines transformational leaders in terms of the leader's influence on followers. Followers are motivated to do more than originally expected because of their feelings of trust, admiration, loyalty, and respect for the leader. Bass believes this motivation occurs when the leader makes subordinates more aware of the importance and values of task outcomes, helps them think beyond their own self-interest to the work team and organization, and activates higher-order needs such as creative expression and self-actualization.[46] Transformational leaders have charisma, but this is not the only factor needed to bring about change. Transformational leaders also perform the roles of coach, trainer, and mentor.

In a recent study of transformational leadership, James Kouzes and Barry Posner asked more than 500 managers first to reflect on all of their leadership experiences and next to focus on one extraordinary experience. Managers were asked to get a clear mental picture of the experience (that is, to see, hear, and feel it again as intensely as possible). They were then asked to respond to a long list of open-ended questions about the situation, the project, their involvement, the leadership actions, and the outcomes. Responses to this "personal bests" study helped the authors to build a new instrument, the *Leadership Practices Inventory*.

The Leadership Practices Inventory is a transformational leadership instrument; it specifically measures the conceptual framework developed in the case studies of managers' personal-best experiences as leaders. The context was the accomplishment of extraordinary things. The original interviews and questionnaire focused on five factors:[47]

1. Challenging the process (search for opportunities, experiment, take risks).
2. Inspiring a shared vision (envision the future, enlist others).
3. Enabling others to act (foster collaboration, strengthen others).
4. Modeling the way (set the example, plan small wins).
5. Encouraging the heart (recognize contributions, celebrate accomplishments).

Summary of Leadership Schools of Thought

Thus far this section has focused on the unique insights provided by scholars who have investigated leadership and its dynamics from different perspectives. Each school of thought, beyond being anchored in a specific discipline, contributed to our holistic understanding of this complex phenomenon. The traits and skills perspective focused our attention on the specific individual skills that are likely to predict leadership effectiveness. The charismatic leadership perspective focused on individuals who by the sheer strength of their personality affect others. The leadership behavior perspective highlighted the leader's behaviors and behavioral dimensions that are likely to predict effectiveness. The situational orientation focused on the contextual elements that can influence the leader's performance. Finally, the transformational perspective drew our attention to the processes and activities of influencing major changes in organizational life and direction.

Some Current Themes and Challenges

Leadership Training

If leaders are not born, but rather are a product of their development with some assist from nature, then what can be done to develop our future leaders? The *Personnel Journal* reported on a 1991 survey conducted by the American Society for Training and Development (ASTD) that 60 percent of all major companies offer leadership training. Of the companies offering leadership training, 93 percent offer it to middle management, 66 percent to top management, 48 percent to executives, 79 percent to supervisors, and 33 percent to nonsupervisors.[48] While the cost of such training is not available, the data suggest that leadership training represents a growing proportion of the more than $45.5 billion spent annually on training in the United States. In addition to numerous in-house programs offered by corporations, *Fortune* magazine reports that more than 600 firms are competing to provide leadership training to individuals and corporations.[49] Jay Conger asserts that leadership can be taught. "But to be successful, training must be designed to (1) develop and refine certain of the teachable skills; (2) improve the conceptual abilities of managers; (3) tap individuals' personal needs, interests, and self-esteem; and (4) help managers see and move beyond their interpersonal blocks."[50] Conger identifies four categories of leadership training: *personal growth, conceptual understanding, feedback,* and *skill building.*

Personal growth experiences tap the needs and interests of the participant to build self-esteem and are linked to the leader's own motivation to lead and formulate a vision. Examples of personal growth experiences include Outward Bound, ropes courses, National Training Labs—Management Workshop, EST, and Lifespring. We address the area of personal growth in more depth in a later module.

Conceptual understanding consists of theory and research designed to give the potential leader a framework for cognitive development. Examples include the Tom Peters Group Leadership Challenge; Covey Leadership Principle-Centered Power and Leadership Seminars; and executive leadership programs at graduate business schools such as Harvard, Wharton, and Stanford.

Feedback approaches focus on a variety of data generated by psychometrics such as Myers-Briggs Type Indicator, Fundamental Interpersonal Relationship Orientation (Firo-B), Leadership Style Indicator (a 360-degree feedback instrument), and the California Psychological Inventory. These approaches also use exercises designed to elicit behavior for videotaping and feedback by skilled observers. The Center for Creative Leadership's Leader Lab and National Training Labs's Leadership Excellence programs are examples of feedback-driven leadership development programs.

Skill building program designers identify key leadership skills that they believe can be taught. An example is the Forum Company's program, which includes interpreting the environment, shaping a vision, and mobilizing employees to reach that vision.

As more corporations are investing in leadership training programs, the need to scientifically assess their effectiveness is growing. Some skepticism is echoed by Conger, who made the following statement: "I believe that radical changes will ultimately have to occur in both content and the process of leadership training if corporations of the future are to ensure an adequate supply of leaders for themselves."[51] The question for students contemplating their own leadership development, if leadership is a choice and leadership skills can be learned, is, What can and must I do to develop my potential?

Learning Leadership from Experience

Warren Bennis in his book *On Becoming a Leader* describes a journey toward self-discovery and understanding that comes through experience and not the classroom or workshop. Bennis's work is based on the following premise: "Leaders are people who are able to express themselves fully. They know who they are, what their strengths and weaknesses are, and how to fully deploy their strengths and compensate for their weaknesses."[52] While Bennis arrives at his position through interviews with leaders and observation, research conducted by the Center for Creative Leadership gives strong empirical evidence to support Bennis's position. In research conducted since 1981 and through continuous refinement of that research, the center has examined key elements in the development of leaders and those factors that have led to the failure (or derailment) of similarly capable managers.[53] Results of that research appear in Figure 3–6. Note that the most significant developmental experience for both men and women came from job assignments.

Figure 3–6
Key Events in Executive Development

	Men	Women
I. Challenging assignments	48%	32%
a. Line to staff	2.1	1
b. Projects/task forces	12.4	7
c. Scope	17	9
d. Fix-it	11	6
e. Scratch	5.6	6
II. Significant other people	17	23
a. Values playing out	9.7	14
b. Role models	7.4	9
III. Hardships	18	28
a. Failures and mistakes	4	9
b. Demotions, missed promotions, lousy job	5	5
c. Breaking a rut	4	4
d. Personal trauma	2	3
e. Employee problems	4	7
IV. Other events	17	16
a. Course work	6	1
b. First supervision	4.9	6
c. Early work	3.3	7
d. Purely personal	2.6	2

Source: E. H. Lindsey, V. Homes, and M. W. McCall Jr., *Key Events in Executives' Lives*, (Greensboro, NC: Center for Creative Leadership, 1987); M. W. McCall Jr., M. M. Lombardo, and A. M. Morrison, *The Lessons of Experience: How Successful Executives Develop on the Job,* (New York: Lexington Books, 1988); A. M. Morrison, R. P. White, and E. Van Velsor, *Breaking the Glass Ceiling: Can Women Reach the Top of America's Largest Corporations?* (Menlo Park, CA: Addison-Wesley, 1992).

The research findings raise the following question for those seeking to be leaders: How do we learn the right things from experience, and how do we get the right experiences? The research community has provided a whole new generation of psychometrics to measure on-the-job development called **360-degree leadership feedback.** These instruments invite the individual, his or her bosses, peers, and subordinates to rate leadership skills based on a specific theory (Hersey and Blanchard's LBO-II), a model of leadership (Carlson Learning Corporation's Dimensions of Leadership Profile), or research findings (the Center for Creative Leadership's Benchmarks). All of these approaches seek to accentuate leadership strengths; some seek to mitigate potential weakness leading to derailment. The trend is to bring the work of assessment centers to the job. Current research now begins to focus on how to discover the developmental opportunities in your current job and stake out learning opportunities without ever having to leave the work site.[54] The answer to Conger's plea for further development of leadership training may be unfolding in what is euphemistically referred to as the *school of hard knocks*.

The work of the Center for Creative Leadership has focused on those factors that positively or adversely affect leadership in the work setting. These factors do not rely on innate traits, but rather on factors that can be learned from experience. These skills and perspectives really matter in a career. The author's review of 360-degree feedback instruments revealed that almost all of these psychometrics measure observable workplace behaviors. The factors described in the Benchmark section of the publication *Feedback to Managers* are the basis for developmental leadership continuums.[55]

Culture and Globalization

The internationalization of business has focused interest in the leadership styles found in different countries. The rise of multinational corporations and the rush to acquire companies and properties is catching worldwide attention. Rapid advances in telecommunications and computers also have aided economic integration among countries. It has been noted that affluent teenagers in different countries wear the same clothes and listen to the same music. Societies are converging.

While trends toward common lifestyles are unmistakable, leadership style is still influenced by cultural values and practices. Some researchers have found it useful to group countries into clusters according to common characteristics.[56] Evidence of an Anglo-American cluster, including Australia, Canada, New Zealand, South Africa, and the United States, is strong. For example, managers in this cluster value the individual and democracy and often have a British heritage. The Scandinavian cluster (Norway, Finland, Denmark, and Sweden) places even more emphasis on democracy in both government and the workplace. It is not surprising that countries in both clusters have welcomed participative management programs or that their employees resist autocratic styles. In contrast, Middle Eastern, Far Eastern, and Germanic clusters favor an autocratic style.

In some cultures leader–follower roles and relationships are quite different. The allocation of responsibilities in the Far Eastern cluster is much less differentiated than in the Anglo-American cluster. For example, Japanese firms do not emphasize job descriptions or other mechanisms of dividing up the work. Japanese leaders are expected to provide *amae* (love) for subordinates, and they will look to subordinates for advice. In turn, Japanese employees have high respect for their supervisors, and this respect extends beyond the workplace. The Japanese are known for participation of the workforce in recommendations for worker activities, and their Quality Circles (worker suggestion and problem-solving groups) have become models of worker participation for U.S. companies. This would appear inconsistent on the surface until we understand the Japanese value of the individual denying one's own need for the good of the group and the need to contribute to the group. So the expectations of management and the employees are that the employee will contribute ideas, but at the same time be highly submissive to the will of management. In their cultural setting an autocratic style is the expectation, but a clearly defined area exists where the employee will participate. In other cultures where the autocratic style of management exists, workers may feel that management should make all decisions and therefore do not expect to participate in any aspect of the managerial function.

Rosabeth Moss Kanter describes global corporate leaders as "being cosmopolitans, those who can integrate and cross-fertilize knowledge; moving capital, ideas, and people where they are needed; creating multiple points of input and output; generating new routes of communication; and managing dispersed centers of expertise, influence, and production."[57] In the past it was sufficient to adapt to cultural differences and not be offensive; now one must be able to leverage those differences for a competitive advantage. Kanter's description of a global leader captures the need for the ability to leverage and learn from the diversity and chaos of the world marketplace. Maxine Dalton asserts that to meet these challenges leaders must possess the ability to master a high level of cognitive complexity, excellent interpersonal skills, the ability to learn from experience, and advanced moral reasoning.[58] The process of mastering this level of complexity is a major challenge for those who will inevitably see a global assignment in their future. Dalton asserts that the best road to success is embedded in obtaining critical job assignments, getting accurate and timely feedback, and developing important relationships such as having a mentor.[59]

Leadership and Diversity

The workplace of the 1990s is consistent with the theme that began in the first module: an arena of great diversity. With the exception of the most recent research, the focus has been on the American white male. What differences might we expect if we were to expand our paradigm of leadership to an international setting with its great ethnic diversity and include women, who constitute a growing proportion of workers?

The work of Geert Hofstede includes a sample population of 116,000 employees from 40 countries. He found that managers and employees vary on four dimensions of national culture: individualism versus collectivism, power distance, uncertainty avoidance, and quality of life. Most important in our discussion of leadership is the concept of power distance. *Power distance* is a national cultural attribute describing the extent to which a society accepts that power in institutions and organizations is distributed unequally. In the United States and Canada, power distance is small; in Mexico and France, power distance is large, with Italy and Japan being in the middle. Missing subtleties such as power distance could adversely affect a leader's effectiveness.[60]

Since the 1970s the number of women in leadership positions has steadily increased. In 1990 women occupied more than 25 percent of the supervisory positions in U.S. industry, and women are increasingly elected to local, state, and national political positions. Another sign of this increase is the enrollment of women in schools of business. In 1990 the number of men and women enrolled in many U.S. business programs was equal. The entrepreneurial spirit is also alive. A rising number of women have started their own businesses, particularly in the service, retailing, and trade industries.[61]

As a result of these employment gains, men's attitudes toward women in the workplace are changing. Recent surveys indicate that executives realize women want to be hired in positions of authority; these same executives also feel comfortable about working for women. Still both men and women executives believe that women have to be exceptional to succeed in business. Women executives believe that they have had to struggle more to attain their positions in the business world and that they have been subjected to discrimination. It is evident that although conditions have improved, women still face disadvantages in opportunities. Some experts believe that corporate discrimination helps explain the explosive growth in small businesses owned by women.

According to Peter D. Heart Research Associates for Shell, the gender of the boss doesn't matter for 63 percent of currently employed adults; only 23 percent favored a male boss, 12 percent a female boss, and 2 percent were not sure.[62]

According to Catalyst, a New York based nonprofit organization, the most highly paid female corporate executives in the United States earn 68 percent of what their male counterparts earn, with a median income of $518,596 as compared to $765,000 for men.[63]

In 1992 women held 17 percent of managerial positions, and this proportion increased to 42.7 percent in 1995.[64] The gains were at lower and middle management, but not in the executive ranks. The glass ceiling appears to have been raised to a higher level, not eliminated as hoped for. Dismantling the glass ceiling requires three key pieces of information: the barriers women face in advancement, successful career strategies, and making corporate leaders aware of the barriers and climatic conditions impeding the advancement of women to top leadership positions.[65]

Barriers to
Advancement

- Lack of significant general management or line experience.
- Women not in the pipeline long enough.
- Male stereotyping and preconceptions.
- Exclusion from informal networks.
- Inhospitable corporate culture.

Successful Career
Strategies

- Consistently exceed performance expectations.
- Develop style that men are comfortable with.
- Seek difficult or high visibility assignments.
- Have an influential mentor.
- Network with influential colleagues.
- Gain line management experience.
- Move from one functional area to another.

Corporate Leader
Awareness

CEOs understand barriers only when they have some direct experience:

- They may have experienced discrimination.
- They are cognizant of gender discrimination through significant others.
- They have had experiential training to heighten their awareness.[66]

Management has long been associated with stereotypical masculine traits and behavior such as competitiveness, willingness to take risks, and task orientation. Early studies indicated women identified with the masculine stereotypes of a successful manager as a way of overcoming the negative stereotypes of the ability of women to lead. However, recent studies indicate that women who are middle and top executives no longer equate management with masculine traits.

While long-held stereotypes of women and men are beginning to loosen, you might recognize stereotypes at work within your discussion group team. Research has shown that although some men are reluctant to assume leadership roles in all-male groups, they will often step forward when the group includes both men and women. Women are often viewed as better communicators and team players than men and are often perceived to be better at group building. But these general tendencies may not hold in your class group. They will be explored in a later module.

Considerable research suggests that early trait differences disappear later in life. Differences between boys and girls, and between male and female college students do not hold up as managers move into upper-level executive positions. Both men and women change with training and managerial experience. On the whole, experienced men and women managers have similar motives. Studies show both men and women executives have a high need for achievement and power, and both groups demonstrate assertiveness, self-reliance, risk taking, and other traits and behaviors associated with leadership. Women who are experienced managers show no differences in leadership ability from their experienced male counterparts. In fact, once men and women have established themselves as leaders in their organizations, women do not behave differently than men.[67]

Sally Helgesen in *The Female Advantage: Women's Ways of Leadership* studied four nationally prominent female leaders and identified their differences from their male counterparts. She characterizes their workplaces as "webs of inclusion," organizations where sharing information is key and where hierarchy is de-emphasized. While male leaders tend to champion vision, their female counterparts concentrate on developing voice. "The woman leader's voice is a means both for presenting herself and what she knows about the world, and for eliciting a response."[68] In finding one's voice, each individual leader in the study had to find her own individual strengths and weaknesses and determine how her uniqueness could contribute to her organization's success.

As global leaders the expectation of flexibility and the ability to affect behaviors as the situation requires is critical to our success. We may also continue to learn from those who are different from us, modeling new behaviors and skills that might serve us well as the workplace continues its pace of rapid change.

Leadership and the Development of Your Class Team

If you are assigned to a permanent class team, you have an excellent opportunity to practice leadership skills. You are presumably working in a "leaderless" group, since the instructor has not designated a formal leader. Leadership functions are still needed if the group is to carry out meaningful problem solving and perform various tasks. It may prove worthwhile to scan the list of roles typically assumed by members during the life of a small group. The module on small group dynamics covers these roles, indicating task- and relationship-oriented behavior needed for successful performance. Take time in your next group meeting to discuss these roles and the value of having a facilitator, recorder, and spokesperson. Some groups find it valuable to rotate these responsibilities so that all members can practice different leadership behaviors. Other groups recognize leadership skills in certain members, and the leadership positions are informally assumed early in the course.

Summary

Leadership is defined as a set of expectations for an individual to use in a leadership position to participate and to involve people in the achievement of results. The definition relates to the historical issue concerning the degree to which management and/or the employees should assume responsibility for planning, organizing, directing, and controlling organizational functions.

A review of the multiple perspectives on leadership revealed that although each school of thought is anchored in a specific discipline, taken together they contribute to our holistic understanding of leadership dynamics. The traits and skills perspective focused our attention on the specific individual skills that are likely to predict leadership effectiveness. The leadership behavior perspective highlighted the leader's behaviors and behavioral dimensions that are likely to predict effectiveness. The situational orientation focused on the contextual elements that can influence the leader's performance. Recent research on leadership training and the value of work experience on shaping or derailing leaders was explored. Finally, the transformational perspective draws our attention to the need to integrate many of the diverse factors of current society, including a highly educated and specialized work force, a vast technology, and rapid environmental change.

Key Terms and Concepts

Achievement-oriented leadership	Participative leadership
Behavioral leadership theory	Path–goal theory
Charismatic leader	Relationship behavior
Consideration	Role behaviors
Directive leadership	Situational leadership
Employee involvement	Supportive leadership
Initiating structure	Task behavior
Leadership	Traits and skills theory
Leadership style	Transformational leadership
Least preferred co-worker (LPC)	360-degree leadership feedback

Study Questions

1. We have described leadership as a set of expectations. What is the advantage of focusing on expectations, attitudes, and philosophy, rather than on actual behavior, when defining leadership?

2. What is the best style of leadership?

3. What is the difference between leadership and management? Would you apply this characteristic to all levels of management? Give reasons for your answer.

4. Are managers born or made? The argument around this question has raged for many years. Many executives will say, You've either got it or you haven't. What are the arguments on both sides? What do you believe?

5. In what way can leadership be regarded as a process? How does this apply to your team activities?

6. Compare and contrast between the trait approach, the behavioral approach, and the situational approach to leadership.

7. What new perspectives are offered by the situational leadership theories?

8. Discuss the relationship between leadership, expectation, learning, and diversity.

9. Describe the leadership dynamics within your team. How would you characterize the team? How effective is it? What can you experiment with to improve your team performance?

Endnotes

1. R. J. House and R. N. Adiya, "The Social Scientific Study of Leadership: Quo Vadis?" *Journal of Management* 23, no. 3 (1997), pp. 409–73.

2. R. M. Stogdill, *Handbook of Leadership: A Survey of the Literature,* (New York: Free Press, 1974).

3. B. M. Bass, *Transforming Leadership,* (New York: Lea Publishers, 1998).

4. G. Yukl, "Managerial Leadership: A Review of Theory and Research," *Journal of Management* 15, no. 2 (1989).

5. G. A. Yukl, *Leadership in Organizations,* (Englewood Cliffs, NJ: Prentice-Hall, 1998).

6. J. K. Hemphill and A. E. Coons, "Development of the Leader Behavior Description Questionnaire," in R. M. Stogdill and A. E. Coons (eds.), *Leader Behavior: Its Description and Measurement,* (Columbus, OH: Bureau of Business Research, Ohio State University, 1957).

7. R. Tannenbaum, I. R. Weschler, and F. Massarik, *Leadership and Organization,* (New York: McGraw-Hill, 1961).

8. D. Katz and R. Kahn, *The Social Psychology of Organizations,* 2nd ed., (New York: John Wiley & Sons, 1978).

9. J. M. Kouzes and B. Z. Posner, *The Leadership Challenge,* (San Francisco: Jossey-Bass, 1995).

10. G. Yukl, *Leadership in Organizations,* 4th ed., (Englewood Cliffs, NJ: Prentice Hall, 1998).

11. K. E. Clark and M. B. Clark, *Choosing to Lead,* 2nd ed., (Greensboro, NC: Center for Creative Leadership, 1996), p. 19.

12. Bass (1998), Ibid.

13. H. Mintzberg, "The Manager's Job: Folklore and Fact," *Harvard Business Review,* July–August, 1975.

14. A. Zaleznik, "Managers and Leaders: Are They Different?" *Harvard Business Review* 55, no. 5 (1977).

15. A. Zaleznik, "The Leadership Gap," *Academy of Management Review* 4, no. 1 (1990).

16. J. P. Kotter, *The Leadership Factor,* (New York: Free Press, 1987).

17. W. Bennis, *On Becoming a Leader,* (Menlo Park, CA: Addison-Wesley, 1998), p. 45.

18. K. E. Clark and M. B. Clark, *Choosing to Lead,* (Greensboro, NC: Center for Creative Leadership, 1996).

19. Ibid., p. viii.

20. See, for example, N. J. Adler, *International Dimensions of Organizational Behavior,* (Belmont, CA: Wadsworth, 1998).

21. R. M. Stogdill, "Personal Factors Associated with Leadership: A Survey of the Literature," *Journal of Psychology* 25 (1948), p. 64.

22. S. A. Kirkpatrick and E. A. Locke, "Leadership: Do Traits Matter?" *The Executive,* 5, no. 2 (May 1991), pp. 48–60.

23. R. J. House and R. N. Aditya, "The Social Scientific Study of Leadership: Quo Vadis?" *Journal of Management* 23, no. 3 (1997), pp. 409–73.

24. J. A. Conger and R. N. Kanungo, "Behavioral Dimensions of Charismatic Leadership," in Conger and Kanungo (eds.), *Charismatic Leadership,* (San Francisco: Jossey-Bass, 1998). J. A. Conger and R. N. Kanungo, "Training Charismatic Leadership: A Risky and Critical Task," in *Charismatic Leadership,* pp. 309–23.

25. E. A. Fleishman, "The Description of Supervisory Behavior," *Personnel Psychology* 37 (1953).

26. J. Taylor and D. Bowers, *The Survey of Organizations: A Machine-Scored Standardized Questionnaire Instrument,* (Ann Arbor, MI: Institute for Social Research, University of Michigan, 1972).

27. F. E. Fiedler, "Engineering the Job to Fit the Manager," *Harvard Business Review,* September–October 1965.

28. F. T. Sepic, L. Manar, and F. E. Fiedler, "Match the Manager and the Milieu," *Cornell HRA Quarterly,* August 1980, pp. 19–23.

29. P. Hersey and K. H. Blanchard, *Management of Organizational Behavior: Utilizing Human Resources,* 6th ed., (Englewood Cliffs, NJ: Prentice-Hall, 1993), p. 215.

30. Ibid., p. 185.

31. Ibid., p. 187.

32. R. J. House, "A Path–Goal Theory of Leadership Effectiveness," *Administrative Science Quarterly* 16 (1971); R. J. House and T. R. Mitchell, "Path–Goal Theory of Leadership," *Contemporary Business* 3 (1974).

33. J. Indvik, "Path–Goal Theory of Leadership: A Meta Analysis," *Proceedings of the Academy of Management Meetings,* 1986.

34. R. Hogan, G. J. Curphy, and J. Hogan, "What We Know about Leadership," *American Psychologist* 49, no. 6 (June 1994), p. 497.

35. Ibid., p. 503.

36. Ibid.

37. Ibid., p. 504.

38. Ibid.

39. Ibid.

40. Ibid., p. 498.

41. C. Fitzgerald and L. K. Kirby, *Developing Leaders: Research and Applications in Psychological Type and Leadership Development,* Davies Black, (1997), pp. 3–59.

42. Clark and Clark, p. 45.

43. B. Shamir, R. J. House, and M. B. Arhur, "The Motivational Effects of Charasmiatic Leadership: A Self-Based Theory," *Organizational Science,* 1993, pp. 577–94.

44. B. Shamir, E. Zakay, E. Breinin, and M. Popper, "Correlates of Charismatic Leader Behavior in Military Units: Subordinate's Attitudes, Unit Characteristics, and Superior's Appraisals of Leader Performance," *Academy of Management Journal* 41, no. 4 (1998), pp. 387–409.

45. G. Yukl, "Managerial Leadership: A Review of Theory and Research," *Journal of Management* 15, no. 2 (1989), pp. 269, 272.

46. Bass, ibid., p. 9.

47. Kouzes and Posner, 1995, ibid.

48. D. Gunsch, "For Your Information—Learning Leadership," *Personnel Journal* 70, no. 8 (1991), p. 17.

49. J. Huey, "The Leadership Industry," *Fortune,* December (1994), p. 54.

50. J. A. Conger, *Learning to Lead: The Art of Transforming Managers into Leaders,* (San Francisco: Jossey-Bass, 1992), p. 34.

51. Ibid., pp. 44–53.

52. W. Bennis, *On Becoming a Leader,* (Menlo Park, CA: Addison-Wesley, 1989), p. 3.

53. E. H. Lindsey, V. Homes, and M. W. McCall Jr., *Key Events in Executives' Lives,* (Greensboro, NC: Center for Creative Leadership, 1987); M. W. McCall Jr., M. M. Lombardo, and A. M. Morrison, *The Lessons of Experience: How Successful Executives Develop on the Job,* (New York: Lexington Books, 1988); A. M. Morrison, R. P. White, and E. Van Velsor, *Breaking the Glass Ceiling: Can Women Reach the Top of America's Largest Corporations?* (Menlo Park, CA: Addison-Wesley, 1992).

54. C. D. McCauley, M. N. Ruderman, P, J. Ohott, and J. Morrow, "Assessing the Developmental Components of Managerial Jobs," *Journal of Applied Psychology* 79, no. 4 (1995), pp. 544–60.

55. E. Van Velsor and J. B. Leslie, *Feedback to Managers, vols. 1 and 2: A Review and Comparison of Sixteen Multi-Rater Feedback Instruments,* (Greensboro, NC: Center for Creative Leadership, 1991), pp. 71–74.

56. S. Ronen and O. Shenkar, "Clustering Countries on Attitudinal Dimensions: A Review and Synthesis," *Academy of Management Review* 10 (1985).

57. R. M. Kanter, *World Class: Thriving Locally in the Global Economy,* (New York: Simon & Schuster, 1995), p. 17.

58. M. Dalton, "Developing Global Leaders," in C. D. McCauley, R. S. Moxley, and E. Van Velsor (eds.), *Handbook of Leadership Development,* (San Francisco: Jossey-Bass, 1998), pp. 379–402.

59. Ibid.

60. G. Hofstede, "Motivation, Leadership, and Organization: Do American Theories Apply Abroad?" *Organizational Dynamics,* Summer 1980, pp. 42–63.

61. Bass, 1990, p. 708.

62. "USA Snapshots," *USA Today,* November 11, 1998, p. 1B.

63. "Pay Gap," *USA Today,* November 10, 1998, p. 1A.

64. "Employed Persons by Occupation, Race and Sex," *Employment and Earnings,* (Washington: U.S. Department of Labor, 1996), p. 171.

65. B. R. Ragins, B. Towensend, and M. Mattis, "Gender Gap in the Executive Suite: CEOs and Female Executives Report on Breaking the Glass Ceiling," *Academy of Management Executive* 12, no. 1 (1998), pp. 28–42.

66. Ibid.

67. Ibid., p. 721.

68. S. Helgesen, *The Female Advantage: Women's Ways of Leadership,* (New York: Doubleday–Currency, 1990), pp. 223–24.

Activity 3–2: Leadership Behavior

Objectives:

a. To examine a behavioral model of leadership.

b. To provide students with an opportunity to evaluate a past boss's leadership behavior.

c. To demonstrate that sound leadership behavior varies with the organizational situation.

Task 1 (Homework):

a. As a homework assignment, complete the Leadership Questionnaire by rating the behavior of a past immediate supervisor.

b. Use the scoring key below to determine high, moderate, and low ratings on each of the five University of Michigan dimensions. Be prepared to discuss the scores and their meaning to the class team.

Enter information and scores below:

Boss rated _____

Type of business _____

Description of the work situation _____

_____

_____

_____ a. *Leadership support.* Behavior that enhances employee feelings of self-worth and importance.

_____ b. *Team facilitation.* Behavior that encourages members of the group to develop close, mutually satisfying relationships.

_____ c. *Work facilitation.* Activities that help achieve goal attainment by doing things such as scheduling; coordinating; planning; and providing resources such as tools, material, and technical advice and knowledge.

_____ d. *Goal emphasis.* Behavior that stimulates an enthusiasm for meeting the group's goals, helps establish priorities, and promotes achievement of excellent performance.

_____ e. *Upward influence.* Behaviors that advance the status of the work group and individuals (for example, acquiring resources needed by the group, securing rewards for group members, and eliminating barriers raised by other organizational units).

Task 2:

a. Meet with your class team. Let each team member describe the work situation and his or her ratings of the leader, without interruption except for clarifying questions. Move around the group until everyone has participated. (Time: 20 minutes)

b. Discuss the following questions:
Do the dimensions cover all the behaviors that you believe are important for a leader in your situation? What dimensions would you add that would more fully describe the leader's actions?
What features of the situation caused the leader to behave the way she or he did? Does job success require the leader to behave in this fashion?
(Time: 10 minutes)

Name _____   Date _____

Leadership Questionnaire*

Instructions:

This short questionnaire on leadership behaviors is based on the University of Michigan model. Identify a current or past manager who was your immediate supervisor. Circle the best choice from the options provided.

1. My supervisor is eager to recognize and reward good performance.
   - *a.* strongly disagree
   - *b.* disagree
   - *c.* not sure
   - *d.* agree
   - *e.* strongly agree

2. To what extent does your supervisor encourage you to think and act for yourself?
   - *a.* not at all
   - *b.* to a small extent
   - *c.* to some extent
   - *d.* to a great extent
   - *e.* to a very great extent

3. Generally, decisions are arrived at by my immediate supervisor with no input from people at lower levels.
   - *a.* strongly agree
   - *b.* agree
   - *c.* not sure
   - *d.* disagree
   - *e.* strongly disagree

4. My immediate supervisor is usually successful in dealing with higher levels of authority.
   - *a.* strongly agree
   - *b.* agree
   - *c.* not sure
   - *d.* disagree
   - *e.* strongly disagree

5. To what extent does your supervisor stress the importance of work goals?
   - *a.* not at all
   - *b.* to a small extent
   - *c.* to some extent
   - *d.* to a great extent
   - *e.* to a very great extent

6. My supervisor is friendly and easy to talk to.
   - *a.* strongly agree
   - *b.* agree
   - *c.* not sure
   - *d.* disagree
   - *e.* strongly disagree

7. To what extent does your supervisor offer new ideas for job-related problems?
   - *a.* not at all
   - *b.* to a small extent
   - *c.* to some extent
   - *d.* to a great extent
   - *e.* to a very great extent

8. How often does your supervisor hold group meetings for his or her employees?
   - *a.* never
   - *b.* rarely
   - *c.* sometimes
   - *d.* rather often
   - *e.* nearly all the time

9. My immediate supervisor is very successful in getting management to recognize the success of the employees he or she supervises.
   - *a.* strongly disagree
   - *b.* disagree
   - *c.* not sure
   - *d.* agree
   - *e.* strongly agree

10. My supervisor encourages people to give their best efforts.
    - *a.* strongly disagree
    - *b.* disagree
    - *c.* not sure
    - *d.* agree
    - *e.* strongly agree

*This instrument is a major modification of a survey initially developed at the Institute of Social Research, University of Michigan, Ann Arbor, Michigan, which was discussed in D. G. Bowers and S. Seashore, "Predicting Organizational Effectiveness with a Four-Factor Theory of Leadership," *Administrative Science Quarterly* 11, (1966), pp. 238–63.

11. To what extent is your supervisor attentive to what you say?
    a. not at all   *d.* to a great extent
    b. to a small extent   *e.* to a very great extent
    c. to some extent

12. To what extent does your supervisor provide the help you need to schedule your work ahead of time?
    a. not at all   *d.* to a great extent
    b. to a small extent   *e.* to a very great extent
    c. to some extent

13. To what extent does your supervisor encourage employees to exchange ideas and opinions?
    a. not at all   *d.* to a great extent
    b. to a small extent   *e.* to a very great extent
    c. to some extent

14. To what extent is your immediate supervisor successful in getting the best possible rewards for his or her employees (for example, merit raises, promotions, challenging work assignments)?
    a. to a very great extent   *d.* to a small extent
    b. to a great extent   *e.* not at all
    c. to some extent

15. To what extent does your supervisor emphasize high standards of performance?
    a. to a very great extent   *d.* to a small extent
    b. to a great extent   *e.* not at all
    c. to some extent

16. To what extent is your supervisor willing to listen to your problems?
    a. not at all   *d.* to a great extent
    b. to a small extent   *e.* to a very great extent
    c. to some extent

17. How would you describe the amount of responsibility delegated by your supervisor?
    a. none   *d.* a considerable amount
    b. a minimum amount   *e.* a maximum amount
    c. a moderate amount

18. To what extent does your supervisor encourage employees to work as a team?
    a. not at all   *d.* to a great extent
    b. to a small extent   *e.* to a very great extent
    c. to some extent

19. How often does your supervisor work with you to set specific goals?
    a. never   *d.* rather often
    b. rarely   *e.* nearly all the time
    c. sometimes

Use the score sheet on the next page to rate the five leadership behavioral dimensions.

Score Sheet for the Michigan-Based Leadership Questionnaire

Score Sheet

Scoring: Enter your answers for each item by circling the alphabetic choice in the scoring grid. Then enter the corresponding numeric score in the right-hand column.

Item #	1	2	3	4	5	
Leadership Support						
1	a	b	c	d	e	_____
6	e	d	c	b	a	_____
11	a	b	c	d	e	_____
16	a	b	c	d	e	_____
				A Total		
				A ÷ 4 =		
Team Facilitation						
3	a	b	c	d	e	_____
8	a	b	c	d	e	_____
13	a	b	c	d	e	_____
18	a	b	c	d	e	_____
				B Total		
				B ÷ 4 =		
Work Facilitation						
2	e	d	c	b	a	_____
7	a	b	c	d	e	_____
12	a	b	c	d	e	_____
17	a	b	c	d	e	_____
				C Total		
				C ÷ 4 =		
Goal Emphasis						
5	a	b	c	d	e	_____
10	a	b	c	d	e	_____
15	e	d	c	b	a	_____
19	a	b	c	d	e	_____
				D Total		
				D ÷ 4 =		
Upward Influence						
4	e	d	c	b	a	_____
9	a	b	c	d	e	_____
14	e	d	c	b	a	_____
				E Total		
				E ÷ 3 =		

Explanation: Total raw scores for each dimension are calculated by summing up scores for individual items. The scoring grid is required be cause several items are negatively worked. Simply total the raw scores from the right-hand column; then divide by the number of items (four except for "upward influence") to produce summary scores for each leadership dimension.

Summary Scores

A	Leadership Support	_____
B	Team Facilitation	_____
C	Work Facilitation	_____
D	Goal Emphasis	_____
E	Upward Influence	_____

Your instructor will provide definitions and discuss the "upward influence" dimension.

**Activity 3–3
Donny Is My Leader**

Objectives:

a. To allow you to examine the leadership process.

b. To provide you and your team with an opportunity to investigate the leadership episode from different theoretical perspectives.

Task 1 (Individual Task):

Read the following case carefully and answer these questions:

a. Which characteristics describe Donny's leadership philosophy and style?

b. What are some of Donny's strengths and weaknesses as a leader? as a manager?

c. What are the likely consequences of Donny's leadership style? What effects does he have on the performance of individual team members (Choc, Herb, Harvey, Harry, Larry, David, Bruce, John, and Bradley)? What effects does he have on the overall performance of the team?

d. How did Donny's absence affect team dynamics?

e. If you were Donny, how would you lead the team? Why?

Task 2 (Class Discussion):

The instructor will lead a class discussion to capture the basic facts in the case.

Task 3 (Team Task):

Teams will examine the case from a specific theoretical perspective assigned by the instructor. Each team is to

- Capture the essence of the assigned theoretical perspective.
- Identify the major facts in the case as viewed by the assigned perspective.
- Conduct the analysis of the facts from the assigned perspective.
- Identify potential problems in the case.
- Identify the most critical problem.
- Provide some alternative solutions.

Task 4:

Each team will present its analysis and findings to the total learning community.

Donny Is My Leader*

　　The first day I joined the team, Donny asked me how far I was going to run. The team had a goal of running 2 miles every Monday, Wednesday, and Friday morning at a fairly fast pace—about 8 minutes a mile. That speed is not fast by any track club's standard, but it's fairly fast for 35- to 45-year-old occasional jocks. I said I'd try for a mile and a half, a distance I had occasionally managed to complete over the past several months of jogging by myself. I ran at the tail end of the team and did, in fact, run the mile and a half. We run on a small inside track at the Y, which has 18 laps to a mile. At the end of 27 laps, a mile and a half, Donny turned and shouted back to me from his place at the front of the group, "OK, Harvey, that's enough!" And I stopped.

*This case was prepared by Professors Harvey F. Kolodny and Robert J. House of the faculty of management studies at the University of Toronto. All rights are reserved by the authors. We are grateful to Professors Kolodny and House for their permission to include the case in this textbook.

When the others finished (some did the 2 miles, others dropped out at different distances—as little as a mile), Donny came over and congratulated me. He told me I'd run well. He suggested I try adding 3 more laps next time, staying at that level for a while, and then add another 3 until I reached the team's 36-lap or 2-mile objective.

The "team" is a very informal collection of people with no formally appointed leader. Donny, however, is referred to as "the coach." The team has existed for a while with a small, hard core and with others who come and go. The regulars comprise Donny, who always runs on the right side of the pacer, who is almost always Choc, and Herb, who runs about fourth and takes over as a leader when Donny is away. Barrie generally runs third and sometimes sets the pace but is sort of an irregular regular, since he occasionally forsakes the groups for a squash game or gets in late after a hard night. Harry and Larry are two recent regulars. Larry always runs last, and Harry runs just ahead of me. Three or four others occasionally join us. On some mornings we are as few as four running. On other mornings there are nine running.

			Rail			
						Choc
Larry	Harvey	Harry		Herb	Barrie	Donny
			Wall			

My second day was a beautiful, warm morning, and we ran outside. I quit after a mile and a quarter. Harry quit after a mile. No one said anything to us—good or bad—about the running.

My third day was my big mistake! I vowed to myself to run 1 mile and 12 laps, 3 better than my previous inside run. At the end of the 11th lap of the 2nd mile, I still had a little left in me, so I sprinted the last lap, passing everyone. I'd noticed that all the finishers usually sprinted for the last one or two laps. However, when he was done, Donny came over and several castigated me. How could I possibly have sprinted? If I could sprint, I must have had some strength left in me and therefore I could have gone for several more laps; in fact, I might even have been able to finish the 2 miles. He verbally lashed out at me several times, both on the track and back down in the locker room. The others joined in, though in a more teasing mode. They said that the next time not only was I going to run the 2 miles but also would set the pace.

Soon after this occurrence Harry became the culprit—and the victim of Donny's wrath. We did each lap in about 28 seconds. Donny was the timekeeper. He shouted out the time for the first lap, and for the 1st mile he counted out every second lap each time we passed the starting point (where a wall clock was mounted). Donny constantly encouraged us to keep going. Herb and Larry did so, too. They called out milestones: "Three-quarters done!" or "Two-thirds done!" or "Five laps to go!" Near the end of the run, they kept up a steady stream of comments to urge those of us who were struggling to keep going and to try to finish the distance. On this particular day, at the end of the first lap Harry said, "Hey, we're going too fast! We did it in 20 seconds." It was a bad day. Quite a few of us didn't finish. Donny was angry. He took it out on Harry repeatedly. He said that Harry's statement was incorrect and, furthermore, had discouraged several of the team members, making them, including me, quit. He carried on all the way down to the locker room, in the showers, and even into the next running day.

An incident somewhat similar to my own experience occurred about 2 years after I joined the team. By this time we were all up to 3 miles a day. A fellow named David joined us on the track. He ran 2 miles at first, while we ran 3, but he soon got up to 2½ miles. Then one day it looked as if he might be able to make the 3 miles, so Donny slowed down and ran with David for the remaining distance. At first Donny harangued David very loudly—you could hear Donny all around the track—for threatening to quit. Then as David came closer to completing the distance, Donny became gentle and encouraging until David made it. David was very excited, and we all congratulated him on his success.

The next time out David was having a hard time repeating the 3-mile distance, so Donny slowed down to urge him on and asked us all to encourage him. We all did, mostly by running slowly with him and talking it up, and David successfully completed the 3 miles that day.

However, on our next run it looked certain that David wouldn't make it. It was hot, and we were all dragging. Donny dropped back to help David along for the last ½ mile while the better runners sprinted ahead to complete the distance. I stayed back, running behind David. Donny told me to go ahead, that it was OK because he would take care of David. But I was exhausted and said that I would just continue running along behind him, slowly, because I just couldn't go any faster. We all finished together, and then David, to everyone's surprise, kept going and ran for several more laps. I was walking slowly with Donny, to settle down after the run, and he was livid. "What does David think he's doing?" Donny exclaimed. "I've got to teach that boy something!"

As David passed us on the track, Donny shouted out at him several times along the lines of "What do you think you're doing?" Then, when David stopped, Donny walked over and chewed off David's ear. "We are all here to run 3 miles," Donny said, "and if you have enough in you to go farther, then you should try and sprint with the others at the end. The goal is to make 3 miles with the rest of us if you can. Don't you understand? I dropped back and ran with you to help you through, and then you just kept running on. Next time, if you have something left in you, just sprint a little harder a little earlier." David apologized.

The Training of Troy

One morning Donny showed up with Troy, a rather corpulent young man. Troy was not a very good runner. Donny said he would spend his time with Troy and not run alongside Choc, the pacer. The first morning, amid a lot of puffing, panting, and perspiring, Troy ran about six laps. Donny ran with him. After six laps he told Troy to stop running and just walk for a bit. Then Donny ran up alongside the rest of us, eventually taking his regular place at the head of the team.

Donny followed this routine for many mornings thereafter. Each morning he set increasingly difficult targets for Troy and mixed them up a bit, for example, "This morning you'll walk five laps after you've run, and then you'll run with us for four more." Then Donny would run ahead to join us after running alongside Troy at a slightly slower pace for the first few laps. After a while we got used to the idea of Donny being all over the track: sometimes behind us, encouraging Troy; sometimes ahead of us, pacing alongside of Choc. Within a month Troy was up to a mile and was running with the rest of us.

Weigh-In

Once a month Donny had us weigh in. At that time we set our objectives for how much weight we would lose by the next weigh-in. The successful ones were not pressed.

The next running day after the weigh-in, there was a great ceremony. Herb received a jersey on which was printed "Doctor D's Track Team." Choc had had them made up and kept them in his locker, waiting for the appropriate occasion to hand one out. Herb was the only recipient. He not only had consistently run the distance but also had made his weight target. Donny let us all know that he wasn't going to be generous about giving out the other jerseys—even though they were all ready and printed. Only consistent demonstrations of performance across several fronts would merit a Doctor D's Track Team jersey.

The Breaking of Bruce

Bruce was a bit younger than most of us, in his late 20s. He had been running with us and had been mocking Donny a bit about how slow he ran. One morning Bruce set out in the first lap, passed Donny and Choc and the others, and finished well ahead of everyone. Donny castigated Bruce for setting so severe a pace that he could not possibly maintain it consistently, even if he had done so on that particular day. Well, that was the beginning of quite a situation. Next time out Donny, Bruce, and John (who joined us occasionally were all running well ahead of the rest of us and lapping us once or twice in the process. John runs well and quickly. Donny had set the pattern for his running by telling him before we started how to pace him, how often to lap us, and so on. Donny stayed with John most of the way, but not all the way all the time. Bruce ran ahead, too. However, he appeared to listen less to Donny's advice, in fact, not to take it at all. At first Bruce was going great guns. He would lap us two and even three times, finishing the 2 miles in as little as 14½ minutes. However, Bruce was running without Donny's help; John, in contrast, was getting better but under Donny's tutelage. Soon John was outperforming Bruce, and Bruce was, in fact, slowing down. He was soon back to running with the team. Donny challenged him almost every day about his pace and pattern of running. Soon he was running regularly with the whole team and then even a little behind the team. I know, because he would run just ahead of me, and I was one of the slower runners.

Donny would harass Bruce quite a bit in the locker room by telling him that he wouldn't last and by telling some of Bruce's buddies, who were also there in the morning but didn't run with us, that they would have to do something about the poor boy because he was getting beyond himself. The criticism appeared to have a significant effect on Bruce, because he kept slowing down, and then one very hot, muggy day near the end of June, when many in the group ran poorly and quit after a mile, Bruce pulled up short of a mile. Donny was sort of gloating in the locker room afterwards. He told everyone, particularly Bruce's buddies, quietly of course, what happened. He told them they would have to get the poor boy's morale up again. He said to me, coming out of the showers, "Well, we broke him, psychologically. Now we'll have to build him up again."

About a year later I asked Donny why he had broken Bruce. He didn't respond immediately, but later, while we were running, he shouted back to me, "I have an answer to your question." And he answered with a question: "Why does a parent discipline a child?"

Emergent Leadership

On a Friday not too long after I joined the team, Donny was absent. Herb took over as leader that day. He asked us each how far we planned to run and assured us that we would run slow enough for everyone to finish. He stressed this goal repeatedly. And we all made it, including two members, and I was one of them, who had never been able to do 2 miles before. Everyone felt great, and we made some joking remarks about how we had to make Herb our new leader.

Herb left for a short holiday that weekend, and Donny reappeared to lead us on the next running day, a Monday. It was a tough run. Several of us quit early, and Donny castigated everyone who quit, particularly Harry. Harry mentioned that he preferred running under Herb. The rest of the week was average, no great performances. Herb returned on the following Monday, and Donny, for the first time in years, failed to show up because he had slept in. Herb took charge, and we all ran the 2 miles again. I looked forward with anxious anticipation to Wednesday, when both Donny and Herb would be there together.

Wednesday turned out to be a strange running day. It happened this way: Donny took the right lead position beside Choc, and Herb was two positions back. After less than a mile, Choc faltered badly and began to slow down. Barrie, running behind, took over as pacer. But as Choc fell back, Herb fell back and kept pace with Choc. Harry, Larry, and I stayed behind. Meanwhile Donny and three others in front moved ahead, and as they continued a normal pace and we kept slowing down, the gap between us widened. We were now two separate groups. Those of us behind Choc and Herb, who were still running side by side, didn't know what to make of it. We muttered about getting farther behind but made no specific effort to pass Choc and Herb and catch up to the front group. Donny kept turning and shouting over his shoulder at all of us to move up, gesturing constantly with his arm and looking very worried about what was happening. In the meantime the gap grew wider.

Then Donny did something unusual. Leaving the front group to fend for itself, he dropped all the way back to our subgroup and urged us to keep running ahead. He commenced with Herb, getting him to leave Choc's side and run ahead. Choc was slowing down more and more. Donny urged us all ahead of Choc, and soon we were all running, not as we normally do in a tight group, but spread out and scattered all along the track.

Then Donny took another assertive action. He dropped all the way back behind everyone to take up a position, his usual one, alongside Choc, who was lagging very far behind now. And though we were all ahead of him, and it was clear he wasn't going to complete the 2 miles in any kind of time, Donny stayed alongside Choc all the way, urging him on in a constant and very audible voice. We all kept going, and we all finished. Donny stayed with Choc, and with Donny's help, Choc finished, although the pace was much slower than normal. After that incident, most of us ran the 2 miles almost every time out, under the original coach's direction.

Challenging the Leader

Larry usually ran in last place with the team. One summer he broke his ankle playing baseball and didn't run with us for most of the year. Then he started running again, sometimes joining us for short periods, sometimes running before or after us, sometimes faster for short spurts, though usually slower. He was slowly getting back into shape.

Then one day he took his usual position at the rear as we were starting. After the first few laps, Donny had not called out the number of laps, and Larry chose to call them out, loudly. Someone kibitzed and said that wasn't his job. I chipped in jokingly and said that I liked it when Larry called the laps. It was like old again, having Larry back. Larry kept calling the laps out as we completed them, and Donny, up front, said nothing.

Then Larry lost count somewhere around the eight or ninth lap. I shouted to Donny to tell us where we were, but he wouldn't answer. I feel kind of lost when I don't know what I've run, so I asked a few more times. "Would someone please say where we are?" Donny didn't answer. Finally, in a loud voice, he said, "Strictly for Harvey, that was 1 mile we just passed." The next mile, he gave us two counts, one at the half mile and one at the end of the 2nd mile. Normally he would count out every two laps, that is, nine times in a mile. In the 3rd mile he gave us three counts.

At the end of the run he muttered something about "teaching you guys respect the hard way."

I was away one week when a new fellow, Bradley, joined the group and ran 2 miles with the team. He showed up on the morning I returned, complaining about his leg. He said the tight corners on the track had bothered him, particularly because we always ran in the same direction.

Choc was on vacation, so Herb took up the pacer position, and Donny ran along side him. After several laps Donny looked back at Bradley and could see why he was hurting. He was doing something wrong. Donny dropped back to run with Bradley and talk to him for quite a while.

Then Donny made some kidding remarks from his position near the back of the group about how Herb was burning up the track and would never have the stamina to keep it up. Someone else made an aside about how leaders shouldn't undermine their subordinates. Donny was running beside me at that point and muttered, "Yeah, but if you don't undermine a subordinate who challenges the leader, you become an ex-leader."

Then he turned to me and said, "That reminds me of the time I was in the office of a chief executive I know. His company normally placed its insurance through my agency, but someone in the organization had placed it with a competitor that year. I found out and went to see him. I was furious; I shouted and yelled at him. And he said, "Don't you think you are overreacting?" I said, "The cemeteries are filled with insurance agents who underreacted."

4

The Organization: A Foundation

Learning Objectives

After completing this module, you should be able to

1. Explain the major features of the organization.
2. State the key elements of open-systems thinking as they apply to understanding and improving effectiveness.
3. Describe a cognitive map of an organization: the formal and human organizations.
4. Describe the major characteristics of the emergent role system.
5. Appreciate the complex dynamics between the formal organization and human organization.
6. Develop conceptual tools useful in diagnosing, understanding, predicting, and influencing behavior in organizations.

Module Outline

Study Questions

Endnotes

Activity 4–2: Values in Business

Optional Activities on the WWW

Activity 4–3W: Diagnosing an Organization—WWW Exploration

Activity 4–4W: Learning from a Manager about an Organization

Premodule Preparation

Activity 4–1: A Comparative Exploration of Two Organizations: Sandlot and Little League[1]

Objectives:

a. To identify the multiple features of an organization.

b. To learn about two types of organizations and their management.

c. To introduce alternative ways to map an organization.

Task 1:

One of the major characteristics of a modern society is the development of numerous and more complex organizations. This activity asks you to draw on your individual and shared experiences to look at the similarities and differences between two forms of athletic organizations: sandlot and Little League organizations. The athletic teams could be two baseball organizations (sandlot and Little League baseball) or basketball or soccer. The comparative analysis forms suggest several dimensions on which you may compare the two types of organizations. Feel free to develop any additional dimensions that you consider relevant.

a. Review the listed dimensions and add supplemental dimensions that you consider relevant.

b. Each individual should complete the individual comparison that follows.

c. Working in teams, develop a group composite of your comparative analysis on the page that follows.

d. Each group selects a spokesperson to present its analysis to the class.

e. The instructor will facilitate a class discussion.

f. Reflecting on this activity, your previous experiences, and your learning thus far, try to define below, in your own words, an organization.

An organization is _____

_____

_____

_____

[1]This activity is a modified version of "Informal and Formal Organizations: Sandlot and Little League Baseball" created by Professors Fremont E. Kast and James E. Rosenzweig. We appreciate the authors' permission to modify and include this activity in this textbook.

Individual Comparative Analysis of Sandlot and Little League

	Sandlot Organization	Little League

1. Who are the participants? How are members of these organizations identified?

2. What are the goals of these organizations? Who identifies the goals?

3. What rules govern these organizations? Who makes the rules?

4. How structured are these organizations?

5. Who performs the managerial functions of planning, decision making, and control in these organizations?

6. How would you describe the relationships among the people in these organizations?

7. What motivates people in these organizations?

8. What are the leadership and influence patterns in these organizations?

9. What are some of the expectations in these organizations?

10. How do these organizations relate to their external environments such as other groups, organizations, competitors, and resources?

11. Who are the customers in these organizations?

12. What is the nature of the technology used (for example, equipment, knowledge)?

13.

14.

15.

Team Comparative Analysis of Sandlot and Little League

	Sandlot Organization	**Little League**

1. Who are the participants? How are members of these organizations identified?

2. What are the goals of these organizations? Who identifies the goals?

3. What rules govern these organizations? Who makes the rules?

4. How structured are these organizations?

5. Who performs the managerial functions of planning, decision making, and control in these organizations?

6. How would you describe the relationships among the people in these organizations?

7. What motivates people in these organizations?

8. What are the leadership and influence patterns in these organizations?

Sandlot Organization　　　　　　　**Little League**

9. What are some of the expectations in these organizations?

10. How do these organizations relate to their external environments such as other groups, organizations, competitors, and resources?

11. Who are the customers in these organizations?

12. What is the nature of the technology used (for example, equipment, knowledge)?

13.

14.

15.

Introduction

Organizational members and managers tend to develop cognitive maps that help them sort out their work experiences. A map is a graphic representation that provides a frame of reference. For geographers a map is a means of depicting the world so that people understand where they are and where they are going.[1] In the organizational context cognitive maps help people make sense of information and at times provide the reasoning behind actions. The broad cognitive map presented in Module 1 introduced organizations as systems composed of subsystems that interact regularly to produce and accomplish a desired goal or goals. Module 2 explored the role that expectations and learning play in organizational settings. In Module 3 management and leadership were charged with the responsibility of making organizations work as they should.

This module focuses on the exploration of the main features of the organization. We begin by inquiring into the work dynamics of two sport-based organizations: Sandlot and Little League. Many models, conceptual road maps, frameworks, and metaphors or images of organizations and how they work can be found in the literature. We have chosen to focus on two complementary cognitive maps as the foundations for the exploration and understanding of what organizations are and how they function: the open-systems view and the "script and actors" metaphor. The open-systems framework is introduced to help understand the environmental context within which organizations function, the complex dynamics between the organization and its environment, and some of the unique features of systems and open systems and how they are used to improve results. Next we introduce the script-and-actors metaphor to help explain the complex dynamics of both the human and formal organization. But first we need to develop a definition of an organization.

What Is an Organization?

An **organization** is an entity created for the basic purpose of accomplishing tasks that individuals cannot accomplish alone.[2] As such an organization is viewed as a coordinated unit consisting of at least two people who function to achieve a common goal or set of goals. They can be viewed as tools that people use to accomplish a wide variety of goals, attempting to obtain something they desire or value. Thus an organization is a response to and a mean of creating value that satisfies human needs.

Organizations exist in the form of agreements between people. As such the nature of the agreements, the process that was developed to arrive at shared agreements, and the need to continuously revisit the agreement are critical for the survival and success of the entity. (See our discussion on dialogue and expectation clarification in Module 2.) If agreements are good—meaning that individuals are fully committed to helping the organization succeed, are able to work together effectively, and have the proper tools and resources—the organization is more likely to adapt to its changing environmental context, survive, and succeed. If agreements are poor, individuals feel compelled to protect their own interests instead of being concerned with the success of the organization as a whole, the result of which is products, services, or both that fail to meet market needs.[3]

The way the organization is designed and organized will have a major effect on the organization's ability to achieve its goals. We devoted a complete module to the design of work and the design of organizations (see Module 13). A few points are important to note at this stage:

- Whereas many kinds of organization designs are possible, only some of the designs are superior.

- Organizational design begins with organizational creation and evolves over time.

- To the extent that this evolution reflects the real demands of the external environment, survival is more likely.

- As of late increasing attention is being given to the view of organizations as teams of teams (the team-based organization).

The Open-Systems View of Organizations

How do organizations create value? The basic premise of the open-systems view of organizations is that value creation takes place through complex dynamics between input, transformation, and output elements and processes in the context of the environment in which the organization operates. Before we go any further, let's explore some of the key notions of systems thinking.

The basic premise of open-systems theory is that organizations have common characteristics with all other living systems—from microscopic organisms to plants to animals to humans. Understanding these characteristics allows us to work with the natural tendencies of an organization rather than struggle against them needlessly. By understanding these similarities, we can apply the survival techniques of living systems to organizations and thereby increase our understanding of why certain organizations thrive while others fail.

For this discussion we shall define a *system* as an organized, unitary whole composed of two or more interdependent parts, components, or subsystems and delineated by identifiable boundaries from its environment. Systems of various parts are all around us. For example, we have mountain systems, river systems, and the solar system as part of our physical surrounding. The body itself is a complex organism including the skeletal system, the circulatory system, and the nervous system. We come into daily contact with transportation systems, communication systems, and economic systems. An **open system** means that the system depends on open interaction with its external environment. All living systems are open systems. Likewise, all organizations are open systems; a consumer purchasing an organization's product is an example of an open interaction of the organization with its external environment.

All systems have a **system boundary** (border) that separates one system from another. The boundary may be physical (building), temporal (a work shift), social (a departmental grouping), or psychological (a stereotyped prejudice). The degree to which the boundary allows interaction with the external environment or other systems is called the *permeability* of the boundary. Excessive permeability can overpower the system with external demands; too little permeability can starve the system for resources. All systems have a *purpose* that guides their existence. In the pursuit of this purpose, systems develop internal targets or goals with which the system measures its progress.

Inputs of materials and energy from the environment to a system are required for the survival and growth of the system. The inputs received into the system are subject to a transformation process, which converts the inputs into an output through a variety of processes. (See Figure 4–1.)

The transformation process yields *outputs* of materials and energy that are exported to the environment. The outputs are the system's attempt to fulfill its purpose. *Feedback* refers to the system's knowledge of how well it is accomplishing its purpose in terms of deviation measurements of the output from the purpose so that a correction can be made. Feedback also measures whether the purpose itself is appropriate in the current environment.

Everything outside the system's boundary is considered the environment. A closed system (mechanical system) does not interact with its environment. An open system (living system) interacts with its environment, but only with those segments of the environment that are relevant to its purpose. The balance between which segments are allowed to interact with the system and which are excluded (or ignored) is unique for each system.

Open Systems and Results

A basic understanding of the tenets of open-systems theory enables you to think in terms of systems when analyzing organizations or organizational issues. Since we all face situations in which we would like our units to respond or perform better, a system-based cognitive map can help us scan our unit and its environment systematically

Figure 4–1   **The Organization: A System-Based Framework**

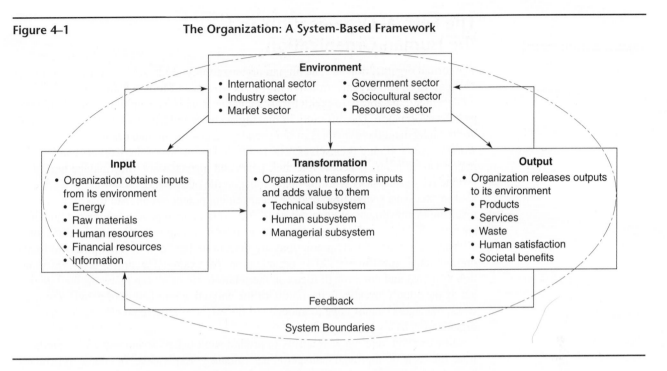

and provide direction for improvements. To understand any unit's functioning, we can begin by asking a few fundamental questions:

■ What is the apparent purpose or goal of the organization that causes activities to be coordinated into a pattern?

■ What are the key outputs and their major boundary transactions?

■ What are the key transformation processes, and how effectively are they balanced in achieving the purpose?

■ What are the key inputs and their major boundary transactions?

■ What is the reactivating feedback (both positive and negative) being delivered?

If the analysis of the diagnostic questions reveals that corrective action is appropriate, the next phase is to diagnose what happens when the system moves or exerts itself. We examine some key processes to determine whether all the parts will still function properly. The following questions can guide this diagnosis:

■ **Information coding.** Does the system obtain the needed information inputs (feedback) and appropriately block out unneeded items?

■ **Steady state.** Can the system maintain its operation within the limits of tolerance related to its targets?

■ **Negative entropy.** Is the system able to import more than it exports by changing purpose, goals, and practices to match emerging environmental demands?

■ **Equifinality.** Is there capacity, self-direction, and spontaneous self-regulation by individuals and groups to achieve the needed results?

■ **Specialization.** Does the system grow and expand appropriately without becoming overspecialized?

A review of the entire analysis will create a picture or map of the organization that clarifies its strengths and weaknesses. Any planned change to improve the organization's performance should likewise be analyzed with the same criteria in mind.

This methodical approach to analyzing and understanding organizations is quite adaptable to all types and styles of organizations and has proven to be a useful tool in enhancing organizational performance.

The Formal Organization and the Human Organization

The formal organization and the human organization provide analytical tools to further examine work and organization dynamics. As we saw in Module 3 on leadership and management, the ability to predict work behavior is an important dimension of managerial performance. The difficulty in making accurate predictions lies partly in the failure to understand the dynamics of the social system—the human organization—that workers create among themselves. The needs and emotions of the workers can be major determinants. If people like their peers and management, they may be highly productive despite poor working conditions; on the other hand, monotonous work can lead to excessive socializing, or poor management practices can lead to irritation, resulting in slowdowns or even sabotage. This statement appears obvious, but understanding the impact of needs and emotions on work-group behavior is most difficult.

Another reason that the predictions are inaccurate lies in the overemphasized focus on individual, specific parts of an organization (for example, technical tasks, information systems) and not enough focus on the relationship of all the pieces as they interact. If they don't investigate the nature of the collective interaction of people and their tasks, managers cannot hope to understand the effect of individual changes on the organization as a whole.

How can you improve your ability to predict work behavior and make your predictions the basis of improved managerial performance? Experience, of course, is primary, but learning to work with analytical tools can yield excellent insights. We will introduce some aspects of the formal organization that give the functional structure to work groups and that create the interrelated job designs and descriptions the work-group members must follow to perform their required functional roles. It is while interacting to perform these required roles that the web of group dynamics begins to spin.

The analytical tools and road maps that we introduce in this module are the open system and the formal and human organization framework. Together they enable us to develop a holistic understanding of the organization. We will be assuming that managers can improve employee performance by going beyond the formal organization to acquire a working knowledge of the many aspects of the human organization. A general development of the script-and-actors approach, which can be applied to the total organization or to smaller work units, follows. Then we discuss the more detailed formal and human organization models: the operational blueprint (Figure 4–2), actors playing their roles (Figure 4–3).

The Script and the Actors

One of the best ways to comprehend the idea of the **formal organization** is to think of it as a **script** that has to be thoroughly understood by the director (manager) before the **actors** (employees) are given their roles to play. The script of a formal organization includes, among other things, the purpose, the functional roles that must be assigned to the actors, the coordination of the interactions between the roles, the nature of the different types of work to be performed, and the status accorded to the different work roles by the actors or the audience (the public). The background in which the play takes place must be known, as must the immediate setting. The types of people available to play the parts plus their character, attitudes, and experience are also important.

If you are a competent director, you will be able to hire the actors, train them in your particular interpretation of the script, and see that the performance of the play achieves the purposes of the script and provides satisfaction to the actors. Under these conditions the formal organization (script) and the **human organization** (actors) are compatible and well integrated. This condition can be achieved only when the director has carefully developed, shaped, and perhaps rewritten the script and the setting so the performance can be predicted. In other words, management can design the work, control the environment in which it takes place, and shape the human organization so that high productivity will result from the achievement of the purposes of both the organization and the people. If management does not carry out this responsibility, a possibly serious consequence is that the actors will spontaneously create and control their own human organization, which may not have the type of climate conducive to high productivity. It may even have an antiorganizational bias in regard to the formal system.

The area of job redesign, which is of widespread current interest in the auto industry, illustrates one aspect of script control of the formal organization. In an early study the Volvo auto plant in Sweden (faced with annual turnover rates of up to 40 percent) experimented with processes such as job rotation, in which the employee changes jobs once or several times a day, depending on the nature of the work of the group. Jobs have also been enriched in that work teams in some cases follow the same auto body through several stations over a 20-minute period. Both strategies to control the script resulted in significant reductions in turnover and higher productivity.

In addition to job redesign, other management technologies and practices can be adopted to develop the human organization; these will be introduced later. Participation of people in the decision-making process is a subject of a later module. However, it is assumed that managers must have a good understanding of how people live and work in organizations in order to write and rewrite the script and direct the performance. Coming modules address the topics of small group dynamics, motivation, communications, and perception to provide you with a set of concepts and theories through which this understanding can be increased. The concepts can also be used as tools of analysis. If, for example, you know Abraham Maslow's *hierarchy of needs,*[4] you can examine any script and attempt to predict what satisfactions and frustrations employees will experience in the performance of the work. Frederick Herzberg's motivation theory is the basis of his idea of *job enrichment,* a method of redesigning work to fulfill the needs of the workers more effectively.[5]

We must now show the utility value of the formal organization and human organization models by moving to a more detailed development, starting with the idea of the operational blueprint.

Operational Blueprint

Just as engineers follow blueprints, managers need **operational blueprints** to guide them when establishing a manufacturing organization or when attempting to understand one that is already in operation. Figure 4–2 provides an operational blueprint depicting major elements of a formal organization and the setting in which it operates. For convenience we will focus on three areas: external environmental factors, internal environmental factors, and the formal organization or script.[6]

Figure 4–2
Operational Blueprint

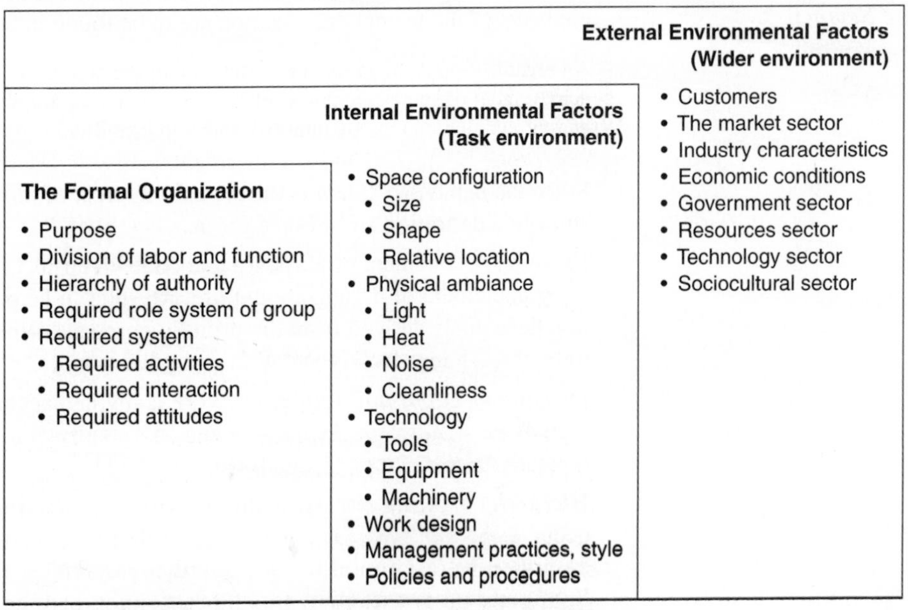

The Formal Organization	Internal Environmental Factors (Task environment)	External Environmental Factors (Wider environment)

• Purpose
• Division of labor and function
• Hierarchy of authority
• Required role system of group
• Required system
  • Required activities
  • Required interaction
  • Required attitudes
	• Space configuration
	  • Size
	  • Shape
	  • Relative location
	• Physical ambiance
	  • Light
	  • Heat
	  • Noise
	  • Cleanliness
	• Technology
	  • Tools
	  • Equipment
	  • Machinery
	• Work design
	• Management practices, style
	• Policies and procedures
		• Customers
		• The market sector
		• Industry characteristics
		• Economic conditions
		• Government sector
		• Resources sector
		• Technology sector
		• Sociocultural sector

External Environmental Factors

When designing a manufacturing company, planners must determine all the factors in the specific setting that will make the endeavor feasible or impinge upon it. These include (1) the market for the product involved; (2) potential competition, both national and international; (3) economic factors such as interest and inflation rates and the value of the dollar; (4) sources of supply; and (5) government regulations and legislation. These and many other factors related to economics, politics, social conditions, and technological development may have varying degrees of importance from case to case.

Our discussion thus far has centered on the use of Figure 4–2 as a guide for developing a new organization; however, its primary value for the reader will be in analyzing ongoing operations in case studies where only limited but essential factors are presented. Thus in the comparison of Sandlot and Little League organizations, we know only that a Little League team is likely to be sponsored by a specific business. We do not know the attitudes of the players and/or public toward the sponsor. Thus the factor of public attitude permits us to make some assumptions about (1) the importance of the sponsor and how that might influence the players and (2) the relationship between the players and coach and how it might affect performance.

Internal Environmental Factors

Internal environmental factors directly relate to designing the formal organization. Examples are (1) ownership; (2) acquisition and layout of physical facilities; (3) finances; (4) technology (selection of equipment, machines, and methods); (5) work design; and (6) work flow. All plans and procedures of the manufacturing process are included here, but the required behavioral roles of the managers and employees are not.

Here is an example of how spatial arrangements can affect the work group. An insurance company was located in an old building where all insurance agents had private offices on the second floor. The clerical and support staffs were scattered in several small rooms on the first floor. A new building was built in which all personnel were located on one spacious floor. The insurance agents were located around the borders of the floor in cubicles separated by waist-high walls. In the vast center area were the desks of the clerical and support personnel. The agents initially complained about lost privacy for their clients. Six months later they expressed satisfaction with the openness of the atmosphere, and privacy was never a problem. More important, the clerical and support personnel showed an increase in productivity of more than 20 percent. Management attributed this increase to the full visibility of the clerical and support personnel to all those agents they were supporting—it was difficult to slack off in front of people waiting for their files to be completed.

Formal Organization (the Script)

Now we move from the background setting into the functioning organization. The basic elements of the formal organization are to be found in Schein's classical definition:

An organization is the rational coordination of the activities of a number of people for the achievement of some common explicit purpose or goal, through division of labor and function and through a hierarchy of authority and responsibility.[7]

Since the behavior system is the primary interest of this text, we shall elaborate to show this definition's relevance for us.

Purpose: A statement of purposes and goals in terms of products and services is an integral element of organizational life. All roles to be performed within the organization have goals derived from the primary purposes. While these purposes change over time, they change slowly and with great difficulty.

Division of Labor and Function: Work is divided according to the specific tasks individuals are to perform. As the size and complexity of a company increase, this division typically becomes more specialized.

Hierarchy of Authority: As planning, staffing, directing, and controlling processes occur, a chain of command (bosses and subordinates) of line positions is established to designate the responsibilities for activities essential to the operation of the business. Staff positions are set up to provide the support and services that help conduct these essential activities.

The Required Role System of the Work Group: Readers sometimes find the term system confusing, so a definition may be helpful at this point. *System* means a regularly interacting or interdependent group of elements that together make up a unified whole.

The **required system** of the formal organization refers to the behavioral requirements of the role an individual plays when performing the tasks of a specific position. These consist of three elements:

1. *Required activities.* Specific sets of activities are usually an integral part of every job. Analysts in an organization, for example, are required to receive data daily from the field depots worldwide and to keep inventory sheets from these data.

2. *Required interactions.* Most positions require interaction with other positions. Thus the same analysts have to provide data to supervisors; however, little or no coordination with fellow workers might be called for in the script.

3. *Required attitudes.* The analysts may be expected to maintain attitudes of conscientiousness, carefulness, and independence in the processing of their data records.

The required role behaviors of a specific position interlock with those of one or more other roles in the basic work group, creating a required role system. It is this **required role system** of the work group and its relationship to other work groups as they interact in the entire system that is our most basic focus in the formal organization.

The Human Organization (Actors Playing Their Roles)

Once an organization is in operation, how do managers and other employees make the formal organization work? As noted previously, people almost always play their roles somewhat differently than the script because it may be incomplete, may not satisfy their needs, may not fit their personality, and so on. The formal organization sets the stage for the creation of the human organization. The human organization is the way that the system actually works rather than the way it is supposed to work. The script, with its rigidly defined purposes, chain of command, and many requirements, gets interpreted, transformed, and acted upon by the people who work in the system. As a result, a new human organization emerges with its own characteristics, values, roles, and social norms as management and workers go about making the formal organization workable and livable. This differentiation of the human system occurs from two perspectives (see Figure 4–3): (1) managers adapting and changing the operational blueprint and (2) workers developing identifiable recurrent ways of acting.

Figure 4–3
The Human Organization
Actors playing their roles

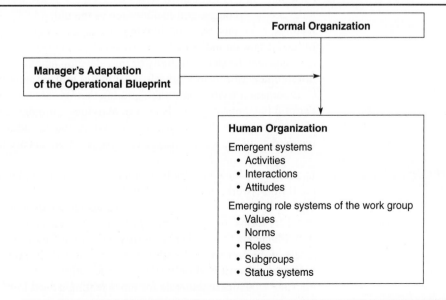

Managers' Adaptations of the Operational Blueprint

Managers often find they must innovate or adjust to the normal dynamics of the company to make plans work. Thinking of the human organization as a living, organic entity, ever adapting to the internal and external changes, provides better insight into the manager's role than limiting our view to the static, rigid positions of the formal organization.

The Emergent Role System of the Work Group

The required system of behavior of the formal organization becomes the emergent system of the human organization when the actors start playing their roles.[8] The **emergent role system** refers to those activities, interactions, and attitudes that spontaneously develop as individuals strive to follow the script but also satisfy their own needs. For example, an insurance analyst is to be at his desk working by 8 A.M. (a required activity). Instead, he arrives on time but goes directly to the washroom, stops off at the coffee machine on the way back to his desk (emergent activities), chats with neighboring workers along the way (emergent interactions), and starts work at 8:10. While analyzing insurance claims, he seeks his neighbor's help for a difficult case (emergent interaction) instead of his supervisor's (the required interaction) because he dislikes his supervisor (emergent attitude, since the required attitude would be favorable feelings toward the boss). He and his neighbor encounter a claim that is not covered by regulations so they improvise a solution (emergent activities and interactions) and submit it to the supervisor for approval (required interaction).

Just as the required system is adapted into the emergent system, the required role system evolves spontaneously into the emergent role system as the actors go about their work. The emergent role system of one work group is linked to the emergent role systems of one or more other work groups; the resulting total structure becomes the human organization. In this sense a manufacturing company is a social system or small community.

The small work group is the primary focus of the study of organizational behavior because it is here that the emergent role systems, which are major determinants of behavior, are spontaneously generated. The development of the emergent role system is the subject of small group dynamics in the next module, where group elements, processes, and attributes (such as values, norms, roles, subgroupings, status, and cohesiveness) will be discussed. At this time, however, emergent attitudes should be defined, since many group elements (for example, norms) are derived from them.

Emergent Attitudes: The work group's emergent attitudes are singled out for study because they are predictors of worker behavior, just as political attitudes are often useful indicators of voter behavior. By *attitudes* we mean an individual's predisposition to respond in a given way toward situations, things, ideas, people, and issues; for example, workers frequently view management as insensitive to employee needs. Attitudes are based on general factors such as the individual's experience, knowledge, feelings, emotions, ways of thinking, needs, and goals. In a given situation they will influence how an individual perceives, acts, and reacts. In the emergent role system, attitudes may be shared initially or may develop among people as they interact and differentiate aspects of work life meaningful to their activities and well-being.

Emergent activities, attitudes, and interactions are not necessarily either helpful or harmful to company goals. However, activities, attitudes, and interactions do tend to affect one another. Some emergent behaviors and attitudes are closely related to required activities and attitudes; as we will see, others are more distant.

Networks and Cliques

In addition to the emergent behaviors closely associated with required behaviors, people form networks and cliques that do not appear in the script. Those that control scarce resources and communication (grapevines) are among the most common. For instance, formal organizational channels are often slow and give incomplete information. Managers and workers typically have a network of friendly contacts at different levels of the organization with whom they informally exchange information. Often this emergent network is closely related to the script requirements but also functions to alleviate anxieties and threats for those feeling a need to know.

Social groupings—either employee or management initiated (for baseball, bridge, and item collection)—are not related to the script, but members may develop acquaintances who are useful back on the job. On the other hand, the only relationship of a covert network running a numbers racket in a factory to the script requirements is to impact them negatively.

Diversity of the Actors

If planners responsible for starting a new company were using the operational blueprint for completing an operating plan, their concern would now turn to locating, recruiting, and hiring the workforce. It would be important to know the backgrounds of the people who are going to work for the company to understand how they will work together and to predict how management might mold them into an effective human organization. Some background factors to consider may include sociological factors such as culture and ethnicity; demographic characteristics such as age and sex; and individual attributes such as knowledge, skills, abilities, values, beliefs, and personality. Furthermore, one may want to explore the occupational mix between professional and managerial, technical, clerical, and blue collar.

Background characteristics of the actors will influence their attitudes toward work, toward team work, and toward managerial policies and practices. Employers must be aware that the whole person comes to work, not just the part that does the job. Employees' immediate attitudes contain many ingredients of their backgrounds as well as their reactions to what is happening to them on the job. Women, ethnic minorities, and handicapped members of our society are intensely aware of equal rights legislation. Companies not heeding their rights can anticipate less than fully productive performance.

Integrating the Two Cognitive Maps

In this module we proposed two cognitive maps that we view as complementary. At the center of the open-systems-based framework we have the "transformation" cluster (see Figure 4–1). The transformation cluster is composed of the formal and human organization components (see Figure 4–3). One way to examine the nature and dynamics of the transformation process is to focus on the many elements of the formal and human organizations and the interactions between them. Figure 4–4 provides a schematic skeleton for such an integrated framework.

**Figure 4–4
An Integrated Roadmap:** Open System, the Formal Organization and the Human Organization

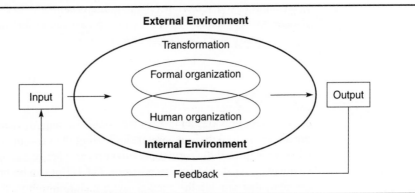

Consequences

Our major emphasis has been on the use of behavioral science models to gain greater understanding of work behavior. But as managers we must go further, using these tools of analysis to improve your effectiveness as decision maker and leader. How can you evaluate your actions in this regard? Are improved worker performance, improved profits, and reduced costs the major criteria? They may or may not be. To answer this question, we need to return to our past view that what constitutes effective leadership depends upon the consequences of your actions. From the perspective of the human organization, we use three primary criteria for evaluating consequences:

1. *Productivity.* Are costs per unit and quality ensuring profits and meeting the competition?
2. *Worker satisfaction.* Does the worker situation maximize satisfactions and minimize frustrations?
3. *Organizational health.* Is the vitality and viability of the human organization being maintained? Does the work culture facilitate individual growth?

Managerial actions need to be evaluated in advance from both long- and short-range views. A well-recognized problem in industry is the tendency of managers to make decisions that maximize short-range profits (the overemphasized bottom line) but damage long-range effectiveness. Examples are avoiding capital reinvestment in new technology and letting working conditions deteriorate, thus stimulating employee resentment.

The following characteristics describe employees of firms that maintain organizational health:

- They are highly productive, results-oriented, and cost-conscious.
- They like to be a part of a team, like to work in the department, identify with the organization, are cooperative with management and each other, and coordinate activities well. They do not overemphasize the goals of their section to the detriment of the department or the organization.
- They like their work, find it interesting and challenging, and are self-directing.
- They develop patterns of interaction that generate good communications, and they confront conflict meaningfully.
- They feel they have opportunities for growth and achievement of their goals.
- They have flexibility in coping with change.

These characteristics are similar to those of the professional-transformational manager organizational model introduced in the previous module.

In concluding, a cautionary note. We have implied that managers can mold the script-and-actor systems into an effective organization. But managers have limits to their powers to change and mold people. Play directors can ask many things that managers cannot. And sometimes the ongoing organization is so rigidly locked in that change is not possible. We are hoping and assuming that there is always some wiggle room—usually more than most of us recognize.

Summary

This module provides an integrative cognitive map, or road map, for understanding organizations and their dynamics. Following the view of organizations as open systems, we depicted the formal organization as a script that tells the actors (the employees) where, what, and how to perform. The script can be broken down into certain elements that provide the manager with insight into how the play is apt to go, where potential problems will arise, and so on. To direct the organization toward desired performance, the manager must have in mind models of how the actors are to interact and perform. Awareness that the actors will not play the roles as the author intended is all-important. The human organization is always different from that called for in the formal organization; however, a manager can design and redesign the script and the environment to maximize the integration of the formal and human systems.

Figure 4–2 and Figure 4–3 are guides for understanding the script-and-actors approach. Finally, an integrative framework that pulls together the formal organization, the human organization, and the open-systems perspective was presented in Figure 4–4.

Key Terms and Concepts

Actors

Emergent role system

Equifinality

External environment

Formal organization

Human organization

Internal environment

Negative entropy

Open system

Operational blueprint

Organization

Required role system

Required system

Script

Steady state

System boundary

Transformation process

Study Questions

1. What is the value for managers of concepts such as the operational blueprint and actors playing their roles?

2. Students frequently do not understand how to apply the operational blueprint to case studies. For instance, Figure 4–2 gives a number of external background factors. How would you use these in analyzing a case? Could you apply them to a company that you are familiar with? Give reasons.

3. In what ways is the formal organization like the script of a play?

4. Why is there a difference between the required role system and the emergent role system of a work group?

5. Is the required role system included in the emergent role system?

6. Most managerial actions have some impact on the human organization or the emergent system. What criteria can be used in evaluating the effectiveness of management's actions?

7. How does the open-systems view of organization complement the human and formal views?

8. Discuss the relationship between expectations, open-systems thinking, and organizational behavior.

9. Apply the formal organization and human organization frameworks to examine your team's effectiveness.

10. Discuss the role of diversity in the human organization.

Endnotes

1. For a good review of maps and managers, see C. M. Fiol and A. S. Huff, "Maps for Managers: Where Are We? Where Do We Go from Here?" *Journal of Management Studies* 29, no. 3 (1992), pp. 267–85.

2. C. Barnard, *The Function of the Executive,* (Cambridge, MA: Harvard University Press, 1938).

3. W. A. Pasmore, *Designing Effective Organizations,* (New York: Wiley, 1988).

4. A. H. Maslow, *Motivation and Personality,* (New York: Harper & Row, 1954).

5. F. Herzberg, "One More Time: How Do You Motivate Employees?" *Harvard Business Review* 46, no. 1 (1968), pp. 53–62.

6. The discussions to follow on the required system and the emergent system and related concepts are adapted from the classical work by G. C. Homans, *The Human Group,* (New York: Harcourt Brace Jovanovich, 1950).

7. E. H. Schein, *Organizational Psychology,* 2d ed., (Englewood Cliffs, NJ: Prentice-Hall, 1970), p. 9.

8. A more complete development of the conceptual scheme described here is to be found in the book by G. C. Homans, *The Human Group,* (New York: Harcourt Brace Jovanovich, 1950). Other adaptations of Homans's required and emergent systems are contained in the following references: A. R. Cohen, S. L. Fink, H. Gadon, and R. D. Willits, "The Work Group," in *Effective Behavior in Organizations,* chap. 5, rev. ed., (Burr Ridge, IL: Richard D. Irwin, 1994).

Activity 4–2:
Values in Business

Objectives:

a. To increase awareness of the importance of values as determinants of organizational behavior.

b. To increase awareness of the differences in team members' perception of values.

c. To experience some of the issues associated with group decision making.

Introduction:

The future-shock era has caused continuous questioning and change of values. The Watergate crisis, the 1976 bicentennial celebration and strong ideological orientation of the Reagan administration, and the Newt Gingrich congressional revolution of 1995 have been times for intensive reexamination of the values of American democracy. Particularly prominent were the negotiations involving the trade of arms for hostages between members of the National Security Council and Iranian officials; the subsequent denial by the White House set off a credibility crisis on honesty. *U.S. News & World Report* did a national survey at that time on lying in America. The responsibilities and roles of business in our society, in the European democracies, and in the communist countries are also constantly debated. Further, the individual American is torn as never before between the values of our past, more stable culture and those of the present world. Marriage, sex, personal commitments, trust in interpersonal relationships, religion, and material wealth are among the primary areas of value conflict.

The need for governments, organizations, and individuals to identify and live by commitment to values is currently recognized as an essential element of effectiveness in living.

The exercise that follows is to help your team evaluate the relative importance of certain values with which business organizations must be concerned. Values can be thought of as existing in a hierarchy in our thought processes, some being given higher importance or priority than others. The whole pattern of values in an organization represents the core of its operating philosophy and its organizational culture. Thus they are major determinants of behavior of management and employees.

Values defined: Things, ideas, beliefs, and acts that are regarded as good or bad, right or wrong, desirable or undesirable, beautiful or ugly, contributing to or detrimental to human welfare, and so on. Societies, organizations, and individuals all have values with priorities of importance. For example, individuals may differ greatly in the values associated with religious beliefs, but a higher-order value that they all presumably would accept is freedom of religious beliefs.

General Exercise:

Assume you are a member of a top-management team of a large corporation. During a team-development retreat, the facilitator-consultant informs the group that she has observed from individual interviews with team members that differences in perception exist as to the values by which they operate. Yet each person seems to be assuming that her or his values are shared by the other team members. As a basis for developing awareness and better consensus in values, the following tasks are undertaken.

Task 1 (Individual Rankings):

Listed in alphabetical order on the accompanying worksheet are 10 values that are among those often discussed in regard to business functioning. Your job is to rank these according the priority you would assign each in terms of importance for conducting business. Do this by writing in the first column next to the value a 1 for the value of highest importance, a 2 for the next, on down to a 10 for the value of lowest importance. In the second column, briefly note the reason for your ranking. Be sure to do this without consulting others; also, be sure your rankings are not observable to team members while completing this task. (*Note:* There is no right or wrong answer and no definite solution to this exercise. The rankings should be based on your own beliefs.)

Task 2 (Team Rankings):

Teams meet outside of class. Members compare their rankings of the values and come to a consensus as to how the team would rank the items from 1 to 10. This ranking should reflect what the team believes, not your estimate of how businesspeople would rank the values. (*Note:* Consensus does not necessarily mean that all agree with the final ranking of the team; it does mean that everyone's views were expressed and understood and that agreement was reached on how the values were to be ranked. In a real situation your personal values may differ from your colleagues', but you may decide to support the team's viewpoint for reasons such as hoping eventually to persuade your co-workers to adopt your views or wanting to be open-minded to see whither you could be wrong. If your values are too different, you may find, after a reasonable period, that you do not fit into the team. The main point of the exercise at this time is to increase your awareness of value issues.)

Task 3 (Classroom):

Teams list on the board the rank ordering of their values. Discuss similarities and differences.

Name _____ Date _____

Worksheet for Activity 4–2

Values	Your Ranking	Reason	Your Team's Ranking	Reason
Career growth and development of personnel	7		4	MAINTAIN employment Moral, need to make employees happy, and they will work harder knowing they can grow as a team
Concern for personnel as people	10		7	WANT HAPPY People + AVOID TURNOVER
Efficiency	2		6	MAKE most profits w/out diseconomy of scale (wasting goods) make use of resource wisely
Ethics (morality)	9		3	why not? unhappy employees— Possible law suit - want to do the right thing
Managerial and organizational effectiveness	1		1	MAINTAIN the structure of the company
Servicing clients' needs (for example, equipment, orders)	4		9	Avoid COGNITIVE DISSONANCE } need to treat others like people as well
Profits	5		2	w/out profits you will not succeed —> services to run + quality
Providing products or services for society	2		10	automatically ingrained in the company will ultimately provide products it produces
Quality of goods or services	6		8	need good quality to sell it w/out quality no one will buy it
Social responsibility	8		5	everyone needs to do their part in order for each link to work properly

Part 2

Managing Teams

Review

Thus far in the course, we have explored the context within which individuals function in organizational settings. Part 1 helped to establish the boundaries and process of the course: The field of study was defined, the learning community was established and expectations were examined, and key characteristics of the organization were discussed.

After the completion of Part 1, we need to step back and recapture some of the learning. Two distinct purposes were established for Part 1: to create the content and the process boundaries for the course and to establish the learning community.

The Learning Community: As managers you will need to assume that your organization is an educational institution for its employees. As an educator you need to foster the learning organization, help build the institution, train the employees, and help develop an appreciative inquiry culture. What we did to build the learning community in the classroom can serve as a model for your work organization. We worked on five aspects:

1. *Content.* In defining organizational behavior, the topic areas were identified. The course objectives were given.

2. *Technology.* Experiential learning methods (that is, involvement learning through interaction activities) were used. A learning sequence for these methods was given that differed from a content learning approach. Skills development and learning competencies were emphasized. Through communication the bonding process emerged.

3. *Roles.* The instructor's role was defined as that of a facilitator, a coach, and a resource person. The participant's role was defined as that of learner and coach who is responsible for the learning of fellow participants.

4. *Climate.* Values of openness, sharing, full participation, appreciation of uniqueness, inquiry appreciative, and seeing conflict as creative were interwoven into the fabric.

5. *Structure.* Teams were formed and are functioning under the guidance of the facilitator.

All of these factors and more are relevant when you are building the learning organization at any work organization; they apply to any level from the basic supervision up to top management.

What did we do to create the learning community? The course started with an exercise in which you defined behavior in organizations with topics such as fair treatment, motivation to work, frustration from work, communication breakdown, relationships with supervisors, supervisory practice, and relationships with fellow workers. The text added a theoretical approach that focused on an organization as a system made up of interacting subsystems, all coordinating people and materials to achieve goals. For the purpose of studying the aspects of this system that are most relevant to management, four levels of behavior were designated: individual, small group, intergroup, and total organization effectiveness. Personality, communication, motivation, and perception were defined as core concepts to be explored at each of these levels. We stated our belief that the most meaningful way to study organizational behavior is by relevant activities exercises or cases that permit the participants to examine their own behavior. This method was described as involvement or process learning, as contrasted with content learning.

The learners were assigned into permanent teams for the duration of the course. As a member of a learning team, appreciative inquiry into some of the content areas began via a set of experiential activities. Expectations, individual learning goals, individual differences, and leadership styles were explored through the sharing of individual experiences and reflections. Some work team norms and roles are evolving as the teams are struggling with the ambiguity of some of the team tasks. Some work teams in the learning community seem to be more effective than others; some seem to have a lot of fun, and some seem to struggle a little.

Preview of Part 2

Teams are a major focus of study throughout this course because teams and work groups are the basic unit of the emerging contemporary enterprises. Interestingly, teamwork is an old idea that is experiencing renewal as a mechanism to carry out complex tasks and integrate work, people, and organizations. The view of organizations as "teams of teams," or team-based organization, seems to be taking hold.

As the course progresses, new aspects of team effectiveness will be introduced so they can be applied to your classroom group. Modules 5, 6, and 7 concentrate directly on the small group and provide material on team skills, small group theory, and team building or team development. Module 8 focuses on the dynamics between teams. We approach the study of work groups and teams with the process-learning model, which first provides an experience from which you can develop theory and concepts.

Thus at the beginning of Module 5, group problem solving is explored in Activity 5–1 ("Mountain Survival Exercise"), Activity 5–1W ("Important Days Task"), and Activity 5–2W ("Task 21"). These exercises are similar, and your instructor will most likely assign only one of them. These activities should help you to understand (1) the difference between a group and a team and (2) why teams are so often used in organizations.

These activities are a good introduction to the subject of team effectiveness and the individual behaviors that help to improve team effectiveness. We then discuss individual versus group decision making as well as the circumstances where group problem solving or participative management is most appropriate. The module examines the role of the manager in facilitating group decision making and problem solving, explores ways in which creativity in problem solving can be enhanced, and shows some specific ways in which organizations use teams.

Module 5 ends with three additional activities that you may be assigned (two in the book and one on the WWW). The "Group Skills Development" activity is followed by "Who Gets the Overtime?" which is an exercise in decision making where there is no single right answer. The third, on the WWW, "Decision Making—Japanese Style," shows the impact of culture on group processes.

Module 6 focuses on group dynamics. It begins with two activities, "An Initial Inventory of Group Dynamics" and "A Card Game Called *Norms,*" that are designed to help you focus on some of the dynamics at work in your classroom group. The module explores in detail the factors that affect group development and performance, including leadership, group structure, and member composition. The phenomena of social loafing and cohesion are also discussed. The module ends with two activities to help you further explore the dynamics of your classroom group: "Individual Role Assessment" and "Status on the Campus." Finally a case study provides an opportunity for you to apply the concepts discussed in the module.

Module 7 describes ways to improve team effectiveness, both before a team starts operating and after it has begun its work. The activities and cases in Modules 5 and 6 should have demonstrated the possibility that dysfunctional behavior can exist in teams and work groups, and now Module 7 briefly examines ways to prevent and cure this behavior in systematic interventions to enhance team performance. The module contains five possible activities. The first provides an opportunity for you to examine your team development goals; the second activity—"Team Building in a Hospital Setting"—illustrates the team-building process via a case study that presents a situation in which team building is needed and gives you the chance to outline an intervention program. The third activity provides three essential tools for teams, and finally two activities on the Web provide conceptual integration via the analysis of two cases.

Finally, Module 8 focuses on the dynamics between teams in organizational settings. As such the module presents a framework that can guide the examination of the dynamics between two or more work teams. Intergroup communication processes and the dynamics of conflict are focal points for the module. A significant portion of the module is devoted to handling conflict. Three activities—"Ambiguity, Conflict, and Interteam Dynamics," "The Prisoners' Dilemma," and "The SLO Corporation"—provide opportunities to have concrete experiences of the complex interteam dynamics and to examine their effect on human behavior and performance.

5

Group Problem Solving and Decision Making

Learning Objectives

After completing this module, you should be able to

1. Understand the differences between teams and groups.
2. Explain the role that synergy and creativity play in group problem solving.
3. Understand the rational group problem-solving process.
4. Understand the consensus process in team activity.
5. State the conditions under which group decision making or participative management is most effective.

Module Outline

Premodule Preparation
    Activity 5–1: Mountain Survival Exercise

Introduction

The Nature of Teams
    Historical Context and Global Competition
    Work Groups and Teams: Toward a Definition
    Discussion of Premodule Preparation's Results
    Individual versus Group Problem Solving

Group Decision Making and Participative Management
    Other Factors

The Manager and Group Decision Making

Consensus and Group Decision Making

Organizational Skills

Creativity and Group Problem Solving
    Brainstorming
    Nominal Group Technique

Premodule Preparation

Activity 5–1:
Mountain Survival*

Objectives:

a. To demonstrate problem solving as a small group skill.

b. To show that group solutions can be superior to those of individuals under certain conditions.

c. To identify the types of behavior on the part of team members that facilitate problem-solving effectiveness.

Task 1:

a. Individuals, working alone, will complete the attached "Mountain Survival" worksheet. (Time: 10–15 minutes)

Task 2:

a. Individuals are to sit with their regular teams; it will not be necessary to appoint a spokesperson for this exercise.

b. Teams are to solve the problem as a team and arrive at a team solution for the problem. In doing so, the team should try to reach consensus and not use majority vote, trading, or averaging in reaching decisions.

Consensus is a decision process for making full use of available resources for resolving conflicts creatively. Consensus is difficult to reach, so not every ranking will meet with everyone's complete approval. Complete unanimity is not the goal—it is rarely achieved. However, each individual should be able to accept the group rankings on the basis of logic and feasibility. When all group members feel this way, you have reached consensus and the judgment may be entered as a group decision. This means, in effect, that a

*Source: Special permission for reproduction of the Mountain Survival activity is granted by the authors, Professors Fremont E. Kast and James E. Rosenzweig, Graduate School of Business Administration, University of Washington. All rights are reserved, and no reproduction should be made without express approval of Professors Kast and Rosenzweig. We are grateful to them.

single person can block the group if he or she thinks it necessary; at the same time, individuals should use this option in the best sense of reciprocity. Here are some guidelines to use in achieving consensus:

1. Avoid arguing for your own rankings. Present your position as clearly and logically as possible, but listen to the other members' reactions and consider them carefully before you press your point.

2. Do not assume that someone must win and someone must lose when discussion reaches a stalemate. Instead, look for the next most acceptable alternative for all parties.

3. Do not change your mind simply to avoid conflict. When agreement seems to come too quickly and easily, be suspicious. Explore the reasons and be sure everyone accepts the solution for similar or complementary reasons. Agree only to positions that have objective or logically sound foundations.

4. Avoid conflict-reducing techniques such as majority vote, splitting the difference, or coin tosses. When a dissenting member finally agrees, don't feel that that person must be rewarded by having her or his own way on a later point.

5. Differences of opinion are natural and expected. Seek them out and try to involve everyone in the decision process. Disagreements can help the group's decision because with a wide range of information and opinions, there is a greater chance that the group will hit upon more adequate solutions.[†]

6. As the teams work on a solution to the problems, no references, books, or other aids are to be used. The group results are to the recorded in the column titled Group Rankings. The individual rankings completed prior to the exercise should not be changed; they will be scored later.

(Time: 30–45 minutes)

Task 3:

a. The correct answer to the exercise will be provided by the instructor.

b. Individuals will calculate a total error score for their own solutions as follows:

If Your Answer Is	If Key Is	Difference between the Two Is
15	4	11
5	7	2
11	2	9
etc., for all items	etc.	etc.

Total Error Score*

*Add up without regard to pluses and minuses.

c. Calculate the team score in the same manner.

d. Calculate the average score for the individuals in your group by adding all scores and dividing by the number of members.

e. The instructor will record and display the results for all teams. Table 5–1 (for "Mountain Survival Exercise") is provided for you to record them.

f. Discussion question: Why were the group solutions in this activity superior to those of the average of the individual team members or, for some teams, superior to the "best" individual member?

[†]Special permission for reproduction of this is granted by the author, Jay Hall, Ph.D., and publishers, Teleometrics International. All rights reserved.

Table 5–1   Error Scores for Individuals and Groups on "Mountain Survival Exercise" for
                                 Your Class

Group	Before Discussion		After Group Discussion			
	Average Error Score of Group Members	Error Score of Most Accurate Group Member	Group Error Score	Gain or Loss over Average Error Score	Individuals in Group Superior to Group Score	Gain or Loss over Most Accurate Individual
1						
2						
3						
4						
5						
6						
7						
8						
Overall Average						

Worksheet for Activity 5–1

Your charter flight from Seattle to Banff and Lake Louise (Alberta, Canada) crash-landed in the north Cascades National Park area somewhere near the U.S.–Canadian border and then burst into flames. It is approximately noon in mid-January. The twin-engine, 10-passenger plane containing the bodies of the pilot and one passenger has completely burned. Only the airframe remains. None of the rest of you has been seriously injured. The pilot was unable to notify anyone of your position before the plane crashed in a blinding snowstorm. Just before the crash you noted that the plane's altimeter registered about 5,000 feet. The crash site is in a rugged, heavily wooded area just below the timberline. you are dressed in medium-weight clothing. Each of you has a topcoat.

After the plan landed and before it caught fire, your group was able to salvage the 15 items listed below. Your task is to rank the 15 items in terms of their importance to your survival. Place the number 1 by the most important item, number 2 by the second most important, and so on through number 15, the least important.

	Step 1: Your Individual Ranking	Step 2: The Group Ranking	Step 3: Survival Experts' Ranking	Step 4: Difference between 1 and 3	Step 5: Difference between 2 and 3
Sectional air map of the area	7	8	12	5	4
Flashlight (four-battery size)	4	10	8	4	2
Four wool blankets	6	1	1	5	0
One rifle with ammunition	5	5	14	9	9
One pair of skis	12	14	13	2	1
Two fifths of liquor	11	12	15	4	3
One cosmetic mirror	13	7	7	6	0
One jackknife	3	6	5	2	1
Four pairs of sunglasses	15	15	10	5	5
Three books of matches	2	3	3	1	0
One metal coffeepot	14	4	6	8	2
First-aid kit	1	9	9	8	0
One dozen packages of cocktail nuts	10	11	11	1	0
One clear plastic tarpaulin (9' × 12')	8	2	2	6	0
One large, gift-wrapped decorative candle	9	13	4	5	9
Total (The lower the score the better)				70 / Your score	36 / Group score

Introduction

Your participation in classroom groups provides an opportunity to gain an understanding of three aspects of small group effectiveness: (1) team skills that facilitate the achievement of group goals, (2) characteristics of a group that influence its ability to solve problems and make decisions effectively, and (3) the dynamics of small groups. Even more important for you, participation in a classroom group provides you with a setting where you can assess and develop your own skills in influencing the activities of groups in which you participate. Group problem solving and decision making are the subject of this module, with an emphasis on the potentially creative forces (**synergy**) in group processes.

We start with a definition of teams. A discussion of team skills is based on the premodule activity, which allows you to explore team problem solving and synergy. Coverage of group versus individual problem solving is followed by a discussion of group decision making, and an exploration of managerial actions that should foster creativity and improve group problem solving and decision making. Finally, the utilization of group problem solving and decision making in organizations is reviewed. A questionnaire is included to aid you in assessing your personal skills in operating as a team member so you can develop these skills in your team activities as the course continues.

The Nature of Teams

Historical Context and Global Competition

Teamwork in organizations seems like a new idea to many people, but as a mode of organizing the work organization it has a long history in the United States, Europe, and Japan. Before we move into the definitions of teams, basic team skills, and team decision making, a brief review of the historical context and the changing global context is needed. The interest in the theory and practice of group-based work stretches back several decades.[1] From the late 1920s Elton Mayo and his associates in the United States pioneering studies of industrial work organization and workers' motivation under what became characterized as the "human relations" school of industrial relations. A central finding of this stream of research emphasized the impact of positive attention from managers on a group's productivity. Kurt Lewin's work in the 1930s and 1940s laid the groundwork for the extensive study of group dynamics and leadership behavior. He was the first researcher to distinguish between participative and authoritarian leadership. Lewin demonstrated the usefulness of a democratic leader on the creativity and effectiveness of the group. A common theme to this early work was the search for an approach that would produce a more satisfying working life and hence greater commitment and motivation within the workforce.

In Britain a more structural orientation emerged. Eric Trist and his associates at the Tavistock Institute led a research program in the late 1940s and early 1950s on the effects of the introduction of new technologies on working practices in the British coal-mining industry. Through multiple studies the researchers found that the creation of small self-regulatory work groups that coordinated with each other within and between shifts resulted in improved individual motivation, improved group productivity, and a dramatic decline of sickness rates. Beyond the development of the basic concept and design principles of semiautonomous work groups, one of the important outcomes of this work was the development of the Sociotechnical System School as a conceptual framework (discussed in some depth in Modules 4 and 13) for linking technological, social, and environmental elements of the work organization.

The increasing concern in the United States, Britain, and the Scandinavian countries with increasing workforce motivation and commitment underlies the many approaches that came together under the rubric of the quality of working life (QWL) movement that emerged in the late 1960s and early 1970s. Work groups were a means of returning autonomy and control to workers involved in automated manufacturing. The continued interest in the work group or team from the 1950s to the 1970s resulted in making groups responsible for a whole product or process and the task of coordinating and managing production and service.

In postwar Japan other ideas about groups emerged. The collective culture orientation coupled with an acute scarcity of resources resulted in the emphasis on harnessing employees' capabilities to collective goals of quality, efficiency, and customer service and less with employee involvement, team autonomy, and quality of working life.

The changing conditions of world markets during the 1980s and 1990s, the increasing commercial pressures of a global nature, and the potential created by new technologies and manufacturing techniques led managers to explore new business strategies and alternative approaches to organize the work organization. In this context team-based designs emerged as key design choices.[2]

Work Groups and Teams: Toward a Definition

Work groups and teams have been referred to as "the building blocks of excellent companies."[3] Committees, task forces, quality circles, product development teams, and self-managed teams are all features of today's organizations.

At the most basic level, a **group** can be defined as "a set of three or more individuals that can identify itself and be identified by others in the organization as a group." Groups in organizations can be either *formal* (that is, a formal part of the organization, created by management) or *informal* (created by the members themselves, largely out of day-to-day interaction between individuals). Alderfer advocated the organizational behavior view of groups, which encompasses both the sociological (external relations) and psychological (internal relations) aspects of group operations in this definition:

A group is a collection of individuals (1) who have significantly interdependent relations with each other, (2) who perceive themselves as a group, reliably distinguishing members from nonmembers, (3) whose group identity is recognized by nonmembers, (4) who, as group members acting alone or in concert, have significantly interdependent relations with other groups, and (5) whose roles in the group are therefore a function of expectations from themselves, from other group members, and from nongroup members.[4]

McGrath, Arrow, and Berdahl regard groups as complex, adaptive, dynamic systems composed of a set of elements: (1) individuals, who become the group's *members;* (2) intentions, which become both *group projects*—and the tasks by which those projects are carried out—and *members' needs* that must be satisfied if the group is going to be able to stay in business effectively over the long run; and (3) resources, which become the group's *technology*—that is, the hardware and software tools (rules, norms, procedures) by which its members do the tasks of its projects.[5]

Katzenbach and Smith define a **team** as "a small number of people with complementary skills who are committed to a common purpose, set of performance goals, and approach for which they hold themselves mutually accountable."[6] They distinguish between work groups such as committees and teams as follows: committee performance is a function of what its members do as individuals, whereas team performance includes both individual performance and what they call "collective work products" that reflect the joint, real contribution of team members and that are greater than the sum of their individual contributions.[7]

The premodule activity highlights this difference between real teamwork and simple group membership and the skills that lead to performance differences in teams.

Discussion of the Premodule Preparation

Table 5–2 summarizes the results of the Mountain Survival Exercise for 12 groups of college students. You should find that these results are similar to the ones you obtained in your groups, although because the exercises are not conducted under controlled conditions, artifacts such as the time allotted for both individual and group decision making may cause results to vary. However, if we use the group average score as an approximation of the individual group members' capability in the situation faced by the group in the exercises, in general the groups did better than the average individual. In many cases the groups performed better than their best individual member. This outcome clearly demonstrates Katzenbach and Smith's notion that a team is more than the sum of its parts and produces performance levels greater than the sum of all the individual bests of team members.[8]

Table 5–2 Summary of Group Performance on the Mountain Survival Activity	Number of Groups	Average Individual Score	Average Group Score	Average Gain	Average Low Score	Number of Group Scores Lower Than Best Individual Score
	12	56.2	40.8	6.6	43.3	4

Why were group scores superior to those of individuals? We must look at several aspects of the exercise in seeking an explanation.

1. Three conditions appear relevant: (a) There was a definite answer to all problems, (b) the problem could be solved by logic or reason in the case of Activity 5–1 and (c) for all problems each person had some relevant information or point of view but no member had it all. More information resources were available to the group—if the group made use of them.

2. A problem-solving process was used. If you followed the experiential learning cycle, your team has been developing some sequence or steps to its problem-solving process. If you followed the **rational problem-solving** process model, steps you might have followed include (1) agreement on goals, (2) shared understanding of what the problem is, (3) shared understanding of ground rules for the way the group will work, (4) shared understanding of the basic assumptions and priority issues in solving the problem, (5) consideration of alternative solutions, (6) development of criteria to evaluate alternatives, (7) choosing the best alternative, and (8) checking the alternative chosen against the problem statement. Some researchers argue that this process has a left-hemisphere focus. If the process that you followed is less orderly, systematic, or linear, you probably followed a more *intuitive problem-solving process* (which some researchers call a *right-hemisphere focus*). Some differences in the scores received by different teams may be attributable to differences in the effectiveness of their problem-solving process.

3. The **consensus process** was used. If you followed the instructions, your team was developing (or improving) communication skills that could augment the problem-solving process. It is often important to (1) get input from all, (2) listen to all views, (3) be willing to change your views if someone else's makes more sense, and (4) assume conflict can be creative in generating ideas.

Thus effective team problem solving involves both effective problem-solving skills and effective **interpersonal skills.** Those interpersonal skills include careful listening plus supporting and encouraging the contributions of all members. For example, a team can adopt a practice whereby, when communication problems arise, members feel comfortable paraphrasing what they hear one another say to make sure that everyone understands what is being said (for example, "Do I hear you saying . . . ?"). This technique involves learning to listen until it is clear what a person is saying and then paraphrasing what is said to the satisfaction of the speaker. Where there is no awareness on the part of the team members that a communication problem has arisen, periodic summaries of what has been discussed can ensure that all are on the same wavelength. Similarly, some individuals have learned that saying something like "Here's the problem *I'm* having with what you said," is a more effective response than "That's a stupid idea." The former response is less likely to generate defensive behavior and is more likely to encourage complete communication and contribution to the group's effort.

Just like problem-solving skills, interpersonal skills can be learned and practiced. Individuals who learn the skills of listening and communicating can apply them in any situation; they become part of the interpersonal skills that improve the person's effectiveness in any group. Differences in group performances on this module's activities may also be a function of how well the group's interpersonal processes operate. Effective teams work on improving their interpersonal processes.

Individual versus Group Problem Solving

In your class's operation of the problem-solving activities, you may have observed instances where the group score was higher than the best individual score. Such was the case with 4 of the 12 groups whose performance is outlined in Table 5–2. There, in four of the groups, the group outcome was worse than that of the best members. Thus while in general groups performed better than the average of their members, and most of the time better than their best member, this case was not always true. Some groups would have been better to use the solution of their best member, *assuming, of course, they knew who that was!*

Thus no generalization can be made that group problem solving is superior to individual effort. Variables such as the type of problem; the talent, ability, education, and experience of the individuals; the time available; organization and national culture; leadership; and group process are all relevant as are many other factors.

There is evidence that the capacity of groups to perform better than their best individual member increases with the time that individuals have worked with each other in teams.[9] Other research has suggested that the superiority of teams is a function of their capacity to develop valid information about the members' relative expertise.[10] Hackman and Morris observe that, in sum, there is substantial agreement among researchers and observers of small task groups that something important happens in group interactions that can affect performance outcomes. There is little agreement about just what that "something" is, whether it is more likely to enhance or depress effectiveness, and how it can be monitored, analyzed, and altered.[11]

One problem in applying research findings to managerial situations concerns the methods used in experimental studies. By necessity they are done in the laboratory, with the necessary controls to examine specific variables. This situation has little comparability to the conditions under which real work teams operate. Real teams can learn to critique and redirect their actions, a flexibility not possible in experimental studies, nor perhaps as likely to occur, given that the stakes, risks, rewards, and punishments for real work teams are significantly different from those for laboratory teams.

In truth, group process can both enhance and detract from team performance. In reality, organizations—for a variety of reasons, some of them discussed below—cannot avoid using groups and teams for problem solving and decision making. Thus the real questions for managers do not involve individual versus group decision making. The real questions are, (1) Where is group decision making most appropriate? and (2) How can teams be made more effective?

One primary factor affecting group performance is the degree of proficiency in team action that a group can develop. This proficiency is aided by effectiveness training for individual members, such as leadership, problem-solving, and communications workshops. It also requires on-the-job training in the use of these skills by the work team after the individuals have had the advantage of separate training. If group effectiveness is to be enhanced, time must be allotted for these activities.

Group Decision Making and Participative Management

The problems involved in Activitiy 5–1 had a "right" or preferred answer. Although organizations face such problems indeed, these are not the only type of problems that exist. Very often, organizations face situations with a number of viable alternative solutions. Activity 5–3 ("Who Gets the Overtime") at the end of the module presents such a situation.

In that activity the leader is instructed to behave in a particular manner. Is that the only way to handle the problem? Is it the best way? What are the alternatives?

Victor Vroom, Phillip Yetton, and Arthur Jago have developed a model that can provide the answers to these questions. They first suggest five ways in which decisions can be made:

1. The manager solves the problem by himself or herself, using the information available at the time (AI style).
2. The manager obtains the necessary information from employees and then makes the decision himself or herself (AII style).
3. The manager consults with subordinates individually, getting their ideas and suggestions, and then makes a decision (CI style).
4. The manager consults with subordinates as a group, again getting their ideas and suggestions, and then makes a decision (CII style).
5. The manager explains the problem to the employees as a group, and the group makes the decision (GII style).[12]

The model suggests five key attributes to problem situations: time, information, quality, employee commitment, and employee development. It lists eight problem attributes that allow these factors to be taken into account in decision making:

1. *Quality requirement (QR).* How important is the technical quality of the decision?
2. *Commitment requirement (CR).* How important is employee commitment to the decision?
3. *Leader's information (LI).* Does the leader have sufficient information to make a high-quality decision?
4. *Problem structure (ST).* Is the problem well structured?
5. *Commitment probability (CP).* If the leader makes the decision alone, will subordinates be committed to the decision?
6. *Goal congruence (GC).* Do employees share the organizational goals to be attained in solving this problem?
7. *Subordinate conflict (CO).* Is conflict among employees over preferred solutions likely?
8. *Subordinate information (SI).* Do employees have enough information to make a high-quality decision?[13]

To decide on a decision-making style, the manager follows a decision tree incorporating the eight problem attributes, asking the question in each attribute of the problem at hand, as shown in Figure 5–1.

Note that only one of the styles in the model is what is conventionally called **participative management.** Others are consultative and autocratic. The model is a contingency model, which seeks to identify the situations under which particular forms of employee influence are most appropriate. In brief, it suggests that full participation is not *always* an appropriate style for the leader to use, although at times it is *very* appropriate. In light of this model, it may be argued that the participative style has been overused, a view supported by recent research results that find low relationships (so low so as to be insignificant) between participation, productivity, and employee satisfaction.[14]

Review the "Who Gets the Overtime?" activity using the Vroom–Yetton–Jago model. Which decision-making style would be appropriate?

Other Factors

Although the Vroom–Yetton–Jago model incorporates a number of important variables, still other variables may affect the choice of decision-making style:

1. *Personality of the manager.* Managers who feel most comfortable making all the decisions and who have difficulty allowing others to be involved should not attempt to use participation. If they do not believe in it, they should assume that employees will detect this and feel they are being manipulated if they are asked to become involved.
2. *Skill and ability of the manager.* The manager's abilities in managing group problem-solving activities and in conflict resolution affect the results of participative management attempts.[15]
3. *Organizational climate.* If the organization's climate and culture are strictly authoritarian, it is difficult for any single manager to follow a participative style.

Figure 5–1   **The Vroom–Yetton–Jago Decicion Model**

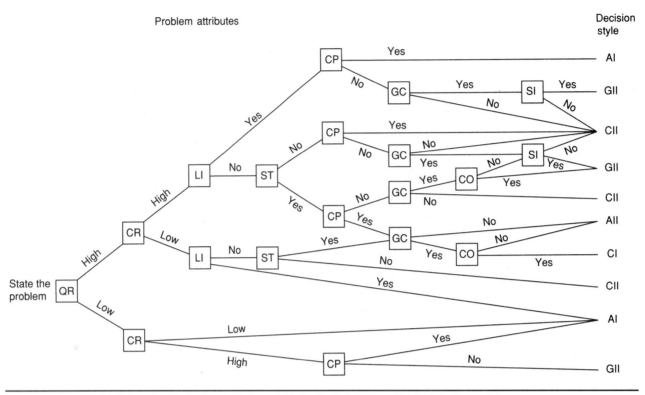

Source: V. H. Vroom and A. G. Jago, *The New Leadership,* (Englewood, NJ: Prentice-Hall, 1988), p. 184. Printed with permission.

4. *Employee personality.* Some employees do not work well in participative situations, but rather prefer to work in highly structured situations where they are told what to do.[16]

5. *Group size and diversity.* Some employees do not work well in large groups. At the same time, the larger the group, the greater the likelihood that the members of the group will be different. Furthermore, demographic diversity enhances the richness and breath of input into the decision-making process. As such the larger the group and the more diverse the group, the more challenging the managerial task of facilitating a participative decision making.[17]

The Manager and Group Decision Making

Although group decision making is not necessary in every problem situation, where it is used, its efficacy rests with the manager who is responsible for facilitating the process. In deciding to proceed with a group decision, the manager has to address several key issues before the group or team can begin to function:[18]

1. *Assignment boundary.* Tasks given to teams are often complex. Therefore, the manager must clearly define the group's task, its responsibility and authority, and the requirements and performance criteria that the team is expected to meet.

2. *Assessment of assignment resources.* Once the assignment boundaries are defined, the manager may need to divide the assignment into manageable tasks and examine the resources available for the assignment. Time, knowledge, skills, and competing system demands are some of the resources that are likely to have an impact on the decision-making process. An attempt to address and resolve the resource issues prior to the formation of the group will aid the team's performance.

3. *Team formation.* Decision-making groups are often formed to deal with complex tasks that are beyond the ability of any one individual. Identifying the individuals who have the needed knowledge and skills as well as the individuals who are likely to be affected by the decision provides the group with the appropriate resources to deal with the task. Appointing a leader at the start of the group or ensuring that the groups selects a leader as a first task is often a good idea.

The role of the manager in group decision making can be that of a chairperson who guides the consensus process while trying not to influence others to adopt his or her solution. In playing the role of the supervisor in "Who Gets the Overtime?" individuals sometimes adopt a completely passive manner. The supervisor in this situation (or similar ones) could choose to be highly active and still permit the employees to make the decision. Here are some ways the manager-as-chairperson can facilitate this process:

1. Set the stage and clarify expectations.
    a. Help the group members get acquainted (at the first meeting of a new group).
    b. Review the agenda for the meeting or, if this is a continuation of prior meetings, review the progress made to date.
    c. Introduce the problem by asking what would be a fair way of deciding who should get the overtime.
    d. Have the group decide what criteria should be used. Explore alternative options.
    e. Let the group decide what method, procedure, or decision-making process to use. Review the alternative methods. Some of the methods discussed below (such as brainstorming and nominal group technique) may be useful.
2. Do not takes sides or give your own views.
3. Make sure all employees have time to express their views.
4. Control conflict by having each person "own" his or her feelings without attacking another person—say where you are without "laying it on" the other person. (It is much more acceptable to say, "I think seniority is a better way to decide this than one's personal needs," than "Chris's ripping us off by contributing to the overpopulation problem.") Also, remember that conflict can be creative when it is focused on issues rather than personalities.
5. Protect those who are verbally attacked. Create a supportive atmosphere.
6. Focus on the agreement about the reasoning and its logic rather than on the agreement about the choice itself.
7. Do not manipulate the process so it will come out the way you would like to have the problem decided. Others usually become aware of your hidden agenda and may resent it.
8. At the end of the meeting, review the task, the agenda, the decision method, and the decision. If the group has a follow-up meeting, spell out the task ahead, its schedule, and the responsibilities of the members to be completed before the next meeting.[19]

When exposed to this type of leadership, employees can learn the team skills implicit in this behavior and, by example, learn to make a decision without the supervisor, if called on to do so.

Consensus and Group Decision Making

The process of consensus refers to arriving at a decision that all members of the group are willing to support and no team member opposes. As Activity 5–1 shows, this approach represents a major challenge to most groups. The decision is not necessarily a unanimous choice, but is acceptable to all the group members. The consensus process seems to enhance the opportunity for creativity, innovation, and high-quality decisions because the group spends a significant amount of time working through alternative solutions until reaching a solution that everyone finds acceptable.[20]

A 1994 report by the U.S. Department of Defense suggests that the "rule of thumb" procedure be followed. Team members use their thumbs to create three signals to show how they feel about an issue. A "thumbs up" signal indicates that a team member favors a proposal. The "thumbs down" sign means that the member is opposed to the idea and in no way can support it. If a team member is not wild about a proposal, but can support it, he/she will turn the thumb sideways. If any member is "thumbs down" on a proposal, it may have to be modified or rewarded in a way that the resistor can buy in. Thus this procedure clarifies what needs to occur as the group progresses on its task of making a decision.

An alternative procedure for reaching consensus differentiates between levels of consensus.[21] Consensus is achieved if all participants indicate that they are at levels 1 to 4 (not at level 5 or 6). The levels of consensus are

1. I am *enthusiastic* about this alternative. I am satisfied that the decision is an expression of the wisdom of the group.

2. I find the decision is the *best choice.* It is the best of the real options that we have available to us.

3. I can *live with* the decision. I'm not especially enthusiastic about it.

4. I do not fully agree with the decision and need to register my view about it. However, I do not choose to block the decision and will *stand aside.* I am willing to support the decision because I trust the wisdom of the group.

5. I do not agree with the decision and feel the need to *block* this decision being accepted as consensus.

6. I feel that we have no clear sense of unity in the group. We need to *talk more* before consensus can be reached.

The consensus decision-making process is advantageous to the extent that the decision is important to the group's performance, there is time available to arrive at the consensus, and it is important to develop members' commitment to the decision. The process can be detrimental in situation that require a quick decision, such as crisis or when a window of opportunity is about to close.

Organizational Skills

A systems approach to organizational effectiveness must provide for the development of the group skills of both individual managers and the teams they direct. Figure 5–2 provides a model of four goal areas for the attainment of these organizational skills. To move in the direction of the goal areas, development is needed in two types of group skills for both individuals and groups: *emotional* and *task skills.*

For the individual, skills related to influencing social and emotional relationships include abilities both to be supportive of others and to confront others when necessary. Communication skills such as listening, paraphrasing, and appropriate expression of feelings and support are examples. For the team, acquiring these skills means developing the climate of relationships in which interactions can be facilitated and the use of all other skills can be optimized.[22]

Task skills are more directly related to getting the group's tasks accomplished. An individual can learn certain roles in a group, such as clarifying what is going on or keeping the discussion on target. (A more complete discussion of group roles can be found in the next module.) In addition to group skills, such as those you experienced in the problem-solving exercises earlier in this module, teams can learn planning and implementation techniques such as Management by Objectives. The critiquing of the

**Figure 5–2
Goals and
Organizational Skills**

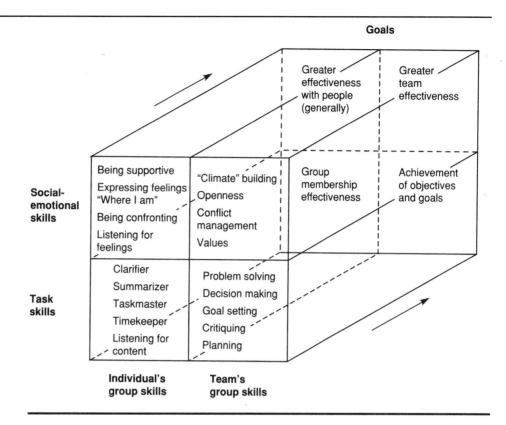

progress achieved at a given moment or after a completed activity has much to offer for future improvement of the group's operation if it is done objectively in a nonthreatening climate.

Some of the techniques for attaining improvement in the four goal areas shown in Figure 5–2 have been discussed or will be in future modules. Module 7 discusses team building, but before focusing on techniques and skills, we attempt to develop a more general understanding of group dynamics in Module 6.

Creativity and Group Problem Solving

An integral element of the synergy process in group problem solving involves creativity. As individuals interact around ideas, an issue, or a problem, a novel solution may emerge that no individual has identified earlier. **Creativity** is defined as an individual's ability to take bits and pieces of seemingly unrelated information and synthesize the pieces into a new understanding or a novel, useful idea. Creativity is discussed in Module 17, which focuses on the phenomena of creativity and innovation in the organizational setting. This section explores two techniques that are likely to foster creativity in group problem solving and decision making: brainstorming and the nominal group technique.

Brainstorming

One well-known method for developing creative ideas and decision alternatives through group participation is **brainstorming.** Here are some general ground rules for brainstorming:

1. Everyone spontaneously expresses all ideas, no matter how extreme they may appear.

2. Ideas belong to the group, and all members are encouraged to rework or elaborate upon them.

3. Evaluation of ideas does not occur until the generation process has been completed.

Nominal Group Technique

The **nominal group technique** is a highly structured group problem-solving process[23] in which the focus is on the rational process of problem solving. Here are some ground rules for nominal group technique:

1. During a period of silence, individuals independently write down their ideas.
2. Each individual in turn shares one of his or her ideas at a time, following a round-robin reporting process. Ideas are written on a chart for all to see. No discussion is allowed during this phase.
3. After all ideas have been recorded, members discuss the ideas only for the purpose of clarification. No criticism is permitted.
4. A preliminary vote takes place to reduce the number of alternatives.
5. An in-depth discussion of the remaining ideas then occurs.
6. An independent silent vote takes place, and the group's solution is determined by the votes.

The nominal group technique is an orderly, efficient, rational process that encourages full participation and meaningful discussion. Research findings suggest that this method seems to have a clear advantage under conditions of high stress and conflict. Other research suggests that although most individuals feel relatively satisfied with their level of involvement, some show resistance to the forced method of decision making.

Problem-Solving and Decision-Making Teams at Work

Organizations use a variety of problem-solving and decision-making teams. Let's discuss three recent applications of teams in organizations: self-managed work teams, new product development teams, and quality control circles.

Self-Managed Work Teams

Self-managed work teams (SMWT) consist of employees who work on relatively whole tasks (such as assembling a car or a major auto component) and are responsible for managing the task that will result in a product or service being delivered. Team members are typically responsible for handling all or most aspects of the work and performing all the technical tasks involved. Technical tasks are typically rotated among team members, as are management responsibilities, such as monitoring the team's productivity and quality.[24]

Many self-managed teams work without direct supervision. One recent survey found that almost half of all *Fortune* 1000 companies were using self-managed work teams, with even more planning their use.[25]

The important characteristics of self-managed work teams are employees with a variety of skills who (1) perform interrelated tasks, are responsible for making a product or delivering a service, and work together closely (face-to-face interaction) and (2) have discretion over decisions such as work assignments, work scheduling, work methods, and sometimes even team member selection and training.[26]

One recent study found that self-managed work teams were rated higher than conventionally managed work groups in quality of work life (QWL) areas such as job satisfaction, personal growth satisfaction, social satisfaction, and organizational commitment. Self-managed work groups were also found to perform better than conventionally managed work groups in terms of both quantity and quality of work.[27]

Cross-Functional Teams

Cross-functional teams have emerged as a viable way to bring together people with knowledge and skills from various functional areas to work on a specific task.[28] Many organizations use cross-functional teams as an effective means for allowing individuals from diverse areas within the organization to exchange information, identify problems, develop new ideas, solve problems, and coordinate complex projects. Cross-functional teams cut across departmental and functional boundaries. A specific example of such teams are new product development teams. Many companies—such as Boeing's 777 development team, Chrysler's Neon subcompact car development team, and Motorola's Iridum project development team—use such teams very successfully. The **new product development teams (NPDT)** have emerged as a viable tool within highly competitive technology-based industries for enhancing the product development process. NPDTs are small groups of employees who collectively have the knowledge and skills needed to solve the problem of developing a new product, from conception through manufacturing and distribution—"from design to delivery." These teams often comprise individuals from a variety of functional areas, such as marketing, finance, design engineering, process engineering, and manufacturing.

Research has shown that NPDTs are highly effective in facilitating the development process,[29] shortening product development time, and increasing cooperation between functional groups within the organization.[30] These teams typically succeed if they effectively obtain information and resources from others (both inside and outside the organization), use the information and resources to create a viable product, and gain support for the product from others (both inside and outside the organization).[31] In a fashion similar to the use of NPDT, organizations can create multidisciplinary teams to service or support a single large customer.

Quality Control Circles

Quality control circles (QCC) are small groups of workers from the same work area who are given training in problem solving, statistical quality control, and group processes. They meet regularly to discuss ways to improve the quality of their work and to solve job-related problems. The concepts of QCC originated in Japan, and are considered by many to be the most famous Japanese organizational innovation to date.[32] Although results of the use of quality circles have been mixed in both the United States and Japan,[33] the most important potential of QCCs is the continuing organizational dialoguing they promote between managers and the workforce.[34]

Computer Technology and Group Decision Making

One of the most rapidly developing fields is the use of computer technology to enhance group problem solving and decision making. (We explore the relationships between technology, information technology, and human behavior in Module 20.) Computer-based forms of brainstorming (electronic brainstorming) have been developed.[35] Computer programs that allow for sharing information via computer networks are called **groupware.** The emerging groupware technology reflects a change in emphasis from using the computer to support record keeping and managerial decision making toward using the computer to facilitate human interaction and team performance.[36] Furthermore, groupware technology allows for the creation of virtual work teams. **Virtual work teams** are groups of people working closely together, even though they may not be working on the same time schedule or at the same physical space. Team members can be separated by many miles and even be on different continents. Johansen created a helpful categorization based on time and space: team members can be working at the same place and at the same time, they can be working at the same time but be working at different places, they can be working at different times at the same place, and they can be working at different times in different places.[37] Though it's still relatively new, this technology has produced impressive productivity gains.[38] Research studies on groupware are just beginning to appear, but one study indicates that its use improves group conflict resolution processes,[39] and another found that groups using electronic communication have more difficulty in reaching consensus than do groups meeting face-to-face and also appear to be more willing to take risks.[40]

Group Decision Making and the Cultural Context

Culture influences the ways that organizations make decisions. When we think of decision making in the global context, the following questions come to mind: Do groups from different cultures perceive problems in the same way? Do they use the same decision-making processes? Do they gather similar types and amounts of information while investigating the problem? Do they follow the same thinking patterns? Do they construct similar types of solutions? Do they use similar strategies for choosing between alternatives? Do they implement their decisions in the same ways? The answer to each question is no.[41]

The cultural context within which groups exist plays a critical role in preference for and the performance of individual versus group problem solving. While some cultures (for example, the United States and Great Britain) have a strong belief in the importance and centrality of the individual, other cultures (for example, China and Taiwan) have a strong belief in the importance of collectivism.[42] Thus we find that a person's choice of either individual or group problem solving and his or her actual behavior and performance are likely to be affected by the individual's cultural heritage. We also find that culture can affect performance in a particular context. One study showed that managers from collectivist cultures performed worse when working alone, as opposed to working in a group with which they identified.[43]

As an example of the impact of culture on decision-making processes, within the Japanese culture, a unique consensual decision-making process exists. The process has two components—*ringi* and *nemawashi*—through which Japanese managers involve subordinates in considering the future direction of their companies. Individuals and groups that have ideas for improvement or change will discuss them widely with a large number of peers and managers. During this extensive informal communication process, some kinds of agreements (*nemawashi*) are hammered out. At this point a formal document is circulated for signatures or a personalized stamp (the seal) of every manager who is considered relevant to the decision (called a *ringi*).[44] Only after all the relevant managers put their seals on the proposal is the idea or suggestion implemented.

Summary

This module has explored aspects of team problem solving and decision making and their differences have been discussed. Behaviors that enhance group problem solving have been outlined as have conditions under which both individual and group decision making (participative management) may be effective. The manager's role in facilitating group decision making was covered as were techniques for enhancing group creativity. Several ways in which organizations use problem-solving teams were outlined.

Key Terms and Concepts

Brainstorming	Nominal group technique
Consensus process	Participative management
Creativity	Quality control circles (QCC)
Cross-functional team	Rational problem solving
Group	Self-managed work team (SMWT)
Group problem-solving process	Synergy
Groupware	Team
Interpersonal skills	Team skills
New product development teams (NPDT)	Virtual work team

Study Questions

1. What is rational group decision making? Why is it useful?

2. What is the consensus process? How is it of value to your teams in this course? What is its relationship to synergy?

3. Athletic coaches train teams in techniques to win the game or to achieve peak performance. In what kinds of skills can managers train work teams? Give specific examples.

4. Students often remember Activity 5–3 ("Who Gets the Overtime?") as an attempt to illustrate the effectiveness of group decision making. Was it effective? Why do you think so?

5. What are some considerations in deciding whether to allow a group to participate in decision making?

6. Assume that you are a manager and have decided to use group decision making for a problem affecting the productivity of your team. What issues should you consider before the first group meeting? How would you go about managing the meeting? What are some pitfalls to avoid?

7. Identify the different phases in the group problem-solving cycle. At which phases did your group encounter problems in the activities in this module? Why? How can you avoid these problems in the future?

8. Identify one method to improve your classroom group's problem-solving effectiveness. What specific steps would you take to facilitate the process?

9. In what ways are quality control circles and new product development teams different? How are they alike?

10. How does culture affect group problem-solving effectiveness? How might U.S. culture affect a team's performance?

Endnotes

1. J. E. Neumann, R, Holti, and H. Standing, *Changing Everything at Once,* (Oxford, England: Tavistock Institute, 1996).

2. S. Lembke and M. G. Wilson, "Putting the 'Team' into Teamwork: Alternative Theoretical Contributions for Contemporary Management Practice," *Human Relations* 51, no. 7 (1998), pp. 927–44.

3. T. J. Peters, *Thriving on Chaos,* (New York: Alfred A. Knopf, 1988).

4. C. P. Alderfer, "An Intergroup Perspective on Group Dynamics," in J. W. Lorch, (ed.), *Handbook of Organizational Behavior,* (Englewood Cliffs, NJ: Prentice-Hall, 1986).

5. J. E. McGrath, H. Arrow, and J. L. Berdahl, *A Theory of Groups as Complex Systems,* (Newbury Park, CA: Sage, 1998).

6. J. R. Katzenbach and D. K. Smith. *The Wisdom of Teams: Creating the High Performance Organization,* (Boston: Harvard Business School Press, 1993).

7. Ibid.

8. Ibid, p. 112.

9. W. Watson, L. K. Michalson, and W. Sharp, "Member Competence, Group Interaction, and Group Decision Making: A Longitudinal Study," *Journal of Applied Psychology* 76 (1991), pp. 803–9.

10. A. N. Hollingshead, "Distributed Knowledge and Transactive Process in Decision-Making Groups," in D. H. Gruenfeld (ed.), *Managing Groups and Teams,* vol. 1, (Stamford, CT: JAI Press, 1998), pp. 103–23; P. W. Yetton and P. C. Bottger, "Individual versus Group Problem Solving: An Empirical Test of a Best-Member Strategy," *Organizational Behavior and Human Performance* 29 (1982), pp. 307–21.

11. J. R. Hackman and C. G. Morris, "T-Group Tasks, Group Interaction Process, and Group Performance Effectiveness: A Review and Proposed Integration," in Leonard Berkowitz (ed.), *Advances in Experimental Social Psychology,* vol. 8, (New York: Academic Press, 1974), p. 49.

12. V. H. Vroom and P. W. Yetton, *Leadership and Decision Making,* (Pittsburgh: University of Pittsburgh Press, 1972), p. 13.

13. V. H. Vroom and A. C. Jago, *The New Leadership,* (Englewood Cliffs, NJ: Prentice-Hall, 1988), p. 184.

14. J. A. Wagner III, "Participation's Effects on Performance and Satisfaction: A Reconsideration of Research Evidence," *Academy of Management Review* 19, no. 2 (1994), pp. 312–30.

15. J. Hall, "Decisions, Decisions, Decisions," *Psychology Today,* November 1971; and A. Crouch and P. Yetton, "Manager Behavior, Leadership Style, and Subordinate Performance: An Empirical Examination of the Vroom–Yetton Conflict Rule," *Organizational Behavior and Human Decision Process* 39 (1987), pp. 384–96.

16. D. Collins, R. A. Ross, and T. L. Ross, "Who Wants Participative Management?" *Group and Organizational Studies* 14 (1989), pp. 422–45.

17. P. M. Elsass and L. M. Graves, "Demographic Diversity in Decision-Making Groups: The Experience of Women and People of Color," *Academy of Management Review* 22, no 4 (1997), pp. 946–73; D. C. Lau and J. K. Murnighan, "Demographic Diversity and Fultlines: The Compositional Dynamics of Organizational Groups," *Academy of Management Review* 23, no. 2 (1998), pp. 325–40.

18. G. P. Hubler, *Managerial Decision Making,* (Glenview, IL: Scott, Foresman, 1980), Chapter 9.

19. W. A. Randolph and B. Z. Poner. *Getting the Job Done! Managing Project Teams and Task Forces for Success,* rev. ed.; (Englewood Cliffs, NJ: Prentice-Hall, 1992).

20. S. E. Yeatts and C. Hyten, *High-Performing Self-Managed Work Teams,* (Thousand Oaks, CA: Sage, 1998).

21. B. Geoff, *Level of Consensus,* (CA: Geoff & Associate Consulting Firm Pub., 1995).

22. S. G. Barsade and D. E. Gibson, "Group Emotion: A View from Top and Bottom," in D. H. Gruenfeld (ed.), *Research on Managing Groups and Teams,* vol. 1, (Stamford, CT: JAI Press 1998), pp. 81–102.

23. A. L. Delbecq, A. H. Van de Ven, and D. H. Gustafson, *Group Techniques for Program Planning: A Guide to Nominal and Delphi Processes,* (Glenview, IL: Scott, Foresman, 1975); J. M. Bartunek and J. K. Murningham, "The Nominal Group Technique: Expanding the Basic Procedure and Underlying Assumptions," *Group and Organization Studies* 9 (1984), pp. 417–32; G. E. Burton, "The 'Clustering Effect': An Idea-Generation Phenomenon during Nominal Grouping," *Small Group Behavior* 18 (1987), pp. 224–38.

24. D. E. Yeatts and C. Hyten, *High-Performing Self-Managed Work Teams,* (Thousand Oaks, CA: Sage Publications, 1998).

25. E. E. Lawler, S. A. Mohrman, and G. E. Ledford Jr., *Employee Involvement and Total Quality Management: Practices and Results in Fortune 1000 Companies,* (San Francisco: Jossey-Bass, 1992).

26. P. S. Goodman, S. Devadas, and T. L. Hutchinson, "Groups and Productivity: Analyzing the Effectiveness of Self-Managing Teams," in J. P. Campbell, R. J. Campbell, and Associates (eds.), *Productivity in Organizations,* (San Francisco: Jossey-Bass, 1988), pp. 295–325.

27. S. G. Cohen and G. E. Ledford Jr., "The Effectiveness of Self-Managing Teams: A Quasi-Experiment," *Human Relations* 47 (1994), pp. 13–43.

28. G. M. Parker, *Cross-Functional Teams,* (San Francisco: Jossey-Bass, 1994).

29. K. B. Clark and S. C. Wheelwright, *Managing New Product and Process Development,* (New York: Free Press, 1993); W. E. Souder, *Managing New Product Innovation,* (Lexington, MA: Lexington Books, 1987).

30. M. Iansiti and A. MacCormack, "Developing Production Internet Time," *Harvard Business Review,* September–October (1997), pp. 108–17; J. R. Hackman and R. E. Walton, "Leading Groups in Organizations," in P. Goodman (ed.), *Designing Effective Work Groups,* (San Francisco: Jossey-Bass, 1986).

31. R. Burgelman, "A Process Model of Internal Corporate Venturing in the Diversified Major Firm," *Administrative Science Quarterly* 31 (1982), pp. 223–44.

32. P. Lillrank and N. Kano, *Continuous Improvement: Quality Control Circles in Japanese Industry,* (Ann Arbor: University of Michigan Press, 1989).

33. R. E. Cole, "Japan Can but We Can't," IAQC Conference Presentation, Louisville, March 1981.

34. P. Lillrank, A. B. (Rami) Shani, B. Stymne, H. Kolodny, J-R. Figuera, M. Liu, "Continuous Improvement: An International Comparative Study," in W. Pasmore and R. Woodman (eds.), *Research in Organizational Change and Development,* (Greenwich, CT: JAI Press, 1999).

35. R. B. Gauupe, L. M. Bastianutti, and W. H. Cooper, "Unblocking Brainstorming," *Journal of Applied Psychology* 76, no. 1 (1991), pp. 137–42.

36. A. D. Shulman, "Putting Group Information Technology in Its Place: Communication and Good Work Group Performance," in R. R. Clegg, C. Hardy, and W. R. Nord (eds.), *Handbook of Organization Studies,* (London: Sage Publication, 1996), pp. 357–74.

37. R. Johansen, *"Leading Business Teams: How Teams Can Use Technology and Group Process Tools to Enhance Performance,"* (Reading MA: Addison-Wesley, 1991).

38. David Kirkpatrick, "Why Microsoft Can't Stop Lotus Notes," *Fortune,* December 22, 1994, p. 142. This article reported returns on investment from use of groupware ranging from 179 to 351 percent.

39. M. S. Poole, M. Holmes, and G. DeSanctis, "Conflict Management in a Computer-Supported Meeting Environment," *Management Science* 37 (1991), pp. 926–53.

40. Sara Kiesler and Lee Sproull, "Group Decision Making and Communication Technology," *Organizational Behavior and Human Decision Processes* 52 (1992), pp. 96–123.

41. N. J. Adler, *International Dimensions of Organizational Behavior,* 3rd ed., (Boston: PWS–Kent, 1997).

42. G. Hofstede, *Culture's Consequences,* (Newbury Park, CA: Sage, 1984).

43. P. C. Earley, "East Meets West Meets Mideast: Further Explorations of Collectivistic and Individualistic Work Groups," *Academy of Management Journal* 36 (1993), pp. 319–48.

44. P. Sethi, N. Namiki, and C. Swanson, *The False Promise of the Japanese Miracle,* (Marshfield, MA: Pittman, 1984).

Activity 5–2:	*Objective:*
Group Skills	
Development	

Activity 5–2: Group Skills Development

Objective:

To help individuals identify specific group skills that they want to develop.

Task 1:

Individuals are to complete the attached Questionnaire on Group Skills Development.

Task 2:

a. Individuals are to share with their group the list of skills to which they assigned top priority.

b. The group should brainstorm about how it can help each individual accomplish his or her goals.

c. Each individual in collaboration with the group is to develop an action plan (for each individual) that will help him or her accomplish these learning goals or team skills.

Questionnaire on Group Skills Development

Below are skill areas in which participants in past courses have indicated an interest in developing greater proficiency. Please indicate the degree to which you have an interest in developing greater skills effectiveness by checking the appropriate position on the scale to the right of each item.

Skills Areas	Not Interested		Somewhat Interested			Very Interested			Highly Interested		
1. Expressing my viewpoints clearly and logically	1		2	3	4	5	6	7	8	9	10
2. Convincing or persuading others of my ideas or views	1		2	3	4	5	6	7	8	9	10
3. Gaining or holding the attention of others	1		2	3	4	5	6	7	8	9	10
4. Listening attentively so I can understand others' ideas and perceptions	1		2	3	4	5	6	7	8	9	10
5. Paraphrasing back what someone says so I can determine if I am "hearing"	1		2	3	4	5	6	7	8	9	10
6. Paraphrasing back what someone says so the other person feels reassured that I'm listening	1		2	3	4	5	6	7	8	9	10
7. Asserting myself more	1		2	3	4	5	6	7	8	9	10
8. Asserting myself without stepping on others' toes	1		2	3	4	5	6	7	8	9	10
9. Getting my share of airtime	1		2	3	4	5	6	7	8	9	10
10. Being less dominating, opinionated, or dogmatic	1		2	3	4	5	6	7	8	9	10
11. Being more open-minded about the views of others	1		2	3	4	5	6	7	8	9	10
12. Feeling less intimidated by the way others express their views	1		2	3	4	5	6	7	8	9	10
13. Feeling less defensive when others don't agree with me	1		2	3	4	5	6	7	8	9	10
14. Being less nervous and more confident in speaking	1		2	3	4	5	6	7	8	9	10
15. Taking criticism better	1		2	3	4	5	6	7	8	9	10
16. Coping with people who are different than I am (for example, differences in age, sex, race, religion, fraternity, sorority)	1		2	3	4	5	6	7	8	9	10
17. Confronting conflict when it arises between myself and another person	1		2	3	4	5	6	7	8	9	10
18. Having a harmonizing influence on the group (for example, helping shy people open up; getting others to listen to each other; getting group members more involved and enthusiastic; helping group members to be more comfortable in their relations)	1		2	3	4	5	6	7	8	9	10
19. Leading the group discussion	1		2	3	4	5	6	7	8	9	10
20. Taking control when the discussion gets out of hand; keeping discussion on target	1		2	3	4	5	6	7	8	9	10
21. Facilitating the group discussion to get maximum output	1		2	3	4	5	6	7	8	9	10
22. Dealing with conflict between group members	1		2	3	4	5	6	7	8	9	10
23. Manipulating the group's interactions so they will come out the way I feel is best	1		2	3	4	5	6	7	8	9	10

Note: When you have finished, review the above items and circle the numbers of those to which you would give top priority.

**Activity 5–3:
Who Gets the
Overtime?**

Objectives:

a. To examine group decision making as a process.

b. To identify some issues concerning participation of employees in decision making.

c. To explore the role of the leader in group decision making.

d. To use role playing as a learning method.

(*Note:* This activity's objective is neither to advocate the use of group decision making nor to demonstrate how it should be done. Rather, we are exploring the issue of group decision making based on your experience in the exercise.)

Task 1:

a. The instructor will briefly discuss role playing. There are a number of ways to role-play, and it is used for a variety of purposes. In this case each member of your team will be given a role in a group decision-making problem. You will be comfortable if you remember that you are not participating in a theatrical production. You are not being asked to take the lead in the school play. All you are asked to do is play yourself as you would feel if you were in the situation described in the role you will be given. For instance, pretend you are taking a final examination and the professor comes up to your desk, picks up your exam paper, tears it up, and says, "You fail the course. You have notes and books on the floor beside you and under your desk, and I've seen you looking down there. Also, you were glancing at the examination paper of the student next to you." You decide to appeal your failure grade to the dean. What are all the possible arguments you could use to defend yourself? (Take 2 minutes now and discuss this situation with two of your fellow students.) This situation could be role-played by you, with someone else playing the role of the dean, whose viewpoint would probably be different from yours. The roles of our exercise are similar in that you will have some idea of how you would behave if you were in the situation described. One more point about role playing: you are role-playing not only for what you can learn from it but also to give the other role player the opportunity to see what it is like to interact with, and learn from, you in this situation. That is, in this course you are responsible for the learning of others.

b. Tear out the instruction sheet "Who Gets the Overtime?" that can be found at the end of the instructions, but be careful not to look at any of the individual role sheets while doing so. The instructor will read this instruction sheet aloud while the class follows it. Participants can refer to this sheet at any time during the role playing.

c. Each team is to arrange itself in a circle and elect the supervisor (Kim) for this specific exercise. (*Note:* If the class is not working in permanent teams, participants are to form groups of six and elect a supervisor for this exercise.) Starting clockwise from the supervisor, the role assignments are as follows:

A woman in the group should assume the role of Sara. (If there is no woman in the group, of course, she has to be played by a man.) If only five members are present, eliminate the role of Fran. If only four are present in the team, a member of a six-person team should be borrowed temporarily for this exercise.

Turn to your own role assignment sheet and tear it from the book. After you have read the role description and understand it, turn it face down and use it as a name card so your team members can identify your role name during the exercise. Do not tell others what your role instructions are. When the exercise begins, play your role naturally, without referring to your sheet. When facts or events arise that are not covered by the roles, make up things that are consistent with the way it might be in a real-life situation.

When Kim has studied and understands the supervisor's role, she will stand. When the supervisors for all groups are standing, the instructor will give the signal to begin the exercise. When Kim sits down, assume Kim has just entered the office and greet Kim with a hearty "Good morning!" Kim will tell you what to do from this point on.

(*Note for Kim:* If you have only five on the team, including yourself, announce to your group that Fran called in sick and read them Fran's role. Fran is to be taken into consideration in arriving at the solution.)

Observers, if there are any, are to be assigned one to a group for the purpose of observing and, possibly, reporting to the class at the end of the session how the decision was made. Observers are not to enter into the process. (Time: for introduction, 10 minutes; for role playing, 20 to 25 minutes; for discussion, 20 minutes or longer. This exercise generates a range of rich data, and it is well to reserve discussion time to extend into the second hour.)

(*Note:* Teams completing role playing before the time has run out should proceed with task 2. Skip task 2 and go directly to task 3 if teams all finish at about the same time.)

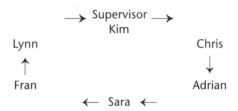

Task 2 (Only for Teams Finishing Task 1 Early):

After deciding who gets the overtime, the team should assume it is reconvening as a committee of supervisors to deliberate and decide the same case. To whom would this committee give the overtime? Why?

Task 3:

a. When the role playing is complete, the instructor will ask each supervisor to give the name of the person in the role play who got the overtime. The names are to be listed on the blackboard for all groups (using the chart form below), but no discussion is to take place at this time. The listing provides the class with information as to which groups agree and disagree with their choice.

Group	Who Got the Overtime?	How Was Decision Made?
#1		
#2		
#3		

b. The instructor will now interview each group on the following:

  a. How was the decision made? (List the elements of these decision processes on the board for each team.) What are the similarities and differences among the decision processes? What criteria were used? (List on the board.) What procedures could be used to bring more objectivity into the process if the group were to start over again—assuming the leader left the problem entirely up to employees to solve?

  b. Was this a good way to make the decision for this particular problem? Why?

  c. What issues (points of controversy) were raised by the group decision making?

  d. How did the supervisor feel about the role she or he was given? How did the employees feel about the role played by the supervisor? How could the supervisor have actively guided and facilitated the process and still let the employees make the decision?

  e. If the supervisor had decided not to let the employees make the decision, what other methods could he or she have used to arrive at the decision? Which of the alternatives, including group decision, would you have preferred?

f. How did each Sara feel about her role? (*Note:* This has to be done from the standpoint of sharing feelings with others. The atmosphere of listening for understanding without confrontation or argument is important. The differing reactions and the way the Saras perceive their roles can provide insight into the area of male–female interface in a work group.)

g. For teams that finished both tasks 1 and 2, were there any differences in the decisions for the two circumstances?

Source: This activity follows the design developed by Norman R. F. Maier's exercise "The New Truck Dilemma," in N. R. F. Maier, A. R. Solem, and Ayesha A. Maier, *Supervisory and Executive Development,* (New York: John Wiley & Sons, 1957). This exercise is printed here with the special permission of Dr. Maier.

Who Gets the Overtime?
(For Activity 5–3)

Five of you are employees of the Customers' Division of the Mountain Power Company's District Headquarters in Green Valley, Virginia. Your job requires monitoring customer accounts for records, billing, payments, and collection purposes. Answering customer inquiries and opening and closing accounts are a major part of your job. All five of you are considered excellent employees, and the atmosphere in the office is one of congeniality and good morale. One reason for this is that Green Valley is a small town in a beautiful area where few good jobs exist. The small local college is the main activity in the town, and Mountain Power's district office offers one of the few good places to work, even though salaries are modest. Students graduating from the local high schools and colleges move out of the area to find permanent jobs.

All five of you are feeling the squeeze for money. Inflation is a problem, and many of the products sold in Green Valley are higher priced than in big cities because of transportation costs and the limited market. All of you moonlight when you can, but the opportunities are scarce. When overtime work is required, Mountain Power's policy is to rotate employee assignments so all have an equal share on an annual basis; however, overtime needs are very low.

Here are some general facts about the employees in your section.

Chris is 22 years of age, has been with the company four years, and has three young children.

Adrian is 27 years of age, has been with the company 10 years, and is the senior person in the office.

Sara is 21 years of age. It is the company's policy to employ two deserving college students half-time and to let them study at the office during times when customer inquiries are low; she is one of these students.

Fran, 25 years of age, is the second half-time student. Fran started work at the same time as Sara two years ago and plans to graduate in one year.

Lynn, 20 years of age, is the newest employee, having decided to make Mountain Power a career after graduating from a two-year college.

Kim is your supervisor. When the instructor gives you the signal to start role playing, the scene is as follows: You have just been called into Kim's office for a discussion. The supervisor will tell you what you are to do. Play your role as if you were in the position described on your role sheet. When facts arise that are not covered by the roles, be creative; make up things that are consistent with the way it might be in a real-life situation.

Note: Return to the instructions of Task 1c, Activity 9–5, before proceeding with the role playing.

Source: This appendix follows the design developed by Norman R. F. Maier's exericse "The New Truck Dilemma," which appears in N. R. F. Maier, A. R. Solem, and Ayesha A. Maier, *Supervisor and Executive Development* (New York: John Wiley & Sons, Inc., 1957). This exercise is printed here with Dr. Maier's permission.

(CUT ON LINE)

FRAN

(CUT ON LINE)

LYNN

KIM THE SUPERVISOR

Your manager has asked you to select one of your employees to work Saturday mornings on a new job in another section of the headquarters office. The manager wants the same person to perform in the job for the next year because it requires technical training in data-processing equipment, and continuous experience will be needed.

Your dilemma is that all five of your people are equally qualified and all need the money. You have recently had a supervision course in which participation of employees in decision making was studied. You decide that this is a case in which they all have an equal interest so you will let them make the decision. You have called them together for this purpose. Tell them what the opportunity is and then tell them to go ahead and decide among themselves who is to get the overtime assignment. Remember, *you are going to let them make the decision.* The team must arrive at a decision.

(CUT ON LINE)

ROLE OF FRAN

You are always pressed for money. You live with your fiancé, also a student, who shares expenses. Your car is old and always requiring repairs. You wish to enter the MBA program at Midwest University next fall; if you can save up for the initial tuition, you might be able to attend classes half-time and work half-time.

(CUT ON LINE)

ROLE OF LYNN

You are married and living with your in-laws so you can save, but you find it most uncomfortable. Your spouse works half-time, having found nothing full-time. The two of you are very frugal because your parents have promised to pay half the down payment on a "starter" house if you can accumulate the other half. You plan no children until this is accomplished. You hope to prove to Mountain Power that your all-around capabilities and two-year community college degree qualify you to work into management. You plan to take a computer course in the near future as part of your personal development program.

CHRIS

(CUT ON LINE)
SARA

(CUT ON LINE)
ADRIAN

M5-31

ROLE OF CHRIS

You and your spouse have had one child after another so money is tight. Your spouse continually presses you to find extra work, which you do whenever you can. Both of you spend much of your spare time raising chickens and vegetables for the family.

(CUT ON LINE)

ROLE OF SARA

You give part of your earnings to the support of your younger brothers because money is scarce for your mother since your father died. You have been borrowing money for your education. You have been able to carry almost a full load at college in your business administration major and maintain a good average in spite of your work; you are starting your junior year. You like Mountain Power and may want to stay on after you graduate if they will give you a job. You have learned in your business courses that professional women have to be better than their male peers to move ahead in the work world. Your personal effectiveness goal is get "your share of the air time," "to hold your own," or "be assertive in a pleasant way" in discussions with male peers.

(CUT ON LINE)

ROLE OF ADRIAN

You give 10 percent of your salary to the church and are highly regarded for your willingness to help with church responsibilities. For two years you have been building a small house in your spare time. Progress is slow because you have to save up to buy building materials. You are single, but you hope to get married as soon as you find the right person. You feel that your seniority entitles you to first consideration when new opportunities arise.

6

Small Group Dynamics

Learning Objectives

After completing this module, you should be able to

1. Explain the basic elements and processes of small group dynamics.
2. Identify the factors affecting the evolution and performance of groups.
3. Discuss the differences between the emergent role system and the required role system.
4. Describe the role that the manager can play in facilitating the development and performance of a group.
5. Appreciate the effect of group cohesion on group performance.
6. Identify the developmental stages of groups.

Module Outline

Premodule Preparation
    Activity 6–1: An Initial Inventory of Group Dynamics
Introduction
    Group Dynamics Defined
Factors Affecting Group Development and Performance
    Context
    Purpose
    Processes
    Composition and Diversity
    Structure
    Role Differentiation
    Leadership
Other Aspects of Small Group Dynamics
    Social Loafing and Free Riding
    Cohesiveness
    Group Development and Group Maturity

_____   ## Premodule Preparation

Activity 6–1:
An Initial Inventory of
Group Dynamics

Objectives:

a. To give you the opportunity to reflect on your group experience thus far in the course.

b. To help you develop an appreciation for the many elements that play a role in the evolution of a group.

c. To help you diagnose the current stage of development of your group so that you can improve its effectiveness.

Task 1:

a. Working alone, jot down as many norms as you can think of that emerged in your group. Briefly describe each norm (not more than one sentence per norm).

b. Reflecting on your experience with your group, identify the different roles that individuals have taken on.

c. List additional elements that you believe influenced the evolution and progress of your team.

Task 2:

a. Each team is to elect a spokesperson.

b. Each team is to compile a list of the norms that emerged that are agreed upon by the team and provide an example of the norm wherever appropriate.

c. Each team is to compile a list of the roles that evolved that are agreed upon by the team.

d. Each team is to compile a list of elements that are agreed upon that influenced the evolution of the team and its effectiveness.

e. The instructor will call upon spokespersons, one at a time, to name the elements, norms, and roles. These will be written on the board. Examples will be requested for clarification.

f. The instructor will give a short lecture on this subject.

Task 3:

a. The teams are to discuss the different norms and roles that emerged in the groups and examine their effects on the groups' effectiveness.

b. Teams are to identify norms and roles that they would like to see change and devise an action plan to execute and monitor the changes.

Introduction

In Module 5 we introduced some characteristics of small group activities, emphasizing the development of group skills for greater team effectiveness. We also discussed several uses of small groups and teams in the work setting. We will now take a closer look at small group processes and characteristics to provide you with knowledge of small group dynamics and an understanding of the social group that develops within the work group. Understanding the dynamics of small group operation should help you improve the operation of your class team and other groups of which you are a member.

As a primary frame of reference in studying group dynamics, remember that *whenever a group of strangers or whenever two or more people come together to perform a task, the web of group dynamics spontaneously begins to spin.* (Sounds magical, and maybe it is!)

Group Dynamics Defined

The small work group is a primary focus of the study of organizational behavior because it is here the social system (what we call the *emergent role system*), which is a primary determinant of behavior, is spontaneously generated.[1] One good definition of **group dynamics** is from Knowles:

[Group dynamics] refers to the complex forces that are acting upon every group throughout its existence which cause it to behave the way it does. We can think of every group having certain relatively static aspects—its name, constitutional structure, ultimate purpose, and other fixed characteristics. But it also has dynamics aspects—it is always moving, doing something, changing, becoming, interacting, and reacting, and the nature and direction of its movement is determined by forces being exerted upon it from within itself and from outside. The interaction of these forces and the resultant effects on a given group constitute its dynamics.[2]

A knowledge of small group dynamics is essential for your understanding of the social system of the group, what we call the *emergent social system.* You will also find this knowledge helpful in analyzing the interactions in your classroom team because whenever a group of individuals comes together to perform a task, predictable patterns of behavior develop. Thus we may also define *group dynamics* as the pattern of interactions among group members as a group develops and achieves goals.[3] The influence of the individual on the group and the group on the individual, and the interrelationships between groups and the interaction of groups with the larger institutions of which they are a part are the primary focus in the study of group dynamics.

Factors Affecting Group Development and Performance

As Activity 6–1 has demonstrated, many factors affect the development and performance of teams. These elements can be clustered into six broad categories: context, purpose, composition and diversity, structure, processes, and leadership. Figure 6–1 shows key components of the six elements.

Context

Context refers to the environment in which groups operate. It refers to both the organizational environment and the environment external to the organization. Contextual factors influence both the evolution of a group and its performance as well as all the other (internal) factors.[4] A group's contextual factors might include (1) *organizational characteristics* such as business strategy, production technology, organization structure, management philosophy and practice, information technology, decision-making processes, reward and punishment systems, control systems, and working conditions; (2) *organizational culture* such as norms, values, attitudes toward strategy and goals, actual operating procedures, and power structure; and (3) the characteristics of the organization's *external environment,* which could include factors such as industry characteristics; competitive pressures; technological change; economic, social, political, and legal expectations and requirements; customers; and suppliers.

Figure 6–1
Factors Affecting
Group Development
and Performance

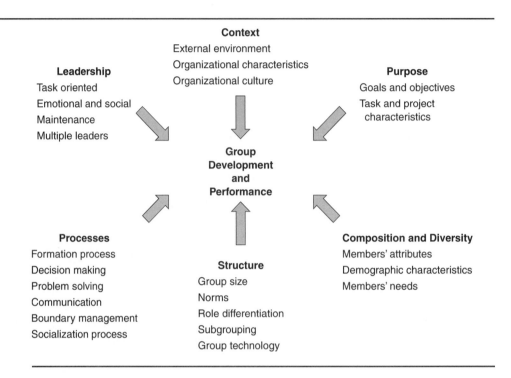

Purpose

All small groups have *goals and objectives* to attain. Groups are always engaged in accomplishing group projects. They are the reason the members have come together and the primary determinants of the interaction of people out of which patterns of behavior will emerge. The purpose of a group can be clearly defined—as would be the case with work teams—or loosely defined (or collectively recognized)—as would occur with a meeting of a group of friends held to satisfy the social needs of the members. Goals are powerful inducements for action. Clearly defined goals are critical for effective group performance.[5] The specific content of the goal and the kind of goal (competitive versus cooperative, for example) influence the evolution and performance of the group.[6] Furthermore, the group's specific *task and project characteristics and requirements or characteristics of the group project* determine its performance. These include required activities and interactions, the required level of interdependence among group members to accomplish the task,[7] and the task's time frame and deadlines.[8] Group projects can vary in several aspects. First is the extent to which their execution requires specific task activities, interpersonal activities, or process activities. Second is the extent to which the projects concern (1) acquisition, processing, and distribution of information; (2) managing conflict and achieving consensus; and (3) motivating, regulating, and coordinating member behavior. Each project is likely to represent some mix of the above requirements and activities.[9] The nature of the group's project will affect the kind of group that is put together. Coupled with group member composition, these set the stage for group performance.

Composition and Diversity

This category includes elements that are related to the characteristics of the individuals who are brought together to work on a task or project. Following McGrath,[10] the different elements can be clustered into three subcategories: members' attributes, members' demographic characteristics, and members' needs. Figure 6–2 summarizes the elements that make up this category.

**Figure 6–2
Composition and Diversity**

Members' attributes
Knowledge, skills, and abilities
Values, beliefs, and attitudes
Personality
Cognitive and behavioral styles
   Learning style
   Problem-solving style

Members' demographic characteristics
Age
Sex
Race

Members' needs
Needs for affiliation
Needs for achievement
Needs for power
Needs for economic or material resources

Members' Attributes

Individuals come to the group with some pattern of values on each of the four sets of attributes: they have basic knowledge, skills, and abilities; they hold values, beliefs, and attitudes; they have distinct personality characteristics (we explore this topic in Module 9); and they have developed cognitive and behavioral styles of learning and problem solving. These attributes are likely to affect the individual's ability to carry out the various activities required by the group's task or project and as such will influence the group's dynamics and performance.

*Members' Demographic
Characteristics*

An individual's basic demographic characteristics, such as age, sex, and race, may affect his or her performance as a group member either by themselves or through their relationships with other attributes. For example, being the only ethnic minority (or the oldest or the only male) in a group may affect the member's attribute (that is, attitude or behavior style) and as such will influence both the individual's behavior and the team's development process and performance. As of late the topic of diversity within groups has received significant attention. While diversity appears to have an effect on group development and performance, the relationship between diversity and group dynamics and outcomes is complex. A recent study of the relationship between diversity and innovation and creativity pointed out the many complex relationships that need to be investigated further by isolating the effects of diversity in age, sex, race-ethnicity, and tenure on the work group dynamics and performance.[11] At this point it is safe to say that much more research is needed into the intricacies of diversity and its role in shaping group dynamics and performance.

Members' Needs

Individuals differ when it comes to their basic needs in the group's context. Individuals come to the group with some pattern of needs that they would like to fulfill via the group's experience. The members' needs affect members' motivation to participate in the group. Although we explore the topic of motivation in Module 12, at this point we must distinguish between four distinct individual needs: needs for affiliation, needs for achievement, needs for power, and needs for economic or material resources. Any group must fulfill its members' needs to some degree to motivate the members to participate and as such will influence the group to carry out its task or project to completion.

As we saw in Module 2, beyond the unique similarities and differences that exist between individuals' personalities and learning styles, research has indicated that all four dominant learning modes are critical for group effectiveness. Thus the extent to which group members are compatible will influence the group's performance. Similar conclusions can be drawn regarding individual problem-solving styles. The particular combination of member styles will affect the group's evolution and its outcomes.[12] For example, a group composed of four strong "accommodators" and one "diverger" is likely to fall short in its ability to objectively analyze the situation, may have difficulty identifying the main issue or problem, will lack insight in the identification and exploration of alternative solutions, and may fall short in the choice of the best solution.

Studies have also shown that a heterogenous group in terms of abilities and experiences can have a positive effect on group performance, particularly when that group's tasks are diverse, because a wide range of competencies are needed. On the other hand, groups with a more homogenous makeup may have less conflict, better communication, more member satisfaction, and lower turnover.[13]

Other individual characteristics that can influence group performance are individual flexibility in terms of task assignments[14] and preference for group work. Individuals who prefer to work in groups tend to be more satisfied and effective in those settings.[15]

Processes

The formation and socialization processes play a critical role in the development of the group and its performance. Regardless of whether the group is a new group or has been working together for a while, most people wonder why they were selected and/or recruited for a specific work group. Yet fulfilling this requirement does not seem to be enough. The formation of new groups, beyond the actual choices based on the skills and competencies needed to accomplish the task/project requires the matching of diverse individuals. A complex socialization process helps to integrate new members into a mature group and/or helps the new group begin to function as a task or project group. For example, recent research suggests that the existing composition of the group, the demographic similarities between newcomers and established group members, and the nature of the newcomer cohort affect the socialization of new group members.[16] Furthermore, it also became apparent that the perception of newcomers and old-timers about how well new members were fitting in sometimes diverged substantially. The role of perception in shaping individual and group behavior is discussed in Module 10.

The process elements of decision making and problem solving were discussed in Module 5. *Boundary management* refers to the management of the relationship between a team and other teams or other organizational entities, a process related in part to context and purpose elements, which have already been discussed. The other major element, communication, is discussed in Module 11, but we consider here the impact on the location of individuals within the channels of communication.

The effects of location on performance and satisfaction have been summarized by Swap[17] in his review of Cartwright and Zander's experimental work on communications networks.[18] According to Swap, an important determinant of a group's decision-making effectiveness is the communication structure of the group—who is allowed to communicate with whom. An extract of that review follows.

We might want to know the answers to a number of questions relating to a network: How *satisfied* will each of the group members be? How *efficiently* will they be able to accomplish a task or make a decision? Will any one member come to be viewed as a *leader*? To answer these questions, let us return to the social psychologist's laboratory.[19]

You are one of five subjects in an experiment. Each of you is given a card with five symbols taken from a group of six (circle, triangle, and so on). Only one of the symbols appears on each subject's card. The task of the group is to determine the identity of that common symbol as quickly as possible. The five subjects sit around a table divided by partitions. In each partition is a slot through which subjects can exchange written messages. Which slots are open or closed determines the nature of the communication network. You may be in a position where you communicate with only one other subject, or two, or perhaps all four corresponding to the patterns shown in Figure 6–3. These are just four of the many possible networks. A double arrow indicates a two-way communication link; that is, a slot permits both sending and receiving messages. (While some networks include one-way channels—such as putting a message in a suggestion box—they are relatively rare and are not be considered here.)

Figure 6–3
Four Communications
Networks

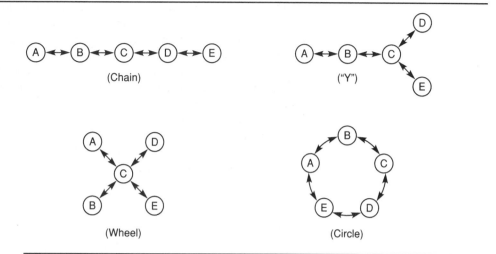

Source: W. C. Swap and Associates, Decision Making, (Beverly Hills, CA: Sage, 1984), p .55. Reprinted by permission of Sage Publications, Inc.

Perhaps the most important characteristics of communication networks are their centrality and the degree of centrality of a given member within the network. Centrality may be viewed as the degree of *connectedness* among the people in the network. In Figure 6–3, the wheel is highly centralized, with C maintaining communications with all other group members. The circle is less centralized as each member maintains but two communication links.

Let's summarize the major findings that have emerged from research on **communication networks.** First, a given member's centrality is strongly related to his or her satisfaction with the group experience. This relationship is particularly strong among people with relatively dominant personalities. Second, people who are placed in central positions in the network come to be viewed as *leaders* by the other group members. Virtually all group members agree that C is the leader in the wheel, but there is no consensus about leadership in the circle. Third, the performance of the group (measured by such factors as speed, accuracy, and rate of learning) is strongly affected by its structure. For simple tasks, such as information gathering described in the preceding experiment, the more centralized networks perform better. For more complex activities such as those requiring somebody (that is, the central person) to operate on the information after it is collected, centralized groups perform more poorly. We might speculate that the result will be particularly pronounced when the central person is basically incompetent. But a further explanation comes from the fourth general finding: decentralized groups as a whole are more satisfied with their group experience than are centralized groups. While the wheel may have one satisfied person (the "leader"), there are four peripheral, unhappy members. Participants in a circle network, on the other hand, are all equally central or peripheral and share equally in the group responsibilities. This higher degree of group satisfaction might contribute to the finding that such decentralized (democratic) groups outperform others on more challenging tasks.

The effectiveness of group decision making should clearly vary with the complexity and nature of the group task and with the type of communication structure. A highly centralized structure should be most effective with simple decisions and when a competent leader holds the central position. For more complex, discretionary tasks, a more decentralized communication structure should produce both better decisions and greater member satisfaction.

Structure

Group Size

Effective team size seems to range from 3 members to a normal upper limit of about 16 members. Yet while the optimal size seems to be correlated with the degree of project complexity and leadership competence, most argue that effective work groups range in size from 7 to 12 members. Advances in computer technology and software, such as groupware, the Internet, and email, are enabling larger teams to work on projects. In a recent study that summarized some of the literature on the relationship between group size and group members' feeling of inhibition, the authors argued that groups of 2 to 7 members feel a "low degree" of inhibition, in groups of 8 to 12 inhibition is "moderate," and groups of 13 to 16 exhibit a "high degree" of inhibition. Furthermore, group "members' tolerance of direction by the leader" seems to be low to moderate for groups of 2 to 7 members, moderate for 8 to 12 members, and high for 13 to 16 members.[20]

Group structure refers to certain psychologically shared properties of the group that result from both formal and informal interactions of its members. Structural elements that influence group performance can be divided into two categories: the formal and the informal. Formal structural elements are those that are imposed by the organization, and the most important is the design of the group's tasks. Informal elements are those that develop out of the group's operation.

Formal Elements—Work Design

Work design is discussed in Module 13. Work design influences the activities and interactions of group members. One recent study shows that the design of group tasks that provide for skill variety, task identity, task significance, autonomy, and feedback have a positive influence on group productivity, satisfaction, and effectiveness.[21] Since the subject of work design is extensively covered in Module 13, we will not discuss additional details here, but merely note that work design is indeed an important element to be considered in understanding group performance and developing enhanced group performance.

Informal Elements

As a group develops, *recurrent patterns* of relationships occur. Furthermore, group technology is developed. Group technology has three dimensions: (1) task predictability, (2) problem analyzability, and (3) interdependence. There are also three properties of group structure: (1) *connectiveness* (the extent to which group members identify with the goals of other members in their group), (2) *vertical differentiation* (the number of different levels of the organizational hierarchy represented in a group), and (3) *horizontal differentiation* (the number of different job areas represented in a group). Beyond the unique recurrent patterns of relationships, group technology and group structure affect overall group performance.[22]

The recurrent patterns are shared psychologically by group members in that all come to know and are influenced by the patterns, whether they are consciously aware of them or not. This psychological sharing may be thought of as being in the general area of emergent attitudes. However, since we need more specific concepts to aid us in analyzing group behavior, we will work with terms such as *norms* and other structural components, including *status* and *role differentiation*.

To understand shared expectations that emerge in the group, we must know the process by which two or more persons spontaneously, often unconsciously, come to share expectations and assumptions of what is appropriate or meaningful behavior. Group members develop and accept these unwritten, informal guidelines without realizing it.

Development of Norms: **Norms** are expectations shared by group members of how they ought to behave under a given set of circumstances. The idea of a norm carries with it a range of behaviors that are acceptable, so there is some variability for individuals. Work attitudes are an example. A work team made up of individuals who believe in giving an honest day's work to their employer could readily develop a high-productivity norm, whereas one composed of individuals who believe business rips off workers could develop a low-productivity norm. One work team having half of each type might have only a shared expectation that "we will never agree on productivity."

Group members are often unaware of their norms and that these norms influence member behavior. Freudians have always assumed that subconscious and unconscious mental processes influence our behavior, and norms often exist at the level of group subconsciousness. When participants in our courses write a term paper on their teams' interactions, it is surprising how few norms they have observed. (Are you making entries in your journal on the norms you assume to be developing in your group? One way to identify norms is to observe behavior of the group, particularly in relation to the behavior of an individual member. Is the group upset by the behavior, for example, of being late or not being prepared? If so, does that identify behavior that the group feels is appropriate or inappropriate? The same can be said for behavior that the group rewards with praise.) We offer this hint because it is important first to become aware of the consequences of certain norms and then to become knowledgeable of how teams can develop and shape their own norms for the purpose of improved effectiveness.

Work groups often spontaneously develop an emergent role system with norms that are contrary to management goals but that satisfy their own needs and reduce their frustrations. If you have analyzed The Slade Company case, you have seen an example of this kind of situation. Integrating the required and the emergent systems so they are compatible is an ever-present management challenge.

Values play a special role in the formation of norms. **Cultural values** provide an example of this. Values tell us what is moral, worthwhile, good, or beautiful. For individuals, values have been developed and reinforced through a lifetime of experiences. When team members in this course meet for the first time, often they espouse values related to democracy, fair treatment, and honesty. They frequently develop such group norms as "Let everyone have a fair share of the airtime," "Let's not play manipulative games," and "Let's be open and level with one another."

So how do values and norms differ? Values may be thought of as "criteria or conceptions used in evaluating things (including ideas, acts, feelings, and events) as to their relative desirability, merit, or correctness."[23] Values can be held by a single individual; norms cannot because they emerge from the interactions in the group. Norms are rules of behavior, but values are critical for evaluating behavior and other things. Further, norms carry sanctions, but values never do. This distinction is important because management teams in particular need to be in agreement on the basic operating values from which their system of norms is derived. We frequently find that management teams are in conflict over values, such as short-run profits versus longer-range organizational viability or rate of return on investment versus market share. Consultants find values clarification is usually a priority need in high-level team-building sessions. You may recall from your own experience with Activity 4–2 ("Values in Business") how emotionally loaded the area can be.

Role Differentiation

Whenever two or more people come together to work on a common purpose, **role differentiation** occurs; that is, patterns of behavior for each individual develop that tend to become repeated as activities progress. Roles can be classified into those that are focused on achieving the tasks of the group, ones that build and maintain favorable relationships among group members, and those that serve individual needs, sometimes at the expense of the group.[24]

Task Roles

Individuals who assume **task roles** are interested in getting the job done. They often emerge as the informal leaders of work groups. Roles that fall in this category include

- *Initiator*—Offers new ideas both on ways to solve problems and on ways for the group to approach its task or organize to do its work.
- *Coordinator*—Coordinates group activities, connects different ideas and suggestions, and clarifies relationships.
- *Information seeker*—Seeks out facts and information and clarifies ideas. *Opinion seekers* are variants of this role.
- *Information giver*—Offers facts and information that are relevant to the group's task. *Opinion givers* are variants of this role.
- *Recorder*—Keeps track of the group's activities and progress to date. May write down ideas. *Summarizers* are a variant of this role and act to provide a verbal summary of activity to date or decisions made by the group.

- *Evaluator/critic*—Offers assessments of the group's operation as well as evaluations of ideas and suggestions made by group members.
- *Timekeeper*—Works to keep the group on schedule and to help ensure that the group makes productive use of the time available to it.

In any group these roles may be played by one or many individuals.

Group-Building and Relationship Maintenance Roles

Individuals who assume relationship roles are often the most popular members of groups because they work to facilitate social and emotional relationships among group members. They are often the social leader of the group. Examples of the types of roles in this category are

- *Encourager*—Supports the activity of other group members, praises contributions, and agrees with suggestions.
- *Gatekeeper/expediter*—Keeps individuals from monopolizing the discussion, encourages participation by everyone, and keeps the discussion moving.
- *Standard setter*—States both output and process standards and goals for the group to achieve; assesses group performance in terms of these standards and goals.
- *Observer/commentator*—Acts as a detached observer, commenting on both group process and outcomes.
- *Followers*—Passive but friendly group members.

Individual Roles

These roles are expressions of individual personalities and individual needs. Sometimes individuals act in a manner that is detrimental to group performance. Individual roles include

- *Aggressor*—Verbally attacks other team members and their contributions.
- *Blocker*—Refuses to concede a point even when confronted with group unanimity; stubborn and unreasonable at times.
- *Dominator*—Attempts to control the group and the discussion.
- *Recognition seeker*—Needs to be the center of attention.
- *Avoider*—Seeks to avoid becoming involved with the group, passive, avoids commitment.

Other types of individual roles include self-confessor, playboy, help seeker, and special-interest pleader. You may be able to think of other classifications based on your group experience. One student saw Wonderwoman, Superman, cynic, cheerleader, white knight, and Florence Nightingale among her team members.

The significance of role differentiation is that these patterned relationships develop in a group and become part of the members' shared expectations of what ought to be done and what is appropriate or acceptable behavior. Knowledge and awareness of different roles provide the manager or team leader with a basis not only for understanding what is taking place but also for developing useful roles and discouraging dysfunctional roles in the group.

Status

Status is defined as the degree of esteem, respect, or prestige an individual commands from others. Status operates in group settings, and group members acquire common perceptions for respecting other members on numerous dimensions. If problem-solving and analytical abilities are important in the group, members will, over time, rank one another from the highest to the lowest ability in this regard. Other dimensions of status include ability to judge the motivation and the capabilities of others, professional knowledge, experience, interpersonal skills, personal appearance, "personality," and any other area valued by the group, including items like a car to transport the group or an apartment where the group can meet comfortably. An overall status that is dependent on a combination of these factors is accorded to group members. One of the most important is the degree to which a person conforms to the norms of the group.

High conformers have high status; low conformers have lower status. However, group pressures toward uniformity vary. Some norms are absolutes, whereas others permit a range of behaviors—what is called *wiggle room*. Group leaders usually have more freedom than the other group members to try new behavior.

Awareness of Status: Participants often write in their papers that there were no differences in status among members of their group. This failure of observation may be because they think it is unfair to label people or to ridicule some. However, status always exists in groups and affects behavior and performance. You need to think of it, first, as the characteristics one brings to the group (such as family background or what course of study the individual is pursuing) and, second, as the degree to which a person conforms to the norms of the group. Another way of thinking about status is that of credibility (What's my credibility in this group?). Acceptability is another dimension (How can I improve my acceptability in this group?). Listening more attentively to others is a possible answer to this question. Good journal entries can enhance your awareness of status factors and have implications for growth in your understanding of how your status can influence others.

Rejection of the Deviant

A **deviant** is an individual whose behavior differs from what is regarded as standard. In a group sense, a deviant is one who does not subscribe to the group's norms. Stanley Schachter conducted laboratory experiments with college students and found some interesting reactions of small groups toward individuals who take an unchanging position in opposition to the majority.[25] In each group he had three "stooges" who played three different roles: one would agree with whatever majority position arose; the second—called the *slider*—would take the opposite position but would change toward the majority gradually; and the third, who was the deviant, took the opposite position and did not change. In those groups where there was high cohesiveness among the members (see the discussion of cohesiveness below) and where the subject under discussion was of high relevance, communications were directed toward the slider and the deviant in attempts to convince and persuade them. Communication toward the deviant fell off toward the end of the meeting; the slider was accepted and the deviant rejected.

The dynamics of deviant behavior in groups is a complex phenomenon that has a significant effect on the development of a group. (Have you ever been in a group in which one member constantly violated accepted norms of behavior? Can you imagine the effect of such behavior on a group?) A *scapegoat* or *covert role player* is an individual in a group who is unconsciously assigned the role of absorbing emotions on behalf of the group. For example, the scapegoat can be blamed for the failures of the group; he or she also allows the group to avoid an unpleasant true examination of its behavior and performance.[26]

Subgroupings of Members

Subgroupings are recurrent patterns of relationships among individuals within the group that become established. Some of these relationships are temporary and some are enduring. These subgroups may be dyads (pairs) or triads (trios). A positive dyad is two persons supporting each other's views; a negative dyad is composed of opposing persons; a third possibility is one person who finds someone attractive but meets with rejection. Such subgroupings are not always readily apparent to members. Triads are supposedly the most unstable of all groups because they almost always break down into a pair and one.[27]

Observers, more often than group members, can identify subgrouping patterns. Greater awareness and sensitivity to this can help team members become more objective. For instance, subgrouping tends to become associated with seating arrangements. A fixed pattern by which each member always sits in the same place or members from one unit always sit next to one another can reinforce any feelings associated with subgrouping.

Participants often write that there were no subgroupings and comment that everyone was equally independent; however, subgroupings always exist to some degree. Sociometric techniques can readily bring out the underlying basis for subgrouping (attraction to or identification with other people or rejection). Ask the question, Which team member would you most like to go to a movie with? Rank all members from "most like to" to "least like to." The responses could be listed on a diagram showing the interrelationships among members. The same ranking could be done with a number of questions relating to different aspects of relationships—for example, Who would you most like to have on your debate team? These underlying feelings can be the basis of subgroupings, though they might not be apparent on the surface or influence the team greatly. See whether you can make journal entries that show an enhanced ability to observe subgroupings and their influences on the team.

Leadership

Leaders in small groups play a critical role in fostering the evolution of the group and its performance. Studies in group dynamics have emphasized the importance of the emergent leader in the accomplishment of group tasks. The group leader or leaders are seen as roles that emerge within the group just like the other differentiated roles discussed earlier in this module. Module 3 provided an overview of leadership orientations and some of the current knowledge about the role of leaders in organizational settings.

In the context of **small group leadership,** we would like to add the following points based on recent research. First, two types of leadership functions in small groups have been found to influence group performance: *monitoring* (obtaining and interpreting data about performance conditions and events that might affect them) and *taking action* (creating or maintaining favorable performance conditions).[28] Second, the performance of both task-oriented and maintenance-oriented leadership roles influence group process and group effectiveness.[29] Third, two categories of behavior—*performance monitoring* (collecting performance data) and *performance consequences* (establishing rewards and punishments for performance)—are required optimal leadership performance in small groups.[30] Finally, effective leaders of effective teams manage the teams' boundaries—defining goals and direction and placing constraints on team behavior.[31] It is also important to note that group leaders greatly influence all the factors that determine group development and performance (summarized in Figure 6–1).

Other Aspects of Small Group Dynamics

Group dynamics is a field that has been intensively studied. Only a few of the concepts associated with it have been touched on so far in this book. In this section we examine several other concepts that have relevance for the manager: social loafing and free riding, cohesiveness, and group development.

Social Loafing and Free Riding

Social loafing is an effect first noted by a German psychologist named Ringleman, who measured individual and group effort on a rope-pulling task. He found that the effort extended by a group was less than the sum of individual efforts. Subsequent psychological experiments have found this effect to exist in other group settings.[32] The term *free rider* refers to a person who obtains benefits from being a member of a group but who does not bear a proportional share of the costs of providing those benefits.[33] These effects have been noted to increase as group size increases.[34]

Social loafing and free riding can be attributed to individual perceptions about other group members' efforts, to individual laziness, and to the fact that individual effort is hidden or less noticeable in a group setting. Other factors that have been identified are an indifferent group climate, unimportant or meaningless group tasks, low expectancy of being able to master the task, the presence of a highly qualified group member, and pressures to conform.[35]

Clearly, social loafing and free riding can be detrimental to group performance. This tendency can be dealt with by attempting to make individual contributions or tasks identifiable or perceived as unique.[36] It can be reduced by controlling the size of groups (with five to seven members generally seen as ideal). Social loafing and free riding can also be controlled by rewarding cooperative behavior and by encouraging the development of norms that encourage all members to make a full contribution to the group effort.

Cohesiveness

The term **group cohesiveness** refers to the attractiveness of the group to its members—the degree to which members desire to stay in the group. Unlike structure and process characteristics, which can be shaped by the team, cohesiveness is an outcome of how group members interact.

Research tends to support the assumption that members of highly cohesive groups, as contrasted to those of low cohesiveness, communicate better, are more cooperative, and are more responsive to group influence; they also tend to achieve accepted goals more efficiently and to have higher satisfaction.[37] Does this outcome mean that cohesive work groups have better performance than less cohesive groups? Although many studies over the past 30 years have demonstrated mixed results in attempting to answer this question,[38] one recent summary study found a consistent, small relationship between cohesion and productivity. The study found that the effect was much stronger in "real" (as opposed to laboratory or experimental) groups.[39]

Cohesiveness leads to trust, confidence, and acceptance among members. The pressures toward conformity give the group more influence over the individual,[40] and the individual shows greater commitment and loyalty.[41] Members of highly cohesive groups tend to have higher self-esteem and are less anxious than those of less cohesive groups.

A **hot team** is an example of a highly cohesive team. Such a team performs extremely well and is dedicated to both the team and to task accomplishment. Members of such a team are turned on by an exciting and challenging goal. Hot teams completely engage their members to the exclusion of almost everything else. Such teams can be characterized as teams with vitality; they are absorbing, full of debate and laughter, and very hard working.[42]

Highly cohesive groups are by definition fulfilling important needs of group members. This situation has several implications:

1. If the group can become more aware of the needs being fulfilled by the group for each member, it can improve its support of those needs.

2. If your team members in this class were more aware of the team skills you desire to develop, they might be more helpful in this regard.

3. One of the goals of team building (discussed in Module 7) is to become aware of the skills, abilities, and strengths of each member so that they can be integrated into the work activities of the group wherever feasible. This has the potential of increasing cohesiveness and individual satisfaction.

Groupthink

Groupthink is a mode of thinking that individuals engage in when pressures toward conformity become so dominant in a group that they override appraisal of alternative courses of action. High cohesiveness, insulation of the group from outsiders, lack of methodological procedures for search and appraisal of alternatives, directive leadership, a complex and changing environment, and high stress with a low degree of hope for finding a better solution than the one favored by the leader or other influential members were found to be conditions that can trigger groupthink behavior.[43] The following are the characteristics and symptoms of groupthink as articulated by Irving Janis:

1. An illusion of invulnerability is shared by all or most members of the group, which creates excessive optimism and encourages high risk taking.

2. Collective rationalization discounts warnings that might lead members to consider their assumptions before they commit themselves to a major policy decision.

3. An unquestionable belief in the group's morality inclines members to ignore ethical or moral consequences of their decisions.

4. There are stereotyped views of the enemy leaders as too evil to warrant genuine attempts to negotiate, or as too weak and stupid to counter whatever risky attempts are made to defeat their purpose.

5. Direct pressure on any member who expresses strong arguments against any of the group's stereotypes, illusions, or commitments makes clear that this type of dissent is contrary to what is expected of all loyal members.

6. Self-censorship of deviations from the apparent group consensus reflects each member's inclination to minimize the importance of self-doubts and counterarguments.

7. There is a shared illusion of unanimity concerning judgments conforming to the majority view (partly resulting from the self-censorship of deviants, augmented by the false assumption that silence means consent).

8. Self-appointed mindguards (members who protect the group from adverse information that might shatter its shared complacency about the effectiveness and the morality of its decision) emerge.[44]

Janis developed groupthink theory in analyzing the failed Bay of Pigs invasion of Cuba. Groupthink has also been implicated in the Nixon White House staff's handling of the Watergate affair and the Air Traffic Controllers Union's approach to the strike in 1981, which resulted in the discharge of most of its members.

One dramatic example of groupthink is NASA's managerial actions associated with the January 1986 accident that destroyed the space shuttle *Challenger*. The mindguarding function has been well documented. Before the launch the engineers voted unanimously to recommend a delay in the launch because the O-rings might not work in low temperatures. In the past Thiokol engineers had been asked to present considerable evidence to support a launch. This time they were asked to prove that no launch should occur. The engineers' recommendation was never relayed by management up to the top level in NASA, where the final decision to launch was made.[45] The presidential commission investigating the accident concluded that space agency officials were at certain critical points ill informed and "mesmerized" (a good synonym for *groupthink*) by past successes. When the Marshall Space Flight Center was criticized, the *Los Angeles Times* reported

"Everybody in a position of responsibility has to ape the boss in order to maintain their position," he said. "They have to have the same noxious attitude. Dissent is a bad word." To some employees at Marshall, the criticism was welcome news. Engineer William C. Bush, a long-time critic of the center's management, said the commission's description of the Alabama facility's isolationism from the rest of NASA was well deserved. "Marshall management has an 'us vs. them' mentality and equates dissent with disloyalty," Bush said.[46]

These highly publicized examples of groupthink may give you the false impression that the phenomenon only happens "out there" and can't or doesn't happen to you. Student team projects frequently get into a groupthink mode that negatively affects their results. One team, in considering its (poor) performance on the Mountain Survival activity, ruefully concluded that it quickly latched onto the idea of walking out, never considered the problems with that alternative, and never considered the alternative of staying at the crash site. A former student recently told us that what she remembers most about her organizational behavior class is the groupthink she experienced with her classroom team. She reported that she sees it often in her work relationships and regards guarding against it as a major responsibility in team management.

Groupthink can be prevented by the following steps:

- Appointing a team member to serve as a *devil's advocate* to question the group's assumptions and actions.

- Bringing in outside experts to evaluate the group's processes.

- Testing the group's ideas on outsiders.

- Having the leader avoid stating his or her position before the group reaches a decision.
- Once a decision is made, carefully reexamining the alternatives.[47]
- Having the leader alleviate time pressures on the group or, if this is not possible, focusing on issues, encouraging dissension and confrontation, or scheduling special meeting sessions.[48]

Group Development and Group Maturity

Group cohesiveness and the operation of norms occur over time. Like individuals, groups develop over time and reach developmental maturity. **Group maturity** has been described as existing when

1. Members are aware of their own and each other's assets and liabilities vis-à-vis the group's task.
2. These individual differences are accepted without being labeled as good or bad.
3. The group has developed authority and interpersonal relationships that are recognized and accepted by its members.
4. Group decisions are made through rational discussion. Minority opinions and/or dissent is recognized and encouraged. Attempts are not made to force decisions or false unanimity.
5. Conflict is over substantive group issues such as group goals and the effectiveness and efficiency of various means for achieving those goals. Conflict over emotional issues regarding group structure, process, or interpersonal relationships is at a minimum.
6. Members are aware of the group's processes and their roles in them.[49]

Group Development

Development is a process by which a system adapts to internal and environmental forces. Throughout this book we have noted that individual development is driven by the interaction of biological, psychological, and social elements. Groups that function in a relatively homogeneous environment tend to progress through similar patterns of development. A number of group development models have been advanced in the literature. These models can be classified into three categories: performance models, emotional climate models, and revolt models.[50] Table 6–1 provides a comparative summary of a representative model from each of the categories.

Table 6–1 **Group Development Models: A Comparison**

	Forming	Storming	Norming	Performing	Adjourning
Tuckman and Jensen (1977) (Performance Model)	Activity to determine nature and parameters of task	Engender emotional responses, resistance, ineffectiveness	Open exchange of relevant interpretations	Constructive task activity	
Schutz (1958) (Emotional Climate Model)	**Inclusion** In or out	**Control** Top or bottom	**Affection** Near or far		
Hartman and Gibbard (1974) (Revolt Model)	**Uncertainty** Revolt	**Group** Fusion-utopia	**Competition** Intimacy	**Termination**	

The *performance models* are based on the assumption that groups resolve issues as preparation to completing task performance. The group develops or moves through a clear hierarchy of stages toward more efficient and effective group work. Not all groups move through all stages; some groups may become stuck at a particular level of development. The *emotional climate* models do not contain stages of task performance but rather describe a progression of emotional concerns in the group. The stages build hierarchically toward closer relationships between members. The *revolt models* are based on the notion that groups proceed predictably toward a rebellion against the leader or leaders. The group develops by working through complex dynamic relationships between the members and the leader(s).

For illustration purposes we describe an emotional climate development model developed by H. J. Reitz.[51]

1. *Orientation.* People wonder how authority and power will be distributed. What is our purpose? How will we carry out the activities? What are the rules? What will my role be? How will I appear to others? How can I influence what is going on? This is a period of getting organized. The function of many of the behaviors is to ward off anxiety. The individuals' needs for status, attention, and acceptance are involved. Some individuals respond by withdrawal, not talking, doodling, or yawning. Others respond by being assertive, overtalkative, or aggressive; others respond by attempting to please. People seek to avoid anxiety by depending on the structure of leadership, rules, goals, and activities.

2. *Conflict.* Even though there is an initial settling in and the group seems somewhat stabilized, individual needs are not satisfied. Eventually this situation results in challenging or testing the leadership, the role structure, or the rules and goals that are developing. Subgroupings are apt to form around these issues, some supporting what has been established so far, others opposing or offering alternative approaches.

3. *Cohesion.* During the conflict phase, emotions are more easily expressed and some tension release takes place. A redistribution of leadership power may occur and members' roles become more clearly defined. Some issues raised during the conflict stage are resolved, so the authority structure and members' role clarification result in feelings of belongingness, feelings that "we have been through this together."

4. *Delusion.* The good feelings of having resolved many of the issues of authority may not last long. Group members still face issues concerning emotional aspects of interpersonal relationships. How intimate are they to become? How much are they willing to reveal about their feelings? Can they accept individual differences? The delusion arrives because the increased group acceptance that members feel around the authority and power issues can lead them to believe—erroneously—that there are no interpersonal problems. Conflict is apt to be smoothed over until the group members realize obstacles do exist and move into the next phase.

5. *Disillusion.* The euphoria of the delusion stage wears off as uncertainties around interpersonal issues remain. Subgroupings may form around the degree of socializing versus task orientation.

6. *Acceptance.* If the group has work to do and faces the pressure of goals and deadlines ahead, these forces will greatly influence the resolution of residual authority and intimacy problems. Such pressures bring rationality into the forefront and provide the base for individuals to play roles furthering problem resolution and acceptance of the group. Achievement of goals can greatly augment the movement toward maturity as described above.

Summary

Some concepts of small group dynamics have been described to demonstrate their applicability to the emergent role system of work groups and to your classroom teams. Group development and group performance are affected by six general factors: the group's purpose, the group's composition, the context within which the group operates, the group's structure, the group's processes, and the group's leadership.

Within groups recurrent patterns of relationships occur that are based on shared expectations. Of particular importance are the group's norms. Individuals follow norms to perform their roles and to ensure status and acceptance in the group. Sub-grouping among members occurs from role interactions and from attraction and rejection. Some group members may not put forth full effort, and social loafing may occur.

Group cohesiveness plays a critical role in high-performance teams. Cohesiveness is associated with the strength of the members' desire to remain in the group and their commitment to the group goals. Mental group ability and the personality of group members have a direct impact on the work-team processes and team effectiveness.[52] To the extent that a match between members' goals and group goals exists and the group composition results in a high general mental group ability, the team is likely to perform well.[53] High cohesiveness is also related to group maturity. Groups go through developmental stages as members struggle with both tasks and interpersonal relationships. Effectiveness requires avoiding hang-ups en route to group maturity. A major hazard faces groups that become highly cohesive. They can develop groupthink, which can lead to inappropriate or incorrect action.

Key Terms and Concepts

Communication network	Groupthink
Cultural values	Hot team
Deviant	Maintenance role
Group cohesiveness	Norms
Group development	Role differentiation
Group dynamics	Small group leadership
Group maturity	Social loafing
Group size	Task role
Group structure	

Study Questions

1. What is group dynamics? Why is an understanding of group dynamics essential for any team manager or group member?

2. In what way can group norms be considered a part of group structure?

3. Leadership is listed as a factor that influences performance. The other factors discussed are also influenced by team leaders. Develop an example of such influence for each of the other factors.

4. The disadvantages of groupthink are outlined in this module. Can you think of any advantages arising from groupthink?

5. What generalizations can be made concerning the relationship between homogeneity/heterogeneity and team effectiveness?

6. Think of any team you now are or have been a member of. How would you rate it on the six points given on group maturity?

7. Reflect on your group experience in this course thus far. Identify the different factors that affected the development of the group. What course of action would you take to improve the group's performance? Why?

Endnotes

1. J. E. McGrath, H. Arrow, and J. L. Berdahl, *A Theory of Groups as Complex Systems,* (Newbury Park, CA: Sage, 1998).

2. M. Knowles and H. Knowles, *The Introduction to Group Dynamics,* (Chicago: Follet, 1972), p. 14.

3. For a more complete definition of this complex subject, see D. Cartwright and A. Zander (eds.), *Group Dynamics: Research and Theory,* 3d ed., (New York: Harper & Row, 1968).

4. D. H. Gruenfeld, *Research on Managing Groups and Teams,* (Stamford, CT: JAI Press, 1998); D. L. Gladstein, "Groups in Context: A Model of Group Effectiveness," *Administrative Science Quarterly* 29, no. 4 (1984), pp. 499–517.

5. R. A. Guzzo and M. W. Dickson, "Teams in Organizations: Recent Research on Performance and Effectiveness," *Annual Review of Psychology* 47 (1996), pp. 307–38; R. A. Guzzo and R. J. Campbell, "Group Performance and Intergroup Relations in Organizations," in M. D. Dunnette and L. M. Hough (eds.), *Handbook of Industrial and Organizational Psychology,* vol. 3, (Palo Alto, CA: Consulting Psychologists Press, 1992), pp. 269–313.

6. R. W. Napier and M. K. Gershenfield, *Groups: Theory and Experience,* 4th ed., (Boston, MA: Houghton Mifflin, 1989).

7. G. P. Shea and R. A. Guzzo, "Group Effectiveness: What Really Matters?" *Sloan Management Review,* Spring 1987, pp. 499–517.

8. C. J. G. Gersick, "Time and Transition in Work Teams: Toward a New Model of Group Development," *Academy of Management Journal* 31, no. 1 (1988), pp. 9–41.

9. J. E. McGrath, "View of Group Composition through a Group-Theoretic Lens," in D. H. Gruenfeld (ed.), *Research on Managing Groups and Teams,* vol. 1, (Stamford, CT: JAI Press, 1998), pp. 255–72.

10. Ibid.

11. C. A. O'Reily III, K. Y. Williams, and S. Barade, "Group Demography and Innovation: Does Diversity Help?" in D. H. Gruenfeld (ed.), *Research on Managing Groups and Teams,* vol. 1, (Stamford, CT: JAI Press, 1998), pp. 183–207.

12. J. E. Diskill, R. Hogan, and E. Salas, "Personality and Group Performance," in C. Hendrick (ed.), *Group Processes and Intergroup Relations,* (Newbury Park, CA: Sage, 1987), pp. 91–122; and D. A. Kolb, I. M. Rubin, and J. M. McIntyre, *Organizational Psychology: An Experiential Approach to Organization Behavior,* (Englewood Cliffs, NJ: Prentice-Hall, 1984).

13. J. A. Pearce and E. C. Ravlin, "The Design and Activation of Self-Regulating Work Groups," *Human Relations* 40 (1987), pp. 751–82; S. E. Jackson, J. F. Brett, V. I. Sessa, D. M. Cooper, J. A. Julin, and K. Peyronin, "Some Differences Make a Difference: Individual Dissimilarity and Group Heterogeneity as Correlates of Recruitment, Promotions, and Turnover," *Journal of Applied Psychology* 76 (1991), pp. 675–89.

14. E. Sundstrom, K. P. DeMuse, and D. Futrell, "Work Teams: Applications and Effectiveness," *American Psychologist* 45 (1990), pp. 120–33.

15. T. G. Cummings, "Designing Effective Work Groups," in P. C. Nystrom and W. H. Starbuck (eds.), *Handbook of Organizational Design,* vol. 2, (New York: Oxford University Press, 1981), pp. 250–71.

16. H. Arrow, "Standing Out and Fitting In: Composition Effects on Newcomers' Socialization," in D. H. Gruenfeld (ed.), *Research on Managing Groups and Teams,* vol. 1, (Stamford, CT: JAI Press, 1998), pp. 59–80.

17. W. C. Swap and Associates, *Group Decision Making,* (Beverly Hills, CA: Sage, 1984), pp. 55–58. The extract given here is reprinted by permission of Sage Publications, Inc.

18. Cartwright and Zander, Group Dynamics.

19. Ibid.

20. D. Hellriegel, J. W. Slocum, R. W. Woodman, *Organizational Behavior,* (Cincinnati, OH: South-Western College Publishing, 1998).

21. M. A. Campion, G. J. Medsker, and A. C. Higgs, "Relations between Work Group Characteristics and Effectiveness: Implications for Designing Effective Work Groups," *Personnel Psychology* 46 (1993), pp. 823–47.

22. F. R. David, J. A. Pearce, and W. A. Randolph, "Linking Technology and Structure to Enhance Group Performance," *Journal of Applied Psychology* 74 (1989).

23. J. W. Vander, *Sociology,* (New York: Ronald Press, 1965), pp. 64–65.

24. K. D. Benne and P. Sheats, "Functional Roles of Group Members," *Journal of Social Issues,* Spring 1948, pp. 41–49; L. R. Hoffman, "Applying Experimental Research on Problem Solving in Organizations," *Journal of Applied Behavioral Science* 15 (1979), pp. 375–91.

25. S. Schachter, "Deviation, Rejection, and Communications," *Journal of Abnormal and Social Psychology* 46 (1951), pp. 190–207.

26. J. Eagle and N. Newton, "Scapegoating in Small Groups: An Organizational Perspective," *Human Relations* 34 (1981), pp. 283–301; G. Gemmill and G. Kraus, "Dynamics of Covert Role Analysis," *Small Group Behavior* 19, no. 3 (1988), pp. 299–311.

27. T. Caplow, *Two against One* (Englewood Cliffs, NJ: Prentice-Hall, 1968).

28. R. J. Hackman and R. E. Walton, "Leading Groups in Organizations," in P. S. Goodman (ed.), *Designing Effective Work Groups,* (San Francisco: Jossey-Bass, 1986), pp. 72–119.

29. D. L. Gladstein, "Groups in Context: A Model of Task Group Effectiveness," *Administrative Science Quarterly* 29, no. 4 (1984), pp. 499–517.

30. J. L. Komaki, M. L. Desselles, and E. D. Bowman, "Definitely Not a Breeze: Extending an Operant Model of Effective Supervision to Teams," *Journal of Applied Psychology* 74, no. 3 (1989), pp. 522–29.

31. J. R. Hackman, ed., *Groups That Work (and Those That Don't),* (San Francisco: Jossey-Bass, 1990), pp. 496–97.

32. B. Latané, K. Williams, and S. Harkins, "Many Hands Make Light the Work: The Causes and Consequences of Social Loafing," *Journal of Personality and Social Psychology* 37 (1979), pp. 822–32.

33. R. Albanese and D. D. Van Fleet, "Rational Behavior in Groups: The Free-Riding Tendency," *Academy of Management Review* 10, no. 2 (1985), pp. 244–55.

34. J. M. Beyer and H. M. Trice, "A Reexamination of the Relations between Size and Various Components of Organizational Complexity," *Administrative Science Quarterly* 24 (1979), pp. 48–64.

35. J. F. Verga, "The Frequency of Self-Limiting Behavior in Groups: A Measure and an Explanation," *Human Relations* 44, no. 8 (1991), pp. 877–94.

36. G. R. Jones, "Task Visibility, Free Riding, and Shirking: Explaining the Effect of Structure and Technology on Employee Behavior," *Academy of Management Review* 9, no. 4 (1984), pp. 684–95; K. H. Price, "Decision Responsibility, Task Responsibility, Identifiability, and Social Loafing," *Organizational Behavior and Human Decision Processes* 40 (1987), pp. 330–45.

37. M. E. Shaw, *Group Dynamics: The Psychology of Small Group Behavior,* (New York: McGraw-Hill, 1976), pp. 232–33.

38. P. E. Mudrack, "Group Cohesiveness and Productivity: A Closer Look," *Human Relations* 9 (1989), pp. 771–85.

39. B. Mullen and C. Copper, "The Relation between Group Cohesiveness and Performance: An Integration," *Psychological Bulletin* 115, no. 2 (1994), pp. 210–27.

40. Cartwright and Zander, *Group Dynamics,* p. 104.

41. P. R. Nail, "Toward an Integration of Some Models and Theories of Social Response," *Psychological Bulletin* 100 (1986), pp. 190–206; G. E. Overvold, "The Imperative of Organizational Harmony: A Critique of Contemporary Human Relations Theory," *Journal of Business Ethics* 6 (1987), pp. 559–65.

42. H. J. Leavitt, "Hot Groups," *Harvard Business Review,* July–August 1995, pp. 109–16; H. J. Leavitt, "The Old Days, Hot Groups, and Managers' Lib," *Administrative Science Quarterly* 41, (1996), pp. 288–300.

43. I. L. Janis and L. Mann, *Decision Making: A Psychological Analysis of Conflict,* (New York: Free Press, 1977); C. Posner-Weber, "Update on Groupthink," *Small Group Behavior* 18 (1987), pp. 118–25.

44. I. L. Janis, *Victims of Groupthink,* 2d ed., (Boston: Houghton Mifflin, 1982).

45. R. Jeffrey Smith, "Shuttle Inquiry Focuses on Weather, Rubber Seals, and Unheeded Advice," *Science,* February 28, 1986, p. 909.

46. M. Dolan, "Fletcher Pledges NASA to Make Technical, Management Reform," *Los Angeles Times,* June 10, 1986, part I, p. 10.

47. I. L. Janis, *Groupthink: Psychological Studies of Policy Decisions and Fiascoes,* 2d ed., (Boston: Houghton Mifflin, 1982).

48. G. Moorhead, R. Ference, and C. P. Neck, "Group Decision Fiascoes Continued: Space Shuttle Challenger and a Revised Groupthink Framework," *Human Relations* 44 (1991), pp. 539–50.

49. L. N. Jewell and H. J. Reitz, *Group Effectiveness in Organizations,* (Glenview, IL: Scott, Foresman, 1981), pp. 14–15. (Based on W. Bennis and H. Shepard *A Theory of Group Development,* (San Francisco: Jossey-Bass, 1974).

50. M. McCollom, "Reevaluating Group Development: A Critique of the Familiar Models," in J. Gilette and M. McCollom (eds.), *Groups in Context,* (Reading, MA: Addison-Wesley, 1990), pp. 134–54.

51. H. J. Reitz, *Group Behavior in Organizations,* (Burr Ridge, IL: Richard D. Irwin, 1981).

52. M. R. Barrick, G. L. Stewart, M. J. Neubert, and M. K. Mount, "Relating Member Ability and Personality to Work-Team Processes and Team Effectiveness," *Journal of Allied Psychology* 83, no. 3 (1998), pp. 377–91.

53. R. A. Guzzo and M. W. Dickson, "Teams in Organizations: Recent Research on Performance and Productivity," *Annual Review of Psychology* 47 (1996), pp. 307–38.

Activity 6–2: Performance Appraisal Task Force	*Objectives:* a. To learn the distinction between process and content in analyzing group dynamics. b. To apply theories of group development in analyzing one group's interactions. c. To observe the processes of leadership influence and coalition formation in group interaction.

Task 1 (Homework):

(*Note to instructor:* Assign one of the two questions below to half the class or to half the teams in the class and assign the other question to the other half so that a range of data will be generated for analysis of this case.)

Read the following case study, "The Plafab Company: The Performance Appraisal Task Force," and prepare a written answer to the following:

a. Analyze the case by paying attention to dynamics relevant to group development, like self-oriented versus group-oriented behavior, task avoidance, dependency, counterdependency, overt and covert conflict, and subgroup formation. Diagnose what stage or phase the group is in. Particular emphasis should be placed on providing specific examples from the case to justify your diagnosis.

b. Analyze the case from the perspective of leadership, authority, and influence. Describe how these dynamics are played out over the course of the meeting.

Task 2 (Classroom):

a. Teams are to decide on appropriate answers to the question assigned in task 1. (Time: 20–25 minutes)

b. Team spokespersons are to report their answers to the class. Open class discussion follows. (Time: 25–30 minutes)

Case Study: The Plafab Company:
The Performance Appraisal Task Force

The general manager of division X of a medium-size plastic fabrication firm has created a task force. Its mission is to recommend a system of performance appraisal (PA) for the entire division. The task force has met twice in the past. At the first meeting the members decided that they needed greater clarification of the task and decided that Eric should ask the general manager exactly what they should be doing. At the second meeting Eric reported that the general manager wasn't much clearer and seemed to simply want the group's best thinking. A rambling discussion followed, and the meeting ended with a decision to meet for an hour the day after next.

(Meeting comes to order as Paul initiates.)

PAUL: I came across a really interesting article on performance appraisal in *Organization Dynamics,* and I made copies for all of you. (*He passes them out.*) It's about how they set it up at Rohm & Hauss, and I thought it made a lot of sense.

ERIC: I'm sure this information will be very helpful, Paul, but before we look at any specific system, I think we should define our objectives more clearly. For example, I was thinking, is this PA system going to be mainly used for promotion decisions, such as making sure that good people move up in the organization? Or is it supposed to be used mainly for salary and merit decisions?

**Exhibit 3
Third Meeting**

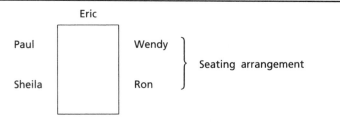

SHEILA: Or how about, Is it supposed to help develop management?

WENDY: It's pretty clear that there are a lot of ways to skin this cat. I've been wondering if we might not be taking on too big a task, especially with our limited knowledge in this area. I guess what I'm saying is that I really think we need to get some outside expertise.

PAUL: Boy, our senior managers are really not on the ball; know what I mean? Just look at this committee. The least they could do is be specific about what they want us to do. Lately they seem to keep blowing it.

ERIC: Oh, I think they do a pretty good job.

WENDY: Personally I find it encouraging that they're thinking of putting in a PA system. I mean it's about time this company started to manage human resources in a systematic way.

PAUL: Well, what about that screwup on the Bently account. Instead of just holding back, working out the bugs, and delaying shipment for a week, they ordered Rodgers to ship a box full of scrap again and the account went down the drain. One thing you have to say about Rohm & Hauss, whatever they ship is 100 percent!

Source: This case study was contributed by Gervase R. Bushe. Special permission for the reproduction of this exercise and case study is granted by the author, Professor Gervase R. Bushe. All rights reserved, and no reproduction should be made without express approval of Professor Gervase R. Bushe, Faculty of Business Administration, Simon Fraser University, Burnaby, British Columbia, Canada V5A, 1S6. We are grateful to Professor Bushe.

SHEILA: Did you hear about what happened with that task force on consolidation? They made a report to the brass last Monday after working their tails off for two months and Dan swears two of them were asleep for most of the presentation. I mean literally asleep.

ERIC: Well, look; we've got a job to do, and I think we should just get down to doing it.

WENDY: There's obviously a lot of ways to look at PA and probably a lot we won't think of, so let's face it—we need some expertise. As it turns out, I have the name of a consulting firm that comes well recommended.

SHEILA: But will the company give us the money to hire a consultant?

WENDY: Good question. Eric should go ask.

PAUL: Hold on a second. Who are these consultants?

WENDY: They're personnel specialists with, apparently, a wide range of expertise. I know they've done work for Celanese and Duo-Plastic and they . . .

PAUL: Celanese!?! They're losing money hand over fist. And they're doing that dumb "quality is free" hype. I don't think I want one of their consultants.

WENDY: Well, we could look into other personnel specialists.

PAUL: Frankly, I don't like asking the company to spend money that way. Obviously management asked us to be a task force because someone thinks we have what it takes, and I'd sure like a shot at it first. I've been reading up on PA, and it seems pretty clear that to make something like this work, it has to be every manager's responsibility.

RON: Maybe we should start by listing all the things we think a PA system could do.

ERIC: Good idea, Ron, but first I just want to know whether the group wants me to ask the general manager about a consultant.

PAUL: I thought we decided to try without one for awhile.

SHEILA: I don't know that anybody decided anything, but I do think it's a good idea to get some additional information and just educate ourselves. But there are lots of ways we could do that.

PAUL: I could distribute other stuff I've read.

ERIC: Great, I'd like to see that.

SHEILA: Me too.

PAUL: Good, I'll have my girl get the stuff out to you.

WENDY: Oh, Paul, I can't believe you still say "my girl." (*general laughter*)

SHEILA: You know, what really bugs me is that the secretaries call themselves *girls.*

PAUL: Well, what does it really matter? Words are just words. You can call me a *boy.* I don't care.

ERIC: You might not say that if you were black. (*general laughter*)

ERIC: Well, this is all good fun, but I think we need to be pushing forward. It seems to me we have to define our objectives here more clearly before we can move ahead.

WENDY: I think it's pretty obvious that the key here is to develop a system that allows us to monitor and rationalize our human resources within the framework of the organization's strategic plan.

SHEILA: But shouldn't it also provide information about the state of human resources that can be fed into strategic planning?

WENDY: Exactly what I mean.

PAUL: Well, I'm not sure what you mean.

SHEILA: All she's saying, Paul, is that the PA system should help management make decisions taking into consideration the manpower implications of them.

WENDY: Well, that's not exactly what I meant.

PAUL: Personally, I want a PA system that's going to give me a clear idea of just what I'm being evaluated on, and I think that's what most people want. They want to know what their boss thinks they should be doing and how well he thinks they're doing.

SHEILA: So you want to see it used mainly as a feedback mechanism.

PAUL: Well, what's wrong with that?

SHEILA: I wasn't saying there's anything wrong with that.

RON: Maybe we should keep a list of all these ideas.

SHEILA: OK. We've got two so far.

ERIC: I think the main point of a good PA system is to make sure that everyone gets treated as fairly as possible, especially when it comes to promotions.

WENDY: Oh yes, I think that's critical.

PAUL: Don't forget the motivational aspects.

WENDY: Which motivational aspects are you referring to?

PAUL: Well, the idea that if people know what the boss expects and get feedback on it, it'll motivate them. The article I'm going to send you talks about tying a PA system into an overall MBO program that really helped increase employee motivation at Terex.

ERIC: What's MBO?

WENDY: MBO—Management by Objectives—and I've heard that that MBO stuff just doesn't work.

PAUL: Why do you say that?

WENDY: Well, they tried at National Semi. I have a friend who works there, and it created such a mess that the company just disbanded it after 10 months.

PAUL: But the article said it worked wonders at Terex. And at other places.

WENDY: You know, Paul, you can't believe everything you read. I'll bet it was written by some consultant trying to generate business. Like do you see all those stories on quality circles these days? But I heard that they're really all falling apart because we're not like Japan.

SHEILA: Yeah, it really bugs me all the stuff we keep hearing about Japan—Japan this, Japan that. If we had their labor rates and government support, we'd be doing just as well if not better.

WENDY: I think that it's true to some extent, but it's also true that they just have a different culture, so different things will work there.

ERIC: I'll say it's different. We spent part of our last vacation in Tokyo, and I couldn't believe how so many people can live in so little space. It'd drive me crazy in short order.

PAUL: Well, I don't know what all this has to do with performance appraisal.

ERIC: Quite right, Paul. We should get back on track. Now . . . what were we doing?

SHEILA: Ron was keeping a list of our ideas.

RON: No, I only suggested we should keep a list.

ERIC: Maybe you ought to be keeping that list for us, Ron.

RON: Frankly, there's so much digression going on here that it's hard for me to stay tuned in.

PAUL: You're not kidding. This meeting seems more like a sewing bee than a business meeting.

WENDY: Well, I wouldn't know, since I've never been to a sewing bee. Have you, Paul?

SHEILA (*laughing*): You know, even when I was a kid, I knew I didn't want to sew and stuff.

PAUL: Look, we're really getting nowhere. Eric, will you please take charge of this meeting and get us moving in some direction.

ERIC: I thought we *were* making some progress on defining objectives.

PAUL: You know, it really pisses me off that senior management hasn't already defined the objectives. If they treated quarterly profit targets the same way, nothing would get done around here. I wonder what would happen if we just told them it's impossible to do this job if they don't take a clear stand.

SHEILA: A stand on what?

PAUL: Well, for example, is the PA system going to be a personnel program or a line-management function?

RON: You think it should be a line function, don't you?

PAUL: Damn right. Don't you agree, Eric?

WENDY: Management has to be involved, but I think it's clear that we would also need personnel specialists to administer and run it and make sure it's working properly. For example, we'd probably need to train managers in how to give constructive feedback, use the system, and all those kinds of things.

PAUL: Oh, just what we need, more training.

SHEILA: But, Paul, whatever system is used, we'll need to teach people how to use it, won't we?

PAUL: I don't want to do any teaching.

SHEILA: I didn't mean that we—this task force—would actually do the teaching. I meant the company will have to teach people.

PAUL: Well, I don't see what's so difficult. You just tell managers to write down their subordinates' objectives, rate them, and then tell them their ratings. What's so tough about that?

WENDY: But can you trust that managers really will give people honest feedback?

PAUL: That's the problem these days—no respect for authority. When guys like Eric and me joined this company, people respected their boss.

WENDY: You haven't said a word yet, Ron. What do you think?

RON: I guess people are a lot less willing to respect someone just because of his or her position than they used to be.

WENDY: No, I mean what do you think the objectives of a PA system should be?

RON: Well, I agree with a lot that's been said. You know, I don't really know.

WENDY: Maybe it'd help us reach some consensus if we talked about what we'd personally want the outcomes of a PA system to be.

SHEILA: OK. I think I'd like to know how I stand compared to other managers in my department.

ERIC: You mean people would know each other's ratings?

SHEILA: Sure, why not?

PAUL (*muttering*): I don't believe it.

ERIC: Hold on a second; I don't know if that's such a good idea. I mean, well, it could be very bad for morale, you know, it . . .

WENDY: Are you advocating management by secrecy?

ERIC: No, of course not. It's just that it could create some very sensitive situations and, anyway, wouldn't it make managers more likely not to give honest feedback? I mean, that's what you're concerned about, isn't it?

WENDY: Maybe it would force them to be more careful and precise in their appraisals.

PAUL: As far as I'm concerned, my rating should be between my boss and me.

SHEILA: But don't you want to know how you're doing in relation to everyone else?

PAUL: I do know. I just have to look at the quarterly reports.

SHEILA: OK, but not everybody's work is directly reflected in profit reports.

RON: I don't think any one person's work is reflected in profit reports.

WENDY: I agree. In fact, if you extend that idea, maybe we should be appraising team performance instead of individual performance.

ERIC: Well, that's a novel idea. And speaking of novel ideas, I could sure use a break to get rid of some of this coffee I've been drinking.

SHEILA: Great—I could use a smoke.

(*Meeting breaks up for 10 minutes.*)

7

Work Team Effectiveness: Team Building

Learning Objectives

After completing this module, you should be able to

1. Explain the relationship between team building and team effectiveness.
2. Describe the potential problems that work teams face.
3. Diagnose the potential problems that your classroom team faces.
4. Describe the phases in team-building intervention.
5. State the variations of team-building activities.
6. Appreciate the roles that team members and team leaders play in improving team effectiveness.

Module Outline

Premodule Preparation
    Activity 7–1: Team Development

Introduction
    Why Team Building?
    Team Building at Team Start-Up

Problems of Work Teams
    Action Orientation
    Use of Time
    Team Style
    Work Habits and Skills
    One-to-One Relationships with the Boss
    Hidden Agendas

Variations of Team-Building Efforts

Goals of Team Building
    Changing the System versus Changing the People
    Planning and Conducting a Team-Building Workshop
    Interview with the Manager

Premodule Preparation

**Activity 7–1
Team Development**

Objectives:

a. To critique the effectiveness of your team in regard to (1) achievement of results in task assignments and (2) achievement of relationships among members that integrate their human resources (abilities, knowledge, views, and so on) into task solutions.

b. To suggest team goals for improved effectiveness.

Task 1:

Individuals working alone are to complete the questionnaire on team development scales on pages 163–165.

Task 2:

Teams meet to discuss the scale items on the questionnaire one at a time. Each member will report the rating he or she made prior to the meeting. The differences in ratings will be discussed to determine why members are perceiving the team's interactions differently. A group consensus rating will be made for each scale after thorough discussion. (*Note:* Avoid majority voting. Instead, seek real understanding to attain agreement.)

Task 3:

Study the comments on team goals at the end of the questionnaire. Teams are then to go back over the consensus ratings for the 15 items completed in task 2. These ratings represent the characteristics of the team at present. Now write a *G* on each scale representing a goal the team would like to attain in its interactions by the end of the course.

Name _____ Date _____

Questionnaire on Team Development Scales

Climate Scales

1. The degree to which my team shows enthusiasm and spirit:

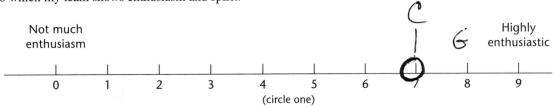

```
Not much                                                    Highly
enthusiasm                                                  enthusiastic

    |     |     |     |     |     |     |     |     |     |
    0     1     2     3     4     5     6     7     8     9
                                (circle one)
```

2. On humor I would rate the team

```
    Not much              Not bad              Funny      Outrageous

    |     |     |     |     |     |     |     |     |
    0     1     2     3     4     5     6     7     8     9
```

3. My team is

_____ Mostly task oriented.

_____ More task oriented than social.

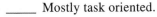 _____ Equally task and social in orientation.

_____ More social than task oriented.

_____ Mostly social.

People Scales (How We Regard One Another as Human Beings)

4. The degree to which we are interested in one another as people is

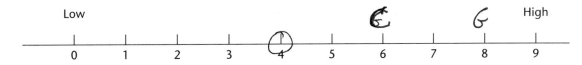

```
    Low                                                    High

    |     |     |     |     |     |     |     |     |     |
    0     1     2     3     4     5     6     7     8     9
```

5. Our regard for each individual as a resource (knowledge, skills, abilities, viewpoints) for group goal achievement is

```
    Low                                                    High

    |     |     |     |     |     |     |     |     |     |
    0     1     2     3     4     5     6     7     8     9
```

Productivity Scales (Goals, Work Accomplishment, Commitment)

6. Team's task achievement goals:

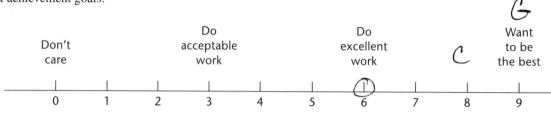

	Don't care		Do acceptable work		Do excellent work		Want to be the best

0   1   2   3   4   5   6   7   8   9

7. Actual quantity of work produced:

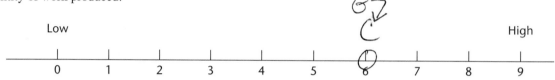

Low   High

0   1   2   3   4   5   6   7   8   9

8. Quality of work produced:

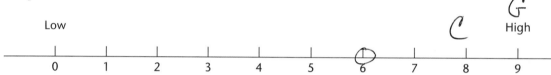

Low   High

0   1   2   3   4   5   6   7   8   9

9. Interest in learning:

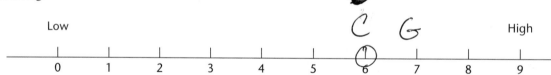

Low   High

0   1   2   3   4   5   6   7   8   9

Process Scales (Participation and Communications)

10. Participation (check one):

_____ One to two members contribute the most.

___✓___ Two to three members contribute regularly.

___C___ Three to four members contribute regularly.

_____ Four to five members contribute regularly.

___G___ All members contribute regularly.

11. An input from all members is sought before decisions are made:

_____ never   ___✓___ sometimes   ___C___ often   ___G___ always

12. Where the team falls on the "handling conflict" scale:

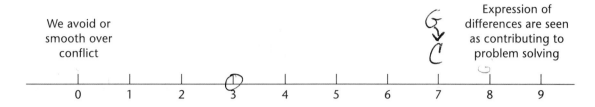

We avoid or smooth over conflict — Expression of differences are seen as contributing to problem solving

| | | | | | | | | | |
|0|1|2|3|4|5|6|7|8|9|

13. Openness in communications:

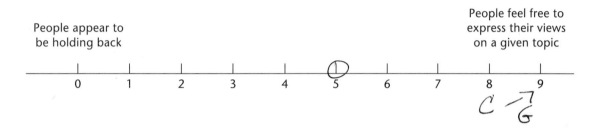

People appear to be holding back — People feel free to express their views on a given topic

| | | | | | | | | | |
|0|1|2|3|4|5|6|7|8|9|

14. Expression of personal feelings:

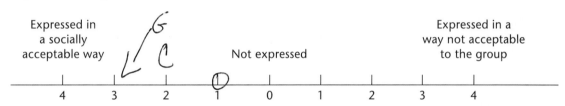

Expressed in a socially acceptable way — Not expressed — Expressed in a way not acceptable to the group

| | | | | | | | | |
|4|3|2|1|0|1|2|3|4|

15. Degree to which we listen and actually hear each other's views:

Low — High

| | | | | | | | | | |
|0|1|2|3|4|5|6|7|8|9|

Comments: Make notes of anything additional you would like to feed back to the team about how members work together or about how effectiveness could be improved.

Team Goals

The scales of this questionnaire pertain to attitudes, processes, and skills that can make a team more or less effective under the conditions in which we work in this course. They thereby suggest goals for improvement of team effectiveness. (*Note:* It should not be assumed that these attributes apply to the effectiveness of all teams under all conditions. Whether the specific goals suggested are appropriate depends on the specific conditions of the situation.)

Scale attributes should be regarded as interacting with and reinforcing one another. The following examples illustrate this point and suggest some of the consequences.

Productivity

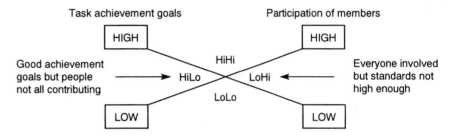

Quality of involvement

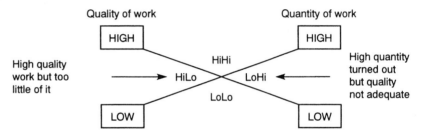

Regard for people

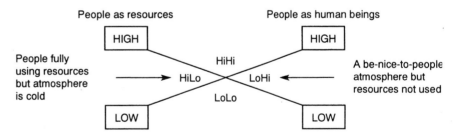

Introduction

Teams and teamwork are currently being championed as a way of replacing inflexible, dehumanized, bureaucratic mechanisms with more humanistic, involving, cultural-ideological methods of productive activity.[1] A recent study identified four types of teams in organizations:

1. **Work teams,** or continuing work units responsible for producing goods or providing services.
2. **Parallel teams,** or people who are pulled together from different work units or jobs to perform functions that the regular organization is not equipped to perform well.
3. **Project teams,** or time-limited teams that have to produce one-time output such as a new product or service to be marketed by the company.
4. **Management teams,** or supervisory teams that are created to provide coordination and direction to the subunits under their jurisdiction, laterally integrating interdependent subunits across key business process.[2]

In Module 5 we identified a variety of teams—such as virtual teams, cross-functional teams, and new-product development teams—that might be charged with any of the tasks listed above. For example, a parallel team, a project team, or a management team can be a virtual team. Although each type of team deals with a different task, regardless of the team type, teams form a critical link between the individual and the organization. They function to accomplish tasks that cannot be performed by one individual or to fulfill individual needs not met by the formal organization. As teams such as top-management teams, product development teams, quality circles, task forces, and project teams become more and more a part of the way organizations operate, understanding the effectiveness and impact of teams becomes increasingly important. Modules 5 and 6 focused on small group behavior and dynamics. This module examines **team effectiveness** from an integrative growth perspective. As we will see, personal growth focuses on the development of interpersonal skills that help an individual be more effective in any situation.

It also stresses the need for personal goal setting to help the individual achieve greater fulfillment. This module focuses on the development of work teams and the ongoing challenge of improving their effectiveness. We start with a look at the evolution of teams via Activity 7–1. An examination of the problems of work teams that call for team-building effort is followed by a review of team-building goals and phases. Finally, we examine the effectiveness of team building within the international context.

Why Team Building?

If you were assigned one of the activities that began Module 5, you should have seen that some teams are more effective than others in solving problems or making decisions. Effective problem solving and effective team operation do not necessarily occur naturally. They have to be worked at. Module 5 suggested a number of ways in which both team members and team leaders can improve team effectiveness. In Module 6 we examined group dynamics and saw that the dynamics of a team are very complex and that at times dysfunctional behavior can occur. The ultimate goal of these modules and the team activities that accompany them is to improve your capacity to work effectively as a team member—initially in your classroom team but ultimately in the organizations in which you will spend your career.

The discussion in those modules focused on improving team performance. Indeed, a continuous improvement focus to team activity should be part of every team's (and team leader's) effort.[3] However, insofar as effective team operation is not necessarily natural and insofar as problems with team operation can indeed develop, **team building,** which can be defined as a process for helping a team to diagnose its problems and become a more effective working unit,[4] is an activity that managers and managers-to-be need to be aware of and understand. This module is designed to further identify problems that work teams can experience and to describe techniques for helping groups solve those problems. The emphasis of team building is the team, and team building is a *collaborative* process.

The use of team building in organizations is not as new as the use of teams. Many team-building methods and techniques were developed in the aerospace industry. That industry was an early user of product development teams, which are limited-duration teams set up for the life of a project. Users of these teams found that assembling groups of individuals from different functional areas and with different disciplines did not automatically create effectively functioning teams. Thus time spent during the group's formation on goal setting and team membership skills was useful in facilitating the team's operation. When teams developed operating problems, time spent on identifying those problems and developing solutions for them improved team performance.

Team Building at Team Start-Up

While team-building efforts aimed at solving teamwork problems are probably more common than efforts aimed at preparing a team to work effectively within itself, such efforts are becoming more frequent, as organizations come to realize that it is often easier to prevent problems from occurring than it is to fix the problems after they have occurred. Thus time is often set aside as a team is formed to help it understand and effectively work through the early stages of group development.

In this type of effort, the likes of Activity 5–1 ("Mountain Survival Exercise") are often used. Such exercises give teams the opportunity to experience and test their problem-solving ability and to understand what types of behavior are necessary to have an effective team. Another type of activity is the Outward Bound Leadership School (and others) in which the team experiences various outdoor activities that require members to work together and learn to trust each other to pass physical tests or accomplish objectives such as crossing a river or climbing a steep mountain. Such activities are analogous to a football team, which engages in play study, practice, and drills and plays intrasquad or preseason games before the regular season starts.

To continue the analogy, such teams continue to practice and work on problems that develop during the season. The same is true in organizations, where even with good preparation, problems may develop with team operation, and team building efforts can be made to solve those problems. Those efforts can be similar to those discussed above. To understand the types of initial team-building efforts that might be useful and the activities that might be used after a team has begun operating, we will examine some problems that work teams can develop.

Problems of Work Teams

Teams typically encounter certain recurring problems if the interaction patterns of the members have not been specifically shaped to avoid them. The problems have been widely described in the management literature, and we have observed that they frequently characterize the behavior of participants of this course, particularly those who undertake the outside team project. Let's discuss some major problems.

Action Orientation

The need to get things under way in organizations and to keep the momentum going frequently results in insufficient time for planning. In executive team-building sessions, this lack becomes evident when the team starts to discuss its goals and objectives. Prior to the meeting, members might have believed they were in accord, but when each person is asked to make a separate list of goals and rank them in order of priority, considerable discrepancies appear. Here it's evident that insufficient time has been allotted to the development of shared goals, and lack of coordination of efforts and problems of overlapping role responsibilities are brought to the surface. In other situations team members are aware of differing views of their goals, but have not faced the conflict.

Some teams that have used the Mountain Survival Exercise at the beginning of Module 5 have experienced some of the problems attached to an **action orientation.** In that exercise some teams immediately start figuring out how to get out of the place they are in, without considering that attempting to leave is an alternative—in fact a better one than attempting to walk out. Similarly, participants who make the outside survey in the self-directed team task exercise described as Plan A often recognize that they have not carefully defined the problem of their survey and have devoted insufficient time to planning. As a result, their survey data is difficult to interpret. The pressures to go right to constructing the questionnaire are so great that team members plan superficially. These faults are true to a lesser degree of executives in workshops; they often do not spend enough time defining the problem of a case study they are assigned and must go back and start over after they are well underway.

An interesting study that illustrates the dominance of task orientation over other considerations is summarized below:

The parable of the Good Samaritan was put to the test recently by two Princeton University psychologists studying bystander behavior in emergencies.

In the experiment . . . 40 unwitting theological students on their way across campus encountered a groaning, coughing "victim" slumped in a doorway.

Sixty percent of the subjects kept right on walking.

Prior to encountering the "victim," subjects in the experiment were asked to prepare a 3- to 5-minute impromptu talk on a specific topic—some on vocations and others on the parable of the Good Samaritan.

Equipped with a map and instructions to go to another laboratory to tape the speech, subjects were told they were either already late for the session (high-hurry condition), that they were expected momentarily (immediate-hurry condition), or that they could take their time (low-hurry condition).

The hurry condition of the subject proved significant as to whether he would stop to help the victim. Of the 16 students (40 percent) who did stop:

Fifty-three percent were low-hurry subjects.

Forty percent were intermediate-hurry subjects.

Seven percent were high-hurry subjects.

A person in a hurry is likely to keep going. Ironically, the individual is likely to keep going even if he or she is hurrying to speak on the parable of the Good Samaritan.[5]

Action orientation frequently leads to inadequate definition of the objectives and problems of the team, poor planning, and lack of consideration for human factors.

Use of Time

Closely associated with action orientation is how the team uses time. Many work groups are concerned about wasting time in meetings. Since planning often involves ambiguity and abstract thinking, there is pressure to get it over with and to get on to something more concrete. Planning requires blocks of time to permit the generation of ideas and allow synergy to take place. Teams must develop the expectation that a 4-hour period, a day, or a weekend might be needed.

The effects of poor distribution of time are perhaps most evident in university life, where the practice is to schedule faculty or committee meetings for 1 hour once a week because teaching schedules and room availability makes it most difficult to arrange longer blocks of time. Meetings in the evening and on weekends are against faculty norms. So each committee meeting, scheduled for an hour, makes little progress because of the long start-up time, which requires recapitulation of what was covered the week before, trying to pick up the continuity of the planning, and carrying it further.

Team Style

Work groups develop a style of operation. (The models presented in Module 6 apply here.) **Team styles** embrace the expectations team members have about meetings. Autocratic-style meetings tend to be avoided except when they are needed to get information out and get reports back; corporate-style meetings are likely to be highly procedural and committee-like and are held for more purposes than are really necessary; permissive-style meetings are apt to be frequent and held just for the conversation; retired-on-the job meetings may never take place; and professional–manager meetings would be of the team-action type discussed in this module. The patterns of member expectations that accompany each of these styles become so frozen in the minds of team members that they cannot be changed without considerable effort, frequently only with the assistance of outside expertise.

Work Habits and Skills

Many organizations are unaware that work groups can develop skills almost like individuals can. Making the improvement of group work habits and skills a goal and providing the time for this purpose is rarely considered.

Only in sports and the military services is training for effective interaction patterns accepted as a necessity. The ideal that time should be devoted to this purpose has come late to business and government organizations.

One-to-One Relationships with the Boss

The rivalries among team members that arise from one-to-one relationships in the managerial hierarchy are extremely difficult to avoid. An effective manager must meet with the team members one at a time for some purposes and with the entire team for others. (This situation was illustrated in the Vroom–Yetton–Jago decision-making model discussed in Module 5.) Determining how to foster maximum trust and keep rivalries low is a continuing challenge. Edgar H. Schein notes:

> The successful manager must be a good diagnostician and must value a spirit of inquiry. If the abilities and motives of the people under him are so variable, he must have the sensitivity and diagnostic ability to be able to sense and appreciate the differences. Second, rather than regard the existence of differences as a painful truth to be wished away, he must also learn to value differences and to value the diagnostic process which reveals differences. Finally, he must have the personal flexibility and the range of skills necessary to vary his own behavior. If the needs and motives of his subordinates are different, they must be treated differently.[6]

Although this view may sound reasonable, it is extremely difficult to practice. The fact that people are complex and need to be treated differently can run contrary to the ideal of fair treatment as perceived by employees. For example, in a team-building session involving an executive and the middle-level managers reporting to her, one manager said that he would like to discuss how money available for management development and training was to be allotted in the coming year. He stated that he had not felt right during the past year when he received $2,400 to attend a 1-week workshop but learned that $5,000 had been spent for another team member. The boss then asked, "But John, didn't you get just what you asked for?" John replied, "Yes, I did, and I was very satisfied with what I gained from the workshop." The boss went on to say that the other employee had also gotten what he had asked for, and that his main concerns had been both satisfying the team members' requests and making sure that the training of each also met organizational needs; following this flexible policy meant that assigning a fixed sum to each individual would not be meaningful.

When the team discussed this situation, it was obvious that all members were concerned about receiving their fair share of the training funds, but they concluded that they would like to have the present policy continued. John said that he felt better about it now that it had been discussed. The boss stated that it had not occurred to her that this flexible policy would be questioned as long as it met the needs of the team members; she then asked whether she was doing other things that were being experienced as perhaps not completely fair; other practices were discussed. If this dialogue had not taken place, the executive might not have become aware that her flexible practices of treating people according to their needs had to take into consideration how team members perceived her actions from the point of fairness. Given that this occurred during a team-building session, we can begin to see how such sessions allow feelings and issues to be addressed—feelings and issues that, if not dealt with effectively, might affect the relationships between team members, with a corresponding impact on the team's operation.

Hidden Agendas

Rivalries; distrust; ambitions; concern about looking bad, foolish, or unknowledge-able; and other factors can cause individuals to avoid saying openly how they feel or what they want. The interactions and communications of individuals in meetings are apt to be complicated by these **hidden agendas.**

Variations of Team-Building Efforts

Organizations, managers, and teams face many issues, and these change continuously. Team-building efforts with different emphases or purposes have emerged over the past several decades. Team-building efforts can be classified into four general types:[7]

1. *Interpersonal processes.* This effort assumes that teams operate best with mutual trust, open communication, and an attempt to build team cohesion. The intervention involves a candid discussion of conflicts and relationships between team members. The purposes are to resolve interpersonal conflict and to create open communication between individuals who work on the same team.[8]

2. *Role definition.* This effort assumes that some major sources of problems within a team are role conflict and role ambiguity. The intervention focuses on clarifying individual role expectations and group norms and the developing shared understanding of the roles and responsibilities that each individual carries in the effort.[9]

3. *Goal setting.* This approach assumes that individual performance in a team setting is influenced to a large extent by the specificity and shared understanding of goals and objectives. The intervention involves clarifying the team's general objectives and goals, defining specific tasks and subgoals to be accomplished within a specific timetable, measuring performance, and using feedback loops.[10]

4. *Problem solving.* This approach is the most often used intervention. Such an activity is generated when someone identifies a problem within the team. What follows is a complete team problem-solving cycle of gathering data, analyzing data, finding causes, understanding solutions, choosing a solution, planning an action, and implementing and evaluating the action.[11]

Team building can be directed at two different types of groups: **family groups** (which are intact, ongoing work teams) and **special groups** (groups that may have a limited life span, such as start-up teams, special project teams, and task forces).

Goals of Team Building

The four types of team-building efforts just listed are likely to be found in any team-building effort. However, "unless one purpose is defined as the primary purpose, there tends to be considerable misuse of energy."[12] If interpersonal problems are great, that may be the central focus. If planning, objectives, and role definition are a major area of confusion, more time will be spent on these. But the major overall purpose of team building is the application of behavioral science knowledge and technology to improve the team's effectiveness. Here are some specific and generic team-building activities:

- Achieving consensus on objectives and goals of the team. This activity may include adding, dropping, or redefining goals.
- Identifying problems preventing the achievement of these goals.
- Developing team-planning, goal-setting, problem-solving, and decision-making skills and improving the work habits of the team, such as the use of time.
- Diagnosing the present team style and determining its preferred operating style. This activity means looking at the system of norms and values that determine the team's manner of interacting and changing it. Moving toward the professional

manager style requires learning and practicing the communication skills of leveling, saying where one is at, listening and paraphrasing, perceptual checking, and so on.

■ Utilizing fully the individual resources of team members. Some members have strengths, expertise, and ideas they do not think are integrated into the group's activities. They may have concerns that should be worked through.

■ Developing action agendas, assigning responsibilities, and setting specific dates for follow-up of the activities identified as important during the session.

Obviously, these activities are too extensive to be covered in a 2- or 3-day work retreat; they can only be regarded as new behavior patterns that are launched in the session and must be practiced and worked into the behavioral system of the team and its members. The permissive-style pitfall of "groupiness" for its own sake must be avoided, and the professional manager's emphasis on goals, results, and high standards through integrated team action has to be understood.

Changing the System versus Changing the People

Changing the norms and interaction patterns within a team, between teams, or within an organization is a primary goal in applying behavioral science methods to organizational life. If a team has norms such as distrust or hidden agendas, it is easy to assume that its members cannot work together—that is, the individuals are at fault. Changing such a team to one that has norms of openness, leveling, and so on may be difficult—the situation has to be right for change, but it can be done. The behavioral scientist has to recognize that there are no bad people, just inappropriate system of norms, values, and interaction patterns. This great oversimplification indicates working assumptions that set the direction of efforts in team building or in organization development programs. This approach does *not* mean that individuals on teams are *never* replaced. It simply is a statement of the assumptions that are in place as team-building efforts are begun.

Planning and Conducting a Team-Building Workshop

Many variations of the generalized model for a team-building workshop are presented here. The specific form will depend on the team members involved and their problems as well as on the consultant's professional orientation. Generally, the format includes four steps: interview with the manager, dialogue with the team, interview with team members, and presentation of the problem data at the workshop.

Interview with the Manager

First, the consultant meets with the manager to discuss the situations that have led the manager to decide to have a team-building workshop. The consultant informs the manager of the general goals of such a workshop and determines how the manager feels about the team examining its own behavior, particularly the manager's willingness to get feedback from the team members on how they feel about his or her style of management and practices. If the manager is not receptive to these ideas, the team-building experience may not have much potential.

Dialogue with the Team

The consultant and the manager meet with all those who are to attend the session, and the consultant describes the goals, agenda, and procedures of the workshop and the agreement with the team manager. An atmosphere of openness and trust must be created at this time, and a commitment of involvement should be obtained from the group.

Interview with Team Members

The consultant interviews each team member privately, assuring each of confidentiality but indicating that problems identified by more than one member will be listed openly for discussion at the workshop. The questions addressed in the interview are designed to diagnose the problems of the team.

Presentation of the Problem Data at the Workshop

The workshop should be held at a site away from the workplace and probably should last 2 or more days, depending on the problems and the number of people involved. Early in the session the consultant provides a feedback summary of problems that have been presented. This is generally put on large flip-chart sheets that are hung on the walls so that all can see and discuss them. From this point on, the consultant designs the progression of the workshop to best suit the needs of the team. For instance, in one workshop of 16 people made up of a division chief, three branch chiefs, and 12 section chiefs, the section chiefs requested that the division and branch chiefs sit in a center circle and openly discuss among themselves how they felt about all the problems they saw on the charts. The section chiefs would listen. After that the section chiefs would discuss the problems among themselves, with the other chiefs listening. A dialogue would follow. The design for the workshop was developed out of this spontaneous beginning.

At some time during the workshop, all six goals of team building may be worked on to some degree, but the design has to be flexible and spontaneous, and the topics are best addressed when the appropriate time arises. The consultant has a variety of techniques to move the team in the direction of the goals. These include using models of leadership styles, case studies, training films, and involvement exercises such as those used in this book. It is helpful for the consultant to have T-group training and experience to assist team members in coping with their feelings and conflicts. The consultant's interviews will have provided considerable data on how the participants feel about each other. Although the consultant is not able to reveal these feelings to the group directly, because of the pledge of confidentiality, if the workshop is successful, the feelings will be brought out by the participants themselves as they become more open. The consultant must be able to be supportive of the members if they need support at that time. Although this set of steps can be found in most team-building programs, practitioners emphasize different phases; Dyer presents a 33-item checklist for identifying whether a team-development program is needed and whether the organization is ready to begin such a program.[13] Burke argues that it is important to use Beckhard's four-purpose list of goal clarification, roles and responsibilities, procedures and processes, and interpersonal processes in the order in which they are listed.[14] Others focus on the interrelationship between process and content of team-building interventions.[15]

Team Building, Diverse Teams, and the Future

The nature of the task and team design (that is, if the team is a self-managed team or if the team is a cross-functional team, or virtual-team) creates an added complexity to the team-building effort. While the basic tenants of the team-building activities are most likely to be followed, some of the team-building process will require a situational adjustment. Gareth Morgan argues that in many organizations teamwork has become trapped by formal team building because, in more ways than one, it has become just a game.[16] Morgan advocates the use of a highly visual method of **imaginization** to explore organizational problems and to find ways for building team cultures in different settings. One of the approaches is for individuals to create whatever images come to mind of their *current team situation*. They are free to capture and express their views through images, feelings, word, drawings, colors, or whatever medium seems appropriate. Next individuals get into small subgroups of up to five members and share whatever they have produced. The subgroup is then required to create a composite image in the form of a picture or a drawing that can be presented to the entire team. As each subgroup presents its composite image, an opportunity is created for everyone to ask for further descriptions and clarifications—without judgments. This activity helps put on the table whatever everyone thinks of the current team situation. Upon the completion of the task, the whole process is repeated with an eye on the future—what members would like the future state of affairs to be in their teams. Once the sharing and probing is completed, team members explore the similarities and differences between the current state and the future. Specific actions steps and a road map are developed to help the team move in the direction of the desired future state. Morgan argues that this approach provides a means of breaking the usual patterns and routines of discourse and of helping new insights, new dialogue, and new action opportunities to emerge.

Recently, toward the end of the module on team building, one of our students asked, "Can one conduct a virtual-team-building workshop with a virtual team?" This intriguing question would not have been asked when the first edition of this book was written 25 years ago. Massive literature research into the topic yields very little results. What became clear is that as this revision is written the empirical research on this issue is at its infancy. Technically, many of the team issues that a virtual team deals with can be addressed without being in the same room at the same time (for example, clarification of some basic expectations about the nature of the task, role clarifications, goal setting, and productivity goals). Yet the question that remains scientifically unanswered has to do with the notion that technology can replace the human interaction and human development that occur in face-to-face team-building activities (for example, a real-time, video-based, team-building session in which people are connected via technology while being at different places at the same time). Even if we examine the recent studies that look at the effectiveness of virtual teams using groupware software, the results are inconclusive. Furthermore, very few studies have begun to investigate the possible relationships between the utilization and effectiveness of groupware technology, and its effects on team performance and team dynamics are inconclusive.[17]

How Effective Are Team-Building Activities?

The results of team-building activities can be classified into three main areas: (1) results specific to individuals, (2) results specific to the team's dynamics and operations, and (3) results that have an impact on the team's relationships with other teams, departments, and so forth. Although most reported results are descriptive in nature, a few empirical studies shed some light on the effectiveness of team-building efforts. In a study conducted with hourly employees in an underground metal mine, team building was found to have a positive effect on the quality of the teams' performance.[18] In a field experiment with command teams of seven combat companies that underwent team-building workshops, researcher D. Eden was able to show that the experimental companies (in comparison to the control companies) significantly improved in teamwork, conflict handling, and communications.[19] Another study with 18 logistics units that went through a team-building workshop demonstrated that team building failed to improve organizational functioning, although subjective reports of the personnel who participated in the workshops were very positive.[20]

An empirical investigation that attempted to compare the effects of team building and goal setting on productivity of hard-rock miners in an underground metal mine resulted in inconclusive results.[21] This study joins an overall inconclusive body of empirical research on the effectiveness of team building. Although positive results were found in 29 of the 36 studies reviewed in one study[22] as well as in 19 of the 30 studies reviewed in another study,[23] both authors concluded that they could make no firm statements regarding the effectiveness of team building with respect to individual and team performance. The challenge as identified by the researchers is in the development of an appropriate research methodology and measures.

An experiment conducted with MBA students who were randomly assigned to four-member teams (half of which received team-building training) and were engaged in complex and interactive decision-making tasks revealed the following results: teams that received team-building training were initially more cohesive and obtained superior economic performance during the early stage of the simulation. As time progressed, teams that did not receive the training became more cohesive and improved their economic performance, but not up to the same level as the teams that received the training.[24] A unique investigation into the performance of 32 teams' teamwork revealed that all except one team had improved attitudes, effectiveness, and performance.[25] Finally, a study that focused on team members' exchange quality in a unionized plant revealed that employees managed under a team-oriented system (following team-building activities) reported higher team member exchange quality than did those managed under a more traditional system.[26]

Summary

The team-building movement has been growing as managers attempt to cope with the explosive changes in technology and the business environment. Types of problems that reduce team effectiveness include too much action orientation at the expense of planning; poor use of and failure to provide adequate time; norms of the autocratic, corporate, and permissive styles; inadequate work habits and team skills; a pattern of one-to-one relationships between the boss and team members; and hidden-agenda game playing. The goals of team building include defining objectives and problems as well as improving group skills and interpersonal relations. A general design for a team-building workshop was described. To avoid the trap of "just playing the game," an alternative way of thinking about a process through which one can help individuals build from their own feelings and experiences and developing the team was presented via the process of imaginization.

Key Terms and Concepts

Action orientation	Project team
Family groups	Special groups
Hidden agenda	Team building
Imaginization process	Team effectiveness
Management teams	Team style
Parallel team	Work teams

Study Questions

1. Describe the relationship between group dynamics and team building.
2. What are some challenges faced by team leaders as they try to facilitate team effectiveness?
3. Discuss the variations of team building.
4. To what extent did the activities your classroom team engaged in help get the team off to a good start? Were the activities adequate for that purpose? What else might have been done?
5. "Every team can use team building." Do you agree or disagree? Why?
6. Identify the reasons that would lead a manager to utilize a team-building intervention.

7. Discuss the phases and activities during a team-building effort.

8. Discuss the merit of the imaginization process for team building.

9. What areas should be considered for evaluating the effectiveness of team building?

10. Discuss the effect of team building on creativity, innovation, and quality improvement.

Suggested Readings

Dyer, W. G. *Team Building: Current Issues and New Alternatives.* 3rd ed. Reading, MA: Addison-Wesley, 1995.

Hirshhorn, L. *Managing in the New Team Environment: Skills, Tools, and Methods.* Reading, MA: Addison-Wesley, 1991.

Kinlaw, D. C. *Developing Superior Work Teams.* Lexington, MA: Lexington Books, 1991.

Yeatts, D. E. and L. Hyten. *High-Performance Self-Managed Work Teams.* Thousand Oaks, CA: Sage, 1998.

Endnotes

1. M. Ezzamel and H. Willmott, "Accounting Teamwork: A Critical Study of Group-Based Systems of Organizational Control," *Administrative Science Quarterly* 43 (1998), pp. 358–96.

2. S. G. Cohen and D. E. Bailey, "What Makes Teams Work: Group Effectiveness Research from the Shop Floor to the Executive Suite," *Journal of Management* 23, no. 3 (1997), pp. 239–90.

3. For a discussion of the difference between team development and team building, and specific programs for team development, see D. C. Kinlaw, *Developing Superior Work Teams,* (Lexington, MA: Lexington Books, 1991).

4. W. G. Dyer, *Team Building, Issues and Alternatives,* 2d ed., (Reading, MA: Addison-Wesley, 1987), p. 6.

5. *APA Monitor,* November 1973.

6. E. H. Schein, *Organizational Psychology,* 2d ed., (Englewood Cliffs, NJ: Prentice-Hall, 1970), pp. 71–72.

7. E. Sundstrom, K. P. DeMeuse, and D. Futrell, "Work Teams: Applications and Effectiveness," *American Psychologist* 45, no. 2 (1990), pp. 120–33; M. Beer, *Organization Change and Development: A System View,* (Santa Monica, CA: Goodyear, 1980).

8. R. E. Kaplan, "The Conspicuous Absence of Evidence That Process Consultants Enhance Task Performance," *Journal of Applied Behavioral Science* 15 (1979), pp. 346–60.

9. W. Bennis, *Changing Organizations,* (New York: McGraw-Hill, 1966).

10. E. A. Locke, K. N. Shaw, L. M. Saari, and G. P. Latham, "Goal Setting and Task Performance," *Psychological Bulletin* 90 (1982), pp. 125–52; E. A. Locke, G. P. Latham, and M. Erez, "The Determinants of Goal Commitment," *Academy of Management Review* 13 (1988), pp. 23–39.

11. P. F. Butler and C. H. Bell Jr., "Effects of Team Building and Goal Setting on Productivity: A Field Experiment," *Academy of Management Journal* 29, no. 2 (1986), pp. 305–28.

12. R. Beckhard, "Optimizing Team-Building Efforts," *Journal of Contemporary Business* 1, no. 3 (1972), pp. 23–32.

13. W. G. Dyer, *Team Building: Issues and Alternatives,* (Reading, MA: Addison-Wesley, 1987).

14. W. W. Burke, *Organizational Development,* (Boston: Little, Brown, 1982).

15. P. G. Hanson and B. Lubin, "Team Building as Group Development," *Organization Development Journal* 4, no. 1 (1986), pp. 27–35.

16. G. Morgan, *Imaginization: New Mindsets for Seeing, Organizing, and Managing,* (San Francisco: Berrett-Koehler Publisher, 1997).

17. U. Essler, *Analyzing Groupware Adoption,* (Stockholm, Sweden: Unpublished doctoral dissertation, 1998); A. B. (Rami) Shani, J. Sena, and M. Stebbins, "Knowledge Work Teams and Groupware Technology: Learning from Seagate's Experience," (San Luis Obispo, CA: Working paper, 1998).

18. P. F. Buller, "The Team Building–Task Performance Relation: Some Conceptual and Methodological Refinements," *Group and Organization Studies* 11, no. 3 (1986), pp. 147–68.

19. D. Eden, "Team Development: Quasi-Experimental Confirmation among Combat Companies," *Group and Organization Studies* 11, no. 3 (1986), pp. 133–46.

20. D. Eden, "Team Development: A True Field Experiment Employing Three Levels of Rigor," *Journal of Applied Psychology* 70 (1985), pp. 94–100.

21. P. F. Buller and C. H. Bell, "Effects of Team Building and Goal Setting on Productivity: A Field Experiment," *Academy of Management Journal* 29, no. 2 (1986), pp. 305–28.

22. K. P. DeMeuse and S. J. Liebowitz, "An Empirical Analysis of Team Building Research," *Group and Organizational Studies* 6 (1981), pp. 357–58.

23. R. W. Woodman and J. J. Sherwood, "The Role of Team Development in Organizational Effectiveness: A Critical Review," *Psychological Bulletin* 88 (1980), pp. 166–86.

24. J. Wolfe and D. D. Bowen, "Team Building Effects on Company Performance," *Simulation and Games* 20, no. 4 (1989), pp. 388–408.

25. C. E. Larson and F. M. J. LaFasto, *TeamWork,* (Newbury Park, CA: Sage, 1989).

26. A. Seers, "Team-Member Exchange Quality: A New Construct for Decision-Making Research," *Organizational Behavior and Human Decision Processes* 43 (1989), pp. 118–35.

Activity 7–2: Team Building in a Hospital Setting

Objective:

To demonstrate the application of team-building activities to improve effectiveness in an organizational setting.

Task 1:

a. Read the following case study, "Time for a Change at Suburban Health Maintenace."

b. Based on the limited information presented, make a list of factors and actors that influence the group's work. (You might want to use the "blueprint" and "script and the actors" described in Module 4 as a guide.)

c. Through what set of activities did the consultants lead and guide the group?

Task 2 (Classroom):

Participants are to share their responses to the questions in task 1 and develop a shared understanding of them. Teams are to discuss the following questions:

a. What are the chances of the group successfully resolving the problems at Suburban Health Maintenace? Why?

b. Is this group the one to which these issues should be addressed? Why or why not?

c. What steps can be taken to resolve the nursing issue? What specific changes will each group have to make? What forces make it likely or unlikely that these changes will occur?

d. What kind of specific team-building activities would you recommend for each group? How would you overcome some of the potential roadblocks?

Team ideas will be shared with the whole learning community and serve as the basis for class discussion.

Case Study: Time for a Change at Suburban Health Maintenance

For centuries the relationship between physicians and nurses has generally been that physicians give orders and nurses carry them out. Only recently, with the increasing professionalization of nursing and nurses' desires to be treated as equals, has the traditional physician–nurse relationship been called into question. These days, it seems, physicians and nurses don't work very well together except when they are in the process of providing care to patients. Nurses often feel overlooked and unappreciated by their professional superiors; physicians, on the other hand, feel that nurses should simply comply with their requests. Often, neither party finds the relationship very satisfactory.

One unusual group of physicians and nurses at Suburban Health Maintenance (SHM) decided to change all that. They were in a unique position to do so; as part of a health maintenance organization (HMO), the same physicians work with the same nurses every day, week in and week out. In most hospitals nurses stay put while physicians dart in and out, leaving a concise but unreadable set of orders for the nurse to follow as they go to their next patient.

Physicians and nurses at SHM faced a different situation—they had to learn to live with one another because they worked together all the time. Like most HMOs, SHM was committed to holding down membership costs for its patients. This goal meant utilizing nurses as much as possible in the delivery of care to help minimize the use of expensive physicians' time. Therefore, the group had to work together smoothly and try to avoid the problems besetting traditional nurse–physician relationships.

Over time, members of each group came to know their counterparts on a first-name basis, a situation they had rarely experienced in other places they had worked. Nevertheless, problems still remained, the worst of which was the inability of SHM to attract and retain good nurses.

SHM had several health centers throughout the city that were coordinated by a central administrative group. The south-side center wasn't located in the best of neighborhoods, but the organization was dedicated to continuing its service to the racially mixed population surrounding the facility. Unfortunately, the location of the south-side center made it difficult to attract qualified nurses, since jobs were plentiful in safer parts of the city.

The chronic understaffing of the south-side facility and the low level of skills possessed by those nurses who could be hired caused physicians to complain to the administration about the quality of nursing care. As time went on and the problem was not resolved, some complaints were made directly to an already frustrated nursing management group. It was rumored that some physicians had reprimanded nurses in front of their peers and patients, deploring the poor quality of care being provided by nursing. Of course, such outbursts caused more nurses to leave the already troubled facility and seek employment elsewhere; a vicious circle was beginning to take form.

In most health care organizations, that would have been it—cold war would have begun. Administration would be called on to solve the problem—but as a third party, it would be almost powerless to act. The administration at SHM did what it could; it raised the pay of nurses, but the problem remained. What made SHM different from other health care organizations, however, was the feeling of "being in it together." Nurses and physicians were not exactly aligned in their views of the situation, but they did agree to sit down and talk about it. Representatives of the nursing management group and a number of key administrative physicians representing the medical group met to hammer out an understanding. Administrators responded to an invitation to attend.

The first few meetings of the group were routine. Consultants had been used to design the meetings, and the roles that were specified for the participants managed to keep the cap on the volcano of misunderstanding long enough for the groups to realize that they were actually in agreement about the problems that faced SHM's south-side facility.

By the third meeting, it was discovered that the physicians really didn't have a very clear idea of what activities nursing management engaged in besides responding to complaints from doctors. It was felt that if physicians had a clearer idea of what nurses did, they would not be so quick to complain about nursing's lack of responsiveness to their needs.

Nursing management agreed to take responsibility for preparing a description of nurses' roles, which they would present at the next meeting. What was uncovered during that meeting left the consultants and administrator of the south-side HMO wondering what action needed to be taken to meet the demands of both groups. Some of the issues discussed at that meeting appear in the following list.

1. *Waste of nursing management time on clerical tasks.* The members of nursing management spend an incredible amount of time doing clerical work. This work consists of such things as making out schedules, providing staff coverage where needed, scheduling vacations, and maintaining records on employee absenteeism and tardiness. Repeated requests have been made to computerize the system so that attention could be paid to more important matters, but the downtown office has decided that the computerization of these things is low in priority compared to other things that need to be done.

At one time the nursing supervisor made a request for a clerical support person to do the work; the request for the position went downtown and came back classified as a union position. This meant that a union employee would be involved in scheduling nursing management time and have access to confidential management information. This situation was clearly unacceptable to the nursing supervisor, and she canceled her request for the position.

Attempts at delegating these functions led to dangerous lack of coordination among the nursing departments. Because each department head was unaware of the schedules of other departments, situations developed that left the health center seriously understaffed.

2. *Discipline problems.* Nursing management itself is overworked and understaffed. The manager can't be everywhere at once. Employees have taken advantage of the situation by coming to work late, leaving early, and taking long breaks in between. Nursing management would like to install time clocks to help control the situation. The facility, which was in use before SHM purchased it, once had time clocks, and they are currently being stored in the building. However, the downtown office will not allow them to be installed because then employee policy would not be the same throughout the area.

3. *Budgeting.* The budgeting process is a nightmare. The process begins in May for the next year and usually doesn't conclude until July of the subsequent year. Until the budget is approved, no capital purchases can be made, so even if capital expenditures are eventually approved, the equipment may not be purchased until over a year after it's needed. The process is long and drawn out because the central office must do a careful evaluation of the requests from all of the health centers and the physicians to determine the priority of needs, taking into account the revenue available. The top administrator has expressed a strong conviction that funds should not be given to the health centers unless the need for them can be justified, since financial resources are tight.

4. *Supply.* Even the procurement of normal usage items can be problematic. Orders are placed through the central warehouse, which purchases large quantities of supplies at discounted prices for the entire organization. If the items requested are out of stock, the ordering party is usually informed within a week's time. If the item is desperately needed, arrangements can then be made to place a special order or borrow supplies from another hospital. This whole process is cumbersome.

5. *Influence.* Nurses in the organization do not receive attention when they raise complaints. For example, when the health center ran out of plaster for making casts,

a nurse was told to contact supply immediately. When she called, she was put on hold several times. The chief of surgery then called personally, and the response was instantaneous. The same situation is repeated when dealing with maintenance, dietary, and other hospital support.

At the end of the meeting, the nurses and physicians agreed that something needed to be done about the situation. Both groups looked to the administrator and the consultants for suggestions.

**Activity 7–3
Three Essential
Process Tools for
Teams Development:
The Eye Pie, Voice Box,
and Power Puzzle***

Objective:

To help group members develop a better understanding of team functioning. These activities can help the team become a high-performing team.

Time:

Each activity takes from 30 minutes to 4 hours, depending on the amount of time desired for discussion and feedback.

Materials:

Paper and pencil.

Procedure:

The instructor can use any or all of the following activities. The use of all three activities is likely to help the team become a high-performing team.

A. The Eye Pie Activity

Task 1:

The instructor assigns a specific team task to the team. The task should take up to 30 minutes. The following are some examples of team tasks: (a) developing a team mission statement; (b) designing and building a paper airplane that can fly 15 feet; (c) designing a paper basket that can hold water.

Task 2:

Upon the completion of the task, each member of the group reflects on the experience and completes a distribution chart in the form of a pie graph showing the amount of eye contact each person received during the just-completed task.

Task 3:

As each member reports his or her perceptions to the team, individuals record the different distributions. The team is to discuss how the estimates compare. What do the differences in perception represent? Are sociocultural influences in action? What types of eye contact occurred? To the extent that individuals, the teams, or both desire some corrective actions, specific actionable strategies should be developed.

B. The Voice Box Activity

(If this activity is carried out alone [without "Eye Pie"], start by following task 1 of the "Eye Pie" activity and then proceed to task 4. If this activity follows the "Eye Pie" activity, proceed to task 4 below.)

*This activity was created by Professor Kenneth Murrell and Todd Smith. All rights reserved, and no reproduction should be made without the expressed approval of Professor Murrell, University of West Florida, Department of Management, 11000 University Parkway, Pensacola, FL 32514. We are grateful to Ken and Todd.

Task 4:

Upon the completion of task 3, individuals are to reflect one more time on how they accomplished task 1. This time, individuals working alone are to complete a distribution chart in the form of a box graph, recording the amount of time each person spent talking during the allotted time for the group task. Individuals are to draw a time block, a square that represents the time the group had to accomplish its task. The block is then subdivided into sections that represent the percentage of time each individual spent talking.

Task 5:

As team members report their perceptions, individuals record the distributions. Then the team is to address the following questions: How do the various estimates compare? What do differences in perception represent? What sociocultural influences are in action? What types of talking were occurring (task, social, or other)? How do the findings compare to the earlier nonverbal "Eye Pie" findings? Are they the same or different? What might that say about the reality of group dynamics? To the extent that individuals, the team, or both desire some corrective actions, specific actionable strategies should be developed.

C. Power Puzzle Activity

(If this activity is carried out alone [without "Eye Pie"], start by following task 1 of the "Eye Pie" activity and then proceed to task 6. If this activity follows the "Eye Pie" and "Voice Box" activities, proceed to task 6 below.)

Task 6:

Upon the completion of the group task 1, each individual—looking back on the group experience—working alone is to complete a "power puzzle" depicting the relationships he or she saw occurring in the group as it went about accomplishing its task. Individuals are to draw the group process interactions, using any combination of shapes, sizes, shading, and interaction representations. The goal is for individuals to create representations of how they feel they fit into the group's power relationships and the group's interactions. Be as creative as you can be in capturing the information.

Task 7:

Each member shares his or her creation and its meaning. The team acts as an appreciative inquiry entity with the goal of arriving at a comprehensive understanding of the picture created. *No critique or criticism about a given individual's creation is permitted!!* The team is to discuss the following questions: What are the individual and shared perceptions of the power relationships and dynamic processes in action? How do estimates compare? What do the differences represent? Are there "hidden" dynamics? To the extent that individuals, the team, or both desire some corrective actions, specific actionable strategies should be developed.

Task 8:

The instructor will facilitate a class discussion about the multiple learning from the activities just completed.

8

Dynamics between Teams and Conflict Management

_____ ## Learning Objectives

After completing this module, you should be able to

1. Describe the basic elements in the dynamics between teams.
2. State how the interactions between teams or groups affect their performance.
3. Identify some basic components of intergroup communication.
4. Recognize barriers to intergroup cooperation and the actions that can be taken to overcome such impediments.
5. Understand the relationships between group problem solving, decision making, group dynamics, and intergroup behavior and performance.
6. Describe several approaches that can be used to foster effective outcomes between teams and groups.

_____ ## Module Outline

Premodule Preparation
    Activity 8–1: Ambiguity, Conflict, and Interteam Dynamics
Introduction
Determinants of Intergroup Performance
The Nature of Conflict Dynamics
    Views of Conflict
    Levels of Conflict
    Conflict within the Individual
    Conflict and Group Identity
    Intergroup Conflict
Dealing with Intergroup Conflict
    Awareness of Intergroup Dynamics
    Recognition of the "Common Enemy"
    Development of Superordinate Goals
    Conflict-Handling Modes

_____   **Premodule Preparation**

Activity 8–1: Ambiguity, Conflict, and Interteam Dynamics

Introduction:

Most of this course's group activities to date involved problem solving and decision making. For each, you were given specific situations and techniques with which to work. Exploring what happens to a group when it is confronted with an ambiguous, less-structured task is the purpose of this exercise. Your team is to meet outside class for 2 hours to complete task 1.

This exercise deals with two subjects: management of diversity and managers promoting competition among employees. These have been controversial issues in business and government organizations for many years. Everyone has opinions on these subjects, which become apparent when they search their minds carefully. This exercise will tap your reservoir of opinion.

In this exercise, please use no books, articles, or other reference material. This task is to be completed entirely from the interaction of minds, through sharing of knowledge and opinions, and via the synergistic development of ideas.

Task 1:

Teams are to meet outside class to examine their knowledge and attitudes on the topic and answer these questions:

a. What are the advantages and disadvantages of diversity at the workplace? To aid you in developing as complete a list as possible, groups might first compare and contrast homogenous and heterogenous units in as many subjects as possible. (*Note:* There are a number of diversity aspects that we have not discussed in this course.)

b. What are the advantages and disadvantages of promoting competition among employees and among teams?

c. Under what conditions should a manager promote competition among his or her employees and teams? When should competition not be used as a management technique?

Prepare your answers on one to three (not more) typewritten pages, using outline (not essay) form; be complete enough so the reader will understand the point you are making. (*Note:* Your team's completed answers should be delivered to the instructor at a designated time prior to the next class meeting so copies can be made. These copies will be used in task 2.)

Task 2:

Your team and another team will be assigned the task of comparing the lists developed in task 1. Each member of your group will be assigned to a dyad with a member of the other group. Dyad partners are to supply each other with copies of their team reports from task 1. Each is to study the other's and contrast it with his or her own. The papers are to be discussed in detail so that complete understanding of the intent of the lists is communicated.

At the conclusion of the discussion, the dyad should reach an agreement as to which team paper represents the better solution for the assigned task. For this purpose each dyad has 20 points to divide up and assign to the papers. Thus one paper could have a 20 and the other a 0 (or any other division of the points), but the judgment cannot be 10 to 10, since a final discrimination must be made. If there are an odd number of teams in the class, representatives from each of the last three teams will meet as triads; they will have 30 points to distribute, but there can be no 10-10-10 final judgments. (Time: 30 minutes)

(*Note:* The *Instructor's Manual* has important guidance on how to conduct this case.)

Task 3:

After all dyads and triads have reached their conclusions, participants are to return to their teams. They will have 2 minutes to discuss their experience. The instructor will list the results on team charts on the board. This will be followed by a discussion and interpretation of the results.

Task 4:

The instructor will give a short lecture on the process involved.

Introduction

The new forms of organizations seem to be based on teams. Some researchers view organizations as "a team of teams." As such one way to think about an organization is to conceptualize it as a collection of interrelated groups operating at various levels of the organizational hierarchy. In any firm a high degree of intergroup interaction is vital to the organization's success. The ability to diagnose and manage interteam interactions is essential to the firm because (1) in most organizations teams need to work with other teams to accomplish their goal, (2) the interdependency between the teams often creates dependency relationships that might foster conflict, and (3) conflicting team goals and the emerging dynamics between teams might influence the effectiveness of the firm.[1] Even in small companies the production group must interact with the marketing/sales group, and both must interface with the accounting, human resources, and finance groups.

In the context of this module, we go beyond the definition of a *group* presented in Modules 5, 6, and 7, which focused on person-to-person relations. In this module a *team* or *group* refers to (1) any one of the types of groups and teams previously mentioned, (2) a department or a business unit, or (3) any formal or informal classification of employees based on geographical location, hourly versus permanent workers, race, gender, ethnic background, religion, occupation, educational background, and so on.[2]

Determinants of Intergroup Performance

Intergroup behavior occurs when two groups interact. As we have seen in Modules 4, 5, and 6, each group is likely to have its own characteristics and uniqueness, but all groups operate within a larger organizational context composed of both the formal and the human organization dimensions. These entail policies, rules and procedures, goals and reward systems, culture, work flow, decision-making processes, and so forth. To fully understand the behavior and performance of the marketing and manufacturing departments in a specific organization, we need to know about their interaction with one another, with the different departments in the organization, as well as the interaction between the organization and its environment.

As a broad skeleton, beyond the nature of the formal and human organizations, intergroup behavior and outcomes are influenced by the following key elements: the nature and characteristics of the task (which will be examined in Module 13), the degree of required group interdependence (the frequency and quality of interactions among groups), the group's time and goal orientations, and the bases for the interaction (such as information flow requirements and integration requirements). Figure 8–1 presents a partial schema of intergroup behavior and performance.[3]

**Figure 8–1
Intergroup Behavior:
A Partial Schema**

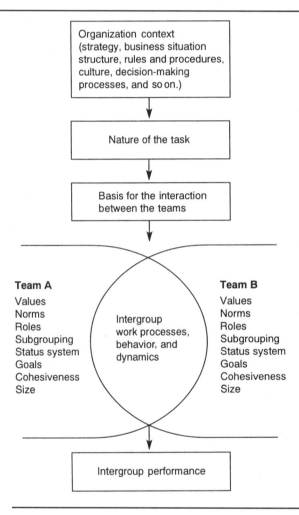

The ability of all parties to the interaction to meet all the requirements influences the quality of the intergroup outcomes. As we have seen in Modules 5 and 6, managing team dynamics is a complex managerial task. Managing intergroup dynamics is more than just managing two teams; it requires the ability to also manage the dynamics between two teams that together form a larger entity with its own complex dynamics.

The Nature of Conflict Dynamics

Special problems of leadership (Module 3), diversity and personalities (Modules 1 and 9), communication (Module 11), self–other perception (Module 10), and win–lose motivation (Module 12) exist in the area of intergroup relationships. Intergroup activities are greatly influenced by the fact that **conflict** is built into both the individual and the society. While this conflict can be destructive, it can also lead to problem solving and creativity when it is understood and coped with appropriately.

Views of Conflict

Conflict dynamics are an integral ingredient of human and organizational life. Three distinct orientations about conflict are reported in the literature. *The traditional view* argues that conflict must be avoided, as it indicates a malfunction within the unit; the *human relations view* argues that conflict is a natural and inevitable phenomenon in any unit and as such serves as an important positive (not evil) force in influencing the unit's performance; and *the system view,* the most recent view, proposes that conflict is not only inevitable but also absolutely necessary for any unit to perform effectively.[4] A few of the general system theory concepts discussed in Module 4—such as entropy, hierarchy, transformation processes, and multiple goals—set the stage for conflict dynamics that may occur at many levels in any system and thus must be managed.

Levels of Conflict

Five primary levels of conflict may be present in any system: intrapersonal (within an individual), interpersonal (between individuals), intragroup (within a group), intergroup (between groups), and interorganizational (between organizations). Our focus in this module is on the conflict dynamics at the individual and team levels.

Conflict within the Individual

The socialization process, by definition, shapes the individual's drives and creates certain needs to make him or her a well-functioning member of society. This means he or she will conform to the group behaviors, values, customs, and standards and will not gratify individual wants and desires totally at the expense of others. This process is not without its toll to the comfort of the individual because it creates lifelong tensions and psychological conflicts.

The psychoanalytic approach to studying this phenomenon has emphasized the internal conflict people experience as they cope with their drives, needs, wants, and fears on the one hand and their internalized "parent" (the society that has been programmed into their mental processes) on the other. People feel compelled to obey society's dictates or suffer self-disapproval and guilt. In the extreme this dynamic conflict results in psychosis, a state in which the individual has been overwhelmed by these opposing forces. Even when adequately coped with, the individual's psychological defense mechanisms can readily be aroused when confronted with certain types of frustration. Once aroused, fear and anger can be available for displacement on available (presumably offending) targets. One indication of mental health is the maintenance of a self-image that facilitates the achievement of needs in a manner acceptable to society as the person has experienced it.

Conflict and Group Identity

By the time an individual is an adult, identity includes an integration of all the groups (family, school, social, work) he or she has been a part of, or has become aware of, that satisfy needs. The values, beliefs, behaviors, and lifestyles of the groups with which the individual has had experience or has admired make up an important aspect of self-image, while the values, beliefs, behaviors, and lifestyles of groups he or she has rejected or not admired are perceived as "not me." Muzafer Sherif uses the concept of *reference groups,* which he defines as "those groups to which the individual relates himself as a member or aspires to relate himself psychologically."[5] Reference groups with which the individual identifies may be thought of as *positive,* whereas those the individual rejects may function as *negative reference points.* As will be discussed in Module 10, perception of an ongoing experience is meaningful primarily because the brain has programmed past experiences into categories, including such reference groups.

Another aspect of this is that the better I know "who I am," the better "who I am not" can be differentiated. Deciding what is "me" and what is "not me" is a continuing mental process. Anything that (1) suggests that what is "not me" might be better than what is "me" or (2) could attack or deprive the individual spontaneously arouses defensiveness. The popularity of the great put-down in contemporary humor reflects the need of individuals to feel superior and put those who are "not like I am" in their place. Reliance upon status, material objects, symbols, and social organization membership is one way of assuring the individual of who he or she is and, moreover, is not. Club bylaws often define not only what "we stand for" but have restrictions against admitting those who are "not us."

One significance of the reference group concept is that it sometimes makes meaningful the actions of an individual that seem completely incongruent with what is known of that person. In one case it was difficult to understand how a high school boy who was from a "good" middle-class family, had excellent school grades, was a church member, and was highly thought of by many teachers could be guilty of vandalizing certain teachers' offices. Then authorities learned that he was a part of a group of boys who believed they had to punish certain male teachers they thought behaved in a sadistic way toward students. The norms of the group included bringing to justice those who had been untouchable in the past in that no suffering student had ever won a grievance against them. A member's status and acceptance in this group could only be maintained by helping vandalize the offices of the offending teachers.

Most frequently, we try to deal with individuals as individuals and are unaware of the forces acting upon them from the groups with which they identify. The informal cliques in which employees participate are excellent examples of this. Rate busters in factories are either deviants from an employee group (a negative reference group for them) or are ignorant of how the group feels about their behavior.

Intergroup Conflict

Intergroup conflict refers to clashes and opposition between two teams or groups. A recent study distinguished between **task-focused conflict** and **relationship-focused conflict** and found that both types of conflicts have an effect on teams' performance.[6] The recent conflicts between management and pilots at Northwest Airlines and American Airlines are examples for disputes over tasks, working conditions, pay, and some even argue over working relations between workers and management.

Both sources of conflict set the stage for four different categories of intergroup conflicts within organizations: **vertical conflict** (refers to clashes between employee groups at different levels), **horizontal conflict** (refers to clashes between groups of employees at the same level), **line-staff conflict** (refers to clashes between advisory/support teams and teams that are responsible for creating the goods or services), and **diversity-based conflict** (refers to clashes between groups due to the nature of diversity, such as race, gender, religion, and ethnicity).[7]

This attachment to groups and the accompanying concern, apprehension, or distrust for other groups can be almost instantaneous. Warren G. Bennis reports the following, which would appear to support this idea.

Jaap Rabbie, conducting experiments on intergroup conflict at the University of Utrecht, has been amazed by the ease with which conflict and stereotype develop. He brings into an experimental room two groups and distributes green name tags and pens to one group, red pens and tags to the other. The two groups do not compete; they do not even interact. They are only in sight of each other while they silently complete a questionnaire. Only 10 minutes are needed to activate defensiveness and fear, reflected in the hostile and irrational perceptions of both "reds" and "greens."[8]

The most famous field experiment on in-group/out-group dynamics and the reduction of intergroup conflict was conducted by Sherif and associates in 1954. At a summer camp they succeeded in creating two groups of boys, each of which developed norms of its own that included hostility to the other group. Then through further experimental arrangements, they succeeded in overcoming both groups' hostility.[9]

Robert R. Blake found a similar outcome when business executives were the subjects.[10] He and his associates brought 20 to 30 executives together in 2-week workshops. They were formed into groups that developed the norms, group structure, and cohesiveness that characterized Sherif's subjects in the first phase. Two executive groups were then given an identical problem for which they were to find the "best" solution; these solutions were later evaluated. Under these conditions, win–lose power struggles spontaneously occurred. Each group enhanced its own position and down-graded its adversary's. Negative stereotypes arose toward the adversary. Intellectual distortion occurred; points upon which the two teams were in agreement were minimized or not recognized, and differences were highlighted. When representatives of the groups met to negotiate, the loyalty of the representatives to their groups became more important than logic. A representative who conceded was seen as a traitor by the group; a winner was a hero.

We have run numerous intergroup exercises in management workshops to provide an experiential base for examining the dynamics of in-group/out-group relationships. The competitive reactions are so spontaneous, demonstrating what past research has documented, that subjects often become too involved to draw back and look at the learning opportunity offered by the situation. Some keep insisting that the other group is wrong without ever understanding the process being illustrated. What better evidence of the process? University students performing the same activity as the executives are much calmer and low key in their reactions. However, the win–lose dynamics are very evident. Most students say they definitely wanted to win for their team, but they did not wish to make the person with whom they were "problem solving" look too bad, so they held out for just enough points to win. For the most part they do show more problem-solving orientation than the more combat-experienced executives. Activities 8–2 and 8–3 illustrate this point.

In the Sherif and Blake research, the conflict is reciprocal between specific adversary groups, which might be thought of as between teams. A similar relationship exists to some degree in the interface of categories, such as male–female, black–white, minority–nonminority, and boss–subordinate. Furthermore, the interface between levels of the hierarchy is characterized by differences in the way the members of the levels perceive their own and others' behaviors. Whenever people of one category perceive themselves or their roles differently than do those with whom they interface, the potential for conflict exists.

Dealing with Intergroup Conflict

Some of the primary determinants of intergroup conflict arise from the greatly augmented rates of change in the general culture. Changing markets, changing technology, and changing availability of resources mean that organizations must be designed to cope continuously with changing circumstances. Changes in emphasis on human values and standards of living are accompanied by rising expectations of the public, which are never more than partially satisfied, leaving a reservoir of tensions and frustrations available for displacement.

Competition for scarce resources is generally agreed to be a major factor in initiating and perpetuating conflict in organizations. The scarce resources may be in innumerable forms, such as materials available, opportunities for promotion, power, recognition and status, attention from the boss, or competent secretaries. Since the scarce-resource condition always exists, how can intergroup conflict in organizations be lessened? How can behaviors facilitating coordination among functionally integrated units be enhanced? A number of theories, strategies, and techniques are relevant to achieving this goal. The following sections discuss several of these.

Awareness of Intergroup Dynamics

It is essential to help people develop both the intellectual and experiential learning necessary to understand the probability that everyone will become spontaneously enmeshed in the win–lose trap. Knowledge alone will not overcome reactions that experience has built into our reflexes, but it may provide the base for preventative measures or for guidance out of the trap once it has been entered. Workshops and education programs are important techniques, but awareness of both causal and remedial measures must become a part of the organizational culture. Future modules discuss organizational change and development methods as a systematic approach to developing organizational value systems and interaction patterns. Values related to avoiding the win–lose trap or groupthink hopefully can be accepted throughout the organization. The ideas discussed in this section also could come to characterize the working climate.

Recognition of the "Common Enemy"

Competition is a part of every American's education. Rivalry for grades or victory in sports—and all the accompanying values and behaviors—are carried from the school right into the organization. Managers often use the word *team* in the same win–lose sense they would use it on the ball field. While the coordination that helps an athletic team win is also needed to help an organization achieve its goals, promoting competition between functionally integrated units of an organization can be highly dysfunctional. Nevertheless, a common view among managers is that competition between employees is healthy because they see competition as one of the more effective motivating forces. The main point is that competition is not "good" or "bad" in itself, and the manager has to determine under what conditions it is functional or dysfunctional.

Some research evidence indicates that intergroup hostility between teams can be reduced when a **common enemy** is introduced.[11] Since all industrial organizations are in competition for their markets, emphasis on the common enemy of the closest competitor provides an opportunity for pitting the organizational team against an outsider as the team to beat.

Some readers will object to this procedure on various grounds, such as ethics or concern over whether the behavior developed against "the enemy" might not be turned back onto the organization. Rensis Likert advocates a more constructive approach, based on research of the management style and performance of the various offices of the sales force of a large company that operates nationally.[12] One finding was that the high-producing offices typically adopted group methods of management; the manager and the salespeople used group problem solving, group coaching, and group goal setting. Likert contrasts this approach with providing contest awards for highest sales by individuals. When the salespeople are pitted against one another this way, they do not share information about markets, leads, techniques, or problems. He concludes, "The best performance, lowest costs, and the highest levels of earnings and of employee satisfaction occur when the drive for a sense of personal worth is used to create strong motivational forces to *cooperate* rather than *compete* with one's peers and colleagues."[13] As an alternative an individual can compete with a past record or strive to achieve goals set individually or group goals set by his work group.

Development of Superordinate Goals

Sherif's experiment illustrated the potential of reducing intergroup conflict through the achievement of goals that are important to both groups. Organizations cannot function without the attainment of **superordinate goals**—primary goals of an organization or competing groups that exceed those of individuals or subgroups—yet intergroup conflict and failure to coordinate are major deterrents to organizational effectiveness. While many reasons for these reactions are irrational in the sense that people are resisting working together, at least a part of the problem can be attributed to a lack of shared understanding as to what the goals are. Consultants who conduct team-building workshops often focus on this. Generally, members of a top-management team assume they all know the objectives and goals toward which they are working, but when they are asked to list the goals and rank their priorities, considerable variance is often found. Subordinates of the team indicate that these confusions are pushed down into the hierarchy and become a factor in interdivisional conflict.

The current surge for the development of shared organizational vision in industrial, government, and educational institutions can be seen as an attempt to identify the superordinate objectives and the objectives of each unit that function to achieve them. When everyone works toward a set of individual, unit, and organizational objectives, the information level of all employees in carrying on their coordinated efforts is systematically raised and perceptual distortion and communication problems are reduced. Fighting can arise spontaneously if two units assume they are working on the same objectives when they are not. The personality–communication–perception–motivation relationship we have been suggesting is directly applicable here.

Conflict-Handling Modes

The notion that intergroup conflict can never be totally resolved or eliminated dictates the need to explore different ways in which groups can deal with such conflict. Kenneth Thomas proposed that two main dimensions underline the intentions of the group to be involved in a conflict situation: (1) **cooperativeness**—the degree to which the group wants to satisfy the concerns of the other group—and (2) **assertiveness**—the degree to which the group wants to satisfy is own concerns.[14] The two dimensions plotted in Figure 8–2 are reflected in five **conflict-handling modes.**

**Figure 8–2
Two-Dimensional
Model of Ways
to Handle Conflict**

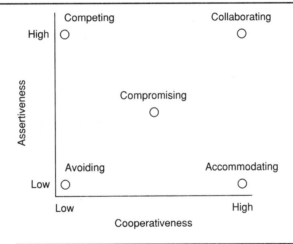

Source: Adapted from T. Ruble and K. Thomas, "Support for a Two-Dimensional Model of Conflict Behavior," *Organizational Behavior and Human Performance* 16 (1976), p. 145.

The **avoidance orientation** implies an unassertive, uncooperative approach in which both groups neglect the concerns involved by sidestepping the issue or postponing the conflict by choosing not to deal with it. The **competitive orientation** implies winning at the other's expense. This orientation is an assertive, uncooperative mode in which the groups attempt to achieve their own goals at the expense of the other through argument, authority, threat, or even physical force. The **accommodating orientation** reflects an unassertive, cooperative position where one group attempts to satisfy the concerns of the other by neglecting its own concerns or goals. The **compromising orientation** reflects the midpoint between the styles. It involves give-and-take by both groups. Both groups gain and give up something they want. The **collaborating orientation** is an assertive, cooperative mode that attempts to satisfy the concerns of both groups. It is different from the compromising orientation in that collaborating represents a desire to satisfy fully the concerns of both groups.

The appropriate mode depends on the nature of the situation, the task, and the people involved. Each mode is used at one time or another. This taxonomy of conflict-handling modes has been interpreted in a number of ways, including behaviors, styles, and strategies. Recent development of this framework suggests that these modes actually represent the strategic intentions of the groups involved in terms of what they attempt to accomplish in satisfying their own and other's goals.[15] Figure 8–3 captures the appropriate situation for each mode, as identified by chief executives.

Figure 8–3
Appropriate Situations for
Five Strategic Intentions

Conflict-Handling Models	Appropriate Situations
Competing	1. When quick, decisive action is vital (for example, emergencies). 2. On important issues where unpopular actions need implementing (for example, cost cutting, enforcing unpopular rules, discipline). 3. On issues vital to company welfare when you know you're right. 4. Against people who take advantage of noncompetitive behavior.
Collaborating	1. To find an integrative solution when both sets of concerns are too important to be compromised. 2. When your objective is to learn. 3. To merge insights from people with different perspectives. 4. To gain commitment by incorporating concerns into a consensus. 5. To work through feelings that have interfered with a relationship.
Compromising	1. When goals are important, but not worth the effort or potential disruption of more assertive modes. 2. When opponents with equal power are committed to mutually exclusive goals. 3. To achieve temporary settlements to complex issues. 4. To arrive at expedient solutions under time pressure. 5. As a backup when collaboration or competition is unsuccessful.
Avoiding	1. When an issue is trivial, or more important issues are pressing. 2. When you perceive no chance of satisfying your concerns. 3. When potential disruption outweighs the benefits of resolution. 4. To let people cool down and regain perspective. 5. When gathering information supersedes immediate decision. 6. When others can resolve the conflict more effectively. 7. When issues seem tangential or symptomatic of other issues.
Accommodating	1. When you find you are wrong—to allow a better position to be heard, to learn, and to show your reasonableness. 2. When issues are more important to others than yourself—to satisfy others and maintain cooperation. 3. To build social credits for later issues. 4. To minimize loss when you are outmatched and losing. 5. When harmony and stability are especially important. 6. To allow subordinates to develop by learning from mistakes.

Source: K. W. Thomas, "Toward Multi-Dimensional Values in Teaching: The Example of Conflict Behaviors," *Academy of Management Review* 2 (1977), Table 1, p. 487.

Social Intervention Approaches

Workshop methods are used to reduce conflict and promote collaboration, such as changing a win–lose condition to a win–win problem-solving situation. One general design can be accomplished in a 1- or 2-day workshop.[16] Representatives of the two groups (such as management–labor, production–sales, or in government, personnel–security or administrative services–line functions) agree that they have serious problems and are committed to exploring thoroughly avenues of better cooperation. First they work in separate team rooms to develop a statement of how each group sees itself as behaving toward the other group. The items from this statement are listed on a large pad. Each group then makes a list of items that outline how it perceives the other group as behaving toward it. The two groups meet and share their lists. The meeting provides an opportunity for them to explore, in an objective setting and under the guidance of a consultant, the problems of perception, communication, and interaction they are having. This process is somewhat similar in function to the organizational dialoguing—Where are you? Where am I?"—used in Module 2.

A second phase might be for each team to work separately on a list of factors it considers essential for an ideal working relationship. These are also shared and explored; an agreed-upon model might be analyzed. A third phase would be preparing a list of tasks the two units would have to accomplish in the future or a list of problems that must be solved. An action agenda is agreed upon; times are set for completion of the items on the agenda, and further meeting arrangements are made to discuss progress. In recognition that interaction skills must be practiced, follow-up meetings are set to maintain the newly improved relationships.

This design can be extended to more than two units, but doing so can become very time-consuming. In a meeting of sales, research and development, and production departments, for example, the three could end with a general contract of how they are to work together, and each could have a separate contract with each of the other two pertaining to matters not involving the third unit.

Richard Beckhard describes a design to work with intraorganizational problems that he refers to as a *confrontation meeting*.[17] In this case the top manager meets with the entire management group and the discussion goes through five phases: climate setting, information collecting, information sharing, priority setting and group action planning, and organization action planning. The top-management team meets immediately after the confrontation to plan actions and then makes its decisions known to the management group. A follow-up meeting with the entire management group should take place 4 to 6 weeks later for feedback and further planning. The success of this model will depend on the degree to which an atmosphere of openness and trust exists in the organization so that actual problems can be fully explored and dealt with.

Team Management

The one-to-one style of management has been characterized as creating conflict, rivalry, and suspicion among those reporting directly to a manager. The atmosphere of distrust provides no incentive for the team members to discuss their relationships when they do meet as a group with the boss; considerable game playing is apt to take place at these meetings. The rivalries among members, who are all managers, generally get pushed down into the hierarchy so that the employees reporting to them also become involved in interdepartment rivalries. Team development methods to overcome this aspect of conflict are covered in Module 7.

Likert advocates the *linking pin* concept as one method of avoiding problems associated with the rigidly traditional, hierarchical, one-to-one arrangement between boss and subordinates in the management structure.[18] Likert's position is that each person in the nonsupervisory structure must be a member of an effective work group and must be skilled in both leadership and membership functions and roles. Each work team needs to develop the type of group skills and means of communicating that will enable members to influence one another and their superior. Each member is a linking pin between the work group of those reporting directly to him or her and the work group consisting of that person's boss and those reporting to the boss. The organization is thus made up of a series of overlapping work groups in which each manager performs a linking function between groups of two levels of the hierarchy.

Likert provides for increased coordination between different functional areas by developing a multiple overlapping group structure through lateral as well as vertical linkage. Vertical linkage may take the form of committees or temporary work projects that provide for the lateral communication between groups.

Intergroup Communications

Perceptual stereotyping, communication barriers, and win–lose motivation are all increased during intergroup relations. Intergroup conflict can be better understood by first considering conflict within the individual. In the socialization process, individuals learn the conforming behaviors of society at the expense of freely fulfilling their own drives and desires; this process can generate internal conflicts that could easily be directed against other people. A second aspect of socialization is that the individual develops a self-identity, which can be thought of as an integration of all the groups he or she has been a member of or has admired; these are termed *positive reference groups*. Groups that individuals have rejected provide negative reference points in perceiving others. Knowing an individual's reference groups makes his or her behavior more understandable. The tendency of people to cluster together when threatened or frustrated tends to make such a group a positive reference group, while outsiders become negative reference points.

Recent research indicates that groups of strangers can develop in-group/out-group attitudes within a very few minutes. Sherif's experiments indicate how easily cohesive groups of boys can fall into the win–lose trap; Blake has shown executives are also highly susceptible. Ways to avoid the win–lose trap include awareness of the dynamics of intergroup conflict, recognition of a common enemy, development of superordinate goals, and certain social intervention strategies, such as workshops set up to solve the conflict. Team management concepts such as Likert's linking pin also are directed at overcoming problems of conflict and increasing coordination.

Summary

Intergroup dynamics is a complex phenomenon and a multilevel concept that can have an impact on behavior at the individual, group, and organizational levels. In this module intergroup dynamics was examined and studied at the interpersonal and intergroup levels within the organizational context. A short review of the determinants of intergroup performance was followed by an exploration of intergroup communication and conflict.

Next we discussed a variety of ways for handling intergroup conflict. Finally, five strategic intentions were presented for handling conflict in a variety of situations. This module's activities—8–1 ("Ambiguity, Conflict, and Interteam Dynamics"), 8–2 ("The Prisoners' Dilemma"), and 8–3 ("The SLO Corporation")—provide an opportunity to develop the ability to diagnose and handle intergroup conflict.

Key Terms and Concepts

Accommodating orientation	Diversity-based conflict
Assertiveness	Horizontal conflict
Avoidance orientation	Intergroup communication
Collaborating orientation	Intergroup conflict
Common enemy	Line-staff conflict
Competitive orientation	Relationship-focused conflict
Compromising orientation	Social intervention approaches
Conflict	Strategic intention
Conflict prevention through change programs	Superordinate goals
Conflict-handling mode	Task-focused conflict
Cooperativeness	Team management
	Vertical conflict

Study Questions

1. Identify and describe some determinants of intergroup performance.
2. Define the term *intergroup conflict.* What makes intergroup conflict a complex phenomenon?
3. Discuss the relationship between intergroup communication and intergroup conflict.
4. What is the relationship between intergroup conflict and groupthink?
5. Identify a group of which you are a member and another group that can affect your group's performance. Describe the two groups. Discuss the interdependences between the groups. How does each group affect the performance of the other group?
6. We discussed a few ways to reduce intergroup conflict. From your own experience, give other methods of coping with conflict that you have used or seen others use meaningfully.
7. Compare and contrast any two of the modes for handling intergroup conflict.

Endnotes

1. See, for example, R. A. Guzzo and G. P. Shea, "Group Performance and Intergroup Relations in Organizations," in M. D. Dunnette and L. M. Hough (eds.), *Handbook of Industrial and Organizational Psychology,* vol. 3, 2nd ed., (Palo Alto, CA: Consulting Psychologists Press, 1992), pp. 269–313.

2. H. C. Triandis, L. L. Kurowski, and M. J. Gelfand, "Workplace Diversity," in H. C. Triandis, M. D. Dunnette, and L. M. Hough (eds.), *Handbook of Industrial and Organizational Psychology,* vol. 4, 2nd ed., (Palo Alto, CA: Consulting Psychologists Press, 1994), pp. 769–827.

3. For a more comprehensive model, see R. M. Steers and J. S. Black, *Organizational Behavior,* (New York: Harper Collins, 1994), pp. 264–68.

4. Conflict is discussed in the C. A. Amason, K. R. Thompson, W. A. Hoachwater, and A. W. Harrison, "Conflict: An Important Dimension in Successful Management Teams," *Organizational Dynamics,* Autumn 1995, pp. 20–35; A. C. Amason, "Distinguishing the Effects of Functional and Dysfunctional Conflict on Strategic Decision Making: Resolving a Paradox for Top Management Teams," *Academy of Management Journal,* February 1996, pp. 123–48; K. A. Jehn, "A Qualitative Analysis of Conflict Types and Dimensions in Organizational Groups," *Administrative Science Quarterly* 42 (1997), pp. 530–57.

5. M. Sherif and C. Sherif, *Social Psychology,* (New York: Harper & Row, 1969), p. 418.

6. Jehn, K. A., A Qualitative Analysis of Conflict Types and Dimensions in Organizational Groups, *Administrative Science Quarterly,* 42 (1997), pp. 530–57.

7. D. Hellriegel, J. W. Slocum Jr., and R. W. Woodman, *Organizational Behavior,* (Cincinnati, OH: South-Western College Publishing, 1998).

8. Verbal communication from Rabbie to Bennis in W. G. Bennis and P. E. Slater, *The Temporary Society,* (New York: Harper & Row, 1968), p. 66.

9. M. Sherif, O. J. Harvey, B. J. White, W. R. Hod, and C. Sherif, *Intergroup Conflict and Cooperation,* (Norman: University of Oklahoma Book Exchange, 1961). Also see Sherif and Sherif, *Social Psychology,* Chapter 11.

10. R. R. Blake, H. A. Shephard, and J. S. Mouton, *Managing Intergroup Conflict in Industry,* (Houston: Gulf Publishing, 1964), Chapter 2.

11. Sherif and Sherif, *Social Psychology,* p. 255.

12. R. Likert, *The Human Organization,* (New York: McGraw-Hill, 1967), pp. 52–59.

13. Ibid., pp. 73–75.

14. K. W. Thomas, "Conflict and Negotiation Processes in Organizations," in M. D. Dunnette and L. M. Hough (eds.), *Handbook of Industrial and Organizational Psychology,* vol. 3, 2nd ed., (Palo Alto, CA: Consulting Psychologists Press, 1991), p. 653; K. W. Thomas, "Conflict and Conflict Management: Reflection and Update," *Journal of Organizational Behavior* 13 (1992), pp. 265–74.

15. Ibid.

16. See H. A. Hornstein, B. B. Bunker, W. W. Burke, M. Gindes, and R. J. Lewicki, *Social Intervention,* (New York: Free Press, 1971), pp. 355–56; R. Beckhard, *Organization Development: Strategies and Models,* (Reading, MA: Addison-Wesley, 1969), pp. 33–35; Blake, Shephard, and Mouton, *Managing Intergroup Conflict in Industry,* App. 1.

17. See Hornstein et al., *Social Intervention,* p. 213.

18. R. Likert, *New Ways of Managing Conflict,* (New York: McGraw-Hill, 1976).

Activity 8–2: The Prisoners' Dilemma: An Intergroup Competition

Objective:

To explore the dynamics of intergroup competition and its effect on performance.

Task 1:

Using your permanent teams, break teams into pairs, designating one team Red and the other Blue. If there are an odd number of teams, members of the extra one should be divided among the other teams, but no Red or Blue should have more than eight members for this activity. The instructor will indicate whether there are to be observers. Be sure that each set of Red and Blue teams is sufficiently isolated from the other sets so everyone can carry on interactions without disturbing the others. Do not communicate with the other team until the instructor indicates the exercise is to start.

Tear out the Prisoners' Dilemma Tally Sheet at the end of the instructions, and study the directions. Your instructor will answer any questions you have about scoring. (Time: 10 minutes)

Task 2:

Your instructor will tell you when to begin. You will have 3 minutes to make a team decision. When the instructor tells you to do so, enter your team's decision on the tally sheet.

Choices of the teams for round 1 will be announced and the scores entered.

Task 3:

After all rounds have been completed, take a moment to note your reactions to the competition.

a. What impact did the ban on communication with the other group have?

b. Did you or others in your team become aggressive? want to compromise? feel frustrated? withdraw?

c. How might a situation like this develop in a working organization?

Task 4:

Your instructor will lead a discussion of the exercise, drawing on the insights of observers and participants' notes. A lecture on intergroup competition will conclude this exercise.

Prisoners' Dilemma Round 10 Prediction Sheet and Tally Sheet*

**Prisoners' Dilemma
Round 10 Prediction Sheet**

Predicting team	Predicted choice	
	Red team	Blue team
Red	◯	
Blue		⊗

*Adapted from: J. William Pfeiffer and John E. Jones, eds., *A Handbook of Structural Experiences for Human Relations Training,* vol. 3 (San Diego, CA: University Associates, 1974). Used with permission.

Prisoners' Dilemma Tally Sheet*

Instructions: For 10 consecutive rounds, the Red Team will choose either an A or a B, and the Blue Team will choose an X or a Y. The score for each team in a round is determined by choices of both teams, according to the following payoff schedule.

AX — Both teams win 3 points.
AY — Red Team loses 6 points; Blue Team wins 6 points.
BX — Red Team wins 6 points; Blue Teams loses 6 points.
BY — Both teams lose 3 points.

Round	Minutes	Scoresheet Choice Red Team	Blue Team	Score Red Team	Blue Team
1	3	A			
2	3	A			
	3				
4**	3 (reps)	A			
	3 (teams)				
5	3	A			
	3				
7	3	A			
8	3	A			
9†	3 (reps)	A			
	5 (teams)				
10†	3 (reps)				
	5 (teams)				

Total Score: Red: Blue:

*Adapted from: J. William Pfeiffer and John E. Jones, eds., *A Handbook of Structural Experiences for Human Relations Training,* vol. 3 (San Diego, CA: University Associates, 1974). Used with permission.

**Payoff points are doubled for this round.

†Payoff points are squared for this round (any minus signs are retained).

**Activity 8–3:
Interdivisional
Competition at the
SLO Corporation**

Objective:

To explore the dynamics of interdivisional competitions and their effect on performance.

Task 1 (Individual):

Read the following case.

Case Study: The SLO Corporation

The SLO Corporation, founded 25 years ago by Mr. Bright, is a success story. Mr. Bright, who is the president and the majority stockholder, rules with a heavy hand and is involved in all company decisions. The two major divisions, manufacturing and marketing/sales, have been in constant conflict. Over the years Mr. Bright assumed the role of the linking pin and arbitrator between the two divisions. Furthermore, at this point on any issue of importance, the two divisions communicate through him. As a successful company SLO has grown at an average annual rate of 9.5 percent in sales, which makes the company an above-average performer in the industry. The management teams of the two divisions are composed of individuals with somewhat different educational background: 65 percent of the manufacturing division managers are engineers, 15 percent with business degrees, 5 percent with some other university degrees, and 15 percent with no college education; 65 percent of the managers of marketing/sales have business-related degrees, 15 percent have engineering degrees, 5 percent have some other university degrees, and 15 percent have no degrees.

Mr. Bright's surprise sale of his stock to Steel Co. Inc. has made SLO Corporation a wholly owned subsidiary that must now operate without Mr. Bright. Known for its participative orientation, Steel Co. Inc. sends its executive vice president, Mr. Aquire, to meet with SLO people and get a clearer picture on the status of affairs, how to proceed in the process of selecting and appointing a new president (that is, should it be a person from within SLO or an outsider), and what kind of person the president should be.

Following a few meetings, Mr. Aquire sends the following short memo to members of the manufacturing and marketing/sales divisions:

I have asked your division heads to call a divisional meeting for the purpose of establishing criteria for choosing the new president. Each one of you should come to the meeting with five criteria on a piece of paper. The outcome of the meeting should be a report listing the criteria with a short description. You are also being asked to rank order the criteria.

Task 2:

The instructor will split the class into an even number of teams, each with the same number of team members. Half of the teams will represent manufacturing, and the other half will represent marketing/sales. Each individual and team is to assume the role of a member from the assigned division. Each team is to meet separately and work on its task. Each member is to make a clear copy of the criteria developed by the team; this copy is to be shared with a member of the other division.

Source: This activity is similar to many that have been developed previously. The original exercise was developed by Sherif, *Intergroup Relations and Leadership,* and further developed by many others, notably Robert Black. This activity is a further modification of one found in D. A. Kold, J. S. Osland, and I. M. Rubin, *Organizational Behavior: An Experiential Approach,* 6th ed., (Englewood Cliffs, NJ: Prentice-Hall, 1995), pp. 291–93.

(Time: 20 minutes)

Task 3:

To review the reports and evaluate them, individuals will be paired with a person from the other division. Each person is to share the report and discuss it with the partner. Your task is to decide which set of criteria is better and assign points accordingly. As a team of two, you have 100 points to assign. You must indicate a preference (for example, 54–46, 52–48, 80–20). Your task is to focus on the content of the criteria that you are evaluating.
(Time: 20 minutes)

Task 4:

a. Go back to your original team and total the number of points that each member brought back.

b. Each individual is to share the process that they have gone through. What occurred between you and the representative from the other division?

c. Brainstorm with the team about an alternative strategy that might work better.

(Time: 20 minutes)

Task 5:

Meet again with your partner from the other group to review and give each other feedback focusing on both content and process.

a. *Content* includes a discussion on your ability to focus on interests or positions, invention of options for mutual gains, and insistence on the use of objective criteria.

b. *Process* includes a reflection on the process that you have used, the way the conflict was handled, the conflict styles that were used, and what kind of negotiations were used.

c. Develop an agreement around a potential repeat of this activity. That is, knowing what you know now, how would you improve the negotiation session?

(Time: 15 minutes)

Task 6:

Meet with your original teams and discuss the following:

a. How did the team operate during the preparation for the first meeting with the representatives from the other division?

b. How did the team handle the outcomes from the first negotiations? What was the climate in the team? What effect did losing or winning have on the team?

c. How willing were you to receive feedback and help from a member of another team? How easy is it for you to work with a member from the other group to develop a winning criteria list?

d. What is the climate in the team now after the activity?

Task 7:

The instructor summarizes the activity, facilitates a class discussion, and presents a minilecture.

Part 3

Managing Individuals

Review

As we advance through the course, we need to stop periodically to examine our progress. Thus far we have explored the context within which individuals and groups function in organizational settings. Part 1 helped to establish the boundaries and process of the course: the field of study was defined; the learning community was established, and expectations were clarified; the role and effect of management and leadership were examined; and the key characteristics of the formal and human organization were discussed. Part 2 concentrated on the understanding of group behavior in organizations: the processes and key elements of group problem solving were examined; group decision making and its effectiveness were investigated; and small group development and its dynamics were reviewed. Before we progress to study the effects of individual, group, and organizational behavior elements on the management of work organizational culture, change development, and learning, we need to investigate four core concepts that are at the root of human behavior in organizational settings: personality, motivation, perception, and communication.

Preview of Part 3

We have briefly touched on the core concepts in almost every subject area we've covered. Each leadership style, for instance, includes assumptions about all four concepts: how managers perceive and understand their personality; how managers perceive their own role and that of the employees; what makes people perform best; and how to communicate with the workforce. Part 3 addresses the core concepts more directly.

Personality and personal growth are considered in Module 9. We review the nature of individual diversity, present two theories of personality, and discuss their implications in the workplace. Motivation theory is considered in Module 10. We review some of the theories of motivation and examine their implications for human behavior. The module discusses applications in the workplace, managerial approaches, and organizational policies and practices that might affect motivation. The role of perception and perceptual differences among individuals are addressed in Module 11. This module also deals with perceptual differences between different organizational levels. Module 12 addresses communications at the interpersonal level, at the small group level, and between groups. The chapter integrates the four core concepts by examining some of the barriers and inducements to interpersonal communication. Personal effectiveness in communication is one of the key skills of a manager. Exercises here help to develop active listening skills and techniques of paraphrasing, feedback, and influencing.

A road map that can aid in understanding the relationship between personality, perception, communication, motivation, and individual effectiveness is presented in the following diagram. Individual personality, diversity, and ability are at the center of understanding individual behavior in the context of the workplace. They play a major role in shaping perception, communication, and motivation. All four core concepts are essential to understanding and managing individual behavior.

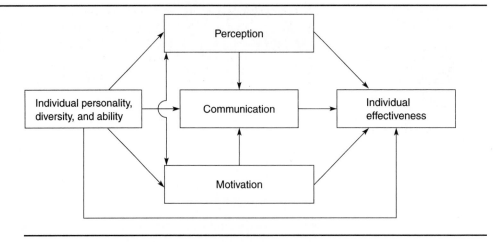

9

Personality and Personal Growth

Learning Objectives

After completing this module, you should be able to

1. Identify the major elements that influence the individual's self-concept and work behavior.
2. Describe the nature and roots of individual differences.
3. Define personality and the basic dimensions of personality differences.
4. Explain the relationship between personal growth and individual effectiveness.
5. Appreciate the role that learners can play in facilitating their own personal growth.
6. Explain the challenges of managing the changing workforce.

Module Outline

Premodule Preparation
    Activity 9–1: Cultural Diversity: An Initial Exploration
Introduction
The Nature of Individual Differences
    Cultural Diversity
    Ethnicity and Race
    Demographic Diversity
Personality
    Personality Theories: An Overview
    Personality Types
    The Big Five Personality Theory
Human Development and Organizational Life
    Themes of Personal Growth

A Model for Continued Growth and Effectiveness

Using the Model for Developing New Behavior Goals

Human Development in the 1990s and Beyond

Summary

Key Term and Concepts

Study Questions

Endnotes

Activity 9–2: Exploring Individual Personality Profile: The Big Five Locator Questionnaire

Activity 9–3: Rough Times at Nomura

Optional Activities on the WWW

Activity 9–4W: Learning about Self and Others: Personal Reflection via "Collage"

Activity 9–5W: Transactional Analysis in the Work Situation

Activity 9–6W: Exploring Individual Personality Profile: The Keirsey Temperament Sorter

Premodule Preparation

Activity 9–1:
Cultural Diversity:
An Initial Exploration

Objectives:

a. To explore the individual's cultural profile.

b. To increase the individual's awareness of cultural diversity.

c. To explore issues associated with the management of diversity.

Task 1:

We all feel that in some way we are different from others. The worksheet for Activity 9–1 asks you to explore the differences. Use the worksheet to take notes.
(Time: 10 minutes for individuals to think about their experience and jot down notes)

Task 2:

Each participant shares these thoughts with a small group. After each has done so, discuss the common elements that seem to emerge. Have a spokesperson make a list.

Task 3:

Spokesperson reports findings to the class.

Source: Adapted and modified from L. Gardenswartz and A. Gowe, *Managing Diversity,* (Burr Ridge, IL: Richard D. Irwin, 1993).

Worksheet for Activity 9–1

The following list identifies different dimensions of culture. Write down some notes about cultural differences you have encountered in each of the dimensions listed.

Dimensions of Culture   **Examples of Ways in Which You Are Different from Others.**

1. Communication and language
   - Language/dialect — Philadelphia Accent
   - Gestures/expressions/tones — Smile
   - ■

2. Dress and appearance
   - Clothing — Whatever is clean/free
   - Hair — Smooth
   - Grooming — brushed once A DAy
   - ■

3. Values
   - Privacy
   - Respect — listen to others
   - ■
   - ■

4. Beliefs
   - Social order/authority
   - ■
   - ■

5. Sense of self and space
   - Distance — I like my space
   - Touch
   - Formal/informal
   - Open/closed
   - ■

6. Time and time consciousness
   - Promptness — laid back
   - Pace
   - ■

7. Work ethics
   - ■
   - ■
   - ■

8. _____

■ _____

■ _____

■ _____

9. _____

■ _____

■ _____

Introduction

Any attempt to learn why people behave as they do in work settings requires some basic understanding of individual differences. When confronted with identical situations, individuals do not necessarily behave in the same way. Managers and employees alike must comprehend and appreciate individual differences in order to be effective.

One of the most dominant features of individual differences is personality. **Personality** is a set of distinctive traits and dimensions that can be used to characterize the individual. Many of the other causes of individual diversity seem to be an integral part of the changing nature of the labor markets. Some argue that individuals who will work together in the future "will be less alike with respect to gender, cultural background, and age."[1] These differences are important because they are associated with differences in perspectives, lifestyles, attitudes, values, behaviors, and thought processes and patterns. This module explores cultural diversity, demographic diversity, and personality as sources of individual differences.

The Nature of Individual Differences

The term **diversity** has multiple interpretations. Here we follow Cox and Beale's definition, which states that "diversity is a mix of people in one social system who have distinctly different, socially relevant group affiliation."[2] A *social system* can be defined in many ways: countries, cities, organizations, work teams, and so on. Furthermore, there are many kinds of group affiliations, such as gender, professional groups, and religious groups. A *socially relevant group* is simply the natural creation and/or construction process of meaning that occurs when a group of people interact. **Cultural diversity** occurs when these group affiliations not only are socially relevant but also have specific cultural significance and are differentiated from other groups based on behavioral norms, values, language, ways of thinking, and so on.

Effective managerial practice requires recognizing and taking into account individual behavior differences when managing individuals, teams, and/or units. Understanding individual differences means that the manager must be able to observe and recognize the differences, understand the sources of the differences, examine the potential relationships between the different elements that influence individual behavior, and take the appropriate action that will result in improved individual and team effectiveness as well as foster personal growth. Many elements seem to have a potential influence on the individual's self-concept and work behavior: the individual's basic demographics such as gender, age, education, and work experience; the individual's abilities and skills such as intellectual ability, physical ability, and work-related competencies; the individual's personality; cultural background such as ethnicity, race, values, and beliefs; family dynamics such as marital status and number of dependents; organizational features such as leadership, structure, and policies; and work design features such as job design, tasks, and rewards. Figure 9–1 provides a partial schema of the elements that influence the individual's self-concept and work behavior. Next we discuss in depth some of the elements. Others are discussed elsewhere in this book.

Cultural Diversity

A diverse workforce typically includes individuals with a variety of cultural backgrounds. Cultural diversity is one of the most noted recent changes in the workforce. As Activity 9–1 illustrated, individuals seem to have diverse cultural profiles. In the North American context, *Workforce 2000* projections indicate that during this decade only 58 percent of new entrants into the labor market will come from the majority population of white people born in the United States; 22 percent of new entrants are expected to be immigrants, and the remainder being mostly African-American and Hispanic-Americans. Meanwhile, the European Community (EC) agreements are likely to change the nature of the workforce throughout the European continent, as people will be able to move easily between countries and search for employment wherever they desire.

Figure 9–1   **The Individual's Work Behavior: A Partial Schematic**

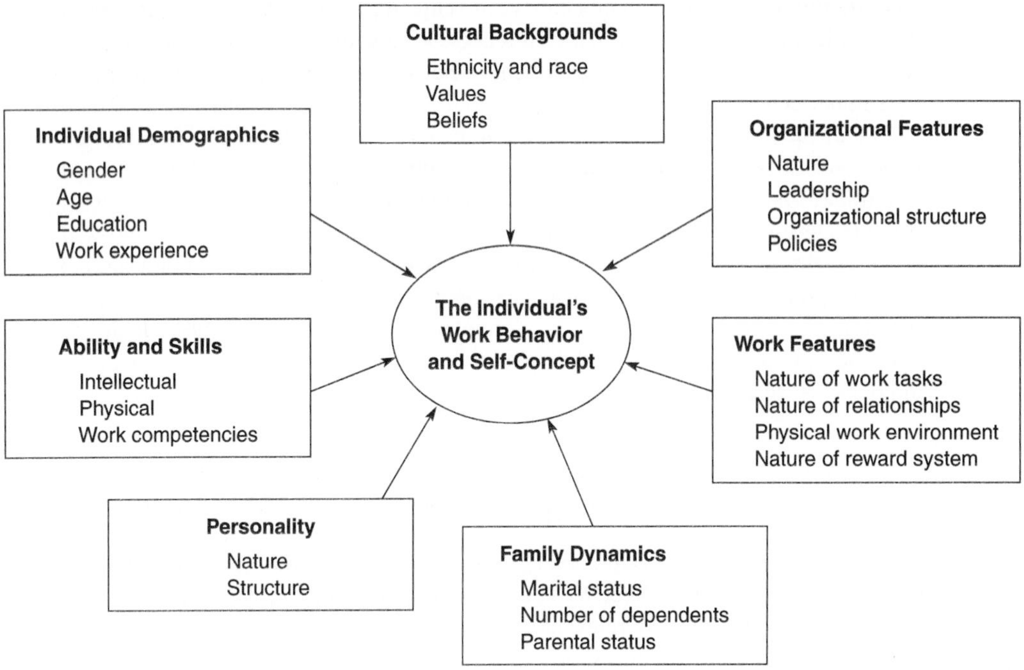

Cultural Backgrounds
Ethnicity and race
Values
Beliefs

Individual Demographics
Gender
Age
Education
Work experience

Organizational Features
Nature
Leadership
Organizational structure
Policies

The Individual's Work Behavior and Self-Concept

Ability and Skills
Intellectual
Physical
Work competencies

Work Features
Nature of work tasks
Nature of relationships
Physical work environment
Nature of reward system

Personality
Nature
Structure

Family Dynamics
Marital status
Number of dependents
Parental status

Cultures have causes that are easily experienced but more difficult to describe. At a surface level the concept of culture invokes images of exotic customs, religions, foods, clothing, and lifestyles. At a deeper level culture includes systems of values, ways of interpreting the world, social structures, and ways of interpersonal relations. By and large, the concept of culture has come to be associated with anthropological thinking. The word **culture** derives in a very roundabout way from the past participle of the Latin verb *colere* (to cultivate) and draws some of its meaning from the association with the tilling of the soil. As such the evolutionary, integrative process within human systems through which values and belief systems are established and mental road maps of the environment are created are likely to have major influences on the behavior of the individual.

The growing diversity of cultural backgrounds that shapes individuals' behavior is one of the major challenges facing today's managers and organizations. When people with different cultural backgrounds, values, and beliefs come together at the workplace, misunderstandings and conflicts inevitably occur. For example, employees who behave according to the cultural adage "the squeaky wheel gets the grease" will behave differently from employees who were taught that "the nail that sticks out gets hammered down."[3] Employees behaving according to the latter adage may be viewed as ineffective by the former group of employees.

Ethnicity and Race

According to the Bureau of Labor Statistics, one-third of the newcomers to the U.S. workforce each year are minority group members. For example, from 1982 to 2005 the Asian female workforce population will increase by 135 percent, the Asian male by 112 percent, the Hispanic female by 164 percent, and the male by 129 percent. Minority group members also face both the glass ceiling and *racism,* the notion that a particular race is superior to all others.

Within the large society and an organization, three basic interrelated forms of racism can be identified: (1) **individual racism**—the extent to which a person holds values, feelings, and attitudes and/or engages in behavior that promotes the person's own racial group as superior; (2) **cultural racism**—the extent to which groups believe that their cultural features and achievements are superior to those of other cultural groups; and (3) institutional racism—the extent to which institutions and organizations create rules, laws, policies and procedures that serve to maintain the dominant status of and control by one group.[4]

Two major factors compound the need for increased attention to cultural diversity. First, the changing nature of the workplace requires that employees interact more with each other and with different external constituencies such as suppliers and customers.[5] Second, the growing competitiveness worldwide requires understanding and sensitivity to an increasing variety of cultures, values, and belief systems in other continents.[6] Activity 9–3 ("Rough Times at Nomura") illustrates some problems that arise in a cross-cultural work environment and the relationship between cultural diversity and employee work behavior.

Demographic Diversity

The demographic composition of the workforce is changing around the world. A sizable amount of research indicates that this broad category labeled *individual demographics* (including basic variables such as gender, age, marital status, number of dependents, and tenure with the firm) has a significant influence on the behavior of individuals at the workplace. Of growing interest are gender and age diversity.

Gender Diversity

In the early 1960s men were receiving about 95 percent of the MBA degrees and 90 percent of the bachelor's degrees awarded in business. Thirty years later the picture is quite different. In 1993 women received approximately 32 percent of the MBA degrees as well as 48 percent of the bachelor's degrees awarded in business. The workforce of the year 2000 is expected to be more balanced than that of 1960 with respect to gender.[7]

Research suggests that few, if any, important differences between males and females affect their job performance. There are, for example, no consistent findings about male–female differences in decision-making and problem-solving abilities, analytical skills, competitiveness, motivation, or leadership.[8] Yet in 1990 women represented 35 percent of the population of management and administrators but held only one-half of 1 percent of the top jobs in major corporations. In a poll of 241 *Fortune* 1000 CEOs, nearly 80 percent of these CEOs said that certain barriers kept women from reaching the top. Of the 80 percent, 81 percent identified stereotypes, preconceptions, and male-dominated corporate culture as problems that women face. Yet while gender-based segregation within organizations seems to gradually decrease, gender inequality seems to be a major managerial challenge that requires continuous improvement.[9]

Age Diversity

In 1983 about one in eight Americans was age 65 or older. In 1993 the ratio was about one in seven. It is estimated that the ratio will fall to nearly one in five in 30 years. The trend that America is aging is clear. Federal legislation has all but wiped out mandatory retirement rules. Most employees do not have to retire at 65. Furthermore, a large proportion of the workforce cannot afford to retire even if a worker so desires. Accordingly, the average age of the American workforce is being pushed up. A recent comprehensive analysis of the research literature found that productivity actually increases as employees grow older.[10]

The combination of changes in the age distribution of employees and new flatter organization structures means that four generations of workers can find themselves working side by side. This potential age diversity of four generations presents a major set of managerial challenges in terms of managing four generations of value sets, belief systems, work norms, work attitudes, and physical and mental functioning, not to mention vast differences of work experiences.

Personality

Individual diversity is also rooted in the person's personality. Personality is an individual difference that lends consistency to a person's behavior. The term *personality* has two quite different meanings.[11] Sometimes it refers to the way a person is perceived by friends, family members, peers, supervisors, and subordinates. This meaning is derived from perception and judgment of the individual by others based on social interactions and reputation. The second meaning refers to the underlying, unseen structures and processes "inside" the person that explain why the individual behaves in a certain manner. The first meaning refers to a person's public reputation whereas the second refers to one's private inner nature.[12] This module is concerned primarily with the inner structures and processes that cause the individual to behave in a certain manner. *Personality* is defined as

a relatively stable set of characteristics, tendencies, and temperaments that have been significantly formed by inheritance and by social, cultural, and environmental factors. This set of variables determines the commonalities and differences in the behavior of individuals (thoughts, feelings, and actions) that have continuity over time and that may not be easily understood as the sole result of the social and biological pressures of the moment.[13]

Sources of Personality Differences

Although many elements contribute to the development of each individual's personality, as can be seen from the preceding definition, two major sources of personality differences can be identified: heredity and environment. The heredity dimension refers to the notion that genetic imprints influence the individual's personality and its development. The environmental dimension refers to the environmental context, such as culture, family, group membership, and life experience, that plays a major role in shaping the individual's personality. Historically, sharp disagreement existed among scholars about which dimension plays a more critical role. Those holding the extreme *nature* position argued that personality is inherited. Those holding the extreme *nurture* position argued that personality is determined by the person's experiences. Recent research suggests a more balanced view, advocating that heredity and environment as well as the interplay between them play critical roles in shaping personality. Yet the scientific controversy is far from over.[14]

Personality Theories: An Overview

Psychological research and practice has produced a wide range of personality theories. It is beyond the scope of this module (and this course for that matter) to review the different theories. Here is an attempt to provide the shell and theoretical context of personality theories and an in-depth examination of two complementary theories. Four major clusters of personality theories seem to influence the study of personality in organizations:

Trait theories state that to understand individuals we must break down behavior patterns into series of observable traits.[15]

Psychodynamics theories emphasize the unconscious determinants of behavior—for example, Sigmund Freud's theory that views personality as the interaction between three elements of personality: the id, the ego, and the superego.[16]

Humanistic theories emphasize individual growth and improvement—for example, Carl Rogers's theory that all people have the basic drive toward self-actualization, which is the quest of the individual to be all he or she can be.[17]

Integrative theories describe personality as a composite of an individual's psychological processes such as emotions, cognitions, attitudes, expectancies, and fantasies.[18]

In the context of organizational studies, many relevant personality characteristics were identified. In recent years few conceptual frameworks for understanding individual differences have become very popular among organizational behavior educators, students, and managers. Two comparable frameworks—the Myers–Briggs model and Keirsey's temperament sorter (both rooted in the personality theory developed by Carl Jung)—have been translated into sets of concepts and tools that have practical applications.

Personality Types

Carl Jung (1875–1961) is second only to Sigmund Freud among modern psychological thinkers. Jung started out as Freud's disciple and broke away to form his own unique ideas, many of which are taken for granted today. Jung's contributions to the field of psychology include his work on psychological types. He coined the terms *introversion* and *extroversion* and is the father of the work continued by Katherine Briggs, who formalized one of the first *type indicators*.

Jung believed that we have an inborn preference for how we function just as we have a preference for using one hand over the other. The preference for how we function is a characteristic, so we may be "typed" by these preferences. Although various researchers have contributed to Jung's work by refining and reorganizing the preferences in various combinations, 16 basic types have been identified from his model. David Keirsey grouped the 16 types into four temperaments, each of which consists of four types that share similar characteristics. The result of this scholarly work is an understandable model of human personality that can be verified by simple observation of friends and family. By reading descriptions of each type, people can identify and predict both the strengths and weaknesses of themselves and others.

Four basic preferences in the way we approach life can be identified (see Figure 9–2). The term *preference* means that we have an inborn tendency to behave a certain way. This does not mean that a preferred way of behaving will be the *only* way we function; it's just the most comfortably favored way. It's the same as being born with a tendency to use either our right or left hand, which results in our developing one over the other. We can only use the nondominant hand in an awkward way while the dominant hand is used without thinking. Some personality functions and behaviors come second nature to us and define our personality type.

Figure 9–2
The Four Pairs of Preferences Based on the Myers–Briggs Type Indicator (MBTI)

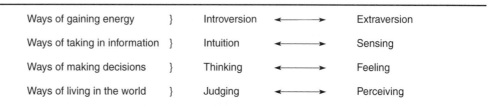

Ways of gaining energy	}	Introversion	⟵⟶	Extraversion
Ways of taking in information	}	Intuition	⟵⟶	Sensing
Ways of making decisions	}	Thinking	⟵⟶	Feeling
Ways of living in the world	}	Judging	⟵⟶	Perceiving

Introversion or Extraversion: The first preference is demonstrated when an individual is *extroverted* and attends more to the outer world of things and people or else is *introverted* and attends more to the inner world of the experience (a private world of ideas, principles, values, and feeling). As in all the personality preferences, one does not exclude the other—a person will attend to both the outer and inner world but will be most at home in one as opposed to the other. An extrovert will use more energy when attending primarily to outside events, while the introvert will use more energy in pondering his own thoughts or feelings.

Extroverts get their batteries charged by being sociable and the "life of the party," while introverts seem to draw their energies from more solitary activities shared with few or no other people. There are three times as many extroverts as there are introverts, which may explain the tendency for pop psychology books to sell extroversion as the "healthy" preference. This conclusion, of course, is false.

Intuition or Sensing: There are two ways to perceive information about the inner and outer world: through one's senses or through one's intuition. A preference to perceive with the senses (touch, smell, sight, hearing, and taste) is especially useful for gathering the facts of a situation. Intuition on the other hand shows meanings, relationships, and possibilities that are beyond the reach of the senses. Intuition is especially useful for perceiving what one might do about a situation. People tend to operate and become expert at one over the other.

Thinking or Feeling: People not only take in information but also make decisions based on how they think and feel about the issues and people involved. Decisions based on thinking utilize judgments that predict the logical results of any particular action in an impersonal and analytical way. Feeling-based decisions do not require logic; only personal values and the impact on others are primarily important. Those who put more confidence in decisions based on feeling typically become sympathetic and skillful in dealing with people as opposed to that part of the world that requires cold-hearted, matter-of-fact decisions.

Judging or Perceiving: As maturation takes place, one of the perceptive preferences (intuition or sensing) will become further developed, and information will be received more confidentially in one of these two ways. Judgments based on this information will also be made by one of two ways (feeling or thinking), and more trust will be put in one over the other.

Not only will an individual favor one of two ways within each of these preferences, but he or she will also rely on one type of preference to deal with the world. Some people will use the taking in of information (perceptive) more often than making decisions (judging). One type will be more comfortable in making judgments (thinking or feeling) before all the information about a situation is completely perceived. This type lives in a planned, decisive, orderly way of life. Others rely mainly on the perceptive process (intuition or sensing) and live in a flexible, spontaneous, reactive way.

The four preferences or tendencies form the basis of the 16 personality categories. If you are interested, most advisement and counseling centers in universities have access to the Myers–Briggs and/or Keirsey instruments. Use of the instruments is controlled through professionally trained people who can administer, score, and interpret the data with you.

A variation of the Myers–Briggs test can be found on the Web at http://www.keirsey.com/cgi-bin/keirsey/newkts.cgi. This variation—the Keirsey Temperament Sorter II is based on the development and the research carried out by Dr. David Keirsey and his associates. The site provides additional information about references and sources of interest.

The Big Five Personality Theory

The past decade witnessed a resurgence of usage and support for a trait theory of personality—the Five Factor Model (FFM).[19] The FFM has received increased attention because it can withstand every kind of statistical analysis. The FFM—popularly referred to as the "Big Five"—is founded on the discovery that people describe themselves and others in terms of five fundamental dimensions of individual differences.[20] Although some differences in the specific labeling of the Big Five are debated in the literature, there is agreement about the Big Five factor structure.[21]

The Big Five factors (and prototypical characteristics for each factor) are extraversion (sociable, talkative, assertive, ambitious, and active); agreeableness (good-natured, cooperative, and trusting); conscientiousness (responsible, dependable, able to plan, organized, persistent, and achievement oriented); adjustment/emotional stability (calm, secure, and not nervous); openness to experience (imaginative, artistically sensitive, and intellectual). Figure 9–3 captures the five dimensions and some of the prototypical characteristics at the end of the continuum of each factor.

In addition to providing a framework to explore personality dimensions, research on the Big Five has also found important relationships between these personality dimensions and job performance. For example, a study that looked at a broad spectrum of occupations found that conscientiousness predicts job performance for all the occupational groups studied. "The preponderance of evidence shows that individuals who are dependable, reliable, careful, thorough, able to plan, organized, hardworking, persistent, and achievement oriented tend to have higher job performance in most if not

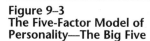

Figure 9–3
The Five-Factor Model of
Personality—The Big Five

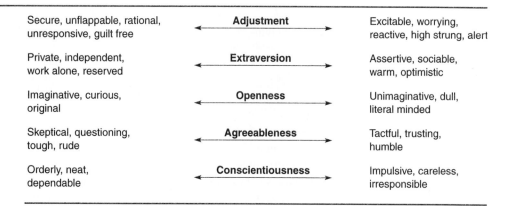

all occupations."[22] For the other personality dimensions, predictability depends on both the occupational group and the performance criteria. This study is one reason that the area of personality testing and employee selection seems to be regaining credibility and increased utilization.[23] Activity 9–3 at the end of the module enables you to use the Big Five model of personality to explore your individual profile.

Human Development and Organizational Life

Self-learning, self-learning competencies, self-management, and self-managed teams are part of personal growth. Some argue that the early 1990s can be characterized as the rebirth of the personal growth movement that was a dominant force during the 1960s and 1970s. The area of **personal growth** involves (1) understanding personality (yours and others) and its influence in the interpersonal communication process, (2) establishing personal goals that make you a winner in the sense of better fulfillment of needs and ambitions, and (3) developing ways of thinking and behavioral skills needed to achieve goals.

Themes of
Personal Growth

Several recurring themes can be found in most of the personal growth approaches, including the New Age human potential movement and the "psychic boom" of the late 1980s.

Theme 1: "If I don't achieve what I want, it's my own damned fault." The idea is that you can achieve almost any realistic goal you set if you concentrate on changing your own behavior and do not blame lack of progress on what is "out there." If your needs are not being satisfied, consider it your own fault. "It is not your family; not your girlfriend, wife, boyfriend, or husband; not your ethnic background; not the 'establishment'; not your boss; not your teacher, or anything else! You are in command! Don't let the world happen to you!" It is essential for the individual to recognize that in all situations, a choice of actions exists if a deliberate attempt is made to think out alternatives.

Theme 2: "I am being programmed by someone else's tape." The idea is that you have been programmed by your early life experience to think in specific patterns, which are not questioned by the individual. The goal is for the individual to become more aware of the nature of the programming and to rewrite it to achieve his or her own goals. Self-determination and choice are relevant.

Theme 3: "I have tremendous potential for growth." Presumably most of us use only a small percentage of our potential talents and abilities. Although everyone is innately creative, few ever consider themselves to be. These forces within us need to be released and nurtured.

Theme 4: "I will never feel good about others until I feel good about myself." The programming we receive in childhood includes all the things we must or must not do to prevent expression of all those terrible, socially unacceptable urges such as lust. Since the urges are lurking beneath the surface, we have some feelings of rejection toward ourselves. We must learn to know, accept, respect, and love ourselves before we can be fully tolerant of and enjoy others. This theme is basic to improved interpersonal relations. "I am my own best friend" is a subtheme.

Theme 5: "What are my true values?" Being aware of and committed to a set of values is necessary for self-acceptance and goal setting.

Theme 6: "Where am I now? Where do I want to be?" The success of personal-growth training is indicated solely by the individual's ability to set new goals and try new behaviors that will make achievement possible. Only by the actual behavior attempts can goals be attained. Intellectual learning alone does not usually lead to change. You must practice swinging the club if you want to lower your golf score.

A Model for Continued Growth and Effectiveness

How could you develop your own behavior change program? The most basic principle to follow is this: The way you think about yourself determines the way you feel and the way you behave. So if you want to change the way you behave, you need to change the way you think about yourself. This interrelationship can be extended to three areas: the cognitive, the communicative, and the behavioral. (See Figure 9–4.)

Cognitive. The cognitive area pertains to the way you think about yourself, the basic beliefs you have and assumptions you make about the way you are, and what you can do. Whatever the structure of this complex interrelated set of thoughts, it has developed over a long time, it is well established, and it is rigid. Changes here can lead to changes in behavior. As we will see, the reverse can also be true.

Figure 9–4
A Model for
Continued Growth

		Change Areas	
	Cognitive	Communicative	Behavioral
Processes	Way you think about yourself and others	Way you talk to yourself	Way you behave
Goal Activities	Imagining television scenes of self/others; changing channel to new script	Directing your new script	Trying specific behaviors from new script

Communicative. You talk to yourself all the time. The way you talk to yourself influences your thinking and behavior. Change the way you talk to yourself, and you can change your behavior. We once knew a real estate developer who carried a card in his wallet that programmed him for the day and its events. He would read it to himself when he started his day: "I will treat every problem that arises not as a source of frustration but as a challenge for new learning or for creative solution making." He would read the card at lunch and critique his morning activities to see to what extent he had followed the programming. He claimed that it and other such personal "programs" had gained him much success.

Behavioral. The way you act determines the way you think about yourself. If you never speak up in a group, you may say to yourself you are shy or do not want to be embarrassed.

Thus one behavior reinforces the other. However, if you change your behavior, you change the way you think about yourself. This interaction was dramatically observed in a young foreign service wife who found that her role required her to be a hostess to foreigners and other Americans of the diplomatic community. At first she resisted and hated the role—it was too much work, she did not have the skills, and so on. After living through this forced role for four years, she was overheard telling a new wife how she would love the role once she learned it. Having been forced to perform in the role, she found the rewards of being an excellent hostess had changed the way she thought about herself and, we presume, the way in which she communicated with herself.

Using the Model for Developing New Behavior Goals

Note that the bottom half of Figure 9–4 describes goal areas that will lead to change. In the cognitive area, it is often suggested that you can set up an imaginary television screen on which you play reruns of your present script, of the way you are behaving with important others or with people in groups, and determine what it is that you don't like or is causing you problems. Now you design a new script to show you on that screen the way you would like to be. Next you select some specific behavior you want to develop and go out and try it. For example, you may be saying, "I see John as constantly belittling my view because he is in accounting [the "real" world], and I am an English literature major [the "unreal" world]. I would like an equal relationship so he respects my views and I respect his. Next time he belittles me, I will tell him how I feel and insist my views are realistic and that he understand what I am saying," and so forth. Once this is done and John has shown respect for the way you stood up for yourself, the way you think of yourself and talk to yourself will change, and it should be easier to stand up for your views.

In another example a student who never talked in class discussions decided her future in the business world would not be advanced by never saying anything in meetings. She resolved to ask one question of the professor in each class for the new week. It did not always work, but she found herself saying to herself, Why didn't you do it, dummy? or What are you going to do in the next class, dummy? She had a number of victories in terms of asked questions and got others in class involved in discussions. This behavior change led to more confidence and a willingness to try other things— all three areas (cognitive, communicative, and behavioral) were interacting to help achieve the goals.

In using the model, remember the following:

1. Be specific about the exact behavior you want to develop or change. Just deciding to be different does not result in success. The more specific you are, the greater your chance of success, and you will be able to adjust your behavior to change other specific behaviors.

2. Don't be too ambitious and try too much. Try a little at a time to increase the chance of positive results.

3. Be patient and tolerant with yourself. Find ways of rewarding yourself for successes.

4. Never stop trying.

Here is a good method to try: The next time you hear yourself complaining, say to yourself, Complaining is only a way of reducing pressure by letting off steam. Now what are you going to do about it? If you're only interested in complaining, I don't want to hear about it. If you want to tell me how you feel and how it hurts, I'll listen as long as you tell me what you are going to do about it. What specific actions are you going to plan and take? Good luck!

Human Development in the 1990s and Beyond

The human potential movement of the 1960s and 1970s emphasized getting in touch with feelings as a way to grow. The movement died down in the late 1970s and early 1980s; but by the late 1980s and early 1990s, it was back in full force riding the crest of the "creativity" wave. The pressures of international competition forced organizations to exploit any lead that might spawn innovations and increased productivity, and the human potential movement was seen as a tool for freeing executives, managers, and professionals to think more creatively and overcome self-defeating attitudes. Personal and interpersonal effectiveness remained an important aspect of human development during the late 1990s.

Summary

Many factors influence the individual's work behavior. The first part of this module provided a partial schema/road map of the factors that influence the individual's self-concept and work behavior. We have explored the nature of individual differences. Of the multiple sources of individual diversity, this module examined the cultural and demographic dimensions. The changing nature of organizations, coupled with the changing nature of the labor force, is likely to present increasing challenges for managers. The road map presented can be used as a way to begin to map out the forces so that a more holistic understanding of the issues will emerge.

One of the key dimensions of the individual's self-concept and work behavior is the individual's personality. The second part of the module focuses on personality theories and models. Following a short overview of personality theories, we focused on Jung's personality theory that provides the basis for two widely used models of personality types—Myers–Briggs and Keirsey–Bates ("Keirsey's temperament sorter"). We also introduced the Big Five theory, which has been gaining empirical research support in recent years, as an alternative and relatively new way to map out personality attributes.

Key Terms and Concepts

Age diversity

Big Five personality theory

Cultural diversity

Culture

Cultural racism

Demographic diversity

Diversity

Ethnic diversity

Four life positions of personality development

Gender diversity

Individual differences

Individual racism

Jung's theory of personality

Personal growth

Personality

Personality types

The four preferences

Study Questions

1. Identify and discuss the nature of individual diversity.
2. Discuss how cultural diversity and demographic diversity influence individuals' self-concept and work behavior.
3. Identify and discuss the key dimensions of individual effectiveness.
4. How can a manager influence individual effectiveness?
5. What are some managerial skills needed to influence an employee's effectiveness?
6. Briefly discuss the four preferences/personality types as identified by Carl Jung.
7. Compare and contrast the Jung and Big Five personality theories.
8. How can the Big Five personality theory be useful in an organizational setting? Provide specific examples.

Endnotes

1. See, for example, S. E. Jackson and E. B. Alvarez, "Working through Diversity as a Strategic Imperative," in S. E. Jackson (ed.), *Diversity in the Workplace,* (New York: Guilford Press, 1992); M. McKendall, "A Course in Work-Force Diversity: Strategies and Issues," *Journal of Management Education* 18, no. 4 (1994), pp. 407–23.

2. T. Cox Jr. and R. L. Beale, *Developing Competency to Manage Diversity,* (San Francisco: Berrett-Koehler Publishers, Inc., 1997).

3. Jackson and Alvarez, "Working through Diversity."

4. J. V. Gallos, V. J. Ramsey, et al., *Teaching Diversity,* (San Francisco: Jossey-Bass, 1996).

5. C. Gardenswartz and A. Rowe, *Managing Diversity,* (Homewood, IL: Richard D. Irwin, 1993).

6. See, for example, J. P. Fernandez, *The Diversity Advantage,* (New York: Lexington Books, 1993).

7. G. N. Powell, *Gender and Diversity in the Workplace,* (Thousand Oaks, CA: Sage, 1994).

8. See, for example, G. N. Powell, *Women and Men in Management,* (Beverly Hills, CA: Sage, 1988).

9. See, for example, J. A. Jacobs, *Gender Inequality at Work,* (Thousand Oaks, CA: Sage, 1994).

10. D. A. Waldman and B. J. Avolio, "A Meta-Analysis of Age Difference in Job Performance," *Journal of Applied Psychology* (1986), pp. 33–38.

11. See, for example, R. T. Hogan, "Personality and Personality Measurement," in M. D. Dunnette and L. M. Hough (eds.), *Handbook of Industrial and Organizational Psychology,* (Palo Alto, CA: Consulting Psychologists Press, 1991), pp. 873–919.

12. R. L. Hughes, R. C. Ginnett, and G. J. Curphy, *Leadership: Enhancing the Lessons of Experience,* (Burr Ridge, IL: Richard D. Irwin, 1993).

13. This definition is based on S. F. Maddi, *Personality Theories: A Comparative Analysis,* (Burr Ridge, IL: Dorsey, 1980), p. 10.

14. M. Snyder and N. Cantor, "Understanding Personality and Social Behavior: A Functionalist Strategy," in D. T. Gilbert, S. T. Fiske, and G. Lindzey (eds.), *The Handbook of Social Psychology,* (New York: McGraw-Hill, 1998), pp. 635–79.

15. Hundreds of traits have been identified over the years. See, for example, R. R. McCrae "Why I Advocate the Five-Factor Model," in D. M. Buss and N. Cantor (eds.), *Personality Psychology: Recent Trends and Emerging Directions,* (New York: Springer-Verlag, 1989), pp. 237–345.

16. S. Freud, *An Outline of Psychoanalysis,* (New York: Norton, 1949).

17. C. Rogers, *On Becoming a Person,* (Boston: Houghton Mifflin, 1970).

18. See, for example, D. D. Clark and R. Hoyle, "A Theoretical Solution to the Problem of Personality-Situational Interaction," *Personality and Individual Differences* 9 (1988), pp. 133–38.

19. J. M. Digman, "Higher-Order Factor of the Big Five," *Journal of Personality and Social Psychology* 73, no. 6 (1997), pp. 1246–56.

20. See, for example, J. M. Digman, "Personality Structure: Emergence of the Five-Factor Model," *Annual Review of Psychology* 41 (1990), pp. 417–40; L. R. Goldberg, "The Development of Markers for the Big-Five Factor Structure," *Psychological Assessment* 4 (1992), pp. 26–42.

21. L. R. Goldberg, "The Structure of Phenotypic Personality Traits," *American Psychologist* 48, no. 1 (1993), pp. 26–34.

22. See, for example, M. R. Barrick and J. P. Strauss, "Validity of Observer Ratings and the Big Five Personality Factors," *Journal of Applied Psychology,* 1994, pp. 272–80; M. R. Marrick and M. K. Mount, "The Big Five Personality Dimensions and Job Performance: A Meta Analysis," *Personnel Psychology* 44 (1991), pp. 1–26.

23. See, for example, C. D. Fisher and G. J. Boyle, "Personality and Employee Selection: Credibility Regained," *Asia Pacific Journal of Human Resources* 35, no. 2 (1998), pp. 26–40; M. C. Ashton, "Personality and Job Performance: The Importance of Narrow Traits," *Journal of Organizational Behavior* 19 (1998), pp. 289–303.

Activity 9–2:
Exploring Individual
Personality Profile:
The Big Five Locator
Questionnaire[1]

Objectives:

a. To investigate a trait model of personality.

b. To enable students to begin to examine their personality profile.

Task 1:

a. Complete the Big Five Locator Questionnaire. On each numerical scale indicate which point is generally more descriptive of you. If the two terms are equally descriptive, mark the midpoint.

b. Complete the scoring sheet, following the instructions.

c. Place your scores on the Big Five Locator Interpretation Sheet.

[1]The Big Five Locator is a quick assessment tool to be used with an instructor and willing learners. Care should be take to follow up this profile with a more reliable personality assessment instrument. This instrument was developed by P. J. Howard, P. L. Medina, and J. M. Howard "The Big Five Locator: A Quick Assessment Tool for Consultants and Trainers," in J. W. Pfeiffer (ed.), *The 1996 Annual* vol. 1, Training (San Diego: Pfeiffer & Company, 1996), pp. 119–22. Reprinted with permission. Copyright by Jossey-Bass Inc., Publishers. All rights reserved.

The Big Five Locator Questionnaire

Instructions: On each numerical scale that follows, indicate which point is generally more descriptive of you. If the two terms are equally descriptive, mark the midpoint.

1.	Eager	5	4	3	2	1	Calm
2.	Prefer Being with Other People	5	4	3	2	1	Prefer Being Alone
3.	A Dreamer	5	4	3	2	1	No Nonsense
4.	Courteous	5	4	3	2	1	Abrupt
5.	Neat	5	4	3	2	1	Messy
6.	Cautious	5	4	3	2	1	Confident
7.	Optimistic	5	4	3	2	1	Pessimistic
8.	Theoretical	5	4	3	2	1	Practical
9.	Generous	5	4	3	2	1	Selfish
10.	Decisive	5	4	3	2	1	Open Ended
11.	Discouraged	5	4	3	2	1	Upbeat
12.	Exhibitionist	5	4	3	2	1	Private
13.	Follow Imagination	5	4	3	2	1	Follow Authority
14.	Warm	5	4	3	2	1	Cold
15.	Stay Focused	5	4	3	2	1	Easily Distracted
16.	Easily Embarrassed	5	4	3	2	1	Don't Give a Darn
17.	Outgoing	5	4	3	2	1	Cool
18.	Seek Novelty	5	4	3	2	1	Seek Routine
19.	Team Player	5	4	3	2	1	Independent
20.	A Preference for Order	5	4	3	2	1	Comfortable with Chaos
21.	Distractible	5	4	3	2	1	Unflappable
22.	Conversational	5	4	3	2	1	Thoughtful
23.	Comfortable with Ambiguity	5	4	3	2	1	Prefer Things Clear-Cut
24.	Trusting	5	4	3	2	1	Skeptical
25.	On Time	5	4	3	2	1	Procrastinate

Scoring The Big Five Questionnaire

Instructions:

1. Find the sum of the circled numbers on the *first* row of each of the five-line groupings (Row 1 + Row 6 + Row 11 + Row 16 + Row 21 = _____). This is your raw score for "adjustment." Circle the number in the ADJUSTMENT: column of the Score Conversion Sheet that corresponds to this raw score.

2. Find the sum of the circled numbers on the *second* row of each of the five-line groupings (Row 2 + Row 7 + Row 12 + Row 17 + Row 22 = _____). This is your raw score for "sociability." Circle the number in the SOCIABIL-ITY: column of the Score Conversion Sheet that corresponds to this raw score.

3. Find the sum of the circled numbers on the *third* row of each of the five-line groupings (Row 3 + Row 8 + Row 13 + Row 18 + Row 23 = _____). This is your raw score for "openness." Circle the number in the OPENNESS: column of the Score Conversion Sheet that corresponds to this raw score.

4. Find the sum of the circled numbers on the *fourth* row of each of the five-line groupings (Row 4 + Row 9 + Row 14 + Row 19 + Row 24 = _____). This is your raw score for "agreeableness." Circle the number in the AGREE-ABLENESS: column of the Score Conversion Sheet that corresponds to this raw score.

5. Find the sum of the circled numbers on the *fifth* row of each of the five-line groupings (Row 5 + Row 10 + Row 15 + Row 20 + Row 25 = _____). This is your raw score for "conscientious." Circle the number in the CONSCIEN-TIOUSNESS: column of the Score Conversion Sheet that corresponds to this raw score.

6. Find the number in the far right or far left column that is parallel to your circled raw score. Enter this norm score in the box at the bottom of the appropriate column.

7. Transfer your norm score to the appropriate scale on the Big Five Locator Interpretation Sheet.

Big Five Locator Score Conversion Sheet

Norm Score	Adjustment	Sociability	Openness	Agreeableness	Conscientiousness	Norm Score
80						80
79			25			79
78						78
77	22					77
76			24			76
75						75
74						74
73	21		23			73
72		25				72
71				25		71
70	20	24	22			70
69					25	69
68				24		68
67		23	21		24	67
66	19					66
65		22		23	23	65
64			20			64
63					22	63
62	18	21	19	22		62
61					21	61
60		20				60
59	17		18	21	20	59
58						58
57		19				57
56			17			56
55	16	18		20	19	55
54		16		19		54
53						53
52		17			18	52
51	15					51
50		16	15	18	17	50
49						49
48	14	15			16	48
47			14	17		47
46		14			15	46
45			13			45
44	13			16	14	44
43		13				43
42			12			42
41				15	13	41
40	12	12	11			40
39						39
38				14	12	38
37		11	10			37
36	11					36
35		10		13	11	35
34			9			34
33	10	9			10	33
32				12		32
31			8			31
30		8			9	30
29	9			11		29
28		7	7		8	28
27				10		27
26		6			7	26
25	8		6			25
24				9	6	24
23						23
22			5		22	22
21	7	5				21
20				8		20

Enter Norm Scores Here: Adj =   S =   O =   A =   C =

(Norms based on a sample of 161 forms completed in 1993–94.)

Big Five Locator Interpretation Sheet

Scores:

Adjustment   _____

Sociability   _____

Openness   _____

Agreeableness   _____

Conscientiousness   _____

Strong Adjustment: secure, unflappable, rational, unresponsive, guilt free	Resilient 35	Responsive 45	Reactive 55 65	Weak Adjustment: excitable, worrying, reactive, high strung, alert
Low Sociability: private, independent, works alone, reserved, hard to read	Introvert 35	Ambivert 45	Extrovert 55 65	High Sociability: assertive, sociable, warm, optimistic, talkative
Low Openness: practical, conservative, depth of knowledge, efficient, expert	Preserver 35	Moderate 45	Explorer 55 65	High Openness: broad interests, curious, liberal, impractical, likes novelty
Low Agreeableness: skeptical, questioning, tough, aggressive, self-interest	Challenger 35	Negotiator 45	Adapter 55 65	High Agreeableness: trusting, humble, altruistic, team player, conflict averse, frank
Low Conscientiousness: private, independent, works alone, reserved, hard to read	Flexible 35	Balanced 45	Focused 55 65	High Conscientiousness: dependable, organized, disciplined, cautious, stubborn

Note: The Big Five Locator is intended for use only as a quick assessment for teaching purposes.

Activity 9–3:
Rough Times at Nomura

Objectives:

a. To introduce the types of problems that arise in a cross-cultural work environment.

b. To explore the relationship between cultural diversity and employees' self-concept and work behavior.

c. To examine the relationship between culture and organizational structure and process.

Task 1 (Individual):

Individuals working alone should prepare the case that follows for class discussion by reading the case and answering the questions at the end of the case.

Task 2 (Group):

Imagine you are a consulting team brought in by Nomura Securities International (NSI) to study the problems in the Japanese Equities Dept. Develop an action plan for resolving the department's immediate problem as well as a long-term plan for improving the situation at NSI's New York office.

Task 3 (Class):

Select one of the teams to present its consulting report to the class, which will serve as NSI's board of directors. Board members will be free to ask questions relating to the nature of problems and the action plans proposed to resolve them.

Source: This activity was contributed by Professor Allan Bird. Copyright © 1995 by Allan Bird. All rights are reserved, and no reproduction should be made without express approval of Professor Bird, College of Business, California Polytechnic State University, San Luis Obispo, CA 93407. We are grateful to Professor Bird.

Rough Times at Nomura

The Problem

George Rosebush sat at his desk pondering the magnitude of the decision that lay before him. He still couldn't quite believe the events that had transpired over the past year. It was July 1988, he had been with Nomura Securities International (NSI), the American subsidiary of Japanese giant Nomura Securities Company Ltd., since July 1986. During that time, George had acquired the skills necessary to be a successful stock trader; however, he now felt prevented from utilizing his skills to the fullest extent.

The management at NSI, all Japanese personnel on assignment from the home office in Tokyo, had refused to give Americans such as George the latitude to aggressively pursue business. Like his predecessors, George was experiencing great frustration at having to cope with Japanese culture and business norms. In particular, the Japanese were very slow to make either decisions or changes—primarily due to their consensus method of decision making.

Nomura was a monolithic machine where decisions emerged from the system with little need for creativity. This was a significant impediment to achieving success in the trading business, where the ability of a trader to respond quickly to customer needs was vital to success. As a pure service industry, the ability to develop strong client relationships was imperative. Here again, Nomura insisted upon doing things the

Japanese way. Among the factors frequently noted as holding Nomura back were adherence to Japanese tradition; inflexibility in negotiations; lack of imagination; little expertise in critical investment banking sectors; and weak relationships with U.S. and European institutional investors. To make matters worse, the business environment in the securities industry was suffering a major recession following the stock market crash of October 1987. Despite this, since the late 1970s, NSI's staff had grown to 750, a 10-fold increase.

In the postcrash era, NSI was experiencing a larger fall in revenues and profits than other firms in the industry. This slump was particularly acute in George's department, Japanese equities, which entailed marketing Japanese stocks to U.S. institutional clients.

Despite the market's downturn, changing Japanese trading habits had accounted for much of the problem. Industry analysts noted that in actuality the Japanese had "severely misjudged the difficulty of mounting major expansion drives overseas." In numerous meetings George had made recommendations to improve business, but management remained unwilling to take the steps necessary to reverse the drop in market share and profits that the department was experiencing.

Business had slowed down so much that George and his colleagues soon found themselves doing crossword puzzles to pass the time. This was occurring in the fast-paced world of global trading.

Each day dragged slowly, and George found himself faced with a decision: He could stay at NSI and continue to develop new plans to improve business at the company, or he could leave the firm. He decided to conduct preliminary discussions about employment opportunities with some other firms. Meanwhile, some of his friends had even suggested that he quit NSI and enroll in a leading business school, to pursue an MBA.

Background

Nomura Securities, the world's largest stockbroker, continued to suffer from both host- and home-country regulatory pressures and related political risks associated with its globalization strategy. The Japanese securities industry, like that of the United States, had undergone extensive liberalization, in terms of deregulation, over the five-year period from 1986 to 1991. Within this ever-changing environment, Nomura had continued with its global expansion policy—aggressively expanding into both the London and New York Markets.

The premise governing Nomura's growth was based on its commitment to opening up international financial markets to Japanese clients and to bringing foreign investors to the Japanese market place. Being the beneficiaries of a society geared toward an unusually high savings rate, Japanese brokerage houses had allowed Japanese investors to seek out higher-yielding foreign investments. This approach was not unique to Nomura, but was pursued by a number of Japanese securities firms. The chairman of European operations for Daiwa Securities, the number 2 securities firm globally, stated, "We started off providing two-way information to U.S. and European clients interested in the Japanese markets and to Japanese clients. We knew that Japan would prove to be an economic force, and we foresaw that brokerage would be profitable."

By the mid-1980s, Japan had become the world's largest creditor nation. Capitalizing on this development, Nomura's expansion was predicated upon its desire to allow borrowers, internationally, to tap into Japan's vast pool of potential investors. Additionally, Nomura was concerned with enhancing its domestic image as a true global market player. Increasing its presence abroad not only boosted its name recognition internationally, but enhanced Nomura's reputation domestically. It generated goodwill and demonstrated the firm's commitment to international markets. In turn, such actions gave evidence of its desire to continue to strengthen its position in the growing Japanese domestic market. In short, Nomura Securities was positioning itself as the preeminent Japanese brokerage firm, able to service the large amounts of Japanese capital targeted for future U.S. investment.

Nomura expanded aggressively into the New York market throughout the early and mid-1980s. The result was an office that underwent rapid growth in terms of staffing, profits, and overall market presence.

Nomura's Growth Phase

Nomura was founded in 1878. Over the years its focus remained on high-quality research and the development of a worldwide financial network. It was the first Japanese securities firm to open an office in the United States (1927), as well as the first to become a member of the New York Stock Exchange. Its American operation suffered a major interruption as a result of World War II. Nomura did not reestablish an American presence until the 1950s. With the improvement of relations between the United States and Japan, and growth of trade between the two countries that occurred in the late 1960s and 1970s, Nomura sought to increase its activities in the U.S. securities markets. Nomura's expansion plans led to the formation of a wholly owned subsidiary in the 1970s, Nomura Securities International.

NSI's expansionary plans required the hiring of a large number of Americans—the intent was to rely upon talented local professionals to further market expansion. Nomura could not afford to rely on nonmanagement personnel from the parent company who were in New York for, at best, two- to three-year rotations.

Because Nomura now planned to serve American clients and compete directly with U.S. firms, it needed Americans who could build the strong client relationships necessary to achieve success in a service industry, particularly in the American securities market. Yoshihisa Tabuchi, president and chief executive of Nomura Securities Company Ltd., stated, "[t]he style and structure Nomura uses to sell securities in Japan cannot work well in the U.S. Nomura's traditional culture is as a Japanese brokerage firm, but, as it expands, it must become multicultural." It is important to develop good working relationships with other firms in the industry. Americans were hired to be on the front lines and, more importantly, to lend credibility to the firm within the U.S. market.

As a critical success factor, the internal working relationships at NSI are as important, if not more so, than its external relationships with clients—the firm cannot hope to properly service its client base, without being able to benefit from the synergies created from internal employee "harmony." Unfortunately, cultural barriers and differences still existed within the firm. All managers were Japanese, with little experience or knowledge about either the American market or, more importantly, American cultural and business values. This created a paradox. The front-line American workers knew how to serve their home market but were not allowed to make the significant and timely decisions needed for success in the American securities marketplace. These decisions were made by Japanese personnel who did not have the working knowledge necessary to properly analyze the situation.

Decisions regarding risk taking and the scope of the firm's operations usually required the consent and approval of Japanese management. However, these managers were often not qualified to make such critical decisions (being unaware of many of the nuances associated with the American market's operation and function). In particular, management was unwilling to delegate to traders the authority to commit the firm's capital. This was a major impediment to "getting a deal done." Traders could not give a quick response to client inquiries. Instead management wanted to discuss the trade under consideration. Only after much deliberation and a consensus had been reached, would the firm be willing to commit capital to a large trade. This slow response time remained unacceptable to customers in the U.S. securities markets. Due to potential rapid changes in prices and investor perceptions, clients expected and demanded quick responses to their inquiries. NSI's failure to make quick decisions severely hampered its ability to effectively compete in the U.S. securities markets. Furthermore, this lack of trust on behalf of Japanese management had a devastating effect upon the morale of the American work force.

George's Tale

In June 1986, George was looking to gain entrance into the securities business. He had just quit his job at an employee benefits consulting firm to seek work in global finance. George had previous work experience selling Individual Retirement Accounts and tax-sheltered annuities in the New England area. Much of that work involved cold calling and building a client base. While his previous jobs had helped him develop strong interpersonal skills as well as given him some familiarity with the stock market,

George did not have any direct experience trading financial securities. He found it very difficult to gain entrance into the trading business without that experience. Most of the opportunities he found were for lower-level operations positions.

George had two brothers who worked in the securities industry. Both knew people who worked, or had worked, at NSI. One of their acquaintances was Mark Blanchard, whom, as it turned out, George would later succeed at Nomura. George learned that Nomura needed to hire traders to replace Mark Blanchard and Steve Montana as well as some traders from the American equities department who had also resigned. George was able to arrange an interview with Nomura to discuss trading opportunities at the firm. Before going on the interview George spoke with Mark Blanchard to get the inside story as to what life at Nomura was actually like.

Prior to the Fourth of July holiday in 1986, George had his first interview at NSI. From the interview's onset, many of the cultural differences George had been fore-warned about became readily apparent. George was greeted by the head of the sales department, Mr. Yoshida, and after a few common pleasantries were exchanged, was whisked into a small conference room. The two were then joined by another Japanese manager and Mike, the head of the Japanese Equity Trading Department. Mike was also a Japanese national. However, rather than go by his last name, as was the custom in Japan, he had adopted the American nickname Mike.

George would later call the interview intense. He was bombarded by questions from each of those present. While George found many of the questions seemingly unrelated to the job at hand (e.g., questions regarding his family as well as his personal views of the work ethic and company allegiance), he nevertheless answered them.

Occasionally there were interruptions to the flow of questions when the interviewers stopped to carry on a conversation among themselves in Japanese. George found these interruptions both rude and unprofessional, but was reluctant to say anything that might ruin his prospects for the job.

After a time, other Japanese men were ushered into the room and took their turn interviewing George. Finally, several American traders from the American equities department were brought in. At this point the interview became more conventional. Specific job duties and the requisite skills were discussed. Finally, the director of personnel (another American) finished the interview. The next day George received a job offer. He started working for NSI on July 14, 1986.

George maintained no illusions of either climbing NSI's ladder of success or of making a lifelong career with Nomura. Furthermore, George held some personal reservations about working for a foreign firm, especially one from such a different culture. He viewed the position as an opportunity to learn the business. If after a few years things were not working out, he knew that he would be able to parlay his newly acquired skills to land a job elsewhere. After trading Japanese stocks for the top Japanese brokerage house, he would be very marketable to the many firms seeking to enter this area of the securities business. For George, the simple fact remained that there were few westerners with experience trading Japanese securities. Should things really go sour, George had a fallback position of returning to school for his MBA.

At the time George started at NSI, the Japanese Equity Department was in a state of disarray. Mark and Steve had been gone for two months and there were no Americans left in the department. Client relationships had deteriorated rapidly, and new traders were desperately needed. George was not the only trader to start work in the Japanese Equity Department on July 14. He was joined by François Boudreau. While growing up, François had lived in both France and the United States and had attended Columbia University in New York. He had spent a month working as a retail broker before coming to NSI, but for all intents and purposes was fresh out of college.

Neither George nor François had the experience necessary to step in and immediately start trading with clients or other firms. To make matters worse, Mike, their boss, was the only other trader in the department. George and François had no western colleagues or mentors. Mike was trying to do as much as he could to keep the business going, which meant that he had little time available to train either George or François.

229

Moreover, Mike was introverted and did not enjoy interacting with clients. The result was that neither the clients nor George and François received much attention.

Mike had been working in the United States for five years. He had been in the New York office for the past three years; prior to that he had spent two years in Nomura's Honolulu branch. Mike was much more westernized than his Japanese colleagues. If they had to have a Japanese boss, both George and François felt fortunate to be working for Mike. Mike was viewed by Japanese management as a renegade of sorts—willing to test the limits of the Japanese business rules and hierarchy. He had an excellent understanding of the underlying forces driving the U.S. securities industry. He, however, did not have the authority to make important policy decisions, which continued to be made by more senior Japanese managers. Senior managers were typically far removed from the daily operations of the firm. Some were even based in Tokyo, 7,000 miles away.

In Japanese corporations, new hires often spend their first year or two on the job in low-level positions that expose them to the fundamental operations of the company's business. In manufacturing firms, this typically involves working on the production line. For financial organizations, the initial period usually involves door-to-door sales solicitations. While NSI could not realistically expect American professionals to go through such a process, at the same time, it was unwilling to let Americans do too much too soon.

Both François and George were initially instructed to sit with the traders in the American Equities Department. There they were supposed to watch and listen in order to learn the fundamentals of stock trading. At first this was a worthwhile activity. However, after a few weeks, they both felt they had learned as much as they were going to learn. François and George were anxious to start trading on their own, and wanted to start assuming more responsibilities. Their superiors, however, did not feel they were ready to get directly involved in the daily trading operations. George thought this particularly odd considering how short-handed the Japanese Equity Department was.

For six months George and François watched the traders from the U.S. Equities Department and did little else. Most of their days were spent answering the telephones and relaying information to the trading desk. George was growing restless and started asking for additional responsibilities. To appease him, Mike allowed him to start trading Japanese ADRs (American depository receipts) on NASDAQ, the over-the-counter market. ADRs represent Japanese stock held by a custodian bank in Japan. Investors cannot actually take delivery of Japanese stock outside Japan, but can take delivery of ADRs. ADRs are denominated in dollars, which further simplifies their purchase, as investors do not have to make foreign exchange arrangements.

NSI used to trade a few hundred thousand ADRs each day. However, that number had recently fallen to just a few thousand. As a market maker in ADRs and other issues, NSI used its own capital to make trades with other market makers and clients. Market makers risk their own capital in the hope of making money on the bid/ask spread. To be successful at doing this, volume is important for two reasons. First, if the spread earned is small, sizable profits can only be made through large volume. More importantly, active market makers attract more client orders because of their ability to provide more liquidity as well as their increased market presence.

Before George could rebuild the client side of the ADR business, he first had to stimulate the firm's trading activity with other market makers on the street. George gradually built good working relationships with the other major market makers of Japanese ADRs. Within a few months, he was making a modest but steady profit for the firm. He often did this by taking advantage of arbitrage opportunities between the ADRs and the underlying Japanese common stock. However, the upside potential on these activities was limited, as the size of position that George could take and the amount of time that he could hold them was restricted. Being a prominent market maker, George was able to attract additional business to NSI. However, he was capturing a larger share of a shrinking market.

10

Motivation

Learning Objectives

After completing this module, you should be able to

1. Gain insight into some managerial viewpoints of motivation.
2. Understand the process and the major factors that affect motivation.
3. Appreciate the difference between the "content" and the "process" approaches to motivation.
4. Describe the behavior modification motivational technique.
5. Gain insights into your own motivation patterns.
6. Identify the basic managerial actions and programs that can foster individual motivation.

Module Outline

Premodule Preparation
    Activity 10–1: Motivation to Work

Introduction

Managerial Viewpoints on Motivation
    Traditional Viewpoint
    Human Relations Viewpoint
    Human Resources Viewpoint
    Alternative Clusters of Motivational Theories

Content Theories of Motivation
    Herzberg's Motivation-Hygiene Theory
    Maslow's Hierarchy of Needs
    McClelland's *n* Achievement and *n* Power

Process Theories of Motivation
    Equity Theory
    Expectancy Theory
    Goal-Setting Theory

Linking Theory and Managerial Practice
    Management by Objectives
    Profit-Sharing Plans
    Skill-Based Pay
    Pygmalion and Motivation
    Behavior Modification

Premodule Preparation

The instructor may assign either one or a combination of the following as a presession activity: task 1 of Activity 10–1 ("Motivation to Work"); 10–2 ("The Slade Plating Department case"); 10–3 ("Alternative Courses of Managerial Action in the Slade Plating Department case"); or 10–4 ("Motivational Analysis of Organization's-Behavior").

Activity 10–1: Motivation to Work

Objectives:

a. To determine your views of what has made you most and least productive in past work situations.

b. To compare your results with some current motivational studies and theories.

Task 1:

Each individual, working alone, is to use the accompanying worksheet for answers to the following:

a. Think back on your work experience to a time when you were performing at your very best. What were the factors that accounted for your high performance? List them on the accompanying worksheet.
(Time: 5 minutes)

b. Think back on your work experience to a time when you were performing less than your best, or poorly. What were the factors that accounted for this performance? List them on the accompanying worksheet.
(Time: 5 minutes)

Task 2:

Each team should select a spokesperson.
List the important factors agreed upon by the group for the two areas of "best" performance and "less than best." Be prepared to give an example from one member's experience for each factor on the list.
(Time: 15 minutes)
The instructor will call upon spokespersons, one at a time, to give one factor from the group's "best" list to be written on the board. Examples should be given for clarification. This exercise will continue until all the best factors from the groups have been presented.
Repeat this procedure for "less than best."
The instructor will give a short lecture.

Worksheet for Activity 10–1

a. Think back on your work experience to a time when you were performing at your very best. What factors accounted for your high performance? List them.
(Time: 3 minutes)

focus
determined
quota

b. Think back on your work experience to a time when you were performing at less than your best or poorly. What factors accounted for this performance? List them.
(Time: 3 minutes)

bored
tired
hungover
wanted to get fired

Introduction

Individual behavior is the result of many factors and motives. A major concern for managers at different levels in organizations centers around effectiveness. Motivation is one of the core concepts that must be studied as we look at the effectiveness of the individual, the small group, intergroup activities, and the organization. We will examine the subject by first giving a case study; second, by providing some philosophical viewpoints that can help managers approach motivation problems such as productivity, satisfaction, absenteeism, and turnover; third, by using a few activities and cases; and fourth, by presenting a few well-known motivation theories.

We will open with a short case study reported by one of our students who had worked in two car washes as a teenager. The car washes were in a small city and operated by different owners. In the first the dripping vehicle would come off the rinse line, where four teenagers waited with towels to wipe it dry. When the wipers were finished, they signaled the car owner by leaving the car door standing open. The car owner would generally walk past a pot placed in his or her path with a sign that read TIPS, THANK YOU, climb into the car, and drive away with the windows still wet and water streaming from some parts of the car. Occasionally, one of the wipers dropped a wet towel on the ground, only to pick it up and continue wiping. One customer complained to the manager that the wet towel could pick up sand from the pavement and scratch the car. Only a few small coins got into the pot. Turnover of wipers was high, and they expressed hostile attitudes toward management.

The second car wash was opened by a vigorous, enthusiastic young owner. A system was established whereby each customer paid for the service when entering the wash. A ticket was handed to the customer (a practice not followed at the first car wash), which was to be given to the final wiper when the car was dry. The car coming off the rinse line was received by four teenage wipers, three of whom would go on to another car after doing the initial work, while the fourth did the final wiping. This individual did everything possible to please because the customer was not inclined to give the ticket to the wiper until the work was done to her or his satisfaction. The customers usually stood beside the wiper pointing out places where more drying was needed. While doing this, the customer generally took change out of his or her pocket or purse and waited for the wiper to ask for the ticket. Tips were generous, and customers drove away in well-dried cars. The manager often got the entire work crew together for pep talks that ran something like this:

> We're the best car wash on the coast. We do the best work, have the most satisfied customers, have the happiest workers, and hopefully make the most money of any car wash of equal size. Your tips will be good if you do a perfect job. I've set up 10 customer chairs alongside the wiping area. This is your audience. Show them how well you can do. When you finish, give your customer a guided tour of the car and ask if everything is all right. With this treatment, your customer standing there waiting to give you the ticket will develop the expectation that you should have a good tip. The "audience" on the sideline will see you get tipped. The audience will also tell other people what a great job we do here.

The owner's practices also included job rotation so workers did all jobs (all got a share of the wiper jobs so they would get tipped), flexibility in choosing work hours, and (on weekends) bonuses if a certain volume was reached. The car wash prospered.

This simple case illustrates many of the basic concepts and approaches to motivation that we discuss in this module. We shall refer to this case during the discussion.

Managerial Viewpoints on Motivation

Global competition, productivity, and *quality* have become buzzwords of this decade. *Productivity* and *quality* have many definitions. Most are related to motivation—where it is "zero defect" ratio in manufacturing, whether it is individual production averaged over a number of people, hours of work and dollar cost of labor, or individual effort and performance, the implied, ever-present question is, How do you get the individual to accomplish more and better-quality work at less cost?

Since this is a management course, we will start with some ways of thinking about motivation that can be helpful in guiding your specific managerial activities.

Ask executives and managers attending workshops what the primary problems of motivation are, and they will place blame on people: workers are not committed; they don't care if they do a good job; they are poorly trained in the school systems; parents don't bring up kids like they used to. Sometimes there is the complaint that you can't get good first-line supervisors who will accept full responsibility. Our answer to this complaint is the same as for problems of personal growth and effectiveness: if you aren't achieving what you want, it's not the fault of your family, teachers, ethnic background, girlfriend, boyfriend, and so on. The only way you're going to achieve goals is to assume full responsibility for your own progress and stop blaming others.

And so it is with management. There is little to be gained by blaming the workers and much to be gained by planning, stimulating, and influencing motivation. A helpful way of focusing on the motivation problem is to assume there are no "bad" people, just bad management practices—that is, management is causing the problem; working conditions are poor; or the architectural, organizational, or work designs are faulty.

Following this logic three general patterns of managerial approaches to motivation were identified: the traditional model, the human relations model, and the human resources model.[1] The basic assumptions made by managers that follow the specific approach guide them in setting up policies, which in turn communicate a set of managerial expectation to their subordinates. Table 10–1 summarizes the managerial approaches and their assumptions, policies, and expectations.

Table 10–1 General Patterns of Managerial Approaches to Motivation*	Traditional Model	Human Relations Model	Human Resources Model
		Assumptions	
*Source: Adapted from R. M. Steers, L. W. Porter, and G. A. Bigley, *Motivation and Learning at Work*, (New York, McGraw-Hill, 1996).	Work is inherently distasteful to most people. What they do is less important than what they earn for doing it. Few want or can handle work which requires creativity, self-direction, or self-control.	People want to feel useful and important. People desire to belong and to be recognized as individuals. These needs are more important than money in motivating people to work.	Work is not inherently distasteful. People want to contribute to meaningful goals which they have helped to establish. Most people can exercise far more creative, responsible self-direction and self-control than their present jobs demand.
		Policies	
	The manager's basic task is to closely supervise and control subordinates. Managers must break down tasks into simple, repetitive, easily learned operations. Managers must establish detailed work routines and procedures and enforce these firmly but fairly.	The manager's basic task is to make each worker feel useful and important. Managers should keep subordinates informed and listen to their objections to his or her plans. Managers should allow subordinates to exercise some self-direction and self-control on routine matters.	The manager's basic task is to make use of "untapped" human resources. Managers must create an environment in which all members may contribute to the limits of their ability. Managers must encourage full participation on important matters, continually broadening subordinate self-direction and control.
		Expectations	
	People can tolerate work if the pay is decent and the boss is fair. If tasks are simple enough and people are closely controlled, they will produce up to standard.	Sharing information with subordinates and involving them in routine decisions will satisfy their basic needs to belong and to feel important. Satisfying these needs will improve morale and reduce resistance to formal authority—subordinates will "willingly cooperate."	Expanding subordinate influence, self-direction, and self-control will lead to direct improvements in operating efficiency. Work satisfaction may improve as a by-product of subordinates making full use of their resources.

Traditional Viewpoint

The *traditional model* (labeled by McGregor as theory X) assumes that for the average worker work is inherently distasteful; that what the individual does is less important than what he or she earns for doing it; that the individual by nature is self-centered, is inclined to be lazy, and prefers to be led rather than take responsibility; and that few individuals want or can handle work that requires creativity, self-direction, or self-control. Therefore the manager's basic task is to closely supervise and control subordinates. He or she must break down tasks into simple, repetitive, easily learned operations; he or she must establish detailed work routines and resources and must enforce these firmly but fairly through rewards and punishments.

Human Relations Viewpoint

The *human relations model* (labeled by McGregor as *theory Y*) assumes that people want to feel useful and important, that people desire to belong and to be recognized as individuals, and that these needs are more important than money in motivating people to work. Therefore the manager's basic task is to arrange organizational conditions so that people can achieve their goals by directing their efforts toward organizational objectives. He or she should make each worker feel useful and important, should keep subordinates informed and listen to their feedback, and should allow subordinates to exercise some self-direction and self-control on routine matters.

Going back to our hothouse analogy, if the prevailing atmosphere in an organization is that of McGregor's theory Y, it could be assumed that individuals feel the need and energy to be productive for themselves and management.

Human Resources Viewpoint

Having made our assumption about people, let us amend it. From the human resource development viewpoint, it is assumed that work is not inherently distasteful, that people want to contribute to meaningful goals that they have helped establish, and that most people can exercise far more creative, responsible self-direction and self-control than their present jobs demand. There may be no "bad" people, but there are those who are unsuitable or less suitable, which brings us to another assumption: People will work well if they have the abilities, aptitudes, interests, attitudes, and temperament that make them most suitable to perform the job—that is, people must be matched with jobs. Therefore the manager's basic task is to make use of "untapped" human resources. He or she should create an environment in which all members can contribute to the limits of their ability, and he or she should encourage full participation on important matters, continually broadening subordinates' self-direction and self-control.

Alternative Clusters of Motivational Theories

As the concerns for productivity and quality are increasing at the global level, so is the search for the "right" theory or the "right" approach to work motivation. Many models have been developed and examined over the past four decades: need models, reinforcement models, equity models, expectancy-based models, and goal-setting models, to mention a few. Furthermore, a variety of definitions emerged as the quest for our understanding of the phenomenon increased.

Although general agreement exists that motivated behavior consists of initiation, direction, persistence, intensity, and termination (any one or any combination of these), different managers and researchers are interested more in one aspect than in others.[2] As a result, several attempts have been made to cluster the many theories of motivation found in the management literature: **content theories of motivation** (emphasizing reasons for motivated behavior or the specific factors that cause it) versus **process theories of motivation** (focusing on how behavioral change occurs); content theories versus process theories versus **reinforcement theories of motivation** (focusing on the elements that will increase the likelihood that described behavior will be repeated); intrinsic theories (emphasizing the drive to perform that results from a person's internalized values and beliefs that the task is rewarding in and of itself) versus extrinsic theories (focusing on the drive to perform that results from a person's expectations that a specific action will result in a desired outcome such as increase in pay); endogenous theories (focusing on the dynamics of the motivational process) versus exogenous theories (focusing on motivationally related elements that can be changed by external agents); and organizational-centered versus individual-centered frameworks, to mention a few.[3]

In this chapter we are using the simplistic broad classification schema of content versus process theories. We believe that this typology not only can help you sort out the many different theories and models of motivation but also can boost understanding of the conditions and practices affecting work motivation.

Content Theories of Motivation

Content theories of motivation strive to understand and explain the elements that arouse, start, initiate, or energize behavior. These theories or models focus on causes that motivate individuals. For example, if we examine the car wash case at the beginning of the chapter, from a content theory point of view the focus would be on what might have motivated the workers to behave the way they did. One can argue that in the more successful car wash, the individuals' needs for money, status, and achievement were more satisfied and served as motivators for their behavior. Representative theories in this cluster include Herzberg's two-factor theory, Maslow's need hierarchy, and McClelland's achievement/power theory.

Herzberg's Motivation-Hygiene Theory

Frederick Herzberg divides morale into two sets of factors: *dissatisfiers* and *motivators*.[4] The **dissatisfiers** include company policy and administration, supervision, relationships with supervisor, working conditions, salary, relationships with peers, personal life, relationships with subordinates, status, and security. These are potential dissatisfiers because employees expect and hope that they will all be good. If they are not good, the employees will be unhappy; if they are good, they only measure up to what the employees expect. The fact that all of these factors are favorable, however, does not make an individual happy or productive. It simply means that the individual is not unhappy. An analogy would be from garbage collection: If the garbage is collected from your home every week, you are almost unaware of it because this is what you expect. You are not unhappy, since conditions are as they should be. If the garbage collector fails to pick it up, you are very much aware of your dissatisfaction and the unhygienic consequences. If all the dissatisfier factors are good in your work life, everything is hygienic.

What really makes you want to work are the motivators. These include achievement, recognition, the nature of the work itself, responsibility, and opportunities for advancement and growth. For college students, the skills and abilities they learn are part of their self-esteem; the opportunity to use these in their first job and to do good work will be a primary motivator. Using their experience and skills remains a primary force throughout their careers.

Figure 10–1 presents results of a study by Herzberg and his colleagues that shows that factors such as achievement, recognition, and the work itself are most frequently mentioned in connection with satisfying work experiences. Dissatisfying work experiences are reported most frequently as arising from company policy and administration, supervision, and other **hygiene factors.** Thus we see more than 40 percent of the workers indicated achievement as a source of satisfaction, while more than 30 percent found company policy and administration were reasons for dissatisfaction.

Figure 10–1 also can be used to discuss Herzberg's assumption that motivation can be thought of as two entirely separate factors. Thus people may be satisfied and dissatisfied at the same time. They can, for example, appreciate the opportunity the job offers for achievement and still be most unhappy about company policy, pay, or working conditions. Figure 10–2 illustrates this concept by showing that the motivators can start at zero (or neutral) and increase to highly satisfied as opportunities for achievement or responsibility improve. The hygiene factors can start at zero and increase to

**Figure 10–1
Comparison of
Satisfiers (Motivators)
and Dissatisfiers**

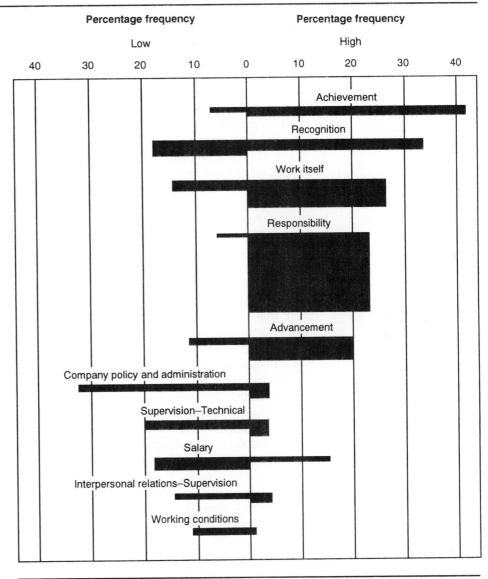

Source: Adapted from F. Herzberg, B. Mausner, and B. Snyderman, *The Motivation to Work,* 2nd ed. Copyright © 1959 by John Wiley & Sons. Reprinted by permission.

**Figure 10–2
Two-Factor Continua**

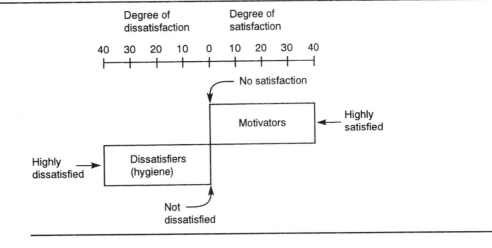

highly dissatisfied as conditions such as bad policy or salary get worse; being at zero on the hygiene scale does not mean you are satisfied. It only means that you are not dissatisfied—the garbage was picked up today so everything is hygienic.

The results college students register in Activity 10–1 generally are similar to Herzberg's findings, which adds a certain amount of apparent validity to his theory. However, some factors Herzberg lists as dissatisfiers are seen by students as motivators. For instance, students enjoy working hard for a boss they like, and they like working hard with peers who are also working hard even if the job is not exciting (possibly reflecting conformity to the social norms of the group). One reason for the basic agreement between Herzberg's findings and students' results may be that the data were selected by a similar method, asking people to recall past experience. This method is subject to criticism, however, because people unconsciously recall unpleasantness as due to things that are not under their control and therefore not their fault (the dissatisfiers). Pride in what they remember as having been achieved or earned (the motivators) can easily be unconsciously attributed to their own good efforts. Because of these psychological factors of recall, we cannot say that the dissatisfiers are really what turn people off; they are only what people *think* turn them off. And what turns people on or off under one set of circumstances may not so do under another; poor pay and working conditions may turn people off during prosperity but not so much during an economic depression when nothing else is available. There is also frequently a discrepancy between what young people say they want and the way they behave. Most will say they want challenge and self-direction, but many find difficulty in performing without considerable guidance and structure. The high turnover rate of young insurance salespersons during their first year provides an example of how the self-direction requirement can be overwhelming.

There has not been sufficient research to show that dissatisfiers and motivators truly account for differences in work performance.[5] Thus it cannot be said that the motivation-hygiene theory has yet provided the evidence that the motivators are what make people perform well. Whether dissatisfaction and satisfaction are two completely different factors also has not been validated. The question might be raised whether the motivators themselves are not potentially the greatest source of dissatisfaction.[6] Is it not possible for talented, educated individuals to be completely frustrated when the job does not provide opportunities for the use of their abilities and achievements? The forecast that there will be more college-educated people than there will be jobs requiring a college education means many people may be dissatisfied because they cannot experience enough of the motivators even though all the dissatisfier factors offering a good life and pleasant working environment are present.

Motivation to work is so complex that it is easy to criticize any specific theory as being an oversimplification. Managers should be aware of the various concepts and determine whether they have utility value in their own working situations. Herzberg's theory is highly important for understanding how people perceive satisfaction and dissatisfaction, realizing that this perception will vary with specific individuals. One person may be saying, I can't work without challenge; another may be saying, Just let me do the routine work so I can think about what I will be doing after work. Most important is Herzberg's position that (1) it is the nature of the work itself that turns on the self-directing generators for accomplishment and (2) emphasis on human relations alone will not result in high productivity or job satisfaction. Herzberg's use of the terms *satisfaction* and *dissatisfaction* in regard to work performance suggests there is a positive relationship between satisfaction and productivity.

Maslow's Hierarchy of Needs

Another way of thinking of patterns of goals is by need categories. Under this concept a need for achievement describes goals the individual is striving to attain in areas such as education, career, and work. Among management theorists, Abraham Maslow's **hierarchy of needs** is the best-known theory of this type.[7] Because his theory is so well-known, we will present only the aspect that will help you use the hierarchy as a tool for analyzing motivation in our case studies.

Figure 10–3
Maslow's Hierarchy of Needs Requiring Fulfillment in a Work Environment

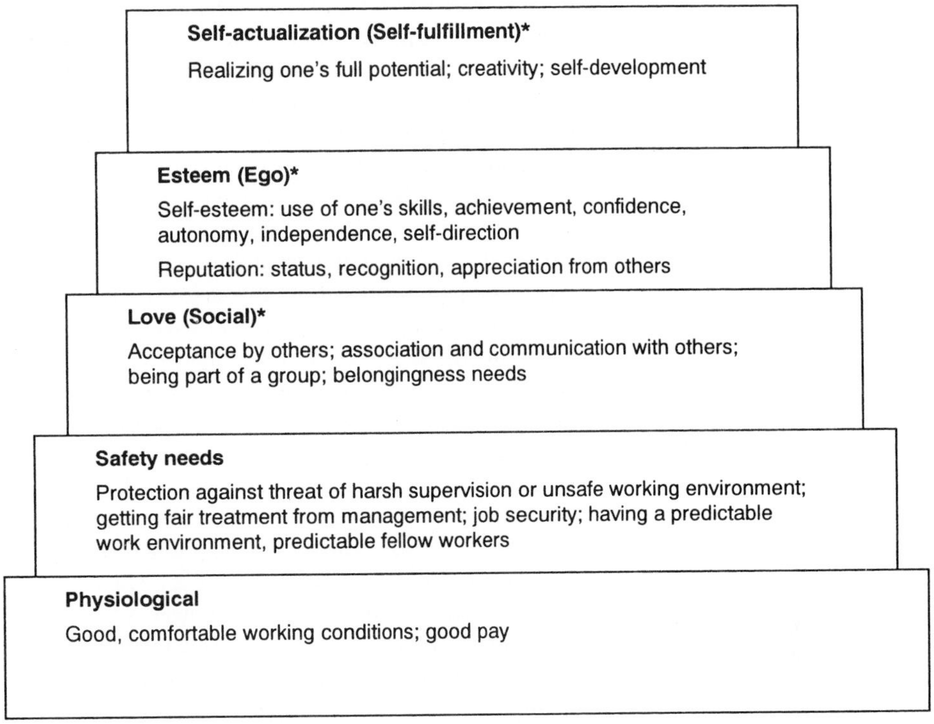

Self-actualization (Self-fulfillment)*
Realizing one's full potential; creativity; self-development

Esteem (Ego)*
Self-esteem: use of one's skills, achievement, confidence, autonomy, independence, self-direction
Reputation: status, recognition, appreciation from others

Love (Social)*
Acceptance by others; association and communication with others; being part of a group; belongingness needs

Safety needs
Protection against threat of harsh supervision or unsafe working environment; getting fair treatment from management; job security; having a predictable work environment, predictable fellow workers

Physiological
Good, comfortable working conditions; good pay

*Terms in parentheses are Douglas McGregor's, which are in common use.

Our adaption of the five levels of the need hierarchy is depicted in Figure 10–3. Maslow assumed that the lower level had to be adequately satisfied before the next higher level became an important motivating force; that is, if the individual was highly concerned about physical needs, the other needs were not going to be the active basis for goal pursuance.

The three lower levels of needs are considered to be *extrinsic* in that satisfaction is initiated from factors external to the individual; the top two levels are considered to be *intrinsic* in that satisfaction is generated from within. The exception, of course, is that one's reputation, an esteem need, depends on the external source. These distinctions become meaningful when one reexamines Herzberg's work: His dissatisfiers are the extrinsic needs, the bottom three levels of Maslow's hierarchy, while his motivators are the intrinsic needs coming from Maslow's top two levels.

McClelland's *n* Achievement and *n* Power

David C. McClelland has made important contributions to need theory, focusing on the needs for achievement, power, and affiliation. He found that salespersons and small business entrepreneurs tended to be high in *n* **achievement** (*n* standing for need), and he concluded they need freedom in the working environment to exercise their strong self-direction tendencies.[8] However, *n* achievement is "a one-man game and need never involve other people." In contrast, managers are not necessarily high in *n* achievement but tend to be high in *n* **power.** The desire to influence, guide, and control others is an important aspect of a manager's motivation. D. G. Winter found, in a limited sample, that business and journalism students were significantly higher in *n* power than those from other occupational categories.[9]

McClelland distinguishes between *p* power (personalized) and *s* power (socialized) and speculates that the former precedes the latter in the development of the individual. The extreme of *p* power is raw control over others expressed in an interpersonal way, whereas *s* power is altruistic and is exercised for the benefit of others. Power fascinates executives; the topics of manipulation, win–lose situations, and Machiavellianism are of top interest when introduced into business workshops.

The concept of *n* power enhances the understanding of Maslow's hierarchy of needs. Persons having power can be assumed to have financial resources for their personal (physiological) needs; control over their environment (safety); considerable interaction with others (social); leeway for self-direction, status, and respect from their position (esteem); and opportunities to excel (self-actualization). Power thus can add considerably to the satisfaction of the person's need pattern and also is a strong reinforcer of managerial role behaviors.

In an extensive review of the research on the relationship between organization structural variables and need and job satisfaction, L. L. Cummings and C. J. Berger found excellent support for the conclusion that satisfaction increases as one moves up the organizational ladder.[10] This conclusion appears to support our analysis of *n* power.

An important aspect of McClelland's work is success in training small business people in India in n achievement behaviors. He reports that many of them changed dramatically after only 5 days of exposure to his workshop methods.[11] Psychologists have traditionally believed that an individual's basic personality structure is formed during the first 5 years of life and is most difficult to change. But McClelland's experience over years of work brings him more to the conclusion that leaders are not so much born as made. The emphasis in this book is that most people can learn leadership types of behaviors; however, we are not saying that everyone will necessarily become a leader—for one thing, *n* power is needed.

Udai Pareek further developed McClelland's work by extending the need for achievement and need for power into six needs or motives that are relevant for understanding the behavior of people in organizations:

1. *Achievement* characterized by concern for excellence, competition with the standards of excellence set by others or by oneself, the setting of challenging goals for oneself, awareness of the hurdles in the way of achieving those goals, and persistence in trying alternative paths to one's goals.

2. *Affiliation* characterized by a concern for establishing and maintaining close, personal relationships, a value on friendship, and a tendency to express one's emotions.

3. *Influence* characterized by concern with making an impact on others, a desire to make people do what one thinks is right, and an urge to change matters and develop people.

4. *Control* characterized by a concern for orderliness, a desire to be and stay informed, and an urge to monitor and take corrective action when needed.

5. *Extension* characterized by concern for others, interest in superordinate goals, and an urge to be relevant and useful to larger groups, including society.

6. *Dependence* characterized by a desire for the help of others in one's own self-development, checking with significant others (those who are more knowledgeable or have higher status, experts, close associates, and so on), submitting ideas or proposals for approval, and having an urge to maintain an "approval" relationship.[12]

Activity 10–4 provides an opportunity to diagnose individual motivation and provide the individual with a motivational profile.

Process Theories of Motivation

Process theories are used to understand and to explain the elements that would foster individual choices of behavioral patterns, the actual motivation process, its direction, and the forces that will increase the likelihood that described behaviors will be repeated over time. In this cluster of theories, the basic assumption is that individuals are capable of calculating costs and benefits and that they use the results of their calculations to choose among alternative courses of action. For example, if we examine the car wash case at the beginning of the chapter, from a process theory point of view the focus would be on the elements and the dynamics between them that foster individuals to put forth more effort in the one car wash than in the other. The better-known theories in this cluster include equity, expectancy, goal setting, and reinforcement. Next we explore equity, expectancy and goal-setting theories.

Equity Theory

Equity theory's basic premise is that individuals want their efforts and performance to be judged fairly relative to others and that individuals engage in a process of evaluating their social relations much like they evaluate economic transactions in the marketplace. Thus equity theory relies heavily both on the assessment of individual inputs and outputs and on social comparison. Figure 10–4 presents a general model of equity theory.

Figure 10–4
Equity Theory
of Motivation

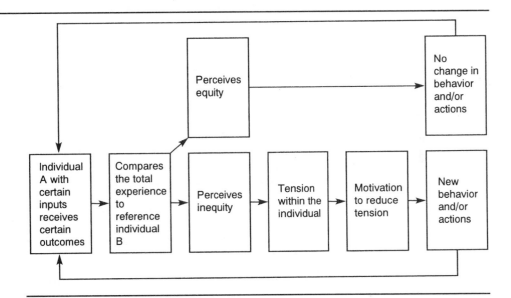

Four key elements are used to explain motivation dynamics in equity theory: input, outcomes, comparative analysis, and action. *Inputs* are what the person brings to the exchange—for example, education, past experience, skills, and knowledge, and these are perceived by the person and/or by others. *Outcomes* are what the individual receives from the exchange (for example, recognition, pay, fringe benefits, promotion, and status). *Comparative analysis* is the comparison of the weights ratio attached by individuals to the perceived inputs and outcomes for themselves versus relevant others who are in the same situation. The comparison to relevant others helps individuals determine the extent to which they feel that they have been treated equitably. Inequity causes tension both within the individual and between individuals. *Action* refers to the specific steps or behavior that the individual takes to reduce the tension that results from the feeling of inequity. The energy source for the individual's motivation is restoring equity. Equity theory further states that an individual is motivated in proportion to the perceived fairness of the rewards received for a certain amount of effort, as compared to the rewards received by relevant others.[13] Perception plays a critical role in the equity theory point of view. We explore the phenomenon of perception in Module 11.

Expectancy Theory

Expectancy-valence motivation theory is perhaps the most researched theory of work motivation.[14] Expectancy theory suggests that individuals consider alternatives, weigh costs and benefits, and choose a course of action of maximum utility. Individuals make decisions among alternatives based on their perceptions of the degree to which a behavior can satisfy a desired want or need. At the most basic level, the expectancy that a specific level of effort will lead to a certain level of performance and the expectancy that a certain level of performance will result in a specific outcome are what facilitate

Figure 10–5
A Basic Model of
Expectancy Theory

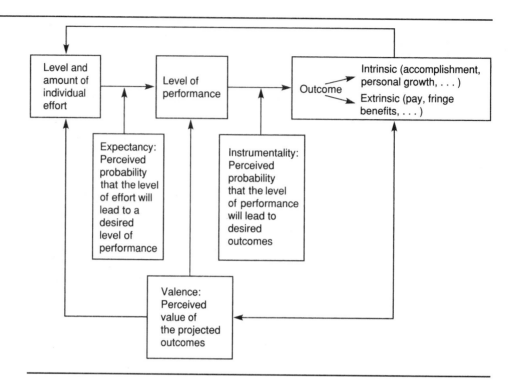

an individual's motivation. Motivation is a function of expectancy, valence, and instrumentality.[15] Figure 10–5 presents a general model of expectancy theory.

The level and the amount of effort that the individual will exert in a given situation is a result of a cumulative effect of (1) the person's perceived probability that the level of the effort will lead to a desired level of performance (*expectancy*), (2) the person's perceived probability that the level of performance will lead to a desired level of outcomes (*instrumentality*), and (3) the person's perceived value of the projected outcomes (*valence*). Although expectancy theory has dominated research in motivation since the early 1970s, because it identifies three useful elements to managers, its complexity has resulted in mixed empirical support.[16] Critics of the theory state that the model is too complex to measure and that the key elements are problematic in terms of definition and operationalization.[17] The comprehensiveness of the theory makes it a useful conceptual guide for understanding and fostering motivation at work.

Porter and Lawler developed expectancy theory one step further by integrating expectancy, equity, and some elements of the content theories.

Porter–Lawler Model

To help understand how people respond differently to work settings, we will turn to an individual approach to motivation, the Porter-Lawler (P–L) model (named for its developers). This model relates a number of different factors to performance and to satisfaction and it highlights how these factors interact. In simplest terms the **P–L model** relates effort to performance. Various factors affect effort, and others affect performance. The outcome or consequences of performance are also affected by individual factors.

In Figure 10–6 we can see that (1) *reward valence,* the value an individual places on a reward, together with (2) *expectancy,* a person's estimate of how probable an outcome is, affect (3) *effort.* An individual simply may not value the awards the organization is offering or may value other outcomes more. The employee who values social relationships with the work group more than potential rewards for outstanding performance will be unlikely to respond to incentives for increased production where group norms restrict performance. A person who believes that no reasonable amount of effort will produce the desired result is unlikely to try to perform. However, a challenging but possible goal is likely to be quite motivating.[18]

Expectancy is the individual's estimate of whether effort will lead to a desired reward (7a or 7b in Figure 10–6). There are several expectancy linkages. First, the

Figure 10–6
The Porter–Lawler
Motivation Model

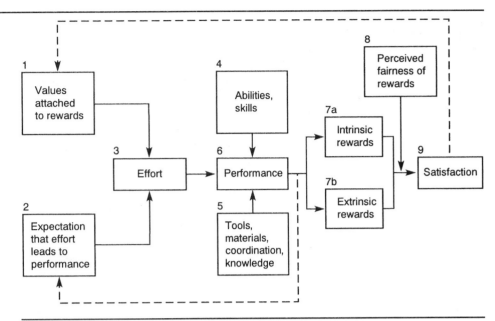

Source: Adapted from L. W. Porter and E. E. Lawler, III. *Managerial Attitudes and Performance,* (Burr Ridge, IL: Richard D. Irwin, 1968).

individual may not believe that effort (3) will lead to performance (6). Where the job standard appears impossible to achieve, workers typically do not put in increasing effort—whether or not management shares workers' impression that the job is impossible. Similarly, if an individual believes the job is impossible, then even if others can do it, for that person effort is unlikely.

Another sort of expectancy concerns performance and outcomes. If I do, in fact, perform, will the desired reward actually come to me? From the manager's perspective, this sort of expectancy concerns the organization's reward system. Where rewards are closely tied to performance and administered fairly, people should have high expectancy that performance will result in the specified reward. Where no such linkage exists or where people believe the system does not operate accurately, people will have very different expectancies. Individuals' self-esteem, their past experiences in similar situations, the present situation, and communications from others (including group norms) will affect both the value they place on rewards (the reward valence) and their expectancies.[19]

In addition to people's values and expectancies, several other factors clearly affect the linkage between effort and performance. A person's abilities (4) clearly affect whether effort leads to performance; so too do the tools, material, and knowledge of when and where to apply effort (5). These factors are of special interest to managers because they seem particularly amenable to managerial change. Employees' skills can be improved by training, and their knowledge of when and where to apply effort can be improved by explicit role descriptions or directions.

The rewards actually received from performance affect both satisfaction and subsequent performance. Two sorts of outcomes can flow from performance: intrinsic rewards (7a) and extrinsic rewards (7b). (Of course, "rewards" can be negative as well as positive. Physical abuse from fellow employees attempting to restrict production or a chewing out from a supervisor constitute negative rewards.) Rewards that others provide (whether positive or negative) include money, praise or recognition, censure, and promotions. These rewards from external sources (outside the individual and the work itself) are extrinsic rewards; they depend upon others' perceptions and assessments of performance. These rewards are like Herzberg's hygiene factors. These are the sorts of rewards most managers think of and most organizations at least partly control. Some of them, most notably those coming from work group members, may be not only outside management's control but also outside the manager's knowledge. But they are no less real or important.

Intrinsic rewards are those that individuals get from the work itself or give to themselves. Herzberg's motivators are intrinsic. A sense of accomplishment; self-esteem; pleasure at a job well done; and the feelings of growth, triumph, and success that may come from a difficult task are all examples of intrinsic rewards. These rewards are profoundly connected both to individual needs and preferences, on the one hand, and to the design of the work, on the other. Thus challenging work creates the potential for this sort of intrinsic reward. But people looking for easy jobs that allow them simply to do the job and go home to really live will not find additional challenge rewarding. Similarly, for many college students, autonomy and self-direction are important values in general—but a part-time job that permits concentration of energies on schoolwork may be preferable.

Equity (8), the perception that rewards are fair or just, is also a factor. It's important to note that we are speaking of perception here and not necessarily fact. A reward system can be perfectly fair in actuality and still be *perceived* as biased (for instance, if employees are not told the basis for decisions about promotion). Where workers believe favoritism or unfairness is the rule, there will be dissatisfaction, especially with extrinsic rewards. (People may also be dissatisfied if they perceive someone was unfairly given a job that's high in intrinsic rewards, while they are left to contend with a less rewarding job.) Another aspect of equity is the balance between effort and reward. Either too little or too much reward will be perceived as inequitable and will be resented. Comparisons of the rewards that others receive for what appears to be equal effort are also a part of equity.

Satisfaction (9) is depicted as the outcome of valences, expectancies, effort, performance, reward, and perceived equity. Of course, this means degree of satisfaction, since individuals might very well be dissatisfied. The feedback loop between satisfaction and earlier factors in the model indicates that motivation is a dynamic, ongoing process. People learn from their experiences and adjust their values, attitudes, and expectations accordingly. Managers must be aware of the feedback loops for two reasons. First, individuals come to the workplace with a prior history or experience (in life if not at work). This past experience colors and affects people's values and expectations no less than their skills do. Managers must deal with people as they are (at least to begin with). Second, people's new experiences in the work setting and with their manager also affect their values and expectations. Therefore, managers will have to live with the results of their behaviors toward individuals and with the results of the organizational script for those individuals.

Goal-Setting Theory

At the most basic level, goal-setting theory is concerned with the effect of goals on individual performance. Some view goal-setting theory as an extension of process theories of motivation. The emphasis is on the intended outcomes and the motivational process that the establishment of the intended outcomes has on the behavior of the individual. Goal-setting theory suggests that goals are associated with enhanced performance because they mobilize effort, direct attention, and encourage persistence and strategy development.[20]

Locke and Latham developed a sophisticated theory of individual goal setting and performance.[21] They claim that an assigned goal influences a person's beliefs about being able to perform that task (labeled *self-efficacy*) and encourages the acceptance of those goals as personal goals. Both factors in turn influence performance. Goals can be implicit or explicit, vague or clearly defined, and self-imposed or externally imposed. Many studies have shown that relative to general do-your-best goals, job performance is enhanced by the setting of specific goals.[22] Some studies suggest that people will accept and work hard to attain difficult goals until they reach the limits of their capabilities. However, as goals become difficult, they may be rejected, and performance will suffer.[23] Activity 10–5W provides an opportunity to experience some powerful notions of goal-setting theory as a motivational mechanism.

Linking Theory and Managerial Practice

Motivation theory is a core concept in the understanding of human behavior. As such it is linked to many aspects of work behavior. The purpose of this section is to discuss some of the linkages and explore managerial practices that are built on the various motivational theories that we reviewed in the earlier part of the module. We will explore the relationship between goal-setting theory and management by objectives, motivation and profit-sharing or stock-ownership programs, motivation and skill-based pay programs, Pygmalion and motivation programs, and motivation programs based on behavior modification.

Management by Objectives

Management by objectives and results (MBO&R) is a system that serves both as a planning tool and a motivational philosophy. This approach reflects synthesis of three areas: goal setting, participative decision making, and feedback. MBO&R is viewed as a participative process whereby managers and employees together set goals for work performance, personal development, and periodic reviews to assess progress. The process allows managers to integrate individual, team, unit/department, and organizational goals.

The process involves four key components: goal setting, mutual involvement of supervisor and employee, implementation, and performance appraisal and feedback. As such, in an MBO&R program, the supervisor and subordinate attempt to reach consensus on the following: the goals the subordinate will strive to accomplish during a specific time period; the means that the subordinate will utilize to reach the goals, and how and when the progress toward the goal accomplishment will be measured and evaluated.

Developed in the 1950s by Peter Drucker,[24] this managerial application has gone through many transformations.[25] While many organizations are using MBO&R successfully, critics have attacked the approach particularly with respect to the ways in which some organizations apply it. Some critics argue that MBO&R places too much emphasis on rewards and punishments; generates an excessive amount of paperwork; places too much emphasis on individual goals versus team goals, and fosters game playing between managers and subordinates.[26]

Profit-Sharing Plans

Employee participation in work-planning programs is frequently reported as a method to link employee compensation with organization profits. It is an old idea that has attracted new interest as a means of increasing productivity and quality. The Scanlon Plan, which goes back to the 1930s, is a program in which employees are involved in making and integrating suggestions into the company's operating processes. A formula is used to distribute a percentage of the resulting cost savings and profits to employees. The plan has been used for many years by the Lincoln Electric Company of Cleveland and has benefited both the company and the employees. A unique and relatively recent development of profit-sharing plans is the **employee stock ownership plan (ESOP).**

Employee Stock Ownership Plans (ESOPs)

ESOP activities have been spreading at an increasing rate over the past decade. It is estimated that 10 million workers, or nearly 10 percent of the private sector workforce, are participating in ESOPs with assets of about $20 billion in 7,500 companies, about 1,500 of which are majority or fully employee owned.[27] There are three main types of ESOPs:

1. *The nonleveraged ESOP.* The company contributes stock or cash to buy stock in a trust that buys workers shares, which workers receive upon retirement or leaving the company.

2. *The leveraged ESOP.* Workers' ownership is established with money the company borrows to invest in company stock for the workers. The company guarantees that it will make periodic payments to the worker-ownership trust to amortize the loan.

3. *The tax-credit ESOP.* The company gets dollar-for-dollar tax credit for stock purchased for workers.

Research indicates that ESOP companies showed an average annual productivity increase, improved employee motivation,[28] and increased growth rate of two to four times that of companies where employees did not own stock.[29]

Skill-Based Pay

Skill-based pay (at times called competency-based pay) has emerged as alternative to job-based pay. Rather than having an individual's job title define his or her pay category, skill-based pay bases pay levels on the number of skills the individual has mastered.[30] Skill-based pay programs motivate employees to learn, expand their skills, and grow. A recent study of *Fortune* 1000 companies found that companies that pay employees for learning skills reported higher job satisfaction, improved product quality, and increased productivity. Furthermore, 75 percent of those companies reported lower operating costs and turnover.[31]

Skill-based pay programs are consistent with many of the process and content motivational theories. For example, acquiring new skills is congruent with McClelland's *n* achievement needs theory because it provides more freedom and flexibility in the work environment and, for high achievers, offers new skills that help them deal successfully with more challenging jobs. Another example that "fits" is equity theory. Individuals are likely to perceive the equity in the program. The more one learns, the more one gets paid. At the same time, tension within the individual might motivate him or her to learn more skills.

From an organization and management perspective, skill-based pay provides clear advantages: It is a way to continually upgrade employees' skills, a way to provide managerial flexibility in terms of grouping people based on changing customer needs and demands, a way to improve communications and understanding across units boundaries, and a way to stay competitive with a dynamic workforce that is current in its knowledge and competencies.

Pygmalion and Motivation

As we saw in Module 2 on expectations and learning, the self-fulfilling prophecy (SFP) or **Pygmalion effect** is a major social phenomenon with far-reaching implications. In a recent study, a unique and practical model that pulls together leadership, expectation, motivation, and performance at work was proposed.[32] (See Figure 10–7.)

The model encompasses five interrelated variables: manager expectations, leadership, subordinate self-expectations, effort, and achievement. The manager's performance expectations for a subordinate influence the leadership dynamics between the manager and the subordinate. As a result, the subordinate raises his or her expectations, which increases the motivation to exert a greater deal of effort on the job, the outcome of which is improved performance and better achievement. Dov Eden's research demonstrated that the combination of raising self-expectations and setting specific, hard goals increases performance. Furthermore, this line of research and its findings provided additional support for the combined effect of Pygmalion and goal setting on motivation. This combined effect appears especially promising in increasing motivation and performance.[33]

Behavior Modification

A very different kind of practical technique that has been attracting much managerial attention is **behavior modification**. Based especially on the work of B. F. Skinner, behavior modification insists that internal states of mind (such as needs) are misleading, scientifically unmeasurable, and in any case hypothetical. Instead, what managers and behavioral scientists need to pay attention to is behavior—the observable outcomes of situations and choices, what people actually do. This approach to behavior rests on

Figure 10–7
A Model of Self-Fulfilling
Prophecy at Work

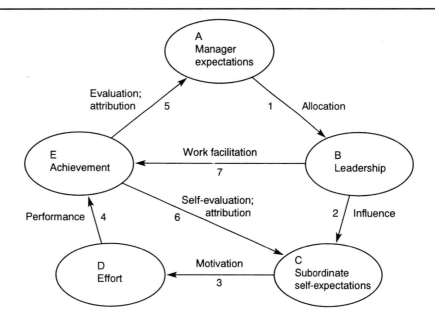

two underlying assumptions. First, human behavior is determined by the environment. Second, human behavior is subject to observable laws (such as the laws of physics or chemistry) and thus can be predicted and changed. Behavior is changed by rewarding it, ignoring it, or punishing people for using it. The behavior modification view says that behavior is a response to a combination of specific stimuli and other environmental factors (such as time and previous experiences).

Continuous reinforcement rewards every occurrence of the desired behavior. (You give your dog a biscuit every time it sits up.) This is the quickest way to get a person to act in the desired way. *Extinction* rewards no behavior; you ignore the behavior (a two-year-old child's tantrum or your dog's chasing its tail instead of sitting up). Behavior receiving no external reward will be less frequent than behavior that is rewarded. *Intermittent reinforcement* rewards some responses but not others according to a preset schedule (rewarding the dog only after five successful sits). Intermittent reinforcement establishes the desired behavior more slowly than continuous reinforcement but has longer-term effects. Moreover, intermittently reinforced behavior is less easily extinguished than continuously reinforced behavior.

In behavior modification (or *operant conditioning,* to use its more formal name), consequences are arranged for some voluntary behavior that is desired. For instance, workers are praised for properly doing their jobs. The most effective reinforcements seem to be specific, detailed, and concrete praise about how and what the employee has done, closely and directly related to the desired behavior. Thus, rather than saying, "Good job, Jones!" the supervisor says something like, "Jones, your use of the new package format has really increased—the record says you're making over 90 percent use on your shipments, and as I watch, I can see you've got a good system."

Behavior modification has had some notable successes. At Emery Air Freight, to use a classic case, managers thought workers were not using containers to combine small package shipments as often as they could. A study showed that containers were deployed in less than half of the cases when they could be used. A behavior modification program resulted in significant improvements in container use that saved the company some $650,000 annually, and the improved behavior persisted over several years. Other companies are also using varied forms of behavior modification, among them General Electric, B. F. Goodrich, and Michigan Bell. Of course, lots of good managers and supervisors (and parents) have used it for years without the fancy name. There are some concerns about *why* it works, however.

While Skinner's reinforcement suggests that the consequences themselves govern behavior, a close look at Emery Air Freight suggests that feedback and goal setting played as much a part of the success story as reinforcement. A high, explicit goal was set, and workers were given training on how to attain it. Employees were provided with timely, accurate reports on their performance, which they monitored themselves. Hence they reinforced themselves by direct access to performance information and always knew where they stood relative to their performance goals.

Most behavior modification programs to date have been applied at operating levels—to clerical help, production workers, or mechanics, for instance. Behavior modification is most easily applied to relatively simple jobs, where critical behaviors can be easily identified and specific performance goals can be readily set. For managerial jobs, these key factors may be more difficult to apply. Further, it's not clear that supervisor praise, recognition, and feedback are enough. After some years Emery had to introduce new reinforcers, such as special luncheons, because the old ones had become routine.

Criticisms of behavior modification include the charge that it's essentially bribery and that workers are already paid for performance. Because it disregards people's attitudes and beliefs, behavior modification has been called misleading and manipulative. Particularly where money is involved, one critic has noted that there is little difference between behavior modification and "some key elements of scientific management presented more than 60 years ago by Taylor."[34] Another criticism is that behavior modification does not take into consideration group norms, which can have an antiorganization character, such as group norms to restrict production. Indeed, behavior modification improperly used can generate much group resistance.

Why does it matter whether behavior modification works because of reinforcement or because of goals? Because you, as a manager, will need to know the essentials for getting the performance you want—whether those essentials are praise or self-administered feedback. Moreover, Emery was careful to avoid setting groups or individuals in competition with one another. Instead, people were encouraged to compete with their own previous records. You, as a manager, should know about this important factor.

Successful behavior modification requires the following:

1. A careful analysis of the job to identify specific key behaviors for targeting.

2. Careful, explicit communication to employees of what is wanted, including both behaviors and concrete, measurable goals.

3. "Reinforcers" to attach consequences to desired behaviors. Most often used are praise and recognition. (Union agreements may make other reinforcers—such as money or promotions—unavailable.)

4. Concrete, continuous feedback or feedback soon after performance that workers can use to check on themselves.

The evidence suggests that behavior modification and goal setting, creatively applied, do seem to improve *some* performance at *some* levels. The thoughtful manager will be wary of any simple solutions and instead pay close attention to the weaknesses and problems of many approaches. He or she may even combine approaches for their strengths.

International Viewpoint on Motivation

Studying theories of motivation can lead us to assume that we are dealing with "human nature"—the way people really are regardless of what part of the world they live in. This assumption would be inaccurate. Motivation, like any other behavioral phenomenon, is culture bound. Many of the motivation theories that we have reviewed in this module were developed in the U.S. context. As Geete Hofstede has shown in his comparative study of 40 modern nations, people carry "mental programs" that are rooted in the family and reinforced throughout the educational system. These mental programs contain a component of national culture that usually is most clearly expressed in the different values that predominate among people of different nations.[35] For example, we must realize that American motivation patterns and social character arise out of unique history; they are not universal—to a degree they differ from those of other cultures. As we have seen earlier, cultural diversity plays an important role in shaping individuals' behavior.

This becomes very relevant when we hear that some managers and companies attempt to apply management practices that were developed in other cultures, assuming that because they worked well in another culture they will work well in their own. Furthermore, industries need to expand the awareness they already have of the cultural differences in motivation that exist between different regions of the United States. This is shown in the relocation from the industrial Northeast, where union practices and attitudes affect productivity, to the Sunbelt states, where past economic conditions have left the population more compliant to rigorous work standards.

The United States is an achievement-oriented society that has historically encouraged and honored individual accomplishment and the attainment of material prosperity.[36] The American dream tells people that with hard work and perseverance, one can attain anything. Individualism, independence, self-confidence, and speaking out against injustice and threat are important elements of American culture. Materialism and the concomitant rewards of living well are basic goal systems in the motivation patterns.

In contrast to American motivation characteristics, Howard, Shudo, and Umeshima found the Japanese motivation and values to be quite different, with obvious implications for management practices.[37] Their research showed that Americans put greater value on individuality, while Japanese place greater value on socially oriented qualities. The social orientation of the Japanese may be traced to Confucianism, which stresses a rigid hierarchy in a collective society, where members are expected to maintain absolute loyalty and obedience to authority. The stress on dependency and security are part of the Japanese upbringing, whereas autonomy and early independence are typically American. In their corporate life Japanese show great dependency and are highly conforming and obedient in return. Japanese management recognizes the inhibiting effects this character has on creativity and innovation; at present they are emphasizing the need to integrate programs into their schools that will free up and develop the creativity and ingenuity they envy in America.

As of late, work motivation in mainland China seems to be an issue of concern. The problem of low work motivation that was identified by foreign researchers and practitioners was a forbidden topic of investigation for Chinese researchers until the end of the Cultural Revolution.[38] Factors that have been postulated as responsible for low motivation and productivity include lack of an effective reward–punishment system, "unscientific" work quotas, the problematic promotion–wage system, lifetime employment, and an ineffective "political work-system."[39]

We discussed McClelland's work on achievement in this module. Adler reviewed the cross-cultural research on achievement and found it relatively robust across cultures.[40] For example, managers in New Zealand appear to follow the pattern developed in the United States. However, the literature would show that the word *achievement* itself is hardly translatable into any language other than English. However, countries characterized by a high need for achievement also have a high need to produce and a strong willingness to accept risk. Anglo-American countries such as the United States, Canada, and Great Britain follow the high-achievement motivation pattern, while countries such as Chile and Portugal follow the low-achievement motivation pattern. (Admittedly, these broad generalizations are based on very limited research data.)

Implications for managerial style, practices, and motivation planning for U.S. firms operating branches in foreign countries are apparent. The social character, the values, and the cultural practices of each country must be taken into consideration when planning and operating the human organization. Corporations operating abroad have long known this but have often not taken it sufficiently into account. Yet as the economic infrastructure and the social fabric of the societies in different parts of the globe change, one needs to pay attention to the actual changes and their nature. The transformations that we have seen during the last decade in the Pacific Rim countries, South American countries, the Middle East, and eastern Europe are challenging the managers of international companies to stay away from making assumptions about human behavior based on the recent past. The indications are that some changes might be occurring in the value base, yet we cannot substantiate this view empirically. At the same time, human expectations and goals in different part of the globe seem to be shifting and as such so should our motivational programs and practices.

Summary

Some understanding of motivation can be gained by examining your own work experience and that of your classmates and then sorting out factors accounting for "best" and "less than best" performance. For this purpose Activity 10–1 yields results similar to Herzberg's dissatisfiers (those factors that make workers unhappy when they are not present) and motivators (those factors that provide opportunities for self-direction and challenge). Motivation is commonly thought of as being inherent in the individual: One either has it or doesn't. When defined as psychological energy directed toward goals, all behavior is motivated; goals are the direction for achievement of wants or avoidance of threats. All "nonproductive" behavior can be viewed as attempts to avoid or counteract threats.

Theories of motivation can be classified as either content or process. The three content theories of motivation—Maslow's need hierarchy, Herzberg's motivation-hygiene theory, and McClelland's achievement—focus on the specific factors that motivate people. The four process theories—expectancy, equity, goal setting, and reinforcement—focus on the elements that foster individual choices of behavioral patterns and the forces that will increase the likelihood that specific behaviors will be repeated over time.

This module focused on understanding motivation dynamics at work; therefore, the last section explored specific managerial implications and programs: management by objectives, profit-sharing plans, employee stock ownership plans, skill-based pay, employee involvement programs, Pygmalion and motivation, and behavior modification. Finally, motivation in the global context of work was discussed.

Key Terms and Concepts

Behavior modification	Motivation theory
Content theories of motivation	*n* achievement
Employee stock ownership plans (ESOP)	*n* power
Equity theory	P–L (Porter–Lawler) model
Expectancy theory	Process theories of motivation
Goal setting	Profit-sharing plans
Hierarchy of needs	Pygmalion effect
Hygiene factors	Reinforcement theories of motivation
Management by objectives	Skill-based pay

Study Questions

1. When this book's authors created the classroom workshop model, which of the following viewpoints did they use: traditional, human relations, or human resources? Give reasons and illustrations to support your answer.

2. Your manager tells you Herzberg's theory applies to himself and other managers he knows, so his advice is to forget about other fancy theories of motivation. If he is the type of manager you can talk to, how would you respond?

3. What are *intrinsic* and *extrinsic* factors in terms of motivation? To what theories do these apply? Why are these important distinctions for a manager to remember in planning for employee motivation?

4. How do Herzberg's dissatisfiers fit into Maslow's hierarchy of needs? How do his motivators fit into the hierarchy?

5. The discussion on leadership asked whether leaders are born or made. How do McClelland's and Eden's works affect the answer to this question?

6. Compare and contrast any one content theory of motivation and any one process theory of motivation.

7. What is the basic management issue when you manage people according to their individual needs, abilities, and experiences? What actions can supervisors take to manage according to individual differences while trying to avoid the problems inherent in such an approach?

8. If you were the human resources manager of a large corporation and the executive office told you to prepare a report on installing an employee profit-sharing program, what major topics would your report include?

9. Explain the phrase "Motivation is culture bound."

10. Thorndike's law of effects states that behavior that appears to lead to positive consequences tends to be repeated, while behavior that appears to lead to neutral or negative consequences tends not be repeated. Which of the theories does this law describe? Give reasons for your answer.

Endnotes

1. R. M. Steers, L. W. Porter, and G. A. Bigley, *Motivation and Leadership at Work,* (New York, McGraw-Hill, 1996).

2. T. S. Pittman, "Motivation," in D. T. Gilbert, S. T. Fiske, and G. Lindzey (eds.), *The Handbook of Social Psychology,* (New York: McGraw-Hill, 1998), pp. 549–90; F. J. Landy and W. S. Becker, "Motivation Theory Reconsidered," in *Research in Organizational Behavior,* vol. 9, L. L. Cummings and B. M. Staw, eds. (Greenwich, CT: JAI Press, 1987), pp. 1–38.

3. R. Kanter and E. D. Heggestad, "Motivational Traits and Skills: A Person-Centered Approach to Work Motivation," in L. L. Cummings and B. M. Staw (eds.), *Research in Organizational Behavior,* vol. 19, (Greenwich CT: JAI Press, 1997), pp. 1–56; R. A. Katzell and D. E. Thompson, "Work Motivation: Theory and Practice," *American Psychologist* 45, no. 2 (1990), pp. 144–53.

4. For the best discussion of this theory, see F. Herzberg, "One More Time: How Do You Motivate Employees?" *Harvard Business Review* 46 (January–February 1968), pp. 53–62.

5. For a critique of Herzberg's work, see E. E. Lawler III, *Motivation in Work Organizations,* (Monterey, CA: Brooks/Cole, 1973), pp. 69–72.

6. The ERG theory discusses frustration of the growth needs. See C. P. Alderfer, *Existence, Relatedness, and Growth,* (New York: Free Press, 1972); C. P. Schneider and C. P. Alderfer, "Three Studies of Measures of Need Satisfaction in Organizations," *Administrative Science Quarterly,* December 1973, pp. 489–505.

7. A. H. Maslow, "A Theory of Human Motivation," *Psychological Review* 50 (1943), pp. 370–96.

8. D. C. McClelland, "Power Motivation and Organizational Leadership," *Power: The Inner Experience,* (New York: Livington Publishers, 1975), pp. 252–71.

9. D. G. Winter, *The Power Motive,* (New York: Free Press, 1973), pp. 108–9.

10. L. L. Cummings and C. J. Berger, "Organization Structure: How Does It Influence Attitudes and Performance?" *Organizational Dynamics* 5 (Autumn 1976), pp. 34–49.

11. D. C. McClelland, "Power Motivation and Organizational Leadership," p. 269. Also see D. C. McClelland and R. S. Steele, *Motivation Workshops,* (New York: General Learning Press, 1972) for the type of training program used.

12. U. Pareek, "Motivational Analysis of Organizational-Behavior (MAO-B)," *The 1986 Annual, Developing Human Resources* (1986), pp. 121–28.

13. J. S. Adams, "Toward an Understanding of Inequity," *Journal of Abnormal and Social Psychology* 67 (1963), pp. 422–36; J. Brockner, J. Greenberg, A. Brockner, J. Bortz, J. Davy, and C. Carter, "Equity Theory and Work Performance: Further Evidence of the Impact of Survivor Guilt," *Academy of Management Journal* 29 (1986), pp. 373–84; R. C. Huseman, J. D. Hatfield, and E. W. Miles, "A New Perspective on Equity Theory: The Equity Sensitivity Construct," *Academy of Management Review* 12 (1987), pp. 222–34; J. Greenberg, "Cognitive Reevaluation of Outcomes in Response to Underpayment Inequity," *Academy of Management Journal* 32, no. 1 (1989), pp. 174–84.

14. See, for example, M. E. Tubbs, D. M. Boehne, and J. G. Gahl, "Expectancy, Valence, and Motivational Force Functions in Goal Setting Research: An Empirical Test," *Journal of Applied Psychology* 78, no. 3 (1993), pp. 361–73.

15. V. H. Vroom, *Work and Motivation,* (New York: John Wiley & Sons, 1964).

16. M. J. Stahl and D. W. Grisby, "A Comparison of Unit, Subjectivity and Regression Measures of Second Level Valences in Expectancy Theory," *Decision Sciences* 18 (1987), pp. 62–72; H. J. Klein, "An Integrated Control Theory Model of Work Behavior," *Academy of Management Review* 14, no. 2 (1989), pp. 150–72.

17. R. J. House, H. J. Shapiro, and M. A. Wahba, "Expectancy as a Predictor of Work Behavior and Attitudes: A Reevaluation of Empirical Evidence," *Decision Sciences* 5 (1974), pp. 481–506; S. T. Connolly, "Some Conceptual and Methodological Issues in Expectancy Theory Models of Work Performance," *Academy of Management Review* 1 (1976), pp. 37–47.

18. L. W. Porter and E. E. Lawler III, *Managerial Attitudes and Performance,* (Burr Ridge, IL: Richard D. Irwin, 1968).

19. For an extensive discussion of the impact of groups on individuals in organizations, see J. Richard Hackman, "Group Influences on Individuals," in M. D. Dunnette (ed.), *Handbook of Industrial and Organizational Psychology,* (Skokie, IL: Rand McNally, 1976), pp. 1455–1525. Hackman pays special attention to the effect of group norms and influences on member performance effectiveness.

20. A. M. O'Leary-Kelly, J. J. Martocchio, and D. D. Frink, "A Review of the Influence of Group Goals on Group Performance," *Academy of Management Journal* 37, no. 5 (1994), pp. 1285–301.

21. E. A. Locke, and G. P. Latham, *A Theory of Goal Setting and Task Performance,* (Englewood Cliffs, NJ: Prentice-Hall, 1990).

22. See, for example, G. P. Latham, and T. W. Lee, "Goal Setting," in E. A. Locke (ed.), *Generalized from Laboratory to Field Settings,* (Lexington, MA: Lexington Books, 1986), pp. 100–17.

23. See, for example, D. E. Terpstra and E. J. Rozell, "The Relationship of Goal Setting to Organizational Profitability," *Group & Organization Management* 19, no. 3 (1994), pp. 285–94.

24. R. G. Greenwood, "Management by Objectives," *Academy of Management Review* 6 (1981), pp. 225–30.

25. See, for example, G. S. Obiorne, *Management by Objectives,* (New York: Pitman Publishing Company, 1965); J. N. Kondrasuk, "Studies in MOB Effectiveness," *Academy of Management Review* 6, no. 3 (1981), pp. 426–31; G. P. Latham, *Increasing Productivity through Performance Appraisal,* (Reading, MA: Addison-Wesley, 1992).

26. C. D. Pringle and J. G. Longnecker, "The Ethics of MBO," *The Academy of Management Review* 7, no. 2 (1982), pp. 177–86; Latham, Ibid; T. H. Poister and G. Streib, "MBO in Municipal Government: Variations on Traditional Management," *Public Administration Review,* January–February 1995, pp. 48–56.

27. Two thoughtful and comprehensive books on the subject have been written by J. R. Blasi, *Employee Ownership: Revolution or Ripoff,* (Cambridge, MA: Ballinger, 1988); *The New Owners* (New York: Harper Business, 1993).

28. T. R. Marsh and D. E. McAllister, "ESOP Table: A Survey of Companies with Employee Ownership Plans," *Journal of Corporation Law* 6, no. 3 (1981), pp. 552–623.

29. *ESOP Survey:* 1990 (Washington, DC: ESOP Association of America, 1990). M. Trachman, *Employee Ownership and Corporate Growth in High Technology Companies,* (Oakland, CA: National Center for Employee Ownership Publications, 1985).

30. For a good review, see E. E. Lawler III, G. E. Ledford Jr., and L. Chang, "Who Uses Skill-Based Pay, and Why," *Compensations & Benefits Review,* March–April 1993, pp. 22–38; G. E. Ledford Jr., "Paying for Skills, Knowledge, and Competencies of Knowledge Workers," *Compensations & Benefits Review,* July–August 1995, pp. 55–62.

31. E. E. Lawler III, S. A. Mohrman, and G. E. Ledford Jr., *Creating High-Performance Organizations: Practice Results in the Fortune 1000,* (San Francisco: Jossey-Bass, 1995).

32. D. Eden, *Pygmalion in Management: Productivity as Self-Fulfilling Prophecy,* (Lexington, MA: Lexington Books, 1990), p. 70.

33. D. Eden, "Pygmalion, Goal Setting, and Expectancy: Compatible Ways to Boost Productivity," *Academy of Management Review* 13, no. 4 (1988), pp. 639–52; D. Eden, "Self-Fulfilling Prophecy as a Management Tool: Harnessing Pygmalion," *Academy of Management Review* 6 (1984), pp. 64–73; D. Eden and A. B. Shani, "Pygmalion Goes to Boot Camp: Expectancy, Leadership, and Trainee Performance," *Journal of Applied Psychology* 67 (1982), pp. 194–99.

34. E. A. Locke, "The Myth of Behavior Mod in Organizations," *Academy of Management Review,* October 1977.

35. G. Hofstede, *Culture's Consequences: International Differences in Work-Related Values,* (Beverly Hills, CA: Sage Publications, 1990).

36. J. T. Spence, "Achievement American Style, The Rewards and Costs of Individualism," *American Psychologist,* December 1985, pp. 1285–94.

37. A. Howard, K. Shudo, and M. Umeshima, "Motivation and Values among Japanese and American Managers," *Personnel Psychology* 36 (1983), pp. 883–98.

38. See, for example, O. Shenkar and S. Ronen, "Structure and Importance of Work Goals among Managers in the People's Republic of China," *Academy of Management Journal* 30 (1987), pp. 564–76; M. M. Yang, "Between State and Society: The Construction of Cooporateness in a Chinese Socialist Factory," *The Australian Journal of Chinese Affairs* 22 (1989), pp. 36–60.

39. See, for example, P. Jin, "Work Motivation and Productivity in Voluntarily Formed Work Teams: A Field Study in China," *Organizational Behavior & Human Decision Processes* 54 (1993), pp. 133–55.

40. N. J. Adler, *International Dimensions of Organizational Behavior,* (Boston: Kent, 1986), pp. 129–30.

Activity 10–2: The Slade Plating Department Case

Objectives:

a. To allow you to examine motivational processes.

b. To provide you and your team an opportunity to investigate motivational issues from different theoretical perspectives.

c. To provide you with the opportunity to integrate many of the content areas covered thus far in the course via the analysis of the case.

Task 1 (Individual Activity):

Read the following case carefully and answer these questions:

a. What background factors are important in understanding the emergent role system that developed in the plating room?

b. Exhibit 6 shows the various subgroups the developed in the plating room. The Sarto and Clark subgroups are the two most important. What are some of the factors or characteristics that probably account for group membership in each subgroup?

c. Make a complete list of the norms of the emergent role system that developed in this case.

d. What are some of the major problems at the Slade Plating Department?

Task 2 (Class Discussion):

The instructor will lead a class discussion to capture the basic facts in the case.

Task 3 (Team Activity):

Teams will examine the case from a specific theoretical perspective assigned by the instructor. Each team is to focus on the following:

- Capture the essence of the assigned theoretical perspective.
- Identify the major facts in the case as viewed by the assigned perspective.
- Conduct the analysis of the facts from the assigned perspective.
- Identify potential problems in the case.
- Identify the most critical problem.
- Provide some alternative solutions.

Task 4:

Each team will present its analysis and findings to the total learning community.

The Slade Plating Department

Ralph Porter, production manager of the Slade Company, was concerned by reports of dishonesty among some employees in the Plating Department. From reliable sources, he learned that a few were punching the time-cards of a number of their co-workers who were leaving early. Porter had only recently joined the Slade organization. From conversations with the previous production manager and other fellow managers, he judged that they were pleased, in general, with the overall performance of the Plating Department.

The Slade Company was a small but prosperous manufacturer of metal products designed for industrial application. Its manufacturing plant, located in central Michigan, employed 500 workers who were engaged in producing a large variety of clamps, inserts, knobs, and similar items. Orders for these products were usually large and came in on a recurrent basis. The volume of orders fluctuated in response to business conditions in the primary industries that the company served. At the time of this case, sales volume had been high for over a year. The bases on which the Slade Company secured orders, in rank of importance, were quality, delivery, and reasonable price.

The organization of manufacturing operations at the Slade plant is shown in Exhibit 1. The departments listed there, from left to right, are approximately in the order in which material flowed through the plant. The die making and set up operations required the greatest degree of skill, which was supplied by highly paid, long-service craftspeople. The finishing departments, divided operationally and geographically between plating and painting, attracted less highly trained but relatively skilled workers, some of whom had been employed by the company for many years. The remaining operations required largely unskilled labor and contained positions characterized by relatively low pay and high turnover of personnel.

The plating room covered the entire top floor of the plant. Exhibit 2 shows the floor plan, the disposition of workers, and the flow of work throughout this department. Thirty-eight people worked in the department, plating or oxidizing the metal parts or preparing parts for the application of paint at another location in the plant. The department's work occurred in response to orders communicated by production schedules that were revised daily. Schedule revisions, caused by last-minute order increases or rush requests from customers, resulted in short-term volume fluctuations—particularly in the plating, painting, and shipping departments. Exhibit 3 outlines the activities of the various jobs, their interrelationships, and the type of work in which each specialized. Exhibit 4 rates the various types of jobs in terms of the technical skill, physical effort, discomfort, and training time associated with their performance.

The activities that took place in the plating room were of three main types:

1. Acid dipping, where parts were etched by being placed in baskets that were manually immersed and agitated in an acid solution.

2. Barrel tumbling, where parts were roughened or smoothed by being loaded into machine-powered revolving drums containing abrasive, caustic, or corrosive solutions.

3. Plating, either manual, where parts were loaded on racks and were immersed by hand through the plating sequence; or automatic, where racks or baskets were manually loaded with parts that were then carried by a conveyor system through the plating sequence.

Within these main divisions of work, there were a number of variables, such as cycle times, chemical formulas, abrasive mixtures, and so forth, that distinguished particular jobs as Exhibit 3.

This case was prepared as the basis for class discussion rather than to illustrate either effective or ineffective handling of an administrative situation.

Exhibit 1   Manufacturing Organization

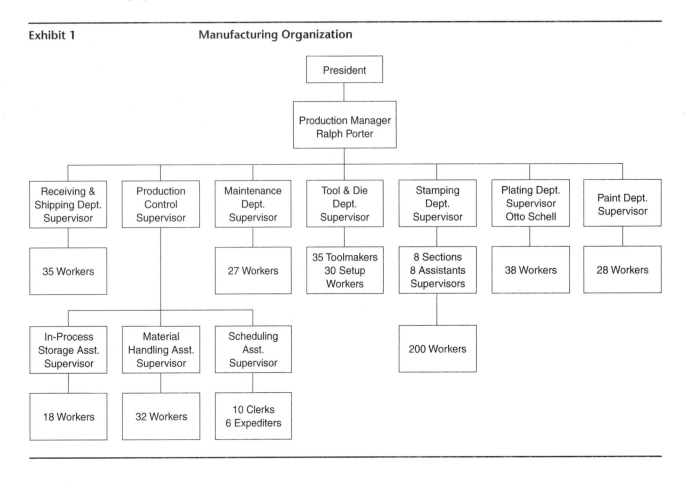

The work of the plating room was received in batch lots averaging 1,000 pieces each. The clerk moved each batch, which was accompanied by a routing slip, to its first operation. This routing slip indicated the operations to be performed and also when each major operation on the batch was scheduled to be completed, so that the finished product could be shipped on time. From the accumulation of orders presented, each worker organized his or her own work schedule so as to make optimal use of equipment, materials, and time. Upon completion of an order, each worker moved the lot to its next work position or to the finished material location near the freight elevator.

The plating room was under the direction of its supervisor, Otto Schell, who worked a regular 8:00 a.m. to 5:00 p.m. day, five days a week. The supervisor spent a good deal of working time attending to maintenance and repair of equipment, procuring supplies, handling late schedule changes, and seeing to it that people were at their proper work locations.

Working conditions in the plating room varied considerably. That part of the department containing the tumbling barrels and the plating machines was constantly awash, alternately with cold water, steaming acid, or a caustic soda. Workers in this part of the room wore knee boots, long rubber aprons, and high-gauntlet rubber gloves. This uniform, consistent with the general atmosphere of the wet part of the room, was hot in the summer, cold in winter. In contrast, the remainder of the room was dry, relatively odorless, and provided reasonably stable temperature and humidity conditions for those who worked there.

The men and women employed in the plating room are listed in Exhibit 5. This exhibit provides certain personal data on each department member, including a productivity skill rating (based on subjective and objective appraisals of potential performance), as reported by the members of the department.

Pay in the department was low for the central Michigan area. Employees typically started at a few dollars over minimum wage, with small increases given over time based on seniority and skill. However, working hours for the plating room were long.

Exhibit 2
Plating Room Layout

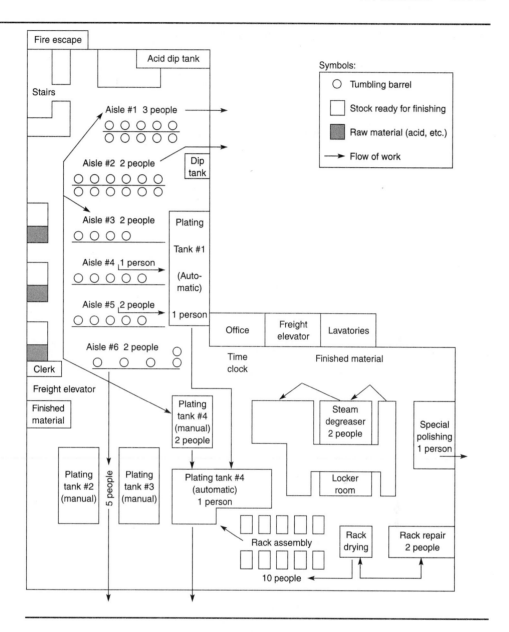

To keep employee training and benefit costs down, the company practice was to increase overtime rather than hire new employees. The typical Monday-through-Friday workweek in the department was 60 hours (except for the rack assembly area, which worked a standard 40-hour week). The first 40 hours were paid for on a straight-time rate basis while the next 20 hours were paid on a time-and-one-half basis. All weekend work was paid on a double-time rate basis.

As Exhibit 5 indicates, Philip Kirk, a worker in aisle 2, provided the data for this case. After he had been a member of the department for several months, Kirk noted that certain members of the department tended to seek each other out during free time on and off the job. He then observed that these informal associations were enduring, built upon common activities and shared ideas about what was and what was not legitimate behavior in the department. His description of the pattern of these associations is diagrammed in Exhibit 6.

The Sarto group, named after Tony Sarto who was its most respected member and the arbiter between the other members, was the largest group in the department. Except for Louis Patrici, Alice Bartolo, and Frank Bonzani (who relieved each other during break periods), the group invariably ate lunch together on the fire escape near aisle 1. On those Saturdays and Sundays when overtime work was required, the Sarto

**Exhibit 3
Outline of Work Flow,
Plating Room**

Aisle 1: Worked closely with Aisle 3 in preparation of parts by barrel tumbling and acid dipping for high-quality* plating in Tanks 4 and 5. Also did a considerable quantity of highly specialized, high-quality acid-etching work not requiring further processing.

Aisle 2: Tumbled items of regular quality and design in preparation for painting. Less frequently, did oxidation dipping work of regular quality, but sometimes of special design, not requiring further processing.

Aisle 3: Worked closely with Aisle 1 on high-quality tumbling work for Tanks 4 and 5.

Aisles 4 and 5: Produced regular tumbling work for Tank 1.

Aisle 6: Did high-quality tumbling work for special products plated in Tanks 2 and 3.

Tank 1: Worked on standard, automated plating of regular quality not further processed in plating room, and regular work further processed in Tank 5.

Tanks 2 and 3: Produced special, high-quality plating work not requiring further processing.

Tank 4: Did special, high-quality plating work further plated in Tank 5.

Tank 5: Automated production of high- and regular-quality, special- and regular-design plated parts sent directly to shipping.

Rack Assembly: Placed parts to be plated in Tank 5 on racks.

Rack Repair: Performed routine replacement and repair of racks used in Tank 5.

Polishing: Processed, by manual or semimanual methods, odd-lot special orders which were sent directly to shipping. Also, sorted and reclaimed parts rejected by inspectors in the shipping department.

Degreasing: Took incoming raw stock, processed it through caustic solution, and placed clean stock in storage ready for processing elsewhere in the plating room.

*High or regular quality: The quality of finishes could broadly be distinguished by the thickness of plate and/or care in preparation. Regular or special work: The complexity of work depended on the routine or special character of design and finish specifications.

**Exhibit 4
Skill indices by Job Group**

Job	Technical Skill Required	Physical Effort Required	Degree of Discomfort Involved	Degree of Training Required*
Aisle 1	10	10	10	10
Tanks 2 to 4	8	9	10	9
Aisles 2 to 6	6	10	10	6
Tank 5	10	6	4	9
Tank 1	3	6	6	4
Degreasing	2	8	4	1
Polishing	5	2	2	4
Rack assembly and repair	1	1	1	1

Note: Rated on scales of 1 (the least) to 10 (the greatest) in each category.
*The amount of experience required to assume complete responsibility for the job.

group operated as a team, regardless of weekday work assignments, to get overtime work completed as quickly as possible. (Few department members not affiliated with either the Sarto or the Clark groups worked on weekends.) Off the job, Sarto group members often joined in parties or weekend trips. with Sarto's summer house being a frequent rendezvous.

Sarto's group was the most cohesive one in the department in terms of its organized punch-in and punch-out system. Since the group's members were regularly scheduled to work from 7:00 a.m. to 7:00 p.m. weekdays, and since all supervisors left at 5:00 p.m., it was possible almost every day to finish a "day's work" by 5:30 p.m. and leave the plant. Moreover, if one of the group's members stayed until 7 o'clock, he or she could punch the time cards of a number of others and help gain them free time without pay loss. (This system operated on weekends also, at which time supervisors were only present, for short periods, if at all.) In Sarto's group the duty of staying late rotated, so that no one did so more than once a week. In addition, the group would punch in a member if he or she were unavoidably delayed. Such a practice never occurred without prior notice from the person who expected to be late and never if the tardiness was expected to last beyond 8:00 a.m., the start of the day for the supervisor.

Sarto explained the logic behind the system to Kirk:

Exhibit 5   **Plating Room Personnel**

Location	Name	Age	Marital Status	Company Seniority (yrs.)	Department Seniority (yrs.)	Education (yrs.)	Familial Relationships	Productivity skill Rating[a]
Aisle 1	Tony Sarto	30	M	13	13	12	Pete Facelli, cousin Louis Patrici, uncle	10
	Pete Facelli	26	M	8	8	12	Tony Sarto, cousin	9
	Joe Iambi	31	M	5	5	10		9
Aisle 2	Herman Schell	48	S	26	26	8	Otto Schell, brother	3
	Philip Kirk	23	M	1	1	16		NA[b]
Aisle 3	Dom Pantaleoni	31	M	10	10	9		9
	Sal Maletta	32	M	12	12	11		8
Aisle 4	Bob Pearson	22	S	4	4	12	Father in tool & die dept.	10
Aisle 5	Charlie Malone	44	M	22	8	8		4
	John Lacey	41	S	9	5	9	Brother in paint dept.	4
Aisle 6	Joyce Martin	27	S	7	7	12		7
	Bill Mensch	41	M	6	2	8		7
Tank 1	Henry LaForte	38	M	14	6	12		5
Tanks 2 & 3	Ralph Parker	25	S	7	7	12		7
	Angela Harding	27	S	8	8	12	Brother in tool & die dept.	7
	George Flood	22	S	5	5	12		6
	Harry Clark	29	M	8	8	12		8
	Tom Bond	25	S	6	6	12		7
Tank 4	Frank Bonzani	27	M	9	9	12		9
	Alice Bartolo	24	M	6	6	12		8
Tank 5	Louis Patrici	47	S	14	14	14	Tony Sarto, nephew Pete Facelli, nephew	10
Rack Assembly	10 women	30–40	9M, 1S	10 (av.)	10 (av.)	8 (av.)	6 with husbands in Co.	7 (av.)
Rack Maintenance	Will Partridge	57	M	14	2	8		4
	Lloyd Swan	62	M	3	3	8		4
Degreasing	Dave Susi	45	S	1	1	12		6
	Mike Maher	41	M	4	4	8		5
Polishing	Russ Perkins	49	M	12	2	12		7
Supervisor	Otto Schell	56	M	35	35	12	Herman Schell, brother	8
Clerk	Bill Pierce	32	M	10	4	12		7
Technician	Frank Rutlage	24	S	2	2	14		5

[a]On a potential scale of 1 (bottom) to 10 (top), as evaluated by the workers in the department.

[b]Kirk was the source of data for this case, and as such, he was in a biased position to report accurately perceptions about himself.

Exhibit 6
Informal Groupings in the Plating Room

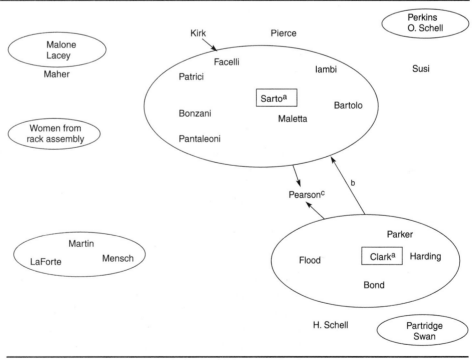

a. The boxes indicate those individuals who clearly demonstrated leadership behavior (most closely personified the values shared by their groups, were most often sought for help and arbitration, and so forth).

b. While the two- and three-person groupings had little informal contact outside their own boundaries, the five-man Clark group did seek to join the largest group in social affairs outside the plant, these were relatively infrequent.

c. Though not an active member of any group, Bob Pearson was regarded with affection by the two large groups.

You know that our hourly pay rate is quite low, compared to other companies. What makes this the best place to work is the feeling of security you get. No one ever gets laid off in this department. With all the hours in the workweek, all the company ever has to do is shorten the workweek when orders fall off. We have to tighten our belts, but we can all get along. When things are going well, as they are now, the company is only interested in getting out the work. It doesn't help to get it out faster than it's really needed—so we go home a little early whenever we can. Of course, some people abuse this sort of thing—like Herman—but others work even harder, and it averages out.

Whenever an extra order has to be pushed through, naturally I work until 7:00 p.m. So do a lot of others. I believe that if I stay until my work is caught up and my equipment is in good shape, that's all the company wants of me. They leave us alone and expect us to produce—and we do.

When Kirk asked Sarto if he would not rather work shorter hours at higher pay in a union shop (Slade employees were not organized), he just laughed and said: "It wouldn't come close to an even trade."

The members of Sarto's group were explicit about what constituted a fair day's work. Customarily, they cited Herman Schell, Kirk's work partner and the supervisor's brother, as a man who consistently produced below level. Kirk received an informal orientation from Herman during his first days on the job. As Herman put it:

I've worked at this job for a good many years, and I expect to stay here a good many more. You're just starting out, and you don't know which end is up yet. We spend a lot of time in here; and no matter how hard we work, the pile of work never goes down. There's always more to take its place. And I think you've found out by now that this isn't light work. You can wear yourself out fast if you're not smart. Look at Pearson up in aisle 4. There's a kid who's just going to burn himself out. He won't last long. If he thinks he's going to get somewhere working like that, he's nuts. They'll give him all the work he can take. He makes it tough on everbody else and on himself, too.

Kirk reported on his observations of the department:

As nearly as I could tell, two things seemed to determine whether or not Sarto's group or any others came in for weekend work on Saturday or Sunday. It seemed usually to be caused by rush orders that were received late in the week, although I suspect it was sometimes caused by the fact that people spent insufficient time on the job during the previous week.

Tony and his group couldn't understand Herman. While Herman arrived late, Tony was always half an hour early. If there was a push to get out an extra amount of work, almost everyone but Herman would work that much harder. Herman never worked overtime on weekends, while Tony's group and the people on the manual tanks almost always did. When the first exploratory time study of the department was made, no one on the aisles slowed down, except Herman, with the possible exception, to a lesser degree, of Charlie Malone. I did hear that the people in the dry end of the room slowed down so much you could hardly see them move; but we had little to do with them, anyway. While the people I knew best seemed to find a rather full life in their work, Herman never really got involved. No wonder they couldn't understand each other.

There was quite a different feeling about Bobby Pearson. Without the slightest doubt, Bob worked harder than anyone else in the room. Because of the tremendous variety of work produced, it was hard to make output comparisons, but I'm sure I wouldn't be far wrong in saying that Bob put out twice as much as Herman and 50% more than almost anyone else in the aisles. No one but Herman and a few old-timers at the dry end ever criticized Bob for his efforts. Tony and his group seemed to feel a distant affection for Bob, but the only contact they or anyone else had with him consisted of brief greetings.

To the people in Tony's group the most severe penalty that could be inflicted was exclusion. This they did to both Pearson and Herman. Pearson, however, was tolerated; Herman was not. Evidently, Herman felt his exclusion keenly, though he answered it with derision and aggression. Herman kept up a steady stream of stories concerning his attempts to gain acceptance outside the company. He wrote country western music that was always rejected by producers. He attempted to join several social and athletic clubs, mostly without success. His favorite pastime was fishing. He told me that fishermen were friendly, and he enjoyed meeting new people whenever he went fishing. But he was particularly quick to explain that he preferred to keep his distance from the people in the department.

Tony's group emphasized more than just quantity in judging a person's work. The group stressed high standards of both quality and inventiveness. A confidence had grown among them that they could master and even improve upon any known finishing technique. Tony himself symbolized this skill. Before him, Tony's father had operated aisle 1 and had trained Tony to take his place. Tony, in turn, was training his cousin Pete. When a new finishing problem arose from a change in customer specifications, the supervisor, the department technician, the plant process engineer or any of the people directly involved would come to Tony for help, and Tony would give it willingly. For example, when a part with a special plastic embossing was designed, Tony was the only one who could discover how to treat the metal without damaging the plastic. To a lesser degree, the other members of the group were also inventive about solving the problems that arose in their own sections.

Herman, for his part, talked incessantly about his feats in design and finish creations. As far as I could tell during the year I worked in the department, the objects of these stories were obsolete or of minor importance. What's more, I never saw any department member seek Herman's help.

Willingness to be of help was a trait Sarto's group prized. The most valued help of all was of a personal kind, though work help was also important. The members of Sarto's group were constantly lending and borrowing money, cars, clothing, and tools among themselves and, less frequently, with other members of the department. Their daily lunch bag procedure typified the "common property" feeling among them. Everyone's lunch was opened and added to a common pile, from which each member of the group chose his or her meal.

On the other hand, Herman refused to help others in any way. He never left his aisle to aid those near him who were in the middle of a rush of work or a machine failure, though this was customary throughout most of the department. I can distinctly recall the picture of Herman leaning on the hot and cold water faucets that were located directly above each tumbling barrel. He would stand gazing into the tumbling pieces for hours. To the passing, casual visitor, he looked busy; and as he told me, that's just what he wanted. He, of course, expected me to act this same way, and it was this enforced boredom that I found virtually intolerable.

More than this, Herman took no responsibility for breaking in his assigned helpers as they first entered the department or thereafter. He had had four helpers in the space of little more than a year. Each had asked for a transfer to another department, publicly citing the work as cause, privately blaming Herman. Tony was the one who taught me the ropes when I first entered the department.

The people who congregated around Harry Clark tended to talk like and imitate the behavior of the Sarto group, although they never approached the degree of inventive skill or the amount of helping activities that Tony's group did. They sought outside social contact with the Sarto group; and several times a year, the two groups went out on the town together. Clark's group did maintain a high level of performance in the volume of work it turned out.

The remainder of the people in the department stayed pretty much to themselves or associated in pairs or threesomes. None of these people were as inventive, as helpful, or as productive as Sarto's or Clark's groups, but most of them gave verbal support to the same values as those groups held.

The distinction between the two organized groups and the rest of the department was clearest in the punching-out routine. The women in rack assembly were not involved. Malone and Lacey, Partridge and Swan, and Martin, La Forte, and Mensch arranged within their small groups for punch outs, or they remained beyond 5:00 p.m. and slept or read when they finished their work. Perkins and Pierce went home when the supervisor did. Herman Schell, Susi, and Maher had no punch-out organization to rely on. Susi and Maher invariably stayed in the department until 7:00 p.m. Herman was reported to have established an arrangement with Partridge whereby the latter punched Herman out for a fee. Such a practice was unthinkable from the point of view of Sarto's group. Evidently, it did not occur often because Herman usually went to sleep behind piles of work when his brother left, or particularly during the fishing season, punched himself out early. He constantly railed against the dishonesty of other people in the department, yet urged me to punch him out on several "emergency occasions."

Just before I left the Slade Company to return to school after 14 months on the job, I had a casual conversation with Mr. Porter, the production manager, and he asked me how I had enjoyed my experience with the organization. During the conversation, I learned that he knew of the punch-out system in the Plating Department. What's more, he told me, he was wondering if he ought to "blow the lid off the whole mess."

Activity 10–3: Alternative Courses of Managerial Action in the Slade Plating Department

Objectives:

a. To use the individual-first, team-second decision-making model to synergistically develop alternative courses of managerial action for the situation described in the Slade case.

b. To use course concepts to make the analysis.

c. To evaluate the consequences of alternative proposals.

Task 1 (Individuals Working Alone)

Alternative 1 (for one-half of the teams in the class):

Working alone, complete the Slade case assignment immediately preceding this exercise.

Assume you are Mr. Porter, the production manager, and have become fully knowledgeable of all the data given in the case study. You are trying to decide on alternative courses of action. Complete the accompanying worksheet for Alternative 1.

Alternative 2 (for the other half of the teams in the class):

Working alone, complete the Slade case assignment immediately preceding this exercise.

Assume you are Tony Sarto and his work group. You have heard that Mr. Porter, the production manager, has become fully knowledgeable of all the data given in the case study. You and your group have an informal meeting outside work to discuss the problem. What actions do you think management might take? How would you respond to these? How do you think management should handle this situation? Complete the accompanying Alternative 2 worksheet for the Sarto group.

Task 2 (Team Activity):

Teams are to meet outside class to analyze the questions on the worksheet for the alternative they have been assigned. At the next class session, turn in to the instructor a one-page typed summary of your analysis. (*Note:* Use a brief outline form in your paper.)

Task 3 (Classroom Activity):

A spokesperson for each team will outline its conclusions on the blackboard and present a rationale to the class. Mr. Porter teams will all report first, followed by Sarto teams. Discussion follows.

Worksheet for Activity 10–3

Alternative 1: Worksheet for Mr. Porter, Production Manager

What are all the possible alternative actions? List them below.	What are the possible consequences that would be expected to be:	
	Favorable	Unfavorable

Which of the above alternatives would you choose? Why?

Name _____   Date _____

Worksheet for Activity 10–3

Alternative 2: Worksheet for Tony Sarto's Work Group

List alternative actions management might take.	List Sarto work group's response to each alternative.

How would Sarto's work group think management should handle this situation? Why?

Activity 10–4:
Motivational Analysis
of Organizations-
Behavior (MAO-B)

Objectives:

a. To examine a behavioral model of motivation.

b. To provide students with the opportunity to diagnose and analyze their own motivation.

c. To compute individuals' operating effectiveness.

Task 1:

Individuals working alone should complete and score the survey.

Task 2:

Individuals in a small group are to share their scores and interpret the results. Each group is to complete the following tasks:

a. Identify common themes.

b. Discuss the implications of individuals' motivation to team performance.

c. Develop an action plan to overcome the motivational issues.

Name _____ Date _____

Motivational Analysis of Organizations-Behavior (MAO-B) Inventory

Instructions: This inventory can help you to understand how different motivations can affect your behavior and your performance at work. There are no "right" or "wrong" responses; the inventory will reflect your own perceptions of how you act at work, so you will gain the most value from it if you answer honestly. Do not spend too much time on any one item; generally, your first reaction is the most accurate.

Read each statement below and decide which of the numbered columns to the right best describes how often you engage in the behavior or have the feeling. Circle the appropriate number next to each statement to indicate your response.

	Rarely/ Never	Sometimes/ Occasionally	Often/ Freqently	Usually/ Always
1. I enjoy working on moderately difficult (challenging) tasks and goals.	1	2	3	4
2. I am overly emotional.	1	2	3	4
3. I am forceful in my arguments.	1	2	3	4
4. I refer matters to my superiors.	1	2	3	4
5. I keep close track of things (monitor action).	1	2	3	4
6. I make contributions to charity and help those in need.	1	2	3	4
7. I set easy goals and achieve them.	1	2	3	4
8. I relate very well to people.	1	2	3	4
9. I am preoccupied with my own ideas and am a poor listener.	1	2	3	4
10. I follow my ideals.	1	2	3	4
11. I demand conformity from the people who work for or with me.	1	2	3	4
12. I take steps to develop the people who work for me.	1	2	3	4
13. I strive to exceed performance/targets.	1	2	3	4
14. I ascribe more importance to personal relationships than to organizational matters.	1	2	3	4
15. I build on the ideas of my subordinates or others.	1	2	3	4
16. I seek the approval of my superiors.	1	2	3	4
17. I ensure that things are done according to plan.	1	2	3	4
18. I consider the difficulties of others even at the expense of the task.	1	2	3	4
19. I am afraid of making mistakes.	1	2	3	4
20. I share my feelings with others.	1	2	3	4
21. I enjoy arguing and winning arguments.	1	2	3	4
22. I have genuine respect for experienced persons.	1	2	3	4
23. I admonish people for not completing tasks.	1	2	3	4
24. I go out of my way to help the people who work for me.	1	2	3	4
25. I search for new ways to overcome difficulties.	1	2	3	4
26. I have difficulty in expressing negative feelings to others.	1	2	3	4
27. I set myself as an example and model for others.	1	2	3	4
28. I hesitate to make hard decisions.	1	2	3	4
29. I define roles and procedures for the people who work for me.	1	2	3	4
30. I undergo personal inconvenience for the sake of others.	1	2	3	4
31. I am more conscious of my limitations or weaknesses than of my strengths.	1	2	3	4
32. I take interest in matters of personal concern to the people who work for me.	1	2	3	4
33. I am *laissez-faire* in my leadership style (do not care how things happen).	1	2	3	4
34. I learn from those who are senior to me.	1	2	3	4
35. I centralize most tasks to ensure that things are done properly.	1	2	3	4
36. I have empathy and understanding for the people who work for me.	1	2	3	4
37. I want to know how well I have been doing, and I use feedback to improve myself.	1	2	3	4
38. I avoid conflict in the interest of group feelings.	1	2	3	4

	Rarely/ Never	Sometimes/ Occasionally	Often/ Freqently	Usually/ Always
39. I provide new suggestions and ideas.	1	2	3	4
40. I try to please others.	1	2	3	4
41. I explain systems and procedures clearly to the people who work for me.	1	2	3	4
42. I tend to take responsibility for others' work in order to help them.	1	2	3	4
43. I show low self-confidence.	1	2	3	4
44. I recognize and respond to the feelings of others.	1	2	3	4
45. I receive credit for work done in a team.	1	2	3	4
46. I seek help from those who know the subject.	1	2	3	4
47. In case of difficulties, I rush to correct things.	1	2	3	4
48. I develop teamwork among the people who work for me.	1	2	3	4
49. I work effectively under pressure of deadlines.	1	2	3	4
50. I am uneasy and less productive when working alone.	1	2	3	4
51. I give credit and recognition to others.	1	2	3	4
52. I look for support for my actions and proposals.	1	2	3	4
53. I enjoy positions of authority.	1	2	3	4
54. I hesitate to take strong actions because of human considerations.	1	2	3	4
55. I complain about difficulties and problems.	1	2	3	4
56. I take the initiative in making friends with my colleagues.	1	2	3	4
57. I am quite conscious of status symbols such as furniture and size of office.	1	2	3	4
58. I like to solicit ideas from others.	1	2	3	4
59. I tend to form small groups to influence decisions.	1	2	3	4
60. I like to accept responsibility in the group's work.	1	2	3	4

Name _____ Date _____

Instructions: Transfer your responses from the MAO-B inventory to the appropriate spaces on this sheet. If you circled the number 2 to the right of item 1, enter a 2 in the space after the number 1 below; if you circled a 4 as your response to item 13, enter a 4 in the space to the right of the number 13 below, and so on until you have entered all your responses in the space below.

A	B	C	D	E	F
1. _____	3. _____	5. _____	10. _____	12. _____	8. _____
13. _____	15. _____	17. _____	22. _____	24. _____	20. _____
25. _____	27. _____	29. _____	34. _____	36. _____	32. _____
37. _____	39. _____	41. _____	46. _____	48. _____	44. _____
49. _____	51. _____	53. _____	58. _____	60. _____	56. _____
A total _____	B total _____	C total _____	D total _____	E total _____	F total _____

a	b	c	d	e	f
7. _____	9. _____	11. _____	4. _____	6. _____	2. _____
19. _____	21. _____	23. _____	16. _____	18. _____	14. _____
31. _____	33. _____	35. _____	28. _____	30. _____	26. _____
43. _____	45. _____	47. _____	40. _____	42. _____	38. _____
55. _____	57. _____	59. _____	52. _____	54. _____	50. _____
a total _____	b total _____	c total _____	d total _____	e total _____	f total _____

Now sum the numbers that you entered in each vertical column and enter the totals in the spaces provided. These totals are your scores for the approach–avoidance dimensions of each of the six primary motivators of people's behavior on the job. Transfer those totals to the appropriate spaces in the two middle columns below.

Achievement	A (approach) _____	a (avoidance) _____	OEQ _____
Influence	B (approach) _____	b (avoidance) _____	OEQ _____
Control	C (approach) _____	c (avoidance) _____	OEQ _____
Dependence	D (approach) _____	d (avoidance) _____	OEQ _____
Extension	E (approach) _____	e (avoidance) _____	OEQ _____
Affiliation	F (approach) _____	f (avoidance) _____	OEQ _____

To compute your operating effectiveness quotient (OEQ) for each motivator, find the value for your approach (capital letter) score for the motivator along the top row of the table that follows and then find your avoidance (lowercase letter) score for that motivator in the left column. The number in the cell that intersects the column and row is your OEQ score for the motivator. Transfer that score to the tally marked OEQ at the bottom of the preceding page. Do this for each motivator.

Avoidance Scores	Approach Scores															
	5	6	7	8	9	10	11	12	13	14	15	16	17	18	19	20
5	0	100	100	100	100	100	100	100	100	100	100	100	100	100	100	100
6	0	50	67	75	80	83	85	87	89	90	91	92	92	93	93	97
7	0	33	50	60	67	71	75	78	80	82	83	85	86	87	87	88
8	0	25	40	50	57	62	67	70	73	75	77	78	80	81	82	83
9	0	20	33	43	50	55	60	64	67	69	71	73	75	76	78	79
10	0	17	28	37	44	50	54	58	61	64	67	69	70	72	74	75
11	0	14	25	33	40	45	50	54	59	60	62	65	67	68	70	71
12	0	12	22	30	36	42	46	50	53	56	59	61	63	65	67	68
13	0	11	20	27	33	38	43	47	50	53	55	58	60	62	64	65
14	0	10	18	25	31	36	40	44	47	50	53	55	57	59	61	62
15	0	9	17	23	28	33	37	41	44	47	50	52	54	56	58	60
16	0	8	15	21	27	31	35	39	42	45	48	50	52	54	56	58
17	0	8	14	20	25	29	33	37	40	43	45	48	50	52	54	56
18	0	7	13	19	23	28	32	35	38	41	43	46	48	50	52	54
19	0	7	12	18	22	26	30	33	36	39	42	44	46	48	50	52
20	0	6	12	17	21	25	29	32	35	37	40	42	44	46	48	50

Operating Effectiveness Quotients

When you have completed this process for all of your scores, you will have a numerical picture of what typically motivates your behavior at work, whether you respond positively (approach) or negatively (avoidance) to each of the six typical motivators, and how your responses to each motivator influence your operating effectiveness.

Source: This questionnaire was designed by Dr. Udai Pareek. The survey is reprinted here with permission of University Associates, San Diego, CA 92121. All rights are reserved.

11

Perception and Attribution

Learning Objectives

After completing this module, you should be able to

1. Describe the perceptual process, and the internal and external determinants of individual perception.
2. Appreciate the impact that perceptual problems have on organizational life.
3. Understand your own perceptual process and barriers to accurate perception.
4. Describe how the attribution process influences perception and individual behavior.
5. Gain insights into the role that Pygmalion and self-fulfilling prophecy can play in the perceptual process at work.
6. Identify the basic managerial actions that can help overcome the barriers for accurate perception.

Module Outline

Key Terms and Concepts

Study Questions

Endnotes

Activity 11–2: Mirroring Gender: Perceptual Exploration

Activity 11–3: Prejudices and Stereotyping

Optional Activities on the WWW

Activity 11–4W: Male–Female Interface on Women in Management

Premodule Preparation

The instructor may assign either one or a combination of the following two as a pre-session activity: task 1 of Activity 11–1 ("Exploring Perceptual Issues via Dan Dunwoodie's Challenge "); and task 1 of Activity 11–4W ("Male–Female Interface on Women in Management").

Activity 11–1: Exploring Perceptual Issues via Dan Dunwoodie's Challenge

Objective:

To have small groups identify and define the problem in a case study so that the process can be studied through the analysis of contrasting results presented by the groups.

Task 1:

Participants are to read the case study "Dan Dunwoodie's Challenge," which follows. Each team is to answer the following three questions on the case study:

a. What is the problem?

b. What is the principal cause?

c. What action should Dan Dunwoodie take?

   (Time: 15 minutes)

Task 2:

Each team first presents its results on problem definition, which the instructor lists on the board. Then the same procedure is followed for causes. After these have been listed, the action recommendations are given and listed. During the process of listing the contrasting results from the various teams, team members are not to challenge or discuss the solutions. Questions may be asked for clarification. When the data are all out, there should be open challenges and discussion of differing points of view and of the feasibility of the suggested actions.

   The class should develop at least one criterion for deciding upon the problem; a decision should be reached as to what would be the best solution from the standpoint of the criteria developed. (Time: 30 minutes)

Case Study: Dan Dunwoodie's Challenge

Up to this point I have been doing very well. At 27 years of age I am chief of an economic analysis branch in the United Automobile Manufacturing Company. I was hired personally by John Roman, my division chief, who interviewed me at the university where I was completing my MBA. John had expressed interest in several of my qualifications: BA in economics from an outstanding university, 4 years of work experience as an analyst in industry, and a specialty in information systems while working on my MBA.

When I came on duty 3 months ago, John gave me guidance as follows:

Economic analysis functions and processing at United need updating. Analysts are substantive experts and do not comprehend the importance of management or the possible application of information systems to managerial decision making. They keep insisting that judgmental processes cannot be automated; they resist suggestions that they can augment their activities by using computers. After you have had 3 to 6 months to learn your job, you are to come up with recommendations for organizational and procedural changes in your branch. You are to keep in close touch with your peers, the other branch chiefs in the division, all of whom have been with the company for 5 or more years.

(Their responsibilities were almost identical to mine except each branch had different economic specialties.)

I assumed my responsibilities with great energy and soon saw many possibilities for developing the effectiveness of my branch. I worked evenings and weekends on a new plan. As I developed ideas, I would try them out on each of the other branch chiefs. They were helpful and responsive. One objection did arise from Carl Carlson, chief of Branch B, who criticized some of the information systems suggestions. (Carl was regarded in the division as the next man in line for John's job. See Exhibit 1.)

At the end of 3 months with United, I presented my plan to my entire branch in a briefing session, complete with a statement of objectives, charts, and expected results. In response to my request for their reactions, two people spoke up. One was Elsie Eden, who was a contemporary of John and the branch chiefs. (I had heard she would have had my job if she had been willing to take an extensive computer training program.) The other was Russ Merrywood, also an old-timer, who had been passed over for advancement. (I had also heard that Russ had money and was not too committed to his job, although I find that his work is excellent.) My plan was well thought out, and further clarification of various details appeared to satisfy all questions raised.

On a Wednesday afternoon I gave the same oral briefing to John (division chief), who showed enthusiasm and pleasure. He promised me an early decision and asked for a copy of my written report for further study. On Thursday afternoon I received the report back with the notation, "Sounds great. Proceed soonest with entire plan with the

Exhibit 1

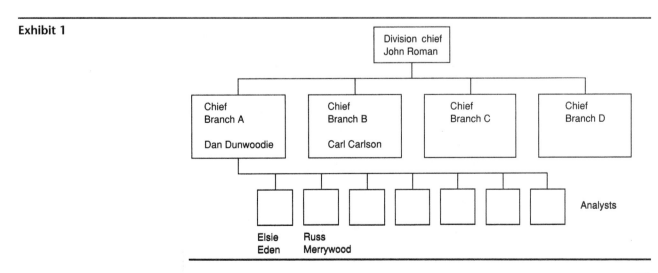

exception of paragraph 6, which I wish to study further." (Paragraph 6 contained an information system suggestion concerning which Carl had expressed disapproval to Dan.)

I spent Friday in meetings with my branch making initial plans for implementing the new program. Over the weekend I continued on my own to make final plans.

Early Monday morning I was asked to come to the division chief's office. I then learned that John had reversed his decision, and no changes were to be put into effect at this time. John appeared rather brusk and said he did not have time to discuss the decision. Later that day, I learned that John had attended a dinner party at Russ's house over the weekend.

Introduction

Perception and attribution, the third of the major core concepts for understanding behavior in organizations (the first two being personality and motivation), provide a framework and a useful tool for understanding effectiveness at the individual, group, intergroup, and organizational levels. The subject has been dealt with indirectly up to this point. Underlying the dialogue process of Module 2 was the question of what differences existed in the way the participants and the professor were perceiving important contextual aspects of the subject to be studied. The study of leadership styles in Module 3 included the question of how managers perceive themselves and how they are perceived by others. Small group membership within the human and formal organizations was seen to provide the basis for self-identity and emergent role system. Understanding motivation involved focus on a person's self-image.

Perception and Perceptual Differences in Daily Life

Perception is a fascinating subject that is being studied in many areas of daily life. Politicians are concerned about how they are perceived by the public and how their images can be improved and maintained; U.S. diplomats want to know how representatives of other nations with whom they will negotiate perceive this country; advertisers must determine how ads and products will be seen by consumers. Students in many law schools are required to take courses in psychology and psychiatry to improve their self-awareness. As one law school dean said, "When you go into the courtroom, you are part of the problem; the better you know what part of it you are, the better you can control and influence the situation." In mental health the therapist attempts to help the patient build a favorable self-concept and change his or her self-image so that it is more consistent with the way the person is perceived by others, thus reducing misunderstandings in interpersonal relations. Intelligence officers must know how their agents perceive themselves in relation to the operation in which they are engaged and how they see the intelligence officer and his or her country in order to understand, predict, and control the agent's activities.

Everyone is aware that we all see things somewhat differently, but in this complicated and difficult area few people are aware of the full extent of the differences. Blind spots develop to obscure specific happenings. Police surrounded a hotel and conducted a shootout with snipers firing from the hotel roof; some police officers were killed. Only one body was found on the roof after the firing stopped; the other suspects presumably escaped during the battle. It was not until some weeks later that the official investigation revealed that only one assailant was ever on that roof. The police and the television reporters, under the pressure of excitement, "saw" several assailants firing. Were police officers actually killed by the ricocheting bullets of other police in this setting, which maximized perceptual distortion?

Often managers, their subordinates, or co-workers perceive the same situation differently. The way individuals perceive their own competencies, skills, and knowledge; the way they perceive their peers and supervisors; the way they perceive their tasks; the way their peers and their supervisors perceive them affect their behavior and performance. As such perceptual differences that are likely to occur in the complex web of relationships and perceptions are likely to have an impact on individuals and their performance.[1] From a management point of view, understanding the perceptual process and the potential barriers for accurate perception is critical.

The Perceptual Process

Perception is an active process by which individuals screen, select, organize, and interpret stimuli. Figure 11–1 captures the key elements of the **perceptual process.** The way an individual perceives a situation is based on what the individual is experiencing at a given moment, which is based on several factors. These include data being received from the five senses (sight, smell, taste, touch, and hearing), data in the memory system, emotions, feelings, needs, wants, and goals. It is important to realize that what individuals experience at any given moment is based primarily upon what goes on inside them (the internal factors affecting perception) rather than what is happening outside them in the external world (physical objects and social interactions).

The degree of influence on the individual of internal and external factors is illustrated in Figure 11–2. It can be assumed that the more pressure the individual is under from physical or mental stress or from external sources (noises, violence, and so on), the greater will be the influence of the internal factors. Figure 11–2 is not intended to be exhaustive; it presents only broad areas relevant to the determinants of perception. The following sections discuss the internal factors listed in the figure.

Figure 11–1 **The Perceptual Process: An Overview**

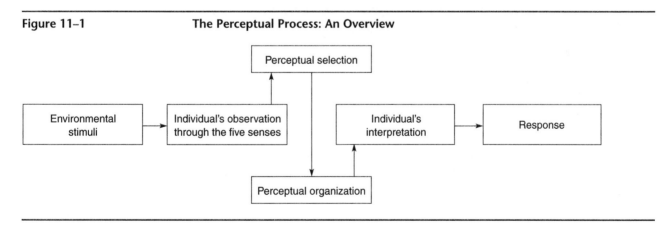

Figure 11–2
Relationship between Factors Determining Perception That Are Internal to the Individual and Those That Are in the External World

Internal factors	External factors
Physiological	Physical objects
Past experience	People
Psychological	Social interactions
Motivation	
Defense mechanisms	

High percentage of influence	Low percentage of influence

Physiological Factors

It is impossible to separate physiological and psychological factors because they are so closely blended. No real purpose could be served by trying to make precise distinctions. We are all aware that the state of our health affects our outlook, abilities, and emotions. The effects of drugs on perception have been widely researched and publicized.

An example of a physiological cause of peceptual differences is color blindness. One student reported his experience of undergoing an army physical examination during induction. Standing in line at a medical station, he could hear those ahead of him calling out "49" as they looked at a printed chart of different-colored circles of various sizes. When his turn came, he looked at the patterns formed among the color spots and called out the number he saw, which was 36. He was pulled out of the line for further testing and learned that he was partially color blind and was not perceiving shades of green and red, although he could identify the vivid basic colors. Thinking back on past experiences, he recalled that he had at times not seen certain aspects of distant scenes reported by others, but he had not thought too much of it. Once the test proved his disability, he became aware that he often was not experiencing what others were experiencing in this regard. Many subtle differences between people exist and influence how they see things, but there may be no awareness of the physiological factors that account for the differences.

Past Experience

It is widely hypothesized that everything experienced by the human being from birth on (some say from in the womb on) is stored in the memory system and is available for recall under certain conditions. Our knowledge in the area of memory and recall is most limited, and we do not know the extent to which, or whether, all experience is recorded in the brain. But it is safe to assume from research that the memory traces are vastly greater than any individual is conscious of, and these traces do affect perceptions and actions even though the individual may not be aware of them.

One mechanistic analogy would be to liken the mind to a computer system in which there is a large memory storage bank. To use the data, a program must give directions to the computer. Instead of programs, the mind has coding systems that organize the memory data into units; these are usable in the perceptual processes when the brain gives the directions for their use.

Codes of Past Experience

"Society" is a meaningfully organized element in the mental context; a complex system of expectations exists in each person's brain of how people should, ought, and must behave under both general and specific circumstances. It does not exist out there in the real world, but only in the expectation system of all members as to how they are to interact with one another. This includes expectations organized around social roles, norms, customs, symbols, and so on. Life around us is automatically meaningful because of this major aspect of the memory system.

Among other important blocks of codes are knowledge, facts, theories, beliefs, attitudes, and language. These codes are widely shared by people in the same society or in subgroupings of that society. There are also many codes of past experience that are unique to the individual and shared with only a few or with no one. The overlap between the coding systems of people with similar experiences is a fundamental requirement of communication. (This concept is explored in Module 12 on communication.)

Psychological Factors

Of the many psychological factors that could be discussed, we will focus on only two: motivation and defense mechanisms. Abilities, skills, intelligence, and the cognitive processes are among others that could be included here.

Motivation

Feelings and Emotions: All experience is accompanied by emotions and feelings, which are integral components of the learning process. The individual is not aware of this most of the time. As you read this text, feelings you have had in the past toward education, classrooms, teachers, or your parents' attitudes toward learning are all present and influence what you are reading. Codes of past experience also have a feeling component. A good classroom demonstration to alert students to this can be done with a dollar bill borrowed from one of the class members. The instructor holds the bill before the group and asks if anyone has any feelings about it. The response is low. He then proceeds to tear the dollar through the center. There are gasps: "You simply don't do that. It's against the law." All of the emotion learned in past experiences with money is brought forth, even though a moment earlier no one felt he or she had any feelings about the dollar.

The attachment of feelings to words becomes evident in learning a foreign language. In English the phrase *I am hot* is a socially acceptable way to express the feeling that the atmospheric temperature is too high. In German, the identical phrase, "*Ich bin heiss,*" means that the person is sexually aroused. An American trying to express the former condition would find the Germans reacting in unexpected ways. (In German, the way to comment on high atmospheric temperature would be "*Es ist mir warm,*" or "It is warm to me.")

As tourists in a foreign country, people frequently find they can spend the local currency like play money; they have not developed the feelings about it that they have about their own currency. American children going to live abroad will learn easily all the dirty words of the new country and shout them about in public, an activity they would not do with opprobrious language in English. When cautioned on this, their reaction could be that it is a fun language; they have not learned the "no-no" feelings they had with such words in their own language.

The point to stress here is that feelings and emotions affect your perceptions all the time, even though you might not be aware of it.

Goals, Needs, and Wants: What your goals and needs are at a specific time are major determinants in perception. The principle that *perception is selective* means that the individual is not experiencing all of the external world to which he or she is exposed at a given moment; the person experiences only those aspects of it (cues) that are being selected out by the internal determinants. Needs demonstrate this nicely. Three people standing on the same street corner perceive the identical street scene selectively. The sailor on shore leave sees only the woman in the miniskirt walking away from him. The businessman, late for an appointment, sees only the clock on a sign above the woman. The third man sees only the restaurant sign above the clock; it's noon, and he is hungry.[2]

Defense Mechanisms	Objects, events, or social interactions that arouse fears or concerns in an individual are often dealt with psychologically in a manner of which the person is unaware. These are defense mechanisms the brain develops to cope with fear or concern.

Denial: One of the most frequent defensive responses is **denial.** Here things that individuals would like to do but that are socially unacceptable are dealt with by the brain processes so that people eventually believe they do not want to do those things. The individual is also opposed to anyone else doing them. This is evident in all the "no-no" areas, such as sex, aggression toward others, envy, and desire for power. A woman may hate a man she loves because she unconsciously realizes she cannot have him, but she really is convinced of the hate. An individual with strong status needs may claim he does not really want any recognition for his deeds. Not being able to make much money may lead to expressions of delight with simple living. The *psychology of opposites* is an apt phrase for denial, which can indeed affect how an individual perceives certain behaviors of self and others.

Projection: We will illustrate projection in terms of a well-known story. A young man visited a psychiatrist, who asked him why he had come for treatment. The man indicated that he did not know, that his parents had sent him because they thought he was acting strangely, but he did not think there was anything wrong. The doctor said maybe he could determine whether there was a problem by asking a few questions. He then took out a piece of chalk and went to a small blackboard in the office and drew a straight vertical line about 10 inches long. He asked, "Tell me, what do you see here that I have drawn?" The young man replied, "It's a naked woman." The doctor said, "Very good. Now what is this?" He then drew an identical vertical line about six inches to the right of the first. The man replied, "It's a naked man." "And now what do you see?" asked the psychiatrist, as he drew a horizontal line between the two lines, forming an H shape. "It is a naked man and a naked woman and they are in bed together making love." The psychiatrist then gave his diagnosis. "I can see you are very sick. You really have some serious sex problems." The young man was upset and said, "Doc, what do you mean, me having all the sex problems? You're the one drawing all those dirty pictures!"

This story illustrates denial, but the main point is that the patient was projecting his own needs onto some external object. **Projection** means interpreting the world and the actions of others in terms of your own wants, needs, goals, desires, impulses, fears, and so on. If you are feeling aggressive and hostile, you may feel that it is those people out there who are hostile and causing all the trouble. If you are in love, you may believe most young couples you see walking on the street are in love. If you are a fearful person, you may perceive everything that happens in negative terms. If you think everyone is unfriendly, chances are you are really unfriendly and are attributing it to others. Of course, you may be unaware of this and immediately deny it if it's brought to your attention. Projecting one's own tendencies onto others and not being aware of it is a natural brain process that operates most strongly when the individual is feeling defensive. Thus projection distorts the perceptual processes in terms of the internal determinants interfering with the reception of what is really out there—the external factors.

A number of other defense mechanisms are useful to know about. You may wish to pursue this topic in your outside reading.

Stereotypes

The term **stereotypes** implies modular (constructed as units) perceptions in which visual, factual, emotional, and feeling elements are all integrated into a fixed pattern of viewing persons, problems, activities, or objects. Within a social cognition framework, stereotypes function to reduce information-processing demands, to define group membership, and to predict behavior based on group membership.[3] The term has a negative connotation in that it implies a closed system in which no new information is taken into the modular unit; it is perceived as a source or excuse for social injustice; it is based on little information; it rarely accurately applies to specific individuals.[4] Also, the strongest stereotypes (such as racial stereotypes) are aggressively biased against a group. Even a positive stereotype (for university graduates), such as a company policy that only university graduates are promotable, shuts out information and educes objectivity. However, stereotyping is not a negative process; rather, it is a neutral, subconscious cognitive process that increases the efficiency of interpreting environmental information that can lead to inaccuracies and/or negative consequences.[5] Stereotyping, prejudice, and discrimination appear to be enduring human traits.[6] The literature identifies three major types of stereotypes: sex role, age, and race.

Sex-role stereotype is the belief that differing traits and abilities make men and women particularly well suited to different roles. Managers may believe that women and men cannot hold the same jobs or that women should be soft spoken and demure and men aggressive and outspoken. Several recent research projects of women managers examined this issue. For example, a survey of 461 female executives in *Fortune* 1000 companies found that 52 percent saw male stereotyping of women's preconceptions about women as the biggest barrier to women's advancement.[7] A recent study compared sex-role stereotypes held by men and women from China, Japan, Germany, the United Kingdom, and the United States. Males in all five countries perceived that successful managers possessed characteristics and traits more commonly ascribed to men in general than to women in general. Among females the same pattern of managerial sex typing was found in all countries except the United States. The U.S. females perceived that males and females were equally likely to possess traits necessary for managerial success.[8] Activities 11–2 and 11–4W provide opportunities to explore this issue a little further.

Age stereotype is the belief that differing traits and abilities make a certain age group more or less suited to different roles or display different behavior toward work. A careful review of empirical research provides inconclusive results about the overall relationship between age, performance, and attitudes. While some studies found age and job performance unrelated, others found that the relationship between age and performance changes as people grow older.[9] A recent review examined 185 different studies of stereotypes. The project revealed that as age increases so do employee job satisfaction, job involvement, internal work motivation, and organizational commitment. Moreover, older workers were not more accident prone than their younger colleagues.[10] The relationship between age and turnover and absenteeism provides some interesting insights. Although one study revealed that the three are not related, another study found that age was inversely related to both voluntary and involuntary absenteeism. Furthermore, the study found that older workers are ready and able to meet their job requirements.

Race stereotype influences how some people might treat others in a variety of work situations. As Module 9 showed, three interrelated forms of racism can be identified: individual, cultural, and institutional. For example, to the extent that an individual holds values, feelings, and/or attitudes and/or engages in behavior that promotes the person's own racial group as superior, the accuracy of the perceptual process will be diminished. A study that examined the relationship of race to employee attitudes across 814 African-American and 814 white managers, demonstrated that African-Americans, when compared with whites, felt less accepted by their peers, perceived lower managerial discretion on their job, reached career plateaus more frequently, noted lower levels of career satisfaction, and received lower performance ratings.[11] Another study uncovered a same-race bias for Hispanics and African-Americans. The Hispanic and African-American interviewers evaluated applications of their own race more favorably than they evaluated applicants of other races.[12]

Recently a cognitive model of stereotyping in the workplace has been proposed by Loren Falkenberg.[13] (See Figure 11–3.)

The classification of individuals and their status assignments provide the background for delineating the processes underlying the maintenance and revision of stereotypes. Inaccurate stereotypes are maintained through interpreting behaviors of minority-status individuals in the workplace that most often lead to actions and behavior expectations that result in enhanced stereotypes. Three processes stimulate the development of more accurate stereotypes: (1) storing distinct or unexpected information in memory, (2) storing personal information on an individual with increased personal interactions, and (3) increasing recognition of individuals working in various occupational roles. Stereotypes can have a self-fulfilling prophecy, such as everyone believing an employee has great potential, and the beliefs come true. Recently the Pygmalion effect has been popular in management as a concept to help managers shape the destiny of employees or to help individuals shape their own personal growth.

The Pygmalion Effect

The Pygmalion effect dramatically demonstrates the influence of perception and expectation on the potential of people to grow, or not to grow, depending upon the labels accorded them.[14] Rosenthal and associates conducted experiments in an elementary school in which all students were given a nonverbal IQ test.[15] The teachers, who were not informed of the experimenter's true purpose, were told the IQ tests identified a number of children who were "intellectual bloomers." Each teacher was given the names of 20 percent of the students in each of their classes who fell into this classification for high intellectual growth. In reality, the 20 percent named were randomly selected and were in the average IQ range for their classes. The general results were that the intellectual bloomer groups did show a significant gain in IQ over the rest of the class. The difference in the students existed only in the minds of the teachers, who assumed they were working with brighter students.

**Figure 11–3
Information-Processing
Strategies Leading to
Maintenance and Revision
of Stereotypes**

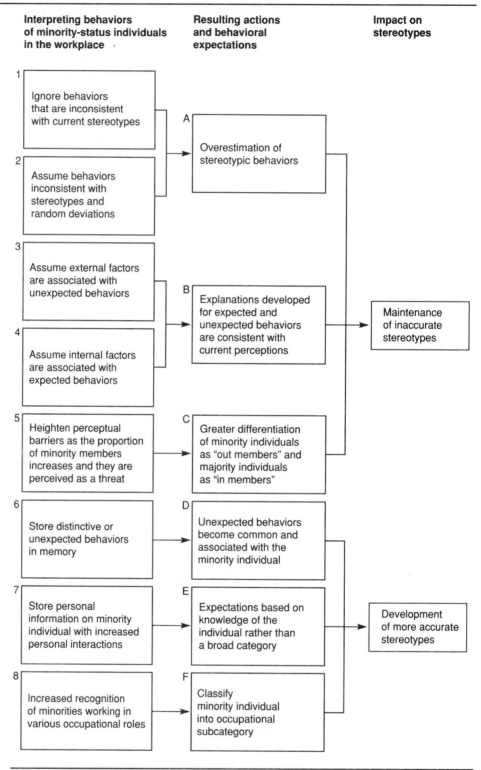

Source: Adopted from L. Falkenberg, "Improving the Accuracy of Stereotypes within the Workplace," *Journal of Management* 16, no. 1 (1990), pp. 107–18.

The experimenters explained the Pygmalion effect, based on their observations, to be due to four factors: The teachers (1) created a warm, supportive learning climate for their special students, (2) gave them more feedback on their performances, (3) gave them more material and more difficult work, and (4) gave them more opportunity to ask questions and respond. This experiment showed that student growth was stimulated by raising the expectations of the teacher that the child could achieve—the expectations were beyond what would have been expected if the teacher had seen these students as average. The point raised earlier that social attitudes and stereotypes generate expectations that are a deterrent to change was also demonstrated by another aspect of the Rosenthal experiments in which there was some tendency for low-income children with high IQs to be viewed negatively by their teachers. When these children passed the expectations of their teachers, they were somewhat resented.

Although Rosenthal's experiments have been evaluated as controversial by reviewers (one reason being that the results have not always been easy to replicate), they will strike a note of truth for many managers who have seen employees sponsored and labeled in order to influence them to move into management positions. To have a high executive label a young professional as a real "comer" can start a career. In Washington, D.C., an Ivy League degree can move one up the ladder of some agencies.

Since the early 1980s, an increasing number of studies attempted to replicate the Pygmalion paradigm with adults. Professor Dov Eden has led the research frontier on the Pygmalion phenomenon with adults.[16] Some of the best studies on the Pygmalion effect among adults have been conducted in military organizations. In one of the studies, military trainees were randomly assigned to three groups and were described to their instructors as possessing high, regular, or unknown "command potential." Data indicated that trainees who had been labeled as having high potential significantly outperformed trainees in each of the other groups on objective measures.[17] In a different study, the same effects were obtained by raising supervisors' expectations toward their subordinates as a group.[18]

At a personnel review board meeting in one company, the executive conducting the meeting described one young professional employee as having outstanding potential and dismissed the individual's mistakes the record showed with the comment, "He needs an opportunity to grow by falling on his face a few times." At a later point, he commented on the mistakes of another subject as "goofing more than you would expect." The record of the second individual actually was stronger in terms of background preparation and achievement in the company, but the comment of the chairperson went unchallenged.

Managers generally pride themselves on their ability and objectivity when judging people. But consider the implications of employee appraisal systems, particularly in large organizations. Some type of a scale is typically used to rate people in their performance, and it is highly probable over a period of time that a manager's employees become typed as outstanding, average, below average, and so on. If we apply what we learned of the Pygmalion effect—as articulated and summarized by Dov Eden and his book *Pygmalion in Management: Productivity as a Self-Fulfilling Prophecy*[19] and in his review article "Leadership and Expectations"[20]—the chances are rather low that the employee labeled as average or below average will ever be perceived as outstanding, even if their performance improves.

The Pygmalion effect has been dramatically described in another form in Maxwell Maltz's book *Psycho-Cybernetics,* which has widespread popularity in management growth workshops.[21] Maltz, a plastic surgeon, noted that some of his patients who underwent a surgical transformation from an ugly face to a beautiful face showed a marked change in their lives; they developed more self-esteem and confidence. However, others continued to experience feelings of inadequacy and inferiority just as if they were still "ugly." From his studies, he concluded that those who had grown through the facial change had also undergone an inner change; they had developed a new self-image to correspond to the new beautiful face. Their expectations of change resulted in new behaviors that "worked" and brought them an increase in satisfaction.

Attribution Theory

One way to understand the relationship between perception and individual behavior is **attribution theory.** Attribution theory focuses on the process by which individuals interpret events around them as being caused by a relatively stable portion of their environment.[22] The underlying assumption is that individuals are motivated to understand the causes of particular events in their environment. According to attribution theory, it is the perceived causes of events, not the actual events, that influence individuals' behavior.

The attribution process includes four phases: (1) A particular behavioral event triggers a cognitive analysis that (2) focuses on what causes the event, (3) followed by a modification or reinforcement of previous assumptions of causality that (4) leads to behavioral choices regarding future behavioral events. For example, an individual who received a bonus will attempt to attribute the bonus to some underlying cause. If the employee perceives the explanation for the bonus to be the fact that he is a hard worker and consequently concludes that working hard leads to rewards in this organization, he will decide to continue to work hard in the future. Another employee may attribute her bonus to the fact that she is a "team player" and decide that it makes sense to continue to be a team player for that reason. In both cases, individuals have made decisions affecting their future behavior based on their attributions.

The attribution process provides insights into the understanding of the behavior of other people. A central question in the attribution process concerns *how* perceivers determine whether the behavior of another person stems from internal causes (such as personality traits, motives, and emotions) or external causes (such as the situation or other people). In making attributions, people focus on three factors:

Consensus—the extent to which others, faced with the same situation, behave in a manner similar to the person perceived.

Consistency—the extent to which the person perceived behaves in the same manner on other occasions when faced with the same situation.

Distinctiveness—the extent to which the person perceived acts in the same manner in different situations.[23]

In the context of managing work and managing others, managers cannot assume that their attributions will be the same as their employees' attributions. The managerial challenge is to understand both the attributions that employees make and the ones that the manager makes of a specific event. This knowledge will enhance the manager's ability to work effectively with others.

Perceptual Challenges in Management

Management research has found large perceptual differences among individuals at different levels of the managerial hierarchy. In a study by N. R. F. Maier and associates, 58 manager and subordinate pairs were asked questions concerning the job duties of the subordinate.[24] Only 46 percent of the pairs agreed on more than half of the topics. More striking was the difference for the obstacles standing in the way of the subordinates' performance; in this category only 8 percent of the pairs were in agreement on more than half of the topics discussed. It would appear that either the subordinates were not fully aware of what their superiors expected of them or the superiors did not know what work the subordinates were required to perform. In either case, the question can be raised as to how much communication occurred between the levels to provide understanding of the job requirements.

Part of the difficulty arises from authority and status differences, which inhibit individuals from communicating freely with their superiors about important job matters. Thus the different perceptions of subordinates and superiors are likely to remain different. Furthermore, there is some tendency at all levels of the hierarchy for supervisors and managers to see themselves as better communicators than their superiors. We have demonstrated this trend in many management workshops, using the following exercise. Participants complete a questionnaire indicating on a 10-point scale (from poor to outstanding) a number of their abilities as a manager, such as administrator, problem solver, and communicator. These rating sheets are picked up; the next day participants are given an identical sheet and asked to rate their bosses on the same abilities. Both questionnaires are completed anonymously to increase the validity of the ratings and protect the individual respondent. Sheets are identified for matching purposes by a code number the individual selects.

The results from one such study of middle managers in the federal government are shown in Table 11–1. The upper part of the table shows that in topics dealing with task completion (problem solver and administrator) the respondents tended to see their bosses as either as good as or better than themselves. In areas of communication (ability to communicate with subordinates, willingness to stand up for subordinates, and candidness), this situation is true to a lesser degree—as many as 46 percent of respondents indicated that they believe they are better than the boss in these attributes.

Table 11–1	Midcareerists' Self-Boss Perceptions of Managerial Abilities ($N = 48$)				
	Solve Problems	Administer	Communicate with Subordinates	Stand Up for Subordinates	Candidness
Percentage saying					
My boss is better	40%	29%	35%	29%	31%
No difference...	29	38	19	31	23
I am better	31	33	46	40	46
	100%	100%	100%	100%	100%
Total number of scale points by which respondent said					
Boss is better	34	26	27	16	38
I am better	37	44	57	62	50

The degree of intensity of feelings on these factors is shown in the lower part of Table 11–1, which gives the total number of scale points, for the total sample, by which respondents felt they exceeded the boss or were exceeded by the boss. The results were quite pronounced. When individuals think their bosses are better than they on a certain ability, they do not see their bosses as much better. But when they see themselves as better, they tend to see themselves as considerably better. This is most apparent on the item "stand up for subordinates," where the 29 percent of the respondents who considered their bosses better gave the bosses a total of 16 points, whereas the 40 percent who considered themselves better allotted themselves 62 points. It is least true in the more task-oriented area of problem solver. The communicate and administer factors all involve more interpersonal relations, which may account for the degree to which individuals felt more intensely why they were better.

The principal point to be made about perceptual differences is that no one perceives with complete objectivity. The determinants of perception are in operation all the time. A positive aspect of this process is that the world can be made immediately meaningful for the individual by his or her codes of past experience. Coding is a normal function of the brain processes, as are the defense mechanisms that protect the individual against being overwhelmed with fears and anxieties.

The disadvantages of perceptual differences are related to the fact that most people rely on the meanings coming from their codes without realizing that the perceptions are primarily from internal determinants rather than from the external world. Stereotyping people, for instance, can shut out new data required to understand others; stereotypes lead to **premature closure,** that is, drawing conclusions too quickly. Identifying someone as a hippie, jock, nerd, frat boy, or minority member provides the already packaged data of what such people are like without bothering to understand the person further.

Stereotypes related to management, employees, unions, and other categories of people serve a similar function in the work world. Stereotypes fulfill the needs of people (particularly when they're frustrated for ready answers) and are major communication problems in organizational life.

Reducing Perceptual Differences and Distortion

The major thrust of this presentation on perceptual differences has been to emphasize the need for people to be more aware of the ever-present distortion and differences in everyone's perceptions. Recognition of the condition is the first step in reducing these differences and the most difficult to learn. Alertness to the differences is required for improvement of effectiveness. It could be said that the theory, concepts, and social technology of this text are generally directed toward helping participants with problems related to this area. For example, a recent study—see Table 11–2—that focused on reducing sex stereotyping identified students' perceptions of how men and women can promote equal ways of relating at work.[25] The second step is to help individuals gain better competencies in gathering factual data in the areas of performance, behavior, and attitudes; reviewing their decision-making assumptions and outcomes; and verifying them for validity and accuracy. A third step is the development of organizational mechanisms that will nurture dialoguing and appreciative inquiry (as discussed in Module 2).

Table 11–2
Student Perceptions of How Men and Women Can Promote Equal Ways of Relating at Work

What women do/can do to promote equal relationships between the sexes:
- Be assertive and confident; take selves seriously.
- Be knowledgeable and well organized.
- Support each other more.
- Network with men; mentor men.
- Push for day care, pay equity, parental leaves (flexibility in workplace).
- Do not ignore or promote sexist behavior at work; don't let it go by.
- Don't negate or undermine selves. (For example, don't play dumb.)
- Aspire to higher positions.
- Break traditional home roles (equality in personal relationship).
- Don't perpetuate stereotypes (male or female)—break the mold.
- Be patient and understanding with men (but challenge them to change).

What men do/can do to promote equal relationships between the sexes:
- Ask women their opinions; take them seriously.
- Don't just look at women as "girls," but see them as partners and team members.
- Involve women in decision making; don't patronize them.
- Delegate responsibility to women; trust them.
- Acknowledge and respect women's talent and ability.
- Complement women on their work and performance.
- Approach women for advice and input.
- Compete with women like they are "one of the gang."
- Listen better; don't interrupt women.
- Share power more readily; mentor women.
- Don't stereotype women.
- Share in child rearing and housework.
- Give more support to women (networks, mentoring); be an ally.
- Accept interdependence in marriage.
- Acknowledge to the organization that family issues are men's issues too.
- Support other men in working through personal change; be patient.
- Don't ignore sexist behavior by male colleagues—"challenge to change."
- Don't "obsess" on work/career success—be willing to let go a little.
- Let go of masculine stereotypes.

Source: M. Maier, "The Gender Prism," *Journal of Managerial Education* 17, no. 3 (1993), p. 306. Used with permission.

As we have seen in this module, overcoming barriers to accurate perception is a major undertaking. Yet if we are to fully utilize human potential, meeting this chalenge is a must. Since workplace diversity is becoming the increasing reality for most organizations, managers are charged with finding ways to reduce distortions such that the potential of the human asset can be realized. Communications theory and techniques are most relevant in this process; these are explored in the upcoming communication module.

Summary

Perceptual differences between people and groups are a major problem area for many fields of study, including foreign affairs, politics, advertising, mental health, and interpersonal relations. In management, perceptual problems are pervasive. Recognition of their existence is of major importance in understanding organizational behavior. The problems are inherent in the nature of the perceptual process.

The determinants of perception are primarily internal to the individual, rather than arising from observed external objects or social interaction. Internal factors can be divided into physiological, past experience, and psychological categories. Codes of past experience and the motivational and defensive processes can filter and greatly distort what the individual is perceiving.

Perceptual differences are normal functions of the brain processes that help make life immediately meaningful. However, they do shut out data that are needed for more objective meaning. Awareness of these processes and particularly of one's own blind spots is seen as a primary need for understanding organizational life and improving all four levels of managerial effectiveness. Approaches to overcoming problems of perceptions and perceptual differences are explored throughout the book via a variety of experiential activities.

Key Terms and Concepts

Age stereotype	Premature closure
Attribution theory	Projection
Denial	Race stereotype
Distortion	Rationalization
Expectancy effects	Sex-role stereotype
Perception	Stereotypes
Perceptual process	

Study Questions

1. Identify and describe the key elements in the perceptual process.

2. "Organizational dialoguing" (see Activity 2–1) is also a model for individual dialoguing between a company representative and a client. Assume you are employed by a major accounting firm and are assigned your first client. Using the individual dialoguing model, what questions are you going to explore that could facilitate your relationship with the client?

3. Why do we emphasize the need to have some understanding of unconscious motivation in the field of OB?

4. Explain the phrase "expectations determine perception." If you are a manager of a number of employees, half of whom have a college education and the other half only a high school background, how can this concept provide you some guidance for supervision?

5. Why are defense mechanisms studied in the field of perception?

6. N. R. F. Maier's findings on differences in perception between bosses and subordinates are so pervasive in organizational surveys that all managers need to understand them. What can be done about these differences?

7. An expert in product quality made the following statement recently: "I've met people who said, 'I've stopped buying South Korean electronics components because the quality seems to have suffered.'" Analyze this statement while illustrating your knowledge of perception.

8. What perceptual errors by managers foster special problems in the assessment of worker performance?

9. Some argue that perception plays a critical role in the problems that women and minorities in management experience at the workplace. State your position and provide your reasons while incorporating what you have learned about perception.

Endnotes

1. B. I. Bertenthal, "Origins and Early Development of Perception, Action, and Representation," *Annual Review of Psychology* 47 (1996), pp. 431–59; D. L. Hamilton and S. J. Sherman, Perceiving Persons and Groups," *Psychological Review* 193 (1996), pp. 336–55.

2. D. Fabun, *Communication,* (Beverly Hills, CA: Glencoe Press, 1968); J. C. Cutting, "Perception and Information," *Annual Review of Psychology* 38 (1987), pp. 61–90; B. M. DePaulo, D. A. Kenny, C. W. Hoover, W. Webb, and P. V. Oliver, "Accuracy of Person Perception: Do People Know What Kinds of Impressions They Convey?" *Journal of Personality and Social Psychology* 52 (1987), pp. 303–15.

3. R. D. Ashmore and F. K. Del Boca, "Sex Stereotypes and Implicit Personality Theory: Toward a Cognitive-Social Psychological Conceptualization," *Sex Roles* 5 (1979), pp. 219–48; D. Christensen and R. Rosenthal, "Gender and Nonverbal Skill as Determinants of Interpersonal Expectancy Effects," *Journal of Personality and Social Psychology* 42 (1982), pp. 75–87; K. Deaux and M. E. Kite, "Gender Stereotypes: Some Thoughts on the Cognitive Organization of Gender-Related Information," *American Psychology Bulletin* 7 (1985), pp. 123–44; A. H. Eagly and V. J. Steffen, "Gender Stereotypes Stem from the Distribution of Women and Men into Social Roles," *Journal of Personality and Social Psychology* 46 (1984), pp. 735–54; M. E. Heilman, M. C. Simon, and D. P. Repper, "Intentionally Favored, Unintentionally Harmed? Impact of Sex-Based Preferential Selection on Self-Perceptions and Self-Evaluations," *Journal of Applied Psychology* 72 (1987), pp. 62–68.

4. B. E. McCauley, C. L. Still, and M. Segal, "Stereotyping: From Prejudice to Prediction," *Psychological Bulletin* 87 (1980), pp. 195–208; G. V. Bodenhausen and R. S. Wyer, "Effects of Stereotypes on Decision Making and Information-Processing Strategies," *Journal of Personality and Social Psychology* 48 (1985), pp. 267–82; J. P. Fernandez, *The Diversity Advantage,* (New York: Lexington Books, 1993); L. Gardenswartz and A. Rowe, *Managing Diversity,* (Burr Ridge, IL: Richard D. Irwin, 1993); U. Hentschel, G. Smith, and J. G. Draguns, eds., *The Roots of Perception,* (Amsterdam: North-Holland, 1986); E. T. Higgins and J. A. Bargh, "A Social Cognition and Social Perception," *Annual Review of Psychology* 38 (1987), pp. 369–425; E. S. Jackson, *Diversity in the Workplace,* (New York: Guilford Press, 1994); G. N. Powell, *Gender and Diversity in the Workplace,* (Thousand Oaks, CA: Sage, 1994).

5. L. Falkenberg, "Improving the Accuracy of Stereotypes within the Workplace," *Journal of Management* 16, no. 1 (1990), pp. 107–18.

6. S. T. Fiske, "Stereotyping, Prejudice, and Discrimination," in D. T. Gilbert, S. T. Fiske, and G. Lindzey (eds.), *The Handbook of Social Psychology,* (New York: Irwin McGraw-Hill, 1998).

7. E. Davis, "Women at the Top," *HR Focus* 73 (May 1996).

8. V. E. Schein, R. Mueller, T. Lituchy, and J. Liu, "Think Manager—Think Male: A Global Comparison," *Journal of Organizational Behavior,* January 1996, pp. 33–41.

9. For a good review of the empirical literature on the topic, see D. A. Waldman, and B. J. Avolio, "Aging and Work Performance in Perspective: Contextual and Developmental Considerations," in G. R. Ferris (ed.), *Research in Personnel and Human Resources Management,* vol. 11, (Greenwich, CT: JAI Press, 1993), pp. 133–62.

10. S. R. Rhodes, "Age-Related Differences in Work Attitudes and Behavior: A Review and Conceptual Analysis," *Psychological Bulletin,* March 1993, pp. 338–67.

11. J. H. Greenhaus, S. Parasuraman, W. M. Wormley, "Effects of Race on Organizational Experience, Job Performance and Evaluation, and Career Outcomes," *Academy of Management Journal,* March 1990, pp. 64–86.

12. T.-R.L Lin, G. H. Dobbins, and J.-L. Farh, "A Field Study of Race and Age Similarity Effects on Interview Ratings in Conventional and Situational Interviews," *Journal of Applied Psychology,* June 1992, pp. 361–71.

13. Ibid., p. 110.

14. According to Greek legend, Pygmalion, a king of Cyprus, created an ivory statue of a maiden known as Galatia. He fell in love with the statue, and at his prayer Aphrodite gave it life. In George Bernard Shaw's *Pygmalion,* a professor polishes the language and manners of a cockney flower girl until he is able to pass her off as a princess, only to fall in love with her. *My Fair Lady* is the musical version of Shaw's play.

15. R. Rosenthal, "The Pygmalion Effect," *Psychology Today,* September 1973, pp. 56–63.

16. D. Eden, *Pygmalion in Management: Productivity as a Self-Fulfilling Prophecy,* (Lexington, MA: Lexington Books, 1990).

17. D. Eden and A. B. Shani, "Pygmalion Goes to Boot Camp: Expectancy, Leadership, and Trainee Performance," *Journal of Applied Psychology* 67 (1982), pp. 194–99.

18. D. Eden, "Pygmalion without Interpersonal Contrast Effects: Whole Groups Gain from Raising Manager Expectations," *Journal of Applied Psychology* 75 (1990), pp. 394–98.

19. Ibid.

20. D. Eden, "Leadership and Expectations: Pygmalion Effects and Other Self-Fulfilling Prophecies in Organizations," *Leadership Quarterly* 3 (1992), pp. 271–305; see also, D. Eden "Implanting Pygmalion Leadership Style through Training, Presented at the 13th Annual Meeting of the Society for Industrial and Organizational Psychology, Dallas, April 24-26, 1998.

21. Maxwell Maltz, *Psycho-Cybernetics,* (New York: Pocket Books, 1966).

22. H. H. Kelley, "The Process of Causal Attributions," *American Psychologist* 28 (1973), pp. 107–28; F. Fosterling, "Attributional Retraining: A Review," *Psychological Bulletin,* November 1985, pp. 495–512.

23. Kelly, "The Process of Causal Attribution."

24. N. R. F. Maier, L. R. Hoffman, J. J. Hooven, and W. H. Read, *Supervisor–Subordinate Communications in Management,* (New York: American Management Association, 1961).

25. M. Maier, "The Gender Prism: Pedagogical Foundation for Reducing Sex Stereotyping and Promoting Egalitarian Male–Female Relationships in Management," *Journal of Management Education* 17, no. 3 (1993), pp. 285–314; A. McKee and S. Schor, "Confronting Prejudice and Stereotypes: A Teaching Model," *Journal of Management Education* 18, no. 4 (1994), pp. 447–67; E. L. Perry, A. Davis-Black, and C. T. Kulik: "Explaining Gender-Based Selection Decisions: Synthesis of Contextual and Cognitive Approaches," *The Academy of Management Journal* 19, no. 4 (1994), pp. 786–820.

Activity 11–2
Mirroring Gender:
Perceptual Exploration

Objectives:

a. To heighten students' awareness of their perception of themselves, their perceptions of members of the opposite sex, and the perceptions of themselves by the opposite sex.

b. To elicit data for improved working relationships between the sexes.

Task 1:

Students are to be divided into same-sex groups of not more than seven students in a group. (Ideal size is five students to a group.) Each group is to respond to two questions:

a. How do you see yourselves as women (or men)? Generate a list on a flip chart, using words or short phrases that describe your characteristics or traits individually as a woman (or man) or as a group of women (or men). For example, I see women as being intuitive, good listeners.

b. Make a second list that describes how you think members of the opposite sex see you as a group or as a member of your sex. For example, I think men see us—as women— as nurturing, chatty, always wanting to shop, . . .

In the development of these lists, students should use a brainstorming process that eliminates the need for agreement or consensus, that includes each individual's contributions, and that does not involve any judgment or evaluation on anyone's part. (Time: 15 minutes)

Task 2 (Class Sharing):

The lists should be taped to the walls of the room for all to see. Each group reads its list aloud to the entire class. The only discussion at this stage should be questions of clarification or explication.
(Time: 10 minutes)

Task 3:

a. The students should look at their lists and silently reflect on what is there. The students are to try to identify and write down some notes about the tone (negative and positive), intensity, patterns, and themes.

b. Individuals are to share their reflections in the groups.

c. The groups are to address the following question: What would be the ideal working relationship with the opposite sex?
(Time: 10 minutes)

Task 4:

a. Spokespersons will report to the class.

b. The instructor will facilitate further discussion related to the work, content, and process of some of the issues that were raised.

(Time: 10 minutes or longer if time is available)

Source: This activity was contributed by Dr. Judith White, California State University, Monterey, Management Department, Monterey, California. All rights are reserved and no reproduction should be made without expressed approval of Dr. White. We are grateful to Dr. White.

Activity 11–3 **Prejudices and** **Stereotyping**	*Objectives:*

Objectives:

a. To heighten learners' awareness of their own prejudices and stereotypes.

b. To develop awareness of the effects of one's own prejudices and stereotypes on one's behavior.

Task 1:

The instructor will facilitate 10 minutes of class brainstorming to generate names of groups and persons the students know to have been targets of some form of prejudice, discrimination, or stereotyping.

Task 2:

The instructor will facilitate 5 to 10 minutes of brainstorming that focuses on the specific characteristics or traits they know to be associated with these groups that contribute to the stereotyping or prejudiced attitude and behavior.

Task 3:

a. Students are to find a group on the board that they can associate themselves with and gather in small similar groups. The students might cluster themselves into a group of African-Americans, Latinos, white males, physically disabled, and so on.

b. Each group selects a reporter who may take notes and who will summarize the discussion and report it to the class. Each group should

   1. Identify (following a few minutes of reflection) a specific time when you experienced some form of discrimination or prejudice because of your identity as a member of this particular stereotyped group.

   2. Describe what occurred, who was there, what you did, and what you felt at the time.

   3. Talk about what you feel now and what you think had happened. What has influenced your feelings and thinking since that particular incident?

Task 4:

In the larger class individuals are asked to share some of their experiences. The instructor will facilitate class discussion around common themes and issues, emphasizing the common and painful experience of suffering from discrimination, prejudice, and stereotyping.

Task 5:

Go back to the same small groups. Each individual will

a. Think of a time when you consciously or unconsciously discriminated against someone, perpetuated a stereotype, or supported some prejudiced attitudes or behaviors.
b. Describe what occurred, who was there, what you did, what you felt and thought at the time, and your current thoughts and feelings.

Task 6:

a. In the larger class individuals are asked to share some of their experiences. The instructor will facilitate class discussion around common themes and issues, emphasizing the importance of awareness as the first step toward understanding and perhaps changing behaviors, and the need to be patient and forgiving as change occurs.
b. The instructor will facilitate a discussion about the application to the workplace.

Source: The basic ideas in this activity are adopted from the work by Drs. Anne MeKee of the Wharton School, The University of Pennsylvania, and Susan Schor of Pace University. The activity in its present form was developed by Dr. Judith White, California State University, Monterey, California. All rights are reserved and no reproduction should be made without expressed approval of Drs. McKee, Schor, and White. We are grateful to Drs. McKee, Schor, and White.

12

Communication

Learning Objectives

After completing this module, you should be able to:

1. Identify and describe the basic elements in the communication process.
2. Appreciate the relationship between diversity, personality, perception, motivation, and communication.
3. Understand the different levels of communication and media richness.
4. State the internal and external determinants of interpersonal communication.
5. Identify the potential barriers in the communication episode.
6. Understand your own barriers in the communication process and some of the actions that you can take to overcome them.
7. Identify some managerial actions that can help overcome the barriers for communication in organizational settings.

Module Outline

Premodule Preparation

    Activity 12–1: Communication, Coaching, and Goal Setting

Introduction

Personality, Motivation, Perception, and Communication

The Communication Process

    Levels of Communication

Barriers to Accurate Communication

    Conflicting Assumptions

    Inadequate Information

    Semantics

    Emotional Blocks

    Nonverbal Communication Barriers

Premodule Preparation

The instructor may assign either one or any combination of the following activities as a presession task: task 1 of Activity 12–1 ("Communication, Coaching, and Goal Setting"), task 1 of Activity 12–3W ("Exploring Communication Barriers"); or task 1 of Activity 12–4W ("Reflections on Communication Episodes").

Activity 12–1: Communication, Coaching, and Goal Setting

Objectives:

a. To develop your awareness of the human resources that you bring to the work situation.

b. To provide an opportunity to practice discussing your own resources with two other persons.

c. To practice listening and paraphrasing.

Task 1:

As homework, complete the "Questionnaire on Coaching and Goal Setting" that follows before coming to class so that you will have notes for participating in this exercise. The questionnaire is intended as a guide, and you may use any other approach or questions you feel would be more helpful to you for performing your role in the triads discussed in the following paragraphs. The questionnaire is for your own use; you will not be asked to hand in any written work on this.

Task 2:

In the classroom the permanent teams are to form into triads.

The roles. During the exercise each participant will have an opportunity to fulfill all three roles. For instance, during the first 15-minute session, participant A will be the teller, participant B will be the listener, and participant C will be the observer. Participants will rotate through the three roles as they complete the sessions as follows:

The role of teller. Individuals will talk about their resources and goals in the way that is most meaningful, using notes from the questionnaire if needed. It is better, however, to speak spontaneously.

The role of listener. Individuals will paraphrase back to the teller what they hear the teller saying. Listeners have to determine how long they should let the teller talk before interrupting to paraphrase. Waiting until the end of the session is too long; interrupting at the end of each sentence is too short. Listeners are not to take notes and are to give the teller their full attention. The paraphrasing must be acceptable to the teller. Questions may be asked for clarification, but remember this is not an interrogation or an interview, so probing is not appropriate. The intent is for people to talk about themselves in a way that is meaningful to them. Questions for any purpose other than clarification can lead the teller into talking about topics that are not really of central concern.

The role of observer. How well do the listeners carry out the role? Do they paraphrase well? How do you feel about the way the teller talked? Make notes if you wish and be prepared to give feedback when the instructor indicates you are to come into the interaction. The observer is not to enter into the discussion until the designated time—this will be difficult for some.

Task 3:

The instructor is to indicate when the exercise is to start. If the time allowed for each session is 10 minutes, the instructor should stop the teller and listener after 7 minutes and allow 3 minutes for the observer to give feedback and for the triad to discuss the activity. If the time allowed is 15 minutes, the teller and listener are to be stopped at 10 minutes, thus leaving 5 minutes for the observer to interact.
(Time for each session: 7 or 10 minutes, depending upon the length of the interval the instructor has chosen. Although 15 minutes is desirable, the time available during the class will be a determining factor.)

The observer gives feedback to the teller and listener in accordance with the role description in task 1. Other possible questions to discuss: How did the talkers feel about their roles? What problems were there with them? How did the listeners feel about their roles? What problems were there with them?
(Time: 3 or 5 minutes, depending upon the length of the interval)

Continue these activities until all three participants have performed all roles. (*Note:* It is important for the instructor to control the timing of the intervals for the teller and listener and for the observer feedback sessions; otherwise, each individual will not get a fair share of airtime.)

Task 4:

Class discussion of the exercise provides a good opportunity for participants to share opinions on these questions:

a. How did you feel about
   1. Talking about yourself?
   2. Listening to someone talk about himself or herself?
   3. Paraphrasing what you heard?
   4. Having someone paraphrase back to you?
   5. Being a listener?
   6. Being an observer?

b. What is the value of being able to talk about one's resources?

c. What other skills are involved in coaching besides (1) understanding how individuals perceive their resources and goals and (2) listening?

Questionnaire on Coaching and Goal Setting

Introduction

The motivation to work may be thought of as the interaction between three areas: (1) the individual as a human resource, (2) the requirements of a particular job, and (3) the character of the work climate. The degree to which individuals are effective and derive satisfaction in their professional assignments depends upon the extent to which these three fit together harmoniously.

Factors in each of these areas that might be relevant to your motivation to work include

1. *The individual as a human resource.* This would include your abilities, skills, experience, education, interests, interpersonal skills, attitudes, temperament, goals, and the broad area of psychological needs such as for achievement, status, recognition, power, acceptance by others, influence, and control. These and many other factors can give you the potential of high performance on certain types of job requirements.

2. *The nature of the job and its specific requirements.* It is assumed there is a range of different types of jobs for which you are suited, depending on your resources. Most of us have some awareness of the nature of work for which we think we are most suited and that encourages us to perform with the highest degree of motivation and involvement.

3. *The work climate.* This can be thought of as, first, relationships between people— between you and your boss, you and your peers, or you and your subordinates. The climate has certain values and norms that characterize the atmosphere and either promote or hinder your effectiveness as an individual.

The Manager as a Coach

A role of the supervisor-manager that is emphasized is that of a coach to employees. This approach is of value because it helps develop the full potential of people and makes the organization fully aware of its human assets. From this knowledge, decisions can be made for selection, placement, assignments, rotation, career planning, promotion, and so on.

The following questionnaire is intended to permit you to practice being both employee and coach as the roles relate to motivation and goal setting. A similar exercise has been used in industrial supervisory training in which trainees complete a questionnaire focused upon the three areas discussed.

Read through the questionnaire and then reread the description of the activity so you will know how you are to use the notes you will make on the questions. (*Note:* This questionnaire is for your own use and is not to be handed in or shown to others unless you so desire. Write your answers on extra sheets of paper if enough room has not been provided on the form.)

Name _____ Date _____

Questionnaire on Coaching and Goal Setting

PART I: YOU AS A RESOURCE (WHAT I BRING TO THE JOB)

In answering this question, think in terms of your human resources as described in the introductory section. Use extra sheets of paper where necessary, since little room is provided here.

1. What do you regard as some of your major strengths: abilities, work habits, needs, goals, temperament, and so on. (Note: Do not try to "sell" yourself. Just state honestly how you see yourself.)

laidback
patient
confident
friendly

PART II: APPLICATION OF YOUR RESOURCES

The first question gives you an opportunity to think of your resources, which might include many assets you do not use frequently. Now think specifically in terms of how you perform in different areas. (You do not have to confine your answers to a work situation—school, recreation, work, church, and so on are fine.)

1. What are some things you do well and would like to do more of? Why?

I try Not to be serious
Persistant

2. What are things you do not do so well, but would like to do better? Why?

Study/taking tests

3. What are things you have done and would prefer not to do more of? Why?

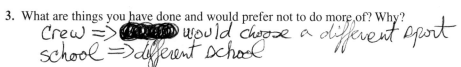
Crew => ~~would~~ would choose a different sport
school =>different school

4. What are some things you have not done, but would like to do?

travel more

5. Can you recall something you have done in the past couple of years that you felt was innovative?

6. What new skill would you like to acquire in the year ahead?

time management

7. Write three brief statements about characteristics that you would like to improve or reinforce.

stress management, listening skills

8. Write three brief statements about characteristics that you would like to minimize or reduce.

critical

9. What I want most out of my job:

To enjoy it

10. What I would like to achieve in the next 5 to 10 years:

MArriage, job

PART III: THE WORK CLIMATE

1. The type of relationship I want with my boss that can provide the support I need to achieve my needs and goals is:

relationship oriented

2. The type of work climate in which I will be most effective is

relAxed => where tAsks are fullfilled at persons own convenience

3. Three things I do that are especially helpful for other people are

listen, lighten the mood, to others ideas

4. Three things I would like to do better to be more helpful to others are

listen, Knowledge on helpful tips,

(Use extra sheets of paper where necessary.)

Notes:

1. This exercise is designed to give you the opportunity to sample an aspect of the broad area of goal setting, coaching. Obviously the times provided for this exercise are unrealistic, and the individual will probably prefer to select some aspect of the questionnaire and concentrate on it. Complete coverage is not the intent here.

2. *If you prefer to discuss questions on the topic of resources and goals not presented here, please feel free to do so.*

Introduction

In all spheres the pressure of competition is forcing organizations and vendors to position their products and/or services by continually relating them to the current needs and interests of their customers. One of the fundamental processes that is the basis for almost all activities in organizations is communication.[1] The complexity of the global business environment and the explosion in information technology have created work environments that use a variety of communication systems, such as electronic boards, teleconferencing, shared files, group screens, and email. But before we proceed any further, we need to explore the basic nature of communication in the work setting.

Communication is one of the primary areas for understanding human behavior. In organizational surveys communication has always been ranked high as a problem by managers. The increasing diversity of the workforce in many parts of the United States coupled with the increasingly global business environment presents many communication challenges to managers. For example, a recent study of high-tech manufacturing companies in California's Silicon Valley found that 16 different languages were spoken on the production floor.[2] Furthermore, the survey of managers in three countries found that 74 percent of the responding companies in the United States, 63 percent in Great Britain, and 85 percent in Japan ranked communication as a key barrier to organizational effectiveness. Another recent study of leading companies concluded that effective managers strategically use communication to manage tough organizational changes.[3] Communicating effectively seems to be an area of increasing concern for most managers.[4]

Communication is the primary area of focus for understanding human interactions and for learning methods of changing one's own behavior and influencing that of others. It is an area in which individuals can make great strides in improving their own effectiveness. Communication is also the point of major conflicts and misunderstandings between two people, between members of a team, between groups, and within the total organization as a system. Communication workshops are probably more widespread than any other type. Sensitivity training deals with helping people communicate better, and family counseling sessions and group therapy are communication oriented. Management workshops deal with communication much as we do in this course.

In the context of information technology and the changing nature of communication systems, four types of work environments were recently identified: same time and same place, same time and different places, different times and same place, and different times and different places.[5] Figure 12–1 captures the nature of the four general types of work environments, the kinds of meetings that they create, and the information technology media that can be used to foster communication within each type. Module 20, on our Web site, develops some of the issues between information technology, communication media, media richness, and human behavior.

In this module we continue to build on previously presented theories of personality, motivation, and perception. We begin with a review of the relationship between

Figure 12–1
Examples of Communication Media and General Types of Work Environments*

	Same Time	Different Times
Same Place	*Face-to-face* Meeting rooms PC projectors Copyboards	*Administration/ data management* Shared files Shift work
Different Places	*Remote meetings* Conference calls Data sharing Video/teleconferencing	*Reliance on coordination* Email Voice mail

*Adapted from Johansen, 1992.

personality, motivation, perception, and communication. An examination of the basic components of the communication process is followed by a review of the different levels of communication. Finally, we explore interpersonal communication, the group's effects on the communication process, and the cross-cultural context of communication.

Personality, Motivation, Perception, and Communication

The nature of the personalities involved, the perceptual process, and motivation deeply affect communication. What two people communicate about is determined by who they are and by how they perceive themselves and the other person in the situation. How they perceive depends on their motivation (goals, needs, defenses) at the given moment. This relationship is illustrated in Figure 12–2.

Figure 12–2
Linkage between Motivation, Perception and Communication

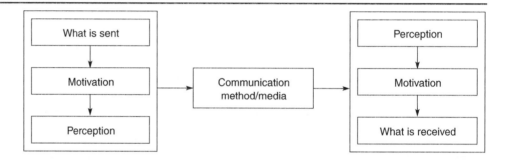

The communicated idea is so closely related to the personality, perceptions, and motivations of both the sender and the receiver that misunderstandings are built into the nature of the process. In addition, the method of communication—face-to-face, telephone, electronically via computer network or via voice-mail technology, meetings, formal reports, and memorandums—is likely to influence the nature of the communication episode. Overcoming the natural barriers to communication is a major objective in communicating meaning. Before we begin to examine some of the barriers to accurate communication, let's review briefly the communication process.

The Communication Process

At the most basic level, **communication** is the transfer of information from one person to another. As such the communication episode entails the transfer of information from one person (the sender) to another (the receiver) by some method (the channel). Yet communication is complex and problematic, as we shall see. The process involves five elements: the sender, the message, the medium, the receiver, and feedback. The sender–receiver link (the channel) can be a telephone wire or computer signal, sound waves (the voice), or a written message, to name a few. One key difficulty is noise or interference in the channel, which distorts the message. Noise can be literally that, as when you try to hold a conversation in the same room with a band or a loud engine. Any other signal in the channel of communication besides the desired message can be thought of as noise. A beautiful symphony that prevents me from hearing a customer's request, static that disturbs a computer signal, or the poor quality of a photocopy that prevents me from reading a memo—all these are noise. However, other sorts of noise originate within the sender and receiver. Communications are heavily interactive with perceptions, attitudes, and interpretations, being both dependent on them and an important factor affecting them. Figure 12–2 outlines some of these connections.

Still another factor affecting communications is the process of encoding and decoding. Any message to be sent must first be encoded. We formulate our meanings in words, for instance, to hold a conversation; in special circumstances, we use special codes. (The signals of the quarterback on the football field; the special language of surgeons during an operation; the slang with which we communicate with our buddies; the specially ordered, cryptic conversation of air traffic controllers and pilots, or the dispatcher and police units all offer examples.) If the sender and receiver aren't using the same code, accurate communication will not take place even if there is no noise in the channel.

Language is one obvious sort of code, and words and their meaning are a significant source of potential miscommunication where sender and receiver understand different meanings for the same word.

Levels of Communication

A variety of classifications of communication levels can be found in the literature. Some make the distinction between verbal and nonverbal communication; some make the distinction between verbal and electronic communication; some make the distinction between different electronic communication media; and some make the distinction among various other types of communication: intraindividual (for example, a message is sent from sensory organ to the brain), interpersonal (for example, a message is sent between two individuals or more within the same group), intraorganizational (for example, a message is sent between two groups or subsystems within the same organization), and interorganizational (for example, a message is sent between two organizations). In this module, we examine communications at the interpersonal levels.

Interpersonal Communication

As we have seen, at the most basic level communication is a process that occurs when an individual sends and receives messages through a chosen method of communication in an effort to create meaning in his or her mind or in the mind of others. Figure 12–2 illustrates the multiple elements that participate in the **interpersonal communication** episode. Each element not only plays a critical role in the communication process but also serves as a source of potential barriers for accurate communications.

Barriers to Accurate Communication

There are many barriers to accurate communication: conflicting assumptions, inadequate information, semantics, emotional blocks, nonverbal communication barriers, cultural barriers, inadequate communication media, and limited communication methods and technology (see Figure 12–3). Four of the barriers that will be presented here have a basis in the factors included in the discussion of perception in Module 11. The barriers become apparent by asking what two people need to have in common to communicate. By way of helping answer this question, we might ask, If you were an explorer in a jungle area and encountered a native who had never had any contact with the world outside of his own isolated tribe, what could you communicate with him about? The answer is that you could exchange meaning—through sign language—

Figure 12–3 Barriers to Accurate Communication: A Partial List

- Perceptual and attributional biases
- Conflicting assumptions
- Inadequate information
- Semantics
- Emotional blocks
- Nonverbal communication barriers
- Cultural barriers
- Inadequate communication media
- Technological barriers

about those things with which both of you had had past experience: food, shelter, temperature, elimination, birth, death, facts about the environment such as where the sun rises and sets, and so on. Both parties must share the codes of past experience before meaning can be exchanged.

Conflicting Assumptions

When one individual sends a communication to another, he or she assumes that the receiver will use the same codes of past experience in interpreting the message that were used in sending it. The receiver, in turn, assumes that the codes he or she uses to give meaning to the message are the same as those used by the sender. This is probably best illustrated by humorous stories that set up a person with one set of assumptions and codes and then switch to an entirely different set in the punch line.

Unfortunately, daily communication between people is frequently distorted because they each use slightly different assumptions and codes but make the assumption that the other is using the same system; there is no punch line to help them out. This *assumed overlap of codes* is incorrect a large percentage of the time, but it is not realized by the participants and the misunderstanding goes undetected.

Organizational life, with its hierarchy of superiors and subordinates, is an ideal culture for nurturing the problems of conflicting assumptions. Employees and bosses perceive many aspects of the subordinate's job duties and the obstacles to performance of them differently as we discussed in the module on perception. The boss may well not be the communicator he or she believes, as indicated in Table 11–1. The organizational climate usually generates an atmosphere in which subordinates fear they might appear to be stupid if they ask too many questions; often they assume they understand what is being passed down but they really do not. Thus conflicting assumptions are apt to abound between levels of the hierarchy, between sections, and between people in the organization.

Figure 12–4 illustrates the problem of conflicting assumptions, or assumed overlap, in the codes of past experience that are active in communication. Each individual's codes of past experience are unique, but to an extent they overlap with those of other individuals in general (as between the explorer and the native) and with those of country, town, social class, family, and so on. The major problem in communications, then, is that each individual is inclined to assume that people with whom he or she interacts are using the same coding systems. That this is not the case often goes undetected.

Inadequate Information

Managers do not always provide enough information for those receiving assignments to do the jobs adequately.

Semantics

Semantics (word usage) is a major source of communication failure. Most words in the dictionary have multiple meanings. An illustration is the word *charge:*

You *charge* someone a fee for doing a service.

You *charge* something you purchase when you want to pay later.

You *charge* a battery when you want it to provide electricity.

You *charge* an official with duties to perform.

You *charge* a horse into battle against an enemy.

You get a *charge* out of something funny.

You place a *charge* of powder into a cannon.

You *charge* a criminal for crimes committed.

You *charge* a rifle when you level it at the enemy.

A favorite word for discussion in management courses is *fast,* which can have meanings that are directly opposite: A color is fast when it won't run, whereas a horse is fast when it runs well.

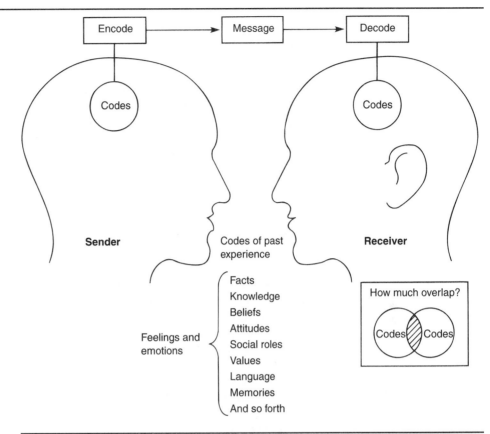

**Figure 12–4
Transfer of Meaning**

Communication between two persons involves transfer of meaning, which assumes that both individuals use the same coding system. Since each individual's codes are unique, there is never the degree of agreement (overlap) between the two coding systems that either party assumes. Thus conflicting assumptions are primary barriers to communications.

When two individuals are using different meanings of the same word and do not realize it, a barrier to meaning exists that may go undetected. The phrase "meanings are in people, not words" is commonly used in management workshops. You cannot assume the meaning you give a word will be the one the receiver uses in decoding the message.

Emotional Blocks

All experiences and all learning have an emotional and feeling component. The recall of past experiences includes not only the event and content but also the feelings that accompanied them at the time they occurred. Figure 12–4 also represents this in the codes of past experience, all of which are learned with a feeling component. The significance of this for communications is that any time the codes of past experience are used, the feelings and emotions are present to influence both sender and receiver at the time the message is exchanged. Most of the time neither is aware of this factor, although the feelings are intense and are a part of the content. Sometimes, however, the content does not indicate the feelings, but the individual is transmitting nonverbal signals of which he or she is not aware though they are being received by others.[6]

Nonverbal Communication Barriers

Activity 12–2 focuses on the critical role that **nonverbal communication** plays in the communication episode that many times serves as a confusing or reinforcement element. Learning to be aware of nonverbal communication can help in understanding the communication episode as well as in setting the stage and deriving a holistic meaning of the communication message. Here are a few basic types of nonverbal communication:

Body motion or **kinesic behavior**—gestures, facial expressions, eye behavior, touching, and any other movement of the limbs and body.

307

Physical characteristics—body shape, physique, posture, height, weight, hair, and skin color.

Paralanguage—voice quality, volume, speech rate, pitch, nonfluencies (for examples, *yaa, um, ah*), laughing.

Proxemics—ways people use and perceive space (for example, seating arrangements and conversational distance).

Environment—building and room design, furniture and interior decorating, light, noise, and cleanliness.

Time—being late or early, keeping others waiting, and other relationships between time and status.

Cultural Barriers

Communication Networks

The nature of the communication network that the individual is a part of might create an additional barrier. Communication can be examined by focusing on how and what individuals communicate as well as by focusing on the communication relationships among individuals. **Communication networks** involve oral, written, and nonverbal signals between two or more individuals. For example, the pattern of signals will flow between a manager of a produce department in a large food store and the other managers while another pattern of signals is flowing between the manager and his or her immediate subordinates and all the other individuals with whom the manager interacts. A manager's network extends laterally (with other managers at the same level) and vertically (with a direct superior or direct subordinates). From this point of view, communication networks can be quite complex, and they have the potential to create barriers to understanding.

Communication Methods and Technology

The method or the tool chosen to transfer the message from the sender to the receiver plays a key role in the communication episode. With the advancement of technology, we are capable of assembling and electronically storing, transmitting, processing, and retrieving words, numbers, and sounds around the globe. Computer networks enhance our communication accuracy not only within the small unit or between two individuals but also between large units located in different geographical areas. Yet limiting the communication episode to the computer's screen—which allows for the use of two of the senses only—can be a major barrier in the communication episode.

Communication, as an exchange of meaning, is bounded by culture. As Figure 12–4 shows, **encoding** describes the producing of a symbol into a message, and **decoding** describes the receiving of a message from a symbol. Furthermore, the message sender must encode her or his meaning into a form that the receiver will recognize. Translating meaning into words and behaviors (that is, into symbols) and translating the words and behaviors back again into meaning is based on a person's cultural background, which is not the same for every person.[7] Since cross-cultural communication occurs between two individuals from different cultures, it can lead to much miscommunication. Recent research indicates that the greater the differences between the sender's and the receiver's cultures, the greater the chance for miscommunication.[8] Miscommunication in this context is the result of misperception, misinterpretation, and misevaluation. The following example was provided by Nancy Adler:

Since in Cantonese the word for "eight" sounds like "faat," which means prosperity, a Hong Kong textile manufacturer Mr. Lau Ting-pong paid $5 million in 1988 for car registration number 8. A year later, a European millionnaire paid $4.8 million at Hong Kong's Lunar New Year auction for vehicle registration number 7, a decision that mystified the Chinese, since the number 7 has little significance in the Chinese calculation of fortune.[9]

Cross-cultural communication occurs when a person from one culture communicates with a person from another culture. Miscommunication in the cross-cultural context occurs when the receiving person (from the "other" culture) does not receive the sender's intended message. Coupling individual diversity with cross-cultural differences dictates that one must assume significant differences between the sender and receiver. Furthermore, cross-cultural perceptions seem to play a role in the cross-cultural communication episode. People from diverse cultures tend to view the world differently while at the same time they stereotype individuals from other cultures. As we have seen in the previous module, perceptual patterns are neither innate nor absolute. They are selective, learned, culturally determined, consistent, and inaccurate.[10] Managing the cross-cultural communication episodes presents a set of challenges for organizations and managers of the multinational corporation. Yet some of the skills that are explored in the next section provide the necessary foundation.

Managers' Role in Managing Communication: Overcoming the Barriers

Managers' role in fostering the communication process is critical. Beyond a self-assessment about their own communication style, methods, and competencies, managers can ensure a work environment in which employees feel that they can communicate openly at all times. A recent study found that two-way communication is a critical element in fostering continuous improvement and organizational learning.[11]

Practicing Communication Skills: Each manager must practice communication skills until they become second nature. *Paraphrasing,* for example, is one of the more useful skills practiced in numerous professions. Diplomats spend considerable (sometimes endless) time making sure they understand views of the representatives of other countries. Television journalists frequently pause in their interviews to feed back what they think they have heard. Supervisors giving instructions to employees find it useful to say, "Now, tell me what you are going to do so we will be sure we are in agreement." One top executive we observed had called six other executives together for a preliminary discussion of a problem area. He asked each person to use 5 minutes to present his initial views on the matter. As each individual finished, he would summarize what he had heard, ask whether he understood correctly, and then ask questions if he had any. After all six had spoken, the executive summarized and integrated their views and then led a discussion concerning what steps should be taken to study the problem.

A middle-level manager informed us that paraphrasing was one of the most meaningful ways to handle a complaint at the initial stage.

Give the person the time needed to fully express the problem. When the person is through, summarize what you have heard and see if there is agreement on the complaint. Then say you will look into the matter and discuss it further at a later date. This has the advantage of not feeling pressured to make an uninformed decision on the spot, of letting the individual know he or she has been heard, and of giving the individual time to cool off.

Paraphrasing is a useful tool when a disagreement arises. One exercise frequently used in communication workshops is to have a group of people sit in a circle and carry on a discussion on a controversial topic such as the Arab–Israeli conflict in the Middle East or arms limitations. After one person has expressed her view, the next person to respond must paraphrase to the last speaker's satisfaction what has just been said before he expresses his own views. This is continued for the entire discussion. Individuals usually find they are so preoccupied with what they are about to say that they forget to listen to what is being said. (Your class might want to try this as an additional exercise if there is time.)

Awareness and Understanding: Learning that communications problems do exist and studying some of the theory and concepts that might account for them is an initial step. This means learning not only at the content level but also at the dynamic level of what goes on between you and other people when you communicate. It is difficult for some people just to understand that others are not perceiving the world as they do.

Social Technology: Knowledge of the techniques and methods available to help administrators in overcoming communications problems is a major objective of this text. Managers must learn what technology is available and how to use it for all four levels of effectiveness. Practice is necessary in dialoguing, listening, paraphrasing, perceptual checking, and so on.

Creating a Supportive Organizational Climate: The organizational atmosphere is all important. If it is threatening and suppresses expression of individuals' feelings, there will be serious breakdowns in communications at all levels of the hierarchy. Modern management theory recognizes that a manager's skills must include the handling of feelings and emotions of employees as much as how to work with logic and rationality. The consequences of not developing these skills are that employees' emotional blocks will divert energy into nonproductive or antiorganizational channels. Supportiveness and two-way communication, as basic values of the organizational culture, can reduce employees' feelings of defensiveness.

Self-Awareness: It is assumed that the more managers are aware of their own needs, goals, feelings, and defenses, the better they will be able to cope with their own growth and behavior. This means being able to communicate with yourself. It means knowing what your strengths are in interaction situations and what part of the problem you represent.

Giving and Receiving Feedback: The impact one person has on another can be a major barrier to communication. Managers need to have some idea of the impact they are having if they are to influence others effectively. Producing an organizational atmosphere in which there is two-way feedback between superior and subordinates is one area of development. Some organizations are having employees fill out anonymous evaluation forms concerning their supervisors and managers. The data become the subject of general discussion between the superior and subordinates as to how the superior's behavior is affecting the progress of the work. Training workshops dealing with communications, leadership, and self-awareness can be helpful in attaining insight into the impact one is having on others; learning how to give others feedback without offending them and learning how to receive feedback without being offended are currently stressed.

Working with the Motivation of Others: In Frederick Herzberg's theory, helping individuals use their own internal dynamos—the motivators—can increase both productivity and satisfaction. A manager can work at the level of trying to produce the conditions in the work situation that augment this result, but he or she also needs to make efforts to understand what motivates each individual. This can be explored in goal setting, in daily conversations when this appears appropriate, and in watching the behavior of the individual. Activity 12–1 focuses on this subject.

Coaching and Goal Setting: Goal setting as an organizationwide practice can help overcome communications barriers. When a boss and a subordinate sit down periodically to define the subordinate's goals, which are part of the organization's goals, many of their perceptual distortions will be greatly reduced. At the same time, the individual's personal goals, what he or she would like to attain careerwise from the present situation and in the coming years, can be an integral part of the process. Discussion of progress and feedback from the supervisor as to how well the individual is doing should be accomplished as the need arises, based on events as they occur. Saving these discussions for yearly review produces barriers to communications; not only does the subordinate lack the information and guidance needed, but unexpressed feelings can build up and interfere with performance. Milestone points for specific review and revision of the goals should be part of the procedure to ensure that nothing is overlooked.

Coaching is a very broad topic, and only two limited aspects of it are considered here. The first concerns developing the manager's attitudes about the employee as a human resource who brings assets to the work situation that need to be nurtured if the employee is to grow and be productive. The manager as a coach needs to know how employees think of themselves in terms of their strengths and what goals they perceive as being meaningful in order to develop and use these strengths. When a manager finds that she and an employee don't agree on these matters, important data for coaching the employee in his or her performance and career become available.

A second aspect of coaching is developing listening skills, which can help the manager determine accurately what the employee is saying about himself or herself. Paraphrasing, as a listening skill, is one way to try to get objective data from others without imposing one's own preconceptions onto what is being said. Asking nonleading questions for clarification is another; "I'm not sure what you are telling me. Could you give me that again more slowly?" does not lead the individual from his or her own trend of thoughts. As an example of a leading question, consider the response to a mother who expressed concern about her teenage son, who had always been a good student, good to his parents, and helpful around the house, but who, during the past 6 months, had shown all the opposite behaviors. The person who was supposed to have been the listener asked, "Do you suppose he might be on drugs?" Even if the mother did not have a problem when she came, she did when she left.

Activity 12–1 ("Communication, Coaching, and Goal Setting") provides an opportunity to further develop your awareness of the critical role that communication plays in facilitating individual goal setting. This activity assumes that the best way to learn to work with human resources is to go through the process of thinking about one's own resources and goals. Most of you will not have formulated your thinking in this regard, and you may feel you are groping. It is better to start thinking about this issue now than to wait until you are confronted with the problem in an actual work situation.

Students in this course sometimes say they do not like to talk about themselves because they may appear to others either to be bragging or to have too few resources to talk about. The fact they have come this far in their education indicates that they do have resources to talk about and they had better think about goals if they are to continue to grow. Recruiters often want the individual being interviewed to talk spontaneously in terms of interests and what he or she does well in an authentic manner that indicates some degree of self-esteem, not just a selling job. Throughout a career, an individual can expect bosses to periodically ask, How do you see yourself in terms of your job? Where do you want to go? What do you want to do? What do you want from your job? Are there abilities you have that are not being used or that you want to develop? Some inhibitions in answering such questions can be overcome by practice in a situation such as we saw in Activity 12–1 earlier in this module.

Media Richness and Communication Effectiveness

Managers can use a variety of media for transmitting messages. Research indicates that media choice has a direct impact on communication effectiveness. Three clusters of media options were identified: written, oral, and electronic.[12] Table 12–1 summarizes the variety of media choices in each of the clusters, their general availability, cost, speed, immediate interactions, impact, and attention.

Media also vary in richness. Recently, **media richness** has received considerable attention in organizational communication. Media richness theory ranks communication media along a continuum in terms of their "richness." In this context *richness* denotes the capacity of the medium to (1) carry a large volume of data and (2) convey meaning.[13] More specifically, media richness refers to the ability of a medium to change human understanding, overcome different conceptual frames of reference, or clarify ambiguous issues in a timely manner. Thus where the mode of communication

Table 12–1
Managers Can Use a
Variety of Media for
Transmitting Messages

Written	Generally Available	Relatively Low Cost	High Speed	Immediate Interaction	High Impact and Attention
Letters	x	x			
Memos and reports			x		x
Telegrams			x		x
Newspapers and magazines	x				
Handbooks and manuals	x	x			
Bulletins and posters	x	x			
Inserts and enclosures	x	x			x
Oral					
Telephone	x	x	x	x	x
Intercom and paging	x		x		x
Conferences and meetings	x			x	
Speeches	x			x	
Electronic					
Fax			x	x	x
Electronic mail			x	x	
Voice messaging			x		x
Computer conferencing			x		x
Audio conferencing				x	x
Videoconferencing				x	x
Groupware				x	

Source: Adapted with permission from D. A. Level Jr. and W. P. Galle Jr., *Business Communications: Theory and Practice,* (Burr Ridge, IL: Business Publications, Inc./Richard D. Irwin, Inc., 1998), pp. 91, 93.

provides new substantial understanding, it is considered "rich"; otherwise, it is "lean." As tasks become more ambiguous, managers should increase the richness of the media they use. For example, simple nonroutine tasks can benefit from a communication medium that is lean, such as a memo, whereas complex nonroutine tasks can benefit from a face-to-face or videoconferencing communication medium that is rich.

Current Challenges

The communication episode is a complex process that involves many different dimensions. New forms of communications have emerged over the past decade. Although face-to-face communication is vital to individual, group, and organizational effectiveness, the major technological leap has introduced alternative advanced communication technology that helps overcome some limitations of interpersonal interaction. The transformation of communication-driven technology has been accelerated as a result of increased global competition and the emerging of the global markets. Email, communication networks (such as local area networks and wide area networks), electronic bulletin boards, real-time videoconferencing, and groupware software that allows individuals and teams located in different places to work together on a problem are likely to become the norms in communication.

While globalization and technological development are driving the emerging new forms of communication, the challenge of understanding the impacts of the new communication technologies and attempting to manage them increases. For example, think of yourself as a part of a team where each member is in a different geographical location. You are linked via a local area network and a groupwide software program. The team is trying to solve a problem but is not able to see each other or talk to each other orally. But you are able to send messages back and forth, and every person on the team is able to take part in the exchange via the computer screen.

Based on what we have covered in this module, what are some of the barriers for accurate communication that your team is likely to experience? What will be the effect

**Figure 12–5
What Do I Do If They Do
Not Speak My Language?**

Verbal behavior

- *Clear, slow speech.* Enunciate each word. Do not use colloquial expressions.
- *Repetition.* Repeat each important idea using different words to explain the same concept.
- *Simple sentences.* Avoid compound, long sentences.
- *Active verbs.* Avoid passive verbs.

Nonverbal behavior

- *Visual restatements.* Use as many visual restatements as possible, such as pictures, graphs, tables, and slides.
- *Gestures.* Use more facial and hand gestures to emphasize the meaning of words.
- *Demonstration.* Act out as many themes as possible.
- *Pauses.* Pause more frequently.
- *Summaries.* Hand out written summaries of your verbal presentation.

Attribution

- *Silence.* When there is a silence, wait. Do not jump in to fill the silence. The other person is probably just thinking more slowly in the nonnative language or translating.
- *Intelligence.* Do not equate poor grammar and mispronunciation with lack of intelligence; it is usually a sign of second-language use.
- *Differences.* If unsure, assume difference, not similarity.

Comprehension

- *Understanding.* Do not just assume that they understand; assume that they do not understand.
- *Checking comprehension.* Have colleagues repeat their understanding of the material to you. Do not simply ask whether they understand or not. Let them explain what they understand to you.

Design

- *Breaks.* Take more frequent breaks. Second-language comprehension is exhausting.
- *Small modules.* Divide the material into smaller modules.
- *Longer time frame.* Allocate more time for each module than usual in a monolingual program.

Motivation

- *Encouragement.* Verbally and nonverbally encourage and reinforce speaking by nonnative language participants.
- *Drawing out.* Explicitly draw out marginal and passive participants.
- *Reinforcement.* Do not embarrass novice speakers.

Source: Adopted from N. J. Adler, *International Dimensions of Organizational Behavior,* (Boston, MA: PWS-Kent, 1996), p. 89. Used with permission.

of this barrier on your team? The scientific community is only beginning to investigate the new advanced communication technology and its impact on the behavior and effectiveness of individuals and teams. In Module 20 on the management of technology and information, we explore further some of these issues.

Communication is also faced with the increased challenge of diversity at the workplace and globalization. As we have seen, diversity and cultural differences can play a major role in creating barriers to accurate communication. Ethnocentrism—the tendency to consider the values, norms, and customs of one's own country to be superior to those of other countries—has been shown to hinder the communication process.[14] Figure 12–5 presents Nancy Adler's suggestions for overcoming cross-cultural barriers to communication.

Summary

Communication is often ranked as a key problem of organizational life. Communication is closely interrelated with the other core concepts of personality, diversity, perception, and motivation previously reviewed. Messages to be communicated are formulated from the sender's motivation (intent) and perception of the relevant context. The meaning of the message to the receiver is filtered through the receiver's perceptual frame of reference and own needs and defenses.

Eight barriers to communication are conflicting assumptions between sender and receiver, cultural differences, nonverbal communication barriers, limited communication methods and technology, inadequate information, semantics, inadequate communication networks, and emotional blocks. The latter area is complicated by the tendency of the receiver to evaluate and judge the message rather than understand the meaning. Listening for logic and rationality, while ignoring the emotional and feeling content, also interferes with the transmission of meaning. Ways to overcome these barriers and improve communications include developing awareness and understanding, social technology applications, a supportive organizational climate, and self-awareness.

A variety of activities were developed to enhance improved communication skills. Activities 12–1 and 12–3W provide the experiential base for understanding the communication process and the development of basic skills of coaching and goal setting. Activity 12–2 provides the opportunity to explore the dynamics of nonverbal communication.

Communication is a complex phenomenon and a multilevel concept that can have an impact on behavior at the individual, group, and organizational levels. In this module, communication was examined and studied at the interpersonal and intragroup levels. As we will see in the advanced modules, communication influences key organizational processes such as creativity, innovation, work design, and the management of quality. Improving the communication process is an ongoing managerial challenge that requires continuous effort.

Key Terms and Concepts

Communication	Kinesic behavior
Communication media	Media richness
Communication networks	Message
Computer networks	Nonverbal communication
Decoding	Paralanguage
Encoding	Proxemics
Interpersonal communication	Semantics
Intragroup communication	Superordinate goals
Intragroup conflict	

Study Questions

1. "In the communication process, meaning is in the mind of the sender and the receiver." Explain this statement.

2. Of the barriers to communication given, which is the most basic? Why?

3. Several methods are given for overcoming barriers to communication. Give examples from your own experience of how these methods worked. Give examples of other methods that have worked for you or others you know.

4. Discuss the relationship between communication and perception.

5. Discuss the relationship between communication, diversity, and expectations.

6. We discussed a few ways for overcoming barriers to communication. Provide an example from your group's experience that illustrates how you overcame communication barriers.

7. What are some of the similarities and differences between interpersonal and intergroup communications?

8. What does goal setting have to do with communication at both the interpersonal and intergroup levels?

9. Discuss the relationship between "media richness" and communication effectiveness.

Endnotes

1. See, for example, R. D'Aprix, *Communicating for Change: Connecting the Workplace with the Marketplace,* (San Francisco: Jossey-Bass, 1996); E. Marlow, and P. O. Wilson, *The Breakdown of Hierarchy: Communicating in the Evolving Workplace,* (Boston:Butterworth-Heineman, 1997).

2. A. B. (Rami) Shani and Y. Mitki, "Creating the Learning Organization," in R. G. Golembiewski (ed.), *Handbook of Organizational Consultation,* (New York: Marcel Dekker, 1999).

3. M. Young and J. E. Post, "Managing to Communicate, Communicating to Manage: How Leading Companies Communicate with Employees," *Organizational Dynamics* 22, no. 1 (1993), pp. 31–43; D. K. Berlo, *The Process of Communication: An Introduction to Theory and Practice,* (New York: Holt, Rinehart & Winston, 1960); P. Burger and B. M. Bass, *Assessment of Managers: An International Comparison,* (New York: Free Press, 1979); G. Cheney, "The Rhetoric of Identification and the Study of Organizational Communication," *Quarterly Journal of Speech* 69 (1983), pp. 143–58; D. Fabun, *Communications,* (Beverly Hills, CA: Glencoe Press, 1968); L. Gibson, J. M. Ivancevich, and J. H. Donnelly Jr., "The Communication Process," in *Organizations: Behavior, Structure, Processes,* rev. ed., (Dallas, TX: Business Publications, 1976), pp. 161–85; G. Goldhaber, M. Yales, D. Porter, and R. Lesniak, "Organizational Communication," *Human Communication Research* 6 (1978), pp. 76–96; W. V. Haney, *Communication and Organizational Behavior,* (Burr Ridge, IL: Richard D. Irwin, 1973).

4. See, for example, W. A. Gudykunst, *Bridging Differences,* (Thousand Oaks, CA: Sage, 1994); L. L. Chu, "Mass Communication Theory: The Chinese Perspective," *Media Asia* 131 (1986), pp. 14–19.

5. R. Johansen, *Leading Business Teams: How Teams Can Use Technology and Group Process Tools to Enhance Performance,* (Reading, MA: Addison-Wesley, 1992).

6. See Carl Rogers's concept of congruence in communication. C. Rogers, *On Becoming a Person,* (Boston: Houghton Mifflin, 1961), pp. 338–46.

7. N. J. Adler, *International Dimensions of Organizational Behavior,* (Boston, MA: PWS–Kent, 1996); R. L. Kohls, *Survival Kit for Overseas Living,* (Yarmouth, ME: Intercultural Press, 1979), pp. 30–31.

8. B. J. Reilly and J. A. DiAngelo, "Communication: A Cultural System of Meaning and Values," *Human Relations* 43, no. 2 (1990), pp. 129–40; T. Prekel, "Multi-Cultural Communication: A Challenge to Managers." Paper delivered at the International Convention of the American Business Communication Association, New York, 1983.

9. N. J. Adler, *International Dimensions of Organizational Behavior,* p. 65.

10. N. J. Adler, Ibid., p. 68.

11. Young and Post, "Managing to Communicate."; J. M. Putti, S. Aryee, and J. Phua, "Communication Relationship Satisfaction and Organizational Commitment," *Group and Organization Studies* 15, no. 1 (1990), pp. 44–52.

12. D. A. Level Jr. and W. P. Galle Jr., *Business Communications: Theory and Practice,* (Burr Ridge, IL: Irwin, 1988), pp. 91, 93.

13. See R. L. Daft and R. H. Lengel, "Information Richness," in L. L. Cummings and B. M. Staw (eds.), *Research in Organization Behavior,* vol. 6, (Greenwich, CT: JAI Press, 1984), pp. 191–233.

14. See, for example, N. J. Adler, *International Dimensions of Organizational Behavior.*

**Activity 12–2:
Nonverbal
Communication**

Objectives:

a. To complete small group tasks without any verbal communication.

b. To explore individual and group reactions when verbal communication is cut off and only nonverbal communication can be used. To test your tolerance for ambiguity.

c. To demonstrate that shared expectations (group norms and roles) are spontaneously generated.

d. To provide behavioral data for a theoretical discussion of communications in this module.

Task 1 (A Structured Task):

Participants are to put their books aside and are not to refer to them again until this exercise and the discussion following it have been completed.

All chairs and tables are moved to the sides of the room. Members of a team or group (five to seven people) stand in a close circle facing one another.

The instructor will ask participants to become completely silent before giving instructions and will ask them not to speak until this exercise in nonverbal communication is completed.

The instructor will present a poster for all to see upon which the "Shoe Store" problem (included in the Instructor's Manual) is written. Teams are to reach a consensus on the correct answer. Only nonverbal (no written or spoken) communication is to be used.
(Time: 5 minutes)

When the instructor indicates the time is up, each team is to report its solution to the class. Three minutes are then allowed for discussion of the results among team members, after which the instructor will provide the correct solution.

Task 2 (An Unstructured Task):

Participants are to remain completely silent until this exercise is completed.

Each group is to carry on, as a team, any activities or conversational topic of its own choosing for seven minutes. No spoken or written communication, only nonverbal communication, is to be used. You might want to start by expressing to each other your feelings about this class and then move on to other activities as a team. Use the space in this room in any way you wish.
(Time: 7 minutes)

Task 3:

The instructor will stop all the activity, asking everyone to remain silent until the next instruction has been given.

Take 1 minute to try to get in touch with your feelings. How are you feeling now, and how were you feeling during the exercise, about the interaction in which you just took part? When the instructor indicates the time is up, you are to speak. Each participant should be given an opportunity to share feelings with the group.
(Time: 1 minute of silence and 3 to 5 minutes for sharing)

Individuals are called on to share how they felt about the experience.
(Time: 10 to 15 minutes)

Task 4:

Each group is to discuss the following:

a. What shared expectations developed in the group as to what was to be done and how members should or could behave? These may be thought of as group norms.

b. What roles developed among the members?

c. Did any subgrouping take place?

(Time: 5 minutes)

Each group is to report its findings. The instructor will add observations of what norms and roles he or she saw evolving in each group.

Part 4

Managing Work Design, Culture, and Change

Review

Managing work design and redesign, culture, and change seems to absorb a significant amount of time and energy in today's organizations. Some managers argue that in reality their job almost entirely consists of managing change. The complexity, amount, and pace of change have increased significantly during the past decade. Most organizations, employees, and managers are struggling to find the optimal path. The management of work design, culture, and change influences organizational behavior and organizational effectiveness.

Part 3 interrelated the four conceptual areas of personality and personal growth, motivation, perception, and communication to key organizational processes. The design of work and organizations fosters organizational dynamics that result in the emergence of organizational culture. Thus the area that remains to be addressed in detail is the interrelationship of "effectiveness" at the individual, team, and organizational levels.

Embedded in organizational efforts to improve effectiveness is continuous improvement or what the Japanese call *Kaizan.* Continuous improvement is a purposeful and explicit set of principles, mechanisms, and activities within an organization designed to achieve positive and continuous change in operating procedures, effectiveness, and systems by the people who actually perform these procedures and work within these systems. *Continuous* means that an improvement activity is explicitly designed and organized for continuity. Improvement projects and episodes should follow each other in the same area or around the same general performance indicators. In this respect continuous improvement is markedly different from sporadic improvement projects, which are undertaken without a view of continuity, and from suggestions systems, where any kind of improvement suggestions are called for without explicit management of the area, quality, or direction of the suggestions. Continuity usually requires permanent support structure. *Improvement* is a planned change in the state of affairs of an organization that results in positive changes in the organizational effectiveness indicators.[1]

Preview of Part 4

Part 4 incorporates much of the material already studied into an overall system approach to individual, team, and organizational effectiveness. This part has three integrated modules: "Work and Organization Design," "Organizational Culture, Symbolism, and Effectiveness," and "Organizational Change, Development, and Learning."

In Module 13 work and organization design is described as a fundamental process that groups people and tasks in a variety of configurations and as such has a major influence on organizational behavior, dynamics, and effectiveness. The design of work and jobs is an ongoing challenge that faces the manager. Routed in the historical context of the organization, its business environment, and evolved culture, the design or redesign of organizations is a complex task. The module provides comprehensive road map for organization design as an ongoing process, describes alternative forms of structures, emphasizes a variety of options for work design at both the individual and team levels, and highlights the important role that the manager must play as the designer.

Choices made about work and organization design set the stage for the formation of organizational culture. Module 14 focuses on the nature of organizational culture and its relationships to organizational effectiveness. As such the module goes beyond an exploration of the different views on the topic; the focus is on symbolism as a way of diagnosing organizational culture in its business and organizational context. Organizational culture is a complex phenomenon to map out, since culture is much like air; it is everywhere we look, and it touches everything that goes on in organizations. Understanding the culture of the organization is critical if the manager is to attempt to manage and or try to shape the culture.

One way for managers to influence organizational culture is via a planned change process. Module 15 focuses on organizational change, development, and learning. Following a brief discussion of organizational learning; its meaning; and its impact on individual, group, and organizational effectiveness, we explore various organizational learning mechanisms. Managing organizational learning, development, and change is a challenge that managers face on an ongoing basis. The module presents two complementary ways to cluster the different change programs that have emerged: target focus and consequence focus change programs.

Managing organizational change and development (OC&D) is described as planned change organizational efforts that attempt to improve effectiveness. We provide an in-depth review and comparison of three commonly used systemwide change programs—reengineering, total quality management, and sociotechnical systems. The comparison provides an insight into the complexity of managing change and development. In concluding the book, we reiterate our view that an integration of important aspects of the traditional and the behavioral models is essential for organizational effectiveness.

Notes

1. For a detailed discussion of continuous improvement, its origin, and current definitions, see P. Lillrank and A. B. (Rami) Shani, "Continuous Improvement: Beyond a Definition," EFI Research Paper (Stockholm, Sweden: Stockholm School of Economics, 1998).

13 Work and Organization Design

Learning Objectives

After completing this module, you should be able to

1. Appreciate the importance of integrating goals, structure, and people through comprehensive organization design.
2. Identify the different ways of grouping people into teams, departments, and organizational units.
3. Describe three types of work teams fostered in private industry.
4. Describe alternative designs for global competition.
5. Identify design-related problems in different organizational settings.
6. Appreciate that there are many successful ways to approach work design at individual, group, and organizational levels.

Module Outline

This module was revised by our colleague Michael Stebbins, Professor of Organization Design, College of Business, California Polytechnic State University, San Luis Obispo, California 93407. We are grateful to Professor Stebbins.

Premodule Preparation

The instructor may assign either one of the following two activities. If time permits both might be used.

Activity 13–1: Designing a Student-Run Organization That Provides Consulting Services

Objectives:

a. To appreciate the importance of the total organization on group and individual behavior.

b. To provide a beginning organization design experience that will be familiar to students.

Background:

The Industry Advisory Council for your school has decided to sponsor a student-run organization that will provide business consulting services to nonprofit groups in your community. The council has donated $20,000 toward start-up costs and has agreed to provide office space, computer equipment, and other materials as needed. The council hopes that the organization will establish its own source of funding after the first year of operation.

Task 1:

The dean of the school wants you to develop alternative designs for the new organization. Your task is to identify the main design dimensions or factors to be dealt with in establishing such an organization and to describe the issues that must be resolved for each factor. For example, you might provide an organization chart to help describe the structural issues involved. Before jumping ahead with your design, you may also have to think about (1) groups in the community that could use your help and (2) problems they face. Remember, though, your task is to create the organization that will provide services, not to provide an in-depth look at the types of services provided.

You and your team are to brainstorm design dimensions to be dealt with and to develop a one- or two-page outline that can be shared with the entire class. You have 1 hour to develop the outline. Select two people to present your design. Assume that you will all be involved in the new organization, filling specific positions.

Task 2:

After the brainstorming period, the spokespersons will present the group designs or preferred design and answer questions from the audience.

Task 3:

The instructor will comment on the designs and discuss additional factors that might be important for the success of this organization.

Activity 13–2: The Woody Manufacturing Company: Start-up Design

Objective:

To apply the concepts learned in the module about work design at the individual, group, and organizational levels in designing the Woody Manufacturing Company.

Task 1 (Individual Assignment):

a. Read the following case study of the Woody Manufacturing Company.

b. Review the module carefully and choose the design orientation that you feel can best guide you in developing the design for Mr. Woody.

c. Write down your thoughts on alternative management structures, pay systems, and allocation of work to individuals and groups.

Task 2 (Team Assignment):

a. Get together in your team and develop a proposal for Mr. Woody that, if followed, would help him fulfill his vision.

b. Prepare a 5-minute presentation. Your typewritten team proposal is due prior to your team presentation in Mr. Woody's conference room.

Case Study: The Woody Manufacturing Company

Mr. Woody, the owner/operator of a small furniture company specializing in the manufacture of high-quality bar stools, has experienced a tremendous growth in demand for his products. He has standing orders for $750,000. Consequently, Mr. Woody has decided to expand his organization and attack the market aggressively. His stated mission is "to manufacture world-class products that are competitive in the world market in quality, reliability, performance, and profitability." He would like to create a culture where "pride, ownership, employment security, and trust" are a way of life. He just finished a set of interviews, and he has hired 32 new workers with the following skills:

Four skilled craftspeople.

Ten people with some woodworking experience.

Twelve people with no previous woodworking experience or other skills.

One nurse.

One schoolteacher.

One bookkeeper.

Three people with some managerial experience in nonmanufacturing settings.

Mr. Woody (with your help) must now decide how to design his new organization. This design will include the management structure, pay system, and the allocation of work to individuals and groups. The bar stool–making process has 15 steps:

1. Wood is selected.
2. Wood is cut to size.
3. Defects are removed.
4. Wood is planed to exact specifications.
5. Joints are cut.
6. Tops are glued and assembled.
7. Legs/bases are prepared.
8. Legs/bases are attached to tops.
9. Bar stools are sanded.
10. Stain is applied.
11. Varnish is applied.
12. Bar stools are sanded.
13. Varnish is reapplied.
14. Bar stools are packaged.
15. Bar stools are delivered to the customer.

Mr. Woody currently manufactures three kinds of bar stools (pedestal, four-legged corner, and four-legged recessed). There is no difference in the difficulty of making the three types of bar stools. Major cost variations have been associated with defective wood, imprecise cuts, and late deliveries to customers. Mr. Woody must decide how to organize his company to maintain high quality and profits.

He has thought about several options. He could have some individuals perform the first step for all types of bar stools; he could have an individual perform several steps for one type of bar stool; or he could have a team perform some combination of steps for one or more bar stools. He wonders whether how he organized would affect quality or costs. He's also aware that while the demand for all types of bar stools has been roughly equal over the long run, there were short periods where one type of bar stool was in greater demand than the others. Because Mr. Woody wants to use his people effectively, he has committed an expert in work design to help him set up an optimal organization.

Introduction

"The limiting factor in achieving society's goals is quite often the manner in which resources are organized."

Jay Galbraith, 1977

Organizations of all sizes have human and other resources that can be used to address the challenges posed by their rapidly changing environments. While managers are often aware of the unique capabilities within their companies, they are seldom sure that resources are used in the best possible ways. This is one reason why it is common to see newly appointed chief executive officers spending time on organizational assessment and redesign. Historically, reorganization and redesign have been viewed as top-management functions, often with help from an outside consulting firm. Today work and organization design is a preoccupation at all organizational levels, and there is debate as to whether it is best approached in a top-down, bottom-up, or compromise way that includes high employee involvement.

In earlier decades managers had a general sense of certainty about where their companies were going and spent a lot of planning time on how to get there. Companies had formulas for success and felt that growth was clearly sustainable. Today the competitive environment is much more turbulent and managers see a world of chaos and uncertainty. Leading companies rise and fall from grace rather rapidly, depending on their abilities to use human capital and technology in flexible and innovative ways. So while there is still emphasis on strategic design, it is being conducted with a greater sense of urgency and opportunity.

Organization and work design can be a key element influencing how well organizations and people perform. The design of work and jobs is an ongoing challenge and is evolving as a specialized field of study in academia and as a tool for change. Organizations have unique histories, purposes, cultures, and environments; they usually evolve through trial and error rather than by being developed all at once through deliberate organizational planning and design. While we might say that companies in an industry are in the same business, they often do not have the same mission and do not pursue the same strategies and ways of organizing. For example, Alpha Health Care Corporation is a relatively new managed care company in the health care industry. Alpha competes with long-established health maintenance organizations (HMOs) such as Kaiser Permanente, but does not build and own hospitals, operate its own medical groups and clinics, or directly provide medical services in the traditional Kaiser Permanente mode. Alpha has a different mission and follows a market-driven strategy that results in faster growth and greater flexibility. The company's strength is marketing and customer relations. Managers at Alpha do not worry about hospital administration or quality-of-care audits. They leave operations matters to community hospitals and other providers that choose to participate in the Alpha network. The point is that organizations take on different tasks and are configured in different ways. The differences in configuration can be explored at the total-organization, department, work group, and job levels to find out how design affects organizational success.

Comprehensive Approaches to Organization Design

Work design at the organizational level has developed over the past 40 years both as a field of academic study and as a process for improving organizations. A recent comparison of organization design perspectives identified 10 design schools of thought or orientations that can be used to guide redesign programs.[1] Three of the orientations are comprehensive; that is, they provide guiding models, they spell out design principles, they provide a redesign process, and they have an empirical track record of applications in different settings.[2] All three approaches have been applied to diverse organizations during the corporate downsizing era. The orientations are *information-processing theory, sociotechnical systems theory,* and *self-design.*

The Information-Processing Design Approach

Jay Galbraith is credited with establishing the information-processing orientation to design. According to information-processing theory, **organization design** is most usefully defined as a decision-making process.[3] The decision-making process includes choices about goals, tasks to be accomplished, technology to be adopted, ways to organize, and ways to integrate individuals into the organization.[4] The key is finding a balance or fit among these decisions and doing it in a way that is in step with the changing environment. Attention to customers, changing market needs, and desired outcomes makes the overall process **strategic organization design.** A comprehensive redesign program might involve strategic-planning activities, reengineering of core work processes through (for example) computer and telecommunications enhancements, creation of a new formal structure, development of management systems to provide better coordination, and finally, efforts to develop a new organizational culture, work-group norms, and values. Increasingly, information technology plays a role in each of these activities.

The growth of information technology (IT) and its pervasive use in all sectors of the economy is a familiar trend at the beginning of the new millennium. **Information technology**—including voice messaging, on-line transaction processing, the intranet, electronic mail, teleconferencing, and other computer and telecommunications advances—are fundamentally changing the nature of the workplace. The potential for IT innovations is exemplified by a recent Andersen Consulting company project at UCAR Carbon of Clarksville, Tennessee. The company was concerned about its ability to respond quickly to changing customer orders. With expert advice from Andersen's consultants, the company eliminated its big assembly line production setup and formed new worker teams in manufacturing, order processing, and other mainstream work areas. Now one employee with a workstation connected to a computer network can respond to a customer's request for price quotes within minutes, in place of an old system that relied on time-consuming information gathering and contacts among affected departments. Workers in the assembly teams gain access to vital order information on the same network, and the new system sets the wheels in motion to replenish customer inventories on demand.[5]

Information technology advances have resulted in a new **macro organization design model.** The model (see Figure 13–1) is an outgrowth of the information-processing theory proposed by Jay Galbraith and further enhanced by David Nadler and Michael Tushman. Briefly, design begins with analysis of the company's business situation. Managerial assessments of the environment and business situation help determine the organization's goals and strategies. Goals and strategies in turn influence decisions about tasks and work processes. Based on these strategic decisions, managers decide the best ways to group employees into departments, coordinate department activities, and provide additional integration by adopting various support systems. Information technology and cultural variables influence or drive all design choices. Emergent behavior and business results are directly tied to the quality of managerial choices made throughout the design chain.

Figure 13–1
Macro Organization Design

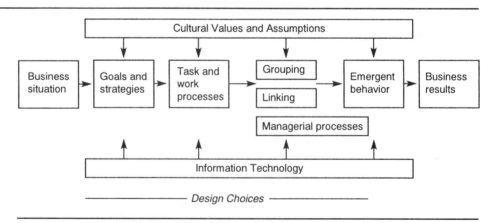

Now that an overall macro organization design model has been explained, we will demonstrate **design dimensions** and relationships with an example. Consider the simple case of a dentist starting a new practice in a small town. He is not the only dentist in town, and he must gradually build a practice in competition with others in a 40-mile district. Initially the dentist does everything himself. That is, he takes appointments, greets patients, provides his own workstation setup, cleans teeth and performs other dental services, cleans the office, orders supplies, and sends out the bills. Soon he is working a 12-hour day, and his wife has taken over the billing. Considerable time passes with other adjustments being made. Five years later he is the leading dentist in the district and has a markedly different operation. Now he has a much larger office facility, an office manager, three dental hygienists to clean teeth, three dental assistants, an information specialist who deals with outside insurance companies and runs an automated billing system, and a part-time dentist who assists with patient overloads. Office cleaning has been contracted out, as have various supply, financial, tax, and legal services. The dentist has a sophisticated electronic data interchange (EDI) with vendors that automatically triggers purchase orders for supplies and speeds billing to major insurance carriers. His entire staff is trained in data entry and inquiry activities. What happened during the 5-year period?

Initially the dentist was content with the idea of doing everything himself. Coordination was easy, since the dentist handled all transactions personally and a single brain did the integration. With increasing patient demand, variety of services needed, and related business activities, the dentist was in an overload situation. At first he made piecemeal decisions, such as hiring a receptionist and contracting a cleaning service. After a time he contacted a business consultant to rethink his entire practice. Over a 1-year period, the dentist, the consultant, and an architect investigated new work design possibilities, did some strategic planning, developed an ideal practice model, created a set of plans for a new office facility, and developed business systems to complement the patient care changes. The dentist's wife and employees were included in the planning activities to contribute ideas and help with practical applications. The processing of information in the expanded practice was also a key consideration. At a predicted high volume of patient demands, the proposed future office required new information-processing capacity. The consultant helped the dentist create new capacity, primarily through new computer systems. The planning work culminated in a move to a new office facility, installation of state-of-the-art equipment, expanded staffing, and employee training activities; these activities occurred over a 3-month period. Computers and IT innovations were used at each step of the way, and the dentist is now poised to adopt new technologies as his practice moves into the 21st century.

This case illustrates that total organization design requires an assessment of information-processing requirements to perform a task that is to be matched by new information-processing capacity. That capacity can include a new structure or hierarchy, new roles and other mechanisms to help integrate the work, and new management systems. In the case of the small dental office, the choices were limited yet profound. While the office retains a pleasant and caring small-office work climate, the volume of work and productivity have leaped ahead. Both people and technical considerations were covered in the organization redesign.

The Sociotechnical Systems Design Approach

Whether the organization is big or small, it must consider people concerns as well as technology during a redesign project. This concept was recognized by founders of the sociotechnical systems (STS) school of design as early as 1948. Eric Trist of the Tavistock Institute in London coined the term *sociotechnical* to describe the interrelatedness of social and technical subsystems within organizations. The principle of joint optimization of these subsystems is the backbone of STS theory. An organization will function best if the social and technical systems are designed to fit the demands of each other and the environment.[6]

STS is a diverse and flexible approach to design. It demands a careful analysis of each situation (contingency perspective) and encourages managers to develop options rather than insisting on the idea that there is one best way to organize. It has strong ties to quality of work life (QWL) experiments and is also associated with autonomous work groups, self-inspection of work quality, job enrichment, team orientations, and other design principles covered in this module. STS programs have been implemented in many countries, notably in British coal mines; in textile mills in India; in diverse

Norwegian, Dutch, and Swedish companies; and in American manufacturing firms. Recent attention has been directed to design programs in high-technology businesses and to knowledge workers.[7] We explore STS theory and planned change process in Module 15.

The Self-Design Approach

Self-design is an outgrowth of STS theory. Thomas Cummings, a leading self-design author, contributed to the STS school of thought in earlier decades. The **self-design approach** encourages managers to plan and to implement their own strategy/structure change programs. The design process is neither simple nor quick. Managers and employees are trained in project planning and in the diagnostic, process, and design skills needed to run the program. Self-design emphasizes the need for practice in design implementation, assessment, and continual modification of the organization. The process is dynamic and cyclical and encourages organizational learning from design experimentation.

Figure 13–2 shows the self-design process model. Briefly, the foundation for self-design is employee and manager training. People must prepare themselves for activities that differ substantially from daily routines. New conceptual and empirical knowledge is needed to conduct a redesign project; otherwise, redesign will be superficial. Also, the values and outcomes the organization is trying to promote must be specified, and the people involved must undertake diagnostic work to determine how well the organization is currently performing. These activities lead to an initial definition of organizational issues and agreement on design criteria. Design criteria are standards that guide design activities by specifying the purposes the new design must satisfy. They will help designers choose among design alternatives and influence the best design. From this point the process is hard to delineate, since the extent of change needed is unknown. The existing design might need fine-tuning, a competitor's design might be imitated, or drastic redesign might be in order. Additionally, there may be a need to have different groups of employees generate designs, test them against design criteria and realities of the workplace, and decide on the best overall design. Even when the designers agree, the job is not over, as different constituents must provide input to the final design. Constituents might force the work back to zero by questioning the original diagnostic work

Figure 13–2   **Self-Design Process Model**

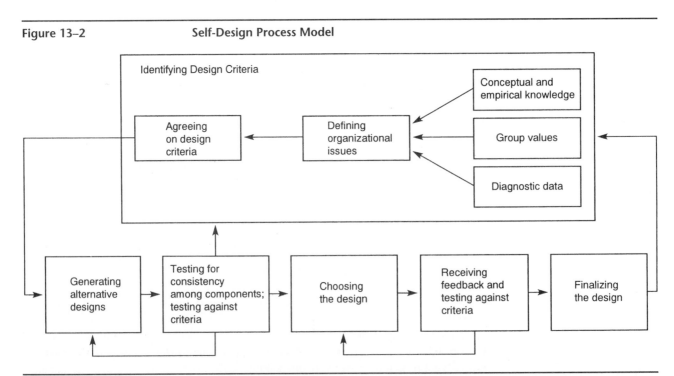

Source: Adapted from S. A. Mohrman and I. G. Cummings, *Self-Designing Organizations,* (Reading, MA: Addison-Wesley, 1989).

and design criteria. Although self-design is still new, it promises to be a fruitful approach for the coming century. Self-design programs have recently been conducted within companies in the telecommunications, aerospace, electronics, software, and pharmaceutical industries.[8]

Activity 13–5W provides additional material on self-design theory plus an opportunity to redesign a small bakery operation using self-design concepts. Organization structure is a major focus in all redesign projects. We turn now to consider forms of structure and related concepts.

Forms of Structure

The term *structure* has many meanings. Research studies on organizations have identified *structural variables* such as the number of levels in the hierarchy, formalization (the amount of written documentation, as in policies and procedures manuals, job descriptions, and the like), standardization (the extent to which activities must be performed in a uniform manner), and degree of centralization. **Form of structure** refers to the method of grouping employees together into work units, departments, and the total organization. Finally, structure includes *organizational processes* such as reward systems that foster cooperation and integration of diverse work activities. Since a comprehensive look at structure is beyond the scope of this book, we provide a brief abstract of common forms of structure and organizational processes.[9]

Simple Form

In our previous dental practice case, a simple form of structure exists. The dentist is owner/operator of a small business and clearly has a hand in all aspects of the enterprise. While he has a modest division of labor through delegation of certain activities to support personnel, he can personally perform every function if needed. The dentist has established the foundation for a functional organization, but the organization will not be the functional form until managers of specialty units are appointed and given some discretion to make decisions. Many small businesses do not grow in size beyond the capabilities of the owners as direct supervisors.

Functional Form

Organizations that group personnel on the basis of function performed; work process; and specialized knowledge, training, or academic discipline have chosen the functional form. Typically, as the organization grows, **differentiation** of specialty units occurs, with managers appointed for each unit. Again, using our dentist example, if activities are delegated, **integration** or coordination must still be achieved. For example, the dentist knows that he must reserve time in his own schedule to check the work of his dental hygienists. Likewise, he must work closely with the support staff on instructions provided to patients so that both patients and providers are aware of what is to take place following the visit. All staff members must know what the others are doing if the patient is to receive integrated dental health care. Figure 13–3 shows a functional form of structure.

Figure 13–3
Function Form of Structure

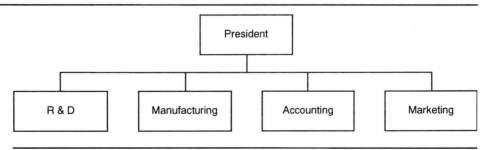

Moving away from the services industry to a manufacturing example, a small production plant will typically have departments with names such as production, sales, finance, engineering, purchasing, information technology, and personnel. As the company grows, additional hierarchy and differentiation is created. For example, as a plant expands from 500 to 2,000 employees, the three-person personnel office may be enlarged to include separate units such as plant security, labor relations, salary and benefits, training, and workers' compensation, each headed by a supervisor. As the personnel department grows, the department manager must ensure that her own supervisors and employees are communicating and must be concerned about how personnel services are being received by managers and employees throughout the plant. The plant manager, as a generalist, will be preoccupied with coordination to a great extent, as departments must cooperate in getting quality products to the customer on time. A similar scenario exists for larger services companies, government offices, and nonprofit organizations.

Certain advantages and disadvantages are associated with the functional form of structure. Functional organizations tend to be efficient and work well when the business situation and outside environment are generally stable. Employees are hired into junior positions and develop skills under the direction of senior workers and managers. Employees then take on increasingly complicated tasks and grow through special assignments and applications of their skills. On the negative side, people in functional organizations often develop parochial viewpoints, and interdepartmental cooperation can be poor. Department goals often differ, and decisions are often pushed up the hierarchy, slowing deliberations and blocking needed changes. As the company's products and customers expand, other forms of structure appear more attractive to top management.

Product or Self-Contained Form

With increasing company size, product divisions or other self-contained units are often created to replace the single-function organization. In our manufacturing example, a new product created at the company's plant may enjoy immediate success, diverting attention from mainstream products. If demand for the new product increases, there will be pressure to retool the factory or construct an entirely new facility. With greater diversification of products and greater diversification in customers and markets served, the company may choose to reorganize according to its major products. When this occurs, each product group gains discretion to design, produce, and distribute its products in ways that are consistent with the competitive environment. If the new product groups are organized in the same basic way (R&D, manufacturing, accounting, marketing), it can be argued that nothing new has occurred. The product groups still appear functional, and people may behave in the same ways. However, if the structure and support processes change to emphasize multispecialty teams or other forms of teamwork, a truly new form might exist. When personnel are grouped according to product line, service performed, or project, then a product or self-contained form of organization has been created.

At the corporate level companies with the product form often have certain functions such as public relations, legal, compensation, and finance units as staff executive offices. These corporate units work with the president and product division personnel to establish certain common policies, practices, services, and controls for the entire company. Cases of staff/line cooperation and conflict are widely experienced in larger organizations. Recently, there have been efforts to decentralize certain corporate and division staff units to operating groups so that the operating groups are better able to manage support services.

Advantages associated with the product form include greater responsiveness to a changing environment, improved cooperation and coordination within each product group, decision making closer to the customer, and improved customer satisfaction. Disadvantages include duplication of resources, difficulties coordinating company activities that cross product lines, and a reduction of knowledge and technical specialization compared to the functional form. Companies that are moving to greater product division independence find it more difficult to integrate activities and standardize across product lines.

Mixed or Hybrid Form

As a practical matter, many organizations have mixed or hybrid forms rather than the pure forms of structure listed above. One of the mixed forms is *matrix* structure (Figure 13–4), which allows a focus on two dimensions at the same time. For example, a pure matrix structure in an aerospace firm has functional engineering departments and project offices. Most employees work in functional departments under the day-to-day supervision of functional bosses, but are also assigned to one or more project teams. Project managers work with functional managers and employees to ensure that projects are accomplished on time with high quality and attention to costs. Changing competitive environments in many industries have pushed companies toward matrix and other experimental forms. For global competition some companies have organized by country and types of products. Other emerging forms of structure are discussed at the end of this module.

**Figure 13–4
SSC Software
Development Division**

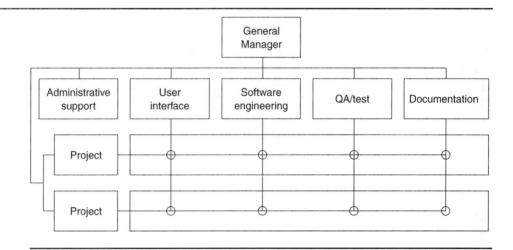

The Horizontal and Flexible Organization

A recent theme in the writings of organization design experts has been the need for greater horizontal or cross-unit coordination and integration within organizations of all types. Jay Galbraith's book *Competing with Flexible Lateral Organizations* shows us how to build *lateral organization capabilities* to match company goals and strategies.[10] Simply put, lateral organization capability means that people get things done by working across organizational units rather than relying on the managerial hierarchy. The organization is decentralized with free flow of information. Galbraith observes that lateral coordination begins with informal, voluntary cooperation. Our dentist office example offers open and continuous sharing of information by the dentist and his employees, usually on a face-to-face basis. In situations that are more complex, such as in an investment bank where people in different departments must implement fast-moving deals for their clients, coordination requirements can be high. The bank might establish formal groups such as new product teams to ensure that diverse inside experts and groups take responsibility for new product success. If there is further need for new product oversight, the bank might also appoint a coordinator or integrator person to strengthen coordination. Creating teams and integrating roles would move the organization toward the matrix organization form. In general, it can be said that many of the concepts underlying the notion of lateral organization capability have been associated with matrix organizations since the 1960s and therefore are not new. In contrast, reengineering and "the process organization" are relatively new developments that make the lateral organization quite unique.

Process Organization

Popular managerial interest in the process organization was sparked by Douglas Smith and Frank Ostroff of McKinsey and Company, a leading management consulting firm.[11] Ostroff and Smith state that hierarchical and functional barriers in companies can be reduced by organizing around core processes such as new product development, sales and order fulfillment, and customer support. The process organization is an enhancement of ideas from sociotechnical systems theory. The object is to improve business results such as quicker time to market, increased focus on customer needs, and lower costs. Teams are the primary organizing focus of process organizations,[12] and there is an emphasis on self-management. Characteristics of autonomous STS teams are evident, as the process team members design their own jobs, schedule work, conduct peer evaluations, measure processes and results, and are involved in extensive training and cross training. The key is that teams now handle broad business activities (core processes) rather than being limited to traditional functional department. Core processes have typically been reengineered to take advantage of advanced IT. The teams work closely with each other, with suppliers, and with customers, and this proximity encourages a spirit of continuous improvement. Traditional boundaries between departments are eliminated in favor of resource sharing that benefits the customer.[13]

The guiding model for design of the process organization is the McKinsey "7S" model. This model refers to strategy, skills, shared values, structure, systems, staff, and style as the critical elements in any complete organization redesign. These elements are similar to those advanced in Galbraith's information-processing model. The process organization is used only where warranted, and the conditions for using it stress high performance pressures from the environment. As with Galbraith's theory, the company's leaders must be concerned with much more than structure in achieving a coherent overall design.

The process organization may evolve to be recognized as a distinct organizational form. However, much more detail is needed regarding the design of work in the process organization, how process activities are integrated (for example, cooperation between autonomous teams), and the unique conditions that call for its use. More empirical research is also needed to determine the advantages and disadvantages associated with this emerging form.

Designs for Global Competition

So far in this module, we have avoided the complexities associated with competing in a global economy. We appreciate that the age we live in demands learning and flexibility. While corporate planning and traditional management functions are still valuable, they must be loosened to recognize changing global business conditions. Leading management theorists and consultants believe that the field of organization design is at a crossroads.[14] The search across the global marketplace for competitive value and new customers leads companies to rethink ways of organizing. The basic options for competing globally have been carefully documented.[15] Companies are showing innovation in allowing business units to seek out new markets for their products and processes, to establish unique relationships with suppliers, and to create strategic alliances and joint ventures that leverage internal strengths. An example of the latter trend is alliances among airlines that vastly extend the reach of a single company's established routes and clientele. The rush to form partnerships has created problems, as shown by recent European Union legal efforts to block the alliance between British Airways and American Airlines.[16] The alliance would have allowed these two airlines to dominate 60 percent of the traffic between London and U.S. destinations. On the other hand, most of the innovations cited above are available to both large and small firms, as seen in the proliferation of small firms conducting international business via the Internet.

Network Organizations

The idea of adopting forms of structure that can flexibly adjust to the global environment has great appeal to executives in leading organizations. One of the new forms, the network structure, blends traditional management concepts such as planning and controls with market concepts such as exchange agreements. Network enterprises rely heavily on contracting out and outsourcing in lieu of owning and operating functions internally. Globalization and rapid improvements in IT have made network organizations popular. We will focus on one of the newer network forms, the "dynamic network," since it so well suited to global competition.

Dynamic network companies operate in fast-paced or chaotic environments. Businesses such as fashion companies, toys, and motion pictures allow extensive outsourcing. The lead company might control few resources directly, or could simply be a broker. A contemporary example of a dynamic network firm is Technical and Computer Graphics (TCG), a privately held IT company in Australia. TCG creates a wide variety of products and services including handheld data terminals and bar-coding systems. TCG is composed of 13 small firms, and each firm has its own purpose and ability to function alone. TCG firms specialize in one or more product categories, in hardware, or in software. Individual TCG firms pursue new product ideas, often by establishing alliances with a major customer, an external development partner (for example, Toshiba), and other member firms within TCG. The TCG firm having the idea takes project leadership and secures advance orders from the principal customer. The development partner(s) provide compatible technology and equity capital. The lead TCG firm acts as entrepreneur, creates self-managing teams, and provides project oversight. The arrangement allows TCG to take on ambitious projects and to leverage ideas into new business opportunities.[17]

The TCG company has shared ownership, so revenues and profits can be monitored to the benefit of partners. Other dynamic network firms operate in the broker mode, and the broker firm may perform only a few functions. For example, Galoob Toys contracts with independent inventors and designers to create toy prototypes. It also contracts out manufacturing and packaging to companies in Hong Kong and China. The toys are shipped to Galoob's commissioned manufacturers in the United States, so distribution is also by contract. In this manner Galoob is able to operate a medium to large size enterprise with only 100 employees.

In other types of network organizations, contracts with partner companies can, of course, be stable and long term or simply reflect temporary market conditions. Nike Corporation is an example of a network firm that has at times invested heavily in partner companies in anticipation of long-term business relationships. Longer-term contracts with companies and the government in China can be altered if competitive conditions change, or Nike can shift production to Thailand or Indonesia to take advantage of higher quality or lower costs. Beyond coordinated contracting, companies can also pursue other legal contracts such as franchising and licensing agreements to increase revenues.

Other Global Influences and Perspectives

Some international observers believe that the future directions for multinational organization design include increased use of matrix formats, transnational organization, Japanese-style **keiretsu,** and global consortia. All of these forms depend to a degree on networks of internal teams and external partners. Most multinational firms need to focus simultaneously on products, functions, country, and business/financial conditions. Clearly, both network and matrix management concepts need to be addressed if multinational firms are to succeed in the future marketplace.

Keiretsu are networks of industrial, transportation, and financial Japanese companies. The cooperation extends beyond vertical and horizontal supply, product, and financial links to include alliances with other companies, research institutions, and universities. Member companies within the *keiretsu* issue their own stock but are interconnected with others in informal and formal ways. One type of *keiretsu* has 20 to 45 companies centered around a bank. The bank owns shares of the member companies, and the companies have interlocking directorships, purchase goods and services from each other, develop products together, cooperate to jointly deal with foreign competitors, and invest in each others' stock.

Western-style forms of *keiretsu* are now being created to take advantage of cooperative arrangements. Consolidation in the global automobile industry might mark a shift toward this form, with the Daimler Benz/Chrysler merger a recent example. The many different businesses of Daimler Benz are interconnected with the activities of Deutsche Bank, which holds a large stake in the Daimler conglomerate. After the merger Daimler Chrysler will have ownership, production, and technology relationships with Beijing Jeep, Eurostar (Austria), Tritec (Brasil), and Ssang Yong (Korea), among others. This approach is not atypical, as BMW, GM, Ford, Toyota, and other major players have similar arrangements.[18] Western-style *keiretsu* hold promise for both political and market advantages and show a trend toward global consortia worth monitoring.

Design and Innovation

Beyond the global, network, and flexibility concepts introduced earlier, much depends upon the firm's ability to innovate. Charles Handy believes that successful companies will stay ahead by constantly reinventing the world rather than by responding to the actions of different players. Companies will accept the notion that the environment is turbulent and will focus on the opportunities that go with discontinuity. They will adopt organizational designs to effectively deal with change and move toward the process organization, high-performance teams, and the learning organization. Emphasis will be on developing positive cultures where shared goals, values, and proactive thinking are nurtured. People will learn how to learn together in a transformational way. Peter Senge states that learning how to "think together" involves high-level skills and cannot be left to chance. It requires creation of a company infrastructure that supports learning. An example of one mechanism is the "learning laboratory." Learning laboratories are practice fields where people can test ideas and learn how to inquire together into complex issues. Learning laboratories have been credited with producing breakthroughs in quality improvements, such as Ford Motor Company's 1995 Lincoln Continental. Warren Bennis believes that the human system of the firm must change. The "social architecture" of the organization must encourage bright people to work together successfully and to deploy their creativity.

Work Design—Emphasis on Processes and Teams

The newer theories of work design focus on processes and teams rather than on the design of individual jobs. Attention is on creating a whole product or service and on producing results that meet customer requirements efficiently, effectively, and consistently. While redesign of cross-functional business processes is beyond the scope of this textbook and module, we will briefly summarize some of the main concepts before turning our attention to work teams.

Business process redesign, or business process reengineering, involves fundamental rethinking of processes to achieve dramatic improvements in performance such as cost, quality, service, and speed. Redesign is not constrained by the existing organizational structure, but instead the analysis focuses on what happens at each step of the process. Time delays, gaps, redundancies, and other inefficiencies are documented, and the designers work together to create a new process that is less complex, shorter, and involves fewer handoffs between people. The new processes include as few non-value-added steps as possible. A non-value-added step is one that fails to produce an identifiable and positive change in the product or service. Checkpoints are built into the process, and are performed by members of work teams as the product or service is created, rather than by second-party inspectors. Where possible, duplication in data entry is reduced to avoid errors and time spent on reconciliation of conflicting data. Full use of available IT enables customers and employees to have access to the records and information needed to handle exceptions and inquiries.

Work groups created during process redesign programs have common goals, are aware of customer needs and requirements, and have all the resources needed to achieve results. The teams either create a whole product or service or own a discrete and meaningful part of a larger process. The teams are staffed by people having the depth and variety of skills needed to plan and control the process and to execute and maintain the process. People are multiskilled where possible so that they can perform each others' work. People have direct contact with customers and thinking and problem solving are integrated with normal role performance.[19]

New organization designs rely on teams of all types. Modules 5, 6, 7, and 8 explore the nature and dynamics of teams. Recent research suggests that more than half of all major U.S. corporations are exploring some form of team-based work system.[20] The team systems in use are grouped into the following categories: *sociotechnical systems (STS) teams, lean production teams,* and *off-line teams* such as quality circles and continuous quality improvement groups.[21]

Competitive Advantage through Teams as a Core Structure Concept

Early efforts to design work around groups can be traced to the experiments conducted by the Tavistock Institute in London in the late 1940s and early 1950s. The research projects led by Trist, Emery, and their colleagues in the coal-mining, textile, and electronics industries found that clustering jobs into work teams yielded better results than did more functional divisions of labor. For example, in coal mining, STS consultants found that newly invented systems and equipment requiring workers to perform specialized jobs and to work together on big coal-extracting platforms failed. Inventors and engineers expected miners to make the switch from small, family-member teams to factorylike working conditions that optimized technology. Downsizing the platforms and returning to other concepts that worked successfully with the traditional small teams eventually generated the expected gains in production.[22]

Sociotechnical Systems Teams

Today **sociotechnical systems teams** are found in diverse industries and nations. Perhaps the most widespread application has been in Scandinavia, stemming in part from Volvo's Kalmar plant success in Sweden and strong government support for STS experimentation in Norway and Sweden. Other widely cited examples of STS design include General Foods in Topeka, Leyland's plant in West London, Procter & Gamble, and Shell Canada.[23] Sociotechnical systems teams, often called *autonomous work groups,* integrate the requirements of social and technical systems. Sociotechnical systems teams feature high worker autonomy in decision making, no first-line supervisors, frequent job rotation, cross-training with an emphasis on learning, and a sound physical work environment. Teams decide specific work assignments, work schedules, work process, quality control procedures, rewards, and other activities that might normally be performed by management or by other departments. For example, at Volvo car assembly team members also participate in design decisions on the next car model. Teams are responsible for reducing costs and negotiating with suppliers on car components and materials. They also stay in touch with customers whose cars they are producing and answer questions about delivery dates.[24] Gulowsen developed the following detailed criteria of work team autonomy:[25]

1. The group has influence on qualitative goals.
2. The group has influence on quantitative goals.
3. The group decides on questions of internal leadership.
4. The group decides what additional tasks to take on.
5. The group decides when it will work.
6. The group decides on questions of production method.
7. The group determines the internal distribution of tasks.
8. The group decides on questions of recruitment.
9. The group members determine their individual production methods.

Theoretically STS is a general framework that should allow for many types of integration among social and technical systems. Technical systems are not viewed as dominant, but rather as equipment and operations to be shaped through worker input.

In practice, nearly all STS design-based organizations have adopted autonomous work groups as a central feature of design, with varying success at modifying technology to meet worker needs.

Lean Production Teams

Japanese influence on the movement toward teams in industry is unmistakable. The label **lean production systems** is synonymous with Japanese manufacturing methods and facilities. Lean production systems feature customer-driven priorities, just-in-time delivery between customers and suppliers, low internal inventory, reduced steps in work operations, high worker participation via work teams, and broad team responsibilities for monitoring quality and planning work activities. The commitment to continuous improvement in all aspects of operations is also strong. In the United States, Nippon-denso Manufacturing of Battle Creek, Michigan, provides a clear example:

We saw machinery tightly packed together, with automated movement of parts from machine to machine such that raw materials flowed quickly through to the loading dock where trucks were dispatched every 12 minutes as part of a just-in-time delivery system. Workers were hustling from station to station; fork lift trucks were moving quickly to deliver raw materials and unload finished product. Despite the hustle, we observed that people also found time to make eye contact, smile, and even briefly converse with us as visitors. There was little inventory visible anywhere in the plant. In each work area, there were highly visible clusters of red, yellow, and green lights to indicate when the line was running (green light) and when workers wanted to consult about a possible quality or inventory problem (yellow light), and when a worker needed to shut down the line (red light). Further, near each part of the production line, a "hot corner" meeting space was provided for each team, featuring a table, chairs, and a filing cabinet. Charts were displayed tracing key "measurables" on quality, safety, productivity, progress in building skills among team members, as well as rewards and communications information.[26]

At Nippondenso Manufacturing people give their own work areas a personal touch with houseplants, pictures, cartoons, and other personal effects—in both production and administrative office environments. The entire Battle Creek plant environment is designed to encourage communications and emphasize common purpose. Early evidence suggests that lean production systems such as the one at Battle Creek are highly dependent on team concepts, although the degree of actual team control over work operations and decision making and employee reaction to the system deserve further research.

Off-line teams such as quality circles (QC), continuous quality improvement (CQI) teams, and total quality management (TQM) teams do not operate on a daily basis. These groups are normally established to identify and address problems that extend beyond regular work teams. Their benefit is probably the ability to solve problems that the formal organization has not resolved. Success depends on training in quality-improvement philosophy and methods and on managerial support for their attempts to implement process improvements.

Work Design— Emphasis on Individuals

As discussed above, modern work design orientations have moved away from individual-focused approaches to group- and organization-focused theories. Historically, however, work design had a strong job engineering foundation and an emphasis on narrowly defined tasks that were easy to perform and monitor. Therefore, it is worthwhile to study both the traditional and newer approaches to job design. We will begin with scientific management.

Job Engineering/ Scientific Management

The **scientific management** approach to job design, often referred to as the **job engineering** approach, was coined by Frederick W. Taylor and further developed by his associates Frank and Lillian Gilbreth.[27] As a supervisor in a shop, Taylor noticed that workers were operating their machines at differing speeds; that workers were devising their own methods to perform their duties; that there was no incentive to increase production; and that many workers did not have the desire, skills, or training to perform their duties appropriately. Trained in mechanical engineering, Taylor set out to develop a way in which management and workers could develop the most efficient work procedures. Through experimentation he was able to determine how tasks were to be performed, the proper tools necessary for maximum efficiency, and the amount of work that an employee could be expected to perform.

Taylor's comprehensive strategy embodies four major ideas about work design. First, work is a cooperative effort by management and workers to ascertain the one best way of performing a job. Second, tasks should be specialized, and work should be designed, wherever possible, so that the individual performs a minimal number of tasks that are easy to master. Third, work should be studied using scientific methods to quantitatively determine how each segment of the work or task should be performed regardless of who actually performs the task. There should be standardization of tasks, methods, and time frames as key work design criteria. And finally, managers should train, develop, and supervise employees so that the work is performed according to scientific methods, and managers should motivate employees by giving monetary bonuses accordingly.

Scientific management was an innovative concept in the early 1900s that led quite naturally to job analysis. The emphasis was to develop efficiency through specialized and standardized tasks. Taylor's work also led to an era of time and motion studies that sought to eliminate wasteful human movements and to simplify work patterns.

Newer Job-Focused Redesign Options

Maximizing efficiency only through time and motion studies and worker–machine interfaces (the scientific management view) creates fractionalized and boring jobs. As characteristics of the workforce changed and employees and unions demanded a better quality of work life, new work design strategies emerged. Job enlargement, job rotation, job sharing, and flexible work schedule strategies emerged to respond to job boredom. By adding more tasks (**job enlargement**), by moving employees among different tasks over time (**job rotation**), and by dividing a job between two or more employees (**job sharing**), individuals had greater job and task variety, skill variety, and freedom and challenge.

Organizations that have a series of routine jobs that cannot be enlarged or enriched might choose to rotate employees from one job to another. Job rotation also is a good work design strategy when the employee does not find the activity challenging. At that point the employee would be rotated to another job at the same level that requires a similar set of skills. An assembly-line worker whose initial job is to install front seats year-round now would rotate every work shift to another task: installing back seats the next shift, door panels the shift after, then electrical panels, and so on.

As the impact of job enlargement was being explored, a new movement started to emerge. Frederick Herzberg, the advocate of *job enrichment,* put forward some work design principles for scientific job enrichment and reported positive results with them. As we saw in Module 10, according to Herzberg, "job enrichment seeks to improve both task efficiency and human satisfaction by means of building into people's jobs, quite specifically, greater scope for personal achievement and its recognition, more challenging and responsible work, and more opportunity for individual advancement and growth."

The theoretical basis for the early formulation of job enrichment, the design principles, the implications, and some of the issues associated with this view can be found in Herzberg's *two-factor theory* of motivation discussed in Module 10. An extension of job enrichment theory, the Job Characteristic Approach, is covered in Exercise 13–4W on the WWW, and your instructor may assign additional reading on this approach.

Flexible Employment Practices

With increasing workforce diversity and greater attention to payroll costs, many companies have adopted flexible employment practices. Some of the practices have origins in social movements of the 1960s and 1970s, while others became common in the recent era of downsizing and restructuring. **Flexible work schedules** give employees the latitude and freedom (often within established parameters) to determine their own work schedule. Four types of work scheduling have been semi-institutionalized: *compressed work week* (for example, a reduction in days per week from 5 days at 8 hours per day to 4 days at 10 hours per day), *permanent part-time employment* (as in sharing a job with another person), *rotated shift work* (such as morning, afternoon, or evening on a rotated basis), and *flextime* (allowing employees to determine when they start and finish work within a given time frame). Employees are usually required to be present during certain daily core hours under flextime.

Some flexible employment practices represent the dark side of human resources management in the 1990s, as viewed by employees and unions. The threat of unemployment resurfaced in the 1980s and continues into the 21st century. Because of the aging baby boom generation, unemployment affects more older workers with higher income loss and greater difficulties obtaining reemployment. Employment cuts in the 1990s affected both blue- and white-collar workers. Restructuring is now regarded as a strategic decision to redeploy the organization's resources. Downsizing continues in the face of prosperity. Part of restructuring involves holding a portion of jobs for **part-time, temporary, and leased employees;** this arrangement allows managers to staff the workplace according to peaks and valleys in work demands, while driving down wage and benefit costs. Recent evidence of this trend is exemplified by a quotation from the *New York Times:*

"People need to look at themselves as self-employed, as vendors who come to this company to sell their skills," explained James Meadows, one of AT&T's vice presidents for human resources, who has helped define the company's new rules of engagement. "In AT&T, we have to promote the whole concept of the workforce being contingent, though most of our contingent workers are inside our walls," Mr. Meadows said. "Jobs are being replaced by 'projects' and 'fields of work,' giving rise to a society that is increasingly 'jobless but not workless.'"[28]

Part-time and temporary employees commonly receive lower wages and fewer benefits than their full-time co-workers receive. Increasingly, employers are also reviewing non-core work activities and administrative services to determine whether contracting out is feasible. Contracting out, or what some call outsourcing, is the use of other firms with specific expertise to perform tasks that the organization chooses not to carry out in-house. Contracting out functions such as information systems support and training reduces overhead and the number of staff support employees. Sometimes contracting out leads to shifting employees from the original firm to the contractor. The contractor might retain some or all of the employees, and they may continue to work at their desks in the same premises. Employees are not "temporary," but they do not have the same human resources benefits or employment security available to "core" employees.[29]

Implications of Flexible Employment

While the political and social implications of unemployment are well-known throughout the world, the trend toward part-time, temporary, and leased employees is just beginning to be studied. Within many European countries the increase in contingent employment has caught many governments by surprise, and there is strong labor union and political interest in pursuing the implications of this trend. During the 1990s many European countries suffered serious unemployment, often in excess of 10 percent. Unemployment had a serious impact on governments' abilities to offer social programs, particularly within countries having comprehensive health, pension, and education benefits. The prospect that employers might exacerbate problems with a shift toward contingent employment has generated some alarm. The main issues are centered on insecurity of employment and employee perceptions of second-class citizenship within the firm. Swedish institutions have already begun to study this trend, and the European Union is reviewing labor union and university proposals for more comprehensive research. Within the United States the use of contingent workers is a hot issue in collective bargaining, and the 1997 UPS employee strike was in part a reaction to UPS's practice of relying on part-time employees.

Summary

Under increasingly competitive conditions, companies will explore more flexible ways of organizing human and other resources. Some of the trends are problematic or contradictory, as with the simultaneous pursuit of positive organizational cultures and contingent employment. Designing the total organization, departments, work units, and jobs is a complex undertaking. We have discussed several design approaches to facilitate organization and work design. The information processing, sociotechnical systems, and self-design approaches are the leading academic design models. They all recognize the importance of information technology advances, and the need for lateral coordination, and the value of team concepts in redesign. Recent emphasis on autonomous teams, reengineering business processes, and the use of quality improvement teams have produced major benefits and are expected to be popular in the 21st century. The emphasis has shifted away from design at the individual-job level, but experimentation will continue with job enrichment, job rotation, and flexible employment practices.

Key Terms and Concepts

Design dimensions

Differentiation and integration

Flexible work schedule

Forms of structure

Horizontal organization

Information-processing design approach

Information technology

Job enlargement

Job rotation

Job sharing

Keiretsu

Lean production system

Macro organization design model

Network organization

Organization design

Part-time, temporary, and leased employees

Process organization

Scientific management

Self-design approach

Sociotechnical systems design approach

Sociotechnical systems (STS) team

Strategic organization design

Study Questions

1. Why is design an important consideration at this point in history?

2. Explain the importance of "fit" in organization design.

3. Compare and contrast the information processing and STS approaches to organization redesign.

4. List the main forms of structure and describe their advantages and disadvantages.

5. What are some major differences between the three types of work team designs?

6. Compare and contrast network organization design and one other approach to organization design.

7. Discuss the relationship between work design, expectations, motivation, and leadership.

Endnotes

1. A. B. (Rami) Shani and M. W. Stebbins, "Organization Design: Emerging Trends," *Consultation: An International Journal* 6, no. 3 (1989), pp. 187–94.

2. M. W. Stebbins and A. B. (Rami) Shani, "Organization Design: Beyond the 'Mafia' Model," *Organizational Dynamics,* Winter 1989, pp. 18–30.

3. D. A. Nadler and M. L. Tushman, *Competing by Design: The Power of Organizational Architecture,* (New York: Oxford University Press, 1997).

4. J. R. Galbraith, *Designing Organizations,* (San Francisco: Jossey-Bass, 1996).

5. M. W. Stebbins, J. A. Sena, and A. B. (Rami) Shani, "Information Technology and Organization Design," *Journal of Information Technology* 10 (1995), pp. 101–13.

6. For additional material on the evolution of STS theory, see W. A. Pasmore, *Designing Effective Organizations: The Sociotechnical Systems Perspective,* (New York: John Wiley, 1988); J. C. Taylor and D. F. Felten, *Performance by Design: Sociotechnical Systems in North America,* (Englewood Cliffs, NJ: Prentice-Hall, 1993); A. B. (Rami) Shani and O. Elliott, "Sociotechnical Systems in Transition," in W. Sikes, A. Drexler, and J. Grant (eds.), *The Emerging Practice of Organization Development,* (La Jolla, CA: University Associates, 1988), pp. 187–98.

7. See, for example, W. A. Pasmore and K. Gurley, "Enhancing R&D across Functional Areas," in R. H. Kilmann (ed.), *Making Organizations Competitive,* (San Francisco: Jossey-Bass, 1991); M. W. Stebbins and A. B. (Rami) Shani, "Organization Design and the Knowledge Worker," *Leadership and Organization Development Journal* 16, no. 1 (1995), pp. 23–30.

8. There is a growing literature on self-design. See, for example, B. Hedberg, P. Nystrom, and W. Starbuck, "Camping on Seesaws: Prescriptions for a Self-Designing Organization," *Administrative Science Quarterly* 21 (1976), pp. 41–65; S. A. Mohrman and T. G. Cummings, *Self-Designing Organizations: Learning How to Create High Performance,* (Reading, MA: Addison-Wesley, 1989); K. E. Weick, "Organization Design: Organizations as Self-Designing Systems," *Organizational Dynamics,* Autumn 1977, pp. 31–46; K. E. Weick, "Organizational Redesign as Improvisation," in G. P. Huber and W. H. Glick (eds.). *Organizational Change and Redesign,* (New York: Free Press, 1993), pp. 346–76.

9. For foundation material on structure and design, see R. L. Daft, *Organization Theory and Design,* (St. Paul, MN: West Publishing, 1998).

10. J. R. Galbraith, *Competing with Flexible Lateral Organizations,* 2nd ed., (Reading, MA: Addison-Wesley, 1994).

11. F. Ostroff and D. Smith, "The Horizontal Organization," *The McKinsey Quarterly,* no. 1, (1992), pp. 148–68.

12. D. Smith, *Taking Charge of Change and Ten Principles for Managing People and Performance,* (Reading, MA: Addison-Wesley, 1996).

13. R. Ashkenas, *The Boundaryless Organization: Breaking the Chains of Organizational Structure,* (San Francisco: Jossey-Bass, 1995).

14. See, R. M. Tomasko, *Rethinking the Corporation: The Architecture of Change,* (New York: Amacor, 1993); D. A. Nadler and M. L. Tushman, *Competing by Design: The Power of Organizational Architecture,* (New York: Oxford University Press, 1997).

15. See, for example, R. J. Kramer, *Organizing for Global Competitiveness: The Matrix Design,* (New York, The Conference Board, 1994), Report 1110.

16. *International Herald Tribune,* November 1, 1998, p. 11.

17. For a closer look at network organizations, see R. Miles and C. Snow, "Organizations: New Concepts for New Forms," *California Management Review* 28, no. 3 (1986); C. C. Snow, R. E. Miles, and J. Coleman, "Managing 21st Century Network Organizations," *Organizational Dynamics,* Winter 1989, pp. 18–30; R. Miles, C. Snow, J. Mathews, G. Miles, and H. Coleman Jr., "Organizing in the Knowledge Age: Anticipate the Cellular Form," *Academy of Management Executive* 11, no. 4 (1997), pp. 7–24.

18. "Globalizzazione: Comunione Planetaria," *Nuovo Auto Capital* 18, no. 10 (October 1998), p. 10.

19. See T. Hupp, C. Polak, and O. Westgaard, *Designing Work Groups, Jobs, and Work Flow,* (San Francisco: Jossey-Bass, 1995); B. Johann, *Designing Cross-Functional Business Processes,* (San Francisco: Jossey-Bass, 1995).

20. P. Osterman, "How Common Is Workplace Transformation and Who Adopts It?" *Industrial and Labor Relations Review* 47, no. 2 (January 1994).

21. J. Cutcher-Gershenfeld and 14 other authors, "Japanese Team-Based Work System in North America: Explaining the Diversity," *California Management Review* 37, no. 1 (Fall 1994).

22. See E. Trist and K. Bamforth, "Some Social and Psychological Consequences of the Long-wall Method of Coal Getting," *Human Relations* 1 (1951), pp. 3–38.

23. F. E. Emery and M. Emery, "Participative Design: Work and Community Life, parts 1–3," in M. Emery (ed.), *Participative Design for Participative Democracy,* (Canberra: Australian National University, Center for Continuing Education, 1989); Taylor and Felton, *Performance by Design.*

24. N. Adler and P. Docherty, "Bringing Business into Sociotechnical Theory and Practice," IMIT Publication, 1997. p. 2.

25. Gulowsen's work is based on P. G. Herbst, Alternative to Hierarchies (Leiden, The Netherlands: Nijhoff, 1976); E. Thorsrud, "Democracy at Work: Norwegian Experiences with Non-bureaucratic Forms of Organization," *Journal of Applied Behavioral Science* 13, no. 3 (1977), pp. 410–21; M. Elden, "Sociotechnical Systems Ideas as Public Policy" in "Norway: Empowering Participation through Worker-Managed Change," *Journal of Applied Behavior Science* 22, no. 3 (1986), pp. 239–55.

26. Cutcher-Gershenfeld et al., "Japanese Team-Based Work System," p. 47.

27. F. W. Taylor, *The Principles of Scientific Management,* (New York: Harper & Row, 1911); F. Gilbreth and L. Gilbreth, *Cheaper by the Dozen,* (New York: Harper & Row, 1947).

28. S. Freeman and K. Cameron, "Organizational Downsizing: A Convergence and Reorientation Framework," *Organizational Science* 4, no. 1 (1993), pp. 10–29.

29. K. Purcell and J. Purcell, "In-Sourcing and the Growth of Contingent Labour as Evidence of Flexible Employment Strategies," *European Journal of Work and Organizational Psychology* 7 (1998), pp. 39–59.

Activity 13–3: SSC Software Development Division Case

Objectives:

a. To learn about problems experienced by software development companies.

b. To explore organization and work design within the software development industry.

c. To involve students in a focused problem and search activity.

Task 1:

Read the SSC Software Development case, with special attention to the company's environment and competitive position. Then work alone to develop a list of ideas, associations, thoughts, and experiences that come to mind as you read the case. This is a preliminary brainstorming phase; free association is encouraged.

Task 2:

a. With the instructor's direction, meet with members of your group to share your list of thoughts. Post all the associations on the board.

b. After listing the thoughts, group them into natural sets or general categories.

c. Poll group members to determine which categories are of greatest interest. What would you like to explore in greater depth?

d. Work with other group members to formulate a problem statement. This statement will be the basis for the group's search efforts under task 3. Does the problem statement provide sufficient focus for your group's search efforts? Is it too narrow?

Task 3:

a. The group is to learn more about the problem identified under task 2 and must decide how to approach the search. Should group members work alone or in subgroups? Should the search include the Web, books, articles, interviews, and so on? Decide and document your learning and search approach.

b. Your instructor will describe the time parameters for this project. Most likely, you will meet one or more times outside class to share your findings. Did the sources provide additional understanding regarding your problem statement? Did the search cause you to alter the problem statement itself?

Task 4:

a. Discuss what you found and evaluate the sources. The group is to prepare a five-page report and include the following elements:

- Problem statement/learning goals.
- Critical evaluation of material and sources.
- Insights, reflections.
- New questions raised.
- Conclusions.
- Comments on this exercise as a learning process.

b. The group is to prepare a 10-minute summary of its report for oral presentation to the rest of the class.

SSC Software Development Division

SSC Corporation's Software Development Division creates backup software in tandem with another leading technology company called MNC. In the course of developing software, engineers must integrate their work with new versions of operating systems created by MNC. The SSC engineers have access to MNC development sites, although fire walls protect MNC's most basic research units. The development task that SSC engineers face is further complicated by the fact that their own products are bundled with utility components created by still other software companies before they reach the ultimate customers. Therefore, SSC has to worry about compatibility in-house, with MNC and with several other development companies. Creation of bug-free software is an obsession at SSC, and this goal is complicated by the uncertainties of the task. SSC is also under pressure to develop products quickly, as cycle time has fallen from 24 months to 12 months for most projects. SSC has a reputation for innovation, although employees have recently reported a tendency to ignore ideas that do not have immediate application to products that are in process.

So far SSC has been effective at holding its market share in the backup-software market, and the market itself is rapidly expanding. SSC employees often spend time away from their primary job sites, since they participate in corporate, division, and interdivision new product development conferences and focused studies. Much of this time is devoted to the definition of the project and the generation of marketing requirement documents (MRDs). These documents provide the basis for all formal project work, and they are periodically updated to reflect new directions or features that might be useful to customers. MRDs are also modified by short-term engineering change orders (ECOs), which can be initiated by marketing personnel or by the developers themselves. Employees view this constant change in the task to be normal, albeit stressful. Stress is highest when the requirements change, but the schedule and launch dates remain the same.

The software division has a matrix structure (see Figure 13–4). Employees are grouped into departments, and each department is headed by a functional supervisor. The supervisor is responsible for recruitment and development of employees and for encouraging innovation in work systems, tools, and quality. For example, the Quality Assurance (QA) Test supervisor takes leadership in the department's use of software quality metrics and testing mechanisms. The supervisor also holds monthly meetings attended by QA/Test personnel staffing all projects. Innovations in QA are explored, and employees share concerns encountered as they work on the various projects. The QA supervisor also has the responsibility for working with her counterparts in other SSC locations, and therefore travels a good deal, attempting to boost QA/Test initiatives at other sites. Other lead people with QA handle day-to-day supervision issues when she is gone.

Within the QA/Test office complex, employees are located according to their assigned projects. That is, members of numerous small QA subteams group their workstations together, allowing face-to-face interaction as required. For example, the Frog project QA subteam has six people, and they are all located within 10 meters of each other. The Frog subteam lead is not a supervisor, but does represent the QA subteam in various meetings called by the overall Frog team project manager.

The project manager for the Frog team has an office in a nearby building. This manager holds twice-weekly meetings of subteam leads, as well as problem-based sessions attended by project personnel involved in the issue at hand. The project manager is the point of contact for MRD, ECO, and marketing changes and has the most responsibility for overall project coordination and scheduling. As software projects move from planning, to definition, to implementation and launch phases, the project manager encourages information sharing and cooperation among the relevant subteams. The project manager, of course, has sophisticated technology support for this coordination as seen in project management software, bug-tracking software, the intranet, and other information and communications systems and tools to support and monitor work. Still much depends on informal cooperation among team members. For example, as the developers finish "builds," they need to communicate changes in direction to the user-interface and documentation teams.

Recently, the Frog project manager has been frustrated because various changes have not been adequately communicated across subteams, slowing down the development process. He is also concerned that deadlines have been regularly missed. He laments, "We seem to always be 2 months from ship." Part of the problem is that target dates are often set before criteria are established. That is, new features are added to the products late in the process, with obvious time consequences. The employee viewpoint is that this type of change does not happen enough, that creativity occurs during development, and project managers need to represent the innovations/ideas to marketing and higher management. Employees feel that they lack clout to change products and that many creative features are left out. Employees value the subteam concept and believe that communication is very high within subteams. But employees also note that several subteam interfaces can be improved, particularly between software engineering and documentation, between software engineering and user interface, and between user interface and quality assurance. Overall, employees report that the Frog team is healthy and that there is a spirit of openness in project communications. They are less sure that interorganizational interfaces are sound, noting more problems recently in getting needed information from other partner sites (other companies including MNC).

The Frog project manager wonders whether there is a better way to organize the Frog resources. he would prefer to have all the team members together in one part of the building, under his direct control. That way, as exceptions come up he could assign employees to perform needed activities as the project moved through the familiar phases. For example, some employees in the QA/Test department were skilled programmers and could be writing code during the implementation phase. In fact, during a past project the QA supervisor had allowed a few people to do this on a short-term basis, but it was a point of argument between the managers. The Frog project manager would welcome some greater flexibility in deploying people. He plans to bring up this idea at his next meeting with the division managers but knows that the manager is firmly committed to the matrix concept.

14

Organizational Culture, Symbolism, and Effectiveness

Learning Objectives

After completing this module, you should be able to

1. Explain the nature of organizational culture.
2. Identify the relationship between symbolism and organizational culture.
3. Articulate the underlying dimensions of organizational culture.
4. Describe the key factors that affect organizational culture.
5. Describe the relationship between organizational culture and organizational effectiveness.

Module Outline

This module was developed in collaboration with our colleague Bill Van Buskirk, Professor of Management, La Salle University. We are grateful to Professor Van Buskirk.

_____ # Premodule Preparation

The instructor may assign one of the following activities as a premodule activity.

Activity 14–1: Exploring the Trouteville Police's Culture	*Objective:* To appreciate the meaning creation process and role of organizational culture in an organization setting. *Task 1 (Homework):* a. Participants are to read and complete the questions assigned at the end of the case. *Task 2 (Classroom):* a. Teams are to reach a shared perception of the major characteristics of the department under John Stage's leadership. b. Teams are to reach a shared perception on the major characteristics of the department under Larry Gaft's leadership. c. Teams are to discuss the process of cultural change. (For example, what were some of the problems in Gaft's approach to change the department culture? What was their impact on individual and group effectiveness? What would have been the ideal process to change the organizational culture)? *Task 3:* a. The instructor will have each team share its perceptions, with the entire class, about the police department's culture under the command of the two leaders. *Task 4:* a. The class will discuss the elements of each culture and examine their similarities and differences. *Task 5:* a. The instructor will give a short lecture on organizational culture and the role that the process plays in fostering or hindering effectiveness.

Case Study: Trouteville Police Department*

Introduction

Trouteville City is located in a rural area of the western United States and has a population of approximately 35,000 people. Within the municipality is the Trouteville Police Department, which is classified as a small department. The department employs 70 people, 55 sworn (police officers) and 15 unsworn.

For the past 17 years, the chief of police has been John Stage, who worked up the ranks from patrolman. Through the years of increased political pressure and stress of the job, Stage became an alcoholic and retired in June 1996. Although most of the people in the community knew about his drinking habits, Stage was nonetheless highly respected. He insisted on a high level of qualified personnel on his staff, and the department did not have any major problems during his tenure. Internally, the men feared his short temper, but he was angry so often that they grew to expect this behavior.

After Stage's retirement the city of Trouteville openly recruited candidates from outside the city. In November 1996, Larry Gaft was appointed as the chief of police. Gaft had previously been a captain in a large metropolitan police department. Several early rumors circulated within the department that Gaft was appointed because of his "tight" control and leadership.

Larry Gaft brought with him the management philosophy known as "team policing" or the "team concept" in police administration. This type of management has been made popular during the last decade in an increasing number of police departments that had changed to this style of management. Team policing has its beginnings in the "team management" style of management. Under team policing a problem or management goal is identified, a staff member is selected to form a committee, and goals are identified and a time table set for their attainment. The committee then attempts to solve the problem through the knowledge and interaction of its members. If the problem is corrected and is not likely to return, the committee is disbanded. If it is a continuous problem or is a specific management goal (that is, reduction of traffic accidents or burglaries), then the committee is made a permanent part of the organization and is called a team.

Soon after Gaft's appointment the department began to experience changes within its organizational structure as teams were added. Gaft solicited the help of all the department's personnel to identify any problems within the department. Some of the major problems were the continuous increase in traffic accidents, obsolete report forms, and the lack of personnel.

Teams were soon organized, a sergeant was appointed as team leader, and members either volunteered or were "asked to volunteer." The Trouteville Police Department now had a traffic team, report writing committee, and a reserve police officers' committee. Officers received no extra pay for the additional responsibility and frequently worked on their own time to complete their assignments.

The Reorganization

In January 1997, the Trouteville Police Department was reorganized to accommodate the new management philosophy of team policing. New employees were hired; others were reclassified; and still others were promoted. The department adapted a goal of "crime prevention," which was the goal behind the reorganization. The following major changes were made:

*Copyright © 1998 by Rolf E. Rogers. All rights reserved, and no reproduction should be made without express approval of Professor Rolf E. Rogers, School of Business, California Polytechnic State University, San Luis Obispo, California 93407.

1. Lieutenants were placed in command of a division.

2. Two levels of sergeants were created. Sergeants under the old organization were reclassified to sergeant II and given the responsibility of a command of a "watch" or shift. Patrolmen were promoted to the level of sergeant I and were responsible for field supervision.

3. The city was divided into four sectors; each sergeant I was assigned the responsibility as sector leader and required to submit a monthly report to the crime prevention leader.

A reorganization manual was prepared and distributed to each employee. The manual defined job duties and responsibilities and detailed the organizational structure and chain of command.

The Case

Several months after the reorganization, the department began to experience an increase in morale problems, as evidenced by a dramatic increase in personnel attrition, grievances, and general complaints made to the president of the Trouteville Police Association, Pete Martin. Pete, a patrolman of 4 years began to notice a specific conflict between the sergeants and patrolmen. One such conflict occurred 2 months after the reorganization. Pete was sent by communications to assist Patrolman Dale White in a minor injury accident. Pete witnessed the following argument between White and Sergeant II Joe Collins.

WHITE: Hello, Sarge, minor injury accident.

COLLINS: So where's the traffic team? You know they investigate all injury accidents.

WHITE: Just a second. Sergeant I Simpson said we could investigate minor injury accidents as well as they can; beside it saves time. It takes them 10 minutes to get here. I can have this investigated by then.

COLLINS: Don't argue with me! Call traffic and get them here now.

WHITE: Yes sir!

Dale, almost completed with the accident investigation, called communications by radio and asked for the traffic team. The team arrived about 5 minutes later. White had the following conversation with Traffic Officer Gary Rice.

WHITE: It's about time you got here, what took you so long?

RICE: We just got the call; it does take some time to drive here, you know!

WHITE: So why weren't you called by communications when the accident happened?

RICE: They want you guys to confirm that there is an injury first. Besides, we're so busy with paperwork, who has time to be in the field?

Dale White left the scene as the traffic team began to investigate the accident (Dale had told them he had not started the investigation).

Later that day Pete was in the department and saw Sergeant Simpson, the field supervisor, reading and correcting crime reports, a responsibility of the watch commander.

Approximately 1 month later, Sergeant Collins was addressing the patrolmen during the role call briefing regarding the lack of citations written during the previous month.

SERGEANT COLLINS: OK, you guys, you know we're attempting to decrease our traffic accidents by an aggressive citation policy. Not one of you is even close to the "right" number. Patrolman Davis, you only wrote five tickets the whole month.

DAVIS: So what's the traffic team for? The only thing they do is sit in the office keeping stats. I'm a member of the reserve officers' committee and report writing committee; how do you expect me to do all that plus write tickets, too?

SERGEANT COLLINS: Your primary duty is law enforcement and that includes traffic enforcement. I'll expect you all to increase your ticket count to a reasonable level this month.

In December 1997, Sergeant Sweigert approached Pete Martin regarding a pay dispute with the city. Apparently, the sergeant IIs believed that they had been promoted when the department was reorganized and their position was reclassified as sergeant II. They were now given the responsibility of "watch commander," a position previously held by a lieutenant. Second, the newly promoted sergeant Is, now "field supervisors," had received an increase in salary below that which the sergeants had been paid prior to the reorganization. Sergeant IIs received no increase in salary.

The sergeants wished to file a formal grievance through the police association. The grievance procedure is as follows:

1. The affected person or group files a written grievance through the association within a reasonable length of time.

2. The association then presents the grievance to the chief of police. If he approves the grievance, it is then routed through the chain of command to the city administrator for approval.

3. If the chief of police disapproves the grievance, the association has two alternatives: They may present the grievance to the city council for adoption or resolve the grievance through other remedies.

As president of the police association, it was Pete Martin's function to present the grievance to Chief Gaft. Pete arranged for an appointment and the following conversation took place.

CHIEF GAFT: Come on in, Pete.

MARTIN: Thanks, chief, I would like to speak to you about the sergeants' pay dispute.

CHIEF: I don't understand why they are so angry. When they accepted their new assignments, they were told what the responsibilities would be; no one griped then.

MARTIN: It's getting to be a real problem—we're having problems between the patrolmen and sergeants already; we don't need anything else to lower morale.

CHIEF: [face reddening, voice rising] It seems every time there is a problem, the association gets involved and blows it way out of proportion. You guys are causing the problems! Another stick in my side! Well, I'm not going to support your grievance; you'll have to take it to court.

Pete left and later that week met with each individual sergeant either in person or by phone and told them what had occurred. Each voiced their support to take the grievance to court.

Six months after Pete Martin's meeting with Chief Gaft, the following events occurred:

1. Personnel attrition continued to increase to approximately 40 percent. (*Note:* None of the officers who resigned sought law enforcement careers after leaving the Trouteville Police Department.)

2. Urged by the police association, the city administrator forced a formal meeting to air and discuss the recent problems within the department. The chief and his staff attended as representatives of the administration, and certain "select" patrolmen were asked to attend to represent the employees. Each patrolman spoke and expressed his concern that the administration was insensitive to employee/employer problems and that the problems began immediately following the chief's appointment.

3. The sergeant's salary grievance was satisfied by the association through its negotiations of wages and benefits during the regular yearly salary negotiations with the city.

Assignment

Prepare notes on the following questions:

1. Based on the limited information presented, identify and briefly describe the major characteristics of the Trouteville Police Department under the leadership of John Stage.

2. Identify and describe the major characteristics of the department after Larry Gaft's appointment as chief of police.

3. Has the Trouteville Police Department culture changes? (If yes, how? If not, why didn't it?)

Activity 14–2:
Symbol Identification

Objectives:

a. To appreciate the symbolic nature of the workplace.

b. To explore the relationship between symbols and organizational culture.

Task 1:

a. Pick one organization with which you are closely associated. It may be your place of employment, a church group where you volunteer, or the college or university that you currently attend.

b. Identify 100 symbols. That's right 100. All you have to do is list them. The point of this activity is twofold: (1) to get you in the habit of seeing the symbolic dimensions of organizational life and (2) to help you appreciate the vastness of culture that we take for granted. If you are stuck, read the discussion in the module about symbols and culture and then proceed with the activity. If you are still having some difficulty, refer to the "symbol generator"—Activity 14–5W on the WWW. It is simply a list of things that people in organizations have found symbolic. Does it give you any ideas? People often get stuck in this exercise because they don't think broadly enough.

Task 2:

a. In your teams read your lists to each other. Hearing other lists often is revealing. Spend 10 minutes each explaining why certain persons, objects, and events are symbolic in your organization.

b. Explore some of the similarities and differences between the lists. Can you see any patterns? What are they? What do they mean?

Task 3:

a. Following some sharing with the learning community, the instructor will lead a class discussion about symbols and organizational culture.

Introduction

The study of organizational culture continues to receive increased attention from managers and scholars alike. One of the main catalysts for the renewed interest in organizational culture seems to stem from the increasing difficulty in executing company mergers once the formal contracts have been signed. The last decade has been characterized as the "company mergers and acquisition decade." As this module is written, the merger between Exxon and Mobil was announced, a merger that according to some observers could forever alter the oil industry. While it is true that the number of merg-

ers and acquisitions has reached record levels, we have also begun to read about the many difficulties that managers run into as they try to transform two entities into one. According to J.P. Morgan (the facilitator behind the merger between Exxon and Mobil), only 1 out of every 10 deals is consummated, and many deals unravel after they are announced. Differences in the nature of the organizations' cultures have been identified as one of the major stumbling blocks.

For example, when management guru Stephen Covey merged his Covey Leadership Center with rival Franklin Quest around the end of 1997, most people predicted that the merging of the two companies was a win-win deal with natural synergies. Yet 18 months later, *USA Today* (in its December 8, 1998 issue) reported that "insiders say that despite similar corporate missions that are supposed to inspire (their) clients to embrace change, Franklin-Covey suffered from having two different company cultures, inertia and indecision about how to transform the two cultures into one." Assessing organization culture and diagnosing the degree of "fit" between the cultures of two companies that are considering a merger might be a necessary step. But before we proceed, we must stop to explore the organizational culture school of thought and its meaning.

The organizational culture theories are based on assumptions about people and organizations that depart significantly, and in more than one way, from those of the "mainstream" schools. First, they challenge the system and the structural schools about, for example, how organizations make decisions and how and why humans behave as they do.[1] While the system and structural schools argue that individuals' personal preferences are restrained by systems of formal rules, authority, and norms of rational behavior, the cultural school advocates that individual preferences are controlled by cultural norms, values, beliefs, and assumptions.[2] Second, from the organizational culture viewpoint, every organizational culture is different, and what "works" for one organization won't necessarily work for another.[3] Third, the organizational culture school believes that qualitative research methods are the better way to fully understand and predict organizational behavior[4] (rather than quantitative research methods using quasi-experimental designs, control groups, and multivariate analyses).

Defining Organizational Culture

An examination of the **organizational culture** school reveals many diverse definitions and elements. For some, organizational culture has something to do with the people and the unique character of the organization; for some, it means shared top-management beliefs about how they should manage themselves and other employees and how they should conduct their business;[5] for some it is the shared philosophies, ideologies, values, assumptions, expectations, attitudes, and norms that knit a community together;[6] for some it is an evolutionary process;[7] and for still others it is a complex pattern of beliefs, expectations, ideas, values, attitudes, and behavior shared by the members of an organization. Furthermore, controversy exists on the role of organizational culture, its effects on organizational life, and the ability to influence and lead corporate culture change.[8]

For our purposes Schein's holistic definition captures the essence, complexity, and uniqueness of the phenomenon: Organizational culture is

(a) a pattern of basic assumptions, (b) invented, discovered, or developed by a given group, (c) as it learns to cope with its problems of external adaption and internal integration, (d) that has worked well enough to be considered valid and, therefore, (e) is to be taught to new members as the (f) correct way to perceive, think, and feel in relation to those problems.[9]

Schein argues further that in analyzing the culture of an organization or group, it is important to distinguish among three fundamental levels at which culture manifests itself: (1) observable artifacts such as physical layout, dress code, the way people relate to each other, company records, statement of philosophy, and reports; (2) values, norms, philosophy, and ideology; and (3) basic underlying assumptions about the organization's relationship to its environment, the nature of reality and truth, the nature of human nature, the nature of human activity, and the nature of human relationships (see Figure 14–1). Figure 14–2 provides an example of specific questions that can guide the exploration of the underlying assumptions around which cultural paradigms emerge.

**Figure 14–1
Organizational Culture:
A Framework for Analysis**

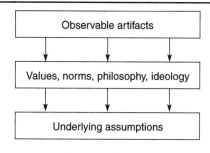

**Figure 14–2
Some Underlying
Dimensions of
Organizational Culture**

Dimension	Questions to Be Answered
1. The organization's relationship to its environment	Does the organization perceive itself to be dominant, submissive, harmonizing, or searching out a niche?
2. The nature of human activity	Is the "correct" way for humans to behave to be dominant/proactive, harmonizing, or passive/fatalistic?
3. The nature of reality and truth	How do we define what is true and what is not true, and how is truth ultimately determined in both the physical and social worlds: by pragmatic test, reliance on wisdom, or social consensus?
4. The nature of time	What is our basic orientation in terms of past, present, and future, and what kinds of time units are most relevant for the conduct of daily affairs?
5. The nature of human nature	Are humans basically good, neutral, or evil, and is human nature perfectible or fixed?
6. The nature of human relationships	What is the correct way for people to relate to each other and to distribute power and affection? Is life competitive or cooperative? Is the best way to organize society on the basis of individualism or groupism? Is the best authority system autocratic/paternalistic or collegial/participative?
7. Homogeneity versus diversity	Is the group best off if it is highly diverse or if it is highly homogeneous, and should individuals in a group be encouraged to innovate or conform?

Source: Adapted from E. H. Schein, *Organizational Culture and Leadership,* (San Francisco: Jossey-Bass, 1985), p. 86. Copyright ©1985 by Jossey-Bass. Adapted with permission.

The Organizational Context of Organizational Culture

Among the many factors that affect the evolution of group and organizational culture are (1) work-group characteristics such as commitment to the group's mission and task, work-group size and composition, and work-group design and autonomy; (2) managerial and leadership styles such as philosophical process and output orientations; (3) dynamics between groups and departments such as degree of dependency, communication processes, and cooperation; (4) organizational characteristics such as mission, product and service requirements, size, technology, policies and procedures, reward system, and organization design; and (5) environmental characteristics such as industry; competitive pressures; and social, political, and legal environments. Figure 14–3 presents graphically some key factors that affect the evolution of culture.

Recently, a guiding framework for maintaining and reinforcing a specific organizational culture was proposed. The framework lists the following dimensions: criteria for hiring individuals who fit the organizational culture; criteria for removing employees who consistently or markedly deviate from accepted behaviors and activities; elements that managers and teams pay attention to, measure, and control; behavioral dimensions that compare how managers react to critical incidents and organizational crises; managerial and team role modeling, teaching, and coaching; criteria for recruitment, selection, and promotion; and organizational rites, ceremonies, and stories. Because every group and organization is an open system that exists in multiple work environments, change in the environment is likely to produce pressure inside the group that forces new learning and the adoption of this learning. To some degree there are pressures for any given culture to continuously change and grow. As such, culture can be seen

as an ongoing evolutionary process. The difficulty of managing the evolution of organizational culture is complex because of the tendency among individuals and groups to resist changes.[10]

As we have seen organizational culture is a dynamic and complex phenomenon. Artifacts, values, assumptions and symbols interact in four cultural processes: manifestation, realization, symbolization, and interpretation. The reminder of this module focuses on mapping the cultural process via symbolization.

Figure 14–3
Some Key Factors
Affecting the Context
of Organizational Culture

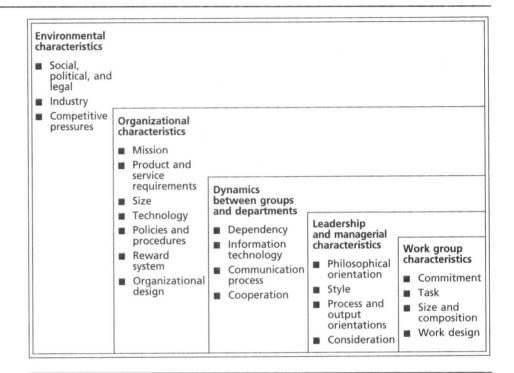

Symbol Sensitivity and the Management of Culture

In 1980s the success of Japanese competition upset much thinking about how business should be conducted and how organizations should be understood. Successive waves of innovation stunned western managers: Just-in-Time inventory management, government/business cooperation in formulating industrial policy, quality circles, market-share-based strategies, global trading companies, *keiretsu* or company groupings, lifetime employment, and a host of other innovations stood behind the "secret" of Japanese competitiveness.

After many years of trying to make sense out of these innovations it occurred to management scholars to ask the question, What kind of people are able to produce one industrial innovation after another? Many researchers began to inquire into the nature of Japanese culture as it played out in the company. Others began to look at the cultures of American firms especially those who had been successful over long periods of time.

The outcome of this research was to discover that culture was a powerful variable that knit companies together. "High culture" companies tended to be more successful in many industries, and this trend was especially true among companies who had "been around" for several decades.[11] These discoveries sparked the search for how to best make use of culture in managing the company. Popular literature is now filled with anecdotes about how a given manager or group of managers successfully managed the culture of a company to achieve corporate goals, to effect turnarounds, or to redirect the attention of their employees. Today, it seems every manager wants to be

a culture manager. For the student of management who wants to explore this area, much of the popular literature does not go deep enough. Laundry lists of dos and don'ts abound. But many researchers take the stand that if you want to change a culture, you have to understand what it is. And to understand a culture, you have to understand how it affects your fellow organization members and how it affects you. In other words, cultural sensitivity should precede culture management.

This approach represents a subtle difference from much management wisdom. The emphasis on **managing culture** assumes that the manager knows what he or she would manage. It assumes that the manager is *outside* the culture and can (and should) act on it. It also assumes a one-way causation—the manager shapes the culture, not the other way around. Although it is true that corporate leaders such as Bill Gates and Sam Walton can have enormous influence on their companies, they are influenced by them as well. Both Bill and Sam are remarkably open to their employees suggestions and take their perceptions and needs into account when redesigning the respective companies.

If it is true that culture management is a two-way street, then awareness of one's company culture is a vital part of changing it. But how do we enhance that awareness? Where do we start? The answer implicit in most culture literature is to start with symbols. Most writes agree that symbols are the "building blocks" of culture. Symbols are also "tools" than can shape underlying values and behavior. However you understand culture—whether in terms of values, rituals, ceremonies, corner offices, gold watches, stories people tell at work, their dreams of the future, and so on—**symbolism** is pretty much at the basis of everything. So cultural awareness is pretty coexistent with awareness of symbols.

The best place to start with symbolic awareness is with yourself. If you can become familiar with the ways in which the symbols in your organization affect you—how they shape your assumptions, how they provide the emotional glue between people who don't know each other, how they influence perceptions of stakeholders—you will be in an excellent position to decide what (if anything) you want to do about them. Culture management will be for you more than a buzzword. It will be a real possibility.

How do we start? Perhaps the best place is with a definition. What is a symbol anyway? Most students can recite a list of common symbols in the companies without much difficulty. Again, corner offices, company jets, and gold watches come to mind. If this were all there were to it, symbols would be trivial ornaments to organizational life. However, company symbolism is much more pervasive than these stock examples would lead us to believe. Perhaps the most useful definition of a symbol comes from anthropology: A *symbol* is any person, object, or event that organizational members invest with personal meanings.

This definition is deceptively simple, First, the word *any* implies that almost anything can be symbolic, including a host of things we think of as "unsymbolic," for example, performance appraisals or sales figures. Yet if we think about an individual waiting anxiously for an upcoming performance review or a CEO wondering what caused a sales shortfall, we recognize that there is more going on here than mere "organizational" thinking. The performance appraisal is "attached" to fantasies about how good life might be if it goes well or about how awful if it does not. Sales numbers trigger doubts in the executive about how well he has prepared the company to weather the storms of a competitive world.

In short these seemingly rather dry artifacts of corporate existence can become "filled" with personal meaning and emotional reactions to that meaning. Moreover, one symbol can trigger another. The employee waiting for the performance appraisal may have trouble sleeping at night because he imagines himself unemployed, out on the street, riding in boxcars, and so on. Similarly, a good speech from a CEO may convince everyone that the company is on the right track or that the future is bright. Symbols may be positive as well as negative, but they are always meaningful.

A final aspect of the symbol is that it is invested with many meanings (go back and look at the definition—*meanings* is plural). Unlike a concept, which contains a one-to-one relationship with that to which it refers, symbols are *bundles of meaning*. Think of the word *chair*. It is most likely a concept in your mind right now. You think of a class

of objects, but the experience is rather neutral. Concepts are useful because they allow us to think rationally about our day-to-day lives. However, if we think of the word *chair* in a different way, symbolic meaning can be added. Think of the phrase *my father's chair.* There is a good chance that the neutral concept has been changed. The chair has been infused with a new, more personal set of meanings. Perhaps you think back to an actual chair that your father sat in when you were a child. Perhaps this symbolic chair triggers some feelings toward that chair and that relationship. In any case it is this characteristic of containing many meanings that makes a person, object, or event a symbol.

Perhaps you are wondering what this discussion has to do with organizational life. Scholars have identified a number of ways symbols, especially when they are unacknowledged, subliminally shape assumptions throughout the organization. Much in organizations is uncertain, yet we need to experience the world in a way that is at least marginally manageable. For example, executives, stakeholders, and competitors of all sorts tend to be very distant from the majority of an organization's members. Even top managers wonder what is going on in the minds of employees or other stakeholders. Often these unseen "zones" of an organization—the nature of certain stakeholders, what is going on in their minds—are mapped by symbols. This is the only way we can "know" certain things about the organization. So images abound about the nature of the CEO—he is a moral person, he is brilliant, he is tough, he is unscrupulous—even though there is often no way for most employees to verify these images. Moreover, the kind of "leadership images" organization members carry around in their heads matters a great deal. Positive images tend to reinforce cooperation of all sorts, whereas negative ones may engender resistance.

So the importance of symbols is that they "define" many vague areas in the organization and its environment, areas of which we can have no direct knowledge. Since this defining is often subliminal, we are unaware that a symbol is at work. We begin to act "as if" something is true, and this as-if action has considerable consequences. For example, Japanese workers tend to act as if the company is a family. They feel an obligation to act in the company's best interest. One result of this trait is that Japanese companies need far fewer first-line supervisors than their western competitors need.

Cultures matter in many ways, Their symbols matter to individuals, to companies, and to their leaders. They shape thinking and behavior. They inspire commitment. They do all this without stirring up much attention or scrutiny. One way to think of culture is as a vast underground text or story that runs throughout the organization, a story that sets the terms for understanding day-to-day experience. Activities 14–2 and 14–3 provide both the opportunity for you to explore the symbols in an organization that you are familiar with and a process to map out a profile of an organizational culture.

Organizational Culture and Organizational Effectiveness

Schein defines *organizational culture* as "a pattern of basic assumptions—invented, discovered, or developed by a given group as it learns to cope with its problems of external adaptation and internal integration—that has worked well enough to be taught to new members as the correct way to perceive, think, and feel in relation to those problems." We argued that a place to start our investigation of culture, its meaning, the management of culture, and the management of culture change is by focusing on symbols. At the most basic level, a symbol was defined as any person, object, or event infused with personal meaning by an individual or a group. Symbols are used to communicate corporate purpose, critique strategic plans, enhance organizational control, harmonize intergroup relations, ease the pain of transitions, support organizational ideologies, and understand subcultures.

Organizational culture seems to play a critical role when it comes to individual, group, and **organizational effectiveness.** Symbols are bundles of meaning that simultaneously tie together emotional and cognitive experience. Sensitivity to symbols involves an awareness of both how they shape cognition and how they function as containers for emotions. As such a symbol-sensitive manager would ideally be able to think about, and constructively manage, the **cognitive and emotional aspects of symbols**—and thus enhance the effectiveness of the individual, the group, and the organization.

As we have seen, in any organization we find a large variety of symbols. The symbols work not in isolation, but in interaction with other symbols. Thus sensitivity to symbols involves sensitivity to interacting groups of symbols in their "larger" forms, such as stories, rituals, myths, and ceremonies. Attention to stories, rituals, myths, and ceremonies enables individuals not only to develop a full understanding of organizational effectiveness but also to work with the larger forms to diagnose and enhance effectiveness.[12]

Organizational culture should be understood in the context of important management issues. The business context, the business strategy, and the business design all influence the evolution of the specific organizational culture. For example, the specific choice that is made about the organization design—the way of grouping people and tasks—is likely to influence the dynamics of the subcultures that will emerge. As mentioned at the beginning of the module, a strategic decision to acquire and/or merge with another company may or may not succeed (be effective) based on management ability to find a high degree of fit between the two cultures and/or the attention that is paid to the cultural aspects of the merger.

Summary

The organizational culture module appears in this section of the book due to the phenomena's comprehensiveness and complexity. The complex nature of culture lends itself to many definitions. Culture is much like air; it is everywhere we look and touches everything that goes on in organizations. It is both a cause and an effect of organizational behavior. The more we learn about organizations, the more elements of culture we discover. Yet at the most basic level, the core components of organizational culture include three elements: (1) the behavior and work patterns that one can observe, (2) the underlying values and assumptions that often cause the behaviors, and (3) the symbols that one can identify.

Managing a cultural change is a complex managerial challenge that requires overcoming many obstacles. The next module in the book addresses the change process and provides several alternative road maps for planned change that might work well for a company that is interested in cultural transformation.

Key Terms and Concepts

Cognitive aspects of symbols

Emotional aspects of symbols

Managing culture

Organizational culture

Organizational effectiveness

Symbolism

Study Questions

1. Identify and discuss the key dimensions of organizational culture based on Schein's definition.

2. Identify and describe the key factors that shape organizational culture.

3. Can organizational culture be taught to organizational members? Explain.

4. Discuss how symbols can help us understand organizational culture?

5. What are some of the ways to manage organizational culture?

6. Discuss the relationship between business strategy, organization design, and organizational culture.

7. Discuss the relationship between organizational effectiveness and organizational culture.

8. What advise do you have for Mr. Covey and Mr. Franklin about managing the merger of their two companies.

Endnotes

1. J. M. Shafritz and J. S. Ott, *Classics of Organization Theory,* (Chicago: Dorsey Press, 1987); R. M. Cyert and J. G. March, *A Behavioral Theory of the Firm,* (Englewood Cliffs, NJ: Prentice-Hall, 1984).

2. R. H. Kilmann, M. J. Saxton, R. Serpa, and Associates, eds. *Gaining Control of the Corporate Culture,* (San Francisco: Jossey-Bass, 1985); G. Hofstede and M. H. Bond, "The Confucius Connection: From Cultural Roots to Economic Growth," *Organizational Dynamics* 16, no. 4 (1988), pp. 4–21; N. M. Tichy, *Managing Strategic Change: Technical, Political and Culture Dynamics,* (New York: John Wiley & Sons, 1983); K. S. Cameron and R. E. Quinn, *Diagnosing and Changing Organizational Culture,* (Reading, MA: Addison-Wesley, 1999).

3. V. Sathe, *Culture and Related Corporate Realities,* (Burr Ridge, IL: Richard D. Irwin, 1985); S. R. Barley, C. W. Meyer, and D. C. Gash, "Culture of Cultures: Academics, Practitioners, and the Pragmatics of Normative Control," *Administrative Science Quarterly* 33 (1988), pp. 24–60; C. A. O'Reilly and J. B. Chapman, "Culture as Social Control in B. M. Staw and L. L. Cummings (eds.), *Research in Organizational Behavior,* vol. 18, (Greenwitch, CI: JAI Press, 1996), pp. 157–200.

4. E. H. Schein, *Organizational Culture and Leadership,* (San Francisco: Jossey-Bass, 1985).

5. J. W. Lorsch, "Managing Culture: The Invisible Barrier to Strategic Change," *California Management Review* 2, Winter 1986, pp. 95–109.

6. R. H. Kilmann, M. J. Saxton, and R. Serpa, "Issues in Understanding and Changing Culture," *California Management Review* 2, Winter 1986, pp. 87–94.

7. M. R. Louis, "Organizations as Culture-Bearing Milieux," in L. R. Pondy, P. J. Frost, G. Morgan, and T. C. Dandridge (eds.), *Organizational Symbolism,* (Greenwich, CT: JAI Press, 1983), pp. 39–54; M. J. Hatch, "The Dynamics of Organizational Culture," *The Academy of Management Review* 18 (1993), pp. 657–93; S. A. Sackman, "Culture and Subculture: An Analysis of Organizational Knowledge," *Administrative Science Quarterly* 37 (1992), pp. 140–61; T. E. Deal, and A. A. Kennedy, *Corporate Cultures: The Rites and Rituals of Corporate Life,* (Reading, MA: Addison-Wesley, 1982).

8. J. Kerr and J. W. Slocum Jr., "Managing Corporate Culture through Reward Systems," *Academy of Management Executive* 1, no. 2 (1987), pp. 99–108; L. K. Trevino, "A Cultural Perspective on Changing and Developing Organizational Ethics," in W. A. Pasmore and R. W. Woodman (eds.), *Research in Organizational Change & Development,* vol. 1, (Greenwich, CT: JAI Press, 1990), pp. 195–230.

9. E. H. Schein, "Organizational Culture," *American Psychologist* 45, no. 2 (1990), p. 109–19.

10. C. Argyris, R. Putnam, and D. M. Smith, *Action Science,* (San Francisco: Jossey-Bass, 1985); R. Beckhard and R. T. Harris, *Organizational Transitions: Managing Complex Change,* 2nd ed. (Reading, MA: Addison-Wesley, 1987); D. P. Hanna, *Designing Organizations for High Performance,* (Reading, MA: Addison-Wesley, 1988).

11. T. J. Peters and R. H. Waterman, *In Search of Excellence,* (New York: Harper and Row, 1982); J. C. Collins and J. I. Porras, *Build to Last,* (New York: Harper Collins Publishers, Inc., 1996); A. De Geus, *The Living Company,* (Boston: Harvard Business School Press, 1997).

12. W. van Buskirk, "Enhancing Sensitivity to Organizational Symbolism and Culture," *Journal of Management Education* 15, no. 2 (1991), pp. 170–92.

Activity 14–3:
The Meaning of
Your Symbols and
the Organization
as a Text

Objectives:

a. To appreciate the patterns and meaning of symbols at the workplace.

b. To read the organization's culture as a complex web of symbols.

Task 1:

a. Go back to the list of symbols that you have generated in Activity 14–2. Pick a few symbols from your list that have particular "juice" for you. These should be more meaningful, vivid, or exciting, or complex than the others.

b. Pick one symbol. Imagine that it is speaking to you. What is it saying? Write a few paragraphs for each one. Try to write as if the symbol itself is talking.

Task 2:

a. Read your paragraphs to one another in your team. How do other team members react to your symbol/script? What are their symbols and meaning like? the same as yours? different? Discuss these different meanings. Are there others in your organization who might react similarly?

b. As you read through your list or as you recite it to someone else, notice the ways you are affected by your symbols.

- Do they contain any assumptions about the organization?

- Are you acting as if certain things are true about the organization, things which might appear doubtful on further inspection?

- Do the symbols inspire you to want to do anything?

- Do the symbols inspire any feelings?

- How do the symbols and what they inspire influence your performance on the job? Do they motivate you? demotivate you?

- Can you observe these symbols influencing others? How do they react? How are they affected?

Task 3 (Reading the Organization as Text [Optional]):

a. After spending some time with your symbol list, identify themes in your organizational symbols. Certain groups of symbols may carry overlapping messages about the organization (that is, some symbols may point to how sophisticated the organization is, how poorly managed it is, or how much it cares/doesn't care about its employees). Try to find five or six themes in your symbols.

b. Write a short paper (five to seven pages) delineating these themes. Your essay can be considered a "snapshot" of the organizational culture as you experience it.

c. Exchange papers with other team members. Read the papers. How are they different from yours? How are they similar? Notice any area where you are surprised or confused. Discuss the differences. (Optional, if time can be set aside for reading and discussion.)

15

Organizational Change, Development, and Learning

Learning Objectives

After completing this module, you should be able to

1. Explain the phenomenon of organizational learning and its underlying dimensions.
2. Describe the alternative organizational learning mechanisms.
3. Describe the relationship among organizational learning, change, development, and effectiveness.
4. Define the field of organizational change and development (OC&D).
5. Compare and contrast any two of the systemwide OC&D interventions.
6. Describe the different types of change problems.
7. Explain some of the challenges that OC&D faces in the global arena.

Module Outline

Premodule Preparation

The instructor may assign the following activity as a premodule assignment.

**Activity 15–1:
Planned Change
at General Electric**

Objective:

To appreciate the complex process and the management of a planned change program.

Task 1 (Homework):

Participants are to read the case that follows and respond to the questions at the end of the case.

Task 2 (Classroom):

a. Individuals are to share their responses to the questions at the end of the case.

b. Teams are to discuss the process of managing change. (For example, What was Welch's approach? How is it different or similar to TQM or STS?)

c. Teams are to discuss the role that organizational learning mechanisms play at GE.

Task 3:

The instructor will have each team share its perceptions with the entire class.

Task 4:

The class will discuss the relationships between organizational learning mechanisms, managing change, and its effects on organizational behavior and productivity.

Task 5:

The instructor will give a short lecture on organizational learning mechanisms, managing change, and the role that the process plays in fostering or hindering effectiveness.

Case Study:
The Transformation at General Electric

Jack Welch Jr. was appointed chairman and chief executive officer of General Electric in April 1981. Recently, Welch announced that he would retire at the end of 2000. His tenure in the job has been characterized by constant strategic and organizational change at GE. Among the initiatives with which Welch is associated are

1. *Changing the shape of the business portfolio.* Welch established two sets of criteria for redefining the business portfolio of GE. The first was to declare, "We will only run businesses that are number one or number two in their global markets—or, in the case of services, that have a substantial position—and are of a scale and potential appropriate to a $50 billion enterprise." Second, Welch defined three broad areas of business for GE: core, high-technology, and service businesses. As a result of these criteria, during the 1980s GE sold or closed businesses accounting for $10 billion in assets and acquired businesses amounting to $18 billion in assets. Divestment included Utah International, housewares and small appliances, consumer electronics, and semiconductors. Additions included RCA; Employers Reinsurance Corp.; Kidder Peabody Group; Navistar Financial; several new plastics ventures; Thomson's medical electronics business; and joint ventures with Fanuc (factory automation), Robert Bosch (electric motors), GEC (major appliances and electrical equipment), and Ericsson (mobile communications).

2. *Changing strategic planning.* Welch largely dismantled the highly elaborate strategic planning system that had been built up at GE over the previous decade. Documentation was drastically reduced, and the planning review process was made more informal—the central element was a meeting between Welch, his two vice chairmen, and the top management of each SBU (Strategic Business Unit), which focused on identifying and discussing a few key themes. By 1984 the 200-strong corporate planning staff had been halved. The broad objective was "to get general managers talking to general managers about strategy rather than planners talking to planners."

3. *Delayering.* The changes in planning were one aspect of a more general change in the role of headquarters staff from being "checker, inquisitor, and authority figure to facilitator, helper, and supporter." This change involved a substantial reduction in reporting and paper generation and an increase in individual decision-making authority. These changes permitted a substantial widening of spans of control and the removal of several layers of hierarchy. In most of GE, levels of management were reduced from nine to four.

4. *Destaffing.* Divesting pressures, removing management layers, reducing corporate staffs, and increasing productivity resulted in enormous improvements. Between 1980 and 1990, GE's sales more than doubled while its numbers of employees fell from 402,000 to 298,000.

5. *Values.* A persistent theme in Welch's leadership was a commitment to values. Welch continually emphasized the importance of the company's "software" (values, motivation, and commitment) over its "hardware" (businesses and management structure). Welch's philosophy was articulated in 10 key principles and values:

Being number one or two in each business.

Becoming and staying lean and agile.

"Ownership"—individuals taking responsibility for decisions and actions.

"Stewardship"—individuals ensuring that GE's resources were leveraged to the full.

Source: This case was written by R. Grant and A. B. (Rami) Shani for classroom use. The case draws heavily on the following sources: N. M. Tichy and S. Sherman, *Control Your Destiny or Someone Else Will,* (New York: Doubleday, 1992); R. Slater, *The New GE: How Jack Welch Revived an American Institution,* (Burr Ridge, IL: Irwin, 1993); R. N. Ashkenas and T. D. Jick, "From Dialogue to Action in GE Work-Out," in W. A. Pasmore and R. Woodman (eds.), *Research in Organization Change and Development,* vol. 6, (Greenwich, CT: JAI Press, 1993), pp. 267–87; "Jack Welch's Lessons for Success," *Fortune,* February 25, 1993, pp. 86–90.

"Entrepreneurship."

"Excellence"—the highest personal standards.

"Reality."

"Candor."

"Open communications"—both internally and externally.

Financial support—earning a return needed to support success.

This emphasis on values was supported by a type of leadership that put a huge emphasis on communicating and disseminating these values throughout the company. Welch devoted a large portion of his time to addressing meetings of employees and management seminars at GE's Crotonville Management Development Institute.

New Culture, New Systems

During his first 5 years in office, Welch's priorities were strategy and structure. GE's business portfolio was radically transformed, and within its main businesses GE's strategies gave a much greater emphasis to local presence and global success and to the development and application of new technology. In terms of organizational structure, Welch's crusade against excess costs, complacency, and administrative inefficiencies resulted in a drastic pruning of the corporate hierarchy and a much flatter organization.

At the root of the "new culture" Welch sought to build at GE was a redefinition of the relational contract between GE and its employees:

Like many other large companies in the United States, Europe and Japan, GE has had an implicit psychological contract based upon perceived lifetime employment. . . This produced a paternal, feudal, fuzzy kind of loyalty. You put in your time, worked hard, and the company took care of you for life. That kind of loyalty tends to focus people inward. . . The psychological contract has to change. People at all levels have to feel the risk-reward tension.

My concept of loyalty is not "giving time" to some corporate entity and, in turn, being shielded and protected from the outside world. Loyalty is an affinity among people who want to grapple with the outside world and win. . . The new psychological contract, if there is such a thing, is that jobs at GE are the best in the world for people who are willing to compete. We have the best training and development resources and an environment committed to providing opportunities for personal and professional growth.[1]

Creating a new attitude requires a shift from an internal focus to an external focus:

What determines your destiny is not the hand you're dealt, it's how you play your hand. The best way to play your hand is to face reality—see the world as it is and act accordingly. . . For me, the idea is: to shun the incremental and go for the leap. Most bureaucracies—and ours is no exception—unfortunately still think in incremental terms rather than in terms of fundamental change. They think incrementally because they think internally. Changing the culture—opening it up to quantum change—means constantly asking, not how fast am I going, how well am I doing versus how well I did a year or two before, but rather, how fast and how well am I doing versus the world outside.[2]

Critical to building a new culture and changing the "old ways" of GE was not just the bureaucracy itself, but the habits and attitudes that had been engendered by bureaucracy:

The walls within a big, century-old company don't come down like Jericho's when management makes some organizational changes or gives a speech. There are too many persistent habits propping them up. Parochialism, turf battles, status, "functionalities" and, most important, the biggest sin of a bureaucracy, the focus on itself and its inner workings, are always in the background.[3]

The Work-Out Program—a Generic View

GE's Work-Out Program was a response to the desire to speed the process of organizational change in GE. Welch conceived the idea of Work-Out in September 1988. Welch conducted a session at every class of GE managers attending Management Development Institute at Crotonville, New York. He was impressed by the energy, enthusiasm, and flow of ideas that his open discussion sessions with managers were capable of generating. At the same time, he was frustrated by the resilience of many of GE's bureaucratic practices and the difficulty of transferring the ideas that individual managers possessed into action. After a particularly lively session at Crotonville, Welch and GE's education director, James Braughman, got together to discuss how the interaction in these seminars could be replicated throughout the company in a process that would involve all employees and would generate far-reaching changes within GE. In the course of a helicopter ride from Crotonville to GE's Fairfield headquarters, Welch and Braughman sketched the concept and the framework for the Work-Out process.

A model for GE's Work-Out was a traditional New England town hall meeting where citizens gather to vent their problems, frustrations, and ideas, and people eventually agree on certain civic actions. Welch outlined the goals of Work-Out as follows:

Work-Out has a practical and an intellectual goal. The practical objective is to get rid of thousands of bad habits accumulated since the creation of General Electric. . . The second thing we want to achieve, the intellectual part, begins by putting the leaders of each business in front of 100 or so of their people, eight to ten times a year, to let them hear what their people think. Work-Out will expose the leaders to the vibrations of their business opinions, feelings, emotions, resentments, not abstract theories of organization and management.[4]

A generic summary of the Work-Out Program reveals three interrelated purposes: to fuel a process of continuous improvement and change; to foster cultural transformation characterized by trust, empowerment, elimination of unnecessary work, and boundaryless organization; and to improve business performance.

The Structure of the Work-Out Process

The central idea of the Work-Out process was to create a forum where a cross-section of employees in each business could speak their minds about how their business was managed without fear of retribution. Because those doing the work were often the best people to recommend improvements in how their work should be managed, such interaction was seen as a first step in taking actions to remove unnecessary work and improve business processes. In January 1989, Welch announced Work-Out at an annual meeting of GE's 500 top executives. A broad framework was set out, but considerable flexibility was given to each of GE's 14 core businesses in how they went about the program. The key elements of Work-Out were

- *Off-site meetings.* Work-Out was held as a forum and to get away from the company environment. Two-to-three–day Work-Out events were held off-site.
- *Focus on issues and key processes.* There was a strong bias toward action-oriented sessions. The initial Work-Out events tended to focus on removing unnecessary work. This is what Braughman referred to as the "low-hanging fruit." As the programs developed, Work-Out focused more on more complex business processes. For example, in GE Lighting, groupwide sessions were held to accelerate new product development, improve fill rates, and increase integration between component production and assembly. In plastics the priorities were quality improvement, lower cycle times, and increased cross-functional coordination.
- *Cross-sectional participation.* Work-Out sessions normally involved between 50 and 100 employees drawn from all levels and all functions of a business. Critical to the process was the presence of the top management of the particular business.
- *Small groups and town meetings.* Work-Out events normally involved a series of small group meetings that began with a brainstorming session followed by a plenary session (or "town meeting") in which the suggestions developed by the small groups were put to senior managers and then openly debated. At the end of each discussion, the leader was required to make an immediate decision: to adopt, reject, or defer for further study.
- *Follow-up.* A critical element of Work-Out was a follow-up process to ensure that what had been decided was implemented.

<table>
<tr><td>

**The Results
of Work-Out**

</td><td>

The results from Work-Out were remarkable. During its first 4 years, more than 3,000 Work-Out sessions had been conducted in GE, resulting in thousands of small changes eliminating "junk work" as well as much more complex and further-reaching changes in organizational structure and management processes. The terms *rattlers* and *pythons* were introduced to describe the two types of problem. Rattlers were simple problems that could be "shot" on sight. Pythons were more complex issues that needed unraveling.

As well as tangible structural changes and performance gains, some of the most important effects were changes in organizational culture. In GE Capital, one of the most centralized and bureaucratized of GE's businesses, one employee described the changes as follows: "We've been suppressed around here for a long time. Now that management is finally listening to us, it feels like the Berlin Wall is coming down."[5]

In 5 years, more than 300,000 employees, customers, and suppliers went through Work-Out sessions. A large variety of impressive and significant performance and efficiency improvements are reported in GE's internal documents, following introduction of the Work-Out processes. For example, the Gas Engine Turbines business unit at Albany, New York, reported an 80 percent decrease in production time to build gas engine turbines; Aircraft Engines at Lynn, Massachusetts, reduced jet engine production time from 30 to 4 weeks. GE's Financial Services Operation reported a reduction in operating costs from $5.10 to $4.55 per invoice, invoices paid per employee were up 34 percent, costs per employee paid fell 19 percent, and employees paid per payroll worker rose 32 percent. The Aerospace plant at Syracuse, New York, reported that as a result of the Work-Out Program, beyond achieving 100 percent compliance with pollution regulations, the production of hazardous waste materials was reduced from 759 tons in 1990 to 275 tons in 1992.

</td></tr>
<tr><td>

Managing Work-Out

</td><td>

Work-Out was intended as a bottom-up process in which (1) employees throughout each business would be free to challenge their leaders and (2) management's role was primarily to perpetuate the program and to ensure that decisions, once made, were implemented. But Work-Out could not be just a populist movement within the corporation. It needed to be directed toward creating the kind of corporation that GE needed to be to survive and prosper in the 1990s. To this extent Jack Welch saw his role as communicating and disseminating the principles, values, and themes that would permit GE's continued success.

In 1989 Welch crystallized his ideas about GE's management around three themes: speed, simplicity, and self-confidence:

We found in the 1980s that becoming faster is tied to becoming simpler. Our businesses, with tens of thousands of employees, will not respond to visions that have sub-paragraphs and footnotes. If we're not simple we can't be fast . . . and if we're not fast, we can't win.

Simplicity, to an engineer, means clean, functional, winning designs, no bells and whistles. In marketing it might manifest itself as clear, unencumbered proposals. For manufacturing people it would produce a logical process that makes sense to every individual on the line. And on an individual, interpersonal level it would take the form of plain speaking, directness, honesty.

But as surely as speed flows from simplicity, simplicity is grounded in self-confidence. Self-confidence does not grow in someone who is just another appendage on the bureaucracy; whose authority rests on little more than a title. People who are freed from the confines of their box on the organization chart, whose status rests on real world achievement—those are the people who develop the self-confidence to be simple, to share every bit of information available to them, to listen to those above, below and around them and then move boldly.

But a company cannot distribute self-confidence. What it can do—what we must do—is to give our people an opportunity to win, to contribute, and hence earn self-confidence themselves. They don't get that opportunity, they can't taste winning if they spend their days wandering in the muck of a self-absorbed bureaucracy.

Speed . . . simplicity . . . self-confidence. We have it in increasing measure. We know where it comes from . . . and we have plans to increase it in the 1990s.[6]

</td></tr>
</table>

Best Practices

One of the Work-Out Program's many impressive outcomes is that it's a catalyst for new improvement programs. One such program, Best Practices, is aimed at increasing productivity. The GE business-development staff focused on 24 credible companies from an initial pool of 200 that had achieved faster productivity growth than GE and sustained it for at least 10 years. From this list one dozen companies agreed to take part in GE's proposal to send its employees to their companies to learn their secrets to success. In exchange, GE offered to share the results of the study as well success stories with the participating companies. This learning for the Best Practices program involved companies such as Ford, Hewlett-Packard, Xerox, and Chaparral Steel plus three Japanese firms.

GE was less concerned with the actual work done at the companies than with management practices and attitudes of the employees. The difference between Best Practices and traditional benchmarking is that the former does not require keeping score. The focus on learning alternative successful management practices and managing processes was identified as the most critical component for long-term productivity improvements. The basic assumption that through multiple exposure to alternative management practices, managers and employees will be stimulated to continuously improve their own practices continues to guide the program. Best Practices has evolved into a formal course taught to at least one dozen employees and managers per month in each business unit.

Assignment (Written)

1. Based on the limited information presented, describe the overall planned change approach and phases led by Jack Welch.

2. Identify and briefly describe the major characteristics of the Work-Out Program.

3. Discuss how the organizational culture changed. What caused the change? What effects did the culture change have on human behavior and organizational performance and effectiveness?

Introduction

Managing change is one of the toughest managerial tasks. In the first module of this book, we argued that the study of organizational behavior looks at the organization as an organic system, ever adapting to the external environment and to the internal dynamic interactions of subunits. As such organizational work design, culture, learning, and change are four integral components of the firm's life. Unique cultures and subcultures emerge as a result of work and organizational design choices; dealing with an ever-changing business environment makes change and planned change a way of survival. Furthermore, from an organizational effectiveness point of view, managers' and organizations' abilities to manage the change process were found to be related to some of the basic criteria of effectiveness (for example, performance, success, improvement, and productivity).[7]

In the context of this text, we briefly define and examine the process of organizational learning; its meaning; and its impact on individual, group, and organizational effectiveness. In our discussion about change, we focus on those changes that are planned—an attempt is made to consciously and deliberately bring about change in the organization's status quo. Two major categorizations of planned change strategies have been articulated. With the first, according to Chin and Benne,[8] planned change can be divided into three basic types of strategies: empirical-rational, normative-reeducative, and power-coercive. The second describes seven "pure" approaches for bringing about change: fellowship, political, economic, academic, engineering, military, and applied behavioral science.[9] In this module we have chosen to focus on the applied behavioral science approach or, more specifically, the organizational development (OD) orientation, to discuss this total-system strategy for improving organizational effectiveness because of its concerns for both macro and micro aspects of change and development.

In this module we define and discuss the nature of organizational learning and the factors that help determine its uniqueness. We discuss the complexity of fostering organizational learning, define organizational development, categorize and review the variety of organizational change and OD interventions, and give examples of the OD approaches designed to influence the total organization. Finally, we discuss results from empirical investigations designed to assess OD's effectiveness.

Organizational Learning*

The view of organizations as adaptive rational systems that learn from experience was first proposed 35 years ago.[10] Sociotechnical system scholars articulated organization design principles that intend to foster the organization's ability to learn.[11] Peter Senge defined a **learning organization** in terms of continuous development of knowledge and capacity.[12] Recently, the focus has shifted to the specific **organizational learning mechanisms** that enhance the organizational capacity of learning.[13,14] The intense interest in **organizational learning** has been documented in many articles in management journals and books. Some critics argue that the wide range of recent publications has helped place "the study of organizational learning firmly on the map of theory and good practice."[15]

Defining Learning Organizations and Organizational Learning

A wide variety of definitions of a learning organization and organizational learning can be found in the literature. A learning organization is an organization characterized by a particular culture, climate, managerial pattern, and capacity that enable the entity to improve itself systematically and over time. As such learning organizations are entities that have the skills of creating, acquiring, and transferring knowledge and have demonstrated the ability to continuously improve their products, services, and financial results and to change themselves as required by the actual and anticipated demands of the marketplace. The intensity and direction of the changes derive directly from the vision, goals, and operating policies of the organization. Organizational learning is a system of principles, activities, processes, and structures that enable an organization to realize the potential inherent in the knowledge and experience of its human capital. Organizational learning incorporates all the activities and processes taking place on the individual, team, and organizational levels. Schein argues that at least three distinctly different types of learning exist: knowledge acquisition and insights (cognitive learning), habit and skill learning, and emotional conditioning and learning anxiety.[16] The concept of a learning organization, then, appears to focus more on the "what," while the concept of organizational learning concentrates on the "how."

As we saw in Module 4, organizations, by their very nature, are social systems that function in an environmental context. As such every organization is a learning entity that develops learning capability in order to survive. Nonetheless, organizations that can be termed *learning organizations* share a number of features. A learning organization is first and foremost an organization that encourages and emphasizes sustained and active learning, one in which organizational learning constitutes an integral part of its business strategy. A learning organization's managerial processes generate an organizational culture that allows for quick response, flexibility, integration, initiative, and innovation. In a learning organization learning stems from and is based on the organization's past experience and accumulated knowledge, that is, on what is commonly termed *organizational memory*. These learning features enable the organization to develop a dynamic and competitive strategy, formulate a shared vision, institute

*This section was adopted and modified from A. B. (Rami) Shani and Y. Mitki, "Creating the Learning Organization: Beyond Mechanisms," in R. T. Golemiewski (ed.), *Handbook of Organizational Consultation*, (New York: Marcel Dekker, 1999).

orderly and permanent systematic thinking, incorporate mapping-systems activities, and create an effective mechanism for adapting to the changes and constraints that arise from operating within a turbulent environment. Organizations with the foresight to adopt the conceptual foundation of organizational learning and to implement it through appropriate procedures have reported significant positive results. Organizations like General Electric, ABB, Rover, and Honda have developed internal mechanisms that facilitate skill development, surface and integrate knowledge within and outside the organizational boundaries, and have become adept at translating the new knowledge and insight into new organizational forms and actions.

Following are two snapshot examples of companies that, after having adopted the organizational learning philosophy, reported improved business and organizational results over time. In 1991 Sir Graham Day, the president of the British company Rover, declared that organizational learning will be the foundation of any company's ability to survive and succeed over time. And indeed, Rover's transformation into a learning organization led to results that speak for themselves: between 1992 and 1996 the company doubled its sales, cut costs of automobile production by half, won every British and European award for quality, and reported a significant increase in employee satisfaction.[17]

In 1990 the management of Kaiser-Permanente (KP), an American company specializing in health products and services, proclaimed that its ultimate goal was to transform the company into a learning organization. As a result of implementing organizational learning techniques, KP has reported that since 1991 the number of service customers has risen by an average of 10 percent annually while the number of customer complaints has dropped by an average of 7 percent.[18]

The Structural Mechanism of Organizational Learning

The experience of the past several years indicates that the idea of organizational learning has captured the imagination of managers and scholars alike. Furthermore, an increasing number of organizations and executives are predisposed to understand and adopt the learning organization concept. Some executives also see this comprehensive concept as a window of opportunity for assimilating advanced managerial approaches.[19] Yet a follow-up study of leading U.S. organizations attempting to assimilate new managerial approaches reveals some failures among those that did not have the foresight to construct a suitable mechanism for organizational learning that incorporated processes, tools, and work patterns. The structural mechanism for organizational learning is viewed as a formal configuration within the organization whose purpose is to develop, improve, and assimilate learning.[20,21] Just as there are many types of formal organizations, there are also various structural forms of organizational learning.

Recently, a continuum of structural learning mechanisms with an **integrated learning mechanism** on the one end and a **parallel learning mechanism** on the other was proposed.[22] The pure integrated learning mechanism is an orientation that takes full advantage of the existing structural configuration by channeling its focus to learning. The pure parallel learning mechanism is based on the orientation of creating a new microcosms-based structure that focuses on learning. Table 15–1 provides a comparative summary of the two organizational learning mechanisms along three dimensions, focus, basic assumptions, and implementation mechanisms, and a partial list of organizations that implemented the approach.

The Integrated Learning Mechanism

The integrated structural mechanism for organizational learning is an organizational structure that is fully integrated with the existing formal structure in the organization. The integrated learning structure is based on the notion that a learning structure gets created and added into the existing structure. The mechanism responsible for organizational learning is established within the existing formal structure. Usually, one of the deputy CEOs or vice presidents is appointed to head the organizational learning unit. The organic teams and units functioning within the organization operate alongside this unit. These teams take on additional activities and responsibilities for improving learning processes within the organization.

	Feature	Integrated Learning Structure	Parallel Learning Structure
Table 15–1 **Integrated Learning Structure and Parallel Learning Structure: A Comparative Analysis**	Focus	■ Taking advantage of the potential inherent in the organization's knowledge and experience by using the existing formal structure to achieve ongoing improvements and to adapt to the changing business environment.	■ Taking advantage of the potential inherent in the organization's knowledge and experience by setting up a parallel organizational structure to achieve ongoing improvements and to adapt to the changing business environment.
	Basic assumption	■ Implementing organizational learning is an inseparable part of existing organizational management activities.	■ Implementing organizational learning requires establishing a structure and creating processes beyond existing organizational management activities.
	Implementation mechanism	■ Executive decision to implement organizational learning. ■ Appointing the CEO or a deputy responsible for organizational learning, with executives serving as the steering team leading the process. ■ Developing an organizational structure in which learning processes are carried out primarily by organic teams (departments) and improvement teams operating within the organization. ■ Reliance on existing processes, structures, and tools for learning.	■ Executive decision to implement organizational learning. ■ Establishing independent steering teams that constitute a microcosm of the formal organization to lead and guide the organizational learning process. ■ Establishing separate learning teams that constitute a microcosm of the organization. ■ Possible development of new processes, structures, and tools for learning.
	Implementing organizations (partial list)	Knight Ridder, Honda, Saab, Fiat, General Electric, Erickson	Komatsu, Rover, ABB, Algoods, Blue Shield of California

Saab, the Swedish automobile company, established an integrated learning structure that included the following components: a primary steering team headed by the vice president of production, quality circles within the permanent work teams on the production floor, and process improvement teams within the organizational units. Information flowed to and from all the teams and was processed and tallied by the steering team. This organizational learning led to significant changes and improvements in work processes, managerial mechanisms and procedures, data processing, and hiring and training procedures.[23]

The Parallel Learning Mechanism

The parallel learning structural mechanism is based on establishing an organizational structure that operates parallel to the existing formal-bureaucratic structure and constitutes a microcosm of the existing organization. The parallel structure comprises of a central steering team and several learning teams. The members of the parallel organization continue to be part of the formal organization as well and to fulfill their managerial and professional roles. In addition, they devote 10 to 25 percent of their time to the parallel organization.

Signetics, a semiconductor manufacturer, set up a parallel learning structure to increase effectiveness and enhance innovation and initiative within the organization. The steering team that was set up constituted a microcosm of the organization's managerial structure. Once the primary objective was formulated and approved by the formal executive body, two 13-member learning teams representing a microcosm of the entire organization were established. One team focused on analyzing the existing organizational structure and work procedures to develop and propose organizational learning procedures for improving organizational performance over time. The second team sought to develop and propose organizational learning procedures for improving and enhancing levels of creativity and innovation. In the 10 years since learning procedures were instituted in the organization, the company has reported on a sustained increase in efficiency and a rise in the number of patents registered at the U.S. Federal Patent Office.

Learning procedures developed in each individual organization must be compatible with its specific goals and specialties. Because of the wide variety of tools, techniques, and processes available for organizational learning, every organization can "tailor" the most convenient and appropriate learning structural mechanism.

Despite the differences between the "pure form" of the structural mechanisms for organizational learning, they do share a number of core processes: (1) establishing a special structural mechanism for learning; (2) developing principles, tools, and procedures for systematic data collection, orderly information flow, and uniform data analysis; (3) creating channels that enable the organization as a whole to collect and analyze its shared "organizational memory" based on firm failures and successes; and (4) providing legitimization for all members of the organization to take advantage of the knowledge and experience accumulated at the individual, team, and organizational levels. Use of these core processes leads to the development of operational methods and solutions to ensure business success over time.

Recent studies on structural learning mechanisms that evolved in organizations reveal a wide variety of mechanisms on the continuum between the pure parallel and integrated. Although the number of reported studies is small, most focus on descriptive case studies about the creation of the learning mechanism and their key features. An interesting finding reveals that in some cases the learning mechanisms that began as parallel evolved into more of an integrated[24] and in others the integrated structural mechanisms evolved into more of a parallel one.[25]

Organizational Change and Development (OC&D)

Probably the most widely quoted definition of **organizational development** (OD) remains Beckhard's from 1969: Organizational development is

an effort (1) *planned, (2) organizationwide, and (3) from the top, to (4) increase organizational effectiveness and health through planned interventions in the organization's "processes," using knowledge.*[26]

We also like Burke's definition because organizational culture, which refers in part to values, norms, and roles as we used them in the emergent system, is the focus of change: Organization development can be defined as a *planned process* of cultural change. This process consists of two phases: **organizational diagnosis** and intervention. OD begins with a diagnosis of the current organizational culture (that is, an identification of the norms, procedures, and general climate of the organization). This identification process becomes more diagnostic as a distinction is made between those standards of behavior, procedures, and so on that seem to facilitate the organization's reaching its objectives (while meeting the needs of its members) from those that do not facilitate the attainment of its goals. Following this diagnostic phase, **interventions** are planned to change those norms seen as barriers to effective individual and organizational functioning.[27]

As OD has been used by professional specialists, it encompasses the following elements:

1. Application of behavioral science knowledge and methods.
2. Improvement or change of interaction patterns (arising from the norms, values, and role expectations) of an ongoing social system.
3. Integration of emotions and feelings into the rational perspective of the formal organization to achieve greater objectivity.
4. A systems focus on affecting individual, team, and organizational interactions concomitantly.

5. Building into the ongoing system the organizational climate and social technology needed to attain both individual and organizational goals.

6. Improvement of the organization design toward an optimal utilization of organizational resources.

7. Integration of organizational strategy and design into a jointly optimized system.

8. A continuing education program for the managerial system.

Organizational development can be better understood by examining what OD specialists do for organizations. This process starts with a diagnosis and continues with the selection of a strategy to achieve the purpose of OD.

Diagnosis

Before a program for change can be formulated, a study of the problems and needs of a particular system should be made. Consultants frequently start with a "presenting problem"—the one that prompted the client to seek their assistance. This problem generally turns out to be a symptom rather than a cause, as shown in the data collected through interviews, recordings, observations, meetings, or survey questionnaires. Information is the most basic ingredient of a change program. The technology of information gathering for OD purposes has been developing rapidly. The variety of collection methods and of alternatives for feedback of data to client systems is a current emphasis of OD practitioners.[28]

Selection of Strategies

Basic to all OD strategies is the assumption that management must ultimately define its own problems and change itself. It is not the role of specialists to change the client system; they are only facilitators or change agents. So strategies are chosen that will permit change to take place and will have the greatest potential for coping with the particular pattern of problems in a specific company.

Where, how, and with whom to start the OD effort is a critical decision. Many theorists and consultants insist that real progress in OD can take place only if it starts with top management. Executives must confront the data from the diagnosis and cope with their own behavior and practices to encourage those lower in the hierarchy to do so. When a company's personnel director initiates the use of OD just because other companies are doing it or because the director thinks the company needs it, the diagnosis and strategy are more complicated. Typically the personnel director will want to start with the supervisory or middle-management level as a step to convincing top management of the value of such a program. The consultant has to decide whether such an OD effort would have sufficient effect. Under some conditions it is possible to "optimize," that is, improve one aspect of an organization's functioning and let this improvement spread to other areas.

Types of Interventions

Considerable literature is appearing that describes social and behavioral strategies, methods, and techniques for achieving change. While few ways of clustering the different change strategies have appeared in the literature, for the purpose of this module we have chosen two complementary typologies. First we will review a typology that groups the change intervention strategies based on their target group. Next we will present a typology that is based on the change intervention emphasis. Together the two typologies provide a holistic picture of change orientations.

Target Group-Based Clustering

This classification of change programs—proposed by Wendell French and Cecil Bell—is based on the primary target of the intervention, for example, individuals, dyads and triads, teams and groups, intergroup relations, and total organization.[29] Table 15–2 shows this classification scheme. Some interventions have multiple targets and multiple uses and thus appear in several places in the table.

**Figure 15–2
Typology of OD
Interventions Based
on Target Groups**

Target Group	Interventions Designed to Improve the Effectiveness
Individuals	Life- and career-planning activities Coaching and counseling T-group (sensitivity training) Education and training to increase skills, knowledge in the areas of technical task needs, relationship skills, process skills, decision making, problem solving, planning, goal-setting skills Grid OD phase 1 Work redesign Gestalt OD Behavior modeling
Dyads/triads	Process consultation Third-party peacemaking Role negotiation technique Gestalt OD
Teams and groups	Team building — Task directed — Process directed Gestalt OD Grid OD phase 2 Interdependency exercise Appreciative inquiry Responsibility charting Process consultation Role negotiation Role analysis technique "Startup" team-building activities Education in decision making, problem solving, planning, goal setting in group settings Team MBO Appreciations and concerns exercise Sociotechnical systems (STS) Visioning Quality of work life (QWL) programs Quality circles Force-field analysis Self-managed teams
Intergroup relations	Intergroup activities — Process directed — Task directed Organizational mirroring Partnering Process consultation Third-party peacemaking at group level Grid OD phase 3 Survey feedback
Total organization	Sociotechnical systems (STS) Parallel learning structures MBO (participation forms) Cultural analysis Confrontation meetings Visioning Strategic planning/strategic management activities Real-time strategic change Grid OD phases 4, 5, 6 Interdependency exercise Survey feedback Appreciative inquiry Search conferences Quality of work life (QWL) programs Total quality management (TQM) Physical settings Large-scale systems change

Source: W. L. French and G. H. Bell Jr., *Organizational Development,* 6th ed., 1999, p. 153. Reprinted by permission of Prentice-Hall, Inc., Englewood Cliffs, New Jersey.

**Consequence-Based
Clustering***

This classification of change programs—proposed by Mitki, Shani, and Stjernberg—is derived from an attempt to understand change programs based on their impact. Three types of change programs holistic, focused, and limited were identified according to their main emphasis. Table 15–3 summarizes the key features of the three orientations.

*This section was adopted and modified from Y. Mitki, A. B. (Rami) Shani, and T. Stjernberg, "A Typology of Change Programs: A Road Map to Change Programs and their Differences from a Global Perspective," in R. T. Golemiewski (ed.), *Handbook of Organizational Consultation,* (New York: Marcel Dekker, 1999).

Table 15–3 Planned Change Programs: Three Orientations		Holistic Change Programs	Focused Change Programs	Limited Change Programs
	Characteristic	Programs that attempt to address simultaneously all aspects of the organization	Programs that identify a few key aspects (such as quality and cycle time) and use these as levers for changing the organization systemwide	Programs that are designed to address a specific problem that is not seen as a lever for a broader change
	Examples of change programs	■ Sociotechnical systems ■ Organization restructuring ■ Lean production ■ Business process reengineering ■ Organizational learning	■ Total quality management ■ Management by objectives ■ Time-based management ■ Dialogue programs	■ Team building ■ Communication improvement ■ Humanization of work ■ Work environment reforms ■ Democratization programs
	Published cases	Kaiser-Permanente Rover Saab Automobile	ABBT-50 GE Work-Out IA Paper Mill	Job rotation, Volvo team building, H-P Communication Workshops, AT&T

Holistic Change Programs

Holistic programs simultaneously try to address all (or most) aspects of organizing. Examples are sociotechnical, lean, downsizing/restructuring, business process re-engineering, and organizational architecture. The logic is that all aspects of an organization are connected. When you change one aspect, you have to take into account the effects on all other subsystems. This sense is captured by concepts such as fit and joint optimization.

Focused Change Programs

Focused programs identify a few key aspects, such as time, quality, and customer value, and then use these as levers for changing the organization systemwide. Some examples of such initiatives are TQM programs, time-based management, and management by objectives. They key concept carries a lot of symbolic value. The logic is that you need a critical mass in a cognitive sense. If you want to influence people, you have to address the same issue again and again. The focused program acts as a schema for understanding and making sense of changes. The change program needs some kind of purpose, change process, change mechanisms, identifiable outcomes, and criteria for success to get legitimacy and momentum. The key concept does not need to be true or proven in any academic sense, but it needs to be "socially valid."

Limited Change Programs

Limited programs are not aimed at affecting broader aspects of the organization. They address a specific problem, which is not seen as a lever for broader change, but may help build a foundation for such change at a later time. The basic logic is decoupling. Examples of such initiatives are work environment programs, ergonomics, career planning, job rotation, and changing the wage structure. Allowing children to live together with their parents in the kibbutzim is an example of a limited program. The change was not conceived as a program in its proper sense—rather, it became a spontaneous movement that affected ultimately all kibbutzim in Israel. It had major long-term effects. It was intended as an isolated change with no planned effects on other aspects of the community. Nonetheless, the practice turned out to trigger a major change of the entire kibbutz movement; that is, the changes toward privatization and the introduction of internal pricing for the distribution of the services within the kibbutz may be seen as consequences of this spontaneous movement.[30,31]

Similarly, the job rotation schemes that were tried in the tapestry department of Volvo's Torslanda plant in the 1960s were intended to solve a limited ergonomic problem. However, in retrospect these job rotation schemes became linked to the wider issue of QWL development—and thus a part in the wider organizational innovations in Volvo during the 1970s and 1980s.[32]

The term *local* means that the changes are not intended to reach other units. With the term *systemwide* we mean that the program, whether limited or holistic or focused, is intended to reach all the relevant units of the company. The word *relevant* is important here—which units are seen as relevant is determined by the other dimension of our classification, that is, whether the changes are holistic, focused or limited.

Some programs may be difficult to characterize into any of these categories. For instance, team building may be seen as a focused program on the systemwide level and, simultaneously, as a holistic program on the local level. On the systemwide level team building may be part of a competence development effort with little links to other changes. On the local level the same program may be part of an effort to reorganize the entire production system.

Systemwide Approaches to Change and Development

The improvement of total organization as the target group with the focus on the management of change is represented in this module in two ways. First, we discuss three comprehensive interventions and their paths to organizational effectiveness. Second, we provide a comparative exploration of the three structural-based interventions: sociotechnical system, reengineering, and total quality management.

The Sociotechnical System (STS) Approach

The **sociotechnical system (STS)** theory, developed at the Tavistock Institute in England by Eric Trist and his colleagues, contends that organizations are made up of people who produce products or services using some technology.[33] As such the STS approach attempts to combine the social subsystem (people), the technical subsystem (machines and technology), and the environmental supersystem into a synergistic system.[34] Joint optimization, the ultimate desire in STS, states that an organization will function optimally only if the social and technological subsystems of the organization are designed to fit the demands of each other and the environment.[35] The STS approach emphasizes the need for compatible integration between the organization's social and technical subsystems to ensure organizational effectiveness.[36] An in-depth discussion of sociotechnical systems as an organizational framework is found in Modules 4 and 13. In this section we focus on the management of change aspects.

Successful STS design focuses on an "open" interface with the environment the organization faces. This implies that the ability of the organization to effectively match its social and technical subsystems relies on the degree of openness or contact the organization maintains with the environment. Organizational competitiveness necessitates the need for organizations to maintain environmental sensing and scanning mechanisms such that the organization will be able to plan and adapt according to anticipated and unanticipated changes.[37] Changes in any one of the subsystems will disturb the status quo and should result in the realignment of the entire organization.

In the context of organizational development, the STS planned change intervention is based on the action research philosophy. **Action research** is defined as an emergent inquiry process in which behavioral and social science knowledge is integrated with existing organizational knowledge to produce new knowledge, which is generalizable and simultaneously usable.[38] As such the STS change endeavor is participatory, co-inquiry–based, client- and organization-owned, and scientifically executed. Figure 15–1 shows a flowchart of the STS planned change process.

The first phase of the intervention involves preparation of the organization and its top-level decision makers for conducting the sociotechnical systems analysis and design activities. This phase includes the consultant's entry, scanning, and contracting with the top-level decision makers; formation of a top-level steering committee; analysis of the business situation (that is, macro environment, industry environment, competition environment, and company environment); analysis of business results (in terms

Figure 15–1
Sociotechnical System
Planned Change Process:
A Flow Design

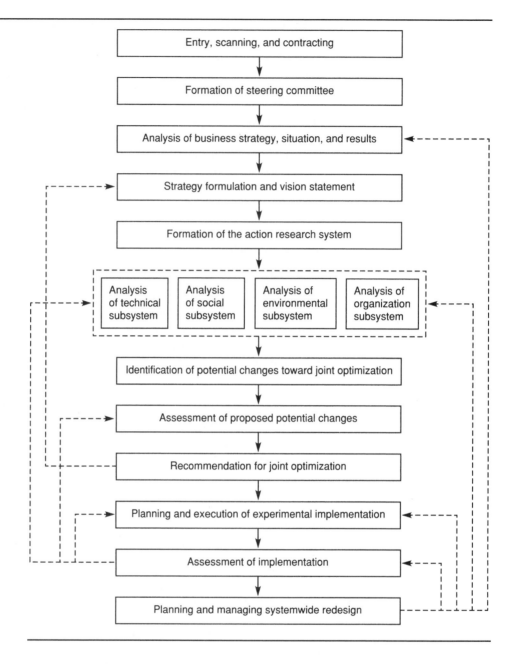

of current and desired profit, volume, cost, and operational purpose); and the formulation of a business vision, a total systems strategy, and a vision statement for the redesign effort.

The second phase consists of formation, education, and analysis by the action research system, which is composed of the steering committee, one or more consultants, and one or more groups representing different parts and levels of the organization. The action research system conducts analyses of the technical, social, environment, and design elements of the organization, which lead to recommendations for organization redesign. The recommendations for joint optimization—once they're approved and prioritized by the top-level management of the organization—will be followed by careful planning of the experimental implementation.

The third phase consists of the experimental execution of the proposed recommendations. The changes are assessed and modified as necessary to fit the unique organizational characteristics. Overcoming some of the difficulties in the experimental implementation process will aid in the formulation and management of the total organization change process.

Finally, based on learning from the experimental implementation of the recommendations for change, the action research system refines the vision statement, formulates the total systems change strategy, and identifies criteria for effectiveness assessments. The action research system might also be utilized in the management of the implementation process. One of the underlying assumptions of the sociotechnical systems change process is the emphasis on organizational learning as key to organizational success. As such, once the implementation of the new organizational design is done, top-level management will reexamine the business situation and likely continue the process of self-examination and refinement.

A review of 134 recorded STS interventions revealed successful results on eight different organizational effectiveness criteria.[39] The studies were conducted over 30 years and were implemented in a variety of organizations. While 87 percent of the studies reported productivity improvements, 89 percent reported cost savings, 81 percent showed reduced absenteeism, 65 percent had reduced turnover, and 54 percent reflected improved attitudes. A special issue of the *Journal of Applied Behavioral Science* was devoted to STS. While the authors represented several different disciplines and theoretical perspectives, all were concerned with the usefulness and effectiveness of the STS approach.[40] In a recent review of two decades of STS interventions in North America, James Taylor illustrates how STS has been expanded to embrace dimensional manufacturing work, service work, nonroutine work, and professional work within increasingly chaotic environments. More than 115 active and successful STS designs or redesigns are currently operating in the United States, of which about a quarter are clearly not continuous process technologies.[41] Continuous process technologies still predominate in STS applications, but the number and proportion of applications to other work systems are increasing.[42] Although space does not permit elaboration, it is important to note that unique applications of STS can be found in many places around the globe—for example, in Scandinavia,[43] the Netherlands,[44] England, Israel,[45] and Italy.

Total Quality Management

Total quality management (TQM) is a managerial approach for improving processes in an organization in order to manufacture products or offer higher-quality services that will satisfy the customer. The approach emphasizes a number of elements: The improvement process is continuous and never ending; the improvement processes are undertaken by teams, some of which are organic and some of which are task specific and ad hoc; each process has an inherent improvement that must be learned in a systematic manner.[46] The analysis, similar to the solution, needs to rest on solid, tested data. An in-depth discussion of the management of quality as a key organizational process is found in Module 19 on the WWW. In this section we focus on the management of change aspects.

Applying TQM in organizations involves a change of organizational culture and the development of quality awareness from the customers' perspective. Likewise, TQM also encompasses "empowerment," which is expressed, on the one hand, in the transfer of responsibility on topics of quality and production to employees, including delegation of authority for decision making in these fields, and on the other hand, in creating workers' commitment to the organization. The approach is applied top-down via a structural mechanism that usually includes a quality council and process action teams (PATs). The quality council is composed of the executive president or vice president plus additional members who represent the whole system insofar as their functions, influence, and level of responsibility. Its main purpose is to determine the framework of the TQM program and to provide a support system. The mechanism for operating TQM is also called the *parallel hybrid organization.*[47] There are those who see TQM solely as a technique or as an integration of tools and systems designed to improve productivity; some who see it as the improvement of a product or service; and others who see TQM as a wider and comprehensive managerial philosophy.[48]

Reports from organizations that adopted TQM indicate that TQM seems to affect customer satisfaction, worker satisfaction, the number of quality or process improvement groups in operation, the percentage of rejected products, the level of exploitation of raw materials, and absenteeism by personnel.[49] Very few firms report radical structural or technological changes resulting from the introduction of TQM. While some argue that TQM affects strategy, little support can be found to confirm this notion.[50]

Reengineering

The reengineering approach emerged at the beginning of the 1990s as a practical orientation (1) to combat worsening corporate business results (mainly in the United States) and corporate difficulties and (2) to establish a competitive edge. The basic assumption of reengineering is that incremental improvement of existing processes within organizations does not provide a sufficient answer to the real existing needs.[51] A drastic cognitive and conceptual turning point—a paradigm shift—is required to allow a breakthrough.

Reengineering is defined as "fundamental rethinking and radical redesign of business processes to achieve dramatic improvements in critical contemporary measures of performance, such as cost, quality, service, and speed."[52] Radical and dramatic changes are fostered when individuals search for answers to the basic question, Why are we doing what we are doing?[53] This approach of reengineering ignores existing processes, structures, organizational culture, and human resources and states that one must begin by pinpointing key organizational processes, which are determined by their conformance to customers' requirements.

Reengineering advocates the design of the required structures and processes based on a customer's requirements. The main structural change necessary is the transfer from organizational structure to process structure.[54] This means breaking down interdepartmental boundaries from "functional departments" to "process teams" or "case teams." The teams have the responsibility for the entire process. The process-teams–based organization design flattens the organizational hierarchy and significantly reduces existing boundaries. Organizations that implement reengineering can use both centralized and decentralized approaches and can enjoy their advantages when managing the processes. Information technology, which is the engine of reengineering, permits organizational units to operate autonomously, while the firm as a total entity enjoys the advantages of system centralization. The function of the new process teams is also to influence the creation of a new system of values and beliefs among employees.

The results of a successful application of reengineering are measured by the radical changes in organizational performance. The most common parameters for testing the results are cost, quality, speed, and service. It must be emphasized that impressive results were expected in the short run within various organizations that reported on the application of this approach. Our current knowledge is limited when it comes to the understanding of reengineering's long-term effects.

A Comparative Examination

The preceding overview shows some striking similarities and differences between the last three orientations to organizational change.[55] Table 15–4 summarizes the essence of the three approaches: their theoretical roots and founders; some of the key principles and assumptions; key elements, phases, and mechanisms of the change process; and outcomes. Our purpose in this section is to explore commonalities and differences between the orientations as related to the change process. A comparison between the other dimensions—although intriguing, as can be seen from the table—is beyond the scope of this module.

For the purpose of this module we will examine four distinct similarities between the three orientations. All require a strategic decision that involves major financial and resource investment and commitment. All three orientations focus on the entire system; they follow both customer and improvement focus; organizational learning is an integral part of the change process; and they all require transformation and/or modification of the organizational culture.

The three orientations share the importance of alignment between the change and the overall business strategy. The decision to pursue any one of the change programs

Table 15–4	Partial Comparison between TQM, STS, and Reengineering		
Dimension	**TQM**	**STS**	**Reengineering**
I. Theoretical roots	Statistical theory (SPC), system theory	Organization theory, applied social and behavioral sciences, system theory, production engineering	Concurrent engineering, production engineering, practice-driven system theory
II. Founders	Deming, Crosby, Juran, Imai, Shewhart, Taguchi, Tshikawa	Cherns Cummings, Davis, Emery, Pasmore, Taylor, Thorsrud, Trist	Champy, Davenport, Hummer
III. Motto	A group of ideas and techniques directed toward enhancing competitive performance through improving the quality of products and processes.	A set of design principles, ideas, and change processes that strive toward best match between organizational, technical, environmental, and social subsystems.	A set of ideas about radical redesign and change in business processes to achieve breakthrough results (major gains in cost, service, or time).
IV. Some basic principles and assumptions	**Organizational Goals**		
	Serving customers' needs to fullest extent possible by supplying goods and/or services of highest quality.	Joint optimization of social, technical, and environmental systems.	Quantum leap in performance by focusing on key processes that really matter, emphasizing strong leadership, technology, and radical change.
	Time Orientation		
	Dynamic. Philosophy of incremental and continuous improvement. Short- and long-term perspectives	Dynamic. Philosophy of innovation, organizational learning, and continuous improvement. Long-term perspective.	Dynamic. Philosophy of radical and rapid changes. Short-term cycle to achieve desired results.
	Coordination and Control		
	Coordination through process action groups (cross-functional). Both control and coordination exercised by managers and employees.	Coordination and control through self-managed groups (autonomous work groups). Both control and coordination exercised by managers and employees.	Coordination and control by reengineering teams, process owner, and steering committee. Both control and coordination exercised mainly by managers.
	Work Design		
	System-based optimization guided by specific design principles. Formation of temporary process action teams.	System-based joint optimization guided by specific work design principles. Formation of functional organic teams.	System-based approach guided by key design processes. Formation of process teams.
	Technology		
	Technology may be a key factor in quality improvement.	Technology is a fundamental factor in work design.	Information technology is an essential factor in work design.
	Customer and Suppliers Orientation		
	Internal and external customers and suppliers are integral parts of the system.	External customers and suppliers are important but are not part of the system.	Processes' customers are an integral part of the system.
	Rewards		
	Individual-, team-, and system-based.	Team- and individual-based.	System- and individual-based.
V. Management of change	**Change Orientation**		
	Led by management and/or a quality council. The effort is mostly guided by ISO 9000 and/or award evaluation processes and/or some combination of specific guidelines provided by quality experts.	Change process led by design team or parallel learning structure. The effort is guided by a modified action research philosophy.	The change is led by top management and the steering committee. The effort is guided by the process owner and reengineering (process design) teams.

(continued)

375

Table 15–4

Partial Comparison between TQM, STS, and Reengineering *(concluded)*

Dimension	TQM	STS	Reengineering
	Change Phases, Mechanisms, and Processes		
	Broadly defined deductive-based phases and basic activities. Team learning and system learning mechanisms.	Clearly defined deductive-based phases, processes, and activities. Team and learning structure mechanisms.	Clearly defined inductive-based phases. Information technology is a key element in team process learning.
	Methods and Tools		
	Quality planning (Hoshin planning). Identifying customers and suppliers (both internal and external) and determining needs. SPC. Develop a process that can produce the quality required. Quality-based systemwide diffusion.	Environmental, technical, and social analysis. Variance and deliberation analysis. Experimentation with alternative design configurations. Systemwide diffusion.	Competitive and customers' needs analysis. Identification of processes that require radical improvements based on specific criteria. Broad understanding of current processes. Radical systemwide or subsystem-based diffusion.
	Change Process Performance Measures		
	Customer- and supplier-based orientation. Processes' improvement against benchmarking. Utilization of both hard (e.g., defect ratios, customer complaints) and soft (e.g., satisfaction, commitment) measures.	Input–throughput–output performance-oriented measures. Utilization of both hard (e.g., productivity, profitability) and soft (e.g., satisfaction, commitment) measures.	Measures of improvements in business processes (e.g., profitability, quality of service) and establishment of business competitiveness and superiority.
VI. Outcomes	**Continuous Improvements**		
	Established.	Established.	Unknown.
	Organizational Learning		
	Specific to quality-related issues.	Systemwide learning mechanism is established.	Learning mechanism based on key organizational processes.
	Organizational Performance Measures		
	1. Customer and supplier satisfaction: Established.	Advocated and at times established.	Advocated.
	2. Quality standards: Established and extensively improved.	Established.	Established quality standards related to process.
	3. Production cost reduction: Advocated.	Established.	Established.
	Organizational Culture		
	New quality-based organizational culture.	New system- and innovation-based culture.	New innovation-based organizational culture.

is strategic. Managers make their determination based on the perceived congruency between the company's strategic goals and what the change program has to offer. Furthermore, the strategic nature of the **planned change** program needs to be emphasized. The investment in each program is viewed as strategic due to its perceived importance (that is, critical value to the firm's overall performance), the substantial resource commitment, the clear time horizon, and the fact that programs are not easily reversible.

Reengineering, TQM, and STS seem to focus on improvement of organizational functioning to better meet changing environmental demands. As such they take a *holistic system* approach that incorporates all the relevant actors (internal and external customers, supplier, and the like). While some variations seem to exist in terms of initial focus and/or targeted unit for the change program, all take into account the entire organization. Furthermore, at some point in each change orientation, the emphasis shifts to the optimal alignment of the different organizational units.

Acquiring new knowledge, skills, and tools seems to be at the heart of each orientation. All three acknowledge in various ways the importance of organizational learning. Specific mechanisms that foster organizational learning and organizational dialogue seem to have evolved in each orientation. Some form of structural support configuration—with different labels—that houses and guides the organizational learning and the change programs provides the source of energy and continuity.

The last striking similarity among the three orientations is the notion that each transforms or modifies the culture of the firm. The involved nature of the orientations; the learning that they generate via the ongoing analysis, data collection, and interpretations; and the paradigm shift that they foster set the stage and momentum for organizational culture change.

The preceding similarities among the three orientations are somewhat surprising due to the nature of their evolution and theoretical foundations. As can be seen in Table 15–4, each orientation is rooted in different scientific disciplines. As such it is relatively easy to identify some of the many differences between them. Now let's discuss some of the differences.

The espoused objectives of each orientation vary. Reengineering focuses on radical changes of key processes; STS focuses on the incremental, gradual, and continuous changes geared toward optimal utilization of organizational resources; and TQM focuses on the continuous quality improvement of products, processes, and services.

As Table 15–4 shows, the three orientations seem to follow somewhat different change processes and phases. STS seems to have a clear analytical road map with specific sequential phases and activities. TQM seems to have broadly defined deductive phases and basic activities. The reengineering change process follows clearly defined inductive-based phases. Furthermore, careful examination of the specific phases and their sequence in each orientation reveals that they vary significantly.

Each orientation incorporates the *technological subsystem* differently. The STS redesign process is based on existing technology and/or new technology. (Most STS projects report on the redesign of the organizations without changing the technology.) Reengineering is mostly concerned with the implementation of new technology with special emphasis on information technology. (Some even argue that information technology is at the heart or the engine of reengineering.) TQM focuses on improvements of processes in general.

Finally, the outcomes and measurements seem to vary. The current scientific literature provides support for significant long-term **continuos improvements** in both STS and TQM. In reengineering, the expectations are that outcomes can be realized in a short time span. Due to the relative newness of reengineering, we have yet to learn about its long-term effects. Organizational structure seems to change mostly in STS and reengineering in an explicit manner. In TQM only minor structural changes take place. Those are mainly changes in internal and external customer linkages.

Toward an Eclectic Planned Change Approach

As can be seen from the comparative examination of the three orientations, the potential for some kind of combination of the three merits exploration. In practice a natural overlap and multiple combinations of bits and pieces of the three approaches can be found in each planned change implementation. This section provides a brief overview

**Table 15–5
Phases in an Eclectic
Planned Change Approach**

Phase 1: Project Initiation
- Define scope and purpose.
- Secure management commitment.
- Establish organizational awareness of the need for radical changes.
- Align with business strategy.
- Create a parallel learning mechanism and educate organization members.

Phase 2: Mapping Customers' Key Processes
- Identify customers' requirements, needs, and potentials.
- Determine the key processes.

Phase 3: The Inquiry Process
- Establish benchmarks.
- Conduct business analysis based on sociotechnical system framework:
  Verify key processes.
  Uncover system pathologies.
- Revise company vision based on analysis, strategic opportunities, and enabling technology (i.e., information technology).
- Identify potential improvements to the existing processes.

Phase 4: Design/Redesign to Modify Existing Processes and Organizational Structure
- Formulate specific alternative sociotechnical-based design solutions. (STS-based design includes the optimal integration of key organizational elements such as rewards, control, structure, information, people, and technology.)
- Explore potential impact of proposed solutions.
- Develop joint optimization of key processes.
- Establish learning processes for continuous improvement.

Phase 5: Implementation and Reconstruction of the Key Processes and Organization
- Foster a climate that is conducive to change.
- Create the implementation and support mechanisms.
- Develop training programs.
- Establish learning loops as an integral part of continuous improvement.

of an **eclectic planned change approach** that pulls together the strengths of each.[56] Table 15–5 summarizes the phases and some key activities in the proposed eclectic framework.

The first phase involves the establishment of the project's foundation. In this phase securing management commitment to the effort is crucial. The scope and purpose of the project is defined by the top-management team/CEO, and the basic project strategy is articulated. Top management needs to make a clear decision about the choice of change orientation based on the compatibility between the business strategic objectives and the change orientation. The next set of activities is geared toward developing shared understanding of the need and companywide awareness for making significant changes. The creation of a parallel learning mechanism and its magnitude signal sincere commitment on management's part for change. Overall, the parallel learning mechanism is charged with the responsibility of housing, guiding, and facilitating the learning and change process. The actual criteria and creation process of the parallel learning mechanism is critical. Various alternatives are available. Management is required to make the choice that best fits the organization.

The second phase builds on the project initiation phase and moves the focus to the key processes to meet customers' needs. Following the establishment of clarity about the role and mission of the learning mechanism, the project shifts to the identification of the customers (both internal and external), their requirements, needs, and potentials. Key business processes that have a direct impact on customers' requirements, needs, and potentials are identified.

Phase 3 focuses on establishing benchmarks and performing systematic business analysis while verifying the key business processes and major business pathologies plus revisiting the business vision, strategic opportunities, and enabling technologies. The challenge in this phase is the collection and assimilation of the data. The data's complexity requires the utilization of multiple human and technological resources that can be found within and outside the company boundaries. At the end of this phase, ideas for improvement of specific processes begin to surface.

Phase 4 is guided by a set of specific design principles that are derived from STS design theory. As such alternative design solutions that strive toward joint optimization of the different business elements are explored. One key challenge during this phase is to strive toward the development of joint optimization between the key business processes. Beyond the tasks of a careful examination of potential impact of the alternative solutions, the goal is also to develop the learning mechanism for continuous improvement.

Implementation and reconstruction of the organization and its key processes are part of phase 5. Implementation planning is treated as a project. Some planned change models treat this kind of planning as a completely new process.[57] Others see this phase as a natural continuation of the change program and, as such, the implementation will be guided by the parallel learning mechanism. The implementation planning calls for the simultaneous execution of both radical and rapid, as well as gradual and ongoing changes. Key processes can be treated either way. The learning mechanism needs to have the know-how that supports the complexity of this deliberation. Of the many challenges during this phase, the most crucial are the creation of support mechanisms, the development of appropriate training programs, and the establishment of learning loops as an integral part of continuous improvement.

Planned Change and Organizational Effectiveness

The field of OC&D and its growth can be best appreciated by the increased number of books, journals, and articles devoted to OD values, philosophies, intervention methods and techniques, evaluation problems, methods for dealing with these problems, and effectiveness criteria and assessment. Organizational change and development, as a field of theory and practice, can have significant positive effects on the total organization, the individual, and the work group in terms of behavioral, attitudinal, and effectiveness changes.[58] In general, the cumulative results of the published empirical investigations point toward the conclusion that OC&D is a successful strategy of planned change.[59] The 12 volumes that have appeared thus far in the JAI series *Research in Organizational Change and Development* (edited by Pasmore and Woodman) reflect a tradition of provocative scholarly work by many contributors. Coupled with the 30 volumes published thus far in the Addison-Wesley organization development series (edited by Beckhard and Schein) for the organization development and change practitioner and the manager, they demonstrate the vitality of the field.

At the same time, the evaluation of change efforts or interventions is a complex and difficult task. OD was defined as "a planned process of organizationwide change," and as such an empirical research methodology that focuses on assessing the dynamic nature of change processes and their effectiveness had to be developed.[60] Published research on OD evaluation was clustered into three categories: (1) identification of general problems and development of guidelines, (2) demonstrations of methods for evaluating change efforts, and (3) identification and resolution of specific methodological issues.[61]

Furthermore, the documentation of OD results reported that studies of a better quality would permit more rigorous comparative examinations. For example, a survey of the OD literature from 1948 through 1982 identified 65 studies that meet a rigorous set of comparative criteria. These studies made the following recommendations: (1) The goals and expected results of the intervention should be stated clearly; (2) the intervention should be clearly defined and clearly described; (3) the intervention should be demarcated from the outcomes; (4) researchers should note why specific dependent variables were selected and how were they measured; and (5) the experimental design utilized, the sequence of observations, the frequency and time span of measurement, and the beginning and termination of the intervention should be described adequately.[62]

Finally, massive reviews of some 800 work improvement efforts by Barry Macy and of 3,200 worldwide work improvement efforts by Frans M. Van Eijnatten show "generally positive conclusions with respect to both performance and worker satisfaction.[63] Taken together, these literature reviews strongly support the conclusion that OC&D programs yield positive improvements at the individual, team, and organizational levels.

Organizational Change and Development in the International Context

The applicability and effectiveness of organizational development and change in different cultural environments are areas of growing interest to managers and practitioners. Reports on OC&D activities on various continents and in many countries (third world countries, northern Europe, Poland, Australia, South Africa, Latin America, Egypt, Israel, India, China, Singapore, and Japan to mention a few) have begun to appear in the literature.[64] Although each study examines one aspect of OC&D, an OC&D program, or a specific intervention in the respective continent or country, comparative empirical studies within a specific country among different interventions, within a specific continent across countries, or across countries on a specific intervention are scarce.

The conceptual and empirical challenges for comparative organizational change, development inquiry, and applications are many. First, the underlying values and assumptions of OD, the values and assumptions of the specific interventions, and the values and assumptions of the practitioners need to be analyzed. Second, the cultural elements and intercultural relations at the country, industry, and corporate levels need to be examined. Third, the degree of congruence needs to be explored, and the line of inquiry developed.

Recently, guidelines with explicit steps for adopting OC&D in different cultural contexts were proposed:

1. Evaluate the ranking of the dimensions of culture in the given situation.
2. Make a judgment as to which values are most deeply held and unlikely to change.
3. Evaluate the "problem appropriate" interventions ranking on the dimensions of culture.
4. Choose the intervention that would clash least with the most rigidly held values.
5. Incorporate process modifications in the proposed intervention to fit with the given cultural situation.[65]

Summary

The field of organizational development and change emerged in the 1950s with the use of T-groups to improve organizational life. It has gradually expanded to include the total organization. It has focused on influencing human interactions to help organizations guide the direction of their evolution and to enhance the cultural elements that are viewed as critical to maintaining the desired effectiveness and outcomes. Examples of contrasting organizational effectiveness strategies include the sociotechnical system approach, the parallel learning structure interventions, total quality management, and reengineering.

Frequently defined as an organizationwide systems approach of planned change, the need for more empirical research remains one of the biggest challenges to the field of organizational learning, managing change, and organization development. Although a significant improvement can be identified in the quality of the reported literature, further advancements are needed. Most organizational change and development specialists view themselves as eclectic change agents pursuing an expert or an action research method and applying a broad range of knowledge and skills suited to the nature of the problems identified by their efforts.[66]

Key Terms and Concepts

Action research	Organizational learning
Continuous improvement (CI)	Organizational learning mechanism
Eclectic planned change approach	Parallel learning structure
Integrated learning mechanism	Parallel learning mechanism
Intervention	Planned change
Learning organization	Reengineering
Organizational change and development (OC&D)	Sociotechnical system (STS)
	Total quality management (TQM)
Organizational development	
Organizational diagnosis	

Study Questions

1. Discuss the powerful notions inherent in the definition of organizational learning.
2. Discuss the relationships between organizational learning, organizational culture, and organizational change and development.
3. Identify and discuss the key elements in the definition of organizational development.
4. Compare and contrast the target-group-based and consequence-based typologies of change programs.
5. What are the major phases of an OC&D program?
6. Compare and contrast any two of the planned change interventions described in this module.
7. Describe an organization that you are familiar with that could use an OC&D intervention. What are some roadblocks that the intervention would likely encounter? How would you overcome them? Describe the phases in the intervention process. How would the intervention affect individual, group, and organizational effectiveness?
8. How effective are planned change interventions?
9. What should be the role of the manager in an OC&D intervention?

Endnotes

1. N. M. Tichy and R. Charan, "Speed, Simplicity, Self-Confidence: An Interview with Jack Welch, *Harvard Business Review,* September–October 1989, p. 120.
2. Ibid., p. 114.
3. *Fortune,* January 25, 1993, p. 87.
4. Tichy and Charan, "Speed, Simplicity, Self-Confidence," p. 118.
5. R. N. Ashkenas and T. D. Jick, "From Dialogue to Action in GE Work-Out: Developmental Learning in a Change Process," Research in *Organizational Change and Development* 6 (1992), p. 271.

6. Jack Welch, "Speed, Simplicity and Self-Confidence: Keys to Leading in the 1990s," speech at annual shareholders meeting, April 1989.

7. K. S. Cameron and D. A. Whetten, *Organizational Effectiveness,* (New York: Academic Press, 1983); R. E. Quinn and K. S. Cameron, *Paradox and Transformation: Towards a Theory of Change in Organization and Management,* (Cambridge, MA: Ballinger, 1988).

8. R. Chin and K. D. Benne, "General Strategies for Effecting Changes in Human Systems," in W. G. Bennis, K. D. Benne, and R. Chin (eds.), *The Planning of Change,* (New York: Holt, Rinehart & Winston, 1969), pp. 32–59.

9. K. E. Olmosk, "Seven Pure Strategies of Change," in J. W. Pfeiffer and J. E. Jones (eds.), *The 1972 Annual Handbook for Group Facilitators,* (La Jolla, CA: University Associates, 1971), pp. 162–72.

10. R. Cyert and J. March, *A Behavioral Theory of the Firm,* (Englewood Cliffs, NJ: Prentice-Hall, 1963).

11. W. A. Pasmore, *Designing Effective Organizations,* (New York: Wiley, 1994).

12. P. M. Senge, *The Fifth Discipline: The Art and Practice of the Learning Organization,* (New York: Doubleday, 1991).

13. G. R. Bushe and A. B. (Rami) Shani, *Parallel Learning Structures: Increasing Innovation in Bureaucracies,* (Reading, MA: Addison-Wesley, 1991).

14. M. Popper and R. Lipshitz, "Organizational Learning Mechanisms: A Structural and Cultural Approach to Organizational Learning," *Journal of Applied Behavioral Science* 34, no. 2 (1998), pp. 161–79.

15. B. Garratt, *The Learning Organization,* (Hammersmith, London: HarperCollins, 1994).

16. E. H. Schein, "How Can Organizations Learn Faster: The Problem of Entering the Green Room," *Sloan Management Review* 34, no. 2, (1993), pp. 85–92.

17. M. Marquardt and A. Reyolds, *Global Learning Orgnaization,* (Chicago, IL: Irwin Publications, 1996).

18. M. W. Stebbins, A. B. (Rami) Shani, W. Moon, and D. Bowles, "Business Process Reengineering at Blue Shield of California: The Integration of Multiple Change Initiatives," *Journal of Organizational Change Management* 11, no. 3, (1998), pp. 216–32.

19. A. C. Edmondson and B. Moingeon "Organizational Learning as a Source of Competitive Advantage," in B. Moingeon and A. Edmondson (eds.), *Organizational Learning and Competitive Advantage,* (Thousand Oaks, CA: Sage, 1996), pp. 7–15.

20. Bushe and Shani, op. cit.

21. E. H. Schein, "Three Cultures of Management: The Key to Organizational Learning," *Sloan Management Review* 38, no. 1, (1996), pp. 9–20.

22. A. B. (Rami) Shani and Y. Mitki, "Creating the Learning Organization: Beyond Mechanism," in R. T. Golemiewski (ed.), *Handbook of Organizational Consultation,* (New York: Marcel Dekker, 1998).

23. A. B. (Rami) Shani, and T. Stjernberg, (1995), "The Integration of Change in Organizations: Alternative Learning and Transformation Mechanisms," in W. A. Pasmore and R. W. Woodman (eds.), *Research in Organizational Change and Development,* vol. 8, (Greenwich, CT: JAI Press, pp. 77–121).

24. M. W. Stebbins, and A. B. (Rami) Shani, "Organizational Learning and the Knowledge Worker," *Leadership and Organization Development Journal* 16, no. 1, (1995), pp. 23–30.

25. Y. Mitki, A. B. (Rami) Shani, and Z. Meiri, "Organizational Learning Mechanisms and Continuous Improvement," *Journal of Organizational Change Management* 10, no. 5, (1997), pp. 426–46.

26. R. Beckhard, *Organization Development: Strategies and Models,* (Reading, MA: Addison-Wesley, 1969), p. 9.

27. W. Warner Burke, "A Comparison of Management Development and Organization Development," *Journal of Applied Behavioral Science* 7, (1971), pp. 569–79.

28. Excellent sources include D. A. Nadler, *Feedback and Organization Development: Using Data-Based Methods,* (Reading, MA: Addison-Wesley, 1977); D. G. Bowers and J. L. Franklin, *Survey-Guided Development, I: Data-Based Organizational Change,* (La Jolla, CA: University Associates, 1977); D. L. Hausser, P. A. Pecorella, and A. L. Wissler, *Survey-Guided Development, II: A Manual for Consultants,* (La Jolla, CA: University Associates, 1977); J. L. Franklin,

A. L. Wissler, and G. J. Spencer, *Survey-Guided Development, III: A Manual for Concepts Training,* (La Jolla, CA: University Associates, 1977).

29. W. L. French and C. H. Bell, *Organization Development,* (Englewood Cliffs, NJ: Prentice-Hall, 1999).

30. Y. Mitki, A. B. (Rami) Shani, and T. Stjernberg, "The Kibbutz in Transition," paper presented at the Fifth International Conference on Communal Studies, May 30–June 2, 1995, Ramat Efal, israel.

31. T. Simons and P. Ingram, "Organization and Ideology: Kibbutzim and Hired Labor," *Administrative Science Quarterly* 42, (1997), pp. 784–813.

32. T. Stjernberg and A. Philips, "Organizational Innovations in a Long-Term Perspective: Legitimacy and Souls-of-Fire as Critical Factors of Change and Viability," *Human Relations* 46, no. 10, (1993), pp. 1193–1219.

33. E. L. Trist, "The Evolution of Sociotechnical Systems," in A. H. Van de Ven and W. F. Joyce (eds.), *Perspectives on Organization Design and Behavior,* (New York: John Wiley & Sons, 1982), pp. 19–75.

34. See, for example, W. A. Pasmore, *Designing Effective Organizations,* (New York: John Wiley & Sons, 1988).

35. W. A. Pasmore and J. J. Sherwood, eds., *Sociotechnical Systems: A Sourcebook,* (La Jolla, CA: University Associates, 1978); E. Emery, *Characteristics of Sociotechnical Systems,* (London: Tavistock Institute, 1959); T. G. Cummings, ed. *Systems Theory for Organizational Development,* (Somerset, NJ: John Wiley & Sons, 1980); T. G. Cummings and S. Srivastva, *Management of Work: A Sociotechnical Systems Approach,* (La Jolla, CA: University Associates, 1977); W. A. Pasmore, *Creating Strategic Change: Designing the Flexible High-Performing Organizations,* (New York: John Wiley & Sons, 1994).

36. A. B. Shani and O. Elliott, "Sociotechnical System Design in Transition," in W. Sikes, A. Drexler, and J. Grant (eds.), *The Emerging Practice of Organization Development,* (La Jolla, CA: University Associates, 1989), pp. 187–98.

37. T. Cummings and S. Srivastva, *Management of Work: A Sociotechnical Systems Approach,* (La Jolla, CA: University Associates, 1978).

38. A. B. Shani and W. A. Pasmore, "Organization Inquiry: Towards a New Model of the Action Research Process," in D. D. Warrick (ed.), *Contemporary Organization Development,* (Glenview, IL: Scott, Foresman, 1985), pp. 438–49.

39. W. A. Pasmore, C. Francis, J. Heldeman, and A. B. Shani, "Sociotechnical Systems: A North American Reflection on Empirical Studies of the Seventies," *Human Relations* 35, no. 12 (1982), pp. 1179–204.

40. W. Barko and W. A. Pasmore, "Introductory Statement to the Special Issue on Sociotechnical Systems: Innovations in Designing High-Performing Systems," *Journal of Applied Behavioral Science* 22, no. 3 (1986), pp. 195–99.

41. J. C. Taylor, "Two Decades of Sociotechnical Systems in North America," paper presented at the annual meeting of the Academy of Management, San Francisco, August 1990; J. C. Taylor and D. F. Felten, *Performance by Design: Sociotechnical Systems in North America,* (Englewood Cliffs, NJ: Prentice-Hall 1993).

42. See, for example, R. Holti, "Sociotechnical Issues in the Software Sector," paper presented at the annual meeting of the Academy of Management, San Francisco, August 1990.

43. See, for example, N. Adler and P. Docherty, "Bringing Business into Sociotechnical Theory and Practice," *Human Relations,* 50, no. 6 (1987); P. H. Engelstad, "The Evolution of Network Strategies in Action Research Support Sociotechnical Redesign Programs in Scandinavia," paper presented at the annual meeting of the Academy of Management, San Francisco, August 1990; B.Denkbaar, "Lean Production: Denial, Confirmation or Extension of Sociotechnical Systems Design," *Human Relations,* 50 no. 5 (1998), pp. 567–84..

44. L. U. De Sitter, J. F. Den Hertog, and B. Dankbaar, "From Complex Organizations with Simple Jobs to Simple Organizations with Complex Jobs," *Human Relations* 50, 5, (1997), pp. 497–534.

45. Y. Mitki, *Sociotechnical Systems: A Comparative Study of 112 Production Units in the Kibbutz Industries,* (Tel Aviv: Tel Aviv University, 1994).

46. R. Grant, A. B. (Rami) Shani, and R. Krishnan, "TQM's Challenge to Management Theory & Practice," *Sloan Management Review* 35, no. 2 (1994), pp. 25–35.

47. P. Lillrank and N. Kano, *Continuous Improvement,* (Ann Arbor, MI: University of Michigan Press, 1989).

48. R. Krishnan, A. B. (Rami) Shani, R. Grant, and R. Baer, "The Search for Quality Improvements: Problems of Design and Implementation," *Academy of Management Executive* 7, no. 4 (1993), pp. 7–20.

49. R. E. Cole, P. Bacdayan, and B. J. White, "Quality, Participation, and Competitiveness," *California Management Review* 35, no. 3 (1993), pp. 68–81.

50. A. B. (Rami) Shani and M. Rogberg, "Quality, Strategy, and Structural Configuration," *Journal of Organizational Change Management* 7, no. 2 (1994), pp. 15–30.

51. G. Hall, J. Rosenthal, and J. Wade, "How to Make Reengineering Really Work," Harvard *Business Review,* November–December 1993, pp. 119–31; P. Lillrnak and S. Holopainen, "Reengineering for Business Option," *Journal of Organizational Change Management* 11, no. 3 (1998), pp. 246–59.

52. M. Hammer and J. Champy, *Reengineering the Corporation,* (New York: HarperCollins, 1993).

53. D. L. Schnitt, "Reengineering the Organization Using Information Technology," *Journal of System Management,* January 1993, pp. 14–42; J. Taylor, "Participative Design: Linking BPR and SAP with STS Approach," *Journal of Organizational Change Management* 11, no. 3 (1998), pp. 233–45.

54. T. Housel, C. Morris, and C. Westland, "Business Process Reengineering at Pacific Bell," *Planning Review,* May–June 1993, pp. 28–34.

55. This section is based on A. B. (Rami) Shani, and Y. Mitki, "Reengineering, TQM and Sociotechnical Systems Approaches to Organizational Change," *Journal of Quality Management* 1 (1996), pp. 131–45.

56. M. Stebbins and A. B. (Rami) Shani, "Moving away from the Mafia Model of Organization Design," *Organizational Dynamics,* Winter 1989, pp. 18–30.

57. Ibid.

58. Many recent review-based studies support this argument. See, for example, J. I. Porras, "Organization Development: Theory, Practice, and Research," in M. D. Dunnette and L. M. Hough (eds.), *Handbook of Industrial and Organizational Psychology,* 2nd ed., vol. 3 (Palo Alto, CA: Consulting Psychological Press, 1992), pp. 719–822; P. J. Robertson, D. R. Roberts, and J. I. Porras, "An Evaluation of a Model of Planned Organizational Change: Evidence from a Meta-Analysis," in W. A. Pasmore and R. W. Woodman (eds.), *Research in Organizational Change and Development,* vol. 7 (Greenwich, CT: JAI Press, 1993), pp. 1–39; B. A. Macy, and H. Izumi, "Organizational Change, Design, and Work Innovations: A Meta-Analysis of 131 North American Field Studies—1961–1991," in *Research in Organizational Change and Development,* vol. 7, pp. 235–313.

59. W. L. French and C. H. Bell, *Organization Development,* 6th ed. (Englewood Cliffs, NJ: Prentice-Hall, 1999); T. D. Jick, *Managing Change,* (Burr Ridge, IL: Irwin, 1993); R. M. Kanter, B. A. Stein, and T. D. Jick, *The Challenge of Organizational Change,* (New York: Free Press, 1992).

60. J. I. Porras and S. J. Hoffer, "Common Behavior Changes in Successful Organization Development Efforts," *Journal of Applied Behavioral Science* 22, no. 4 (1986), pp. 477–94.

61. A. A. Armenakis, A. G. Bedian, and S. B. Pond, "Research Issues in OD Evaluation: Past, Present, and Future," *Academy of Management Review* 8, no. 2, (1983), pp. 320–28.

62. J. M. Nicholas and M. Katz, "Research Methods and Reporting Practices in Organization Development: A Review and Some Guidelines," *Academy of Management Review* 10, no. 4 (1985), pp. 737–49.

63. See B. A. Macy, "An Assessment of Improvement and Productivity Efforts: 1970–1985," paper presented at the National Academy of Management, August 1986, Chicago; F. M. Van Eijnatten, *The Sociotechnical Systems Design Paradigm,* (Eindhoven, The Netherlands, 1986).

64. M. N. Kiggundu, "Limitations to the Applications of Sociotechnical Systems in Developing Countries," *Journal of Applied Behavioral Science* 22, no. 3 (1986), pp. 341–54; Z. Chroscicki, "Conceptualization of OD Process Measures in Poland," *Organization Development Journal* 4, no. 3 (1986), pp. 62–67; M. Rikuta, "Organization Development within Japanese Industry: Facts and Prospects," *Organization Development Journal* 5, no. 2 (1987), pp. 21–32; J. Benders, R-J Van den Berg, and M. Van Bitsterveld," Hitch-Hiring on a Hype: Dutch Consultants Engineering Re-Engineering," *Journal of Organizational Change Management,* 11, no. 3 (1998), pp. 201–15.

65. A. M. Jaeger, "Organization Development and National Culture: Where's the Fit?" *Academy of Management Review* 11, no. 1 (1986), pp. 178–90.

66. A. B. Shani and G. R. Bushe, "Visionary Action Research: A Consultation Process Perspective," *Consultation: An International Journal* 6, no. 1 (1987), pp. 3–19; M. W. Stebbins and C. C. Snow, "Process and Payoffs of Programmatic Action Research," *Journal of Applied Behavioral Science* 18 (1982), pp. 69–86; A. Werr, "Managing Knowledge in Management Consulting," paper presented at the Academy of Management Conference, San Diego, 1998; R. T. Golemiewski, ed. *Handbook of Organizational Consultation,* (New York: Marcel Dekker, 1999).

Activity 15–2: The Management of Change at FoodCo, Inc.

Objective:

To increase the understanding of the concepts of organizational culture, development, and change by applying them to the FoodCo case.

Task 1 (Homework):

Read the FoodCo case that follows and answer the questions at the end of the case.

Task 2:

The instructor will facilitate class analysis and discussion of the case.

Case Study: FoodCo, Inc.*

FoodCo, Inc., is a national supplier of specialty food products sold through grocery stores. Its headquarters are in Chicago, Illinois; its food-processing plants are spread throughout the country. FoodCo maintains a reputation as a well-managed, profitable company in an extremely competitive industry. As is common in the food products industry, most of FoodCo's top executives have marketing backgrounds.

In January of last year, Tom Hawkins, a consultant specializing in organizational design, received a call from Don Stevens, a top-level staff member in the FoodCo plant in Cleveland, Ohio. Don was interested in talking to Tom about some recent developments at the Cleveland plant. During their brief telephone conversation, Don told Tom that the plant manager, Mr. Williams, had become increasingly uncomfortable with the pressure he was under from corporate management to implement sociotechnical systems changes in the Cleveland facility. Don was anxious to hear Tom's advice on how to deal with the situation, since Mr. Williams had made him responsible for preparing a statement on the situation for corporate management.

When they met, Don explained to Tom that FoodCo was organized on a divisional basis around products and that each division was capable of operating as a separate business. However, given the competitive nature of the industry, corporate management felt that it needed to make decisions quickly to maintain an advantage over other firms; this meant that FoodCo's top management became involved in many local decisions. Plant managers throughout the corporation were required to clear even minor changes in operations with their superiors and were expected to implement changes directed from above.

In the past rapid changes had created some difficulties at the Cleveland plant. Product life cycles were short (3 to 5 years in many cases); each cycle was accompanied

*Source: This case was contributed by Professor William A. Pasmore, Weatherhead School of Management, Case Western Reserve University, Cleveland, Ohio 44106. All rights are reserved and no reproduction shall be made without expressed approval of Professor Pasmore. We are grateful to him.

by the hiring and letting go of employees. Shutdowns and retoolings had hit the Cleveland plant more frequently than others, creating dissatisfaction and mistrust on the part of employees. Don described the situation to Tom:

People come here looking for work and we say, "Great! We're glad to have you! Welcome to the company!" Then a couple of years later, we say, "Sorry—we can't use you for a while." That's bad enough; but the trouble is, we never know when the cutbacks will occur, because people in Chicago make those decisions for us based on how well the product is doing in the market, whether they think another plant could produce it for less, or whether they think they have a hotter product for us to make. So we're as much in the dark as anyone—but the employees don't believe us. They think we know, but we just aren't telling them. They say, "You're management, aren't you? If you don't know, who does?" I understand that these people have families and lives of their own to plan for and that this situation makes it hard for them. It's hard for all of us—but it's just the nature of the business. I can even understand why they voted in a union—I get pretty frustrated myself at times—but the union is only making things worse. Now, in addition to dealing with Corporate, we have to fight the union every step of the way. We can't make any changes around here without someone second-guessing us. If we give in to the union, Corporate screams. But if we follow Corporate's orders, union members become upset—and then it just gets harder to get them to go along the next time.

People at Corporate are market oriented. They have to be, I guess. But it seems like at times they don't think very much about what impact their decisions will have on people. We're the ones who have to live with these people day after day. Most of the time, we wind up going along with those corporate executives, since we can't risk losing our jobs or the business for the plant; but we sure would like those corporate executives to be a little more sensitive to the problems they create for us. The demand to implement sociotechnical systems changes here is just the latest bug of theirs. They really don't appreciate the difficulties we would have in making it work here.

Following the Tampa Example

Don explained to Tom that corporate management had gotten excited about sociotechnical systems design after its success in the corporation's newest plant, located in Tampa, Florida. Here are some of its features.

Autonomous Work Groups: Self-managed production teams were given primary responsibility for major segments of the production process. Each team was composed of multiskilled members who could perform one another's job as well as do most of the maintenance and quality work. The teams were free to decide on their own job assignments, to select new team members, and to discipline members who didn't meet their standards.

Integrated Support Functions: Team members were able to perform most work that would be performed by separate maintenance and quality control departments in a typical plant. The teams were also able to schedule their own production runs, plan product changeovers, determine their own overtime, and even do minor process engineering.

Challenging Job Assignments: Jobs were designed to meet human needs for growth, challenge, and learning. Routine tasks were rotated among all team members.

Job Mobility and Rewards for Learning: Pay increases were given in accordance with the number of tasks employees could perform. All employees were encouraged to learn new jobs throughout the plant.

Facilitative Leadership: The plant operated with a minimum of supervision; those supervisors who were present were chosen on the basis of their ability to work effectively with groups in making decisions and their ability to help team members to develop.

Managerial Information for Employees: Employees were provided with a full range of productivity and cost data that allowed them to make decisions about the effective use of their team resources.

Self-Government for the Plant: No rules were specified in advance; employees were allowed to develop their own rules as they saw fit.

Congruent Physical and Social Context: Status symbols that would separate managers from employees were avoided; common cafeterias and parking lots were used. In addition, rooms were provided for work teams to hold meetings, and the plant itself was designed to facilitate discussion among teams that were responsible for interdependent processes.

Learning and Evolution: A commitment was made to continual improvement in the way the organization operated. Employees would have a major influence on changes that would take place.

Plans for the Cleveland Expansion

According to Don, the issue confronting the Cleveland plant was that the corporation wanted the Cleveland plant to follow Tampa's example in designing its new dairy products line. Because Tampa had been successful, corporate management was pressuring the Cleveland plant to adopt the sociotechnical systems approach in managing its operation as well. In fact, the dairy products division manager had already appointed Dick Harold, a manager from the Tampa plant, to head up the new dairy operation in Cleveland. Since the Cleveland plant was part of another division in the company, this move caught Mr. Williams by surprise:

We're not opposed to new ideas here. I've been in this business for 25 years, and I've tried a lot of new ideas in my time. In fact, we did a lot here before we ever heard of Dick Harold—our employees keep their own work areas clean—and we even have them rotate jobs in one area. So these ideas aren't really that new to us. Still, I think the corporation is trying to push this thing on us too quickly. Dick Harold was in town buying a house before I even knew he was coming to work here. What's worse, they never told him that he would be working for me. He thought he would have a free hand in the new dairy products unit, since it's part of another division. I straightened that out—anything that happens at this plant is under *my* control. I made a phone call to Chicago, and my boss made sure that Harold would be working for me.

As I said, I'm not opposed to new ideas. But I think we have a different setup here than Tampa does. They handpicked the best people to work in that plant—we can't do that. They weren't unionized—we are. They didn't have a history of ups and downs that created mistrust— we do. And they built from scratch—we have to make use of our existing building. Besides, we've done all right here using our own way of getting things done. Some of my managers have been with the company for as long as I have, and they don't like the sound of some of Harold's ideas. I've made them hold a tough line in the past, and they've held it. They're afraid of what would happen if we turned the place over to the employees to run. They've also heard that Tampa operates with fewer managers than we do and that makes them nervous.

I suppose that with the corporation behind this thing, we don't have much choice but to try it. But I'm pretty sure it won't work here. Maybe when they see that, they'll back off. At least I've gotten them to agree that we should check it out with our people first to see what they think of it. I doubt that they'll go for it—there's been too much change here already—but we'll see.

The Survey

Tom worked with Don Stevens to prepare a survey to be given to employees to find out how they felt about the new management concept. Tom also met with the president and vice president of the local union to discuss the reasons for giving the survey. He explained to them that not all employees would be affected by the proposed changes but that the survey would be an opportunity for people throughout the plant to comment on how the plant was being run. The union leaders seemed in favor of the proposed changes and agreed that the survey should be given as long as individuals would not be identified with their answers. The results of the survey indicated that attitudes toward management were negative and that communication between management and employees was viewed as practically nonexistent. Although a few employees had written notes on their surveys indicating that the new management concept was a strategy to get more work out of employees for the same pay, the overall reaction to the concept was more positive than Mr. Williams had imagined.

Mr. Williams's Dilemma

Tom discussed the results of the survey with Don Stevens. Don told Tom that Mr. Williams had been surprised by the findings but still was not convinced that employees would really accept the changes associated with the new management concept. What's more, Williams was fairly certain that if the concept was put into practice, it wouldn't work—at least not for long. If Williams went ahead, he would look foolish to the employees, which would make things worse in the future; if he didn't proceed, the corporation would be on his back to explain why, and Williams knew that the people from Chicago weren't good listeners.

Williams decided to put the concept to an employee vote. He figured that if they said yes and it didn't work, they would have no one to blame but themselves; if they said no, he might at least have some reason when Corporate asked him why he hadn't gone ahead with its plan. Williams knew that management had the legal right to design work any way it pleased, so the corporation would not be bound by the results of the vote. Williams arranged to have the union take the vote at the local union hall quickly, since construction on the new unit was being held up by the corporation until the situation at Cleveland was clear. The corporation was anxious to get this work started, since it would lose market share if the product didn't go into production soon.

Questions

1. Describe the culture of the corporation.
2. Is the corporation justified in its position regarding the management of the Cleveland plant?
3. How will the vote turn out? What steps should be taken afterward?
4. What advice should Tom give to Mr. Williams?

Activity 15–3: Custom Nests Simulation

Objectives:

a. To help participants become aware of the differences between sociotechnical design principles and traditional bureaucratic principles.

b. To develop participants' appreciation for the sociotechnical systems approach to organizational development and effectiveness.

Task 1 (Homework):

Participants are to read the following organization description of Custom Nests. (Do not read beyond the basic description of the organization.)

Task 2 (In-class Activities):

a. The instructor will assign roles and give name tags to participants.

b. The instructor will then assign participants to their workstations and ask them to begin their work as it is described in their role descriptions.

c. Production will be stopped after about 25 minutes and participants will be asked to leave the room for about 10 minutes.

d. The instructor will then lead a brief discussion about the experience of work in the phase just completed. Discussion themes might be

1. What was it like being a stapler, a supervisor, and so on?
2. How was this organization like others that you have worked for?
3. What kind of organizational development strategy would you utilize to improve effectiveness?
4. How would you go about implementing the change?

Task 3 (In-class Activities):

Participants will be assigned to new work groups and asked to start production. Production will be stopped after about 25 minutes.

Task 4:

The instructor will lead a class discussion on the following themes:

a. How was the work design in the second phase different/similar to that of the first phase?

b. What would be the implications of the second work design phase to your own experience?

c. Discuss the relationship between the social, technological, and environmental subsystems.

d. What are some challenges for implementing sociotechnical system change in organizations?

e. How would the sociotechnical system intervention be similar to or different from the other organizational development approaches discussed in this module?

(*Note to the instructor.* Be sure to read the *Instructor's Manual* before using this exercise.)

Source: This activity was contributed by Dr. Barry Morris. All rights are reserved and no reproduction should be made without express approval of Dr. Morris. We are grateful to him.

Case Study: Custom Nests Simulation

Organization Description

Custom Nests was founded in 1951 by Mr. Jay Blue. The company began as a small operation consisting of six workers and a manager. Everyone in the company worked as a craftsperson making birdhouses from beginning to end. The explosion in the housing market that followed World War II created massive demand for birdhouses for the displaced birds of this period. As a result Custom Nests grew considerably in a short period of time. Today it continues to be the primary manufacturer of birdhouses, providing the American public with a wide range of quality birdhouses for every occasion and climate. One birdhouse in particular, however, has remained the company's primary and most marketable item and has allowed the business to expand into other birdhouse markets with little risk to overall sales.

The structure of the organization has changed dramatically since its inception. Only the people in research and development actually have the opportunity to build a birdhouse from the bottom up. The majority of the company's products are manufactured in a highly specialized assembly line–type of process in which few people actually have hands-on opportunities to see how the whole product gets made. Wages for hourly workers are determined based on years with the organization and the complexity of the task. For many years the company had been paying minimum wage wherever possible. In 1969, the company was unionized. Wages are currently slightly less than the standard for similar industrial settings. The relationship between union and management is adversarial. There is a fairly high number of grievances written on a regular basis, and neither group has as yet been willing to sit down and iron out their differences in a way that meets both groups' needs. For the most part decisions in the organization are made by managers, while hourly workers are expected to do as they are told.

The company currently employs approximately 175 people. Of these, 140 are hourly employees; the remainder are engineers or managers of one sort or another. The various hourly roles in the organization include cutters, tapers, staplers, and maintenance/supply personnel. The salaried staff includes quality control, supervisors, research and development, and accounting clerks.

The plant's layout has the various specialties spread out and separated from one another in a large single-floor facility. (See the diagram.) Many structural barriers to effective communication between work groups/areas exist. The technology in much of the plant is simple yet antiquated. There is a long history of broken or unuseful tools and inadequate processes for keeping the technology in good working order.

Custom Nest Floor Plan

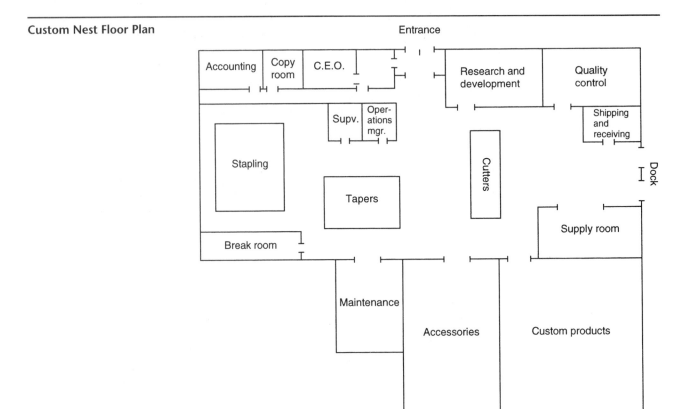

Custom Nests Simulation: Roles

Supervisor

The supervisor's job at Custom Nests is considered the most important job in the plant. In all, there are three supervisors, but there is little need for interaction among them. The supervisor in this company is considered to be the expert, the conflict manager, the scheduler, the communicator, and the quality control representative, to name a few roles.

You, however, have a very special supervisory role in that you are personally responsible for the production of Custom Nests's standard birdhouse. You are directly responsible for all production and maintenance functions within your product line. Your immediate superior is the only operations manager for all products. Although he recognizes the importance of your product, he prefers to give you total responsibility for operations in your area. From his perspective, when problems arise, you are to blame.

The relationships between you and your direct reports are good for the most part. Sometimes you are put in the middle and therefore are thought to be the bad guy, but most people know that you are between a rock and a hard place. You basically do what you have to do to get the job done and to keep your job.

Like all of the other supervisors, you have moved up through the system over the years. You know almost all the jobs from personal experience and got the supervisor's job because of your knowledge of technical processes and your apparent desire to move up in the organization. In addition, you seem to be able to get people to work hard and fast.

Your specific responsibilities include the following:

1. Scheduling, monitoring time cards, and establishing production speeds.
2. Communications from department to department and from management to hourly employees.
3. Supervising maintenance work.
4. Supervising materials handling.
5. Supervising production.
6. Conflict management.
7. Employee counseling and coaching.
8. Handling first-step grievances.
9. Daily and weekly production reports.
10. Managing the absenteeism program.
11. Providing technical skills training.

Source: Contributed by Dr. Barry Morris.

Quality Control

The quality control (QC) department was created in the early 1960s. As the company's products have diversified, the need for a QC department has grown even more essential. Unskilled hourly employees could not possibly understand the importance of quality to the success of the business or keep track of all of the standards and specifications required for each of the company's 33 birdhouse styles and accessories.

Finished products are delivered to the QC department from each product section. The largest group of QC personnel is assigned to Custom Nests's standard birdhouse, which has been the company's primary product since the company was established in 1951 when only six workers built the birdhouses by hand and cared about the results of their labor.

The QC department is located in the back corner of the plant, far removed from the production department. QC personnel, who tend to have very little contact with the workers on the line, communicate primarily with the manager of operations and occasionally the supervisor, who also does a lot of the QC work. Under normal circumstances QC does not usually talk to the supervisor, but the manager of operations prefers to let the supervisor from the standard birdhouse production area manage most of the area's operations-related issues.

The QC personnel are primarily engineers. They tend to be young people who have recently graduated from local colleges. Some of them began with the company as co-op students and, following graduation, continued their work for Custom Nests. The QC engineers responsible for the company's standard birdhouse must examine hundreds of birdhouses a week. They don't have the time to look at every birdhouse unless there is a production breakdown, which gives them an opportunity to catch up. The work they do is very repetitive and boring. On occasion they get an opportunity to work on technological problems causing consistent quality problems. For the most part, however, their skills are not needed or used, since the manager of QC prefers to handle any of the really challenging work. As a result of boredom and lack of challenging work, there is a lot of turnover in this department. Aside from the manager of QC, the average tenure of QC personnel is 3 1/2 years.

QC personnel are responsible for determining the quality of the finished birdhouse based on a set of quality standards on the Quality Standards and Specifications List. (See next section.) They make the final decision to keep a finished birdhouse or to throw it away. They also prepare reports for the operations manager and accounting department.

Quality Standards and Specifications List

Custom Nests's standard birdhouse quality standards and specifications are

1. No lines are to be on the outside surfaces of the birdhouse.
2. All staples must face the inside of the birdhouse; the flat side of the staple should be on the outside surfaces of the birdhouse.
3. Tape should thoroughly cover the roof's center connection.
4. The stapler's employee number should appear on the bottom of the birdhouse.
5. There should be no gaps in any of the corners and connections.
6. The bottom width of the birdhouse should be as close to 3 1/2 inches as possible.
7. The sides should be between 3 and 3 1/4 inches high.
8. The length of the birdhouse should be between 5 1/2 and 6 inches.
9. The perch should stick out 1 1/2 to 2 inches from the front of the birdhouse.
10. The entry hole on the front panel should center 1 to 1 1/4 inches above the birdhouse floor.
11. The diameter of the entry should be between 2 and 2 1/4 inches.
12. No creases should appear in any of the flat surfaces of the birdhouse.
13. All folds in the front and rear panels should be very close to 1/4 inch.
14. All cuts made to prepare front and rear panels for folding should be close to 1/4 inch.
15. The finished birdhouse should sit flat on a table.

Research and Development

The research and development department is involved in the design of new products, the improvement of old products, customer relations, and marketing. This department was established in 1976. The housing market was declining and a new line of birdhouses was needed to meet the needs of apartment dwellers. In addition, the traditional Custom Nests product was becoming less effective. More and more home owners and distributors were complaining that the birdhouses were not squirrel proof. Ways had to be found to keep squirrels from climbing up the birdhouse pole or down from the trees above to steal birdseed from the beaks of hungry baby birds.

Members of the research and development (R&D) department spend most of their time at the drafting tables or out in the field talking with the customers and distributors of birdhouses. Little if any time is spent in the plant. Any design changes are decided upon by R&D personnel along with management, and these are communicated through the manager of operations, to the supervisor, and so forth. R&D reports directly to the owner, Mr. Jay Blue.

The R&D function is relatively new to the organization, and its personnel were hired from the outside. The turnover in the department is high. It seems to be a place where young designers get a chance to learn about the real world just after they have finished their engineering degrees. You therefore have probably been with the company for about 2 years. The pay is less than you expect to be able to make in the future, and the extent to which you are challenged in your work is unsatisfactory. It's just a job and a possible step to a better future.

Accounting

The accounting position was established in 1971 when two major developments occurred: (1) The company had been growing, and the owner was no longer able to manage the books and keep up with the growth of the business and (2) you married the boss's younger sister. You are fairly secure in your position, since you have been doing it for so long. In addition, your relationship with your brother-in-law is good. He confides in you a great deal, since he sees you as his friend and somebody concerned about the business. You must, however, work very hard because you have something to prove to the rest of the employees (that you are not a freeloader). You also know something your brother-in-law doesn't know—your wife is unhappy with your marriage, and you are worried about how that might affect your future, even though you know that your brother-in-law likes you better.

You have major responsibility for much of the management work in the plant. In addition to your accounting responsibilities, you order all materials and manage the shipping department. Recently you took over responsibility for employee relations when the employee relations manager was hospitalized for cardiac problems. You expected to have the job for a month or so, but that was 5 months ago, and the man's health is still uncertain. All you can really handle is some of the administrative trivia required by the union; you have had little time to talk with the employees about their grievances or their benefits.

Some of your specific accounting responsibilities include

1. Purchasing.
2. Supplying raw materials to maintenance/supply personnel.
3. Collecting data gathered by the material/supply department and the quality control department.
4. Analyzing the above collected data in six areas: total number of 4×6 cards distributed; total number of 4×6 cards used; number of birdhouses produced; number of birdhouses accepted; perches distributed and used; and waste.

You can use this data analysis worksheet for your analysis.

Accounting
Data Analysis Worksheet

Raw materials data

Total number of 4×6 cards distributed.   _____

Total number of 4×6 cards used.   _____

Total number of perches distributed.   _____

Total number of perches used.   _____

Waste.   _____

Quality control data

Number of birdhouses produced.   _____

Number of birdhouses accepted.   _____

Waste.   _____

Maintenance/Supply

Maintenance and supply personnel are primarily production people who have moved their way up through the system. None of you have any formal training in machine maintenance and repair, though your experience with the company has provided you with the skills to make simple repairs on the equipment used in the plant.

In an effort to cut costs, 2 years ago the supply function merged with maintenance. You consequently have the responsibility for maintaining equipment, supplying raw materials to all functions in the plant, and moving components from one function to another. You move throughout the plant and probably have the best information about the "goings on" in the plant. Unfortunately, there is little you can do with all of this information. You must report to and take orders from the supervisor in charge of production.

Your work is anything but boring, since you always have plenty to do. The problem is that you are spread too thin and are unable to do any single job to the best of your ability. This bothers you, since you have been with the company for a long time and know that product quality and employee morale have been better in the past.

The majority of the maintenance/supply personnel have been with the company for 25 years or more. Many of you are waiting for the opportunity to retire. Your wages and benefits are fair, but not as good as your counterparts in similar industries. Some of you could potentially leave Custom Nests in pursuit of maintenance jobs in other companies, but you know that the skills required here may be inadequate in another organization. Besides, you have been here for a long time, and you like the people. As a matter of fact, your ability to see and talk to a lot of people in the plant is one thing that motivates you to come to work.

Maintenance/Supply: Job Description

Your job is (1) to provide raw materials to each function in the plant: 4×6 cards to tapers and cutters, staples and straws to staplers, tape to tapers; (2) to transport finished components of the birdhouse to the next stage in the assembly process: transport front and rear panels from the cutters to the staplers, roofs and side/bottom components from the tapers to the staplers, and finished products from the staplers to quality control; (3) to repair or replace equipment used by cutters, staplers, and tapers; and (4) to maintain records of materials being supplied and components being transported from department to department and of finished birdhouses being transported to quality control.

Maintenance/Supply Inventory Sheet

Raw materials

4×6 cards supplied to tapers.   _____

4×6 cards supplied to cutters.   _____

Straws applied to staplers.   _____

Completed components (record finished sets)

Sets transported from taping to stapling
(a set consists of one completed roof and   _____
one completed side/bottom panel).

Sets transported from cutting to stapling
(a set consists of a front and rear panel   _____
cut and folded).

Completed birdhouses

Number of completed birdhouses transported   _____
to quality control.

Stapler

The stapler position, in the production area, is one of the most complex and highest-rated positions in the company. Most workers in this area have been with the company for 20 years or more and have worked in this area for at least 9 years. Most of you have worked your way up through the lower-skill positions, and one stapler was one of the original employees of the company. Because of your seniority, it is possible that a few of you will be retiring in a few years. Movement in this position means potential advancement for people in less-skilled positions. The position has the highest pay rate for production workers at Custom Nests, yet your wages are lower than your counterparts in similar industries. As a result, many of you are involved in the union's fight for higher wages. The fact that many of you grew up in the union movement has made you staunch union supporters.

The stapler's job is most dependent on the workmanship of the cutters and tapers who build the pieces of the birdhouse that you must assemble. For the most part, however, you will assemble the parts that you receive, and those you manufacture (perches) regardless of their condition. It is not your job to determine whether a part is good enough to use.

The technology that you utilize in the stapling function is rather simple, yet numerous technological problems arise on a regular basis. Parts are often hard to find, and maintenance is a challenge.

Although the work is more complex than other production jobs, you have found that with some experience, the work becomes simple and repetitive, and as a result it is often boring. The fact that you perform the final production function means that problems in other areas create work slowdowns or shutdowns for you.

Stapler: Job Description

Your job is (1) to staple the sides and bottom of the birdhouse to the front and rear panels, (2) to staple the roof to the front and rear panels of the birdhouse, and (3) to prepare and attach the perch to the birdhouse door.

Specific instructions and responsibilities are:

a. Attach the bottom/side component to the folds in the front and rear panels of the birdhouse.

b. Attach the roof component to the folds in the front and rear panels of the birdhouse.

c. Cut a 2 to 2 1/2-inch piece of straw.

d. Bend and attach the straw to the door of the birdhouse so that the perch extends out from the door 1 1/2 to 2 inches.

e. Make sure that all staples face inward. That is, the flat part of the staples should be on the outside surface of the final product, except for the staples in the bend at the floor. These should face the ground.

f. Place your employee number on the very bottom of the assembled product.

g. Transport the completed birdhouse to quality control.

Cutters

The cutters' position is one of the lower-paying hourly positions in the company. The majority of the workers in this area have been with the company for at least 13 years and have been in the cutting area for a minimum of 7 years. Over that time most of you have moved up through the organization, learning as you went and bidding on new jobs as they came open.

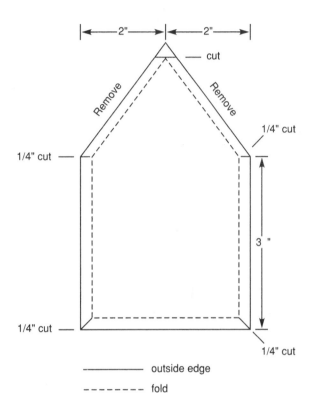

The cutting job tends to be rather boring once you have learned the work. It really takes little thinking for you to do what is expected of you.

Custom Nests pays a little less than other companies in the area. Your union has been pushing for the last couple of years to have wages raised to comparable standards. The company just says that the demand for birdhouses is expected to drop as a result of Japanese competition. The only way for you to make more money is to move to stapling or maintenance, but these jobs are hard to come by. The way you see it, cutting is going to be your job for the next few years.

Cutter: Job Description   The job of a cutter is (1) to cut and fold, from 4×6 cards supplied by the maintenance/supply personnel, the front and rear panels of the Custom Nests standard birdhouse and (2) to cut the birdhouse door in all front panels.

Specific responsibilities and panel design include:

a. Front and rear panels should be made consistent with the above drawing.

b. On all front panels a 2 to 2 1/4-inch hole must be cut 1 to 1 1/4 inches from the bottom of the front panel, and the hole should be centered.

c. The worker's number must be put on the back of each finished piece.

d. Finished goods (completed front and back panels) must be sent to the stapling department.

e. Panels should be identified as front or back on the lined side of the panel.

Tapers

The taper's job receives the lowest pay rate in the organization. People in this work area have been with the company for the least amount of time. Like other work areas, your pay rate is lower than most industries in similar markets, and you have been fairly active in the pursuit of higher wages. Unlike some people who have been with the company for several years, you have been fortunate enough to have received a full high school education and some of you have been to college. The job market in the past few years, however, has forced you to take work that underutilizes your abilities.

The perceived stability but no growth position in the birdhouse business means that there is likely to be little advancement for you in this business unless people in higher-ranked jobs either retire or die. As a result you come to work to make a living, to receive your benefits, and to kill time. The work is boring and simple, and it requires little thought.

Taper: Job Description

The job of taper requires that you (1) tape together two 4×6 cards to make the roof of the Custom Nests standard birdhouses and (2) tape together and fold three 4×6 cards to make the sides and bottom of the birdhouses.

Job specifications are listed below:

a. Two cards taped together at their longest side make the roof. The tape should be applied so that no water can leak into the birdhouse.

b. The three cards utilized for the sides and bottom must be folded and taped together so that the bottom is 3 1/2 inches wide and the sides are 3 to 3 1/4 inches tall. Two seams requiring one long strip of tape each are all that are needed based on the original design of the birdhouse. Tape is a most expensive material and must be used with cost in mind.

c. Tapers' numbers should be put on the underside of each roof and floor/side structure produced in your department.

d. Your finished products must be transported to the stapling department.

e. Tapers should identify each part as a roof or floor. All identification markings should be written on the lined side of the 4×6 card.

**Activity 15–4:
Analyzing the
Team Climate**

This activity should be the most interesting and important learning experience in the course and requires a large block of time. One or two evenings could be valuably devoted to it.

Objectives:

a. To apply the team-building approach to your own work team.

b. To generate the data for completion of the individual or team term paper on team development.

Task 1:

a. Each team member, working alone, is to complete the Climate Attribute Scales that follow prior to coming to the team meeting, which is to be held outside of class.

b. Review your journal analysis of how course concepts and team skills have applied to your team's interactions as the team evolved during the course. Be prepared to present your observations at the team meeting.

Task 2:

Team members are to meet and discuss the climate attributes one at a time. Each member will report the rating made prior to the meeting. The differences in ratings will be discussed to determine why members are perceiving the team interactions differently. After thorough discussion a group consensus rating will be made for each scale. The group consensus rating sheet will be included and discussed in the final team development report.

The rating sheet given here is only a device to help introduce this session. Now make an analysis of how course concepts and theories applied to your team as it evolved during the course. How did team skills develop? Having reviewed your journals before the meeting, a synergistic exchange should result in added insight into these processes. One approach that might be used is for members to call out in rapid succession all possible topics the group might want to discuss. One member should list these for the group. After members have exhausted ideas for the list, the items can be taken up one at a time for discussion. Conclude this portion of the session by answering the following: If this team were to work together in the future, how could it improve its effectiveness? Be specific.

Feedback Session (an Optional Activity): Teams are to give each member feedback as to what they perceive to be the individual's strengths and the areas where the individual could be stronger in team interactions. If the team members are supportive of one another and an openness-to-learning, concern-for-growth atmosphere exists, this experience can be valuable. Knowing what impact one is having on others and how one is coming across is important in one's effectiveness. But the atmosphere must be right so that the individuals hear what others say without becoming defensive. As we have seen throughout this course, being able to receive feedback from one's superiors, peers, and subordinates is widely advocated as an area for improved effectiveness for managers. Feedback sessions are one of the best sources of data for your team paper. But remember, the team feedback is optional—only the team can decide if it wishes to complete it. No individual should be pressured. If an individual decides not to participate in this portion of the exercise, he or she should not do so.

Task 3:

Your team will have an opportunity to discuss this team-building session in a later class and to hear the other teams discuss theirs. These sessions are best when they are spontaneous and all team members participate, so do not prepare.

Name _____   Date _____

Climate Attribute Scales

Climate Attribute

Write an X on the scale to indicate the degree to which the attribute characterizes your team's activities and members.

To a low degree   *To a high degree*

Climate Attribute	Scale
Commitment to the task	0 1 2 3 4 5 6 7 8 9
Openness to learning	0 1 2 3 4 5 6 7 8 9
Retired-on-the-job attitudes	0 1 2 3 4 5 6 7 8 9
Candor and forthrightness	0 1 2 3 4 5 6 7 8 9
Attentive listening for understanding	0 1 2 3 4 5 6 7 8 9
Conviction to stand up for honestly held views	0 1 2 3 4 5 6 7 8 9
Defensiveness or lack of trust	0 1 2 3 4 5 6 7 8 9
Being too polite, being too considerate, smoothing over differences	0 1 2 3 4 5 6 7 8 9
Avoidance of conflict	0 1 2 3 4 5 6 7 8 9
Experimental, innovative	0 1 2 3 4 5 6 7 8 9
Attempts to dominate	0 1 2 3 4 5 6 7 8 9
Cutting people off	0 1 2 3 4 5 6 7 8 9
Interest in one another as people	0 1 2 3 4 5 6 7 8 9
Consideration for others	0 1 2 3 4 5 6 7 8 9
Willingness to express feelings, each person saying "where he or she is"	0 1 2 3 4 5 6 7 8 9
Expressing feelings in a way acceptable to others	0 1 2 3 4 5 6 7 8 9
Paraphrasing for better understanding	0 1 2 3 4 5 6 7 8 9
Perceptual checking	0 1 2 3 4 5 6 7 8 9
Willingness to confront differences in ideas	0 1 2 3 4 5 6 7 8 9

Climate Attribute Scales (concluded)

Write in any other attributes that you believe characterize your team.

Climate Attribute

Write an X on the scale to indicate the degree to which the attribute characterizes your team's activities and members.

To a low degree   *To a high degree*

_____

| 0 | 1 | 2 | 3 | 4 | 5 | 6 | 7 | 8 | 9 |

_____

| 0 | 1 | 2 | 3 | 4 | 5 | 6 | 7 | 8 | 9 |

_____

| 0 | 1 | 2 | 3 | 4 | 5 | 6 | 7 | 8 | 9 |

**Activity 15–5:
Team Feedback
Discussion**

Objective:

To allow each team to share its learning experience in small group dynamics with the other teams.

Task 1:

The instructor will select one team to sit in a circle in the center of the class. Members of the team will spontaneously discuss, without the benefit of notes, what types of group dynamics learning they gained from the team project exercise. Topics that could be covered include how the group dynamic concepts applied to their team, how conflict was handled, how each member felt about his or her role and the role of others in the group, how the group could be more effective if it were to continue, and anything else that seems important to the group. The team should not be interrupted by outside questions at this time.

Time for questions from the other teams should be provided when the team has completed the discussion.

Each team will have its allotted time in the circle.

Task 2:

The instructor will comment at the end of each team discussion and summarize at the end of the session.

(*Note to instructor:* Be sure to read *Instructor's Manual* before using this exercise.)

**Activity 15–6:
Feedback on
Effectiveness of
the Course and
the Instructor**

Objectives:

a. To reinforce learning by participants sharing what they perceive to be course strengths.

b. To provide the instructor with data for improved effectiveness.

Task 1:

The instructor is to leave the room.

Teams that have met throughout the course are each to appoint a spokesperson who will record the team's answers to the following questions:

a. What are the course's strengths? How could it be improved?

b. In what ways is the instructor effective? How could he or she be more effective?

Any member of the team can give an evaluative comment to the spokesperson. His or her identity will be protected; the spokesperson's report is the anonymous judgments of the team members. However, objectivity is urged. Some teams may conclude on their own that a comment will be included only if the majority of the members agree on its validity.
(Time: 20 minutes)

Task 2:

The instructor is to return to the classroom.

Class participants are to arrange themselves in a giant circle around the room, with team members sitting in adjacent seats. The instructor should take a seat on the circle where he or she is able to make eye contact with all class members.

The instructor calls on each spokesperson to discuss the strengths of the course. On the second round, the spokesperson should discuss how the course should be improved; on the third round, discuss the instructor's effectiveness; and on the last round, discuss how the instructor should improve. After each round the instructor should ask whether anyone other than the spokesperson wishes to comment.

The role of the instructor is to hear what the participants are saying. Periodic paraphrasing of what has been said will help ensure understanding. Avoid trying to justify or explain what has taken place in the course because participants might interpret that as a defensive response.

Glossary

A

accommodating orientation   a conflict-handling mode where one group attempts to satisfy the concerns of the other by neglecting its own concerns and goals.

achievement-oriented leadership   a path–goal leadership style where the leader is preoccupied with setting challenging goals for the work group.

action orientation   a focus on doing or acting as opposed to planning.

action research   an emergent inquiry process in which behavioral and social science knowledge is integrated with existing organizational knowledge to produce new, usable knowledge.

actors   employees or the human organization.

administrative school   a classical management approach led by Henry Fayol; focused on the five basic functions of management-planning, organizing, commanding, coordinating, and controlling.

adult learner   individual beyond adolescence engaged in learning.

age diversity   a broad age distribution in organizations.

age stereotype   belief that differing traits and abilities make a certain age group more or less suited to different roles or display different behavior toward work.

appreciative inquiry   focus on appreciating and valuing the best of what is, envisioning what might be, and dialoguing on what should be. Viewed as a cycle composed of four basic elements: discovery, dream, design, and destiny.

assertiveness   the degree to which the group wants to satisfy its own concerns.

attribution theory   relationship between perception and individual behavior.

avoidance orientation   a conflict-handling approach in which both groups neglect the concerns involved by sidestepping issues or postponing conflict by choosing not to deal with it.

B

behavior modification   an attempt to change behavior by operant conditioning, that is, voluntary behavior is rewarded and incorrect behavior is ignored or punished.

behavioral leadership theory   an approach that attempts to identify what good leaders do.

behavioral science school   a neoclassical management approach that was an outgrowth of the human relations school; focused on individual behavior within work groups.

Big Five personality theory   theory postulating that there are five factors of personality—extraversion, agreeableness, conscientiousness, emotional stability and openness to experience—that can serve as a meaningful taxonomy for classifying personality attributes.

brainstorming   a group thought-generation process that revolves around the spontaneous, uncontained expression of ideas.

C

charismatic leaders   individuals who, by sheer strength of their personality, effect strong influence over others.

classical era   period of management thought from 1880s to 1930s; early studies centered on the search for alternative ways to organize and structure the industrial organization and the ways to motivate people who work within the emerging organizational structures.

collaborating orientation   a conflict-handling mode that attempts to satisfy the concerns of both groups.

common enemy   an organization's closest competitor that can often inspire teams that are in conflict to work together.

communication   the transfer of information from one person to another.

communication dialoguing   open exchange of views, beliefs, and when appropriate, feelings, between individuals or groups; it implies hearing each other out and listening for understanding.

communication media   the means by which messages are conveyed, such as conversation, computers, and body language.

communication network   the flow, pattern, and pathway of signals or codes between two or more individuals.

competitive orientation   a conflict-handling mode in which the groups attempt to achieve their own goals at the expense of the other through argument, authority, threat, or even physical force.

compromising orientation   a conflict-handling mode that involves give-and-take from both groups.

computer networks   the software, hardware, logistics, and connection between computers that allow and facilitate the conveyance of information (electronic impulses) between them.

conflict   opposing thoughts, actions, or feelings.

conflict-handling mode   methods of resolving or eliminating opposing thoughts, actions, or feelings.

consensus process   a group process in which the ideas of all individuals are contributed and evaluated fully in arriving at a decision.

consideration   a leadership behavior that creates mutual respect by focusing on group members' needs and desires.

content learning   learning based on knowledge, facts, and theory, which serve as the database for analysis and reasoning.

content theories of motivation   a cluster of theories that emphasize understanding reasons for motivated behavior or the specific factors that cause it.

contingency school   decisions made or actions taken after considering all of the most relevant factors in a situation; in other words, management is situational.

continuous improvement   ongoing effort and commitment to producing quality products and services.

cooperativeness   the degree to which the group wants to satisfy the concerns of the other group.

creativity   an individual's ability to take bits and pieces of seemingly unrelated information and synthesize the pieces into new understanding or useful ideas.

cross-functional teams   an alternative viable way to bring together people with knowledge and skills from various functional areas to work on a specific task. Many organizations use cross-functional teams as an effective means for allowing individuals from diverse areas within the organization to exchange information, identify problems, develop new ideas, solve problems, and coordinate complex projects. Cross-functional teams cut across departmental and functional boundaries.

cultural diversity   individual differences in behavior, values, beliefs, and motivation based on cultural heritage.

cultural racism   extent to which groups believe that their cultural features and achievements are superior to those of other cultural groups.

cultural values   personal beliefs (about such things as morality, worthiness, or beauty) that have been reinforced through lifelong learning.

culture   a pattern of basic assumptions and beliefs proved valid over time and taught to new group members as correct reactions to certain problems and opportunities.

D

decoding   the interpretation of encoded information once communicated and received.

demographic diversity   individual differences based on characteristics such as gender, age, marital status, number of dependents, and tenure with a firm.

denial   a defense mechanism in which an individual is not aware of his or her own needs or concerns and denies they exist.

design dimensions   the elements that are considered in configuring an organization including information processing requirements, the roles and mechanisms that integrate the work, and management systems.

deviant   an individual who refuses to conform to the group norms and is consequently rejected by members.

differentiation   an aspect of the organization's internal environment created by job specialization and the division of labor.

directive leadership   characterized by a leader who informs subordinates of what is expected of them, gives specific guidance as to what should be done, and shows how to do it.

distortion   the misrepresentation of the meaning of a fact, feeling or experience.

diversity   a mix of people in one social system who have distinctly different, socially relevant group affiliation.

diversity-based conflict   clashes between groups due to the nature of diversity, such as race, gender, religion, and ethnicity.

E

eclectic planned change approach   an orientation to organization change that pulls together the strengths of total quality management (TQM), sociotechnical systems (STS), and reengineering.

effectiveness   the ability to define goals and objectives then accomplish them. Efficiency, in contrast, pertains to the ratio of output to input.

emergent role system   the activities, interactions, and attitudes that spontaneously develop as individuals strive to follow the organization script but also satisfy their own needs.

employee involvement   the participation of employees in interactions with managers, in decision making, and problem solving.

employee stock ownership plans (ESOP)   a type of profit-sharing plan wherein employees acquire company stock with the benefit of company subsidization.

encoding   the forming of information to be communicated into codes or symbols that are meaningful to the sender, and ideally to the receiver.

equifinality   a principle that states there are many avenues to the same outcome, and not just one best way.

equity theory   the premise that individuals want their efforts and performance to be judged fairly relative to other individuals.

expectancy effects   the results or consequences of beliefs about one's abilities or performance.

expectancy theory   a person's perceived probability that the level of the effort will lead to a desired level of performance.

expectation   a judgment of the likely consequence that a behavior will produce.

experiential learning   learning based on or from experience, such as interaction, involvement, or process learning.

external environment factors   also called "wider environment" refers to the factors that can be found outside the firm. They include (1) the market for the product involved; (2) potential competition, both national and international; (3) economic factors such as interest and inflation rates and the value of the dollar; (4) sources of supply; and (5) government regulations and legislation. These and many other factors related to economics, politics, social conditions, and technological development may have varying degrees of importance in the functioning of an organization.

F

family group   an intact, ongoing work team.

flexible work schedule   work schedules that give employees the latitude and freedom to determine their work hours.

formal organization   a script which includes the purpose and functional roles of the employees, the coordination of the interactions between the employees' roles and the nature of the different types of work to be performed, and the status accorded to the different work roles by the employees or public.

forms of structure   the method of grouping employees together into work units, departments, and the total organization.

four life positions of personality development   four perspectives on life that adults develop as a result of the treatment they received from the parents: (1) I'm not OK, you're OK; (2) I'm not OK, you're not OK; (3) I'm OK, you're not OK; and (4) I'm OK, you're OK.

G

gender diversity   a mixture of both men and women in organizations.

goal setting   goals are associated with enhanced performance because they mobilize effort, direct attention, and encourage persistence and strategy development.

group   a set of three or more individuals that can identify itself and be identified by others in the organization as an entity.

group cohesiveness   the attractiveness of the group to its members; the degree to which members desire to stay in the group.

group development   the process by which a group adapts to internal and environmental forces.

group dynamics   the patterns of behaviors of interacting members as a group develops and achieves goals.

group maturity   a developmental state of a group that is inclusive of several attitudes and skills, such as the acceptance of individual differences, development of interpersonal relationships, and others, that indicate a highly functional group with wisdom about the group-decision process.

group problem-solving process   the phases a group goes through in solving problems (can be either rational and/or intuitive).

group size   effective team size ranges from 3 members to a normal upper limit of about 16 members; optimal size seems to be correlated with the degree of project complexity and leadership competence, most argue that effective work groups range in size from 7 to 12 members.

group structure   reference to certain psychologically shared properties of the group that result from the interaction of its members.

groupthink   the mode of thinking when pressure toward conformity (concurrence seeking) becomes so dominant in a group that members override realistic appraisal of alternative courses of action.

groupware   computer programs that allow for sharing information via computer networks.

H

hierarchy of needs   Maslow's theory that psychological needs have a hierarchical interrelationship; those lower in the hierarchy (physiological needs) have to be satisfied before those in higher categories (safety, social, self-esteem, and self-actualization) become activated.

hidden agenda   a purpose that the individual or group does not wish to reveal; the intent is to manipulate others so this purpose can be achieved.

horizontal conflict   clashes between groups of employees at the same level.

horizontal organization   a type of design that is organized around processes and adoption of information technology.

hot team   example of a highly cohesive team; such a team performs extremely well and is dedicated to both the team and to task accomplishment; members of such a team are turned on by an exciting and challenging goal; hot teams completely engage their members to the exclusion of almost everything else; such teams can be characterized as teams with vitality; they are absorbing, full of debate and laughter, and very hard working.

human organization   employees or "actors."

human relations school   a classical management approach that viewed organizations as cooperative systems and not the product of mechanical engineering; early studies illustrated the importance of workers' attitudes and feelings.

hygiene factors   characteristics of the workplace, such as company policies, working conditions, pay, and supervision that make a job more satisfying.

I

imaginization process   a highly visual method to explore organizational problems and to find ways for building team cultures in different settings; individuals are free to capture and express their views through images, feelings, words, drawings, colors, or whatever medium seems appropriate.

individual differences   differences based on behavior, demographics, cultural background, personality, and ability or skills.

individual learning   change of skills, insights, knowledge, attitudes, and values acquired by a person through self-study, technology-based instruction, insight, and observation.

individual racism   extent to which a person holds values, feelings, and attitudes and/or engages in behavior that promotes the person's own racial group as superior.

information-processing design approach   a decision-making process that includes choices about goals, tasks to be accomplished, technology to be adopted, ways to organize, and ways to integrate individuals into the organization.

information technology   technologies dealing with computers, communications, user interfaces, storage, software, artificial intelligence, robotics, and manufacturing.

initiating structure   a task-related leadership dimension covering a wide variety of behaviors including role definition and the guidance of subordinates toward attainment of work group goals.

integrated learning mechanism   organizational structure and processes that focus on improving the organization's learning capacity, that is fully integrated with the existing formal structure in the organization.

integration   the degree to which differentiated work units work together and coordinate their efforts.

intergroup communication   message transmission between groups.

intergroup conflict   opposing thoughts, feelings or actions between work units.

internal environment factor   also called "task environment" refers to factors that can be found within the organization. They include (1) ownership; (2) acquisition and layout of physical facilities; (3) finances; (4) technology (selection of equipment, machines, and methods); (5) work design; and (6) workflow. Plans and procedures of the manufacturing process are included here, but the required behavioral roles of the managers and employees are not.

interpersonal communication   message transmission between individuals.

interpersonal skills   human or people skills; the ability to lead, motivate, and communicate effectively with others.

intervention   method or technique for achieving change, which is targeted at the individual, group, or organizational level.

intragroup communication   message transmission within a group.

intragroup conflict   opposing thought, action, or feelings between group members.

involvement-process learning   places primary emphasis on the process of interaction and thinking, rather than on memory of factual content of the area being studied.

J

job engineering   a term synonymous with scientific management. Seeks one best way of performing a job, scientific methods of work performance, production, standards, rigid time frames, and motivation by monetary reward.

job enlargement   increasing the variety of activities in a job to stimulate interest and reduce fatigue and monotony.

job rotation   rotation among jobs to stimulate interest and reduce fatigue and monotony.

job sharing   dividing a job between two or more employees.

Jung's theory of personality   theory postulating that individuals have four basic preferences in the way they approach life: (1) introversion or extraversion; (2) intuition or sensing; (3) thinking or feeling; and (4) judging or perceiving.

K

keiretsu   networks of industrial, transportation, and financial Japanese companies; cooperation extends beyond vertical and horizontal supply, product, and financial links to include alliances with other companies, research institutions, and universities.

kinesic behavior   body motion, such as gestures, facial expression, eye behavior, and touching.

L

leadership   the behavior of an individual when he or she is directing the activities of a group toward a shared goal.

leadership style   an individual's expectation about how to use a leadership position to involve himself or herself and other people in the achievement of results.

lean production system   an operation that strives to achieve the highest possible productivity and total quality cost effectively, by eliminating unnecessary steps in the production process and continually striving for improvement.

learning   the process whereby new skills, knowledge, ability, and attitudes are created through the transformation of experience.

learning community   classroom interactions shaped to create norms, values, and roles conducive to a supportive and stimulating learning climate.

learning organization   an organization characterized by a particular culture, climate, managerial pattern, and capacity that enable the entity to improve itself systematically and over time.

least preferred co-worker (LPC)   description of an individual with whom a manager has worked least well.

line-staff conflict   clashes between advisory/support teams and teams that are responsible for creating the goods and services

M

macro organization design model   an outgrowth of information processing theory where all design choices are driven by information technology and cultural variables.

maintenance role   a functional role that develops spontaneously and allows a group to develop constructive interpersonal relationships.

management   the process of working with people and resources to accomplish organizational goals.

management by objectives   a system that serves both as a planning tool and a motivational philosophy; this approach reflects synthesis of three areas: goal setting, participative decision making, and feedback.

management science school   a classical management approach that applied scientific methods to analyze and determine the "one best way" to complete production tasks.

management teams   supervisory teams that are created to provide coordination and direction to the subunits under their jurisdiction, laterally integrating interdependent subunits across key business processes.

managing culture   assumes that the manager knows what he or she would manage; assumes that the manager is outside the culture and can (and should) act on it; also assumes a one-way causation—the manager shapes the culture, not the other way around.

media richness   ability of a medium to change human understanding, overcome different conceptual frames of reference, or clarify ambiguous issues in a timely manner.

message   what is communicated.

modern era   the current period of management thought; views organizations as systems composed of interrelated and interdependent components that function within an environmental concept.

motivation theory   psychological energy directed toward goals.

N

n achievement   need for achievement; a need characterized by a strong orientation toward accomplishment and a high focus on success and goal attainment.

n power   need for power; a need characterized by a desire to influence or control other people.

negative entropy   the conscious changing of purpose, goals and practices to match emerging environmental demands.

neoclassical era   a period of management from the 1930s to 1960s that posed a direct challenge to the classical school; focused on the dimension of human interaction with the setting and other individuals in a group.

network organization   an organizational form that blends traditional management concepts such as the value or management planning and controls with market concepts such as exchange agreement.

new product development teams (NPDT)   small groups of workers that collectively have the knowledge and skills needed to facilitate the introduction of new products from conception to production.

nominal group technique   a structured group problem-solving process in which individuals first write their ideas independently, discuss them for clarification, vote on them, discuss them again, and finally vote on them silently (nominal in the sense of being little more than a group by name alone).

nonverbal communication   message transmission without the exchange of words, such as body language.

norm   expectations shared by group members of how they ought to behave under a given set of circumstances.

O

open system   a perspective that expands the study of management to include the interaction between the organization and its environment.

operational blueprint   guide for managers when establishing a manufacturing organization or when attempting to understand one that is already in operation.

organization   entity created for the basic purpose of accomplishing tasks that individuals cannot accomplish alone.

organization design   work design at the organizational level; a decision process.

organization learning   principles, activities, processes, and structures that enable the organization to create, acquire, and transfer knowledge to continuously improve products, services, practices, processes, and financial results.

organizational behavior (OB)   (1) the study of the interactions of people as they carry out functional activities in organizations; (2) tools of analysis, applications, and skills development, including theories, concepts, models, and technologies. OB involves the application of the behavioral sciences (for example, sociology, social psychology, and social anthropology) to organizational activities. A "micro" approach starts with the focus on the individual and expands to interactions, groups, intergroup activities, and so on. A "macro" approach begins at the organizational level—or even the interorganizational, industrial, or institutional level—to improve understanding and the ability to predict and influence behavior. The emphasis is on improved effectiveness of individual, group, intergroup, and organizational activities.

organizational change and development (OC&D) program   a program or organization diagnosis and intervention that addresses the norms seen as barriers to effective individual and organizational functioning.

organizational culture   the pattern of basic assumptions that a given group has invented, discovered, or developed in learning to cope with problems of external adaptation and internal integration.

organizational development   an effort planned, organizationwide, and managed from top down, to increase organizational effectiveness and health through planned interventions in the organization's processes using behavioral, social, and economic science knowledge.

organizational diagnosis   an identification of the norms, procedures, and general climate of the organization.

organizational learning   a system of principles, activities, processes, and structures that enable an organization to realize the potential inherent in the knowledge and experience of its human capital.

organizational learning mechanisms   structural and process configurations that enhance the organizational capacity of learning.

P

P–L (Porter–Lawler) model   an individual approach model of motivation that relates effort to performance.

paralanguage   a type of nonverbal communication consisting of voice quality, volume, speech rate, pitch, nonfluencies (e.g., yaa, um, and ah) and laughing.

parallel learning mechanism   based on establishing an organizational structure that operates parallel to the existing formal-bureaucratic structure and constitutes a microcosm of the existing organization.

parallel learning structure   a specific division and coordination of labor that operates in tandem with the formal hierarchy and structure and has the purpose of increasing the organization's learning.

parallel teams   people who are pulled together from different work units or jobs to perform functions that the regular organization is not equipped to perform well.

participative leadership   a path–goal leadership style that emphasizes consultation with subordinates before decisions are made.

participative management   an employee's involvement in decisions relevant to his or her work.

part-time, temporary, and leased employees   employees who work only part-time or on a nonpermanent basis allowing managers to staff the workplace according to peaks and valleys in work demands, while driving down wage and benefit costs.

path–goal theory   a theory that concerns how leaders influence subordinates' perceptions of their work goals and the paths they follow toward attainment of those goals.

perception   patterns of meaning that come to the individual through the five senses.

perceptual process mental and cognitive processes that enable people to interpret and understand their surroundings.

personal growth the process of understanding personality and its influence in the interpersonal communications process, establishing personal goals, and developing the thinking and behavioral skills needed to achieve those goals.

personality the compilation of emotions, thoughts, background, and behavior that give a person his or her identity.

planned change an attempt to consciously and deliberately bring about change in the organization's status quo.

premature closure forming expressions on limited data, such as in stereotyping.

prescientific era period of management thought before the 1880s characterized by trial and error and includes practices of ancient Chinese, Greeks and Romans.

process organization an enhancement of ideas from sociotechnical systems theory in which the object is to improve business results such as quicker time to market, increased focus on customer needs and lower costs.

projection defense mechanism of interpreting the world or action of others in terms of one's own needs and concerns; unawareness of one's needs is implied.

project teams time-limited teams that have to produce one-time output such as a new product or service to be marketed by the company.

process learning learning that arises from interacting or thinking; see experiential learning.

process theories of motivation theories that attempt to understand and explain the elements that foster individual choices of behavior patterns and the forces that increase the likelihood the behaviors will repeat.

profit-sharing plans benefit programs that link employee compensation with organization profits.

proxemics a type of nonverbal communication comprised of the ways people use and perceive space (e.g., seating arrangements and conversational distance).

psychological contract the understanding between the worker and the organization in which each is aware of the other's expectations concerning important issues such as rights, privileges, obligations, etc.

Pygmalion effect self-fulfilling beliefs that influence a favorable change in behavior.

Q

quality control circles (QCC) a group of employees who meet periodically to study and solve job-related problems.

R

race stereotype belief that differing traits and abilities make a certain individual, cultural, or institutional group more or less suited to different roles or display different behavior toward work.

rational problem solving a methodical, systematic approach to a solution (described by some as left-hemisphere focus).

rationality based on logic and reason; contrast with irrationality, which emphasizes feelings, faith, emotions, impulses, and intuitions.

rationalization finding a good reason rather than the real reason for your action.

reengineering the fundamental rethinking and radical redesign of business processes to achieve dramatic improvements in critical contemporary measures of performance such as cost, quality, service, and speed.

reinforcement theories of motivation an approach that concentrates on behavior (rather than needs, for example) and the ability to change behavior by reward, avoidance, or punishment.

relationship-focused conflict clashes between groups over working relations.

relationship behavior actions whereby a leader engages in two-way or multiway communication.

required role system the interlocking of the role behaviors of a specific position with those of one or more other roles in the basic work group to form a system.

required system the behavioral requirements of the role an individual plays when performing the tasks of a specific work position, it can refer to the entire network of interacting roles that make up the total formal organization, but is frequently used synonymously with required role system.

role behavior pattern of behavior an individual learns in order to perform tasks and relate to people while fulfilling the responsibilities of a given position.

role differentiation patterns of behavior that develop for individual group members, and are repeated as the activities of the group process.

S

scientific management approach see job engineering.

scientific management school an innovative concept of the early 1900s that emphasized developing efficiency through specialized and standardized work tasks.

script a set of requirements the individual must perform to complete tasks and interact with others.

self-design approach an approach to job design that encourages managers to plan and to implement their own strategy/structure and change programs.

self-efficacy a judgment of one's capability to accomplish a certain level of performance in a situation.

self-fulfilling prophecy (Pygmalion) beliefs that influence the direction of the outcome.

self-learning competency the capability to learn actively in a variety of situations.

self-managed work team (SMWT) consists of employees who work on relatively whole tasks (such as assembling a car or a major auto component) and are responsible for managing the task that will result in a product or service being delivered; team members are typically responsible for handling all or most aspects of the work and performing all the technical tasks involved; technical tasks are typically rotated among team members, as are management responsibilities, such as monitoring the team's productivity and quality.

semantics word meanings; particularly various meanings for the same word.

sex-role stereotype belief that differing traits and abilities make men and women particularly well suited to different roles.

skill-based pay alternative to job-based pay that bases pay levels on the number of skills the individual has mastered.

situational leadership management whose direction is guided by its response to the existing conditions.

small group leadership an emergent role within groups that may include monitoring, taking action, and could be task- or maintenance-oriented.

sociotechnical systems (STS) organizations are comprised of a social subsystem (people) and technical subsystems (machines, technology) and the environmental suprasystem. The goal is to optimize the "fit" among the systems to ensure organizational effectiveness.

sociotechnical systems design approach an approach to job design that attempts to redesign tasks to optimize operation of a new technology while preserving employee's interpersonal relationships and other human aspects of the work.

sociotechnical systems school a modern management approach that considers every organization to be made up of a social subsystem (the people) using tools, techniques, and knowledge (the technical subsystem) to produce a product or a service valued by the environmental subsystem.

social intervention approaches   workshop methods that are used to reduce conflict and promote collaboration between groups.

social loafing   an effect where total effort expended by a group is less than the sum of individual efforts.

special groups   work groups that have a limited life span, such as start-up teams, special project teams and task forces.

steady state   maintaining the operations of a system within the limits of tolerance related to its targets.

stereotypes   beliefs assumed to apply to a particular group.

strategic intention   what a group attempts to accomplish in satisfying their own and others' goals.

strategic organization design   a decision-making process that focuses on customers, changing market needs, and desired outcomes.

structuralist school   a classical management approach led by Max Weber; focused on the basic tenets of the ideal type of organization, the bureaucratic model, as the most effective way to organize and manage organizations.

superordinate goals   primary goals of an organization or competing groups that exceed those of individuals or subgroups.

supportive leadership   characterized by a leader who creates mutual respect by focusing on group members' needs and desires; see consideration.

synergy   a group solution or decision in which the total effect is greater than the sum of the individual inputs, or 2 + 2 = 5.

system   a regularly interacting or interdependent group of activities or objects that forms a whole. Dynamics are involved in that a change in one aspect an effect change in other aspects.

system boundary   a physical, temporal, social or psychological border that separates one system from the other.

systems school   a modern management approach anchored in general system theory, views the organization as a system composed of subsystems or subunits that are mutually dependent on one another and that continuously interact.

T

task behavior   actions whereby a leader engages in spelling out duties and responsibilities of an individual or group.

task-focused conflict   clashes between groups over tasks, working conditions, and pay.

task role   a functional role assumed spontaneously that helps a group to define, clarify, and pursue a common goal.

team   a small number of people with complementary skills who are committed to a common purpose, set of performance goals, and approach for which they hold themselves mutually accountable.

team building   a process for helping a team diagnose its problems and become a more effective working unit.

team effectiveness   the performance and viability of a work team. Performance is the acceptability of output to customer within and outside the organization. Viability refers to team members' satisfaction and continued willingness to contribute.

team learning   alludes to the increase in knowledge, skills, and competencies that is accomplished by and within groups.

team management   a style of management in which each person in the nonsupervisory structure must be a member of an effective work group and must be skilled in both leadership and membership functions and roles.

team style   a method of preparation that a work group develops over time.

total quality management (TQM)   an integrative approach to management that supports the attainment of customer satisfaction through a wide variety of tools and techniques that result in high quality goods and services.

360-degree leadership feedback   psychometric instruments designed to measure on-the-job development; individuals are rated by themselves, their peers, bosses, and employees on theory-based leadership skills.

traits and skills theory   an approach that focuses on individual leaders and attempts to determine the personal characteristics and abilities that great leaders have.

transformation process   the conversion of materials and energy from the environment into outputs.

transformational leadership   the process of influencing major changes in the attitudes and assumptions of the organization's members and building commitment for the organization's mission or objectives.

V

vertical conflict   clashes between employee groups at different levels.

virtual work team   group of people working closely together, even though they may not be working on the same time schedule or at the same physical space; team members can be separated by many miles and even be on different continents.

W

work teams   continuing work units responsible for producing goods or providing services.

Index

Deaux, K., 11-16
Decision making, 6-6
  theory, 1-12
Decoding, 12-12
De Geus, A., 14-13
Delbecq, A. L., 5-20
Del Boca, F. K., 11-1
DeMeuse, K. P., 7-18, 7-19
DeMuse, K. P., 6-18
Den Hertog, J. F., 15-27
Denkbaar, B., 15-27
DePaulo, B. M., 11-16
DeSanctis, G., 5-21
Design, 2-11
Design dimensions, 13-6
De Sitter, L. U., 15-27
Desselles, M. L., 6-19
Destiny, 2-11
Devadas, S., 5-21
Deviant, 6-10
Devil's advocate, 6-14
Dewey, J., 2-13
DiAngelo, J. A., 12-19
Dickson, M. W., 6-18, 6-20
Dickson, W., 1-15
Differentiation, 13-9
Digman, J. M., 9-15
Directive leadership, 3-12
Discovery, 2-11
Diskill, J. E., 6-18
Dissatisfiers, 10-8
Diversity, 9-5
Diversity-based conflict, 8-6
Dobbins, G. H., 11-16
Docherty, P., 13-21, 15-27
Dolan, M., 6-20
Dominator, 6-10
Donnelly, J. H., Jr., 12-19
Dream, 2-11
Drucker, Peter, 10-17
Dyer, W. G., 7-15, 7-18

E

Eagle, J., 6-19
Eagly, A. H., 11-16
Earley, P. C., 5-21
Eclectic planned change approach, 15-21-15-23
Eden, D., 2-13, 7-16, 7-19, 10-18, 10-19, 10-25, 11-11, 11-17
Edmondson, A. C., 15-26
Effectiveness, defined, 1-7
Elden, M., 13-21
Elliott, O., 13-20, 15-27
Elsass, P. M., 5-20
Emergent role system, 1-14
Emergent social system, 6-3
Emery, E., 15-27
Emery, F. E., 1-15, 13-15, 13-21
Emery, M., 13-21
Emery Air Freight, 10-19, 10-20
Emotional climate models, 6-15-6-16

Employee stock ownership plan (ESOP), 10-17-10-18
Encoding, 12-12
Encourager, 6-10
Engelstad, P. H., 15-27
Equifinality, 4-9
Equity theory, 10-13
Essler, U., 7-19
European Economic Community (EEC), 9-5
Evaluator/critic, 6-10
Expectancy theory, 10-13-10-14
Experiential learning, 2-8, 2-10
Exxon, 1-5, 1-6, 14-6, 14-7
Ezzamel, M., 7-18

F

Fabun, D., 11-16, 12-19
Falkenberg, L., 11-9, 11-16
Family groups, 7-13
Farh, J. L., 11-16
Fayol, H., 1-10, 1-11, 1-15
Feedback, 3-16, 4-8
Feedback to Managers, 3-18
Felten, D. F., 13-20, 15-27
The Female Advantage: Women's Ways of Leadership (Helegsen), 3-20
Ference, R., 6-20
Fernandez, J. P., 9-15, 11-16
Fiedler, F., 3-10, 3-11, 3-23
Fiedler's contingency model, 3-10-3-11
Figuera, J. R., 5-21
Financial Times, 9-28
Fink, S. L., 4-18
Fiol, C. M., 4-17
Fisher, C. D., 9-15
Fiske, S. T., 11-16
Fitzgerald, C., 3-14, 3-23
Five Factor Model (FFM), 9-10-9-11
Fleishman, E. A., 3-23
Flexible work schedules, 13-18
Focused change programs, 15-14
Followers, 6-10
Ford Motor Company, 2-9
Formal organization, 4-10-4-15
  actors, 4-10
  integrated road map, 4-15
  operational blueprint, 4-11-4-15
  the script, 4-12-4-13
  script and actors, 4-10-4-11
Forms of structure, 13-9-13-11
Fortune, 3-16
Fortune 1000, 5-16, 9-7, 10-18
Forum Company, 3-16
Franklin, J. L., 15-26
Franklin-Covey, 14-7
Franklin Quest, 14-7
Freeman, S., 13-21
Free riding, 6-12-6-13
French, W., 15-12, 15-13, 15-27, 15-28
Freud, Sigmund, 9-9, 9-15
Frink, D. D., 10-24
Futrell, D., 6-18, 7-18

Holistic change programs, 15-14
Hollingshead, A. N., 5-20
Holmes, M., 5-21
Holopainen, S., 15-28
Holti, R., 5-19, 15-27
Homans, G. C., 4-17, 4-18
Homes, V., 3-17, 3-24
Honda, 15-9
Hooven, J. J., 11-17
Hoover, C. W., 11-16
Horizontal conflict, 8-6
Hornstein, H. A., 8-13
Hot team, 6-13
House, R. J., 3-22, 3-23, 3-31, 10-24
Housel, T., 15-28
Howard, A., 10-21, 10-25
Hoyle, R., 9-15
Hubler, G. P., 5-20
Huey, J., 3-24
Huff, A. S., 4-17
Hughes, R. L., 9-15
Human organization, 4-10-4-15
   actors, 4-13
   integrated road map, 4-15
   operational blueprint, 4-11-4-15
   script and actors, 4-10-4-11
Human relations school, 1-11
Hupp, T., 13-20
Hutchinson, T. L., 5-21
Hygiene factors, 10-8
Hyten, C., 5-20
Hyten, L., 7-18

I

Iansiti, M., 5-21
IBM, 2-9, 3-11
Imaginization, 7-15
Individual effectiveness, 1-8
Individual racism, 9-6-9-7
Indvik, J., 3-23
Information giver, 6-9
Information seeker, 6-9
Information technology (IT), 13-6, 13-12, 13-14
Ingram, P., 15-27
Initiator, 6-9
Inputs, 4-8
Institutional racism, 9-7
Integrated learning mechanism, 15-9-15-10
Integration, 13-9
Intel, 2-9
Intergroup communications, 8-11-8-12
Intergroup conflict, 8-6-8-7
   dealing with, 8-7-8-12
Intergroup effectiveness, 1-8
Intergroup performance, determinants of, 8-3-8-4
Interpersonal skills, 5-9
Interventions, 15-11
   types of, 15-12
Involvement-process learning, 2-9-2-10

Ivancevich, J. M., 12-19
Izumi, H., 15-28

J

J. P. Morgan, 14-7
Jackson, E. S., 11-16
Jackson, S. E., 6-18, 9-15
Jacobs, J. A., 9-15
Jaeger, A. M., 15-29
Jago, A., 5-10, 5-12, 5-20
Janis, I. L., 6-19, 6-20
Jehn, K. A., 8-13
Jewell, L. N., 6-20
Jick, T. D., 15-3, 15-25, 15-28
Jin, P., 10-25
Job engineering approach, 13-16-13-17
Job enlargement, 13-17
Job enrichment, 3-11
Job rotation, 13-17
Job sharing, 13-17
Johann, B., 3-20
Johansen, R., 5-21, 12-7, 12-19
Jones. G. R., 6-19
Journal of Applied Behavioral Science, 15-17
Julin, J. A., 6-18
Jung, Carl, 9-9

K

Kahn, R., 3-22
Kaiser-Permanente, 13-5, 15-9
Kano, N., 15-28
Kanter, R. M., 3-18, 3-19, 3-24, 10-23, 15-28
Kanungo, R. N., 3-23
Kaplan, R. E., 7-18
Kast, Fremont, E., 4-2
Katz, D., 3-22
Katz, M., 15-28
Katzenbach, J. R., 5-8, 5-9, 5-20
Keiretsu, 13-13-13-14, 14-9
Keirsey, David, 9-10
Keirsey's temperament sorter, 9-9, 9-10
Kelley, H. H., 11-17
Kennedy, A. A., 14-13
Kenny, D. A., 11-16
Kerr, J., 14-13
Kiesler, Sara, 5-21
Kiggundu, M. N., 15-28
Kilmann, R. H., 14-13
Kinesic behavior, 12-11
Kinlaw, D. C., 7-18
Kirby, L. K., 3-14, 3-23
Kirkpatrick, David, 5-21
Kirkpatrick, S. A., 3-23
Kite, M. E., 11-16
Klein, H. J., 10-24
Knowles, H., 6-18
Knowles, M., 2-13, 6-3, 6-18
Kolb, D., 2-8, 2-13, 2-14, 6-18, 8-17

McIntyre, J. M., 6-18
McKee, A., 11-17
McKendall, M., 9-15
McKinsey and Company, 13-12
Meadows, James, 13-18
Media richness, 12-15-12-16
Medsker, G. J., 6-18
Meiri, Z., 15-26
Mencken, H. L., 2-12
Merton, Robert K., 2-13
Mesmerizing factor, 1-9
Meyer, C. W., 14-13
Michalson, L. K., 5-20
Michigan, University of, 3-8, 3-9
Michigan Bell, 10-19
Miles, G., 13-20
Miles, R., 1-15, 13-20
Mintzberg, H., 3-5
Mitchell, T. R., 3-23
Mitki, Y., 2-13, 12-19, 15-8, 15-13, 15-26, 15-27, 15-28
Mobil Oil, 3-11, 14-6, 14-7
Modern era, in management theory, 1-12
Mohrman, S. A., 5-20, 13-20
Moingoen, B., 15-26
Moon, W., 15-26
Moorhead, G., 6-20
Morgan, G., 7-15, 7-16, 7-19
Morris, Barry, 15-33, 15-35
Morris, C., 5-20, 15-28
Morrison, A. M., 3-17, 3-24
Morrow, J., 3-24
Motivation
    content theories of, 10-8-10-12
    humans relations model, 10-7
    international viewpoint, 10-20-10-22
    and managerial practice, 10-17-10-20
    managerial viewpoints, 10-5-10-8
    process theories, 10-12-10-16
    traditional viewpoint, 10-7
Motorola, 5-17
Mount, M. K., 6-20, 9-15
Mouton, J. S., 8-13
Mudrack, P. E., 6-19
Mueller, R., 11-16
Mullen, B., 6-19
Murningham, J. K., 5-20
Murrell, Kenneth, 2-8, 7-22
Myers-Briggs Type Indicator (MBTI), 3-14, 3-16, 9-8, 9-10

N

n achievement, 10-11
Nadler, D. A., 1-15, 13-6, 13-20, 15-26
Nahan, B., 2-13
Nail, P. R., 6-19
Namiki, N., 5-21
Napier, R. W., 6-18
Neck, C. P., 6-20
Negative entropy, 4-9
Nemawashi, 5-18
Neoclassical era, in management theory, 1-11-1-12

Network organizations, 13-12-13-13
Neubert, M. J., 6-20
Neumann, J. E., 5-19
New product development team (NPDT), 5-17
Newton, N., 6-19
New York Times, 13-18
Nicholas, J. M., 15-28
Nominal group technique, 5-16
Nonverbal communication, 12-11-12-12
Northwest Airlines, 8-6
n power, 10-11
Nystrom, P., 13-20

O

Obiorne, G. S., 10-24
Observer/commentator, 6-10
Ohio State University, 3-8, 3-9
Ohott, P. J., 3-24
O'Leary-Kelly, A. M., 10-24
Oliver, P. V., 11-16
Olmosk, E., 15-26
On Becoming a Leader (Bennis), 3-17
Open system, 4-8
Operational blueprints, 4-11-4-15
O'Reilly, C. A., 14-13
O'Reily, C. A., III, 6-18
Organizational behavior
    historical evolution, 1-10-1-12
    macro view, 1-13
    mesmerizing factor, 1-9
    micro view, 1-13
    rational vs. irrational forces, 1-8-1-9
    systems approach, 1-7-1-8
    working definition of, 1-13
Organizational change and development (OC&D), 15-11-15-15
Organizational characteristics, 6-3
Organizational culture, 6-3-6-4, 14-7-14-9, 14-11-14-12
    defined, 14-7
Organizational development (OD), 15-7-15-8
    defined, 15-11
Organizational diagnosis, 15-11
Organizational effectiveness, 14-11-14-12
Organizational learning, 15-8-15-11
    defined, 15-8
Organizational learning mechanisms, 15-8
Organizational skills, and goals, 5-15
Organization design
    comprehensive approaches, 13-5-13-9
    horizontal and flexible organization, 13-11-13-14
    structure forms, 13-9-13-11
Organization learning, 2-7
Organizations
    defined, 3-7
    open-systems view, 4-8-4-9
    system-based framework, 4-9
Osland, J. S., 8-17
Osterman, P., 13-21
Ostroff, F., 13-12, 13-20
Ott, J. S., 14-13

Roberts, D. R., 15-28
Robertson, P. J., 15-28
Roethlisberger, F. J., 1-15
Rogberg, M., 15-28
Rogers, C., 9-15, 12-19
Rogers, Rolf E., 14-3
Role behaviors, 3-6-3-7
Role differentiation, 6-9-6-12
Ronen, S., 3-24, 10-25
Rosenthal, J., 15-28
Rosenthal, R., 11-9, 11-16, 11-17
Rosenweig, James E., 4-2
Ross, R. A., 5-20
Ross, T. L., 5-20
Rover, 15-9
Rowe, A., 9-15, 11-16
Rozell, E. J., 10-24
Rubin, I. M., 6-18
Ruble, T., 8-9
Ruderman, M. N., 3-24
Runbin, I. M., 8-17

S

Saari, L. M., 7-18
Sackman, S. A., 14-13
Salas, E., 6-18
Sathe, V., 14-13
Saxton, M. J., 14-13
Schachter, S., 6-19
Schein, E. H., 2-5, 2-13, 4-12, 4-18, 7-12, 7-18, 14-7, 14-8, 14-13, 15-8, 15-26
Schein, V. E., 11-16
Schneider, C. P., 10-23
Schnitt, D. L., 15-28
Schon, D., 2-14
Schor, S., 11-17
Schutz model, 6-15
Scientific management approach, 13-16-13-17
Scientific management school, 1-10, 1-11
Script, 4-10
Seers, A., 7-19
Segal, M., 11-16
Self-design approach, 13-8-13-9
Self-fulfilling prophecy (SFP), 2-6-2-7
Self-learning competency, 2-7-2-8
Self-managed work teams (SMWT), 5-16
Semantics, 12-10
Sena, J., 7-19, 13-20
Senge, P., 15-8, 15-26
Sepic, F. T., 3-23
Serpa, R., 14-13
Sessa, V. I., 6-18
Sethi, P., 5-21
Sex-role stereotype, 11-8
Shafritz, J. M., 1-15, 14-13
Shamir, B., 3-14, 3-23
Shani, A. B., P4-2, 2-13, 5-21, 7-19, 10-25, 11-17, 12-19, 13-20, 15-3, 15-8, 15-13, 15-26, 15-27, 15-28, 15-29
Shapiro, H. J., 10-24
Sharp, W., 5-20
Shaw, K. N., 7-18

Shaw, M. E., 6-19
Shea, G. P., 6-18, 8-13
Sheats, P., 6-19
Shell, 13-15
Shenkar, O., 3-24, 10-25
Shephard, H. A., 8-13
Sherif, C., 8-13
Sherif, M., 8-5, 8-7, 8-11, 8-13
Sherman, S., 15-3
Sherwood, J. J., 7-19
Shudo, K., 10-21, 10-25
Shulman, A. D., 5-21
Simon, M. C., 11-16
Simons, T., 15-27
Situational leadership, 3-11-3-12
Skill-based pay, 10-18
Skill building, 3-16-3-17
Skinner, B. F., 10-18, 10-20
Slater, P. E., 8-13
Slater, R., 15-3
Slocum, J. W., 6-18, 8-13, 14-13
Small group leadership, 6-12
Smelser, N., 1-15
Smith, Adam, 1-10, 1-11
Smith, D., 13-12, 13-20
Smith, D. K., 5-20
Smith, D. M., 14-13
Smith, R. Jeffrey, 6-19
Smith, Todd, 7-22
Snow, C., 13-20, 15-29
Snyder, M., 9-15
Social loafing, 6-12-6-13
Sociotechnical systems (STS), 15-15-15-17, 15-18-15-21
    design approach, 13-7-13-8, 13-12, 13-15
    school, 1-12
    teams, 13-15-13-16
Socrates, 1-10, 1-11
Solem, A. R., 5-26, 5-27
Special groups, 7-13
Spence, J. T., 10-25
Spencer, G. J., 15-27
Sproull, Lee, 5-21
Srivastva, S., 2-14, 15-27
Stahl, M. J., 10-24
Standard setter, 6-10
Standing, H., 5-19
Stanford University, 3-16
Starbuck, W., 13-20
Steady state, 4-9
Stebbins, M., 7-19, 13-20, 15-26, 15-28, 15-29
Steele, R. S., 10-24
Steers, R. M., 8-13, 10-23
Steffen, V. J., 11-16
Stein, B. A., 15-28
Stereotypes, 11-8-11-9
Stewart, G. L., 6-20
Still, C. L., 11-16
Stjernberg, T., 15-13, 15-26, 15-27
Stogdill, R. M., 3-14, 3-22, 3-23
Strategic organization design, 13-5
Strauss, J. P., 9-15
Streib, G., 10-24